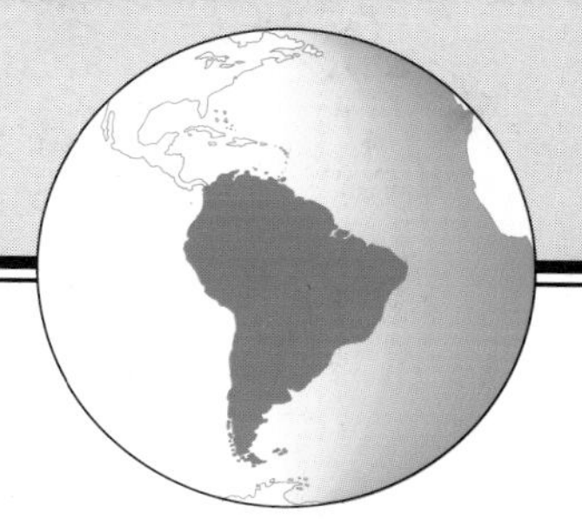

SOUTH AMERICA

EUROPE

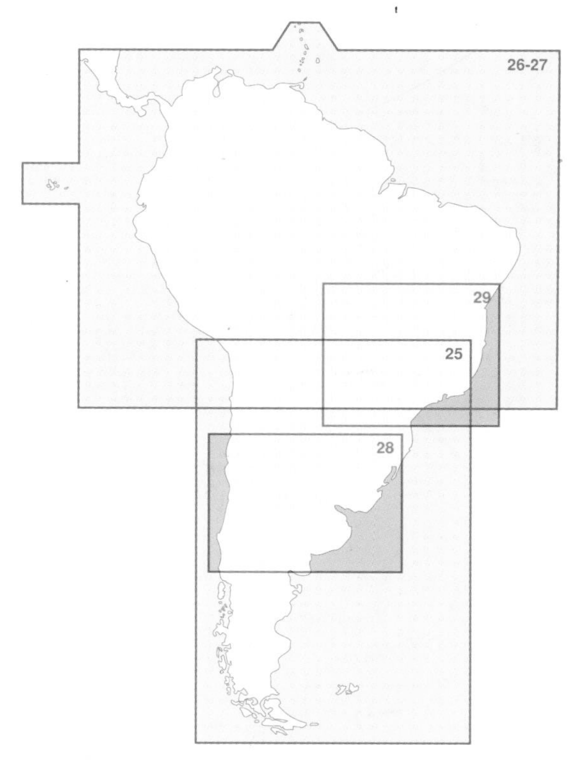

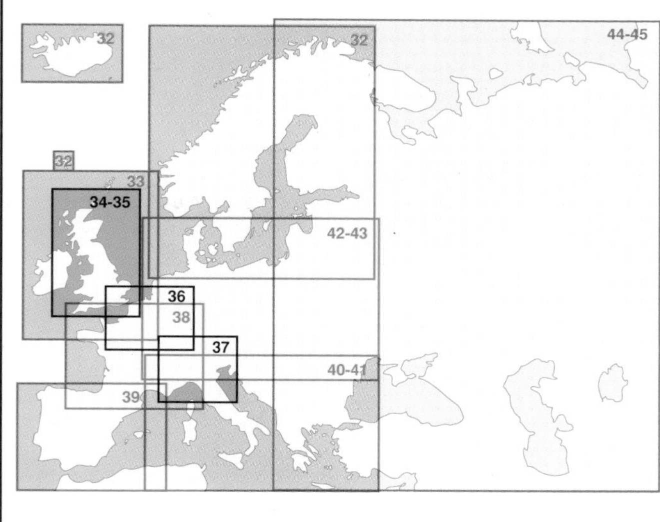

• Bartholomew •

ILLUSTRATED
WORLD
ATLAS

Bartholomew
A Division of HarperCollins*Publishers*

Bartholomew
A Division of HarperCollins Publishers
Duncan Street, Edinburgh EH9 1TA

First published by Bartholomew 1987
Revised edition 1993

© Bartholomew 1993

A CIP catalogue record for this book is available from the British Library

ISBN 0-7028-2373-2

Printed in Great Britain by Bartholomew, The Edinburgh Press Limited.

Details included in this atlas are subject to change without notice. Whilst every effort is made to keep information up to date Bartholomew will not be responsible for any loss, damage or inconvenience caused by inaccuracies in this atlas. The publishers are always pleased to acknowledge any corrections brought to their notice, and record their appreciation of the valuable services rendered in the past by map users in assisting to maintain the accuracy of their publications.

F/B6483

Acknowledgements

The Publishers acknowledge the assistance of the following in the preparation of material used in this publication: Dr Walter Stephen, Senior Adviser, Curriculum, Dean Education Centre, Edinburgh; Alister Hendrie, Assistant Headteacher, Portobello High School, Edinburgh; Andrew Grant, Principal Teacher, Geography, Wester Hailes Education Centre, Edinburgh; Stephen Hamilton, Principal Teacher, Geography, Broughton High School, Edinburgh.

The Publishers are grateful to the following for providing the photographs used in this atlas:
(picture number(s) shown in italics)
Travel Photo International: pages xxii-xxiii, savanna, rain forest, prairie, northern forest; page xxii, *7;* page xviii, *2;* page xv , *11;* page xvi , *4, 5, 13, 14;* page xx , *7;* page xxi , *2;* page vi , *3, 4;* page viii,*3,4. Photographers' Library:* page xxii-xxiii, scrub *Chris Knaggs photograph,* desert *Oliver Martel photograph;* page x , *8 Clive Sawyer photograph;* page xiv, *8 Ian Wright photograph;* page xvii, *9 Tom Hustler photograph;* page xx , *4 Robyn Beeche photograph. Biofotos:* page x , *5 Heather Angel photograph;* page xx , *6 Andrew Henley photograph;* page xxi , *3 Soames Summerhays photograph. The Photo Source:* page xii ,*10;* page xviii, *4;* page xiv, *7. Wade Cooper Associates,* Edinburgh: page xvi , *12;* page xvii, *10;* page vi , *1. Pictor International:* page xiv, *6;* page vi , *2. B. and C. Alexander:* page xxii , tundra. *Bruce Coleman Ltd:* page viii, *6 WWF/Eugen Schuhmacher. Mepha:* page xviii, *1 C. Osborne photograph. Michael Scott:* page xxii , woodland and grass. *Yorkshire and Humberside Tourist Board:* page xi, *2. Spectrum Colour Library:* page xiii, *12, 14.*

CONTENTS

Major Cities by Continent

Africa	Pop. '000
Cairo *Egypt*	9000
Lagos *Nigeria*	7700
Alexandria *Egypt*	3700
Kinshasa *Zaire*	3500
Casablanca *Morocco*	3200
Alger *Algeria*	3000
Cape Town *South Africa*	2300
Abidjan *Ivory Coast*	2200
Tarābulus *Libya*	2100
Ādīs Ābeba *Ethiopia*	1900
Khartoum *Sudan*	1900
Dar es Salaam *Tanzania*	1700
Johannesburg *South Africa*	1700
Luanda *Angola*	1700
Maputo *Mozambique*	1600
Tunis *Tunisia*	1600
Dakar *Senegal*	1500
Nairobi *Kenya*	1500

North and Central America	'000
México *Mexico*	20 200
New York *USA*	16 200
Los Angeles *USA*	11 900
Chicago *USA*	7000
Philadelphia *USA*	4300
Detroit *USA*	3700
San Francisco *USA*	3700
Toronto *Canada*	3500
Dallas *USA*	3400
Guadalajara *Mexico*	3200
Houston *USA*	3000
Monterrey *Mexico*	3000
Montréal *Canada*	3000
Washington *USA*	2900
Boston *USA*	2800
Atlanta *USA*	2200
San Diego *USA*	2200
Santo Domingo *Dominican Rep.*	2200
La Habana *Cuba*	2100
Minneapolis *USA*	2000
Phoenix *USA*	2000
Baltimore *USA*	1900
Miami *USA*	1900
St. Louis *USA*	1900
Cleveland *USA*	1700
Pittsburgh *USA*	1700
Denver *USA*	1600
Seattle *USA*	1600
Vancouver *Canada*	1500

South America	'000
São Paulo *Brazil*	17 400
Buenos Aires *Argentina*	11 500
Rio de Janeiro *Brazil*	10 700
Lima *Peru*	6200
Santiago *Chile*	5000
Bogotá *Colombia*	4900
Caracas *Venezuela*	4100
Belo Horizonte *Brazil*	3600
Pôrto Alegre *Brazil*	3100
Recife *Brazil*	2500
Brasília *Brazil*	2400
Salvador *Brazil*	2400
Fortaleza *Brazil*	2100
Curitiba *Brazil*	2000
Guayaquil *Ecuador*	170
Cali *Colombia*	160
Medellín *Colombia*	160
Montevideo *Uruguay*	120

Asia	'00
Tōkyō *Japan*	18 10
Shanghai *China*	13 40
Calcutta *India*	11 80
Bombay *India*	11 20
Sŏul *South Korea*	11 00
Beijing *China*	10 80
Tianjin *China*	940
Jakarta *Indonesia*	930
Delhi *India*	880
Manila *Philippines*	850
Ōsaka *Japan*	8
Karachi *Pakistan*	770
Bangkok *Thailand*	720
Tehrān *Iran*	680

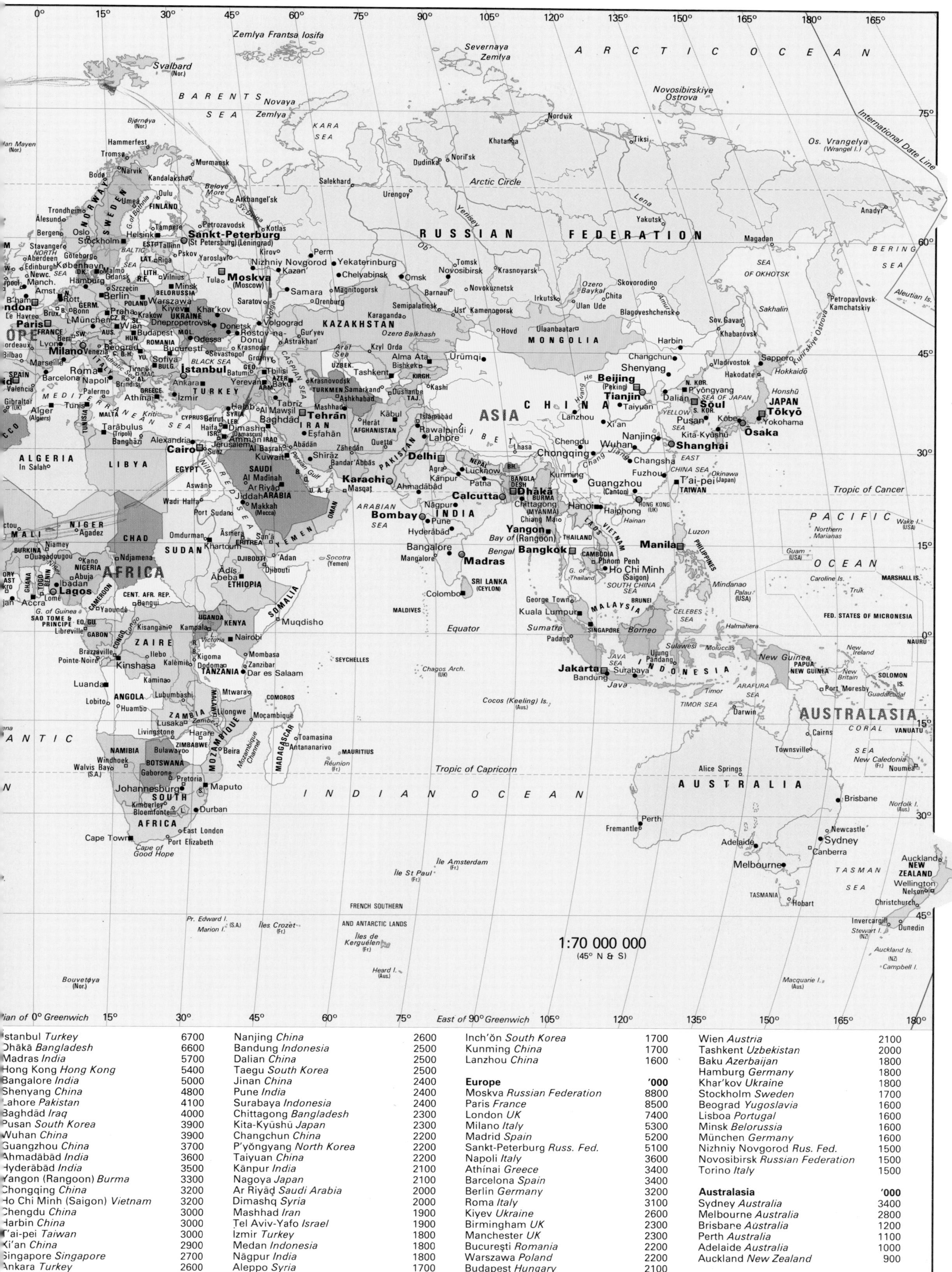

1:70 000 000
(45° N & S)

		Nanjing *China*	2600	Inch'ŏn *South Korea*	1700	Wien *Austria*	2100
Istanbul *Turkey*	6700	Bandung *Indonesia*	2500	Kunming *China*	1700	Tashkent *Uzbekistan*	2000
Dhākā *Bangladesh*	6600	Dalian *China*	2500	Lanzhou *China*	1600	Baku *Azerbaijan*	1800
Madras *India*	5700	Taegu *South Korea*	2500			Hamburg *Germany*	1800
Hong Kong *Hong Kong*	5400	Jinan *China*	2400	**Europe**	**'000**	Khar'kov *Ukraine*	1800
Bangalore *India*	5000	Pune *India*	2400	Moskva *Russian Federation*	8800	Stockholm *Sweden*	1700
Shenyang *China*	4800	Surabaya *Indonesia*	2400	Paris *France*	8500	Beograd *Yugoslavia*	1600
Lahore *Pakistan*	4100	Chittagong *Bangladesh*	2300	London *UK*	7400	Lisboa *Portugal*	1600
Baghdād *Iraq*	4000	Kita-Kyūshū *Japan*	2300	Milano *Italy*	5300	Minsk *Belorussia*	1600
Pusan *South Korea*	3900	Changchun *China*	2200	Madrid *Spain*	5200	München *Germany*	1600
Wuhan *China*	3900	P'yŏngyang *North Korea*	2200	Sankt-Peterburg *Russ. Fed.*	5100	Nizhniy Novgorod *Rus. Fed.*	1500
Guangzhou *China*	3700	Taiyuan *China*	2200	Napoli *Italy*	3600	Novosibirsk *Russian Federation*	1500
Ahmadābād *India*	3600	Kānpur *India*	2100	Athínai *Greece*	3400	Torino *Italy*	1500
Hyderābād *India*	3500	Nagoya *Japan*	2100	Barcelona *Spain*	3400		
Yangon (Rangoon) *Burma*	3300	Ar Riyāḍ *Saudi Arabia*	2000	Berlin *Germany*	3200	**Australasia**	**'000**
Chongqing *China*	3200	Dimashq *Syria*	2000	Roma *Italy*	3100	Sydney *Australia*	3400
Ho Chi Minh (Saigon) *Vietnam*	3200	Mashhad *Iran*	1900	Kiyev *Ukraine*	2600	Melbourne *Australia*	2800
Chengdu *China*	3000	Tel Aviv-Yafo *Israel*	1900	Birmingham *UK*	2300	Brisbane *Australia*	1200
Harbin *China*	3000	Izmir *Turkey*	1800	Manchester *UK*	2300	Perth *Australia*	1100
T'ai-pei *Taiwan*	3000	Medan *Indonesia*	1800	Bucureşti *Romania*	2200	Adelaide *Australia*	1000
Xi'an *China*	2900	Nāgpur *India*	1800	Warszawa *Poland*	2200	Auckland *New Zealand*	900
Singapore *Singapore*	2700	Aleppo *Syria*	1700	Budapest *Hungary*	2100		
Ankara *Turkey*	2600						

NORTH AMERICA

1:35M

0   250   500   750   1000 km
0   250   500   mils

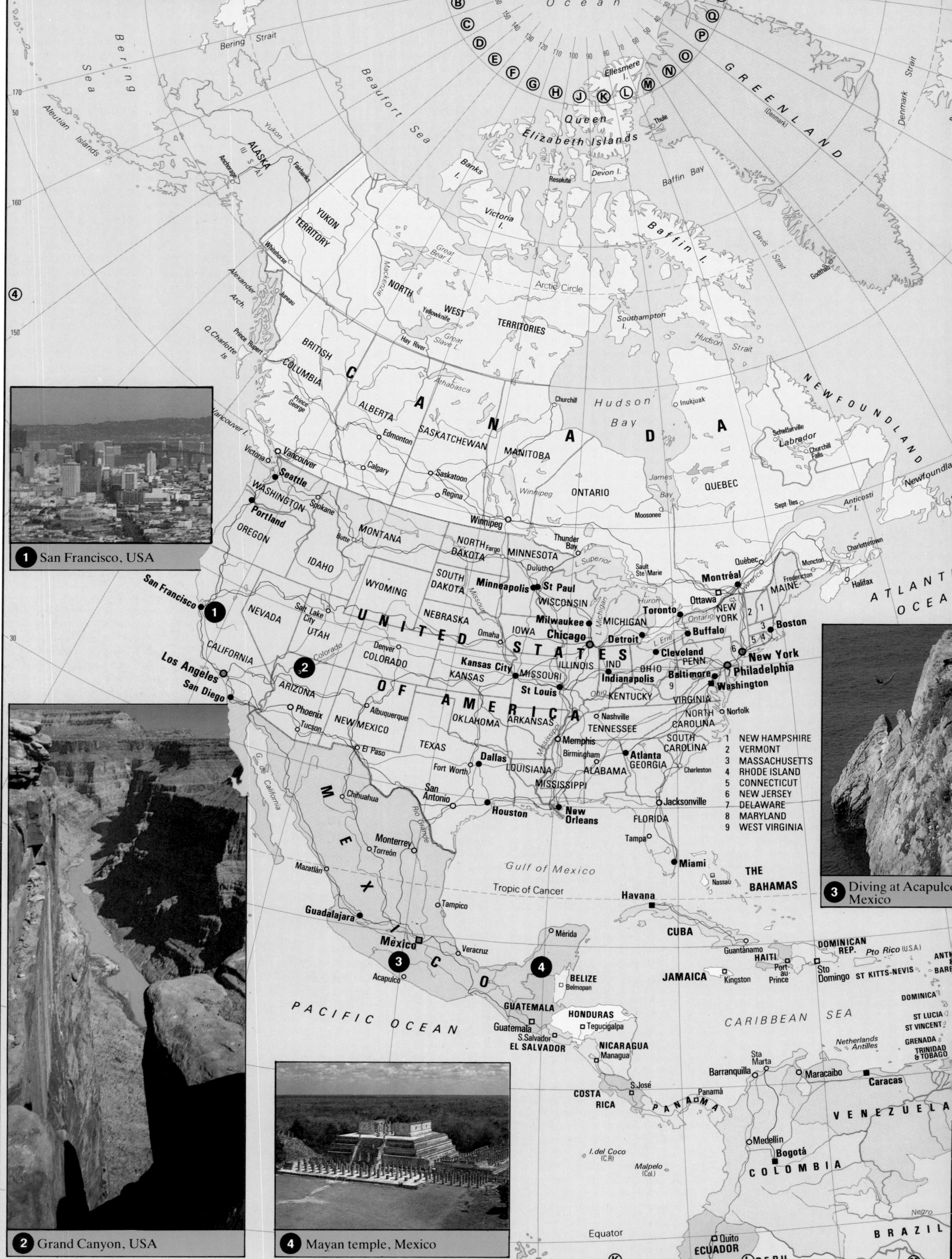

RUSSIAN FEDERATION

Bering Sea

Aleutian Islands

Bering Strait

Beaufort Sea

Arctic Ocean

GREENLAND (Denmark)

Ellesmere I.

Queen Elizabeth Islands

Banks I.

Devon I.

Baffin Bay

Thule

Resolute

Victoria I.

Southampton I.

Davis Strait

Denmark Strait

Godthåb

ALASKA (U.S.A.)

Yukon

Anchorage

Fairbanks

Whitehorse

YUKON TERRITORY

Mackenzie

Great Bear L.

NORTH WEST TERRITORIES

Yellowknife

Arctic Circle

Great Slave L.

Hay River

Hudson Strait

Inukjuak

N E W F O U N D L A N D

Juneau

Alexander Arch.

Prince Rupert

Q. Charlotte Is.

BRITISH COLUMBIA

Prince George

Vancouver I.

C A N A D A

ALBERTA

Edmonton

Calgary

Athabasca

SASKATCHEWAN

Saskatoon

Regina

MANITOBA

Churchill

Hudson Bay

James Bay

Moosonee

ONTARIO

Winnipeg

L. Winnipeg

QUEBEC

Schefferville

Labrador

Churchill Falls

Sept-Îles

Anticosti I.

Newfoundla

Victoria

Vancouver

Seattle

WASHINGTON

Spokane

Portland

OREGON

Butte

IDAHO

MONTANA

WYOMING

San Francisco

NEVADA

Salt Lake City

UTAH

CALIFORNIA

Los Angeles

San Diego

Colorado

COLORADO

Denver

ARIZONA

Phoenix

Tucson

NEW MEXICO

Albuquerque

El Paso

G. of California

MEXICO

Chihuahua

TEXAS

Fort Worth

Dallas

Rio Grande

San Antonio

Houston

Monterrey

Torreón

Mazatlán

Tampico

Guadalajara

México

Veracruz

Mérida

Acapulco

C O

NORTH DAKOTA

Fargo

SOUTH DAKOTA

NEBRASKA

Omaha

IOWA

Missouri

KANSAS

Kansas City

OKLAHOMA

ARKANSAS

MINNESOTA

Duluth

Minneapolis   St Paul

WISCONSIN

Milwaukee

Chicago

ILLINOIS

St Louis

MISSOURI

Nashville

Memphis

TENNESSEE

Birmingham

LOUISIANA

MISSISSIPPI

ALABAMA

New Orleans

Thunder Bay

L. Superior

Sault Ste Marie

L. Michigan

MICHIGAN

Detroit

L. Huron

Toronto

Buffalo

L. Erie

Cleveland

IND

Indianapolis

OHIO

Ohio

KENTUCKY

GEORGIA

Atlanta

FLORIDA

Jacksonville

Tampa

Miami

Nassau

Ottawa

Montréal

St Lawrence

Québec

Moncton

Fredericton

Charlottetown

MAINE

Halifax

NEW YORK

PENN.

Baltimore

Washington

VIRGINIA

Norfolk

NORTH CAROLINA

SOUTH CAROLINA

Charleston

New York

Philadelphia

Boston

ATLANTIC OCEAN

1 NEW HAMPSHIRE
2 VERMONT
3 MASSACHUSETTS
4 RHODE ISLAND
5 CONNECTICUT
6 NEW JERSEY
7 DELAWARE
8 MARYLAND
9 WEST VIRGINIA

U N I T E D   S T A T E S   O F   A M E R I C A

M E X I C O

Tropic of Cancer

Gulf of Mexico

Havana

CUBA

Guantánamo

THE BAHAMAS

HAITI

Port-au-Prince

DOMINICAN REP.

Sto Domingo

Pto Rico (U.S.A.)

JAMAICA

Kingston

ST KITTS-NEVIS

ANT

BARB

DOMINICA

ST LUCIA

ST VINCENT

GRENADA

TRINIDAD & TOBAGO

Netherlands Antilles

CARIBBEAN SEA

BELIZE

Belmopan

GUATEMALA

Guatemala

S.Salvador

EL SALVADOR

HONDURAS

Tegucigalpa

NICARAGUA

Managua

COSTA RICA

S.José

PANAMA

Panamá

Sta Marta

Barranquilla

Maracaibo

Caracas

VENEZUELA

PACIFIC OCEAN

I. del Coco (C.R)

Malpelo (Col.)

Medellin

Bogotá

COLOMBIA

Equator

Quito

ECUADOR

PERU

B R A Z I L

Negro

1 San Francisco, USA

2 Grand Canyon, USA

3 Diving at Acapulco Mexico

4 Mayan temple, Mexico

VI

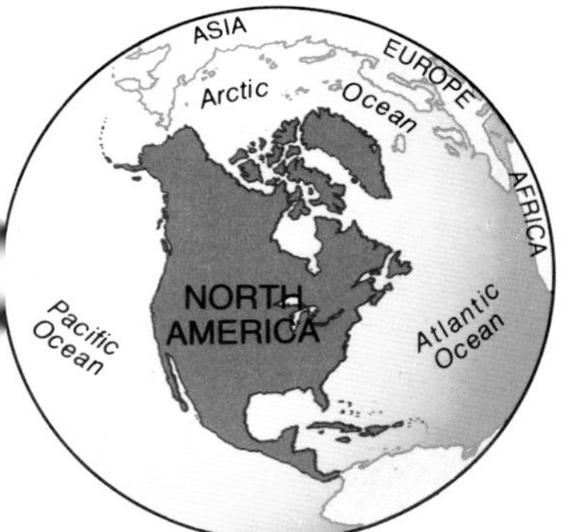

FACTS ABOUT NORTH AMERICA

1 The city of San Francisco was almost destroyed by an earthquake in 1906, and there could be another one soon. Right under the city runs the San Andreas fault, where two of the 'plates' which make up the earth's crust slide against one another. When they get jammed together at any point, pressure builds up, until finally they break apart. This causes an earthquake because of the sudden release of so much energy. The longer the plates stay jammed together, the greater the strength of the final earthquake: in 1906, the plates under San Francisco slid 6 m (20 feet) in a few minutes. Some parts of the fault have not moved for years – and scientists think there will be another big earthquake soon.

2 The huge Grand Canyon in Arizona, USA, was gouged out of the rock by the Colorado River. It is 1.6 km (1 mile) deep, a maximum of 29 km (18 miles) wide and no less than 446 km (227 miles) long! The Grand Canyon is still being carved deeper (though very slowly) by the river.

3 At La Questrada, Acapulco, Mexico, divers often swoop 36 m (118 feet) down into the sea. This is the highest dive which people do regularly.

4 The Maya were a tribe who lived in southern Mexico and Guatemala 1400 years ago. They built great cities with stone temples, public buildings and palaces. The picture shows one of their buildings which can be seen today. It was built without help from any modern machinery.

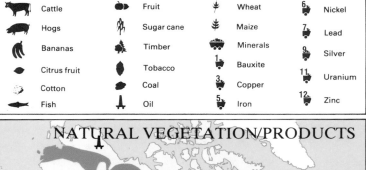

Cattle · Hogs · Bananas · Citrus fruit · Cotton · Fish · Fruit · Sugar cane · Timber · Tobacco · Coal · Oil · Wheat · Maize · Minerals · Bauxite 1 · Copper 3 · Iron 5 · Nickel 6 · Lead 7 · Silver 9 · Uranium 11 · Zinc 12

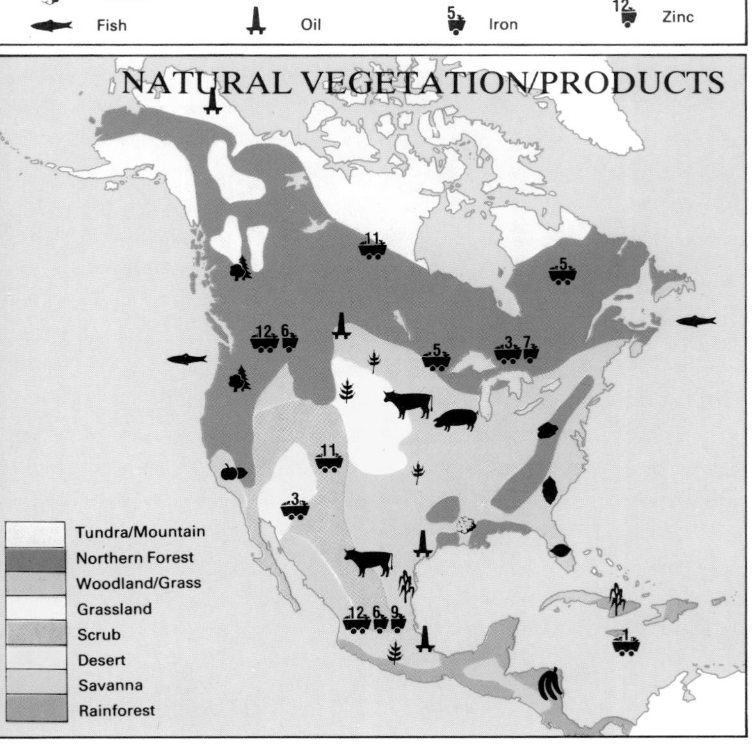

NATURAL VEGETATION/PRODUCTS

Tundra/Mountain
Northern Forest
Woodland/Grass
Grassland
Scrub
Desert
Savanna
Rainforest

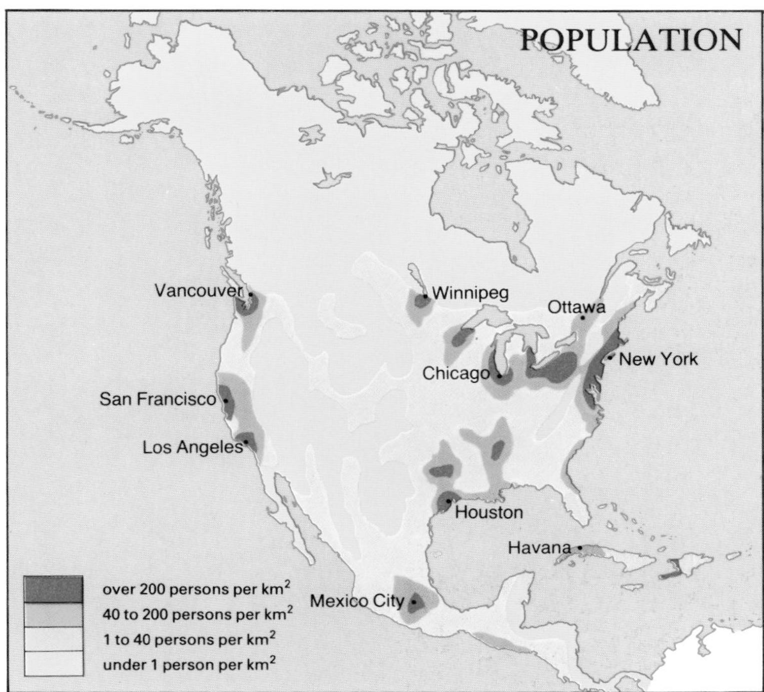

POPULATION

Vancouver · Winnipeg · Ottawa · Chicago · New York · San Francisco · Los Angeles · Houston · Havana · Mexico City

over 200 persons per km²
40 to 200 persons per km²
1 to 40 persons per km²
under 1 person per km²

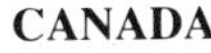

CANADA

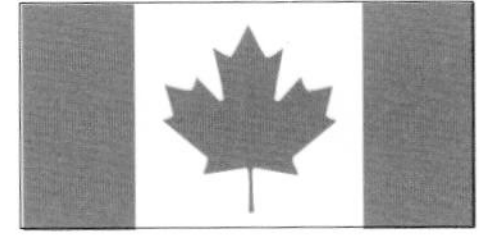

Area: 9 976 147 sq km (3 851 790 sq miles)
Population: 26 500 000
Capital: Ottawa
Languages: English, French
Currency: Canadian Dollar

JAMAICA

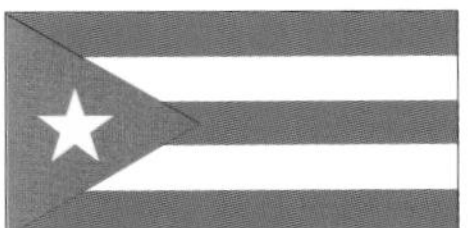

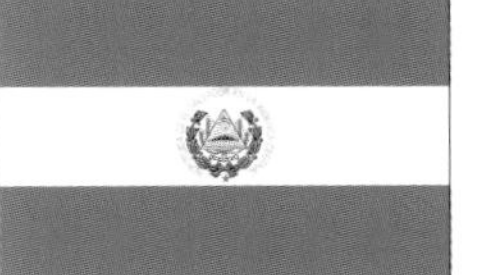

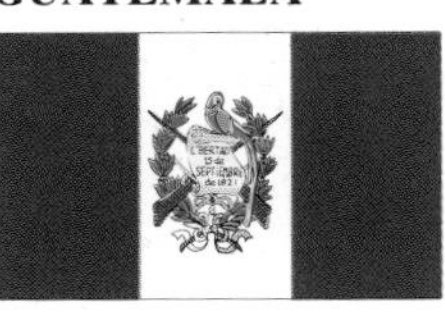

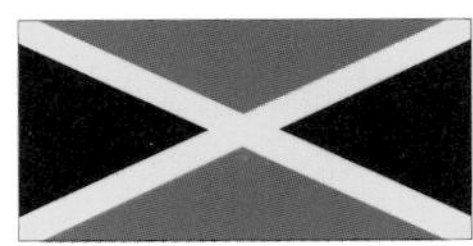

Area: 11 424 sq km (4411 sq miles)
Population: 2 500 000
Capital: Kingston
Language: English
Currency: Jamaican Dollar

CUBA

Area: 114 524 sq km (44 218 sq miles)
Population: 10 600 000
Capital: Havana
Language: Spanish
Currency: Cuban Peso

MEXICO

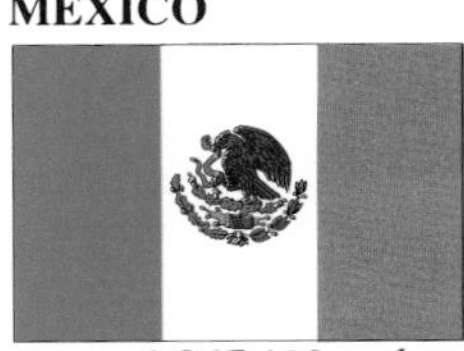

Area: 1 967 180 sq km (759 528 sq miles)
Population: 88 600 000
Capital: Mexico City
Language: Spanish
Currency: Mexican Peso

EL SALVADOR

Area: 20 865 sq km (8056 sq miles)
Population: 5 300 000
Capital: San Salvador
Language: Spanish
Currency: Colon

NICARAGUA

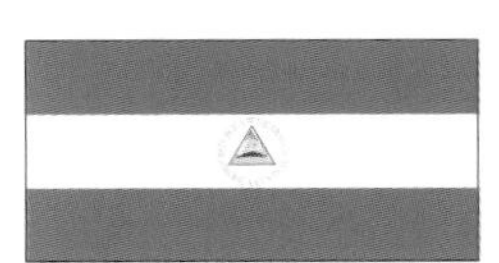

Area: 139 000 sq km (53 668 sq miles)
Population: 3 900 000
Capital: Managua
Language: Spanish
Currency: Cordoba

GUATEMALA

Area: 108 888 sq km (42 042 sq miles)
Population: 9 200 000
Capital: Guatemala
Language: Spanish
Currency: Quetzal

UNITED STATES OF AMERICA

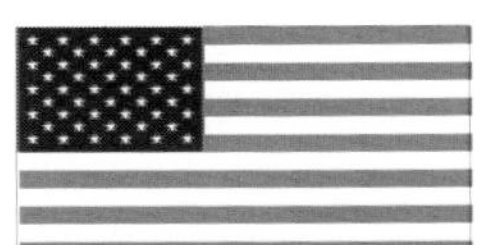

Area: 9 363 130 sq km (3 615 104 sq miles)
Population: 249 200 000
Capital: Washington
Language: English
Currency: U.S. Dollar

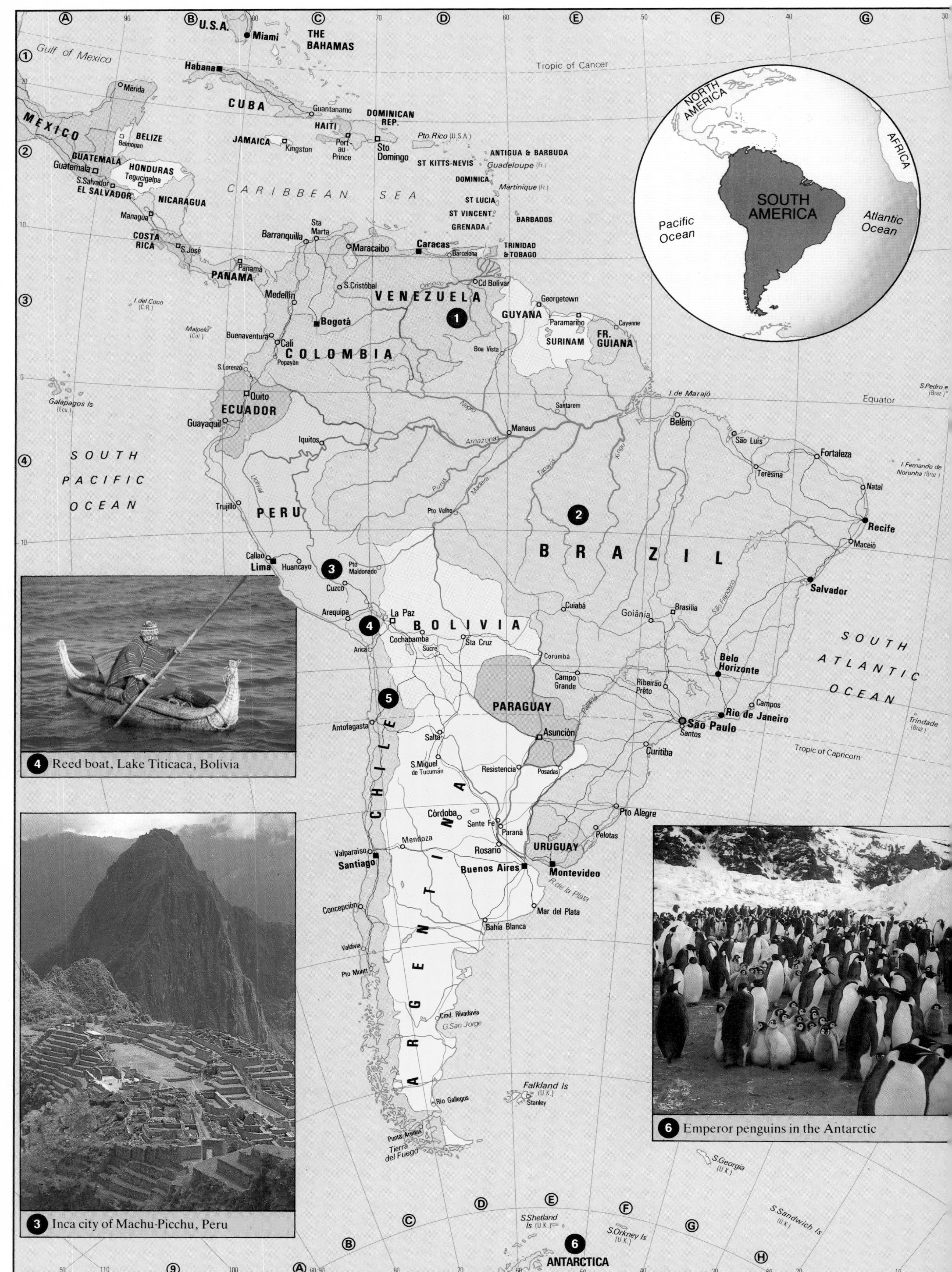

1:35M

0 250 500 750 1000 km
0 250 500 mls

NORTH AMERICA

AFRICA

SOUTH AMERICA

Pacific Ocean

Atlantic Ocean

Gulf of Mexico

Miami

THE BAHAMAS

U.S.A.

Habana

Mérida

CUBA

Tropic of Cancer

MEXICO

BELIZE
Belmopan
GUATEMALA
Guatemala
S.Salvador
EL SALVADOR
HONDURAS
Tegucigalpa

Guantanamo

HAITI
Port-au-Prince
DOMINICAN REP.
Sto Domingo

JAMAICA
Kingston

Pto Rico (U.S.A.)

ANTIGUA & BARBUDA
ST KITTS-NEVIS
Guadeloupe (Fr.)
DOMINICA
Martinique (Fr.)
ST LUCIA
ST VINCENT
GRENADA
BARBADOS

CARIBBEAN SEA

NICARAGUA
Managua

COSTA RICA
S.José

PANAMA
Panamá

Barranquilla
Sta Marta
Maracaibo
Barcelona
Caracas

TRINIDAD & TOBAGO

I. del Coco (C.R.)

Medellín

S.Cristóbal

VENEZUELA

①

Cd Bolívar

Georgetown
GUYANA
Paramaribo
SURINAM
FR. GUIANA
Cayenne

Malpelo (Col.)

Bogotá

COLOMBIA

Orinoco

Buenaventura
Cali
Popayán

Boa Vista

S.Lorenzo

Quito

ECUADOR

Guayaquil

Galapagos Is (Ecu.)

Iquitos

Negro

Santarem

I. de Marajó

S.Pedro e (Braz.)

Equator

SOUTH PACIFIC OCEAN

Amazonas

Manaus

Belém

São Luís

Fortaleza

I. Fernando de Noronha (Braz.)

PERU

Trujillo

Callao
Lima
Huancayo

③ Pto Maldonado
Cuzco

Pto Velho

Madeira

Tapajós

Xingu

②

B R A Z I L

Teresina

Natal

Recife

Maceió

Salvador

São Francisco

Arequipa

④ La Paz
Cochabamba
Sucre
BOLIVIA
Sta Cruz

Cuiabá

Goiânia

Brasília

Arica

Corumbá

SOUTH ATLANTIC OCEAN

Antofagasta

⑤

Campo Grande

Paraná

PARAGUAY

Belo Horizonte

Ribeirão Prêto

Campos

Rio de Janeiro

São Paulo
Santos

Trindade (Braz.)

Asunción

Curitiba

Salta

S.Miguel de Tucumán

Resistencia

Posadas

Tropic of Capricorn

C H I L E

A R G E N T I N A

Córdoba

Santa Fe
Paraná

URUGUAY

Pto Alegre

Pelotas

Mendoza

Rosario

Valparaíso
Santiago

Buenos Aires

Montevideo

R de la Plata

Concepción

Mar del Plata

Bahía Blanca

Valdivia

Pto Montt

Cmd. Rivadavia
G.San Jorge

Falkland Is (U.K.)
Stanley

Rio Gallegos

Punta Arenas
Tierra del Fuego

S.Georgia (U.K.)

S.Shetland Is (U.K.)
S.Orkney Is (U.K.)
S.Sandwich Is (U.K.)

⑥ ANTARCTICA

④ Reed boat, Lake Titicaca, Bolivia

③ Inca city of Machu-Picchu, Peru

⑥ Emperor penguins in the Antarctic

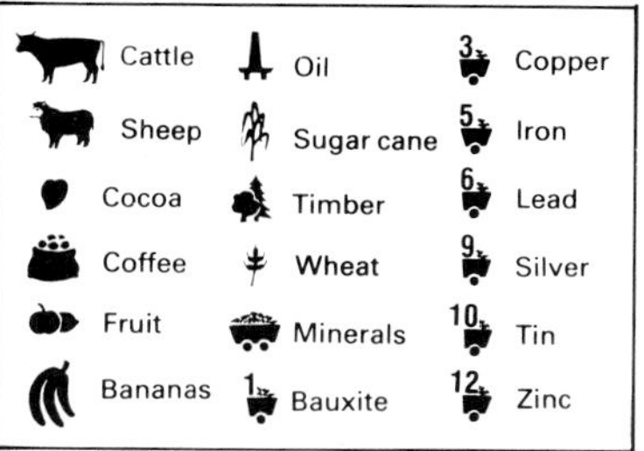

Cattle	Oil	3 Copper
Sheep	Sugar cane	5 Iron
Cocoa	Timber	6 Lead
Coffee	Wheat	9 Silver
Fruit	Minerals	10 Tin
Bananas	1 Bauxite	12 Zinc

FACTS ABOUT SOUTH AMERICA

1 The Angel Falls, Venezuela, are the highest waterfalls in the world, at 979 m (3212 feet).

2 Deforestation is a major problem in South America. About 1 per cent of the total area of forest is lost each year. Often trees are cut down to clear land for agriculture. On hillsides, the soil soon becomes too poor to grow crops and the land is abandoned. Trees cannot grow again, and so soil is eroded away by rain and wind. Trees are also lost when lakes are made for hydro-electric dams; when new towns are built; and as a result of the way people live – they take too much wood for fuel and timber, allow animals to graze on foliage, and light fires which get out of control.

3 In the Andes Mountains, in the north-west of South America, there are ruins of cities built by the Incas. They ruled the Indians in the area 500 years ago. The Incas had well-developed political and religious systems. They built their cities on terraces engineered from the mountain side. The Spanish, the first Europeans to discover these cities, killed the Incas to seize the gold and silver which they had mined, and their cities were abandoned.

4 The highest navigable lake in the world is Lake Titicaca, on the Peru/Bolivia border. It is no less than 3811 m (12 503 feet) above sea level. The local Indian people make boats from bundles of reeds tied together, to use for fishing. The reeds grow around the edge of the lake.

5 Although in the rain forests of the Amazon Basin it rains every day, in the Atacama Desert, Chile, hundreds of years can pass between one rain storm and the next. A storm in 1971 was the first for 400 years. The desert is the driest place in the world.

6 The Emperor Penguin, found in the Antarctic, does not make a nest. Instead, a single egg is carried on top of the male penguin's feet. It is kept warm by a fold of skin which hangs down and covers it. The penguin does not eat during the two months it takes for the egg to hatch out.

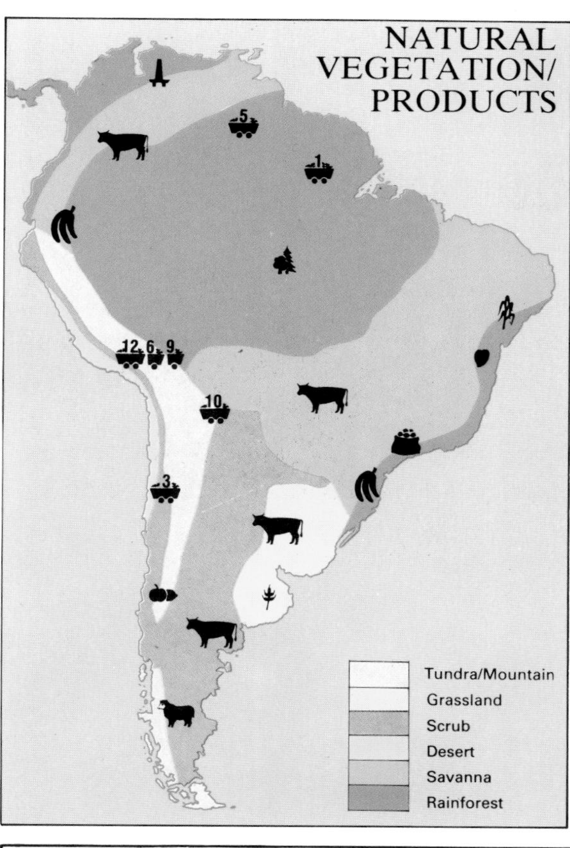

NATURAL VEGETATION/PRODUCTS

	Tundra/Mountain
	Grassland
	Scrub
	Desert
	Savanna
	Rainforest

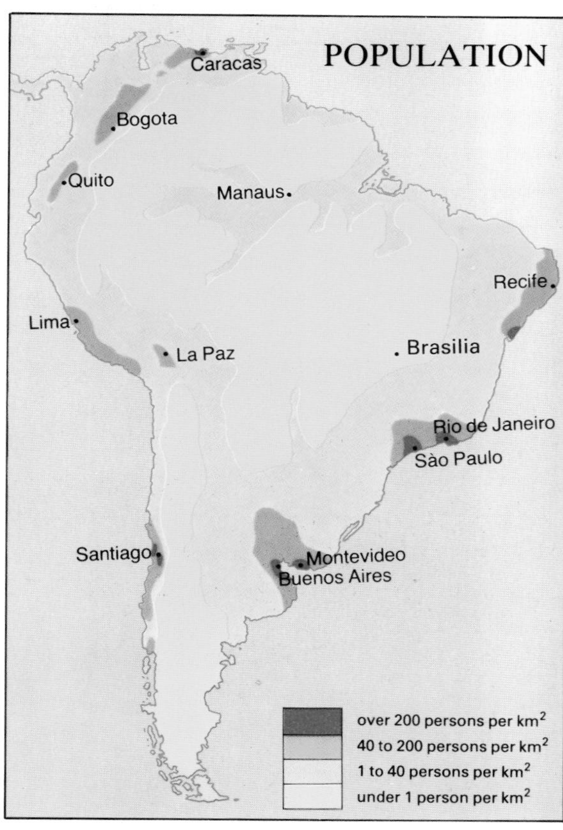

POPULATION

	over 200 persons per km²
	40 to 200 persons per km²
	1 to 40 persons per km²
	under 1 person per km²

ARGENTINA
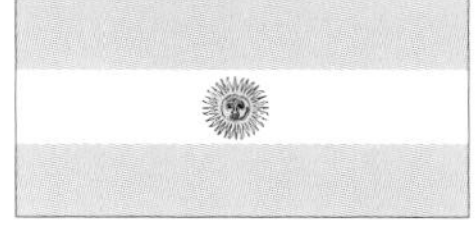

Area: 2 777 815 sq km (1 072 514 sq miles)
Population: 32 300 000
Capital: Buenos Aires
Language: Spanish
Currency: Argentine Peso

BOLIVIA
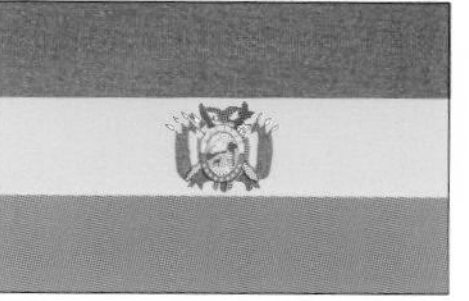

Area: 1 098 575 sq km (424 160 sq miles)
Population: 7 300 000
Capital: La Paz
Languages: Spanish, Aymara, Quechua
Currency: Bolivian Peso

BRAZIL
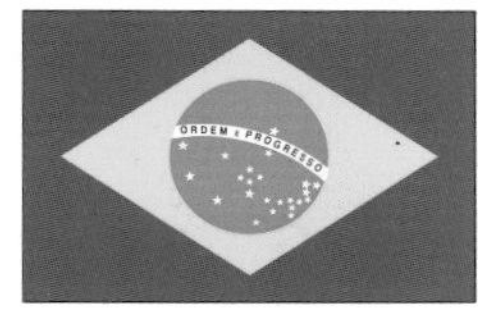

Area: 8 511 968 sq km (3 286 471 sq miles)
Population: 150 400 000
Capital: Brasilia
Language: Portuguese
Currency: Cruzeiro

CHILE
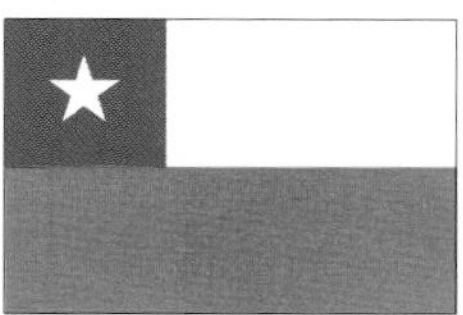

Area: 756 943 sq km (292 256 sq miles)
Population: 13 200 000
Capital: Santiago
Language: Spanish
Currency: Chilean Peso

COLOMBIA
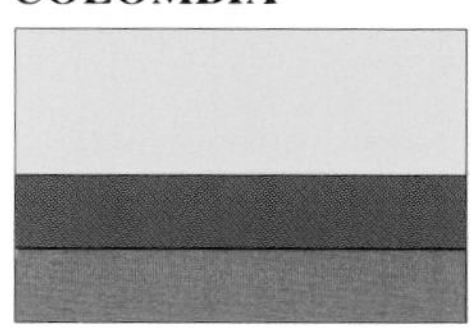

Area: 1 138 907 sq km (439 732 sq miles)
Population: 33 000 000
Capital: Bogota
Language: Spanish
Currency: Colombian Peso

ECUADOR
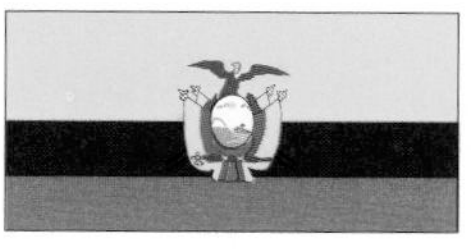

Area: 455 502 sq km (175 869 sq miles)
Population: 10 600 000
Capital: Quito
Language: Spanish
Currency: Sucre

GUYANA
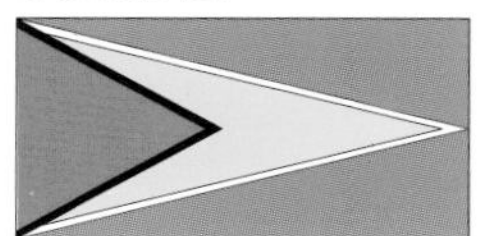

Area: 214 969 sq km (83 000 sq miles)
Population: 800 000
Capital: Georgetown
Language: English
Currency: Guyanese Dollar

PERU
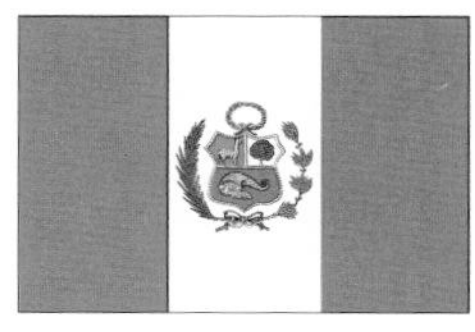

Area: 1 285 215 sq km (496 222 sq miles)
Population: 21 600 000
Capital: Lima
Languages: Spanish, Aymara, Quechua
Currency: Sol

VENEZUELA
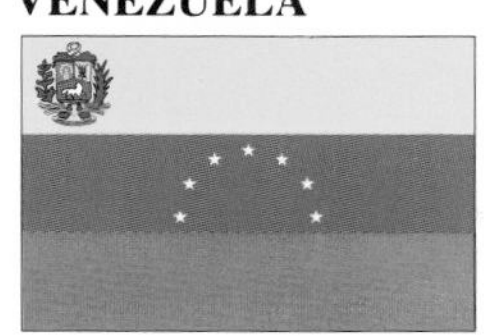

Area: 912 047 sq km (352 141 sq miles)
Population: 19 700 000
Capital: Caracas
Language: Spanish
Currency: Bolivar

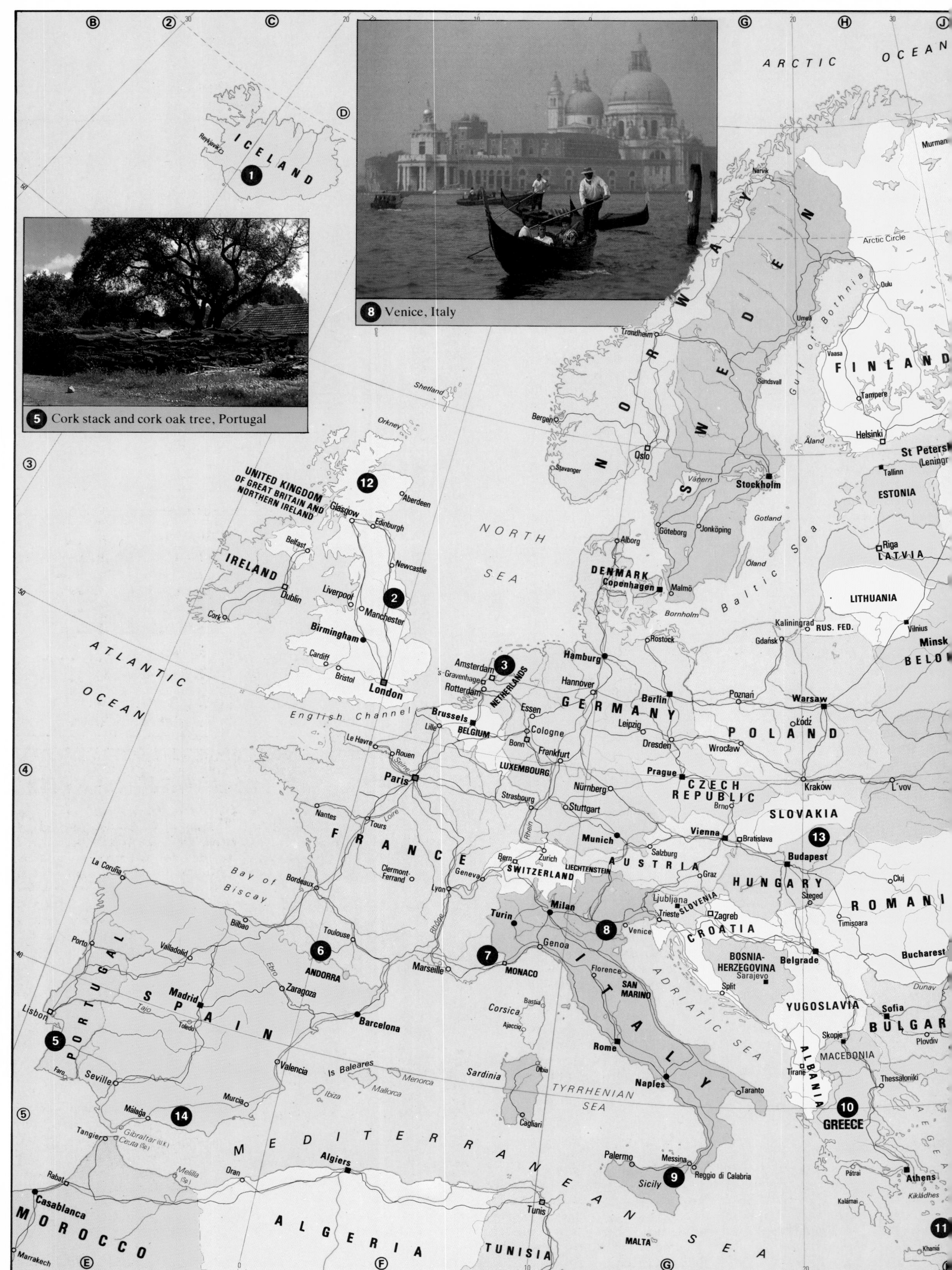

1:15M

ARCTIC   OCEAN

ICELAND
Reykjavik
① ①

8 Venice, Italy

NORWAY   SWEDEN

Narvik

Arctic Circle

Murmansk

FINLAND
Oulu
Vaasa
Umeå
Tampere
Helsinki
St Peters (Leningr)

Trondheim

Shetland

Bergen

Sundsvall

5 Cork stack and cork oak tree, Portugal

Orkney

③

Stavanger

Oslo

Göteborg
Jönköping

Gotland

ESTONIA
Tallinn

Stockholm

Vänern

Öland

Riga
LATVIA

UNITED KINGDOM
OF GREAT BRITAIN AND
NORTHERN IRELAND

12

Glasgow
Aberdeen
Edinburgh

DENMARK
Ålborg
Copenhagen
Malmö
Bornholm

LITHUANIA

NORTH
SEA

Belfast
Newcastle

IRELAND

Dublin
Liverpool
Manchester
2

Hamburg
Rostock

Kaliningrad
Gdańsk
RUS. FED.
Vilnius
Minsk
BELO

Cork

Birmingham

Cardiff
Bristol

Amsterdam
3
's-Gravenhage
Rotterdam
NETHERLANDS

Hannover

GERMANY
Berlin
Poznań
Warsaw
Łódź
POLAND

ATLANTIC
OCEAN

London

English Channel

Brussels
BELGIUM
Lille
Essen
Cologne
Bonn
Frankfurt

Leipzig
Dresden
Wrocław

Prague
CZECH
REPUBLIC
Kraków
L'vov

Le Havre
Rouen
Seine

LUXEMBOURG

④

Paris

Nantes
Tours
Loire

Strasbourg
Nürnberg

Brno

SLOVAKIA
Vienna
Bratislava
13

F R A N C E

Clermont-
Ferrand

Stuttgart

Munich
Salzburg

AUSTRIA
Graz

Budapest
H U N G A R Y

ROMANI

Cluj

Bay of
Biscay

Bordeaux

Lyon

Bern
Zurich
SWITZERLAND
Geneva
LIECHTENSTEIN

Ljubljana
Trieste
SLOVENIA
Zagreb
CROATIA

Szeged
Timişoara

La Coruña

Bilbao

Toulouse

6
ANDORRA

Marseille

Turin
Milan
Venice

BOSNIA-
HERZEGOVINA
Sarajevo

Bucharest

Belgrade

Dunav

Porto

Valladolid
Zaragoza

7
MONACO

Genoa

Florence

Split

PORTUGAL
Madrid
SPAIN
Tajo
Toledo

Barcelona

I T A L Y

SAN
MARINO

ADRIATIC

YUGOSLAVIA

Sofia

Lisbon
5

Corsica
Ajaccio

Rome

Bastia

Skopje
MACEDONIA
BULGAR
Plovdiv

Faro
Seville

Valencia
Is Baleares
Menorca

Sardinia

Olbia

Naples

Tirane

Thessaloniki

Murcia

Mallorca

Ibiza

SEA

Taranto

ALBANIA
10
GREECE

Málaga
14

Cagliari

TYRRHENIAN
SEA

Tangier
Gibraltar (U.K.)
Ceuta (Sp.)

Palermo
Messina
Reggio di Calabria

Pátrai

Athens

Rabat
Melilla
(Sp.)
Oran

Algiers

M E D I T E R R A N E A N   S E A

Sicily
9

Kalámai

Kikládhes

Casablanca

MOROCCO

Marrakech

A L G E R I A

Tunis

TUNISIA

MALTA

Khaniá

11

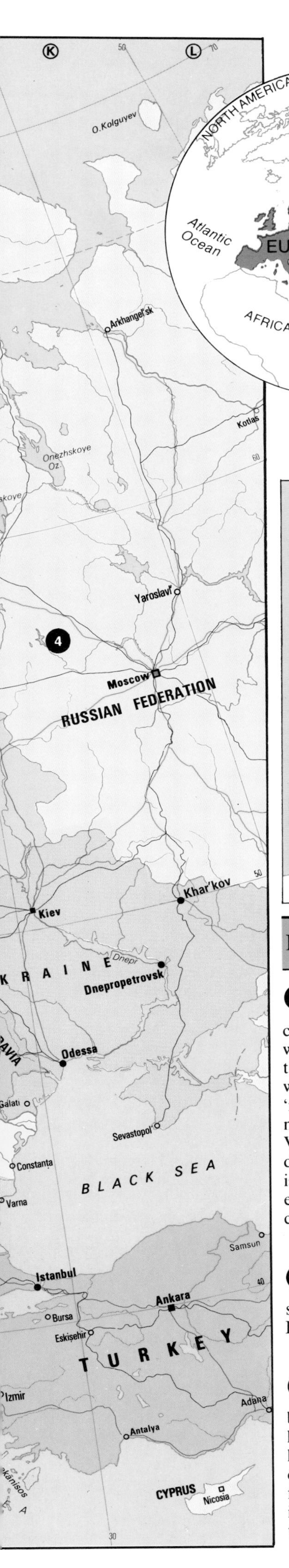

POPULATION

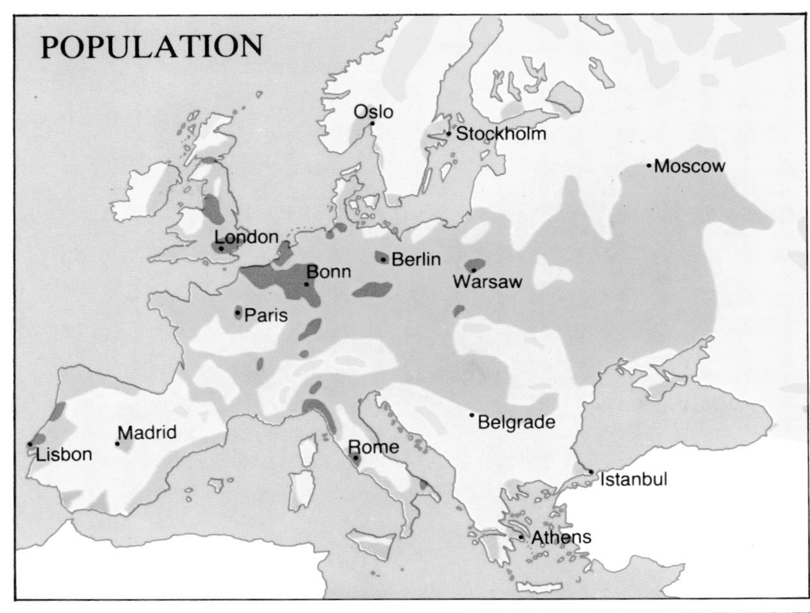

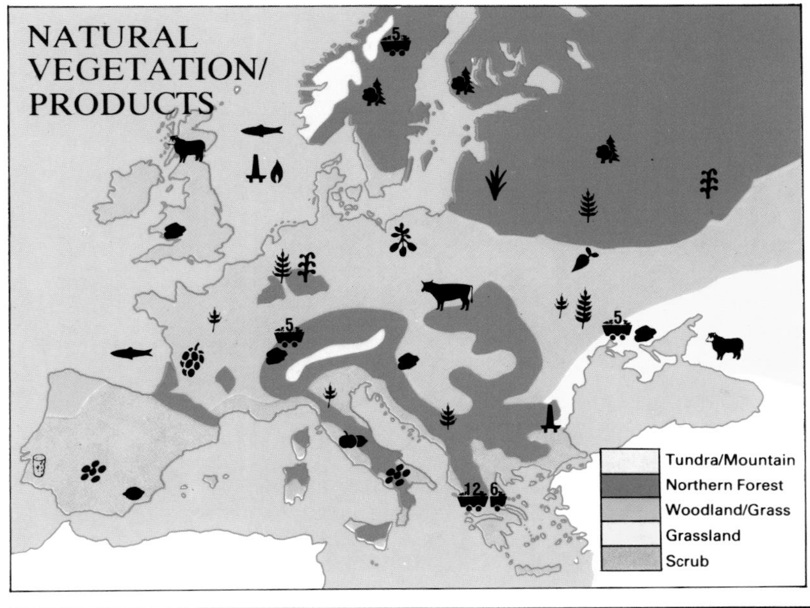

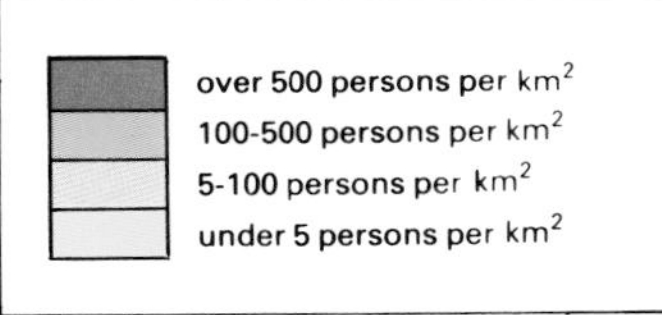

over 500 persons per km²
100-500 persons per km²
5-100 persons per km²
under 5 persons per km²

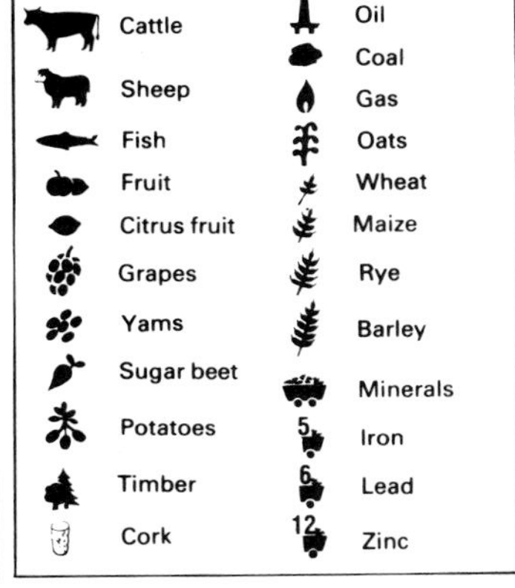

NATURAL VEGETATION/PRODUCTS

Tundra/Mountain
Northern Forest
Woodland/Grass
Grassland
Scrub

Cattle	Oil
Sheep	Coal
Fish	Gas
Fruit	Oats
Citrus fruit	Wheat
Grapes	Maize
Yams	Rye
Sugar beet	Barley
Potatoes	Minerals
Timber	5 Iron
Cork	6 Lead
	12 Zinc

FACTS ABOUT EUROPE

1 In Iceland, ice and fire exist side by side. Many active volcanoes and geysers (hot springs which shoot a column of water into the air at intervals) can be seen, while glaciers (continually moving 'rivers' of ice) and ice sheets cover much of the land. One volcano – Vatnajokull – is particularly dangerous for an unusual reason: it is underneath a glacier and when it erupts, the ice melts very quickly, causing terrible floods.

2 The Humber Bridge, England, has one of the longest single spans of any bridge in the world. It stretches for 1410 m (4626 feet).

3 More than a third of the land area of the Netherlands has been reclaimed from the sea. These lands (the *polders*) are below sea level and the sea is kept out by dykes. Drainage ditches divide the fertile fields. The water from them is pumped into canals and rivers, then out to sea.

4 The longest river in Europe is the Volga, which runs for 3690 km (2292 miles) from the forests north west of Moscow all the way to the Caspian Sea.

5 Portugal is an important source of cork, which is actually the bark of a tree. The cork oak produces cork bark up to 15 cm (6 inches) thick and this is stripped off the trees every 10 to 15 years. Cork oaks grow throughout the western and central Mediterranean region.

6 The Pierre Saint Martin Cavern in the Pyrenees mountains, France, is the deepest cave system yet discovered in the world. It goes 1330 m (4364 feet) into the heart of the mountains.

7 The principality of Monaco is one of the most crowded countries in the world: 28 000 people live on 1.9 sq km (467 acres) of land! By contrast, most of Scandinavia has fewer than 40 people per square kilometre.

8 Venice, Italy, is built on no less than 118 islands. Instead of roads, there are canals, and boats are used for transport. Venice is sinking at a rate of 12 inches each century. Some of the reasons for this include water being extracted from wells, and the compression of the mud on the floor of the lagoon.

9 Mount Etna, Sicily, is the highest volcano in Europe (about 3323 m, 10 902 ft) and is still very active. Despite this, many people live on its lower slopes. This is because the soil there is very fertile and grows good produce.

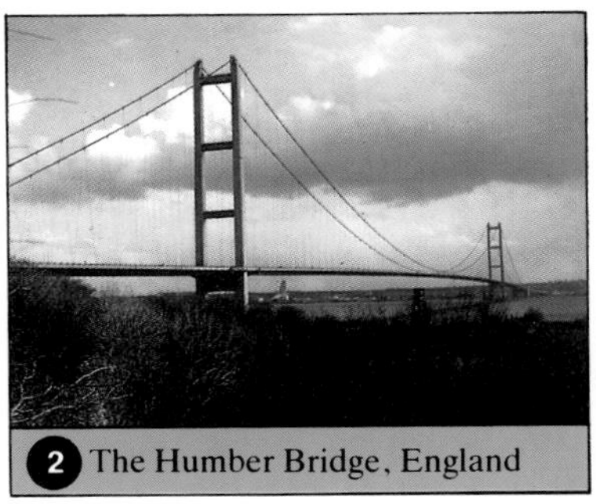

2 The Humber Bridge, England

ALBANIA

Area: 2 732 sq km
(1 055 sq miles)
Population: 3 200 000
Capital: Tirana
Languages: Albanian
(Tosk and Gheg)
Currency: Lek

BELGIUM

Area: 30 512 sq km
(11 781 sq miles)
Population: 9 900 000
Capital: Brussels
Languages: Flemish, French
Currency: Belgian Franc

DENMARK

Area: 43 030 sq km
(16 614 sq miles)
Population: 5 100 000
Capital: Copenhagen
Language: Danish
Currency: Krone

FRANCE

Area: 551 000 sq km
(212 741 sq miles)
Population: 56 100 000
Capital: Paris
Language: French
Currency: Franc

HUNGARY

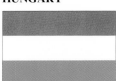

Area: 93 030 sq km
(35 919 sq miles)
Population: 10 600 000
Capital: Budapest
Language: Magyar
Currency: Forint

ANDORRA

Area: 453 sq km
(175 sq miles)
Population: 47 000
Capital: Andorra-la-Vella
Language: Catalan
Currency: French Franc
and Spanish Peseta

BULGARIA

Area: 110 911 sq km
(42 822 sq miles)
Population: 9 000 000
Capital: Sofia
Language: Bulgarian
Currency: Lev

ESTONIA

Area: 45 100 sq km
(17 413 sq miles)
Population: 1 600 000
Capital: Tallinn
Language: Estonian
Currency: Ruble, Kroon
proposed

GERMANY

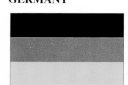

Area: 357 868 sq km
(138 173 sq miles)
Population: 79 000 000
Capital: Berlin, Bonn
Language: German
Currency: Deutschmark

ICELAND

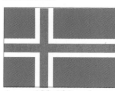

Area: 102 828 sq km
(41 131 sq miles)
Population: 250 000
Capital: Reykjavík
Language: Icelandic
Currency: Króna

AUSTRIA

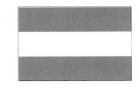

Area: 83 848 sq km
(32 374 sq miles)
Population: 7 600 000
Capital: Vienna
Language: German
Currency: Schilling

CZECH REPUBLIC

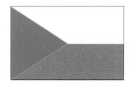

Area: 78 864 sq km
(30 449 sq miles)
Population: 10 300 000
Capital: Prague
Languages: Czech
Currency: Koruna

FINLAND

Area: 337 032 sq km
(130 128 sq miles)
Population: 5 000 000
Capital: Helsinki
Languages: Finnish, Swedish
Currency: Mark

GREECE

Area: 131 955 sq km
(50 948 sq miles)
Population: 10 000 000
Capital: Athens
Language: Greek
Currency: Drachma

IRELAND

Area: 70 282 sq km
(27 136 sq miles)
Population: 3 700 000
Capital: Dublin
Languages: Irish (Gaelic),
English
Currency: Irish Pound
(Punt)

10 Monasteries on rock pillars, Greece

10 Near Kalabaka, Greece, are a group of monasteries built for monks with no fear of heights! They are perched on top of pillars of rock, called meteora, 300 m (1 000 ft) high. The only way up was by ladders or baskets slung on the end of ropes. Now stairways have been constructed so that tourists can visit the buildings.

11 The island of Santorini (Thira) in Greece is the site of the world's largest natural disaster. About 1500 BC this volcanic island erupted leaving a *caldera* (hollow basin shape where the top of the volcano had been) about 13 km (8 miles) across. Many people believe that the destruction of this island is the origin of the story of Atlantis. The people of Atlantis are mentioned by the Greek writer Plato. Crime and corruption spread throughout their island as they became wealthier, until finally the Athenians conquered them. Later the island disappeared into the sea in a single day and night.

7 Monte Carlo, Monaco

12 Loch Ness, in the Highlands of Scotland, is one of the most famous freshwater expanses in the world. Its length and depth are so great that it could accommodate the population of the earth three times over. Its greatest mystery is the world-famous Loch Ness Monster which was first recorded in the 6th century by the Abbot of Iona. 'Nessie', as the monster is affectionately known, has been sighted by many people but evidence of the monster's existence is inconclusive. If it does exist, the most popular theory is that the monster is one of a small colony of unknown creatures which have descended from marine animals trapped in the loch at the end of the last Ice Age 12,000 years ago.

12 Loch Ness, Scotland

13 The stalactite caves of Aggtelek in Hungary form one of the largest cave systems in Europe. They are 23km (14 miles) long and extend over the border into Slovakia. The stalactites and stalagmites in the cave make a spectacular impact. Stalagmites on the floor of the Aggtelek caves bear a clear resemblance to the human form. Others resemble animals, temples, waterfalls, a 'Great Organ' and even a 'Butcher's Shop'.

14 The spectacularly beautiful Alhambra in Spain is situated on a hill overlooking Granada. From the outside, the fortress walls look plain but they belie the complex and colourful interior. Visitors find the intricate stonework, the sumptuous halls and the attractive gardens with their many fountains quite breathtaking. The Palace of the Alhambra was built as a home for the Moorish rulers in the 14th century and is a well-preserved example of the very best of Moorish art.

14 The Alhambra, Spain

ITALY
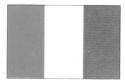
Area: 301 245 sq km (116 311 sq miles)
Population: 57 100 000
Capital: Rome
Language: Italian
Currency: Lira

LITHUANIA

Area: 65 200 sq km (25 170 sq miles)
Population: 3 700 000
Capital: Vilnius
Language: Lithuanian
Currency: Ruble, Litas proposed

NORWAY
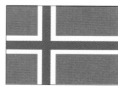
Area: 324 218 sq km (125 180 sq miles)
Population: 4 200 000
Capital: Oslo
Language: Norwegian
Currency: Krone

ROMANIA

Area: 237 500 sq km (91 699 sq miles)
Population: 23 300 000
Capital: Bucharest
Language: Romanian
Currency: Leu

SWITZERLAND

Area: 41 287 sq km (15 941 sq miles)
Population: 6 600 000
Capital: Bern
Languages: German, French, Italian, Romansch
Currency: Franc

LATVIA
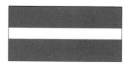
Area: 63 700 sq km (24 595 sq miles)
Population: 2 700 000
Capital: Riga
Language: Latvian
Currency: Ruble, Lat proposed

LUXEMBOURG

Area: 2 587 sq km (999 sq miles)
Population: 400 000
Capital: Luxembourg
Languages: Letzeburgish, French, German
Currency: Franc

POLAND
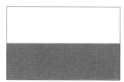
Area: 312 683 sq km (120 727 sq miles)
Population: 38 400 000
Capital: Warsaw
Language: Polish
Currency: Zloty

SPAIN

Area: 504 745 sq km (194 882 sq miles)
Population: 39 200 000
Capital: Madrid
Language: Spanish
Currency: Peseta

UNITED KINGDOM

Area: 244 104 sq km (94 249 sq miles)
Population: 57 200 000
Capital: London
Language: English
Currency: Pound Sterling

LIECHTENSTEIN

Area: 161 sq km (62 sq miles)
Population: 28 000
Capital: Vaduz
Language: German
Currency: Swiss Franc

NETHERLANDS

Area: 33 940 sq km (13 104 sq miles)
Population: 15 000 000
Capital: Amsterdam & The Hague
Language: Dutch
Currency: Guilder

PORTUGAL

Area: 91 671 sq km (35 394 sq miles)
Population: 10 300 000
Capital: Lisbon
Language: Portuguese
Currency: Escudo

SWEDEN

Area: 449 791 sq km (173 664 sq miles)
Population: 8 400 000
Capital: Stockholm
Language: Swedish
Currency: Krona

YUGOSLAVIA

Area: 91 285 sq km (35 245 sq miles)
Population: 10 600 000
Capital: Belgrade
Languages: Serbo-Croatian
Currency: Dinar

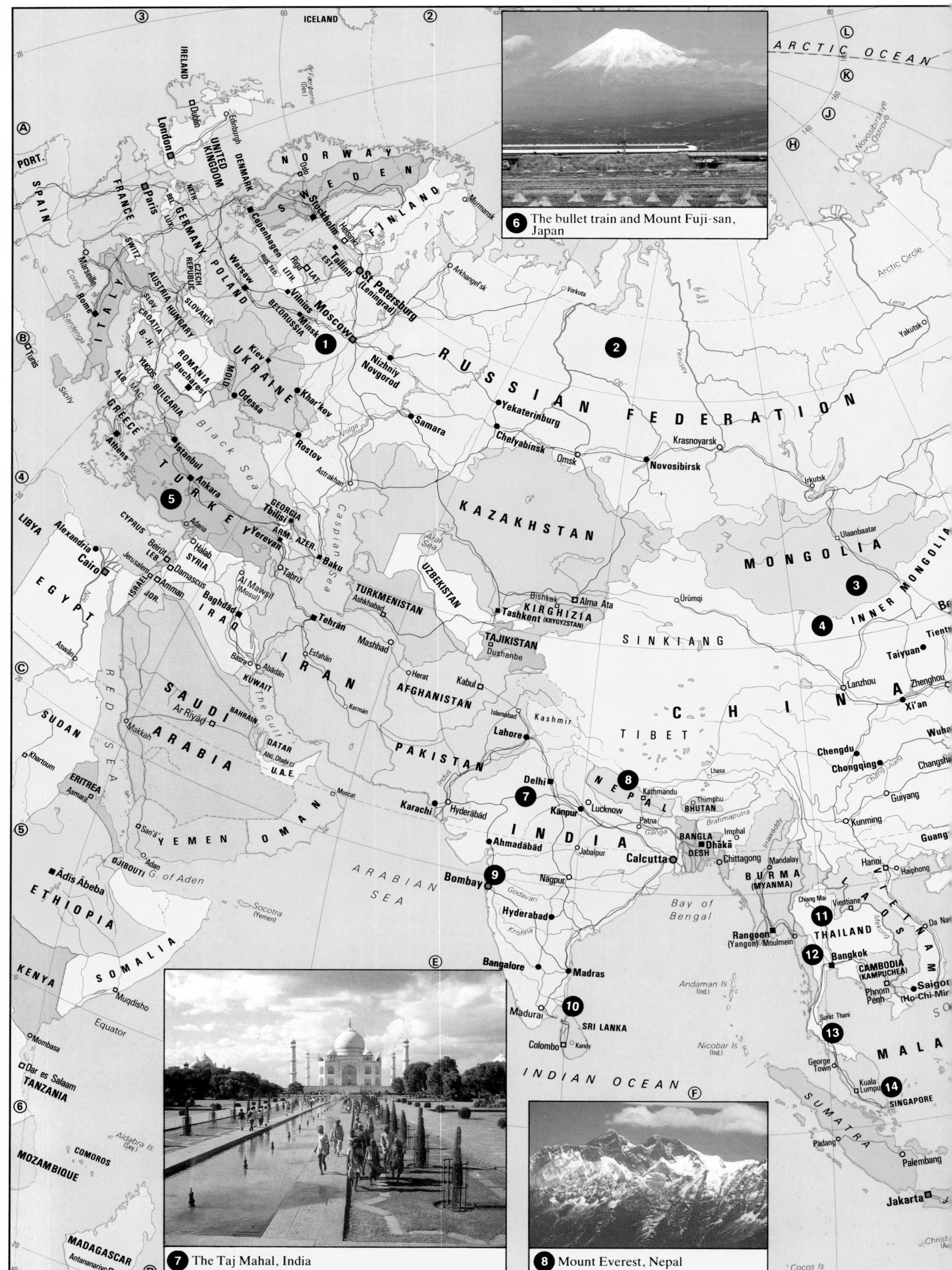

400   800   1200   1600 km

400   800 mls

6 The bullet train and Mount Fuji-san, Japan

7 The Taj Mahal, India

8 Mount Everest, Nepal

ARCTIC OCEAN

Arctic Circle

PORT.

SPAIN

IRELAND

UNITED KINGDOM

London

Dublin

Edinburgh

FRANCE

Paris

Marseille

ITALY

Rome

Corse (Fr.)

Sardegna

Tunis

GREECE

Athens

LIBYA

Alexandria

Cairo

EGYPT

Aswân

SUDAN

Khartoum

ERITREA

Asmara

Âdis Âbeba

ETHIOPIA

DJIBOUTI

Adan

G. of Aden

Muqdisho

SOMALIA

KENYA

Mombasa

Equator

TANZANIA

Dar es Salaam

MOZAMBIQUE

COMOROS

Aldabra Is (Sey.)

MADAGASCAR

Antananarivo

NORWAY

Oslo

DENMARK

Copenhagen

SWEDEN

Stockholm

FINLAND

Helsinki

Tallinn

Riga

Vilnius

Minsk

BELORUSSIA

Moscow

St Petersburg (Leningrad)

Murmansk

Arkhangel'sk

Vorkuta

RUSSIAN FEDERATION

Nizhniy Novgorod

Yekaterinburg

Chelyabinsk

Omsk

Novosibirsk

Krasnoyarsk

Irkutsk

Yakutsk

Lena

Yenisey

Ob

KAZAKHSTAN

MONGOLIA

Ulaanbaatar

INNER MONGOLIA

Ürümqi

SINKIANG

CHINA

TIBET

Lhasa

Lanzhou

Chengdu

Chongqing

Xi'an

Zhengzhou

Taiyuan

Tients

Wuha

Changsha

Guiyang

Kunming

Guang

NEPAL

Kathmandu

BHUTAN

Thimphu

BANGLA-DESH

Dhākā

Chittagong

Imphal

Mandalay

BURMA (MYANMA)

Chiang Mai

Rangoon (Yangon)

Moulmein

THAILAND

Bangkok

CAMBODIA (KAMPUCHEA)

Phnom Penh

Saigon (Ho-Chi-Min

LAOS

Vientiane

Hanoi

Haiphong

Da Na

VIETNAM

Surat Thani

George Town

Kuala Lumpur

SINGAPORE

MALA

SUMATRA

Padang

Palembang

Jakarta

INDIAN OCEAN

SRI LANKA

Colombo

Kandy

Madurai

Madras

Bangalore

Hyderabad

Bombay

Ahmadābād

Nāgpur

Jabalpur

Calcutta

Patna

Ganga

INDIA

Delhi

Kānpur

Lucknow

Lahore

Islamabad

Kashmir

PAKISTAN

Karachi

Hyderābād

Indus

AFGHANISTAN

Kabul

Herat

Kermān

IRAN

Tehrān

Mashhad

Esfahān

Abādān

Basra

IRAQ

Baghdād

Al Mawsil (Mosul)

KUWAIT

SAUDI ARABIA

Ar Riyād

Makkah

BAHRAIN

QATAR

Abū Dhabi

U.A.E.

The Gulf

Muscat

OMAN

YEMEN

San'a'

Socotra (Yemen)

ARABIAN SEA

RED SEA

TURKMENISTAN

Ashkhabad

UZBEKISTAN

TAJIKISTAN

Dushanbe

KIRGHIZIA (KRYGYZSTAN)

Tashkent

Bishkek

Alma Ata

Aral Sea

Caspian Sea

Astrakhan

Baku

AZER.

Tabriz

Yerevan

ARM.

Tbilisi

GEORGIA

Ankara

TURKEY

Istanbul

Adana

CYPRUS

Halab

SYRIA

Damascus

Beirut

LEB.

Jerusalem

ISRAEL

Amman

JOR.

Black Sea

Kiev

UKRAINE

Khar'kov

Odessa

Rostov

Samara

Volga

Bucharest

ROMANIA

MOL.

BULGARIA

YUGOS.

Alb.

MAC.

B-H.

CROATIA

SLOV.

HUNGARY

AUSTRIA

SWITZ.

GERMANY

Warsaw

POLAND

CZECH REPUBLIC

SLOVAKIA

NETH.

BEL.

LUX.

ICELAND

Færøerne (Tórs.)

Andaman Is (Ind.)

Nicobar Is (Ind.)

Bay of Bengal

Cocos Is (Aust.)

Chang Jiang

Irrawaddy

Mekong

Brahmaputra

Godavari

Krishna

XIV

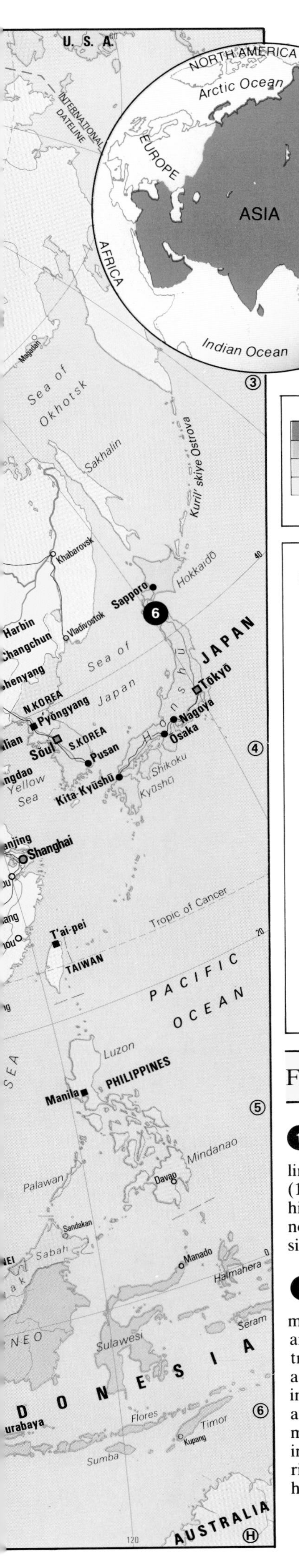

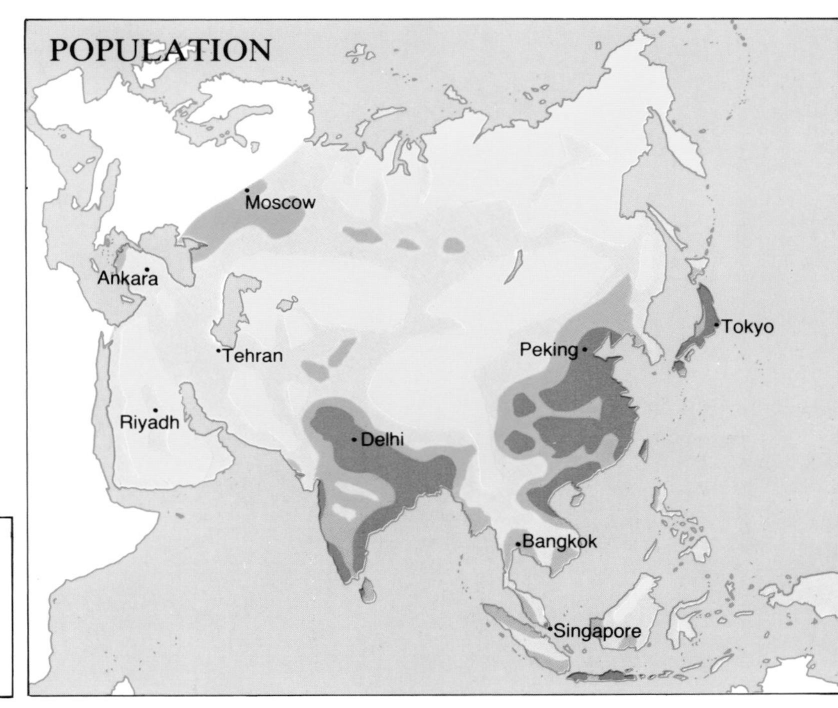

POPULATION

▓	over 500 persons per km²
▒	100-500 persons per km²
░	5-100 persons per km²
□	under 5 persons per km²

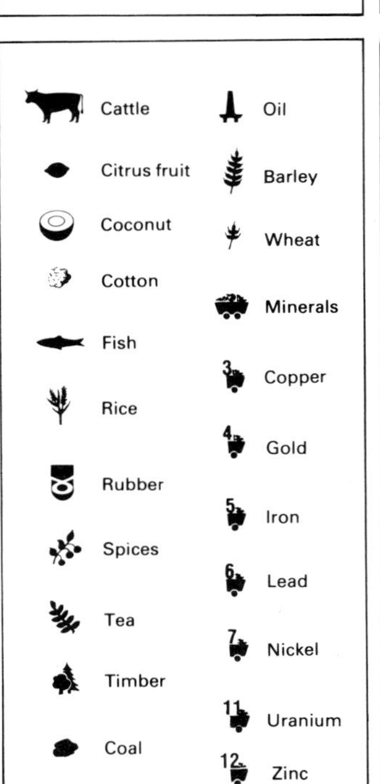

🐄	Cattle	⛽	Oil
🍋	Citrus fruit	🌿	Barley
⊚	Coconut	🌾	Wheat
❀	Cotton	⛏	Minerals
🐟	Fish	3	Copper
🌱	Rice	4	Gold
♣	Rubber	5	Iron
✴	Spices	6	Lead
🌿	Tea	7	Nickel
🌲	Timber	11	Uranium
◆	Coal	12	Zinc

NATURAL VEGETATION/PRODUCTS

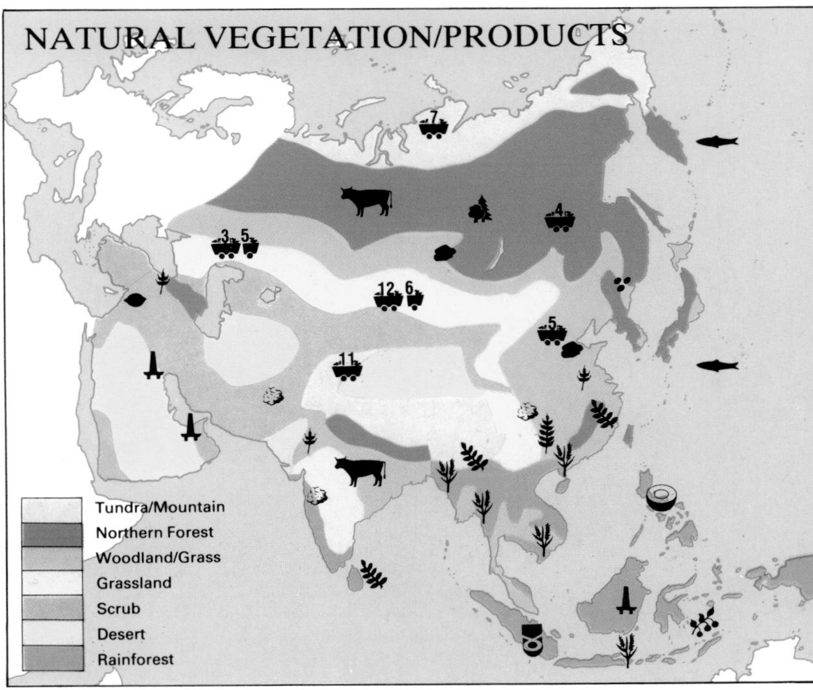

	Tundra/Mountain
	Northern Forest
	Woodland/Grass
	Grassland
	Scrub
	Desert
	Rainforest

FACTS ABOUT ASIA

❶ The world's heaviest bell is the *Czar Bell* in Moscow's Kremlin. It weighs a massive 196 tonnes (193 tons) and is 5.87 m (19 ft 3 in) high. The bell was cast in 1735. It is now cracked, and hasn't been rung since 1836.

❷ In Siberia, there is a huge forest called the *taiga*, which makes up a quarter of the total area of forest in the world. The trees are mostly coniferous - pine and larch. Few people used to live in the taiga, as it is a very cold area, but because it is rich in minerals more people are moving into the forest. They live in industrial towns being built deep in its heart, to exploit the minerals.

❸ The huge Gobi Desert covers much of Mongolia. The Gobi is a cold, barren region of rocky plains and hills. Water is very scarce and only a few nomads live here. They exist mainly by cattle raising and live in an unusual tent called a *yurt*, which is shaped like an upside-down bowl.

❹ The Great Wall of China stretches for 3460 km (2150 miles), making it the longest in the world. It was built for defence in the 3rd century BC and kept in good repair until 400 years ago. Although part of the wall was blown up to make a dam in 1979, the many remaining sections of the wall are still impressive.

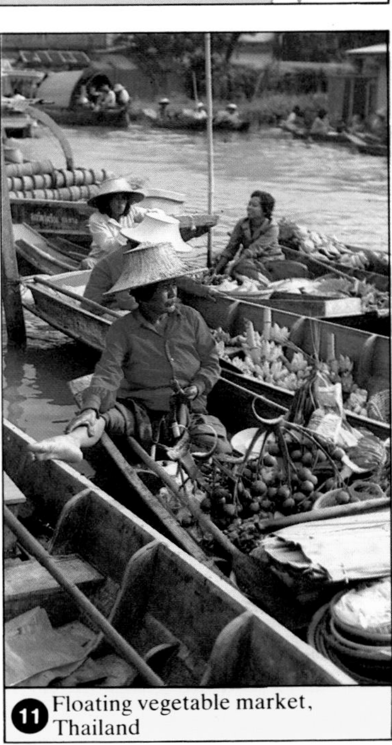

❶❶ Floating vegetable market, Thailand

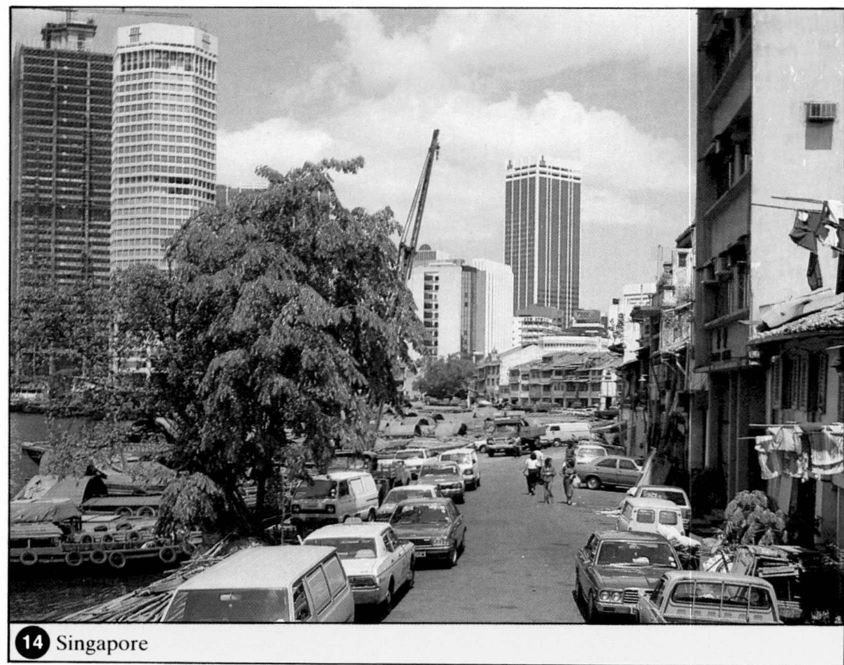

14 Singapore

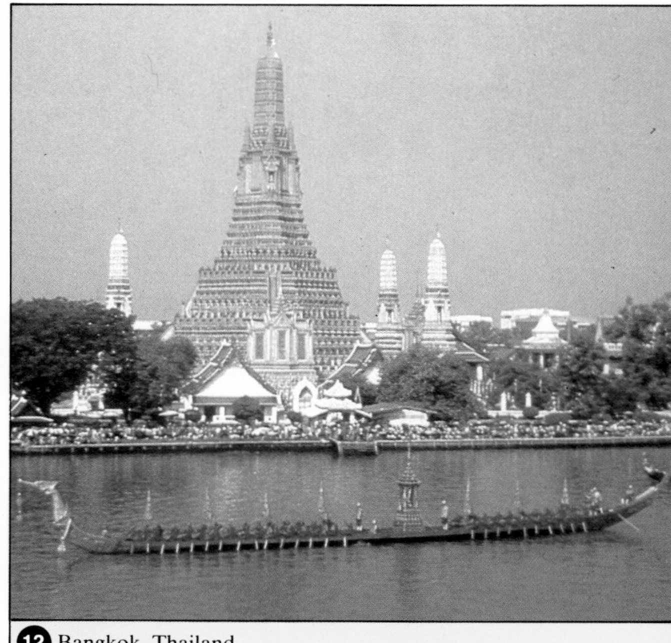

12 Bangkok, Thailand

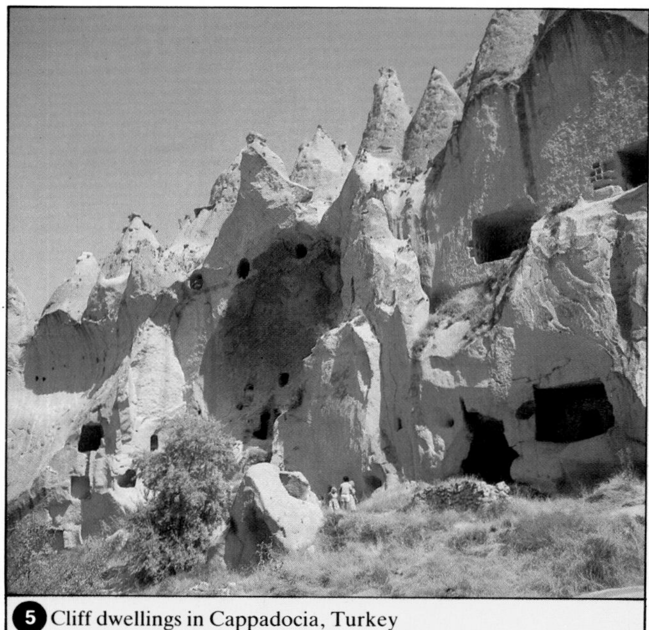

5 Cliff dwellings in Cappadocia, Turkey

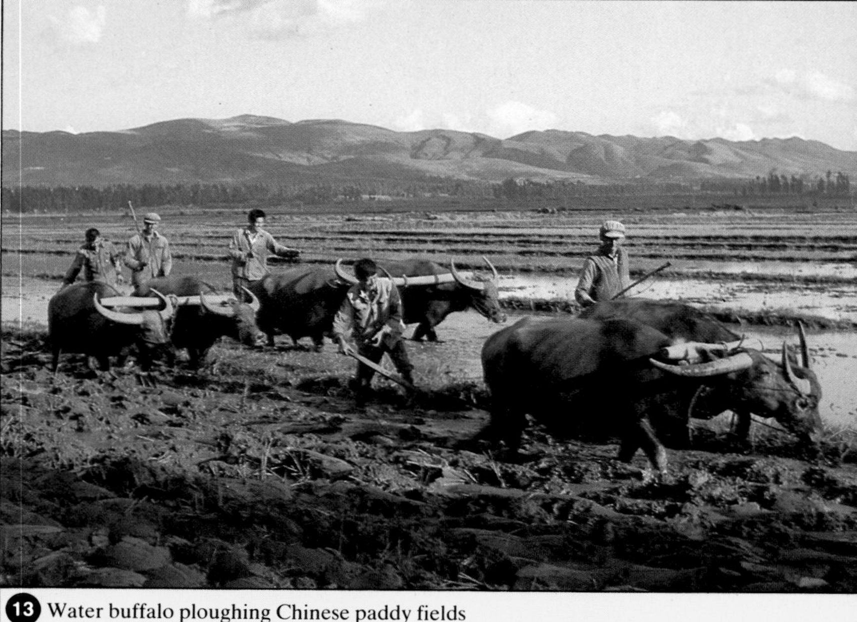

13 Water buffalo ploughing Chinese paddy fields

FACTS ABOUT ASIA

5 In central Turkey, near Urgup in the region called Cappadocia, an extraordinary landscape can be seen. There was once a plateau here, made up of layers of rock, some hard and some much softer. Over thousands of years the softer rocks have been eroded by the weather, by streams and even by men digging out caves to live in. The rocks are now shaped into strange cones, towers and 'mushrooms', with 'hats' of harder rock balancing on top. There are also complete 'villages' of caves connected to each other by passageways cut through the rock. Each cave has 'cupboards' and 'shelves' cut into its walls. Here many centuries ago people hid from religious persecution. Over 300 churches which they dug out of the rock have been found. Some people still live in caves in this region, today.

6 The Seikan Tunnel in Japan is the longest tunnel in the world. It is an underwater tunnel, stretching for 54 km (34 miles). It was built for Japan's famous *bullet train*, the first passenger train to travel at 200 kph.

7 There should have been two Taj Mahals in India – a black one and a white one. In 1648, Emperor Shah Jahan completed the present Taj Mahal. It was a tomb for his wife, and made of white marble. He then began building a tomb of black marble for himself. Before work had got very far, he was overthrown.

8 At 8848 m (29 028 ft) the peak of Mt Everest in the Himalayas is the Earth's highest point. In May 1953, New Zealander Sir Edmund Hillary was the first man to climb Everest. Twenty two years later, in 1975, the first woman to reach the summit was Junko Tabei of Japan.

9 In India cows are sacred animals and are allowed to wander freely, even in the centre of big cities! Drivers are used to going round cows lying peacefully in the middle of the road.

10 Banyan trees can be seen in India and Sri Lanka. They are very unusual to look at, because what seems to be several trees growing close together, is actually just one tree! Aerial roots grow down from the banyan's branches and root in the ground. They become extra 'trunks' and support a huge canopy of leaves, which gives a lot of shade, very useful in such a hot climate.

11 Throughout Asia there are areas where many people live on boats – because there is not enough room for them to live in houses or land (or they cannot afford to) or because they just prefer to live on water. In these places, even the shops are on boats.

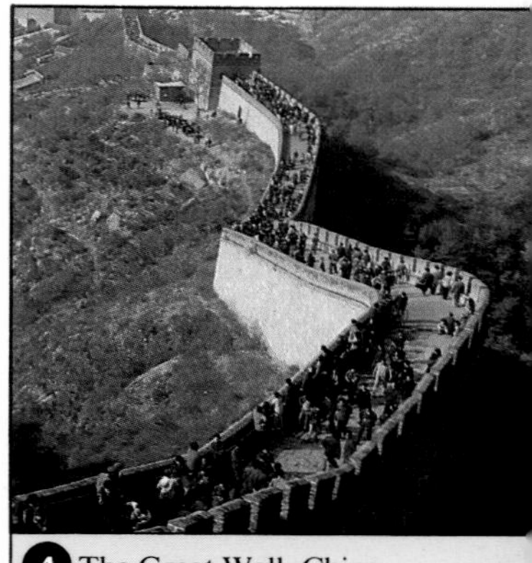

4 The Great Wall, China

10 Banyan tree, India

9 Street in India

2 Bangkok, Thailand, once had many canals, called *klongs*, instead of roads. (The city was called the 'Venice of the East' because the klongs reminded visitors of the canals in Venice, Italy.) They were used for transport and also helped to drain the land during the rainy season. After cars and lorries began to be used for transport, many of the klongs were filled in to make roads. Now Bangkok has problems with flooding when the monsoons come.

3 Paddy fields, the irrigated fields in which rice is grown, get their name from *padi*, the Malayan word for rice. Rice is grown throughout Asia in the fertile lowlands near the equator. Millions of people live in these areas, and rice is very important to them as it yields more food per acre than any other crop.

14 Over half the population of the world lives in Asia – that is 3 113 000 000 people. Some parts of Asia have many people living in a small area. One of the most densely populated countries is Singapore, which has an average of 4 420 people for each square kilometre of ground.

AFGHANISTAN

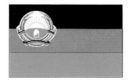

Area: 674 500 sq km (260 424 sq miles)
Population: 16 600 000
Capital: Kabul
Languages: Pashtu, Dari, Uzbek
Currency: Afghani

INDONESIA

Area: 1 919 263 sq km (741 027 miles)
Population: 185 000 000
Capital: Jakarta
Language: Bahasa (Indonesian)
Currency: Rupiah

ISRAEL

Area: 20 770 sq km (8019 sq miles)
Population: 4 600 000
Capital: Jerusalem
Languages: Hebrew, Arabic
Currency: Shekel

PAKISTAN

Area: 803 941 sq km (310 402 sq miles)
Population: 122 600 000
Capital: Islamabad
Language: Urdu
Currency: Pakistan Rupee

SINGAPORE

Area: 616 sq km (238 sq miles)
Population: 2 700 000
Capital: Singapore
Languages: Chinese, Malay, Tamil, English
Currency: Singapore Dollar

CHINA

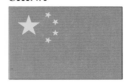

Area: 9 561 000 sq km (3 691 502 sq miles)
Population: 1 118 800 000
Capital: Beijing
Language: Chinese (Mandarin)
Currency: Yuan

IRAN

Area: 1 648 184 sq km (636 364 sq miles)
Population: 54 600 000
Capital: Tehran
Language: Persian (Farsi)
Currency: Rial

JAPAN

Area: 371 000 sq km (143 243 sq miles)
Population: 123 500 000
Capital: Tokyo
Language: Japanese
Currency: Yen

PHILIPPINES

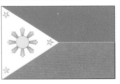

Area: 299 765 sq km (115 739 sq miles)
Population: 62 400 000
Capital: Manila
Language: Philipino
Currency: Philippine Peso

THAILAND

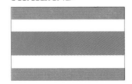

Area: 513 517 sq km (198 269 sq miles)
Population: 55 700 000
Capital: Bangkok
Languages: Thai, Chinese
Currency: Baht

INDIA

Area: 3 287 593 sq km (1 269 340 sq miles)
Population: 853 100 000
Capital: Delhi
Languages: Hindi, English
Currency: Indian Rupee

IRAQ

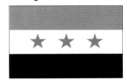

Area: 434 924 sq km (167 924 sq miles)
Population: 18 900 000
Capital: Baghdad
Language: Arabic
Currency: Iraqi Dinar

MALAYSIA

Area: 330 669 sq km (127 671 sq miles)
Population: 17 900 000
Capital: Kuala Lumpur
Language: Malay
Currency: Ringgit (Malaysian Dollar)

SAUDI ARABIA

Area: 2 400 930 sq km (927 000 sq miles)
Population: 14 100 000
Capital: Riyadh
Language: Arabic
Currency: Riyal

TURKEY

Area: 780 576 sq km (301 380 sq miles)
Population: 55 900 000
Capital: Ankara
Language: Turkish
Currency: Turkish Lira

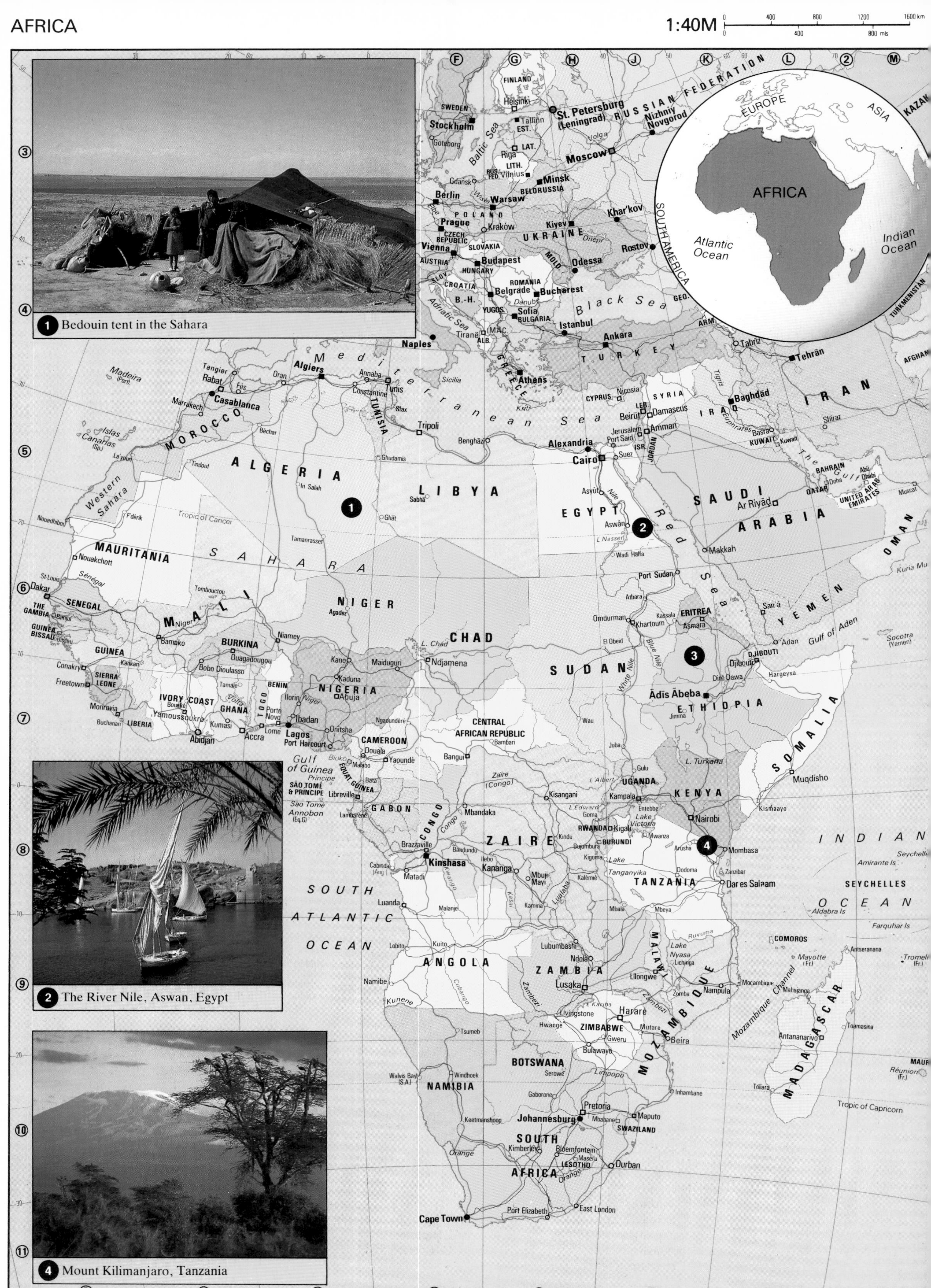

AFRICA

1:40M

1 Bedouin tent in the Sahara

2 The River Nile, Aswan, Egypt

4 Mount Kilimanjaro, Tanzania

EUROPE
ASIA
KAZAK

AFRICA

Atlantic
Ocean

Indian
Ocean

SOUTH AMERICA

FINLAND
Helsinki
SWEDEN
Stockholm
St. Petersburg (Leningrad)
Göteborg
Baltic Sea
EST.
Tallinn
RUSSIAN FEDERATION
Nizhniy Novgorod
Volga
LAT.
Riga
Moscow
LITH.
Vilnius
RUS. FED.
Berlin
Gdansk
Minsk
BELORUSSIA
Wisła
Warsaw
POLAND
Khar'kov
Prague
Kraków
CZECH REPUBLIC
Kiyev
UKRAINE
Dnepr
Vienna
SLOVAKIA
AUSTRIA
Budapest
HUNGARY
MOLD.
Rostov
Odessa
SLOV.
CROATIA
ROMANIA
Belgrade
Bucharest
GEO.
B.-H.
Danube
YUGOS.
Sofia
BULGARIA
Black Sea
Tirana
Naples
M.AC.
ALB.
Istanbul
Ankara
Tabriz
Tehrān
Athens
TURKEY
ARM.
AFGHAN.
Kríti
CYPRUS
Nicosia
SYRIA
LEB.
Beirut
Damascus
IRAQ
Baghdād
IRAN
Shīrāz
Jerusalem
Amman
Euphrates
Basra
Tigris
Port Said
ISR.
JORDAN
KUWAIT
Kuwait
Madeira (Port.)
Tangier
Algiers
Mediterranean Sea
Alexandria
Cairo
Suez
SAUDI
Ar Riyād
BAHRAIN
Abū
QATAR
Doha
Dhabi
The Gulf
Rabat
Fès
Oran
Annaba
Tunis
Sicilia
UNITED ARAB EMIRATES
Muscat
Marrakech
Casablanca
Constantine
TUNISIA
Tripoli
Benghāzi
Asyūt
EGYPT
Nile
ARABIA
OMAN
Kuria Mu
Islas Canarias (Sp.)
MOROCCO
Béchar
Ghudamis
Aswān
L Nasser
Makkah
La'youn
Tindout
ALGERIA
In Salah
LIBYA
Wadi Halfa
Red Sea
YEMEN
San'ā
Socotra (Yemen)
Western Sahara
F'dérik
Tropic of Cancer
Sabha
Ghāt
Port Sudan
Nouâdhibou
SAHARA
Tamanrasset
Atbara
Omdurman
Khartoum
Kassala
ERITREA
Asmara
Adan
Gulf of Aden
MAURITANIA
Nouakchott
El Obeid
Blue Nile
DJIBOUTI
Djibouti
Hargeysa
St Louis
Dakar
SENEGAL
Sénégal
Niger
NIGER
Agadez
L. Chad
CHAD
Ndjamena
SUDAN
White Nile
Dire Dawa
THE GAMBIA
Banjul
Bamako
MALI
Tombouctou
Kano
ETHIOPIA
Ādīs Ābeba
GUINEA BISSAU
Bissau
GUINEA
BURKINA
Ouagadougou
Niamey
Kaduna
Maiduguri
Wau
Jimma
SOMALIA
Conakry
Kankan
Bobo Dioulasso
BENIN
Ilorin
Niger
Abuja
Ngaoundéré
Juba
SIERRA LEONE
Freetown
Tamale
NIGERIA
Bambari
CENTRAL AFRICAN REPUBLIC
Gulu
UGANDA
L. Turkana
IVORY COAST
GHANA
TOGO
Ibadan
Onitsha
L Albert
Kampala
KENYA
Muqdisho
Monrovia
Yamoussoukro
Bouaké
Volta
Porto Novo
Lagos
Port Harcourt
Douala
Bangui
Zaire (Congo)
Kisangani
L Edward
Goma
Entebbe
Lake Victoria
Nairobi
Kismaayo
Buchanan
LIBERIA
Kumasi
Accra
Lome
CAMEROON
Yaoundé
Bata
Mbandaka
RWANDA
Kigali
Mwanza
INDIAN
Abidjan
Bioko
Malabo
EQUAT. GUINEA
Libreville
ZAIRE
Kindu
BURUNDI
Bujumbura
Arusha
Mombasa
Seychelle
São Tomé
Principe
SÃO TOMÉ & PRINCIPE
São Tomé
Annobon (Eq.G)
GABON
Lambaréné
CONGO
Congo
Bandundu
Kananga
Kigoma
Lake Tanganyika
Dodoma
Zanzibar
Amirante Is
SEYCHELLES
Aldabra Is
Brazzaville
Ilebo
Mbuji Mayi
Kalemie
TANZANIA
Dar es Salaam
Kinshasa
Cabinda (Ang)
Matadi
Kwango
Kasai
Kamina
Lake
Farquhar Is
SOUTH
Luanda
Malanje
Luatuba
Mbala
Mbeya
COMOROS
ATLANTIC
Lobito
Kuito
Lubumbashi
Ndola
Ruvuma
Lake Nyasa
Antseranana
Mayotte (Fr.)
Tromeli (Fr.)
OCEAN
Namibe
ANGOLA
Cubango
ZAMBIA
Zambezi
MALAWI
Lichinga
Nampula
Walvis Bay (S.A.)
Kunene
Lusaka
Lilongwe
MOZAMBIQUE
Mahajanga
MADAGASCAR
Réunion (Fr.)
L Kariba
Harare
Zumba
Mozambique Channel
Livingstone
ZIMBABWE
Gweru
Mutare
Beira
Antananarivo
MAUR.
Namibia
Hwange
Bulawayo
Toamasina
Tsumeb
NAMIBIA
Windhoek
BOTSWANA
Serowe
Limpopo
Toliara
Keetmanshoop
Inhambane
Tropic of Capricorn
Walvis Bay
Gaborone
Pretoria
Maputo
Johannesburg
Mbabane
SWAZILAND
Orange
SOUTH
Kimberley
Bloemfontein
Maseru
Durban
Cape Town
AFRICA
LESOTHO
Orange
Port Elizabeth
East London

POPULATION

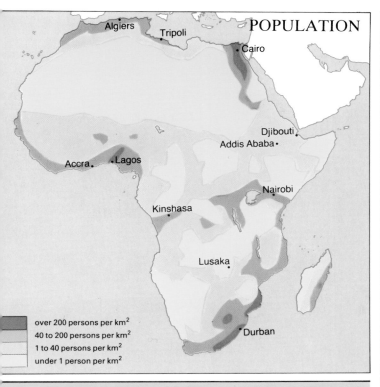

Algiers
Tripoli
Cairo
Djibouti
Addis Ababa
Accra
Lagos
Nairobi
Kinshasa
Lusaka
Durban

over 200 persons per km²
40 to 200 persons per km²
1 to 40 persons per km²
under 1 person per km²

NATURAL VEGETATION/ PRODUCTS

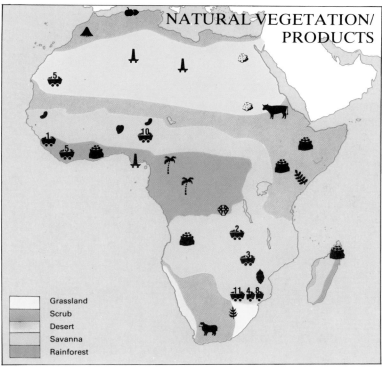

Grassland
Scrub
Desert
Savanna
Rainforest

🐂 Cattle	🌰 Peanuts	🌴 Phosphates	**4** Gold
🐑 Sheep	🌴 Palm oil	🌿 Maize	**5** Iron
🍫 Cocoa	🍃 Tea	Minerals	**8** Platinum
☕ Coffee	🍂 Tobacco	**1** Bauxite	**10** Tin
Cotton	💎 Diamonds	**2** Cobalt	**11** Uranium
🍎 Fruit	Oil	**3** Copper	

ACTS ABOUT AFRICA

The largest desert in the world is the Sahara, but only about % of it is sand. The rest is rocky aste. People live mainly near ses, where the land is watered by rings rising to the surface and ops can be grown. The desert is ry hot and dry, but there are a w plants and animals (like mels) specially adapted to these nditions.

The Nile is the longest river in the world and flows for 6650 m (4160 miles) through North frica to the Mediterranean Sea.

The Nile used to flood its banks each year, but now the High Dam at Aswan controls the floods. When the dam was built, the temples of Abu Simbel (3000 years old) were moved to a higher site to stop them being flooded.

3 Some parts of Africa have had no rain, or very little, for several years. Food crops have failed and many people have died from malnutrition and starvation. A further problem has been wars, which have driven many people from their homes and fields. Even if part of a country can grow food, it is difficult to move that food into areas where none can be grown. There are few lorries and, where people are at war, transporting food may be dangerous. Although western countries have sent food supplies, there is still not enough to feed the hundreds of thousands of people who are starving. Governments are trying to find ways of growing more food and distributing it more quickly.

4 Kilimanjaro (now renamed Uhuru, meaning 'freedom') is the highest mountain in Africa (5895 m; 19 340 feet) and its peaks are always covered in snow.

EGYPT

Area: 1 000 250 sq km (386 197 sq miles)
Population: 52 400 000
Capital: Cairo
Language: Arabic
Currency: Egyptian Pound

ETHIOPIA

Area: 1 104 318 sq km (426 377 sq miles)
Population: 46 626 000
Capital: Addis Ababa
Language: Amharic
Currency: Birr

KENYA

Area: 582 644 sq km (224 959 sq miles)
Population: 24 000 000
Capital: Nairobi
Languages: English, Swahili
Currency: Kenya Shilling

LIBYA

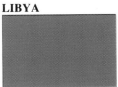

Area: 1 759 530 sq km (679 355 sq miles)
Population: 4 500 000
Capital: Tripoli
Language: Arabic
Currency: Libyan Dinar

NIGERIA

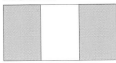

Area: 923 769 sq km (356 667 sq miles)
Population: 108 500 000
Capital: Lagos
Language: English
Currency: Naira

SOUTH AFRICA

Area: 1 221 038 sq km (471 443 sq miles)
Population: 35 300 000
Capital: Pretoria
Languages: Afrikaans, English
Currency: Rand

SUDAN

Area: 2 505 792 sq km (967 486 sq miles)
Population: 25 200 000
Capital: Khartoum
Language: Arabic
Currency: Sudanese Pound

ZAIRE

Area: 2 344 885 sq km (905 360 sq miles)
Population: 35 600 000
Capital: Kinshasa
Language: French
Currency: Zaire

1:60M

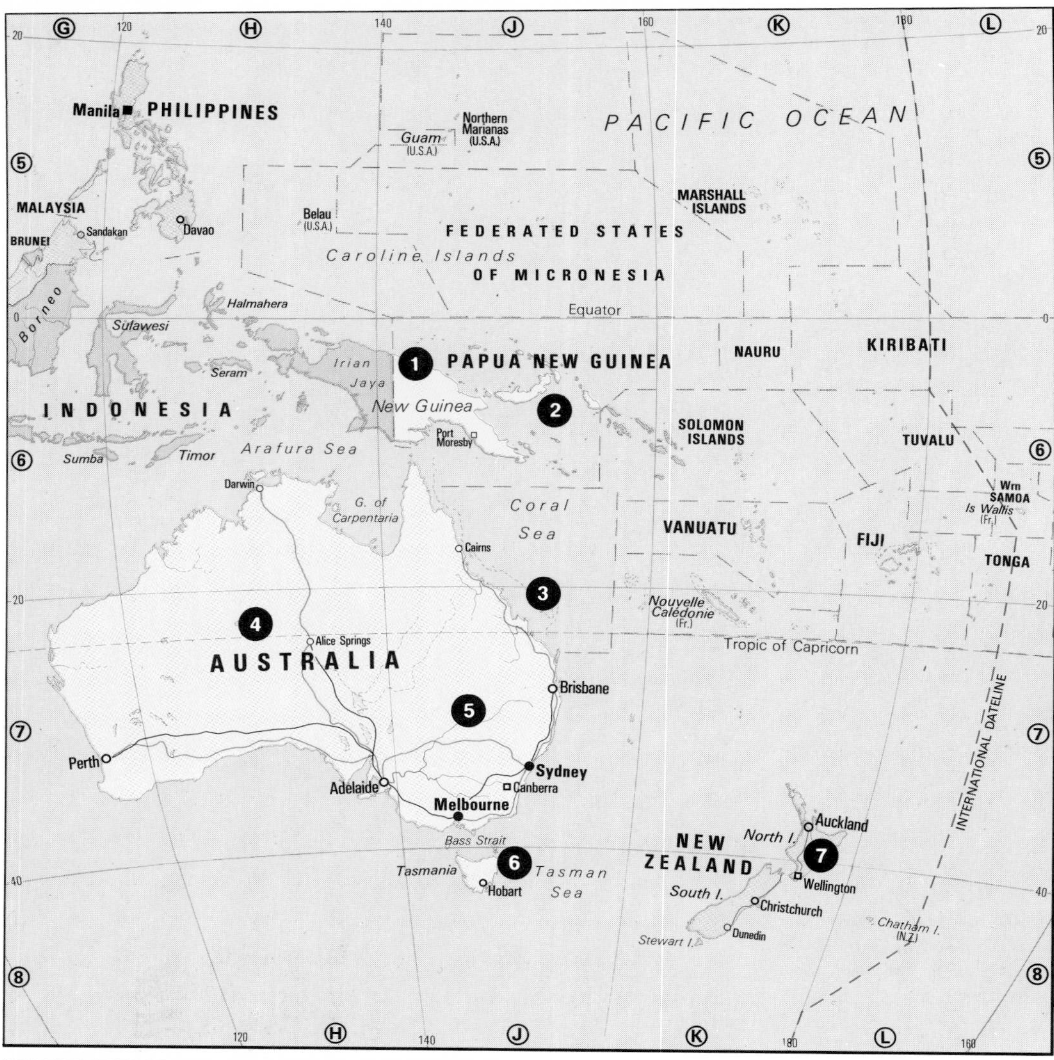

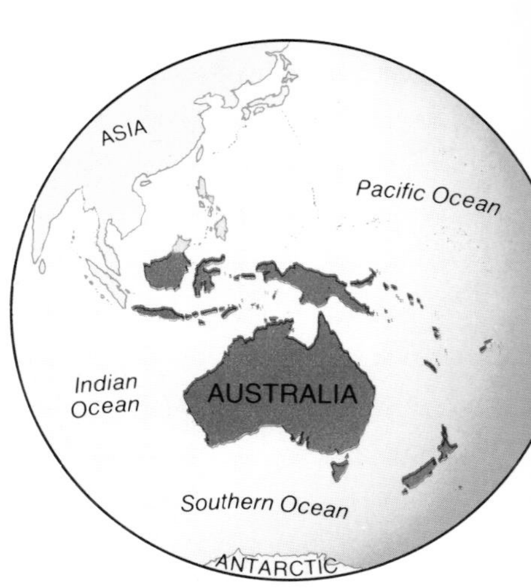

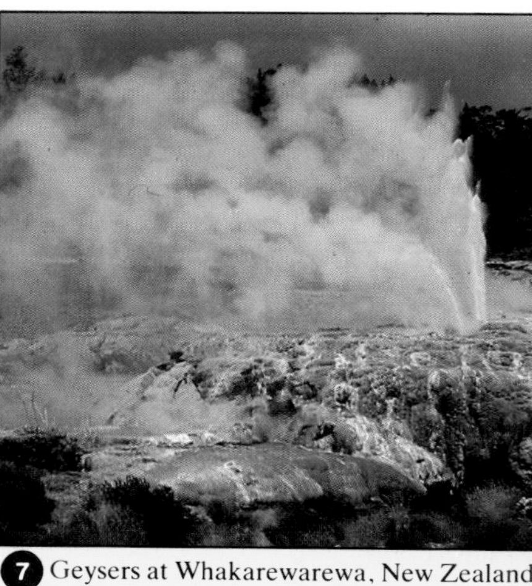

7 Geysers at Whakarewarewa, New Zealand

FACTS ABOUT AUSTRALASIA

1 Over 700 languages are spoken in Papua New Guinea. That is more than a quarter of all the languages spoken in the world. Papua New Guinea's mountains, thick forests and islands meant that different tribes did not mix, so they did not share a common language, but instead each developed its own. Today, Pidgin English and Police Motu have become the languages which the different tribes use to talk to each other.

2 No less than 38 different species of the beautiful Bird of Paradise are to be seen in Papua New Guinea. Another 5 species are found on neighbouring islands and in northern Australia. Their tail feathers are a traditional part of Papua New Guinea tribal costume, although the birds are now protected from hunting to a great extent.

3 Australia's Great Barrier Reef is formed from the shells of millions of tiny sea creatures. It is 2000 km (1250 miles) long and is the world's biggest coral reef. There are many thousands of coral islands or *atolls* in the Pacific region.

4 Ayers Rock is a huge sandstone rock formation which rears up abruptly from the desert in central Australia. The rock is special because it changes colour with the light. Australia's native *aborigine* people believe there is something magical about the rock.

5 Australia is the driest of all the continents in the world. Rainfall is also very unevenly distributed: even though the tropical north has about 2000 mm (79 inches) a year, the centr[al] deserts have less than 150 m[m] (6 inches). Irrigation is importa[nt] for agriculture, and rivers an[d] artesian wells are used as a sour[ce] of water. The Snowy Mountai[n] reservoir and irrigation scheme ha[s] brought water from the mountai[n] to irrigate farmland in the east [of] Australia.

6 A Tasmanian Devil is a litt[le] bear-like creature found onl[y] in Tasmania. It is just 60 cm (2 f[eet]) long, with a big bushy tail. It ha[s] very sharp teeth and eats othe[r]

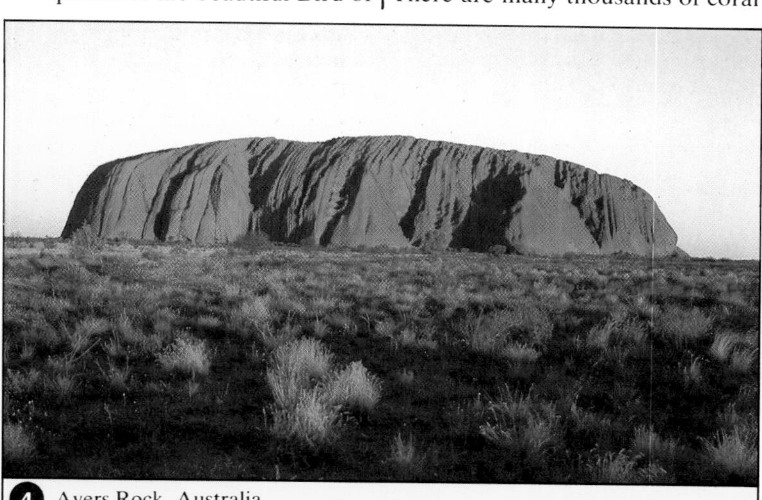

4 Ayers Rock, Australia

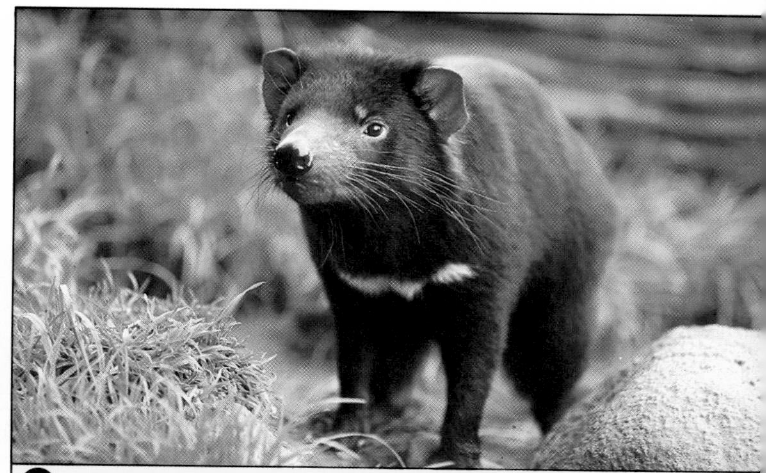

6 Tasmanian Devil

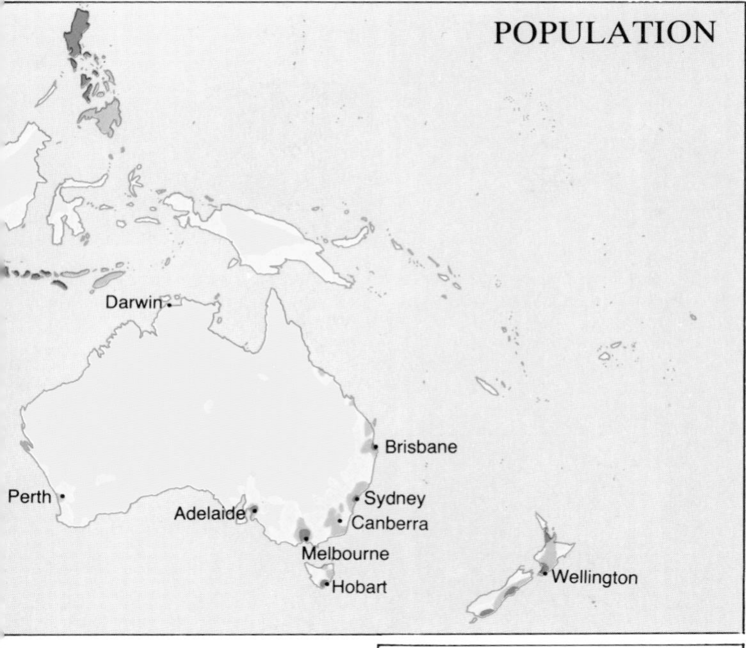

POPULATION

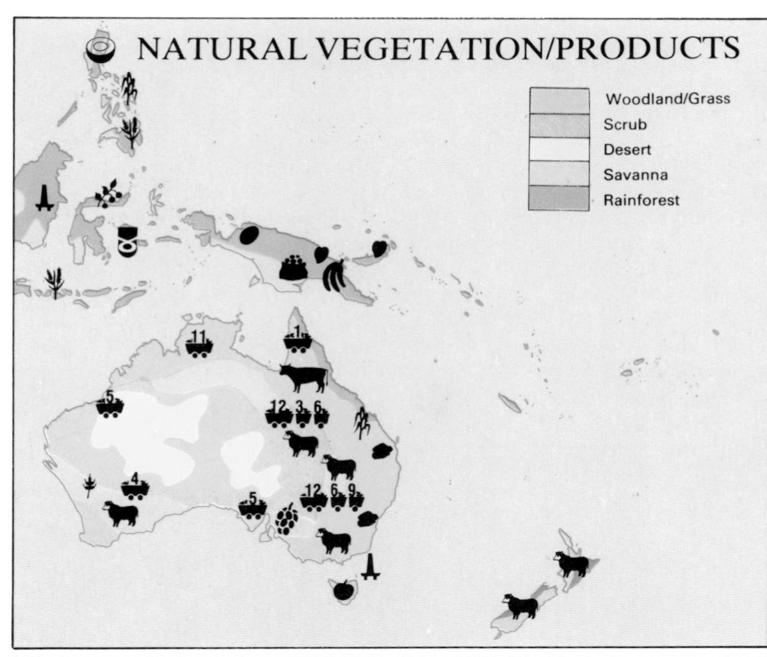

NATURAL VEGETATION/PRODUCTS

Woodland/Grass
Scrub
Desert
Savanna
Rainforest

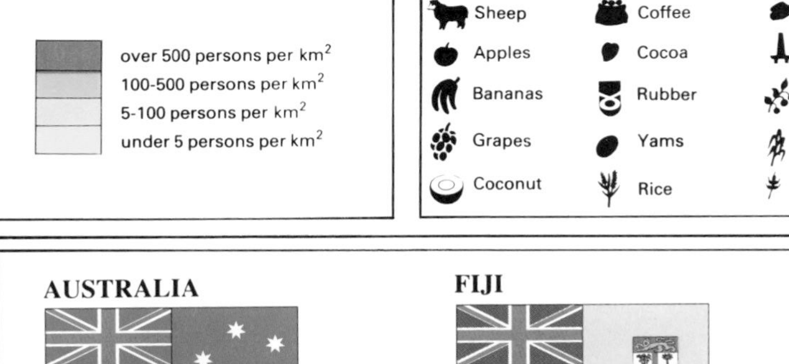

over 500 persons per km²
100-500 persons per km²
5-100 persons per km²
under 5 persons per km²

Sheep	Coffee	Coal	Minerals	6 Lead
Apples	Cocoa	Oil	1 Bauxite	9 Silver
Bananas	Rubber	Spices	3 Copper	11 Uranium
Grapes	Yams	Sugar cane	4 Gold	12 Zinc
Coconut	Rice	Wheat	5 Iron	

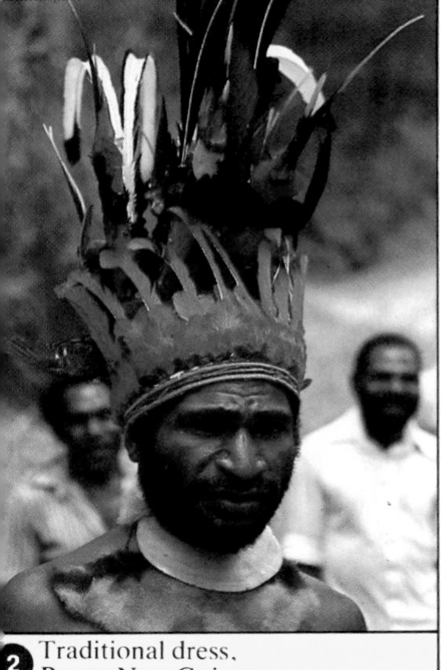

2 Traditional dress,
Papua New Guinea

nimals and small birds when it
omes out at night. The Tasmanian
evil is a *marsupial*. This means it
arries its young in a pouch.

7 The tallest geyser ever to have
erupted was the Waimangu
eyser in New Zealand. In 1904 it
ose to a height of 457 m (1500 ft).
last erupted in 1917, killing four
eople. Today, steam from New
ealand's hot springs and geysers is
arnessed to generate electricity.

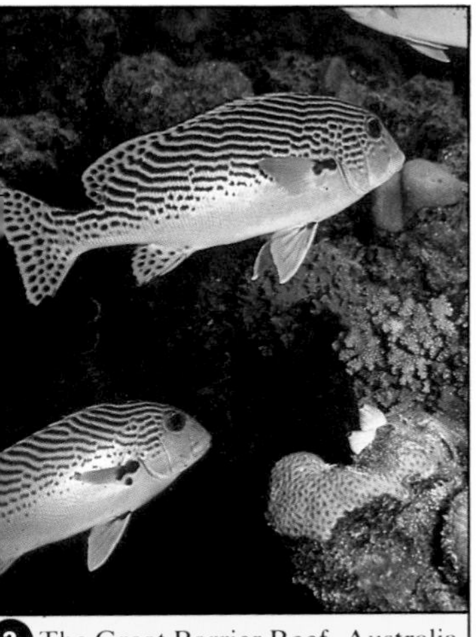

3 The Great Barrier Reef, Australia

AUSTRALIA

Area: 7 682 300 sq km
(2 966 136 sq miles)
Population: 16 900 000
Capital: Canberra
Language: English
Currency: Australian Dollar

NEW ZEALAND

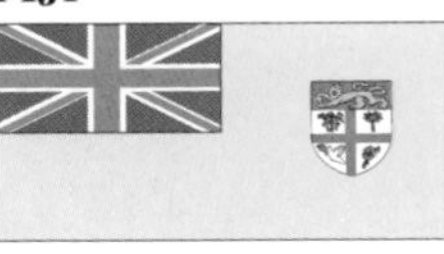

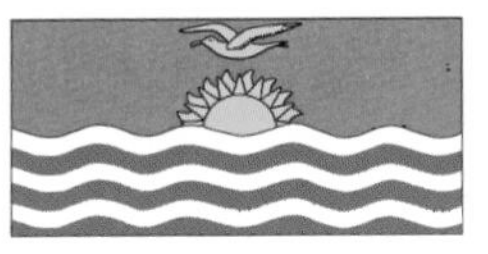

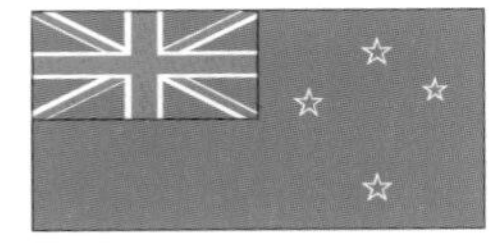

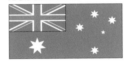

Area: 268 675 sq km
(103 735 sq miles)
Population: 3 400 000
Capital: Wellington
Language: English
Currency: New Zealand
Dollar

TONGA

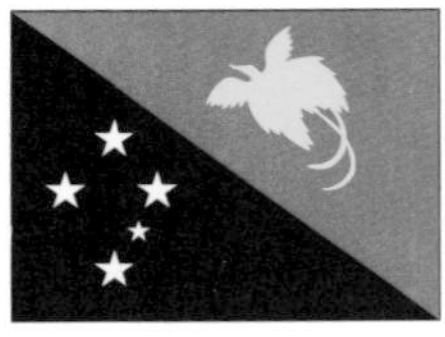

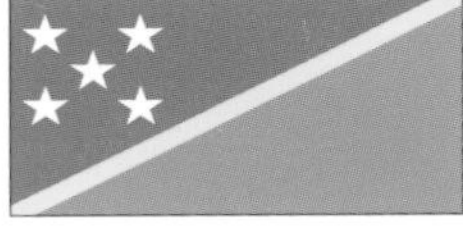

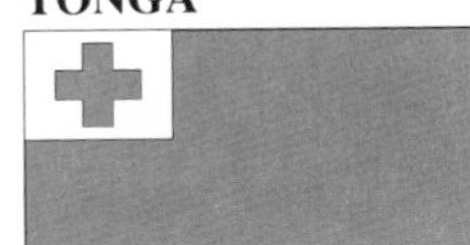

Area: 699 sq km
(270 sq miles)
Population: 100 000
Capital: Nuku'alofa
Languages: English,
Tongan
Currency: Pa'anga

FIJI

Area: 18 272 sq km
(7055 sq miles)
Population: 800 000
Capital: Suva
Languages: English, Fijian
Currency: Fiji Dollar

PAPUA NEW GUINEA

Area: 461 692 sq km
(178 259 sq miles)
Population: 3 900 000
Capital: Port Moresby
Languages: English,
Melanesian Pidgin
Currency: Kina

VANUATU

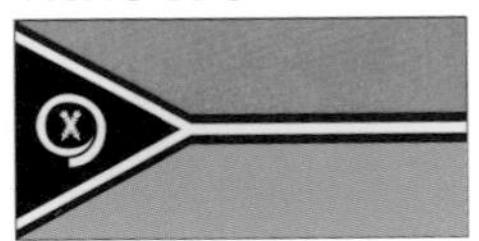

Area: 14 763 sq km
(5700 sq miles)
Population: 160 000
Capital: Vila
Languages: Bislama,
English, French
Currency: Australian Dollar,
Vatu

KIRIBATI

Area: 800 sq km
(309 sq miles)
Population: 66 000
Capital: Tarawa
Languages: English,
I Kiribati
Currency: Australian Dollar

SOLOMON ISLANDS

Area: 29 785 sq km
(11 500 sq miles)
Population: 320 000
Capital: Honiara
Languages: English, Pidgin
Currency: Solomon Islands
Dollar

WESTERN SAMOA

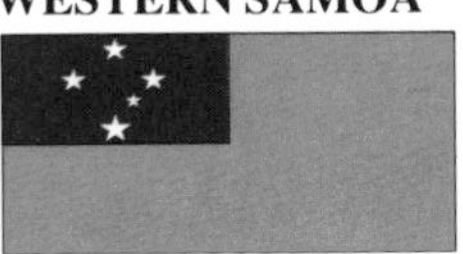

Area: 2831 sq km
(1093 sq miles)
Population: 170 000
Capital: Apia
Languages: Samoan, English
Currency: Tala

WORLD ENVIRONMENT

The world can be divided into 8 broad 'climatic zones' (these are areas with a particular sort of weather). The natural types of plants and animals found in each zone are different and depend on the weather the zone has. This map shows which parts of the world are in each zone. The colour of the strip at the top of each zone description (for example, Desert, Rainforest) is the same as the colour used for the zone on the big map. The little map beside each zone description pinpoints where that type of habitat is found in the world. (For example, the Desert strip is orange/yellow. The little sketch map shows you where on the big map to look for this colour. You will find this colour in the north of Africa, the west of North America and in parts of Asia and Australia. All these places have deserts. The description tells you what the natural countryside looks like and what plants and animals live there.)

SCRUB OR MEDITERRANEAN

Areas of long, hot, dry summers and short, warm winters. The land used to be covered with trees, but man cleared it for crops and grazed his animals on it. Now there is evergreen scrub – vines and olive trees.

TUNDRA OR MOUNTAIN

Polar areas which are usually frozen over. During the short summers the top layer of soil thaws, creating vast marshes. Compact, wind-resistant plants and lichens and mosses are found here. Animals include lemmings and reindeer.

NORTHERN FOREST (TAIGA)

Forests of conifers growing over a large area. Winters are very cold and long. Summers are short. Trees include spruce and fir. Animals found here include beavers, squirrels and red deer.

WOODLAND AND GRASS

Temperate areas (where the weather is seldom very cold or very hot). Deciduous trees (which lose their leaves in winter) grow in the woodlands. They include oak, beech and maple. Man uses these areas most of all, for farming, building towns and villages, and industry.

GRASSLAND

Hot summers, cold winters and moderate rainfall. Huge area of grassland and 'black' (very fertile) soils. Grain crops grow well, and so does rich pasture for beef cattle. Names for this kind of grassland include steppe, veld, pampas and prairie.

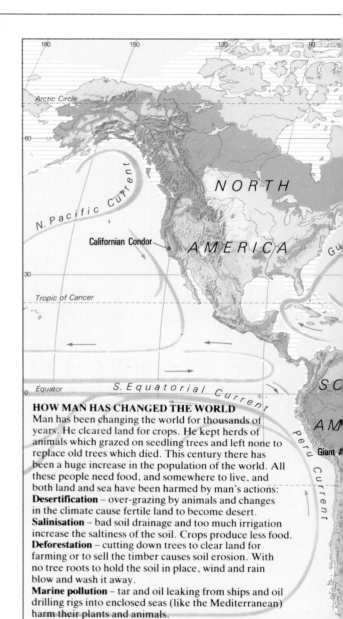

HOW MAN HAS CHANGED THE WORLD
Man has been changing the world for thousands of years. He cleared land for crops. He kept herds of animals which grazed on seedling trees and left none to replace old trees which died. This century there has been a huge increase in the population of the world. All these people need food, and somewhere to live, and both land and sea have been harmed by man's actions:
Desertification – over-grazing by animals and changes in the climate cause fertile land to become desert.
Salinisation – bad soil drainage and too much irrigation increase the saltiness of the soil. Crops produce less food.
Deforestation – cutting down trees to clear land for farming or to sell the timber causes soil erosion. With no tree roots to hold the soil in place, wind and rain blow and wash it away.
Marine pollution – tar and oil leaking from ships and oil drilling rigs into enclosed seas (like the Mediterranean) harm their plants and animals.

SAVANNA

Tall grasses with thick stems, and flat-topped thorny trees grow here. Animals grazing here include giraffes and zebras. There is a short rainy season. Often it does not rain for a long time (a drought). Fires burn the dried out plants but they have adapted to survive this and grow again.

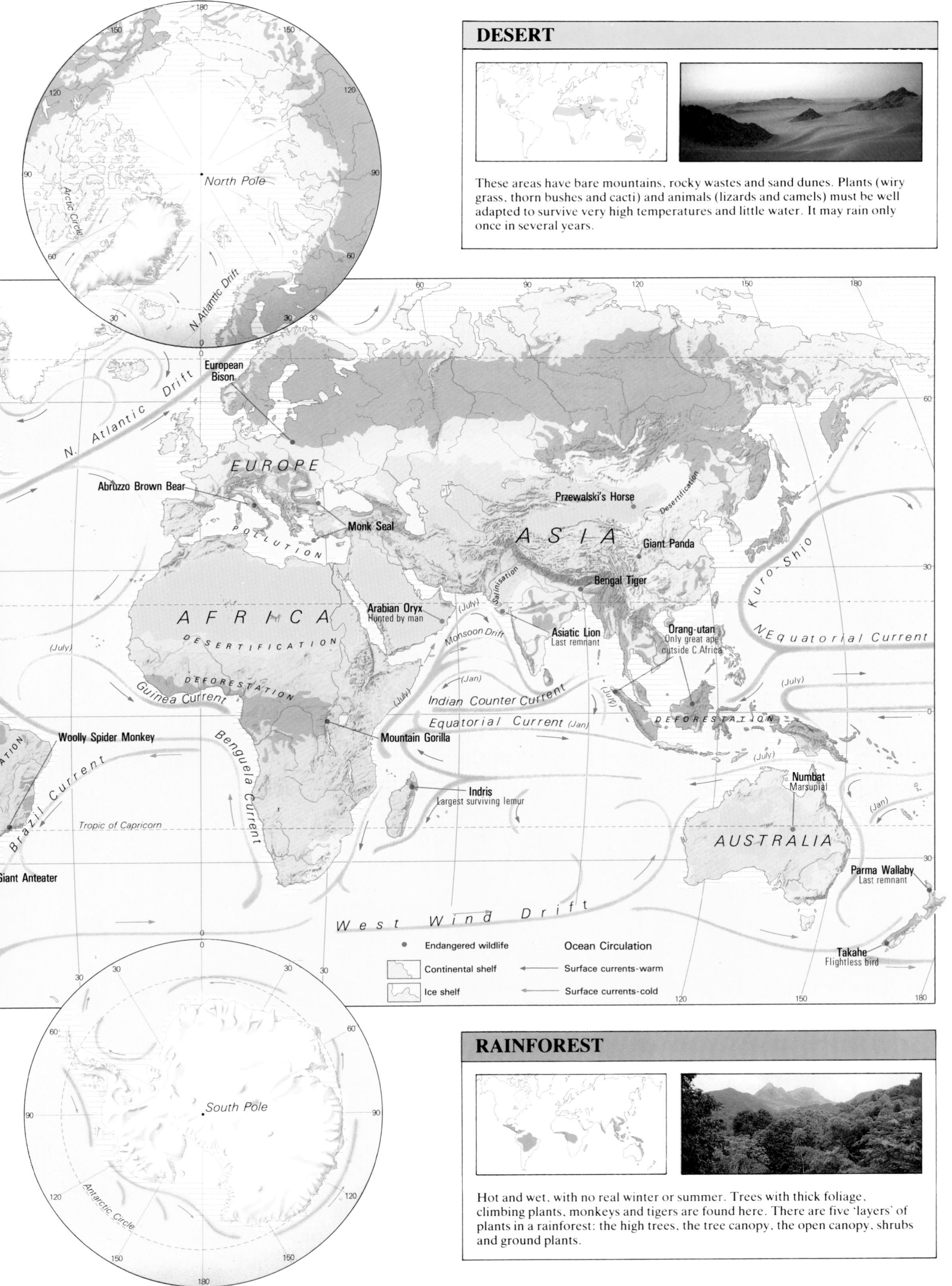

DESERT

These areas have bare mountains, rocky wastes and sand dunes. Plants (wiry grass, thorn bushes and cacti) and animals (lizards and camels) must be well adapted to survive very high temperatures and little water. It may rain only once in several years.

RAINFOREST

Hot and wet, with no real winter or summer. Trees with thick foliage, climbing plants, monkeys and tigers are found here. There are five 'layers' of plants in a rainforest: the high trees, the tree canopy, the open canopy, shrubs and ground plants.

North Pole

Arctic Circle

N. Atlantic Drift

European Bison

Abruzzo Brown Bear

EUROPE

POLLUTION

Monk Seal

N. Atlantic Drift

Przewalski's Horse

ASIA

Giant Panda

Desertification

Kuro-Shio

Bengal Tiger

Arabian Oryx
Hunted by man

(July)

Salinisation

Monsoon Drift

AFRICA

DESERTIFICATION

DEFORESTATION

Asiatic Lion
Last remnant

Orang-utan
Only great ape
outside C.Africa

N. Equatorial Current

(July)

Guinea Current

Woolly Spider Monkey

(July)

(Jan)

Indian Counter Current

Equatorial Current (Jan)

DEFORESTATION

Mountain Gorilla

(July)

Benguela Current

Brazil Current

TATION

Tropic of Capricorn

Giant Anteater

Indris
Largest surviving lemur

Numbat
Marsupial

AUSTRALIA

(Jan)

Parma Wallaby
Last remnant

West Wind Drift

Takahe
Flightless bird

● Endangered wildlife

Continental shelf

Ice shelf

Ocean Circulation

→ Surface currents-warm

→ Surface currents-cold

South Pole

Antarctic Circle

WORLD CLIMATE

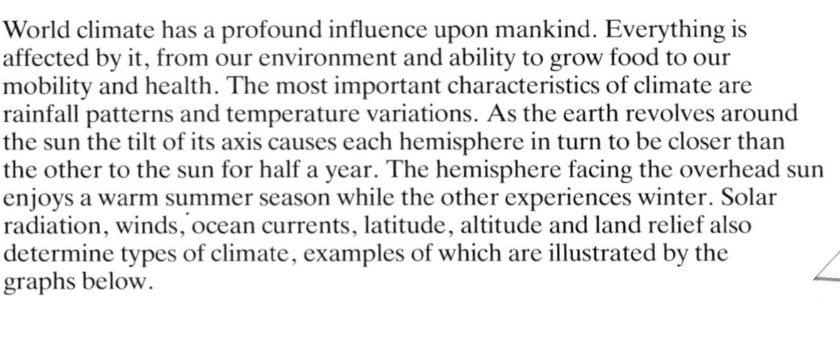

World climate has a profound influence upon mankind. Everything is affected by it, from our environment and ability to grow food to our mobility and health. The most important characteristics of climate are rainfall patterns and temperature variations. As the earth revolves around the sun the tilt of its axis causes each hemisphere in turn to be closer than the other to the sun for half a year. The hemisphere facing the overhead sun enjoys a warm summer season while the other experiences winter. Solar radiation, winds, ocean currents, latitude, altitude and land relief also determine types of climate, examples of which are illustrated by the graphs below.

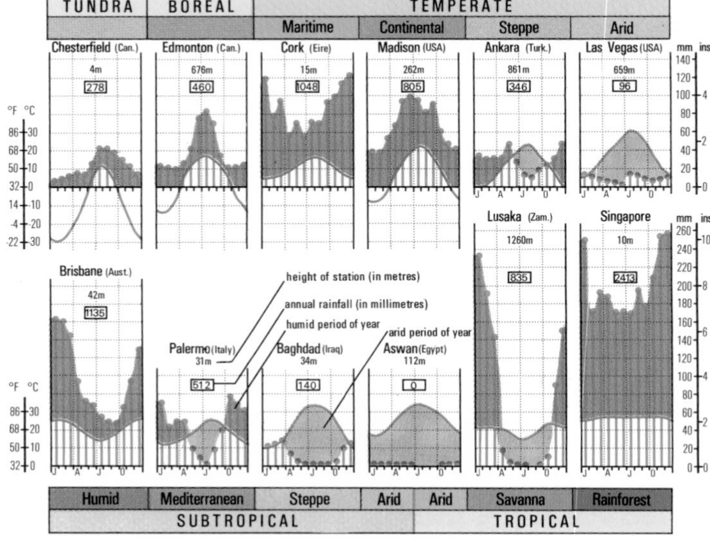

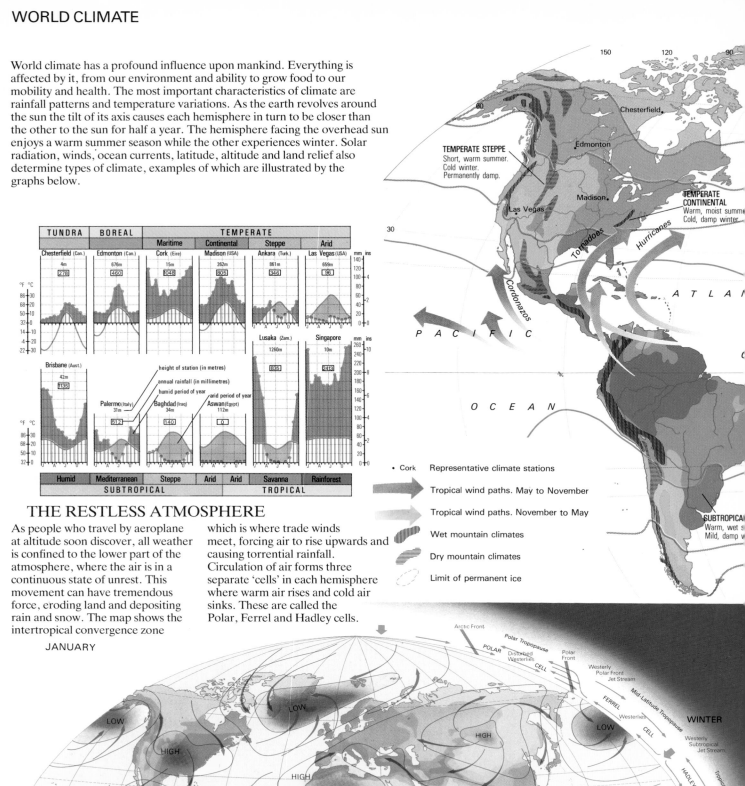

THE RESTLESS ATMOSPHERE

As people who travel by aeroplane at altitude soon discover, all weather is confined to the lower part of the atmosphere, where the air is in a continuous state of unrest. This movement can have tremendous force, eroding land and depositing rain and snow. The map shows the intertropical convergence zone which is where trade winds meet, forcing air to rise upwards and causing torrential rainfall. Circulation of air forms three separate 'cells' in each hemisphere where warm air rises and cold air sinks. These are called the Polar, Ferrel and Hadley cells.

JANUARY

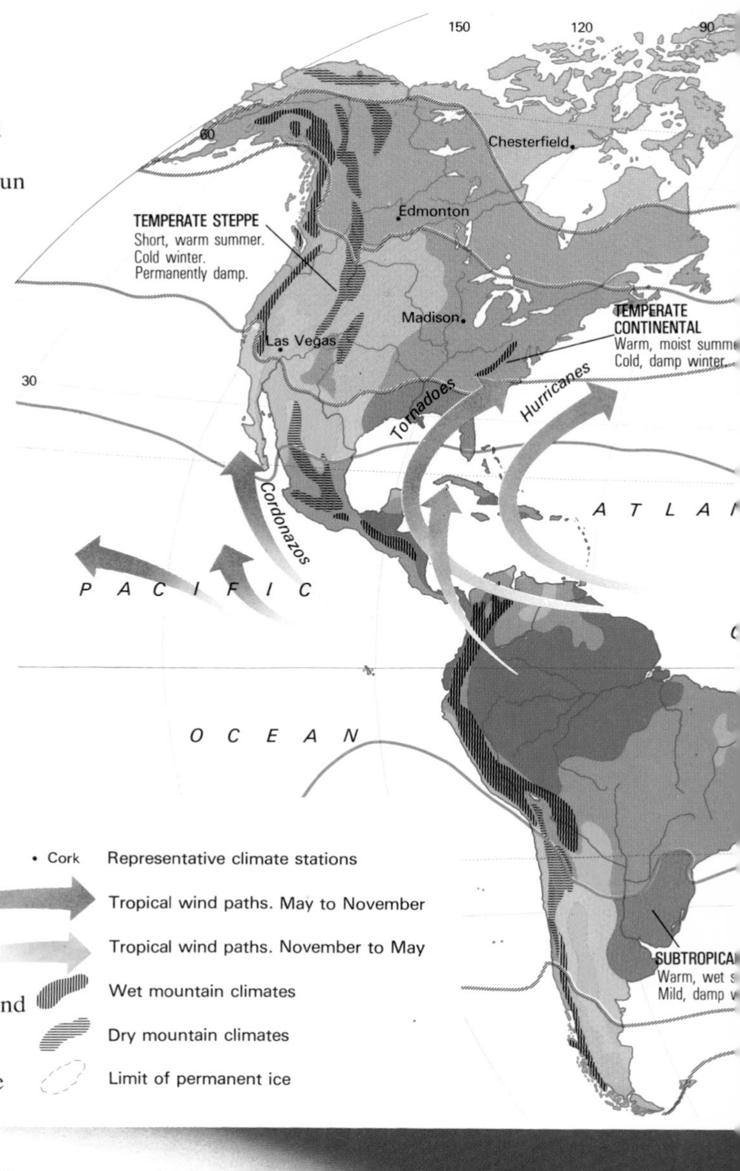

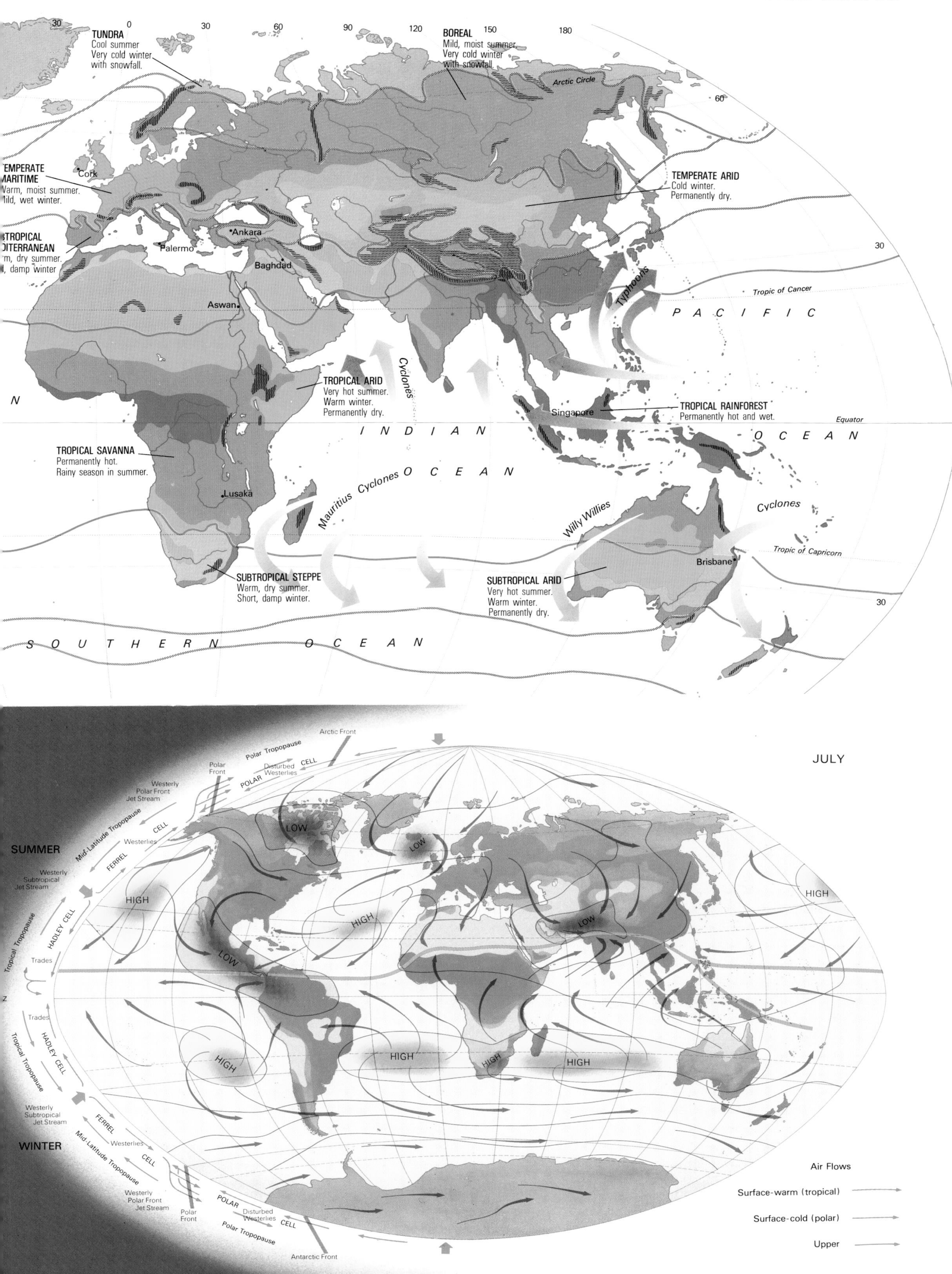

TUNDRA
Cool summer.
Very cold winter
with snowfall.

BOREAL
Mild, moist summer.
Very cold winter
with snowfall.

Arctic Circle

TEMPERATE ARID
Cold winter.
Permanently dry.

EMPERATE
MARITIME
Warm, moist summer.
Mild, wet winter.

Cork

TROPICAL
DITERRANEAN
rm, dry summer.
, damp winter.

Ankara

Palermo

Baghdad

Aswan

Typhoons

Tropic of Cancer

P A C I F I C

TROPICAL ARID
Very hot summer.
Warm winter.
Permanently dry.

Cyclones

TROPICAL RAINFOREST
Permanently hot and wet.

Singapore

Equator

I N D I A N

O C E A N

TROPICAL SAVANNA
Permanently hot.
Rainy season in summer.

Lusaka

Mauritius Cyclones O C E A N

Cyclones

Willy Willies

SUBTROPICAL STEPPE
Warm, dry summer.
Short, damp winter.

SUBTROPICAL ARID
Very hot summer.
Warm winter.
Permanently dry.

Brisbane

Tropic of Capricorn

S O U T H E R N   O C E A N

Arctic Front

Polar Tropopause

Polar
Front

Westerly
Polar Front
Jet Stream

Disturbed
Westerlies

POLAR   CELL

JULY

SUMMER

Mid-Latitude Tropopause

Westerlies

FERREL   CELL

LOW

LOW

HIGH

Westerly
Subtropical
Jet Stream

HIGH

HIGH

HIGH

LOW

Tropical Tropopause

HADLEY CELL

Trades

LOW

Z

Trades

Tropical Tropopause

HADLEY CELL

HIGH

HIGH

HIGH

HIGH

Westerly
Subtropical
Jet Stream

FERREL

WINTER

Mid-Latitude Tropopause

Westerlies   CELL

Westerly
Polar Front
Jet Stream

Polar
Front

POLAR

Disturbed
Westerlies   CELL

Polar Tropopause

Antarctic Front

Air Flows

Surface-warm (tropical)

Surface-cold (polar)

Upper

CLIMATE INDICATORS

Listed from north to south, is a selection of places from different climate zones of the world (see pp xxiv/xxv), indicating their mean monthly temperatures (in °C and °F) and rainfall (in mm and inches). Also shown are their average temperatures and total rainfall for the year.

REYKJAVIK Iceland 64.1°N 21.9°W — TUNDRA

	J	F	M	A	M	J	J	A	S	O	N	D	Year
°C	-0.2	0.2	1.5	3.5	6.7	9.7	11.3	10.8	8.5	5.2	3.0	0.4	5.0
°F	32	32	35	38	44	49	52	51	47	41	37	33	41
mm	89	64	62	56	42	42	50	56	67	94	78	79	779
ins	3.5	2.5	2.4	2.2	1.6	1.6	2.0	2.2	2.6	3.7	3.1	3.1	30.7

ANCHORAGE U.S.A. 61.2°N 150.0°W — BOREAL

	J	F	M	A	M	J	J	A	S	O	N	D	Year
°C	-10.4	-7.6	-4.8	2.0	7.7	12.2	14.1	13.1	8.7	1.8	-5.6	-10.2	1.7
°F	13	18	23	36	46	54	57	56	48	35	22	14	29
mm	20	18	13	11	13	25	47	65	63	47	26	24	372
ins	0.8	0.7	0.5	0.4	0.5	1.0	1.8	2.6	2.5	1.8	1.0	0.9	14.6

STOCKHOLM Sweden 59.3°N 18.1°E — TEMPERATE Continental

	J	F	M	A	M	J	J	A	S	O	N	D	Year
°C	-3.0	-3.1	-0.5	4.6	10.2	15.0	18.5	16.6	12.3	7.1	2.7	0.0	6.6
°F	27	26	31	40	50	59	65	62	54	45	37	32	44
mm	43	30	25	31	34	45	61	76	60	48	53	48	554
ins	1.7	1.2	1.0	1.2	1.3	1.8	2.4	3.0	2.4	1.9	2.1	1.9	21.8

EDINBURGH U.K. 55.9°N 3.2°W — TEMPERATE Maritime

	J	F	M	A	M	J	J	A	S	O	N	D	Year
°C	3.3	3.5	5.1	7.4	9.9	12.9	14.8	14.4	12.5	9.4	6.4	4.6	8.6
°F	38	38	41	45	50	55	59	58	54	49	43	40	47
mm	57	39	39	39	54	47	83	77	57	65	62	57	676
ins	2.2	1.5	1.5	1.5	2.1	1.8	3.3	3.0	2.2	2.6	2.4	2.2	26.6

MOSKVA Russian Federation 55.7°N 37.6°E — TEMPERATE Continental

	J	F	M	A	M	J	J	A	S	O	N	D	Year
°C	-12.7	-9.6	-3.8	5.7	13.3	15.8	17.8	16.9	11.8	5.9	-0.9	-7.0	4.4
°F	9	15	25	42	56	60	64	62	53	43	30	19	40
mm	39	38	36	37	53	58	88	71	58	45	47	54	624
ins	1.5	1.5	1.4	1.5	2.1	2.3	3.5	2.8	2.3	1.8	1.8	2.1	24.6

VANCOUVER Canada 49.2°N 123.2°W — TEMPERATE Maritime

	J	F	M	A	M	J	J	A	S	O	N	D	Year
°C	2.8	4.1	6.4	9.4	12.6	15.5	17.8	17.2	14.4	10.3	6.3	4.2	10.0
°F	37	39	43	49	55	60	64	63	58	50	43	40	50
mm	214	161	151	90	69	65	39	44	83	172	198	243	1529
ins	8.4	6.3	5.9	3.5	2.7	2.6	1.5	1.7	3.3	6.8	7.8	9.6	60.2

PARIS France 48.8°N 2.3°E — TEMPERATE Maritime

	J	F	M	A	M	J	J	A	S	O	N	D	Year
°C	3.4	4.3	7.9	11.0	14.6	17.8	19.5	19.1	16.5	11.7	7.2	4.3	11.5
°F	38	40	46	52	58	64	67	66	62	53	45	40	53
mm	56	46	35	42	57	54	59	64	55	50	51	50	619
ins	2.2	1.8	1.4	1.6	2.2	2.1	2.3	2.5	2.2	2.0	2.0	2.0	24.3

BUCUREŞTI Romania 44.5°N 26.0°E — TEMPERATE Steppe

	J	F	M	A	M	J	J	A	S	O	N	D	Year
°C	-4.2	-1.5	6.2	12.4	17.3	21.2	23.5	22.9	18.2	13.0	6.4	0.6	8.2
°F	24	29	43	54	63	70	74	73	65	55	43	33	47
mm	46	26	28	59	77	121	53	45	45	29	36	27	592
ins	1.8	1.0	1.1	2.3	3.0	4.8	2.1	1.8	1.8	1.1	1.4	1.1	23.4

NEW YORK U.S.A. 40.7°N 74.0°W — TEMPERATE Continental

	J	F	M	A	M	J	J	A	S	O	N	D	Year
°C	0.7	0.8	4.7	10.5	16.3	21.2	24.1	23.3	19.8	14.3	8.1	2.2	12.2
°F	33	33	40	51	61	70	75	74	68	58	47	36	54
mm	89	74	104	89	91	86	102	119	89	84	89	84	1100
ins	3.5	2.9	4.1	3.5	3.6	3.4	4.0	4.7	3.5	3.3	3.5	3.3	43.3

TŌKYŌ Japan 35.7°N 139.8°E — TEMPERATE Continental

	J	F	M	A	M	J	J	A	S	O	N	D	Year
°C	3.3	4.2	7.2	12.5	16.9	20.8	24.7	26.1	22.5	16.7	10.8	5.8	14.4
°F	38	40	45	54	62	69	76	79	72	62	51	42	58
mm	48	74	107	135	147	165	142	152	234	208	96	56	1565
ins	1.9	2.9	4.2	5.3	5.8	6.5	5.6	6.0	9.2	8.2	3.8	2.2	61.6

TANGER Morocco 35.8°N 5.8°W — SUBTROPICAL Mediterranean

	J	F	M	A	M	J	J	A	S	O	N	D	Year
°C	11.9	12.5	13.6	14.4	17.2	20.0	22.2	23.0	21.4	18.6	14.7	12.4	16.7
°F	53	54	56	58	63	68	72	73	70	65	58	54	62
mm	114	107	122	89	43	15	2	2	23	99	147	137	897
ins	4.5	4.2	4.8	3.5	1.7	0.6	0.1	0.1	0.9	3.9	5.8	5.4	35.3

JERUSALEM Israel 31.8°N 35.2°E — SUBTROPICAL Steppe

	J	F	M	A	M	J	J	A	S	O	N	D	Year
°C	8.9	9.4	13.0	16.4	20.5	22.5	23.9	24.1	23.0	21.1	16.4	11.1	17.2
°F	48	49	55	61	69	72	75	75	73	70	61	52	63
mm	132	132	63	28	2	1	0	0	1	13	71	87	528
ins	5.2	5.2	2.5	1.1	0.1	0.0	0.0	0.0	0.1	0.5	2.8	3.4	20.8

NEW ORLEANS U.S.A. 30.0°N 90.2°W — SUBTROPICAL Humid

	J	F	M	A	M	J	J	A	S	O	N	D	Year
°C	12.5	13.9	16.3	19.9	23.5	26.7	27.6	27.7	25.7	21.3	15.5	13.0	20.3
°F	54	57	61	68	74	80	82	82	78	70	60	55	68
mm	97	102	135	114	112	112	170	135	127	71	84	104	1363
ins	3.8	4.0	5.3	4.5	4.4	4.4	6.7	5.3	5.0	2.8	3.3	4.1	53.7

BAHRAIN 26.2°N 50.5°E — SUBTROPICAL Arid

	J	F	M	A	M	J	J	A	S	O	N	D	Year
°C	16.9	18.0	20.5	25.0	29.4	31.7	33.3	33.6	31.4	28.0	24.2	18.6	25.8
°F	62	64	69	77	85	89	92	92	88	82	75	65	78
mm	8	18	13	8	1	0	0	0	0	0	18	18	79
ins	0.3	0.7	0.5	0.3	0.1	0.0	0.0	0.0	0.0	0.0	0.7	0.7	3.2

HONG KONG 22.3°N 114.2°E — SUBTROPICAL Humid

	J	F	M	A	M	J	J	A	S	O	N	D	Year
°C	15.5	15.0	17.5	21.7	25.5	27.5	28.0	28.0	27.2	25.0	20.8	17.5	22.5
°F	60	59	63	71	78	81	82	82	81	77	69	63	72
mm	33	46	74	137	292	394	381	361	256	114	43	30	2161
ins	1.3	1.8	2.9	5.4	11.5	15.5	15.0	14.2	10.1	4.5	1.7	1.2	85.1

MIAMI U.S.A. 25.8°N 80.3°W — TROPICAL Savanna

	J	F	M	A	M	J	J	A	S	O	N	D	Year
°C	19.3	19.9	21.4	23.4	25.3	27.1	27.6	27.9	27.4	25.4	22.4	20.1	23.9
°F	67	68	70	74	77	81	82	82	81	78	72	68	75
mm	51	48	58	99	163	188	170	178	241	208	71	43	1518
ins	2.0	1.9	2.3	3.9	6.4	7.4	6.7	7.0	9.5	8.2	2.8	1.7	59.8

BANGKOK Thailand 13.7°N 100.5°E — TROPICAL Savanna

	J	F	M	A	M	J	J	A	S	O	N	D	Year
°C	25.8	27.5	28.9	30.0	29.4	28.6	28.3	28.3	28.0	27.5	26.4	25.3	27.7
°F	78	81	84	86	85	83	83	83	82	81	79	77	82
mm	8	20	36	58	198	160	160	175	305	206	66	5	1397
ins	0.3	0.8	1.4	2.3	7.8	6.3	6.3	6.9	12.0	8.1	2.6	0.2	55.0

COLOMBO Sri Lanka 6.9°N 79.9°E — TROPICAL Rainforest

	J	F	M	A	M	J	J	A	S	O	N	D	Year
°C	26.1	26.4	27.2	27.7	28.0	27.2	27.2	27.2	27.2	26.6	26.1	25.8	26.9
°F	79	80	81	82	82	81	81	81	81	80	79	78	80
mm	89	69	147	231	371	223	135	109	160	348	315	147	2344
ins	3.5	2.7	5.8	9.1	14.6	8.8	5.3	4.3	6.3	13.7	12.4	5.8	92.3

NAIROBI Kenya 1.3°S 36.8°E — TROPICAL Savanna

	J	F	M	A	M	J	J	A	S	O	N	D	Year
°C	18.6	19.4	19.4	19.2	17.7	16.4	15.5	16.1	17.5	18.6	18.3	18.0	18.0
°F	65	67	67	67	64	61	60	61	63	65	65	64	64
mm	38	63	124	211	157	46	15	23	30	53	109	86	958
ins	1.5	2.5	4.9	8.3	6.2	1.8	0.6	0.9	1.2	2.1	4.3	3.4	37.7

LIMA Peru 12.1°S 77.0°W — TROPICAL Arid

	J	F	M	A	M	J	J	A	S	O	N	D	Year
°C	23.3	23.8	23.6	21.9	19.4	17.2	16.7	16.1	16.9	18.0	19.4	21.1	20.0
°F	74	75	74	71	67	63	62	61	62	64	67	70	68
mm	1	1	1	1	5	5	8	8	8	2	2	1	41
ins	0.1	0.1	0.1	0.1	0.2	0.2	0.3	0.3	0.3	0.1	0.1	0.1	1.6

RIO DE JANEIRO Brazil 22.9°S 43.2°W — TROPICAL Savanna

	J	F	M	A	M	J	J	A	S	O	N	D	Year
°C	25.8	26.1	25.3	23.6	21.9	21.1	20.5	21.1	21.1	21.9	23.0	24.7	23.0
°F	78	79	77	74	71	70	69	70	70	71	73	76	73
mm	124	122	130	107	79	53	41	43	66	79	104	137	1085
ins	4.9	4.8	5.1	4.2	3.1	2.1	1.6	1.7	2.6	3.1	4.1	5.4	42.6

JOHANNESBURG S. Africa 26.2°S 28.1°E — SUBTROPICAL Steppe

	J	F	M	A	M	J	J	A	S	O	N	D	Year
°C	20.0	19.7	18.3	16.1	12.5	10.3	10.5	13.0	15.8	18.3	18.9	19.7	16.1
°F	68	67	65	61	54	50	51	55	60	65	66	67	61
mm	114	109	89	38	25	8	8	8	23	56	107	124	709
ins	4.5	4.3	3.5	1.5	1.0	0.3	0.3	0.3	0.9	2.2	4.2	4.9	27.9

PERTH Australia 31.9°S 115.8°E — SUBTROPICAL Mediterranean

	J	F	M	A	M	J	J	A	S	O	N	D	Year
°C	23.3	23.3	21.7	19.2	16.1	13.9	13.0	13.3	14.7	16.4	19.2	21.7	17.8
°F	74	74	71	66	61	57	55	56	58	61	66	71	64
mm	8	10	20	43	130	180	170	145	86	56	20	13	881
ins	0.3	0.4	0.8	1.7	5.1	7.1	6.7	5.7	3.4	2.2	0.8	0.5	34.7

WELLINGTON New Zealand 41.3°S 174.8°E — TEMPERATE Maritime

	J	F	M	A	M	J	J	A	S	O	N	D	Year
°C	16.9	16.9	15.8	13.9	11.4	9.7	8.9	9.7	10.8	12.2	13.6	15.8	12.8
°F	62	62	60	57	52	49	47	48	51	54	56	60	55
mm	81	81	81	97	117	117	137	117	97	102	89	89	1205
ins	3.2	3.2	3.2	3.8	4.6	4.6	5.4	4.6	3.8	4.0	3.5	3.5	47.4

Civilisation depends on trade for growth and travel makes this possible. Shipping is the most important method of world transport but economic progress and moblity are constantly being improved by the development of new routes and new modes of transport.

ROAD AND RAIL

Integrated road and rail networks are the basis of industrial society. Extended highway systems and improved containerisation techniques have made the whole road and rail system much more flexible.

Roads—comparative lengths (Log scale)

	Vehicles/km	Country
68 / 277	24	USA 6366
49 / 23	1	India 1604
16 / 115	7	Brazil 1399
296 / 95	34	Japan 1118
9 / 9	1	China 890
9 / 367	14	Canada 884
11 / 552	9	Australia 817
146 / 149	27	France 803
28 / 24	11	Russian Federation 620
172 / 78	54	Germany 613
154 / 63	49	UK 353
96 / 83	10	Poland 299
98 / 51	64	Italy 294
7 / 74	20	Argentina 208 —(000's km)

Network Densities

○ Vehicles/km of road

— Motorways (bar length = 1% of network)

High	Medium	Low

km/100km²
100km/million popl.
km/100km²

	Country
3 / 8	UK 18 ———(000's km)
4 / 7	Italy 20
7 / 8	Poland 24
2 / 7	Japan 26
3 / 0·4	Brazil 31
6 / 6	France 34
12 / 2	Argentina 35
27 / 0·5	Australia 40
5 / 13	Germany 41
1 / 0·5	China 50
1 / 2	India 61
28 / 7	Canada 68
6 / 0·5	Russian Federation 86
14 / 3	USA 320

Railways—comparative lengths (Log scale)

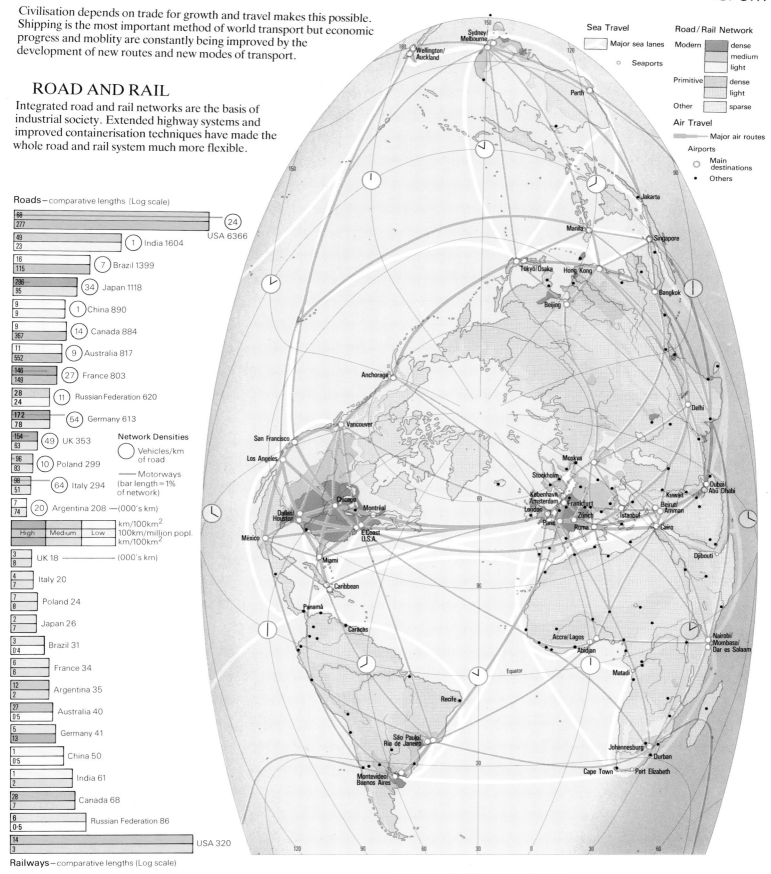

AIR AND SEA ROUTES

A complex network of primary air routes centred on the Northern Hemisphere provides rapid transit across the world for mass travel, mail and urgent freight. Ships also follow these principal routes, plying the oceans between major ports and transporting the commodities of world trade in bulk.

JOURNEY TIME

The Suez canal cuts 3600 miles off the London-Singapore route, while Concorde halves the London-New York journey time.

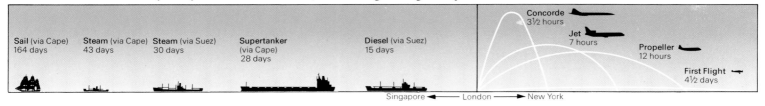

Sail (via Cape) 164 days
Steam (via Cape) 43 days
Steam (via Suez) 30 days
Supertanker (via Cape) 28 days
Diesel (via Suez) 15 days

Concorde 3½ hours
Jet 7 hours
Propeller 12 hours
First Flight 4½ days

Singapore ◄— London —► New York

1:60M

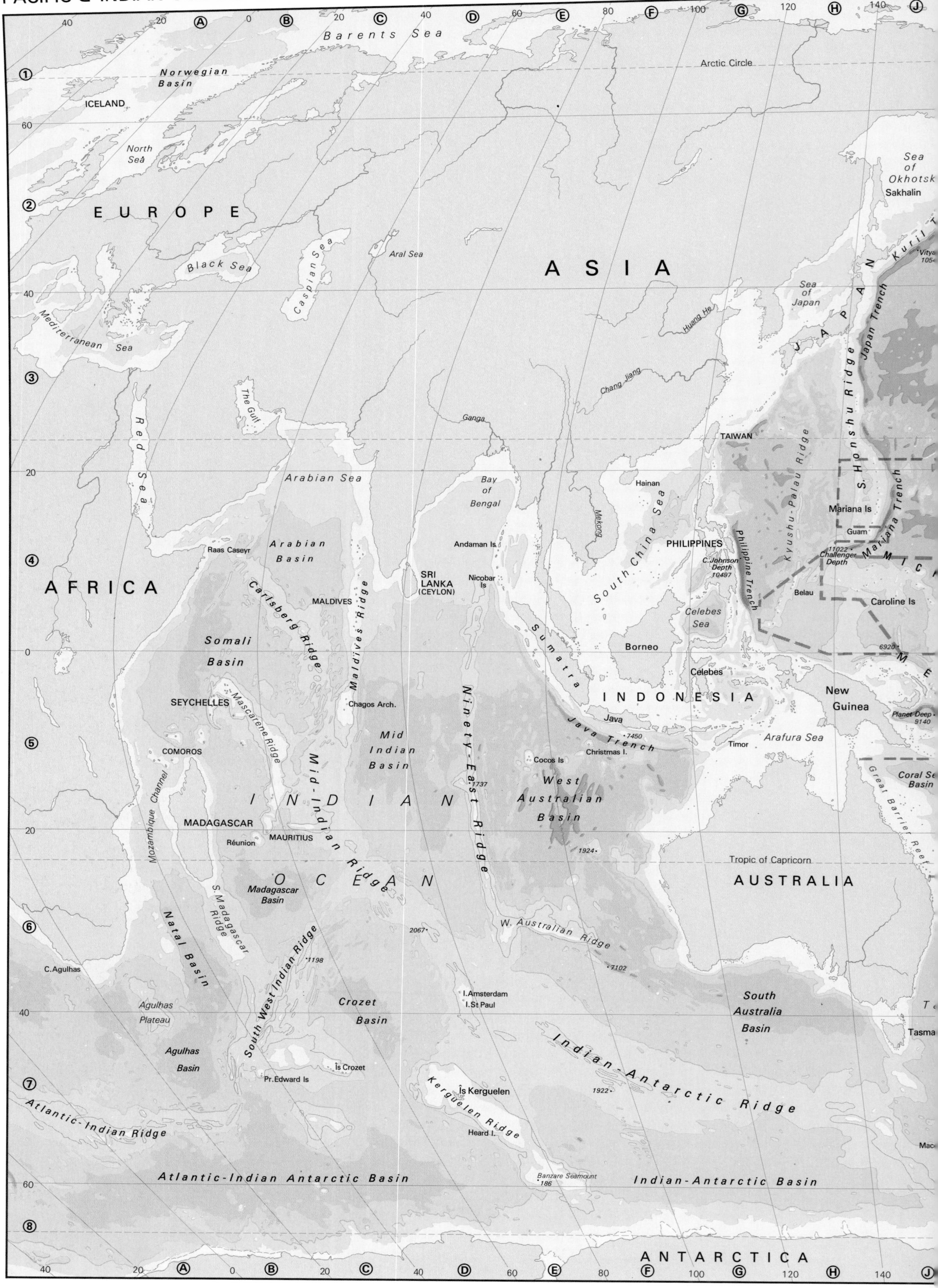

600 1200 1800 2400 km
600 1200 mils

Barents Sea

Arctic Circle

Norwegian
Basin

ICELAND

North
Sea

EUROPE

ASIA

Sea of
Okhotsk

Sakhalin

Black Sea

Caspian Sea

Aral Sea

Sea of
Japan

Mediterranean
Sea

Huang He

Chang Jiang

Ganga

TAIWAN

Red Sea

The Gulf

Arabian Sea

Bay
of
Bengal

Hainan

Mekong

South China Sea

PHILIPPINES

Kyushu-Palau Ridge

S. Honshu Ridge

Japan Trench

Kuril T.

Vitya
1054

Mariana Is

Guam

Mariana Trench

AFRICA

Raas Caseyr

Arabian
Basin

Carlsberg Ridge

Maldives Ridge

SRI
LANKA
(CEYLON)

Andaman Is

Nicobar
Is

Philippine Trench

C.Johnson
Depth
10497

11022
Challenger
Depth

MIC

Belau

Caroline Is

MALDIVES

Celebes
Sea

6920

ME

Somali
Basin

SEYCHELLES

Mascarene Ridge

Chagos Arch.

Mid
Indian
Basin

Ninety-East Ridge

Sumatra

Java Trench

Borneo

Celebes

INDONESIA

Java

New
Guinea

Planet Deep
9140

COMOROS

INDIAN

Mid-Indian Ridge

7450

Cocos Is

1737

West
Australian
Basin

Christmas I.

Timor

Arafura Sea

MADAGASCAR

Mozambique Channel

Réunion

MAURITIUS

OCEAN

1924

Tropic of Capricorn

AUSTRALIA

Great Barrier Reef

Coral Sea
Basin

Natal Basin

S. Madagascar Ridge

Madagascar
Basin

South West Indian Ridge

2067

W. Australian Ridge

7102

South
Australia
Basin

C.Agulhas

Agulhas
Plateau

1198

Crozet
Basin

I.Amsterdam
I.St Paul

Indian-Antarctic Ridge

Tasma

Agulhas
Basin

Îs Crozet

Pr.Edward Is

Îs Kerguelen

1922

Kerguelen Ridge

Heard I.

Atlantic-Indian Ridge

Atlantic-Indian Antarctic Basin

Banzare Seamount
186

Indian-Antarctic Basin

Mac

T

ANTARCTICA

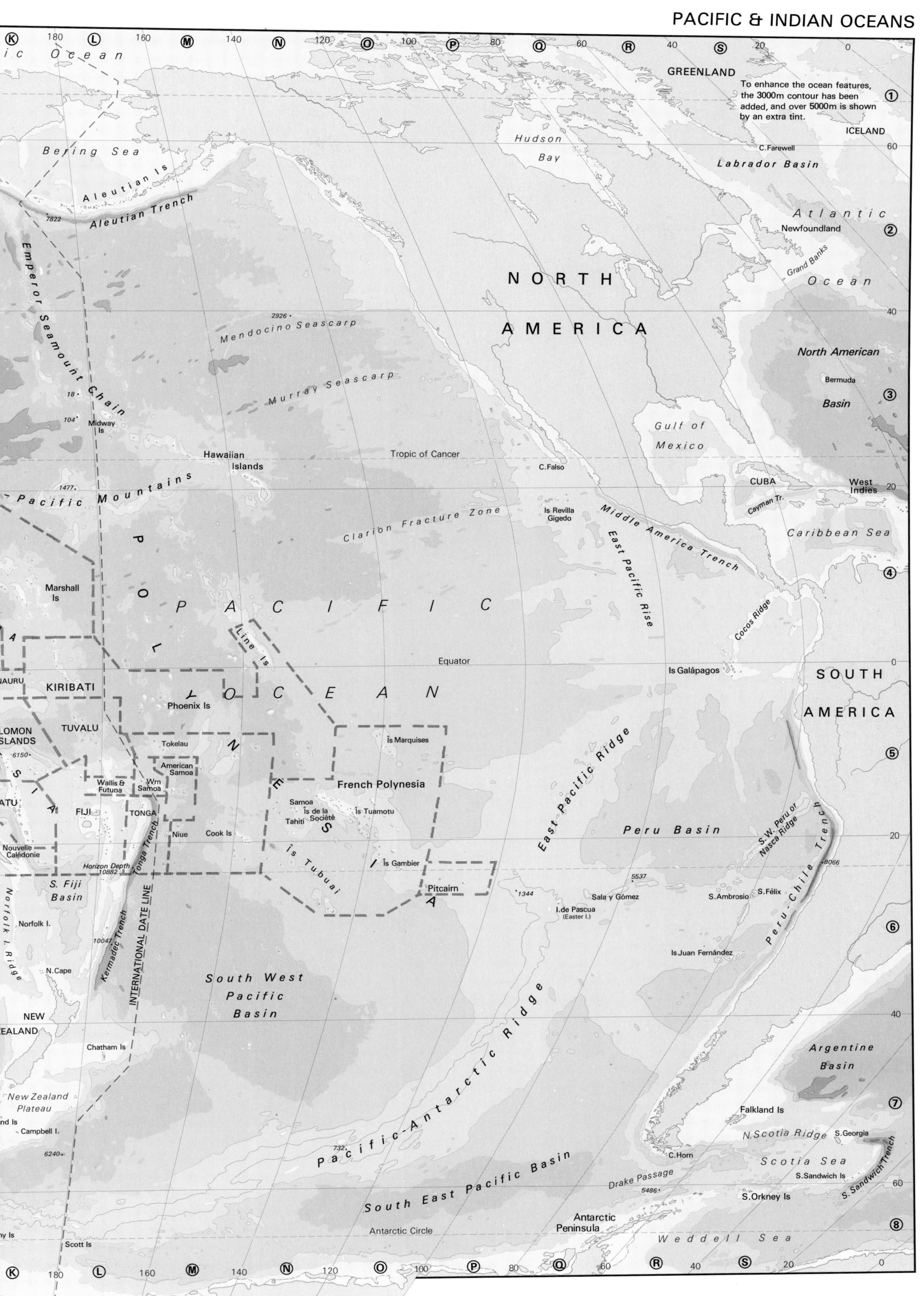

ic Ocean

To enhance the ocean features, the 3000m contour has been added, and over 5000m is shown by an extra tint.

GREENLAND

ICELAND

Bering Sea

Hudson Bay

Aleutian Is

Aleutian Trench

7822

Labrador Basin

C.Farewell

Atlantic

Emperor Seamount Chain

Newfoundland

NORTH

AMERICA

Mendocino Seascarp

2926

North American

Ocean

Grand Banks

Bermuda

Basin

18

104

Murray Seascarp

Midway Is

Pacific Mountains

1477

Hawaiian Islands

Tropic of Cancer

C.Falso

Gulf of Mexico

CUBA

West Indies

Cayman Tr.

Clarion Fracture Zone

Is Revilla Gigedo

Middle America Trench

Caribbean Sea

Marshall Is

PACIFIC

East Pacific Rise

Cocos Ridge

P O L Y N E S I A

Line Is

Equator

Is Galápagos

SOUTH

AMERICA

NAURU

KIRIBATI

Phoenix Is

OCEAN

TUVALU

Tokelau

Îs Marquises

6150

American Samoa

Wallis & Futuna

Wrn Samoa

French Polynesia

East Pacific Ridge

Peru Basin

S.W. Peru or Nasca Ridge

ATU

FIJI

TONGA

Niue

Cook Is

Samoa

Îs de la Société

Tahiti

Îs Tuamotu

Nouvelle Calédonie

Îs Tubuai

Îs Gambier

1344

5537

S.Ambrosio

S.Félix

Horizon Depth 10882

Tonga Trench

Pitcairn

Sala y Gómez

Peru-Chile Trench

8066

Norfolk I.

S. Fiji Basin

I.de Pascua (Easter I.)

Is Juan Fernández

Norfolk I. Ridge

10047

Kermadec Trench

INTERNATIONAL DATE LINE

N.Cape

South West Pacific Basin

Argentine Basin

NEW ZEALAND

Chatham Is

Falkland Is

New Zealand Plateau

N.Scotia Ridge

S.Georgia

and Is

Campbell I.

Pacific-Antarctic Ridge

Scotia Sea

6240

732

South East Pacific Basin

Drake Passage

S.Sandwich Is

S.Sandwich Trench

S.Orkney Is

5486

any Is

Scott Is

Antarctic Circle

Antarctic Peninsula

Weddell Sea

C.Horn

ATLANTIC OCEAN

1:60M

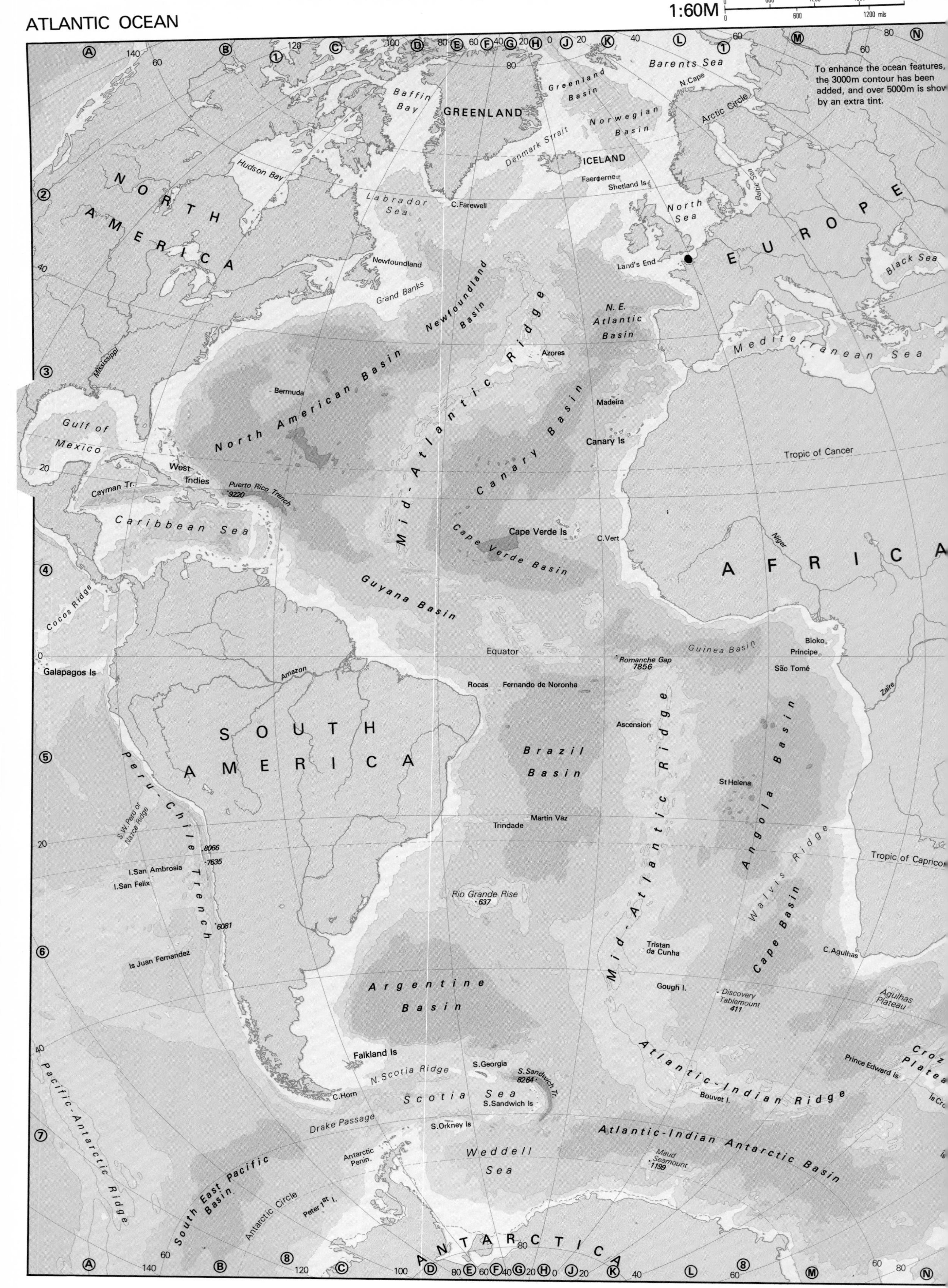

To enhance the ocean features, the 3000m contour has been added, and over 5000m is show by an extra tint.

NORTH AMERICA

Baffin Bay

GREENLAND

Greenland Basin

Barents Sea

N. Cape

Arctic Circle

Hudson Bay

Labrador Sea

C. Farewell

Denmark Strait

ICELAND

Norwegian Basin

Faerøerne
Shetland Is

North Sea

EUROPE

Newfoundland

Grand Banks

Newfoundland Basin

Mid-Atlantic Ridge

Land's End

N.E. Atlantic Basin

Azores

Mediterranean Sea

Bermuda

North American Basin

Madeira

Black Sea

Gulf of Mexico

West Indies

Canary Basin

Canary Is

Tropic of Cancer

Cayman Tr.

Puerto Rico Trench
9220

Caribbean Sea

Cape Verde Basin

Cape Verde Is

C. Vert

AFRICA

Cocos Ridge

Guyana Basin

Niger

Galapagos Is

Equator

Guinea Basin

Bioko
Príncipe

São Tomé

Amazon

Rocas

Fernando de Noronha

Zaïre

SOUTH AMERICA

Brazil Basin

Ascension

Mid-Atlantic Ridge

Angola Basin

St Helena

Peru - Chile Trench

S.W. Peru or Nazca Ridge

8066
7635

I.San Ambrosia
I.San Felix

Trindade

Martin Vaz

Rio Grande Rise
637

Walvis Ridge

Tropic of Capricorn

6081

Cape Basin

C. Agulhas

Is Juan Fernandez

Tristan da Cunha

Gough I.

Discovery Tablemount
411

Agulhas Plateau

Argentine Basin

Falkland Is

S. Georgia

S. Sandwich Tr.
8264

Atlantic-Indian Ridge

Prince Edward Is

Crozet Plateau

C. Horn

N. Scotia Ridge

Scotia Sea

S. Sandwich Is

Bouvet I.

Is Cro

Pacific-Antarctic Ridge

Drake Passage

S. Orkney Is

Weddell Sea

Atlantic-Indian Antarctic Basin

South East Pacific Basin

Antarctic Peninsula

Maud Seamount
1199

Antarctic Circle

Peter 1st I.

ANTARCTICA

MOUNTAIN HEIGHTS

Metres	Feet	
8848	29 028	Everest (Qomolangma Feng) *Nepal-Tibet*
8611	28 250	K2 (Godwin Austen) *Kashmir-Sinkiang*
8586	28 168	Kangchenjunga *Nepal-India*
8475	27 805	Makalu *Tibet-Nepal*
8172	26 810	Dhaulagiri *Nepal*
8126	26 660	Nanga Parbat *Kashmir*
8078	26 504	Annapurna *Nepal*
8068	26 470	Gasherbrum *Kashmir*
8013	26 291	Xixabangma Feng (Gosainthan) *Tibet*
7890	25 885	Distaghil Sar *Kashmir*
7820	25 656	Masherbrum *Kashmir*
7817	25 645	Nanda Devi *India*
7780	25 550	Rakaposhi *Kashmir*
7756	25 447	Kamet *India-Tibet*
7756	25 447	Namcha Barwa *Tibet*
7728	25 355	Gurla Mandhata *Tibet*
7723	25 338	Muztag (Ulugh Muztagh) *Sinkiang*
7719	25 325	Kongur Shan (Kungur) *Sinkiang*
7690	25 230	Tirich Mir *Pakistan*
7590	24 903	Gongga Shan (Minya Konka) *China*
7546	24 757	Muztagata (Muztagh Ata) *Sinkiang*
7495	24 590	Pik Kommunizma *Tajikistan*
7439	24 407	Pik Pobedy (Tomur Feng) *Kirghizia-Sinkiang*
7313	23 993	Chomo Lhari *Bhutan-Tibet*
7134	23 406	Pik Lenina *Kirghizia-Tajikistan*
6960	22 834	Aconcagua *Argentina*
6908	22 664	Ojos del Salado *Chile-Argentina*

Metres	Feet	
6870	22 541	Bonete *Bolivia*
6800	22 310	Tupungato *Argentina-Chile*
6770	22 211	Mercedario *Argentina*
6768	22 205	Huascarán *Peru*
6723	22 057	Llullaillaco *Argentina-Chile*
6714	22 028	Kangrinboqê Feng (Kailas) *Tibet*
6634	21 765	Yerupaja *Peru*
6542	21 463	Sajama *Bolivia*
6485	21 276	Illampu *Bolivia*
6425	21 079	Coropuna *Peru*
6402	21 004	Illimani *Bolivia*
6388	20 958	Ancohuma *Bolivia*
6310	20 702	Chimborazo *Ecuador*
6194	20 320	McKinley *USA*
6050	19 850	Logan *Canada*
5895	19 340	Kilimanjaro *Tanzania*
5700	18 700	Citlaltepetl *Mexico*
5642	18 510	El'bruz *Russian Federation*
5452	17 887	Popocatepetl *Mexico*
5199	17 057	Kirinyaga (Kenya) *Kenya*
5165	16 946	Ararat *Turkey*
5140	16 864	Vinson Massif *Antarctica*
5110	16 763	Stanley *Zaire-Uganda*
5030	16 500	Jaya (Carstensz) *Indonesia*
4808	15 774	Mont Blanc *France*
4508	14 790	Wilhelm *Papua New Guinea*
4201	13 784	Mauna Kea *USA*

RIVER LENGTHS

Km	Miles	
6695	4160	Nile *Africa*
6570	4080	Amazon *South America*
6380	3964	Yangtze *Asia*
6020	3740	Mississippi-Missouri *North America*
5410	3360	Ob-Irtysh *Asia*
4840	3010	Huang He (Yellow River) *Asia*
4630	2880	Zaïre (Congo) *Africa*
4500	2796	Paraná *South America*
4440	2760	Irtysh *Asia*
4416	2745	Amur *Asia*
4400	2730	Lena *Asia*
4240	2630	Mackenzie *North America*
4180	2600	Mekong *Asia*
4100	2550	Niger *Africa*
4090	2540	Yenisey *Asia*
3969	2466	Missouri *North America*
3779	2348	Mississippi *North America*
3750	2330	Murray-Darling *Australia*
3688	2292	Volga *Europe*
3240	2013	Madeira *South America*
3058	1900	St. Lawrence *North America*
3030	1880	Rio Grande *North America*
3020	1870	Yukon *North America*
2960	1840	Brahmaputra *Asia*
2896	1800	Indus *Asia*

Km	Miles	
2850	1770	Danube *Europe*
2820	1750	Salween *Asia*
2780	1730	São Francisco *South America*
2655	1650	Zambezi *Africa*
2570	1600	Nelson-Saskatchewan *North America*
2510	1560	Ganges *Asia*
2430	1510	Euphrates *Asia*
2330	1450	Arkansas *North America*
2330	1450	Colorado *North America*
2285	1420	Dnieper *Europe*
2090	1300	Irrawaddy *Asia*
2060	1280	Orinoco *South America*
2000	1240	Negro *South America*
1870	1160	Don *Europe*
1859	1155	Orange *Africa*
1799	1118	Pechora *Europe*
1609	1000	Marañón *South America*
1410	876	Dniester *Europe*
1320	820	Rhine *Europe*
1183	735	Donets *Europe*
1159	720	Elbe *Europe*
1094	680	Gambia *Africa*
1080	671	Yellowstone *North America*
1014	630	Vistula *Europe*
1006	625	Tagus *Europe*

LAKE AND INLAND SEA AREAS

Areas are average and some are subject to seasonal variations.

Sq. Km	Sq. Miles	
371 000	142 240	Caspian *Central Asia (salt)*
82 900	32 010	Superior *USA-Canada*
68 800	26 560	Victoria *Kenya-Uganda-Tanzania*
59 580	23 000	Huron *USA-Canada*
58 020	22 480	Michigan *USA*
36 500	14 100	Aral *Central Asia (salt)*
32 900	12 700	Tanganyika *Tanzania-Zambia-Zaire-Burundi*
31 330	12 100	Great Bear *Canada*
30 500	11 800	Baykal *Russian Federation*
28 570	11 030	Great Slave *Canada*
25 680	9910	Erie *USA-Canada*
24 390	9420	Winnipeg *Canada*

Sq. Km	Sq. Miles	
22 490	8680	Nyasa (Malawi) *Malawi-Mozambique*
19 400	7490	Ontario *USA-Canada*
18 390	7100	Ladoga *Russian Federation*
17 400	6700	Balkhash *Kazakhstan*
10-26 000	4-10 000	Chad *Nigeria-Niger-Chad-Cameroon*
9600	3710	Onega *Russian Federation*
0-8900	0-3430	Eyre *Australia*
8340	3220	Titicaca *Peru-Bolivia*
8270	3190	Nicaragua *Nicaragua*
6410	2470	Turkana (Rudolf) *Kenya-Ethiopia*
5780	2230	Torrens *Australia (salt)*
5580	2160	Vänern *Sweden*

GREATEST OCEAN DEPTHS

Metres	Feet	Location	Metres	Feet	Location
		PACIFIC OCEAN			**ATLANTIC OCEAN**
11 022	36 160	Marianas Trench	9220	30 249	Puerto Rico Trench
10 882	35 702	Tonga Trench	8264	27 113	South Sandwich Trench
10 542	34 586	Kuril Trench	7856	25 774	Romanche Gap
10 497	34 439	Philippine Trench	7500	24 600	Cayman Trench
10 047	32 962	Kermadec Trench			
9810	32 185	Izu-Bonin Trench			**INDIAN OCEAN**
9165	30 069	New Hebrides Trench	7450	24 442	Java Trench
9140	29 987	South Solomon Trench	7440	24 409	Weber Basin
8412	27 598	Japan Trench	7102	23 300	Diamantina Trench
8066	26 463	Peru-Chile Trench			
7822	25 662	Aleutian Trench			**ARCTIC OCEAN**
6662	21 857	Middle America	5570	18 274	Nansen Fracture Zone

THE WORLD IN FIGURES

STATES AND DEPENDENCIES

COUNTRY	Area (sq. km)	Population ('000)	Capital
North and Central America			
Anguilla (UK)	91	7	The Valley
Antigua and Barbuda	442	76	St. John's
The Bahamas	13 864	253	Nassau
Barbados	430	255	Bridgetown
Belize	22 965	187	Belmopan
Bermuda (UK)	53	58	Hamilton
Canada	9 976 147	26 521	Ottawa
Cayman Is. (UK)	259	25	George Town
Costa Rica	50 899	3 015	San José
Cuba	114 524	10 608	La Habana (Havana)
Dominica	751	82	Roseau
Dominican Republic	48 441	7 170	Santo Domingo
El Salvador	20 865	5 252	San Salvador
Grenada	344	85	St. George's
Guadeloupe (Fr.)	1 779	343	Basse Terre
Guatemala	108 888	9 197	Guatemala
Haiti	27 749	6 513	Port-au-Prince
Honduras	112 087	5 138	Tegucigalpa
Jamaica	11 425	2 456	Kingston
Martinique (Fr.)	1 101	341	Fort-de-France
Mexico	1 967 180	107 233	Mexico
Montserrat (UK)	102	12	Plymouth
Netherlands Antilles (Neth.)	993	188	Willemstad
Nicaragua	139 000	3 871	Managua
Panama	75 648	2 418	Panamá
Puerto Rico (USA)	8 897	3 480	San Juan
St. Kitts-Nevis	260	44	Basseterre
St. Lucia	616	150	Castries
St. Vincent	389	116	Kingstown
Trinidad and Tobago	5 128	1 281	Port of Spain
United States of America	9 363 130	249 224	Washington
South America			
Argentina	2 777 815	32 322	Buenos Aires
Bolivia	1 098 575	7 314	La Paz
Brazil	8 511 968	150 368	Brasília
Chile	756 943	13 173	Santiago
Colombia	1 138 907	32 978	Bogotá
Ecuador	455 502	10 587	Quito
French Guiana (Fr.)	91 000	98	Cayenne
Guyana	214 969	796	George Town
Paraguay	406 750	4 277	Asunción
Peru	1 285 215	21 550	Lima
Surinam	163 820	422	Paramribo
Uruguay	186 925	3 094	Montevideo
Venezuela	912 047	19 735	Caracas
Europe			
Albania	28 752	3 245	Tiranë (Tirana)
Andorra	453	47	Andorra-la-Vella
Austria	83 848	7 583	Wien (Vienna)
Belgium	30 512	9 845	Bruxelles (Brussels)
Belorussia (Belarus)	207 600	10 200	Minsk
Bosnia-Herzegovina	51 130	4 400	Sarajevo
Bulgaria	110 911	9 010	Sofiya (Sofia)
Croatia	56 540	4 700	Zagreb
Cyprus	9 251	701	Nicosia
Czech Republic	78 864	10 300	Praha (Prague)
Denmark	43 030	5 143	København (Copenhagen)
Estonia	45 100	1 573	Tallinn
Faroes (Den.)	1 399	47	Tórshavn
Finland	337 032	4 975	Helsinki
France	551 000	56 138	Paris
Germany	357 868	79 070	Berlin,Bonn
Gibraltar (UK)	6	30	Gibraltar
Great Britain and N. Ireland, see United Kingdom			
Greece	131 955	10 047	Athinai (Athens)
Greenland (Den.)	2 175 600	56	Godthåb
Hungary	93 030	10 552	Budapest
Iceland	102 828	253	Reykjavik
Ireland	70 282	3 720	Dublin
Italy	301 245	57 061	Roma (Rome)
Latvia	63 700	2 681	Riga
Liechtenstein	161	28	Vaduz
Lithuania	65 200	3 690	Vilnius
Luxembourg	2 587	373	Luxembourg
Macedonia	25 713	2 090	Skopje
Malta	316	353	Valletta
Moldavia (Moldova)	33 700	4 341	Kishinev
Monaco	1.8	28	Monaco
Netherlands	33 940	14 951	Amsterdam/'s-Gravenhage
Norway	324 218	4 212	Oslo
Poland	312 683	38 423	Warszawa (Warsaw)
Portugal	91 671	10 285	Lisboa (Lisbon)
Romania	237 500	23 272	Bucuresti (Bucharest)
Russian Federation	17 075 000	147 386	Moskva (Moscow)
San Marino	61	23	San Marino
Slovakia	49 035	5 300	Bratislava
Slovenia	7 815	1 900	Ljubljana
Spain	504 745	39 187	Madrid
Sweden	449 791	8 444	Stockholm
Switzerland	41 287	6 609	Bern
Ukraine	603 700	51 704	Kiyev
United Kingdom	244 104	57 237	London
Vatican City	.4	1	Vatican City
Yugoslavia	255 803	23 807	Beograd (Belgrade)
Asia			
Afghanistan	674 500	16 557	Kabul
Armenia	29 800	3 283	Yerevan
Azerbaijan	86 600	7 029	Baku
Bahrain	660	516	Al Manāmah
Bangladesh	144 020	115 593	Dhaka (Dacca)
Bhutan	46 620	1 516	Thimphu
Brunei	5 765	266	Bandar Seri Begawan
Burma (Myanmar)	678 031	41 675	Yangon (Rangoon)
Cambodia	181 035	8 246	Phnom Penh
China	9 561 000	1 118 760	Beijing (Peking)
Georgia	69 700	5 449	Tbilisi
Hong Kong (UK)	1 062	5 851	
India	3 287 593	853 094	New Delhi
Indonesia	1 919 263	185 020	Jakarta
Iran	1 648 184	54 607	Tehrän
Iraq	434 924	18 920	Baghdād
Israel	20 770	4 600	Jerusalem
Japan	371 000	123 460	Tōkyō
Jordan	97 740	4 009	Amman
Kazakhstan	2 717 300	16 538	Alma Ata
Kirghizia (Kyrgyzstan)	198 500	4 291	Bishkek (Frunze)
Korea, North	121 248	21 773	P'yŏngyang
Korea, South	98 447	42 793	Sŏul (Seoul)
Kuwait	24 300	2 039	Kuwait
Laos	236 798	4 139	Vientiane
Lebanon	10 399	2 701	Beirut
Macau (Port)	16	479	Macao
Malaysia	330 669	17 891	Kuala Lumpur
Maldives	298	215	Malé
Mongolia	1 565 000	2 190	Ulaanbaatar (Ulan Bator)
Nepal	141 414	19 143	Kathmandu
Oman	212 379	1 502	Masqat (Muscat)
Pakistan	803 941	122 626	Islamabad
Philippines	299 765	62 413	Manila
Qatar	11 437	368	Ad Dawḩah
Saudi Arabia	2 400 930	14 134	Ar Riyāḍ
Singapore	616	2 723	Singapore
Sri Lanka	65 610	17 217	Colombo
Syria	185 179	12 530	Dimashq (Damascus)
Taiwan	35 980	20 300	T'ai-pei
Tajikistan	143 100	5 112	Dushanbe
Thailand	513 517	55 702	Bangkok
Turkey	780 576	55 868	Ankara
Turkmenistan	488 100	3 534	Ashkhabad
United Arab Emirates	83 600	1 589	Abū Ẕabī
Uzbekistan	447 400	19 906	Tashkent
Vietnam	329 566	66 693	Hanoi
Yemen	528 038	11 687	San'ā'
Africa			
Algeria	2 381 731	24 960	Alger (El Djezair)
Angola	1 246 694	10 020	Luanda
Benin	112 622	4 630	Porto Novo
Botswana	582 000	1 304	Gaborone
Burkina	274 122	8 996	Ouagadougou
Burundi	27 834	5 472	Bujumbura
Cameroon	475 499	11 833	Yaoundé
Cape Verde	4 033	370	Praia
Central African Republic	622 996	3 039	Bangui
Chad	1 284 000	5 678	N'Djamena
Comoros	1 862	550	Moroni
Congo	342 000	2 271	Brazzaville
Djibouti	21 699	409	Djibouti
Egypt	1 000 250	52 426	Cairo
Equatorial Guinea	28 051	352	Malabo
Eritrea	117 600	2 614	Äsmera (Asmara)
Ethiopia	1 104 318	46 626	Ädis Äbeba
Gabon	267 667	1 172	Libreville
The Gambia	10 688	861	Banjul
Ghana	238 538	15 028	Accra
Guinea	245 855	5 755	Conakry
Guinea-Bissau	36 125	964	Bissau
Ivory Coast	322 463	11 997	Yamoussoukro
Kenya	582 644	24 031	Nairobi
Lesotho	30 344	1 774	Maseru
Liberia	111 370	2 575	Monrovia
Libya	1 759 530	4 545	Tripoli
Madagascar	587 042	12 004	Antananarivo
Malawi	94 100	8 754	Lilongwe
Mali	1 240 142	9 214	Bamako
Mauritania	1 030 700	2 024	Nouakchott
Mauritius	1 865	1 082	Port Louis
Morocco	459 000	25 061	Rabat
Mozambique	784 961	15 656	Maputo
Namibia	824 293	1 781	Windhoek
Niger	1 267 000	7 731	Niamey
Nigeria	923 769	108 542	Abuja
Réunion (Fr.)	2 510	598	Saint-Denis
Rwanda	26 338	7 237	Kigali
São Tomé and Principe	964	121	São Tomé
Senegal	196 722	7 327	Dakar
Seychelles	443	69	Victoria
Sierra Leone	71 740	4 151	Freetown
Somalia	637 539	7 497	Muqdisho (Mogadishu)
South Africa	1 221 038	35 282	Pretoria/Cape Town
Sudan	2 505 792	25 203	Khartoum
Swaziland	17 366	788	Mbabane
Tanzania	942 000	27 318	Dodoma
Togo	56 785	3 531	Lomé
Tunisia	164 148	8 180	Tunis
Uganda	236 036	18 794	Kampala
Western Sahara	266 000	178	-
Zaire	2 344 885	35 568	Kinshasa
Zambia	752 617	8 452	Lusaka
Zimbabwe	390 308	9 709	Harare
Oceania			
American Samoa (USA)	197	38	Fagatogo
Australia	7 682 300	16 873	Canberra
Fiji	18 272	764	Suva
French Polynesia (Fr.)	4 198	206	Papeete
Guam (USA)	549	118	Agaña
Kiribati	800	66	Tarawa
Marshall Islands	181	40	Dalap-Uliga-Darrit
Nauru	21	9	Yaren
New Caledonia (Fr.)	19 104	167	Nouméa
New Zealand	268 675	3 392	Wellington
Niue (NZ)	259	3	Alofi
Federated States of Micronesia	1 300	99	Kolonia
Papua New Guinea	461 692	3 874	Port Moresby
Solomon Islands	29 785	320	Honiara
Tonga	699	95	Nuku'alofa
Tuvalu	25	9	Funafuti
Vanuatu	14 763	158	Vila
Western Samoa	2 831	168	Apai

This page explains the main symbols, lettering style and height/depth colours used on the reference maps on pages 2 to 79. The scale of each map is indicated at the top of each page. Abbreviations used on the maps appear at the beginning of the index.

BOUNDARIES

—————	International
– – – –	International under Dispute
· · · · · · ·	Cease Fire Line
—————	Autonomous or State
—————	Administrative
– –– – ––	Maritime (National)
– – – – –	International Date Line

COMMUNICATIONS

—————	Motorway/Express Highway
=========	Under Construction
—————	Major Highway
—————	Other Roads
– – – –	Under Construction
– – – –	Track
→––––←—	Road Tunnel
– – – –	Car Ferry
—————	Main Railway
—————	Other Railway
– – – –	Under Construction
→–––←—	Rail Tunnel
– – – –	Rail Ferry
┴┴┴┴	Canal
⊕	International Airport
✈	Other Airport

LAKE FEATURES

	Freshwater
	Saltwater
	Seasonal
	Salt Pan

LANDSCAPE FEATURES

	Glacier, Ice Cap
	Marsh, Swamp
	Sand Desert, Dunes

OTHER FEATURES

	River
	Seasonal River
≍	Pass, Gorge
	Dam, Barrage
	Waterfall, Rapid
	Aqueduct
	Reef
▲4231	Summit, Peak
.217	Spot Height, Depth
ᴗ	Well
∆	Oil Field
▲	Gas Field
Gas / Oil	Oil/Natural Gas Pipeline
Gemsbok Nat. Pk	National Park
∴UR	Historic Site

LETTERING STYLES

CANADA	Independent Nation
FLORIDA	State, Province or Autonomous Region
Gibraltar (U.K.)	Sovereignty of Dependent Territory
Lothian	Administrative Area
LANGUEDOC	Historic Region
Loire **Vosges**	Physical Feature or Physical Region

TOWNS AND CITIES

Square symbols denote capital cities. Each settlement is given a symbol according to its relative importance, with type size to match.

▣	◉	**New York**	Major City
■	●	**Montréal**	City
▫	○	Ottawa	Small City
■	●	**Québec**	Large Town
▫	○	St John's	Town
▫	○	Yorkton	Small Town
▫	○	Jasper	Village
			Built-up-area

Height

	6000m
	5000m
	4000m
	3000m
	2000m
	1000m
	500m
	200m
0	0 Sea Level

	200m
	2000m
	4000m
	6000m
	8000m

Depth

1:35M

0 250 500 750 1000 1250 km
0 250 500 750 mls

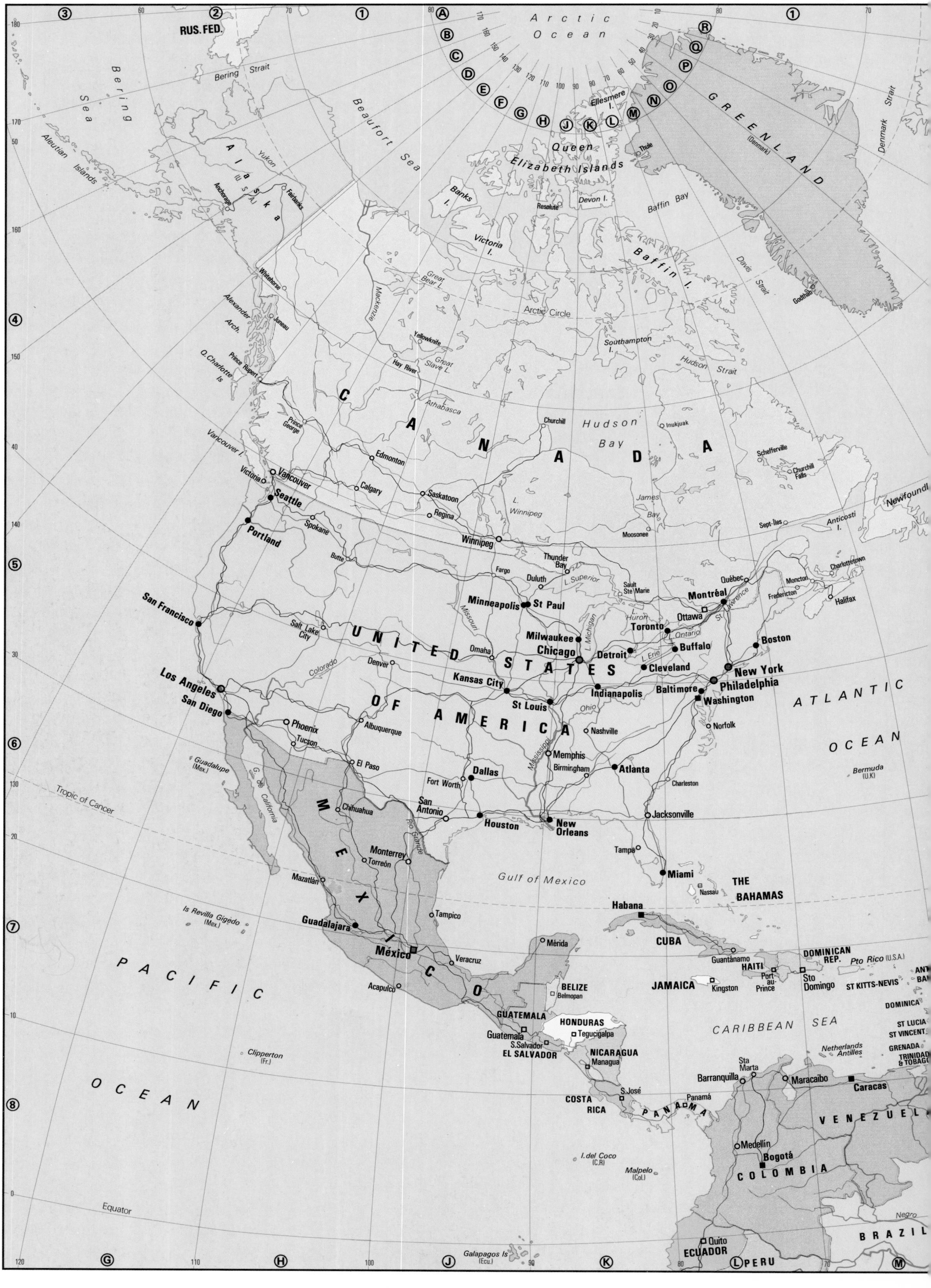

Arctic Ocean

RUS. FED.

③ 60 ② 70 ① 80 Ⓐ 170 Ⓡ 80 ① 70

Ⓑ 160
Ⓒ 150 Ⓠ
Ⓓ 140 Ⓟ 60
Ⓔ 130 Ⓞ
Ⓕ 120 Ⓝ

GREENLAND (Denmark)

Bering Sea

Ⓖ 110 Ⓜ
Ⓗ Ⓙ 100 Ⓚ 90 Ⓛ

Ellesmere I.

Thule

Bering Strait

Beaufort Sea

Aleutian Islands

A l a s k a (U.S.A.)

Yukon

Anchorage
Fairbanks

Whitehorse

Banks I.

Victoria I.

Queen Elizabeth Islands

Resolute
Devon I.

Baffin Bay

Denmark Strait

Juneau

Alexander Arch.

Prince Rupert

Q. Charlotte Is

Vancouver I.

Prince George

C A N A D A

Great Bear L.

Mackenzie

Yellowknife

Hay River

Great Slave L.

Athabasca

Arctic Circle

Southampton I.

Churchill

Hudson Strait

Baffin I.

Davis Strait

Godthåb

Newfoundl

Victoria
Vancouver
Seattle

Edmonton

Calgary

Saskatoon

Regina

L. Winnipeg

Winnipeg

Hudson Bay

Inukjuak

James Bay

Moosonee

Schefferville

Churchill Falls

Sept-Îles

Anticosti I.

Charlottetown

Spokane

Portland

Butte

④ 40

⑤ 30

San Francisco

Salt Lake City

Thunder Bay

Fargo
Duluth

L. Superior

Sault Ste Marie

Québec

Moncton

Fredericton

Halifax

U N I T E D   S T A T E S

Minneapolis St Paul

Milwaukee
Chicago

Detroit

L. Huron
L. Michigan

Toronto

Ottawa

Montréal

L. Ontario

Buffalo

Boston

Omaha

Cleveland

L. Erie

New York

Denver

Colorado

O F   A M E R I C A

Kansas City

St Louis

Indianapolis

Ohio

Baltimore

Washington

Philadelphia

ATLANTIC

Los Angeles

San Diego

Phoenix

Tucson

Albuquerque

Nashville

Norfolk

OCEAN

⑥

El Paso

Dallas

Fort Worth

Memphis

Birmingham

Atlanta

Charleston

Bermuda (U.K.)

Tropic of Cancer

M E X I C O

Chihuahua

Rio Grande

San Antonio

Houston

New Orleans

Jacksonville

Tampa

Guadalupe (Mex.)

G. of California

Monterrey
Torreón

Gulf of Mexico

Miami

THE BAHAMAS

Nassau

Mazatlán

Tampico

Habana

CUBA

Is Revilla Gigedo (Mex.)

⑦

Guadalajara

Mérida

Guantánamo

DOMINICAN REP.

Pto Rico (U.S.A.)

México

Veracruz

HAITI

Port-au-Prince

Sto Domingo

ST KITTS-NEVIS

ANT BA

DOMINICA

Acapulco

BELIZE

Belmopan

JAMAICA

Kingston

ST LUCIA
ST VINCENT

PACIFIC

GUATEMALA

HONDURAS

Tegucigalpa

CARIBBEAN   SEA

GRENADA

TRINIDAD & TOBAGO

Clipperton (Fr.)

Guatemala

S.Salvador

EL SALVADOR

NICARAGUA

Managua

Sta Marta

Netherlands Antilles

OCEAN

⑧

COSTA RICA

S.José

Panamá

P A N A M A

Barranquilla

Maracaibo

Caracas

VENEZUEL

I.del Coco (C.R)

Malpelo (Col.)

Medellín

Bogotá

COLOMBIA

0
Equator

Quito

ECUADOR

PERU

BRAZIL

Negro

120 G 110 H 100 J 90 K 80 L 70 M

Galapagos Is (Ecu.)

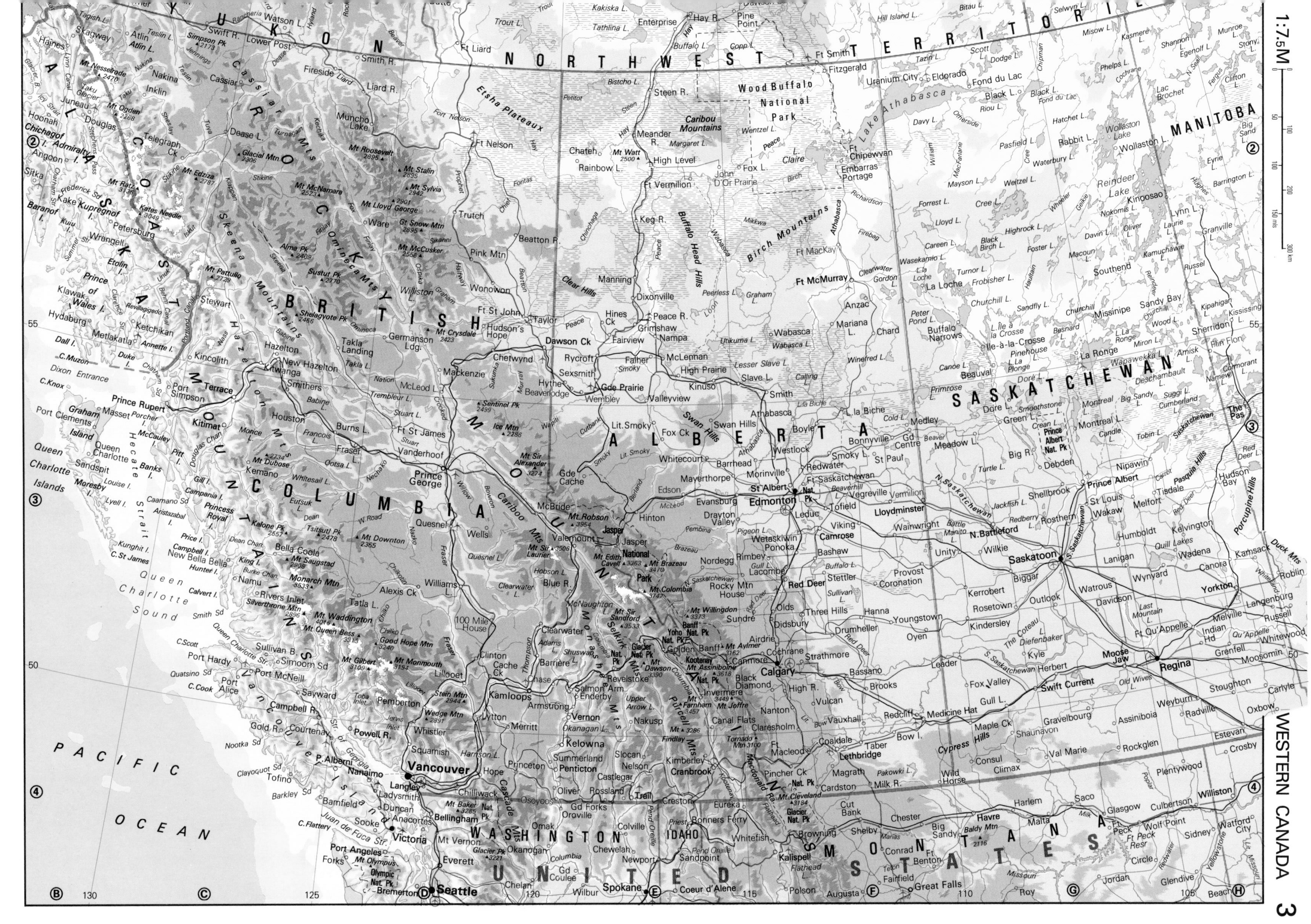
NORTHWEST TERRITORIES
MANITOBA
SASKATCHEWAN
ALBERTA
BRITISH COLUMBIA
YUKON
ALASKA
UNITED STATES
MONTANA
WASHINGTON
IDAHO
PACIFIC OCEAN
ROCKY MOUNTAINS
COAST MOUNTAINS
Vancouver
Victoria
Seattle
Calgary
Edmonton
Regina
Saskatoon
Prince George
Kamloops
Spokane
Lethbridge
Medicine Hat
Moose Jaw
Prince Albert
Prince Rupert
Lake Athabasca
Wood Buffalo National Park
Queen Charlotte Islands
Vancouver I.

1:7.5M

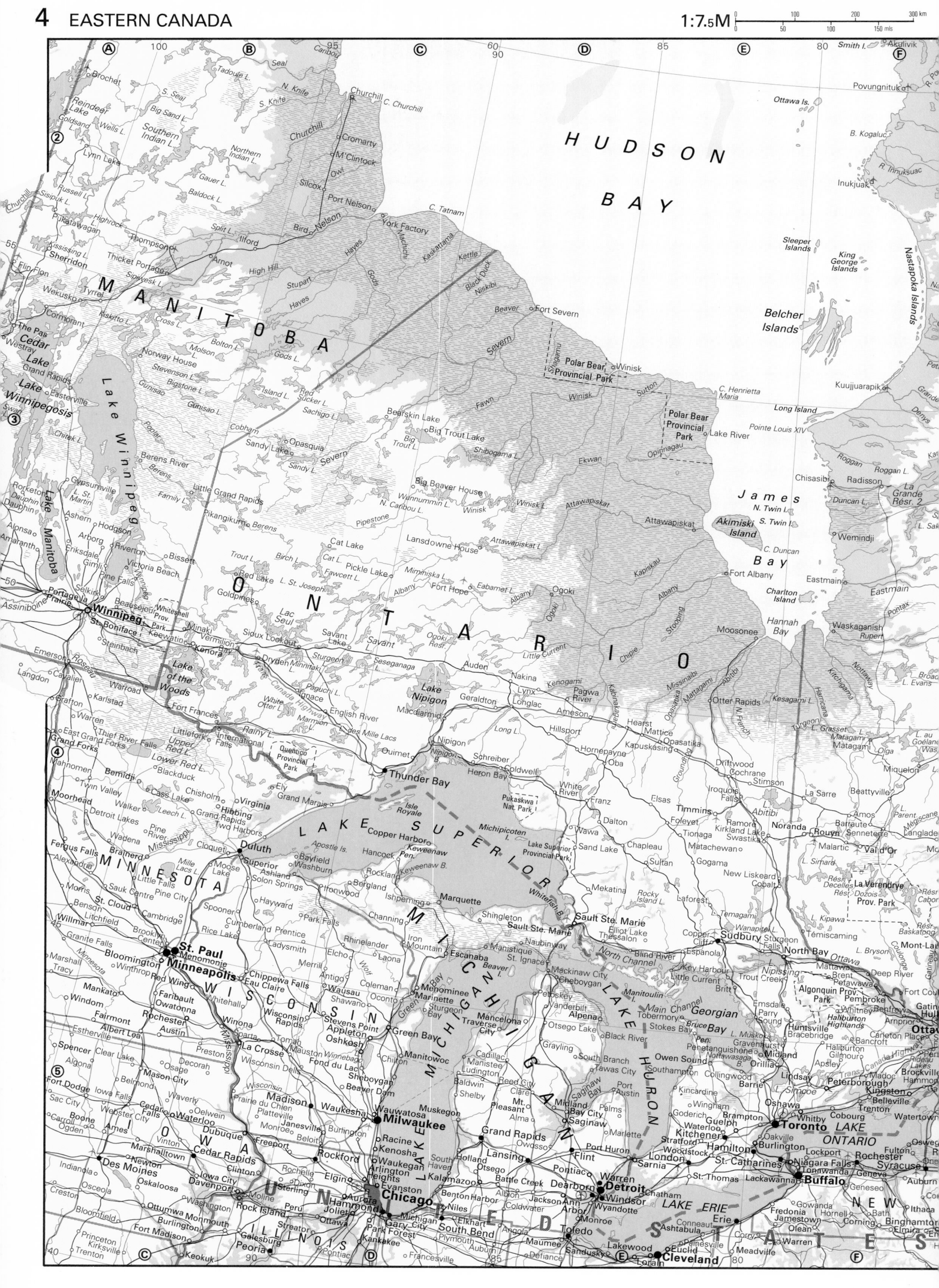

HUDSON BAY

MANITOBA

ONTARIO

JAMES BAY

LAKE SUPERIOR

LAKE MICHIGAN

LAKE HURON

LAKE ERIE

LAKE ONTARIO

MINNESOTA

WISCONSIN

IOWA

ILLINOIS

UNITED STATES

NEW

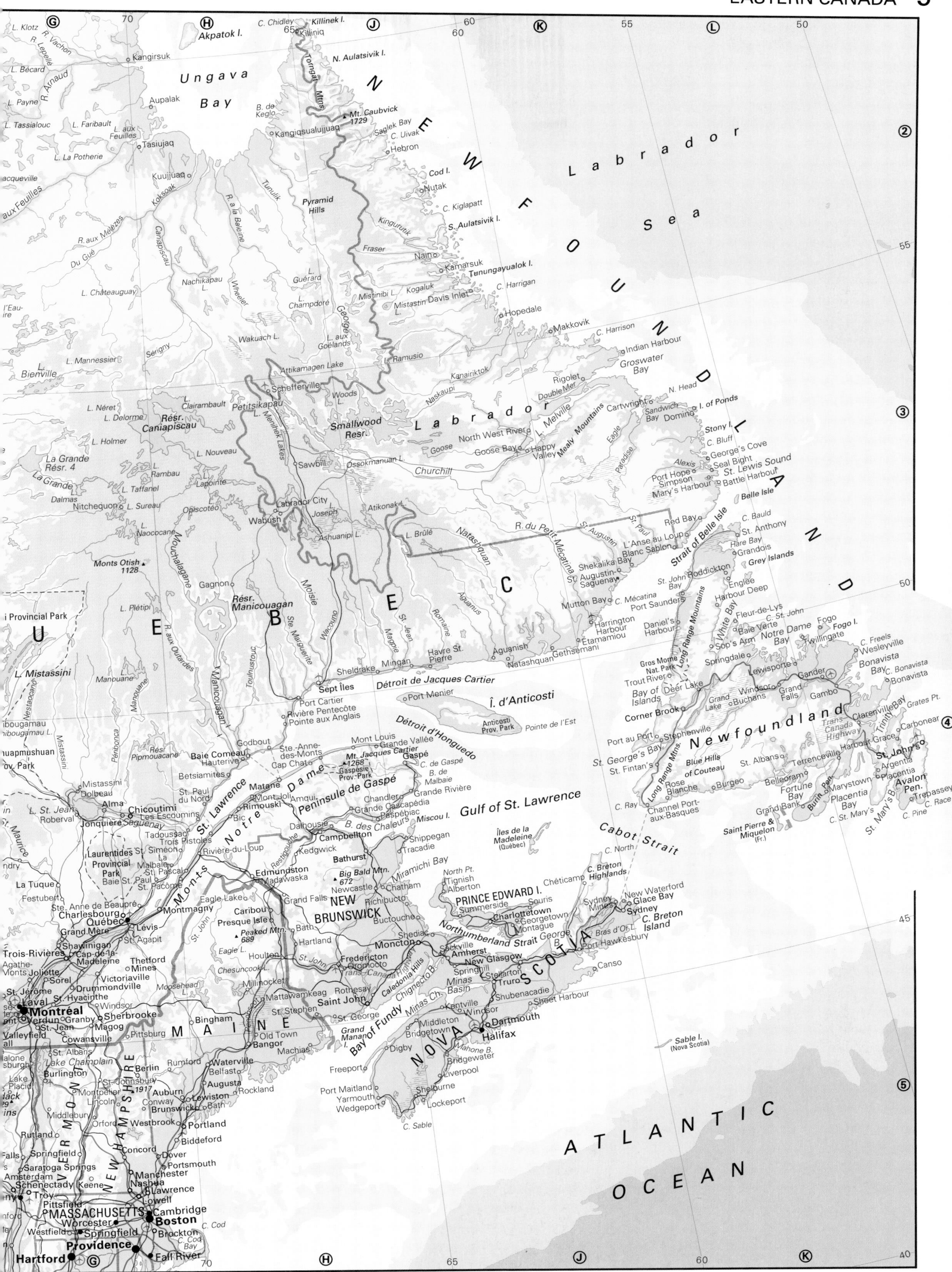
Ungava Bay
Labrador Sea
NEWFOUNDLAND
QUEBEC
Labrador
Newfoundland
Gulf of St. Lawrence
Cabot Strait
Strait of Belle Isle
Détroit de Jacques Cartier
Détroit d'Honguedo
Î. d'Anticosti
Péninsule de Gaspé
NEW BRUNSWICK
NOVA SCOTIA
PRINCE EDWARD I.
MAINE
VERMONT
NEW HAMPSHIRE
MASSACHUSETTS
Bay of Fundy
Northumberland Strait
ATLANTIC OCEAN
Smallwood Resr.
Résr. Caniapiscau
Résr. Manicouagan
Montréal
Québec
Halifax
Boston
St. John's
Sept Îles
Labrador City
Goose Bay
Charlottetown
Fredericton
Saint John
Moncton
Sydney
Corner Brook
Gander
Providence
Hartford
Sable I. (Nova Scotia)
Saint Pierre & Miquelon (Fr.)
Mt. Caubvick 1729
Torngat Mtns.
Long Range Mountains
Mealy Mountains

1:15M

| 0 | 200 | 400 | 600 km |
| 100 | 200 | 300 mls |

Major regions and features

ARCTIC OCEAN

BEAUFORT SEA

PACIFIC OCEAN

Gulf of Alaska

Bering Sea

ALASKA (U.S.A.)

YUKON TERRITORY

NORTH WEST TERRITORIES

BRITISH COLUMBIA

ALBERTA

SASKATCHEWAN

MANITOBA

WASHINGTON

OREGON

IDAHO

MONTANA

WYOMING

NORTH DAKOTA

SOUTH DAKOTA

RUS. FED.

Brooks Range

Mackenzie Mountains

Selwyn Mountains

Rocky Mountains

Coast Mountains

Queen Charlotte Islands

Victoria Island

Banks Island

Kodiak Island

Aleutian Ra.

Alexander Archipelago

Prince of Wales I.

Selected cities

Anchorage, Fairbanks, Juneau, Whitehorse, Yellowknife, Edmonton, Calgary, Saskatoon, Regina, Winnipeg, Vancouver, Victoria, Seattle, Tacoma, Spokane, Portland, Salem, Boise, Helena, Great Falls, Billings, Bismarck, Prince Rupert, Prince George, Kamloops, Kelowna, Medicine Hat, Lethbridge, Moose Jaw

Names underlined indicate Province/State capitals

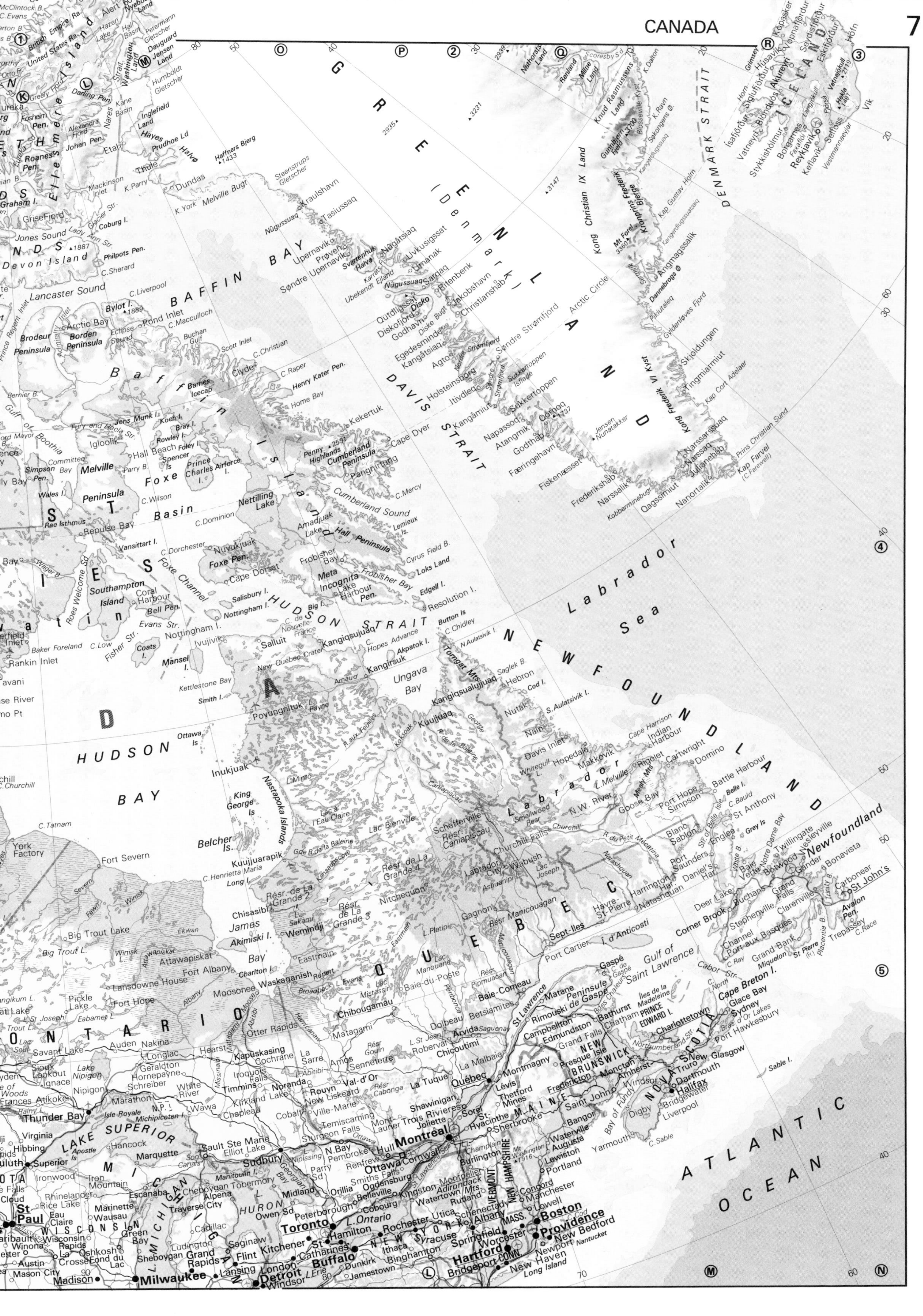
GREENLAND
(Denmark)
BAFFIN BAY
Baffin Island
DAVIS STRAIT
DENMARK STRAIT
ICELAND
Reykjavík
Labrador Sea
HUDSON STRAIT
Ungava Bay
HUDSON BAY
James Bay
Foxe Basin
Foxe Channel
Melville Peninsula
Southampton Island
Devon Island
Ellesmere Island
Lancaster Sound
Cumberland Sound
Frobisher Bay
NEWFOUNDLAND
Newfoundland
St John's
Labrador
QUEBEC
ONTARIO
Gulf of Saint Lawrence
NEW BRUNSWICK
NOVA SCOTIA
PRINCE EDWARD I.
Cape Breton I.
Halifax
Charlottetown
Fredericton
Québec
Montréal
Ottawa
Toronto
Boston
Providence
Hartford
Buffalo
Detroit
Milwaukee
St Paul
Thunder Bay
LAKE SUPERIOR
L. Michigan
L. Huron
L. Ontario
L. Erie
MAINE
VERMONT
NEW HAMPSHIRE
MASS.
CONN.
NEW YORK
MICHIGAN
WISCONSIN
Bay of Fundy
Arctic Circle
ATLANTIC OCEAN
Sable I.

1:12.5M

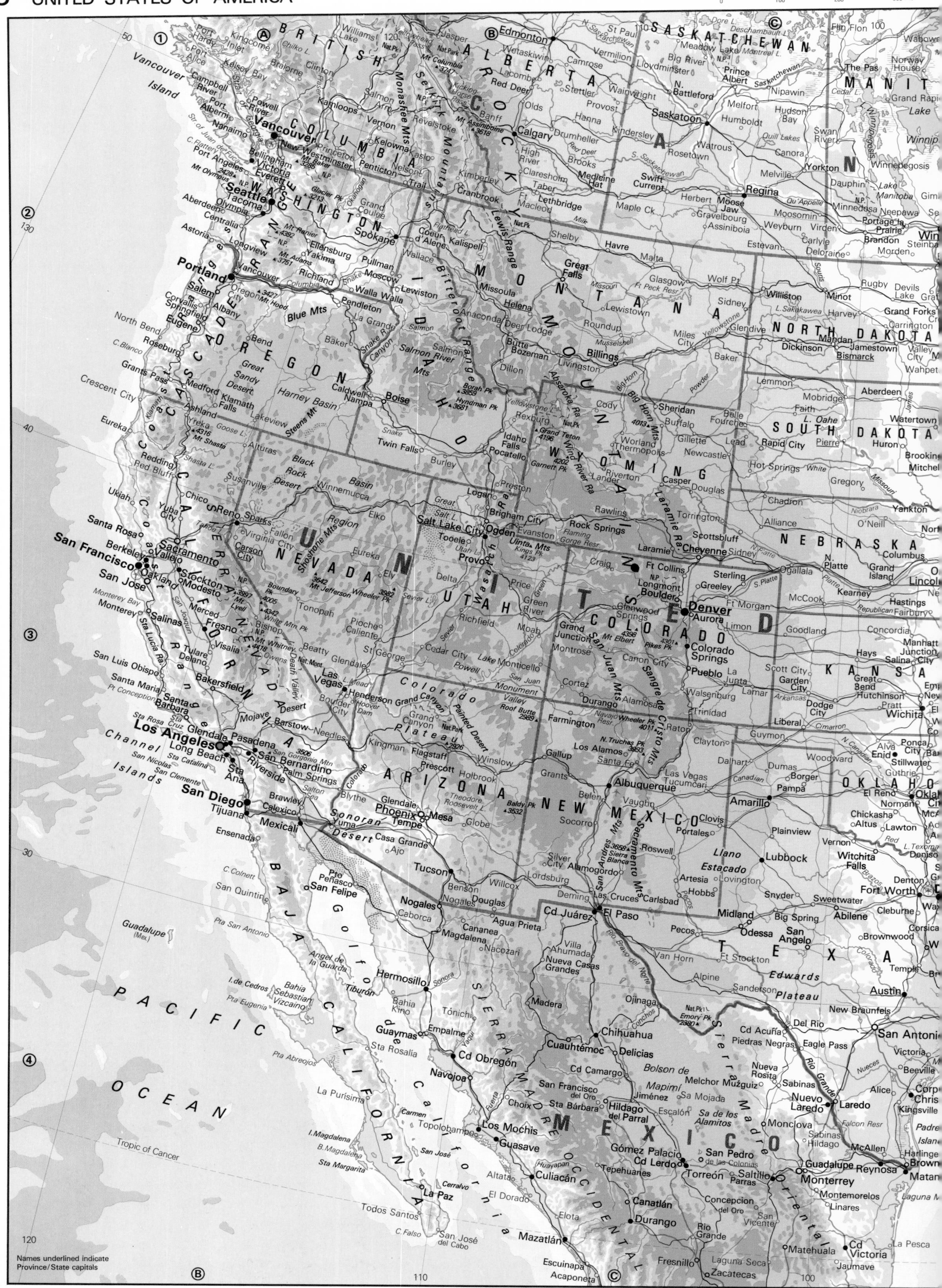

Names underlined indicate
Province/State capitals

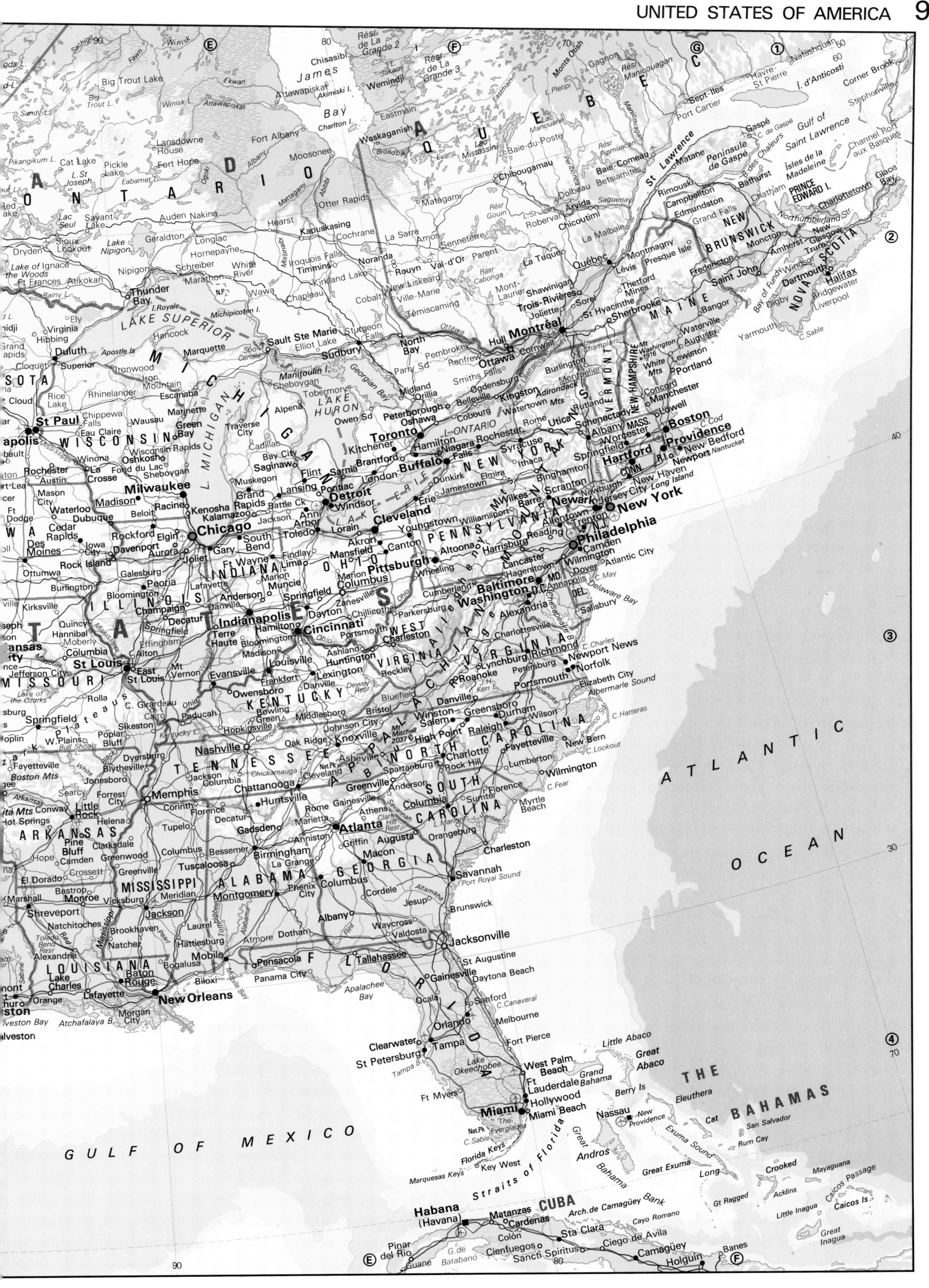
ATLANTIC OCEAN
GULF OF MEXICO
THE BAHAMAS
CUBA
Straits of Florida
Gulf of St Lawrence
James Bay
LAKE SUPERIOR
LAKE HURON
L. MICHIGAN
L. ONTARIO
LAKE ERIE
ONTARIO
QUEBEC
NEW BRUNSWICK
NOVA SCOTIA
PRINCE EDWARD I.
MAINE
VERMONT
NEW HAMPSHIRE
MASS.
CONN.
R.I.
NEW YORK
N.J.
PENNSYLVANIA
DEL.
MD
D.C.
OHIO
MICHIGAN
WISCONSIN
INDIANA
ILLINOIS
MISSOURI
KENTUCKY
WEST VIRGINIA
VIRGINIA
TENNESSEE
NORTH CAROLINA
SOUTH CAROLINA
GEORGIA
ALABAMA
MISSISSIPPI
ARKANSAS
LOUISIANA
FLORIDA
APPALACHIAN MOUNTAINS
Montréal
Ottawa
Toronto
Québec
Halifax
Boston
Providence
Hartford
New York
Philadelphia
Baltimore
Washington
Pittsburgh
Cleveland
Buffalo
Detroit
Chicago
Milwaukee
Indianapolis
Cincinnati
Columbus
St Louis
Louisville
Nashville
Memphis
Atlanta
Charleston
Jacksonville
Tampa
Miami
New Orleans
Habana (Havana)

1:10M

100 200 300 400 km
100 200 mls

ARCTIC OCEAN

NORTHWEST TERRITORIES

YUKON TERRITORY

BRITISH COLUMBIA

Beaufort Sea

Mackenzie Bay

Richardson Mts

Ogilvie Mountains

Wernecke Mountains

Mackenzie Mountains

Pelly Mountains

Cassiar Mountains

Skeena Mountains

St Elias Mountains

Wrangell Mts

Chugach Mountains

Alexander Archipelago

Gulf of Alaska

Brooks Range

North Slope

Endicott Mts

Baird Mountains

De Long Mts

Seward Peninsula

Norton Sound

Kuskokwim Mts

Alaska Range

Mt McKinley

Bristol Bay

Shumagin Islands

Kodiak

Kenai Peninsula

Cook Inlet

Prince William Sd

Chukchi Sea

Bering Strait

Bering Sea

RUSSIAN FEDERATION

Chukotskiy Poluostrov

Anadyrskiy Zaliv

St Lawrence I.

Nunivak I.

St Matthew I.

Pribilof Is

Aleutian Islands

Near Islands

Fox Islands

Unalaska

Unimak I.

INTERNATIONAL DATE LINE

Arctic Circle

Trans-Alaska Pipeline

Fairbanks

Anchorage

Nome

Barrow

Prudhoe Bay

Whitehorse

Dawson

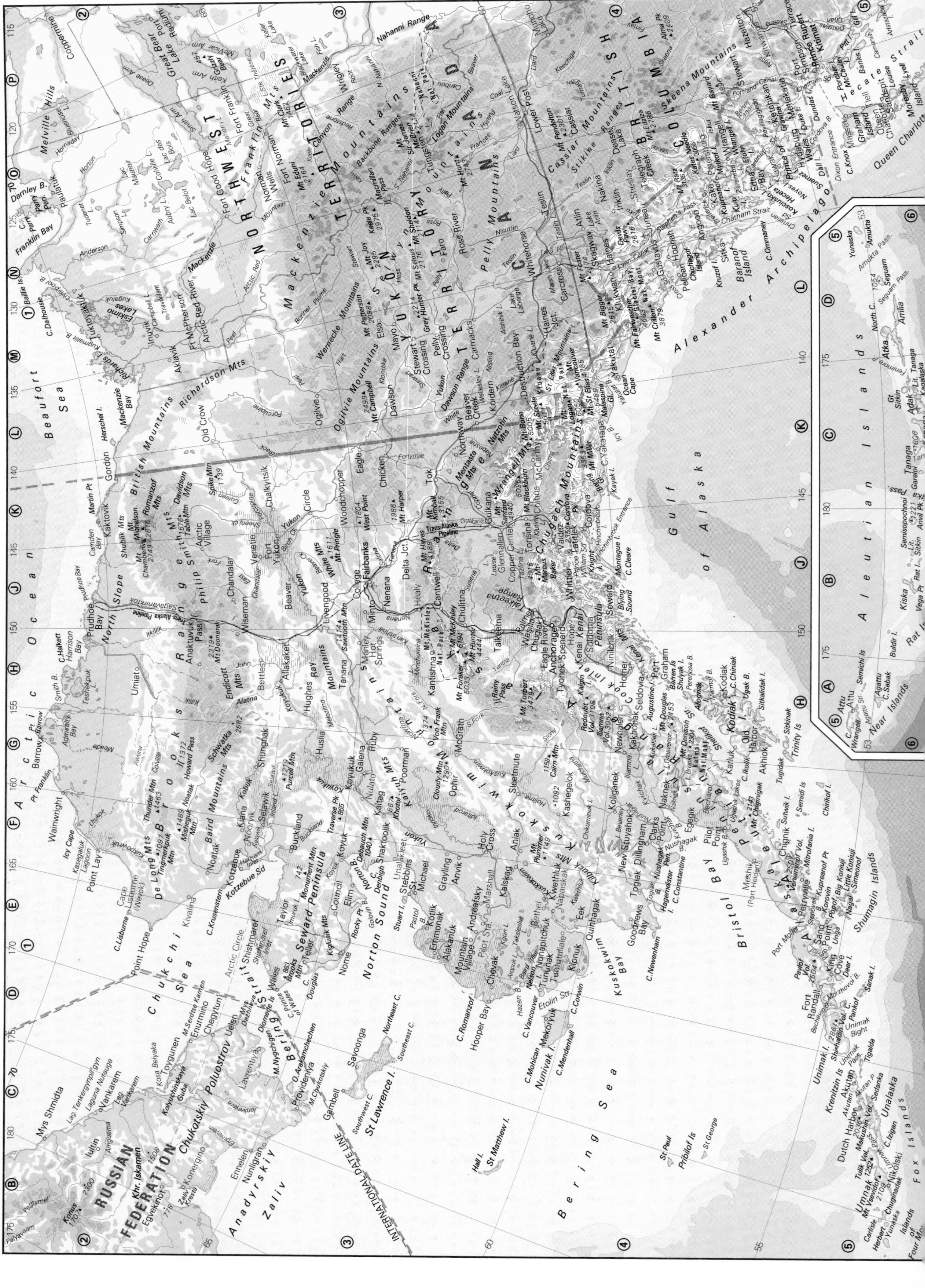

1:5M 0 50 100 150 200 km 0 50 100 mls

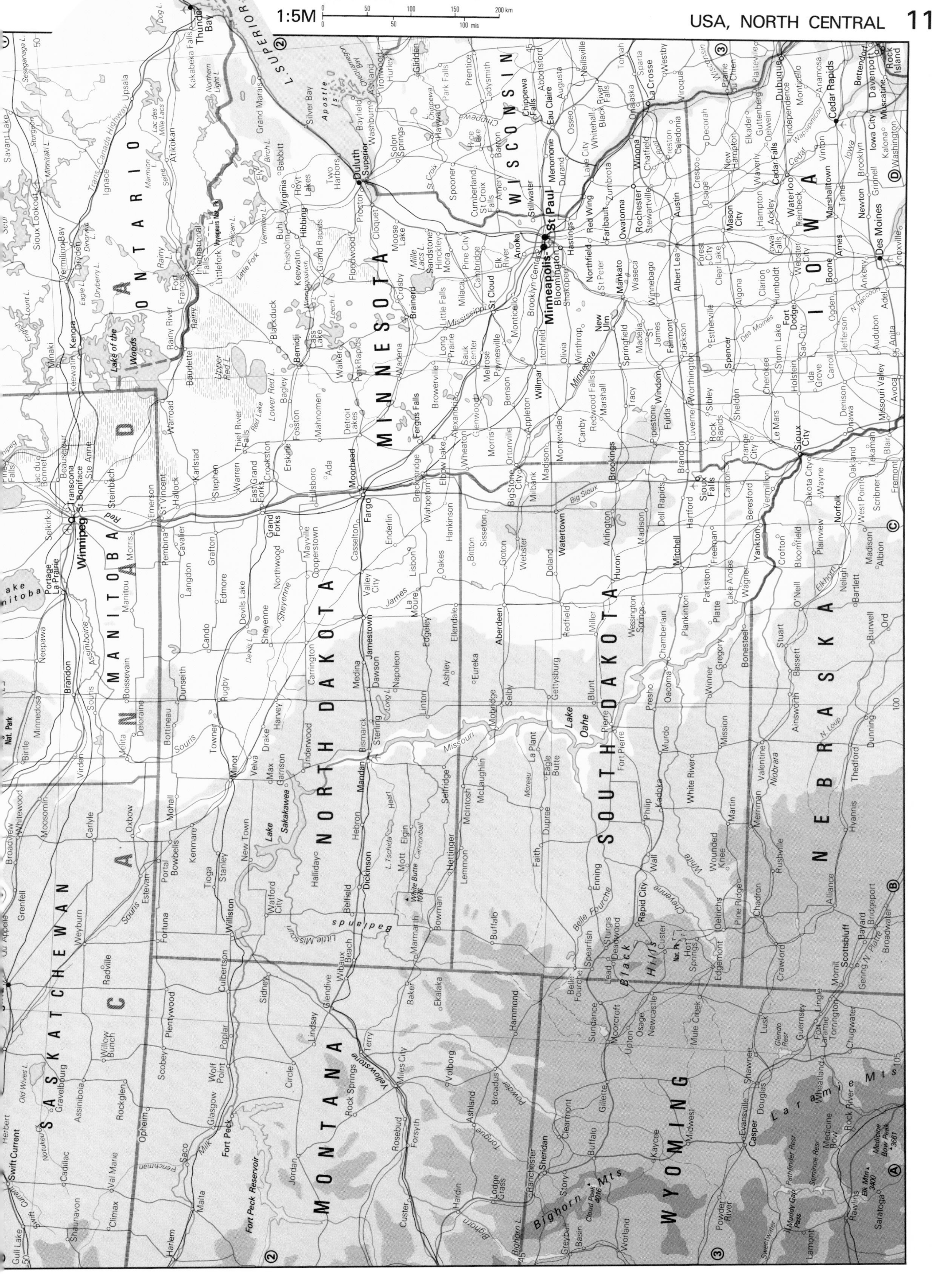
ONTARIO
MANITOBA
SASKATCHEWAN
CANADA
MINNESOTA
WISCONSIN
IOWA
NORTH DAKOTA
SOUTH DAKOTA
NEBRASKA
MONTANA
WYOMING
L. SUPERIOR
Lake of the Woods
Lake Sakakawea
Lake Oahe
Black Hills
Bighorn Mts
Laramie Mts
Fort Peck Reservoir
Winnipeg
Minneapolis
St Paul
Duluth
Fargo
Bismarck
Pierre
Sioux Falls
Des Moines
Cedar Rapids
Thunder Bay

1:5M

LAKE SUPERIOR

LAKE MICHIGAN

LAKE HURON

LAKE ERIE

MINNESOTA

WISCONSIN

IOWA

ILLINOIS

MISSOURI

INDIANA

MICHIGAN

OHIO

KENTUCKY

TENNESSEE

ARKANSAS

WEST VIRGINIA

ONTARIO

St Paul

Duluth
Superior

Milwaukee

Chicago

St Louis

Madison

Indianapolis

Columbus

Cincinnati

Detroit

Cleveland

Thunder Bay

Grand Rapids

Toledo

Akron

Canton

Youngstown

Louisville

Lexington

Nashville

Fort Wayne

Peoria

Springfield

Decatur

Champaign

Evansville

Sault Ste Marie

Green Bay

Appleton

Oshkosh

Fond du Lac

Sheboygan

La Crosse

Eau Claire

Rochester

Cedar Rapids

Davenport

Rockford

Dubuque

Lansing

Flint

Saginaw

Bay City

Kalamazoo

Battle Creek

Ann Arbor

Dayton

Kettering

Hamilton

Marietta

Parkersburg

Huntington

Charleston

Bowling Green

Ozark Plateau

Cumberland Mountains

Allegheny Plateau

Apostle Is.

Isle Royale Nat. Pk.

Keweenaw Pen.

Georgian Bay

Manitoulin I.

Bruce Pen.

Straits of Mackinac

Mississippi

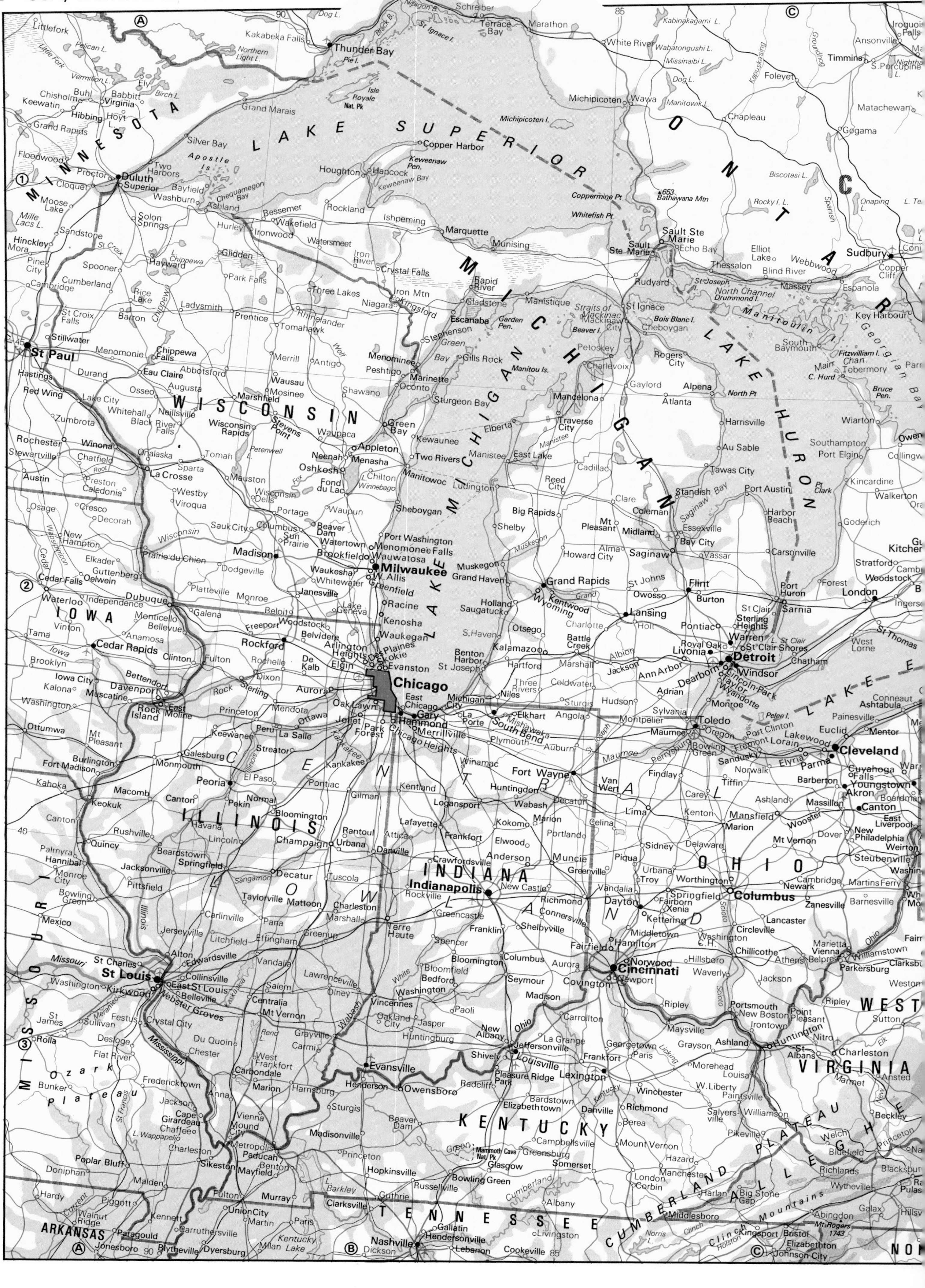

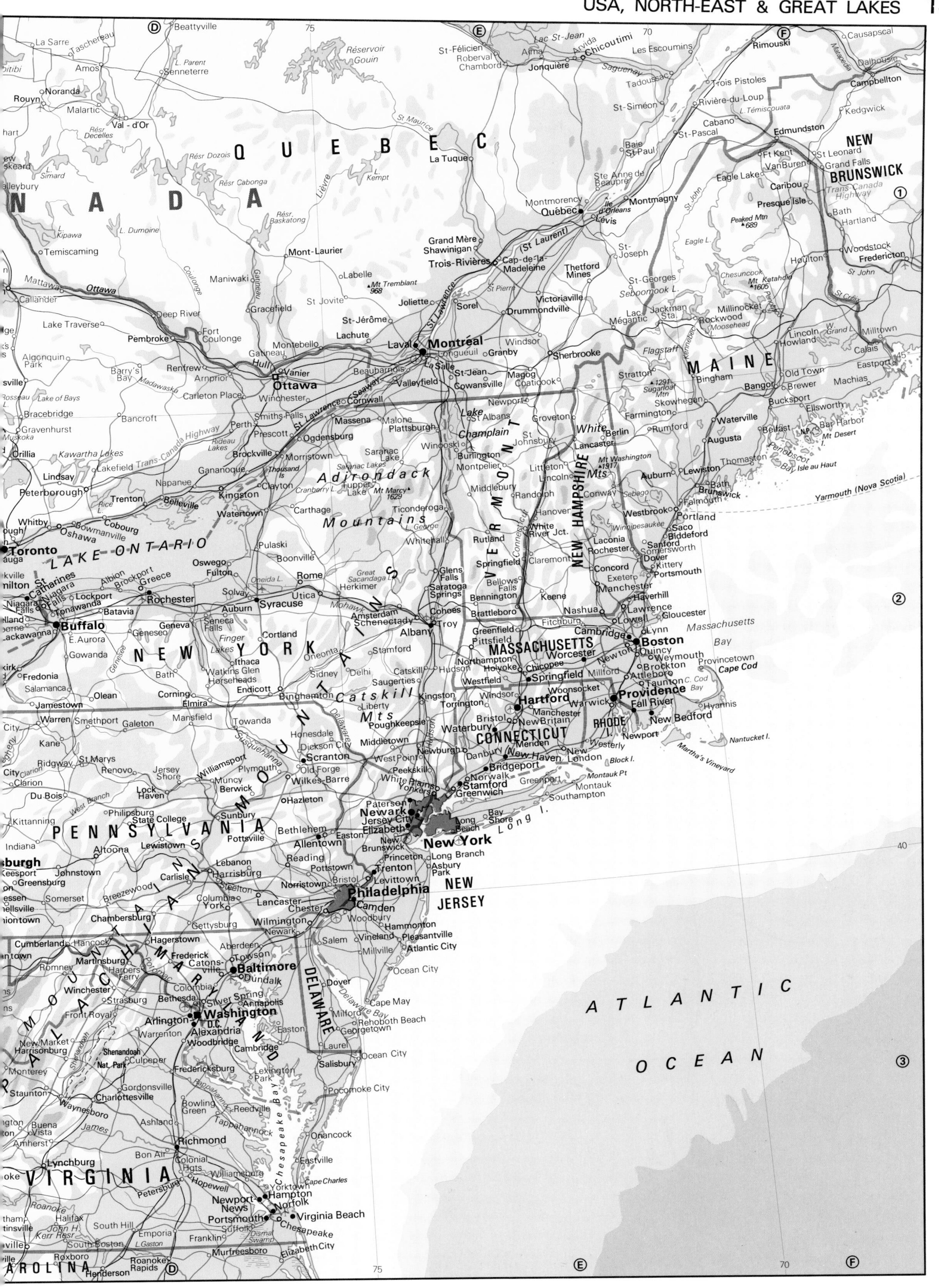
QUEBEC
CANADA
NEW BRUNSWICK
MAINE
VERMONT
NEW HAMPSHIRE
MASSACHUSETTS
CONNECTICUT
RHODE I.
NEW YORK
PENNSYLVANIA
NEW JERSEY
DELAWARE
MARYLAND
VIRGINIA
LAKE ONTARIO
ATLANTIC OCEAN
Adirondack Mountains
Catskill Mts
APPALACHIAN MOUNTAINS
Massachusetts Bay
Cape Cod
Chesapeake Bay
Delaware Bay
Long I.
Martha's Vineyard
Nantucket I.
Block I.
Montauk Pt
Lake Champlain
Finger Lakes
Thousand Is
Trans-Canada Highway
St Lawrence Seaway
St Laurent
Réservoir Gouin
Lac St-Jean
Beattyville
La Sarre
Amos
Rouyn
Noranda
Malartic
Val - d'Or
Temiscaming
Mont-Laurier
Maniwaki
Ottawa
Hull
Gatineau
Pembroke
Deep River
Kingston
Toronto
Oshawa
Whitby
Peterborough
Orillia
Bracebridge
Trois-Rivières
Québec
Lévis
Chicoutimi
Jonquière
Rimouski
Rivière-du-Loup
Edmundston
Campbellton
Fredericton
Woodstock
Sherbrooke
Granby
Montréal
Laval
Longueuil
Sorel
Drummondville
Victoriaville
Thetford Mines
Cornwall
Brockville
Ogdensburg
Massena
Plattsburgh
Burlington
Montpelier
Rutland
St Johnsbury
Berlin
Lancaster
Mt Washington 1917
White Mts
Bangor
Augusta
Waterville
Lewiston
Auburn
Portland
Bar Harbor
Mt Desert I.
Calais
Eastport
Machias
Presque Isle
Caribou
Houlton
Mt Katahdin 1605
Concord
Manchester
Nashua
Portsmouth
Keene
Laconia
Lowell
Lawrence
Haverhill
Gloucester
Lynn
Boston
Cambridge
Quincy
Brockton
Worcester
Springfield
Pittsfield
Hartford
New Haven
Bridgeport
Stamford
Waterbury
New London
Providence
Fall River
New Bedford
Newport
Hyannis
Provincetown
Albany
Schenectady
Troy
Saratoga Springs
Utica
Syracuse
Rochester
Buffalo
Niagara Falls
Binghamton
Elmira
Ithaca
Scranton
Wilkes-Barre
Harrisburg
Allentown
Bethlehem
Reading
Lancaster
Philadelphia
Camden
Trenton
Princeton
Newark
Jersey City
Elizabeth
Paterson
Yonkers
New York
Atlantic City
Cape May
Wilmington
Dover
Baltimore
Annapolis
Washington D.C.
Alexandria
Arlington
Richmond
Fredericksburg
Charlottesville
Lynchburg
Norfolk
Newport News
Hampton
Portsmouth
Virginia Beach
Chesapeake
Petersburg
Williamsburg
Yarmouth (Nova Scotia)
75
70
40
45
D
E
F
1
2
3

1:2.5M

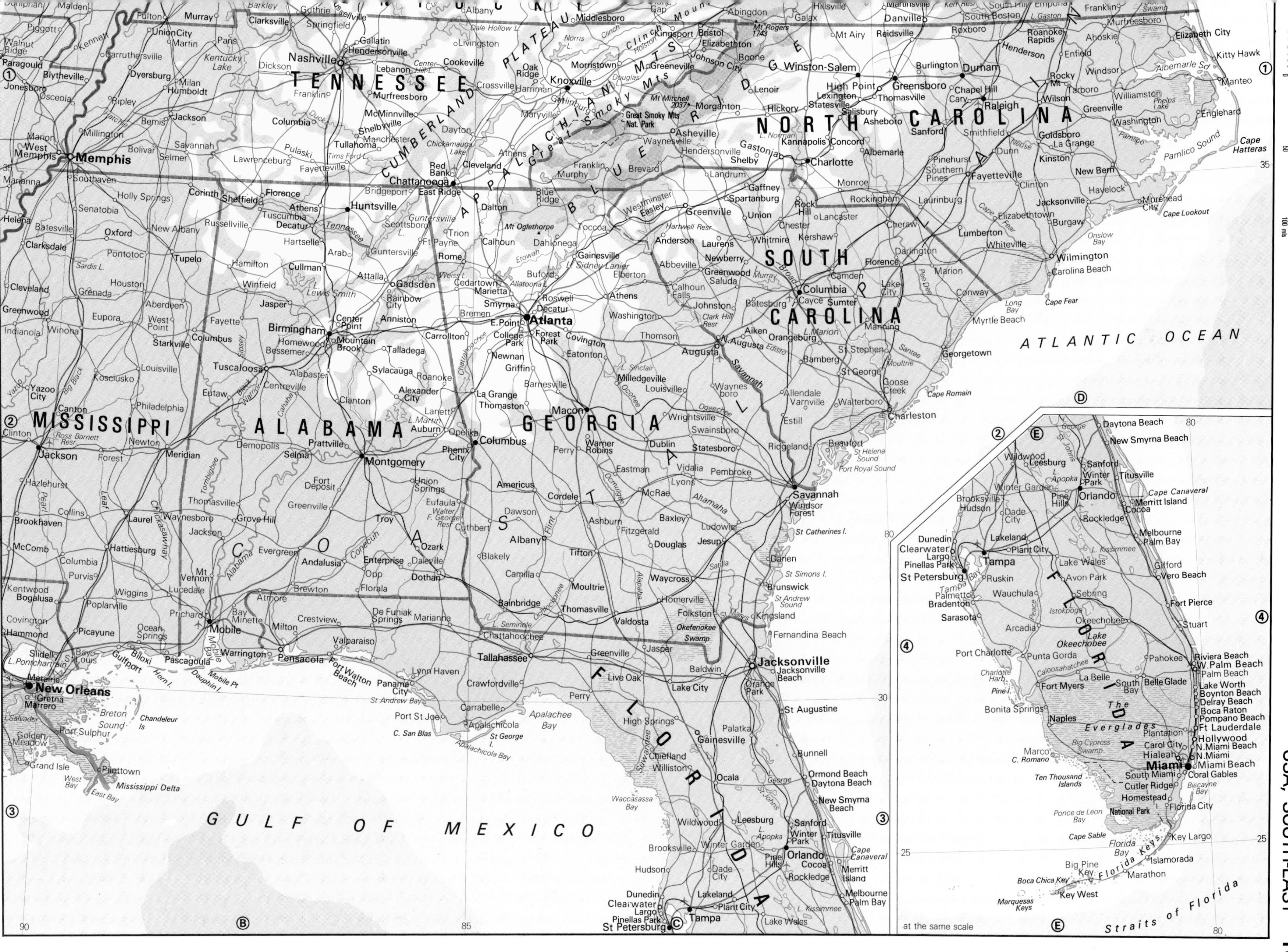
ATLANTIC OCEAN
GULF OF MEXICO
Straits of Florida
NORTH CAROLINA
SOUTH CAROLINA
GEORGIA
FLORIDA
ALABAMA
MISSISSIPPI
TENNESSEE
Memphis
Nashville
Knoxville
Chattanooga
Atlanta
Birmingham
Montgomery
Jackson
New Orleans
Mobile
Tallahassee
Jacksonville
Savannah
Charleston
Columbia
Charlotte
Raleigh
Greensboro
Winston-Salem
Durham
Wilmington
Tampa
St Petersburg
Orlando
Miami
Cape Hatteras
Cape Lookout
Cape Fear
Pamlico Sound
Albemarle Sd
Mississippi Delta
Great Smoky Mts Nat. Park
Okefenokee Swamp
The Everglades
Lake Okeechobee
Florida Keys
Key West
at the same scale

1:5M 0 50 100 150 200 km
0 50 100 mls

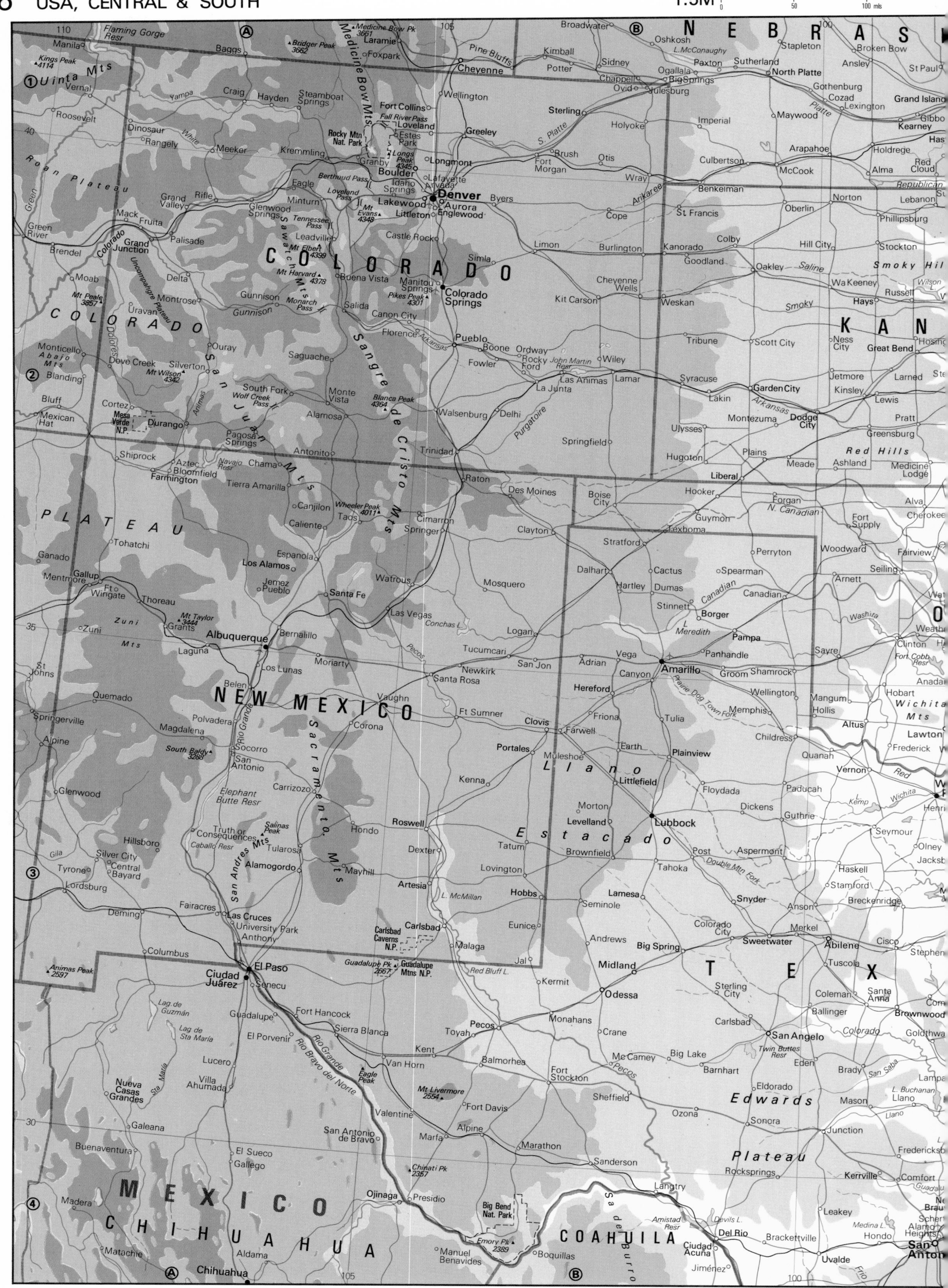
NEBRASKA
COLORADO
KANSAS
OKLAHOMA
NEW MEXICO
TEXAS
MEXICO
CHIHUAHUA
COAHUILA
Uinta Mts
Roan Plateau
COLORADO PLATEAU
San Juan Mts
Sangre de Cristo Mts
Sawatch Mts
Medicine Bow Mts
Sacramento Mts
San Andres Mts
Zuni Mts
Llano Estacado
Edwards Plateau
Smoky Hills
Red Hills
Wichita Mts
Sa del Burro
Denver
Aurora
Englewood
Lakewood
Littleton
Boulder
Longmont
Loveland
Fort Collins
Greeley
Cheyenne
Laramie
Colorado Springs
Pueblo
Trinidad
Raton
Santa Fe
Albuquerque
Los Alamos
Las Vegas
Roswell
Carlsbad
Las Cruces
El Paso
Ciudad Juárez
Chihuahua
Amarillo
Lubbock
Midland
Odessa
Abilene
San Angelo
Del Rio
Ciudad Acuña
Garden City
Dodge City
North Platte
Grand Junction
Durango
Farmington
Gallup
Grants
Tucumcari
Clovis
Hobbs
Alamogordo
Deming
Silver City
Pecos
Fort Stockton
Big Spring
Sweetwater
Plainview
Pampa
Borger
Dalhart
Liberal
Lamar
La Junta
Alamosa
Gunnison
Montrose
Delta
Moab
Vernal
Rocky Mtn Nat. Park
Mesa Verde N.P.
Carlsbad Caverns N.P.
Guadalupe Mtns N.P.
Big Bend Nat. Park
Mt Elbert 4399
Mt Harvard 4378
Pikes Peak 4301
Blanca Peak 4364
Wheeler Peak 4011
Mt Taylor 3444
Kings Peak 4114
Guadalupe Pk 2667
Emory Pk 2389
Mt Livermore 2554
Chinati Pk 2357
Rio Grande
Rio Bravo del Norte
Pecos
Arkansas
Canadian
S. Platte
Colorado
Red

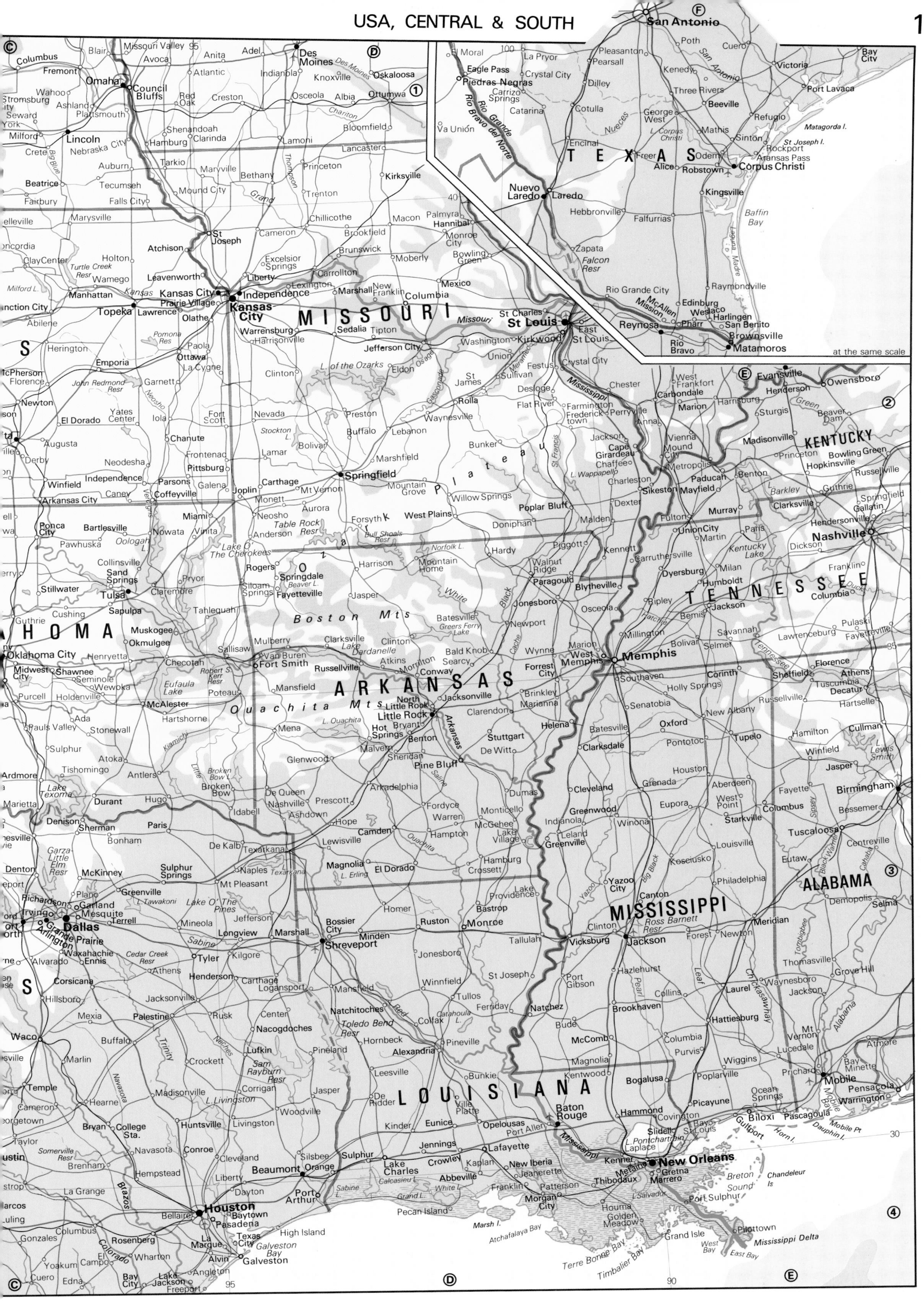

San Antonio F

TEXAS

MISSOURI

KANSAS ... **OKLAHOMA**

ARKANSAS

KENTUCKY

TENNESSEE

MISSISSIPPI

ALABAMA

LOUISIANA

Omaha, Council Bluffs, Lincoln, Nebraska City, Des Moines, Knoxville, Oskaloosa, Ottumwa, Columbus, Fremont, Blair, Missouri Valley, Anita, Adel, Indianola, Albia, Bloomfield, Lamoni, Lancaster, Princeton, Trenton, Kirksville, Hannibal, Macon, Palmyra, Chillicothe, Brookfield, Brunswick, Moberly, Columbia, Bowling Green, Mexico

Kansas City, Independence, Topeka, Lawrence, Olathe, Manhattan, Emporia, Sedalia, Jefferson City, Warrensburg, Clinton, St Charles, St Louis, East St Louis, Kirkwood, Union, Washington, Festus, Crystal City

Springfield, Joplin, Carthage, Mt Vernon, Monett, Aurora, Neosho, Tulsa, Bartlesville, Muskogee, Okmulgee, Fort Smith, McAlester

Oklahoma City, Shawnee, Ada, Sulphur, Durant, Sherman, Denison, Paris, Texarkana

Little Rock, Hot Springs, Pine Bluff, Conway, Searcy, Jonesboro, Fayetteville, Springdale, Rogers, Harrison, Mountain Home

Memphis, West Memphis, Jackson, Nashville, Clarksville, Paducah, Evansville, Owensboro, Henderson, Madisonville, Hopkinsville, Bowling Green

Birmingham, Tuscaloosa, Bessemer, Meridian, Jackson, Vicksburg, Greenville, Greenwood, Columbus

Dallas, Fort Worth, Arlington, Garland, Mesquite, Plano, Richardson, Irving, Waco, Temple, Tyler, Longview, Shreveport, Bossier City, Monroe, Ruston

Houston, Galveston, Beaumont, Orange, Port Arthur, Lake Charles, Lafayette, Baton Rouge, New Orleans, Baytown, Pasadena

Corpus Christi, Laredo, Nuevo Laredo, Brownsville, Matamoros, McAllen, Reynosa, Harlingen, Kingsville, Victoria, Eagle Pass, Piedras Negras

Mobile, Biloxi, Gulfport, Pascagoula, Pensacola

Scale bar: 0 50 100 150 200 km / 0 50 100 mls

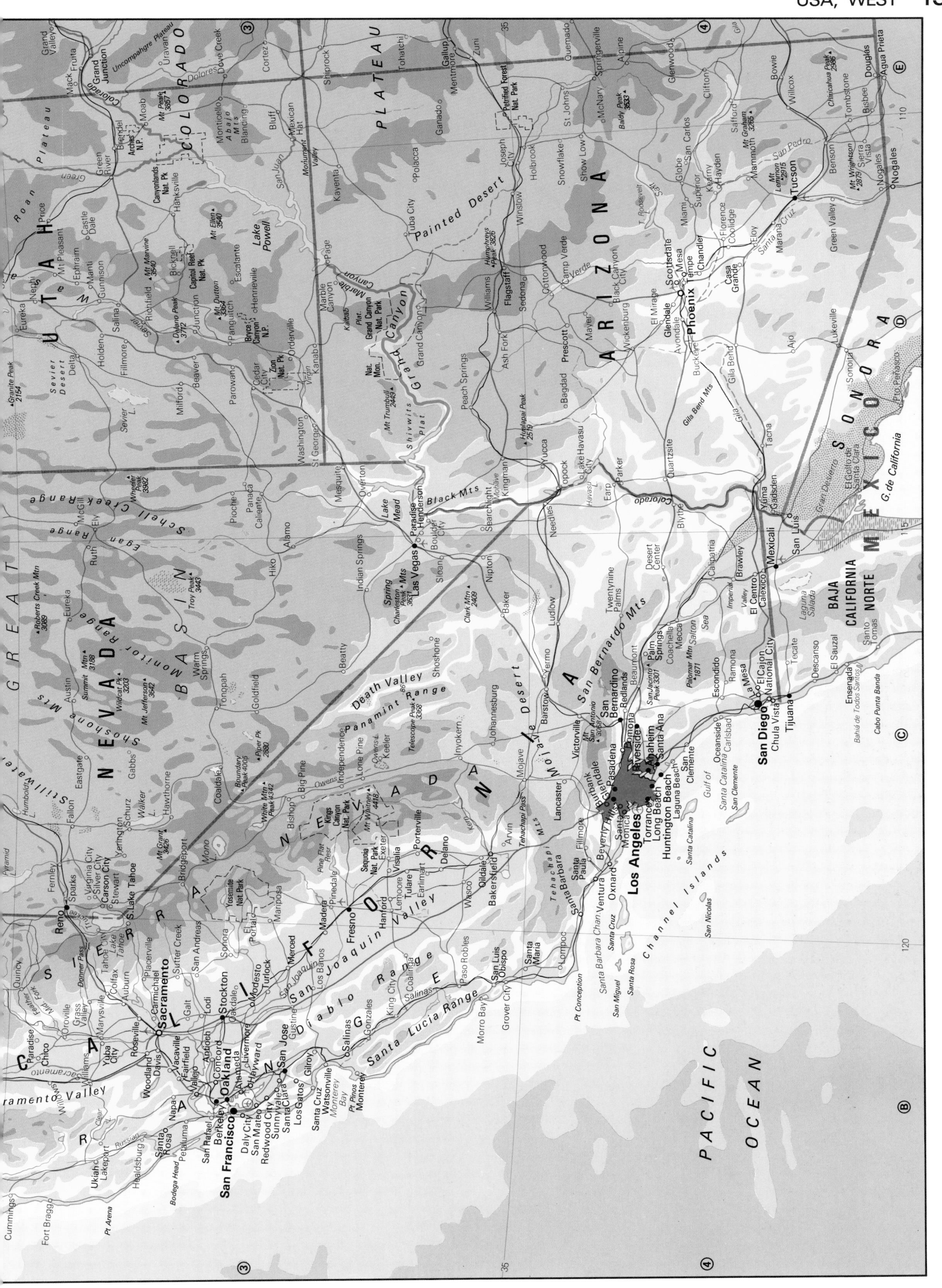
PACIFIC OCEAN
CALIFORNIA
NEVADA
UTAH
ARIZONA
COLORADO PLATEAU
GREAT BASIN
SIERRA NEVADA
SONORA
MEXICO
BAJA CALIFORNIA NORTE
Mojave Desert
Death Valley
Painted Desert
Grand Canyon
San Joaquin Valley
Sacramento Valley
Channel Islands
Santa Lucia Range
Diablo Range
San Bernardino Mts
Lake Mead
Lake Powell
Lake Tahoe
Los Angeles
San Francisco
San Diego
Sacramento
Las Vegas
Phoenix
Tucson
Fresno
San Jose
Oakland
Reno
Stockton

1:2.5M

0 25 50 75 100 km
0 25 50 mls

A | B | 122 | B | 118 | C | D

NEVADA

Cloverdale, Lower Lake, Guinda, Zamora, Lincoln, Auburn, Georgetown, S. Lake Tahoe, Minden, Gardnerville, Mason, Schurz, Gabbs
Lytton, Calistoga, L. Berryessa, Woodland, Roseville, Folsom, Camino, Pacific, Woodfords, Markleeville, Wellington, Smith, Luning, Paradise Peak 2637, Arc Dome 3092
Healdsburg, Winters, Davis, Placerville, Diamond Springs, Highland Pk 3333, Coleville, Topaz, E. Walker, Mt Grant 3426, Hawthorne, Round Moun
Forestville, St Helena, Yountville, Vacaville, Elk Grove, Plymouth, Mokelumne, West Pt, Bear Valley, Dardanelle, Sonora Pass 2933, Bridgeport Resr, Benton, Basalt, Coaldale, Tonopah, Lone Mtn 2776
Santa Rosa, Sonoma, Napa, Fairfield, Dixon, Galt, Jackson, Mokelumne Hill, San Andreas, Arnold, Pinecrest, Excelsior Mtn 3790, Mono Lake, Montgomery Pass 2184, Pilot Pk 2800, Goldfield, Montezuma Pk
Petaluma, Novato, Vallejo, Pittsburg, Antioch, Oakley, Stockton, Manteca, Angels Camp, Bellota, Murphys, Sonora, Groveland, Mather, Lee Vining, Mt Dana 3978, Boundary Pk 4005, Oasis, Lida

San Francisco, Berkeley, Oakland, Richmond, Mt Diablo 1173, Brentwood, Byron, Ripon, Modesto, Coulterville, El Portal, Yosemite National Park, Mt Lyell 3997, Mt Ritter 4010, Devil Postpile N.M., White Mtn Peak 4342, Piper Pk 2880, Deep Springs, Gold Pt
Alameda, San Leandro, Hayward, Tracy, Patterson, Turlock, Snelling, Wawona, Mariposa, Fish Camp, Bass Lake, Huntington L., Mt Goddard 4132, Big Pine, N. Palisade 4341, Bishop, Aberdeen, Eureka Valley, Magruder Mtn 2757
San Mateo, Redwood City, Palo Alto, Fremont, Mountain View, Sunnyvale, Santa Clara, San Jose, Los Gatos, Morgan Hill, Gilroy, Mt Hamilton 1284, Gustine, Los Banos, Dos Palos, Madera, Firebaugh, Mendota, Herndon, Clovis, Fresno, Sanger, Minkler, Kings Canyon National Park, Independence, Lone Pine, Keeler
San Gregorio, Pescadero, Boulder Creek, Davenport, Santa Cruz, Watsonville, Soquel, Hollister, Tres Pinos, San Juan Bautista, Chowchilla, Berenda, Raymond, Pinedale, Piedra, Reedley, Dinuba, Badger, General Grant Grove Section, Mt Whitney 4418, Owens Lake, Cartago, Olancha Pk 3699

PACIFIC OCEAN

Monterey Bay, Pacific Grove, Carmel, Monterey, Seaside, Salinas, Castroville, Gonzales, Soledad, Greenfield, King City, San Lucas, San Ardo, Bradley, San Miguel, Paso Robles, Templeton, Atascadero, Cambria, San Simeon, Morro Bay, San Luis Obispo, Pismo Beach, Grover City, Oceano, Nipomo, Guadalupe, Santa Maria, Orcutt, Lompoc, Buellton, Solvang, Los Olivos, Los Alamos, Santa Ynez, Goleta, Santa Barbara, Carpinteria, Ventura, Oxnard, Port Hueneme, Camarillo

Coalinga, Avenal, Kettleman City, Lost Hills, Wasco, Shafter, Buttonwillow, McKittrick, Taft, Maricopa, Ford City, Bakersfield, Oildale, Delano, Richgrove, Porterville, Terra Bella, Tulare, Corcoran, Tipton, Pixley, Earlimart, Ducor, Hanford, Visalia, Exeter, Lindsay, Woodlake, Three Rivers, Sequoia National Park, Camp Nelson, Kernville, Isabella Resr, L. Isabella, Weldon, Onyx, Inyokern, China Lake, Ridgecrest, Trona, Searles

Los Angeles, Hollywood, Glendale, Burbank, Pasadena, Monrovia, Santa Monica, Beverly Hills, Inglewood, Whittier, Pomona, Ontario, Upland, San Bernardino, Colton, Redlands, Riverside, Corona, Torrance, Redondo Beach, Lakewood, Garden Grove, Santa Ana, Anaheim, Orange, Fullerton, Long Beach, Huntington Beach, Newport Beach, Costa Mesa, Laguna Beach, San Clemente, Oceanside, Carlsbad, Encinitas, Del Mar, La Jolla, **San Diego**

San Gabriel Mts, Mt Wilson 1740, Mt San Antonio 3068, Wrightwood, Hesperia, Victorville, Adelanto, Apple Valley, Lancaster, Palmdale, Littlerock, Acton, Castaic, Fillmore, Santa Paula, Newhall, San Fernando, Moorpark, Thousand Oaks, Gorman, Tejon Pass, Lebec, Mt Pinos 2692, Frazier Park, Grapevine, Wheeler Ridge, Mojave, Rosamond, Edwards, Boron, Helendale, California Aqueduct

Mojave Desert

Santa Barbara Channel, San Miguel, Santa Rosa, Santa Cruz, Anacapa Is, Channel Islands, Santa Monica Bay, San Pedro Channel, Santa Catalina, Avalon, Gulf of Santa Catalina, San Clemente, Outer Santa Barbara Channel

---

0 50 100 150 200 km
0 50 100 mls

160 | 122 | A | 160 | B | 34 | 120 | 155

Kauai, Hanalei, Mana, Kapaa, Lihue, Koloa, Niihau, Kaulakahi Channel
Oahu, Waialua, Kahuku Pt, Wahiawa, Kaena Pt, Nanakuli, Kaneohe, Kailua, **Honolulu**, Pearl City, Pearl Harbor, Kauai Channel
Molokai, Kalaupapa, Kaunakakai, Kaiwi Chan., Kalohi Chan., Pailolo Chan.
Lanai, Lanai City
Maui, Waihee, Kahului, Wailuku, Nat. Pk 3055, Hana, Kahoolawe, Alenuihaha Channel, Upolu Point, Hawi, Kapaau, Honokaa, Honomu, Hakalau, Papaikou
Hawaii, Kawaihae, Waimea, Mauna Kea 4201, Hilo, Kiholo, Kailua, Kealakekua, Kilauea Crater 1243, Mauna Loa 4165, Pahoa, Kalapana, Hawaii Volcanoes Nat. Park, Milolii, Naalehu, Ka Lae (South Cape)

PACIFIC OCEAN

20N | 20N

A | B | C | D | E

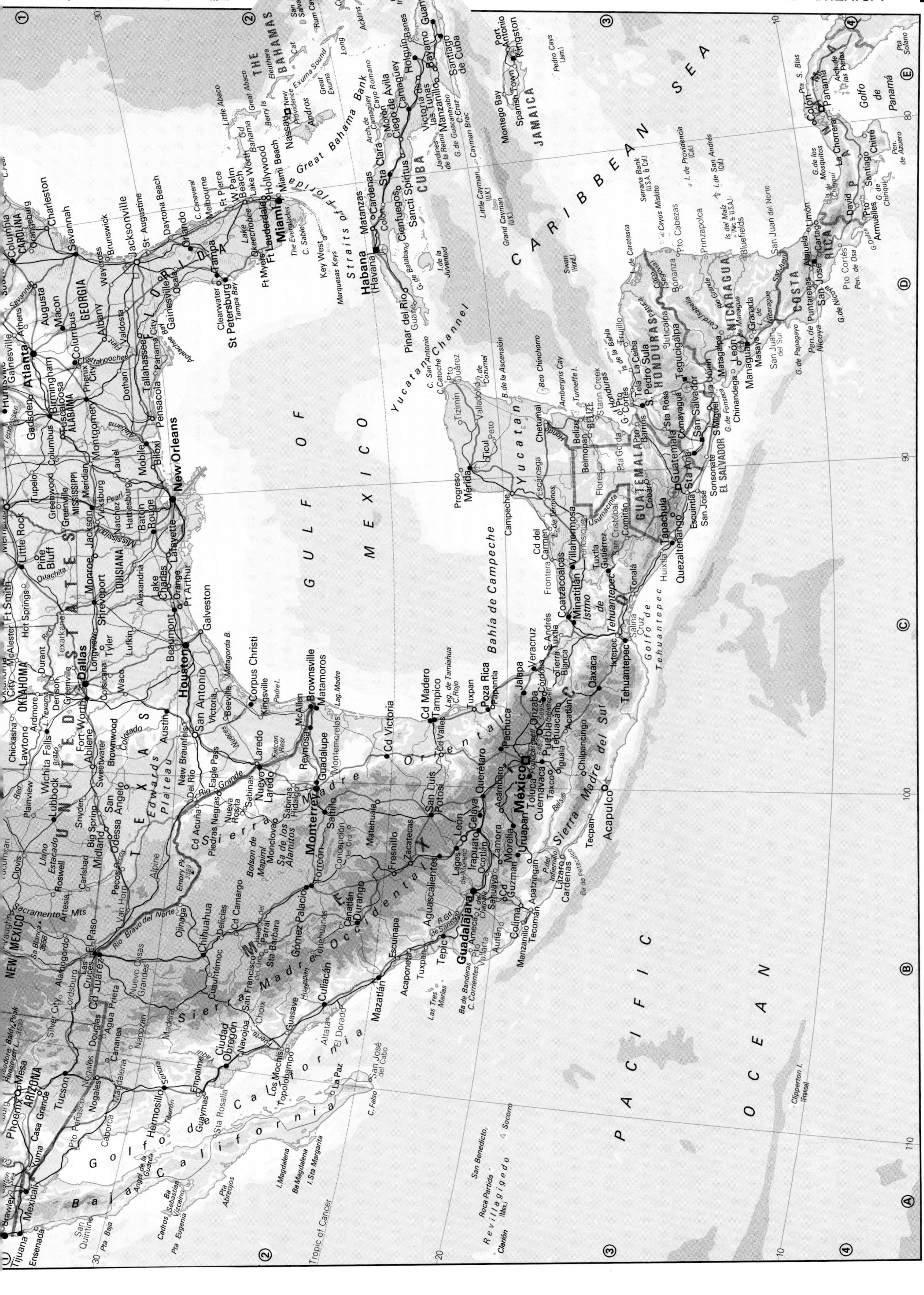

1:15M

200 400 600 km
100 200 300 mls

Map labels:

THE BAHAMAS — Little Abaco, Great Abaco, New Providence, Nassau, Andros, Berry Is, Cat I, Eleuthera, Exuma Sound, Great Exuma, Long I, Crooked I, Acklins, Rum Cay, San Salvador, Great Inagua

CUBA — Habana (Havana), Pinar del Rio, Matanzas, Cárdenas, Sta Clara, Cienfuegos, Sancti Spíritus, Morón, Ciego de Avila, Camagüey, Victoria de las Tunas, Holguín, Bayamo, Manzanillo, Santiago de Cuba, Guantánamo

JAMAICA — Montego Bay, Spanish Town, Kingston, Port Antonio

Grand Cayman, Little Cayman (U.K.), I. de la Juventud

CARIBBEAN SEA

GULF OF MEXICO

STRAITS OF FLORIDA, Key West, Florida Keys, The Everglades

FLORIDA — Miami, Miami Beach, Ft Lauderdale, Hollywood, W Palm Beach, Ft Pierce, Melbourne, C. Canaveral, Daytona Beach, St Augustine, Jacksonville, Orlando, Tampa, St Petersburg, Clearwater, Tallahassee, Pensacola, Lake Okeechobee

GEORGIA — Atlanta, Columbus, Macon, Augusta, Savannah, Albany, Valdosta

ALABAMA — Birmingham, Montgomery, Mobile, Tuscaloosa

MISSISSIPPI — Jackson, Meridian, Vicksburg, Hattiesburg, Biloxi

LOUISIANA — New Orleans, Baton Rouge, Shreveport, Alexandria, Lake Charles, Lafayette

TEXAS — Houston, Dallas, Fort Worth, San Antonio, Austin, Corpus Christi, Brownsville, Galveston, Beaumont, Waco, Abilene, Midland, Odessa, Lubbock, Amarillo, El Paso, Laredo

OKLAHOMA — Oklahoma City, Tulsa, Lawton

ARKANSAS — Little Rock, Fort Smith, Hot Springs, Pine Bluff

NEW MEXICO — Roswell, Carlsbad, Las Cruces, Alamogordo

ARIZONA — Phoenix, Tucson, Nogales, Douglas

UNITED STATES

MEXICO — México, Guadalajara, Monterrey, Puebla, León, Querétaro, Torreón, Chihuahua, Durango, Culiacán, Mazatlán, Acapulco, Tampico, Veracruz, Oaxaca, Mérida, Campeche, Villahermosa, Tuxtla Gutiérrez, Ciudad Juárez, Tijuana, Mexicali, Hermosillo, Ensenada, La Paz, Cd Obregón, Los Mochis, Cuernavaca, Toluca, Morelia, Aguascalientes, Zacatecas, San Luis Potosí, Cd Victoria, Matamoros, Reynosa, Nuevo Laredo, Saltillo, Coatzacoalcas, Poza Rica, Tehuantepec, Minatitlán

Sierra Madre Oriental, Sierra Madre Occidental, Sierra Madre del Sur

Baja California, Golfo de California

Bahía de Campeche, Golfo de Tehuantepec

Yucatán, I. de Cozumel, Chetumal

BELIZE — Belmopan, Belize

GUATEMALA — Guatemala, Quezaltenango, Cobán, Flores

EL SALVADOR — San Salvador, Sta Ana, San Miguel, Sonsonate

HONDURAS — Tegucigalpa, S. Pedro Sula, La Ceiba, Tela, Juticalpa, Comayagua

NICARAGUA — Managua, León, Granada, Matagalpa, Chinandega, Masaya, Bluefields, L. de Managua, L. de Nicaragua

COSTA RICA — San José, Puntarenas, Limón, Alajuela, Cartago

PANAMA — Panamá, Colón, David, La Chorrera, Santiago, Golfo de Panamá

PACIFIC OCEAN

Tropic of Cancer

Clipperton I. (France)

Revillagigedo Is (Mex.)

1:5M

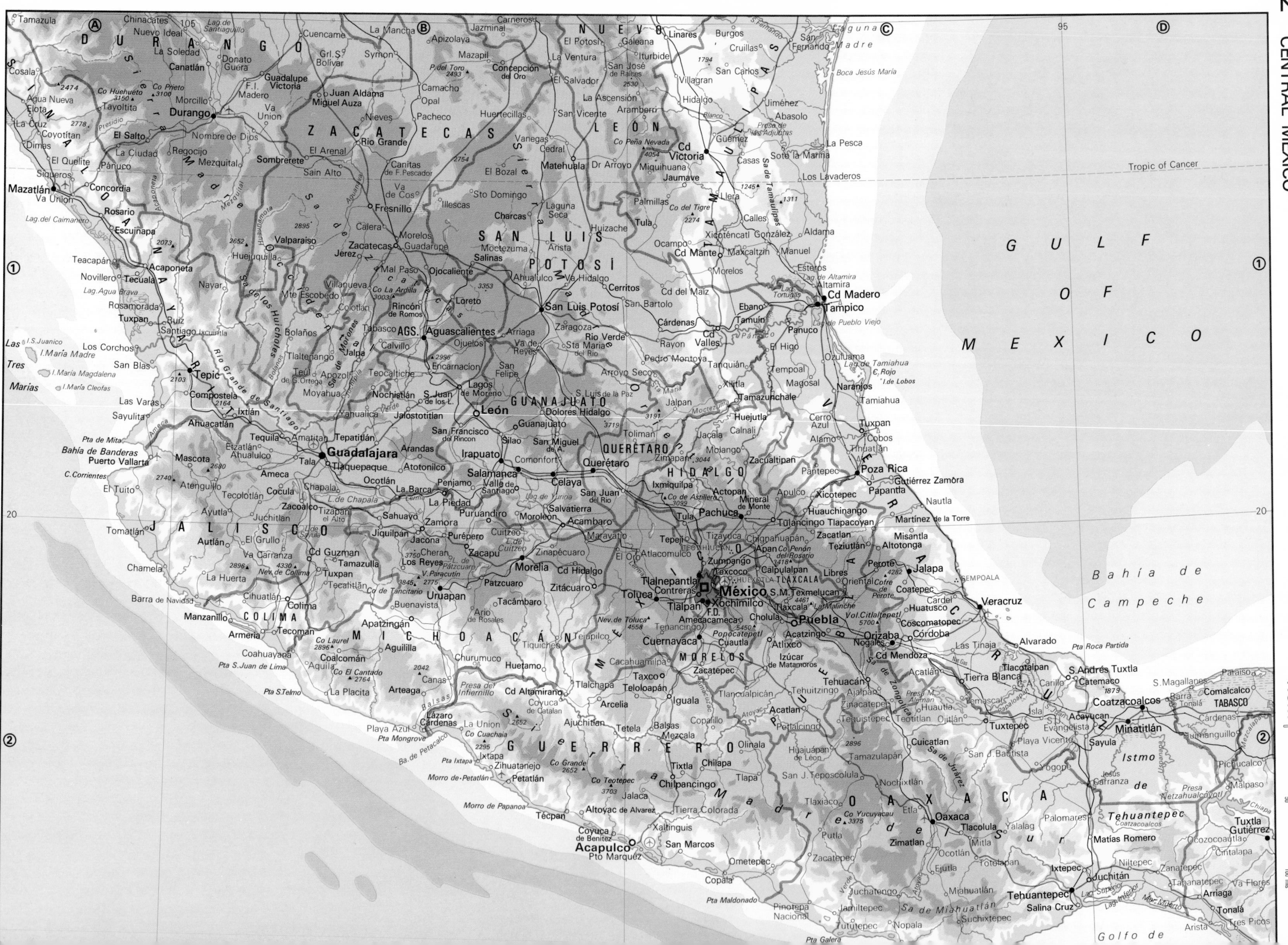
G U L F O F M E X I C O
Bahía de Campeche
Tropic of Cancer
Golfo de
Istmo de Tehuantepec
Cd Madero
Tampico
Cd Victoria
Linares
San Luis Potosí
Aguascalientes
Zacatecas
Durango
Mazatlán
Tepic
Guadalajara
León
Querétaro
Pachuca
México
Puebla
Tlaxcala
Veracruz
Jalapa
Orizaba
Córdoba
Oaxaca
Acapulco
Chilpancingo
Cuernavaca
Toluca
Morelia
Uruapan
Colima
Manzanillo
Puerto Vallarta
Celaya
Irapuato
Salamanca
Poza Rica
Coatzacoalcos
Minatitlán
Tehuantepec
Salina Cruz
Juchitán
Z A C A T E C A S
S A N L U I S P O T O S Í
G U A N A J U A T O
Q U E R É T A R O
H I D A L G O
M O R E L O S
J A L I S C O
C O L I M A
M I C H O A C Á N
G U E R R E R O
O A X A C A
N U E V O
L E Ó N
D U R A N G O
TABASCO

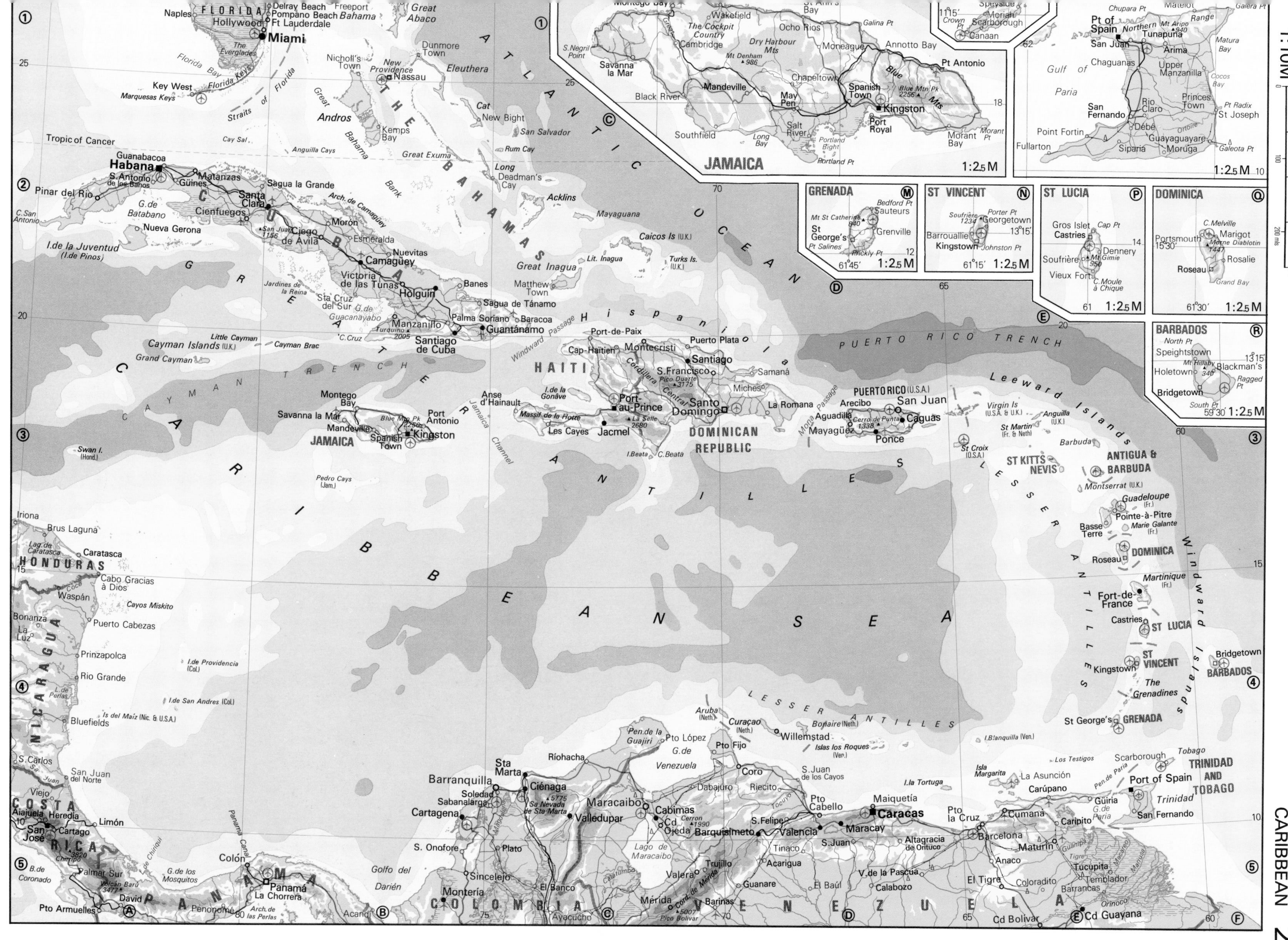
ATLANTIC OCEAN
CARIBBEAN SEA
THE BAHAMAS
CUBA
JAMAICA
HAITI
DOMINICAN REPUBLIC
PUERTO RICO (U.S.A.)
PUERTO RICO TRENCH
Leeward Islands
Windward Islands
LESSER ANTILLES
VENEZUELA
COLOMBIA
PANAMA
COSTA RICA
NICARAGUA
HONDURAS
CAYMAN TRENCH
Jamaica Channel
Windward Passage
GRENADA 1:2.5M
ST VINCENT 1:2.5M
ST LUCIA 1:2.5M
DOMINICA 1:2.5M
BARBADOS 1:2.5M
TRINIDAD AND TOBAGO

1:35M

0 250 500 750 1000 1250 km
0 250 500 750 mls

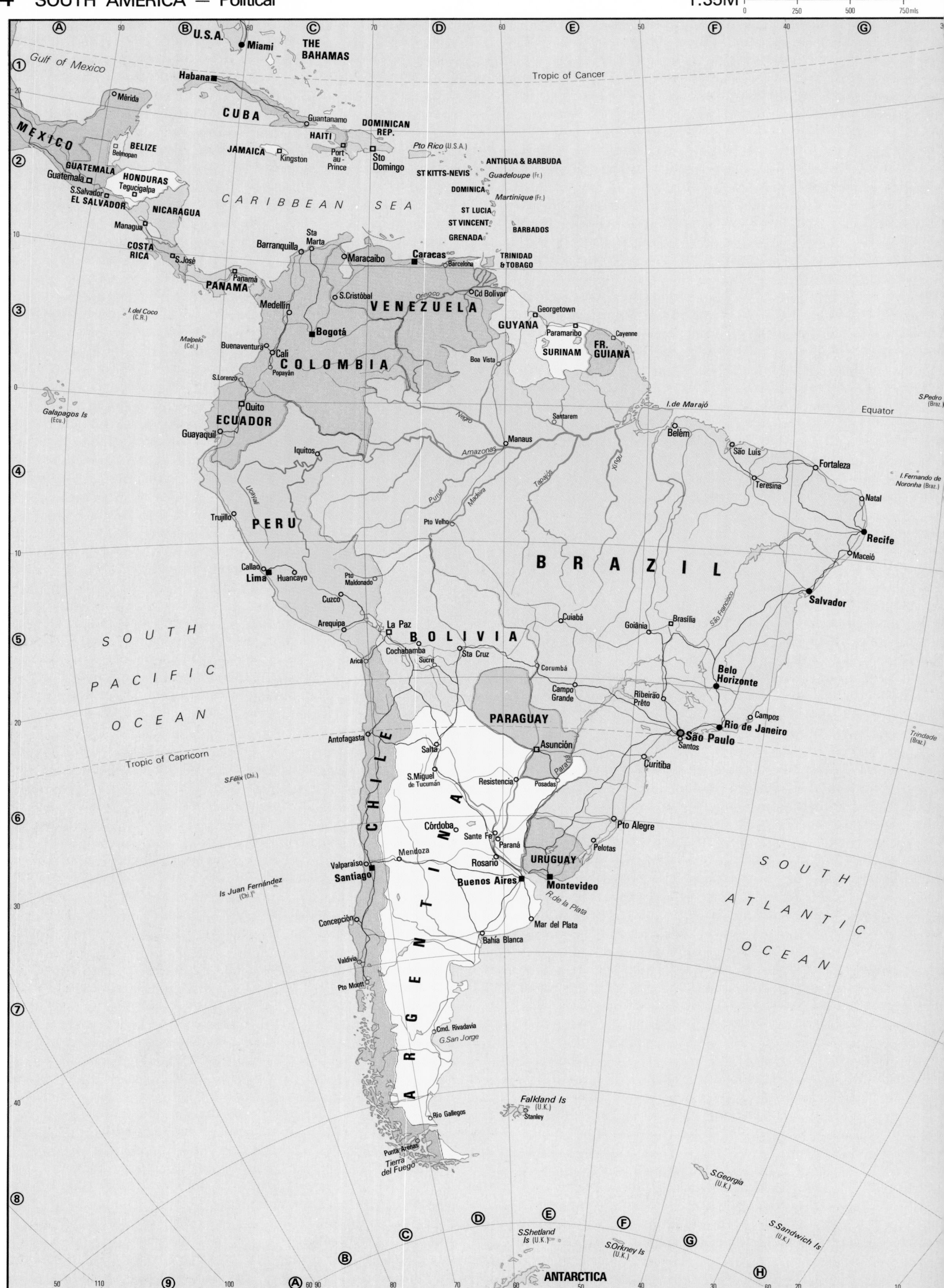

Gulf of Mexico

Tropic of Cancer

U.S.A.
Miami

THE BAHAMAS

Mérida

MEXICO

CUBA
Habana

Guantanamo

DOMINICAN REP.

BELIZE
Belmopan

HAITI
Port au Prince
Sto Domingo

Pto Rico (U.S.A.)

GUATEMALA
Guatemala

HONDURAS
Tegucigalpa

JAMAICA
Kingston

ANTIGUA & BARBUDA

ST KITTS-NEVIS
Guadeloupe (Fr.)

S.Salvador
EL SALVADOR

NICARAGUA
Managua

DOMINICA
Martinique (Fr.)

ST LUCIA

COSTA RICA
S.José

ST VINCENT
GRENADA

BARBADOS

CARIBBEAN SEA

Sta Marta
Barranquilla

TRINIDAD & TOBAGO

PANAMA
Panamá

Maracaibo
Caracas
Barcelona

I. del Coco (C.R.)

Medellín

S.Cristóbal

Cd Bolívar

VENEZUELA

Orinoco

Georgetown

GUYANA

Paramaribo
Cayenne

Malpelo (Col.)

Buenaventura
Cali
Popayán

Bogotá

COLOMBIA

SURINAM
FR. GUIANA

Boa Vista

S.Lorenzo

S.Pedro (Braz.)

Galapagos Is (Ecu.)

Quito

ECUADOR

Equator

Santarem

I. de Marajó

Guayaquil

Negro

Belém

Iquitos

Manaus

São Luís

Fortaleza

Ucayali

Amazonas

Teresina

I.Fernando de Noronha (Braz.)

Trujillo

Purus

Madeira

Tapajós

Xingu

Natal

PERU

Pto Velho

Recife

B R A Z I L

Callao
Lima
Huancayo

Pto Maldonado

Maceió

Cuzco

Salvador

Arequipa

La Paz

Cuiabá

Brasília

Goiânia

São Francisco

S O U T H

Cochabamba
Sucre

BOLIVIA

Sta Cruz

Corumbá

Belo Horizonte

Arica

P A C I F I C

Campo Grande

Ribeirão Prêto

Campos

O C E A N

PARAGUAY

Rio de Janeiro

São Paulo
Santos

Trindade (Braz.)

Antofagasta

Asunción

Curitiba

Tropic of Capricorn

Salta

S.Félix (Chi.)

S.Miguel de Tucumán

Resistencia

Paraná

Posadas

Córdoba

Pto Alegre

Is Juan Fernández (Chi.)

Sante Fe
Paraná

Pelotas

C H I L E

Mendoza

Rosario

URUGUAY

Valparaíso
Santiago

A R G E N T I N A

Buenos Aires

Montevideo

R.de la Plata

Mar del Plata

S O U T H

Concepción

Bahía Blanca

A T L A N T I C

Valdivia

O C E A N

Pto Montt

Cmd. Rivadavia
G.San Jorge

Falkland Is (U.K.)

Río Gallegos
Stanley

S.Georgia (U.K.)

Punta Arenas
Tierra del Fuego

S.Shetland Is (U.K.)

S.Orkney Is (U.K.)

S.Sandwich Is (U.K.)

ANTARCTICA

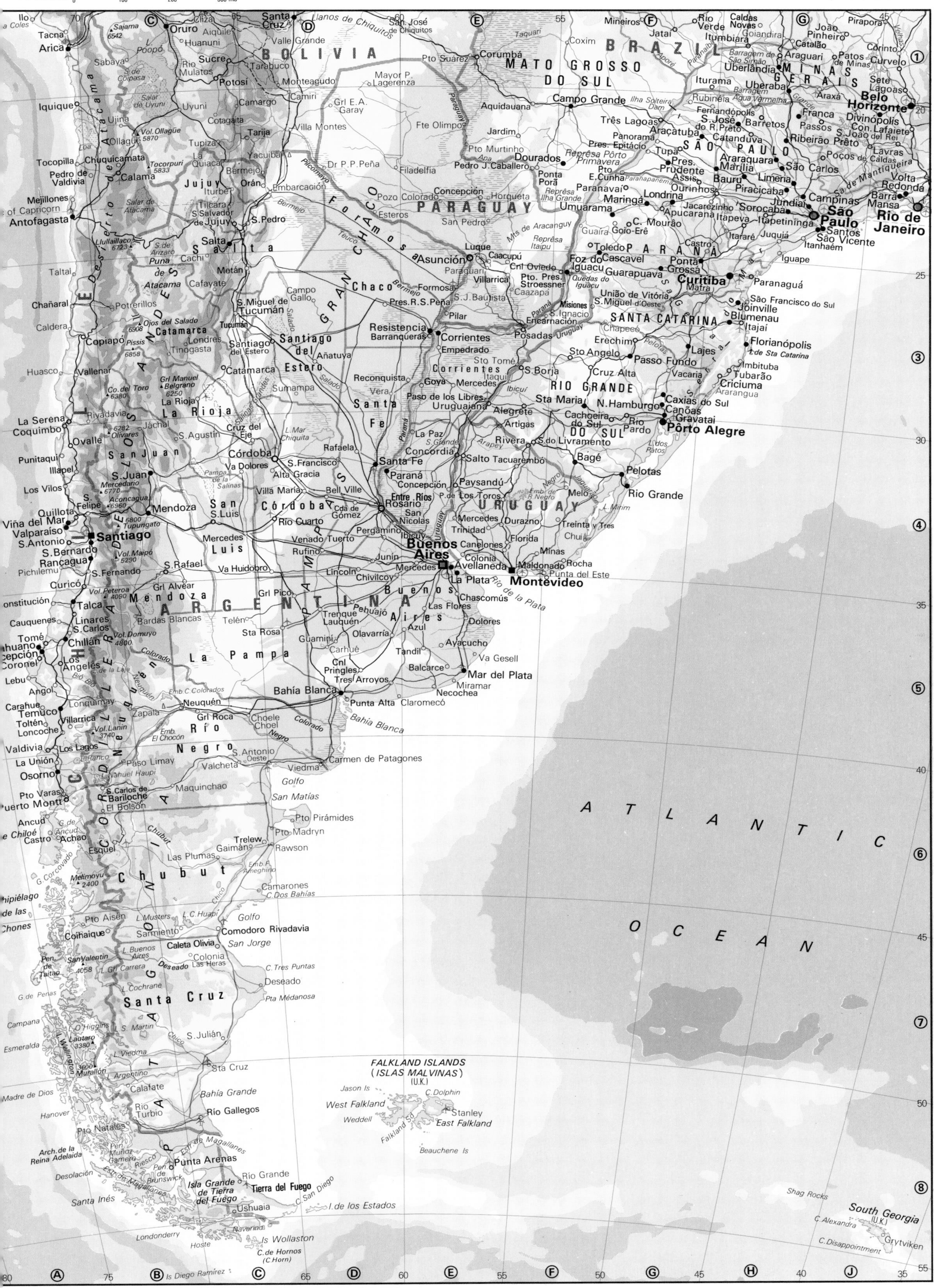
BOLIVIA
BRAZIL
MATO GROSSO DO SUL
MINAS GERAIS
SÃO PAULO
PARANÁ
SANTA CATARINA
RIO GRANDE DO SUL
PARAGUAY
URUGUAY
ARGENTINA
ATLANTIC OCEAN
FALKLAND ISLANDS (ISLAS MALVINAS) (U.K.)
West Falkland
East Falkland
Stanley
South Georgia (U.K.)
Grytviken
Tierra del Fuego
Ushuaia
Punta Arenas
Río Gallegos
Comodoro Rivadavia
Bahía Blanca
Mar del Plata
Buenos Aires
Montevideo
La Plata
Rosario
Santa Fe
Córdoba
Mendoza
Santiago
Valparaíso
Tucumán
Salta
Asunción
Curitiba
São Paulo
Rio de Janeiro
Belo Horizonte
Pôrto Alegre
Florianópolis
Campo Grande
Corumbá
Sucre
Potosí
Oruro
Arica
Iquique
Antofagasta
Concepción
Temuco
Valdivia
Osorno
Neuquén
Viedma
Trelew
Rawson

1:15M

200   400   600 km
100   200   300 mls

PACIFIC OCEAN

NICARAGUA
Managua
Masaya
Granada
L. de Nicaragua
Rivas
S. Carlos
S. Juan
Bluefields
Pto Cabezas
Siguatepeque
Comayagua
Tegucigalpa
San Miguel
Somoto
Esteli
La Unión
Choluteca
Chinandega
León
Matagalpa

COSTA RICA
San José
Cartago
Alajuela
Heredia
Limón
Puntarenas
Pen. de Nicoya
G. de Nicoya
Chirripó 3815
Pto Armuelles
Santiago
David
Barú 3475
G. de Chiriquí
Pen. de Azuero
I. Coiba
I. Pta Mariato
Chitré
G. de Panamá

PANAMA
Panamá
Colón
La Chorrera
La Palma
Arch. de las Perlas
G. de Urabá
I. del Coco (C.R.)

COLOMBIA
Barranquilla
Cartagena
Sta Marta
Ciénaga
Riohacha
Maicao
Valledupar
Sincelejo
El Banco
Magangué
Montería
Quibdó
C. Corrientes
Turbo
Caucasia
Yarumal
Barrancabermeja
Bello
Pto Berrío
Itagüí
Medellín
Manizales
Pereira
Cartago
Armenia
Ibagué
Buga
Palmira
Cali
Buenaventura
G. de Tortugas
Santander
Popayán
Huila 5750
Neiva
Girardot
Villavicencio
Bogotá
Chocontá
Tunja
Sogamoso
Orocué
Granada
Pto Rico
Pitalito
Florencia
Belén
Mocoa
Pto Asís
Pasto
Ipiales
Tulcán
El Diviso
S. Lorenzo
Tumaco
Yari
Calamar
Mitú
Vaupés
Apaporis
Cucuí
Içana
Guainía

VENEZUELA
Maracaibo
Cabimas
Cd Ojeda
Machiques
Coro
Pto Fijo
Pen. de Guajira
Aruba
Curaçao (Neth)
Bonaire
Willemstad
Neth. Antilles
Pta Gallinas
G. de Venezuela
L. de Maracaibo
Mérida
Cord. de Mérida
Bolívar 5775
San Cristóbal
Cúcuta
Pamplona
Bucaramanga
Málaga
Ocaña
Valera
Trujillo
Barinas
Guanare
Acarigua
Barquisimeto
Valencia
Maracay
Caracas
Pto Cabello
Maiquetía
La Guaira
Barcelona
Anaco
El Tigre
Zarara
V. de la Pascua
Cd Bolívar
Cd Piar
Emb. de Guri
El Dorado
Salto del Angel
Cumaná
Pto la Cruz
Carúpano
Güiria
Maturín
Upata
Cd Guayana
Pen. de Paria
G. de Paria
I. de Margarita
La Asunción
La Tortuga
Is Los Roques (Ven)
Orinoco
Meta
Arauca
Casiquiare
Negro
RORAIMA
Sa Pacaraima
Sta Elena
Boa

ECUADOR
Quito
Cotopaxi 5896
Ambato
Riobamba
Chimborazo 6310
Guaranda
Babahoyo
Milagro
Guayaquil
La Libertad
Playas
I. Puná
G. de Guayaquil
Tumbes
Machala
Zaruma
Loja
Zamora
Cuenca
Azogues
Gualaceo
Macas
Esmeraldas
S. Lorenzo
Cojimíes
Jama
Manta
C. San Lorenzo
Jipijapa
Chone
Otavalo
Ibarra
Lago Agrio
Coca
Tena
Napo
Putumayo
Leguízamo

PERU
Iquitos
Leticia
Tabatinga
Caxias
Elvira
Yavarí (Javari)
Marañón
Talara
Negritos
Paita
Pta Aguja
Piura
Catacaos
Sullana
Chulucanas
Huancabamba
Jaén
Moyobamba
Chachapoyas
Tarapoto
Yurimaguas
Cruzeiro do Sul
Feijó
Lambayeque
Chiclayo
Ferreñafe
Chepén
Pacasmayo
Cajamarca
Cajabamba
Huamachuco
Otuzco
Trujillo
Chimbote
Casma
Huaraz
Huascarán 6768
Huallanca
La Unión
Huánuco
Tingo María
Pucallpa
Pomabamba
Huarmey
Pativilca
Barranca
Huacho
Cerro de Pasco
Oxapampa
La Merced
Tarma
La Oroya
Jauja
Acobamba
Huancayo
Huancavelica
Ancón
Callao
Lima
Chincha Alta
Pisco
Ica
Pen. de Paracas
Nazca
Chala
Andahuaylas
Ayacucho
Abancay
Quillabamba
Cuzco
MACHU PICCHU
Parque Nac. de Manu
Pto Maldonado
Pto Heath
Madre de Dios
Sicuani
Ayaviri
Juliaca
Puno
Arequipa
Misti 5822
Coropuna 6425
Majes
Camaná
Matarani
Mollendo
Ilo
Moquegua
Pta Coles
Tacna
Arica
Lago Titicaca
Huanay
Sta Ana
Coroico
Chulumani
Juli
Guaqui
La Paz
Ancohuma 6388

BOLIVIA
Coroico
Cochabamba
Santa Cruz
Quillacollo
Oruro
Huanuni
Sajama 6542
Sucre
Potosí
Poopó
Rio Mulatos
Salar de Coipasa
Salar de Uyuni
Uyuni
Cotagaita
Tupiza
Tarija
Villa Montes
Camiri
Monteagudo
Valle Grande
Llanos de ...
Montero
Camargo

BRAZIL
AMAZONAS
SELVAS
Téfé
Içá
Japurá
Coari
Lábrea
Humaitá
Purus
Bôca do Acre
Porto Velho
ACRE
Sena Madureira
Rio Branco
Brasiléia
Cobija
Porvenir
Riberalta
Guajará-Mirim
RONDÔNIA
Serra ...
Abunã
Madeira
Mamoré
Guaporé
Itonamas
Rurrenabaque
Trinidad
Beni
Pto Acosta

CHILE
Antofagasta
Mejillones
Tocopilla
Pedro de Valdivia
Chuquicamata
Calama
Tocopuri 5833
Vol. Ollagüe 5870
Ollagüe
Llullaillaco 6723
Desierto de Atacama
Cordillera de los Andes
Iquique
Tropic of Capricorn

ARGENTINA
Jujuy
Salta
S. Pedro
S. Salvador de Jujuy
La Quiaca
Yacuiba
Orán
Embarcación
Bermejo
Tarija

PANAMA
PACIFIC OCEAN

Islas Galápagos (Archipiélago do Colón) (Equ.)
Culpepper
Wenman
Pinta
Marchena
Genovesa
Fernandina
Isabela
San Salvador
Santa Cruz
Baltra
Baquerizo Moreno
San Cristóbal
Santa María
Española
Santa Fé
at the same scale

Islas Juan Fernández (Chile)
Alejandro Selkirk
Robinson Crusoe
Sta Clara
at the same scale

F Roseau
Fort-de-France
Martinique (Fr)
St Lucia
Castries
St Vincent
Kingstown
The Grenadines
GRENADA

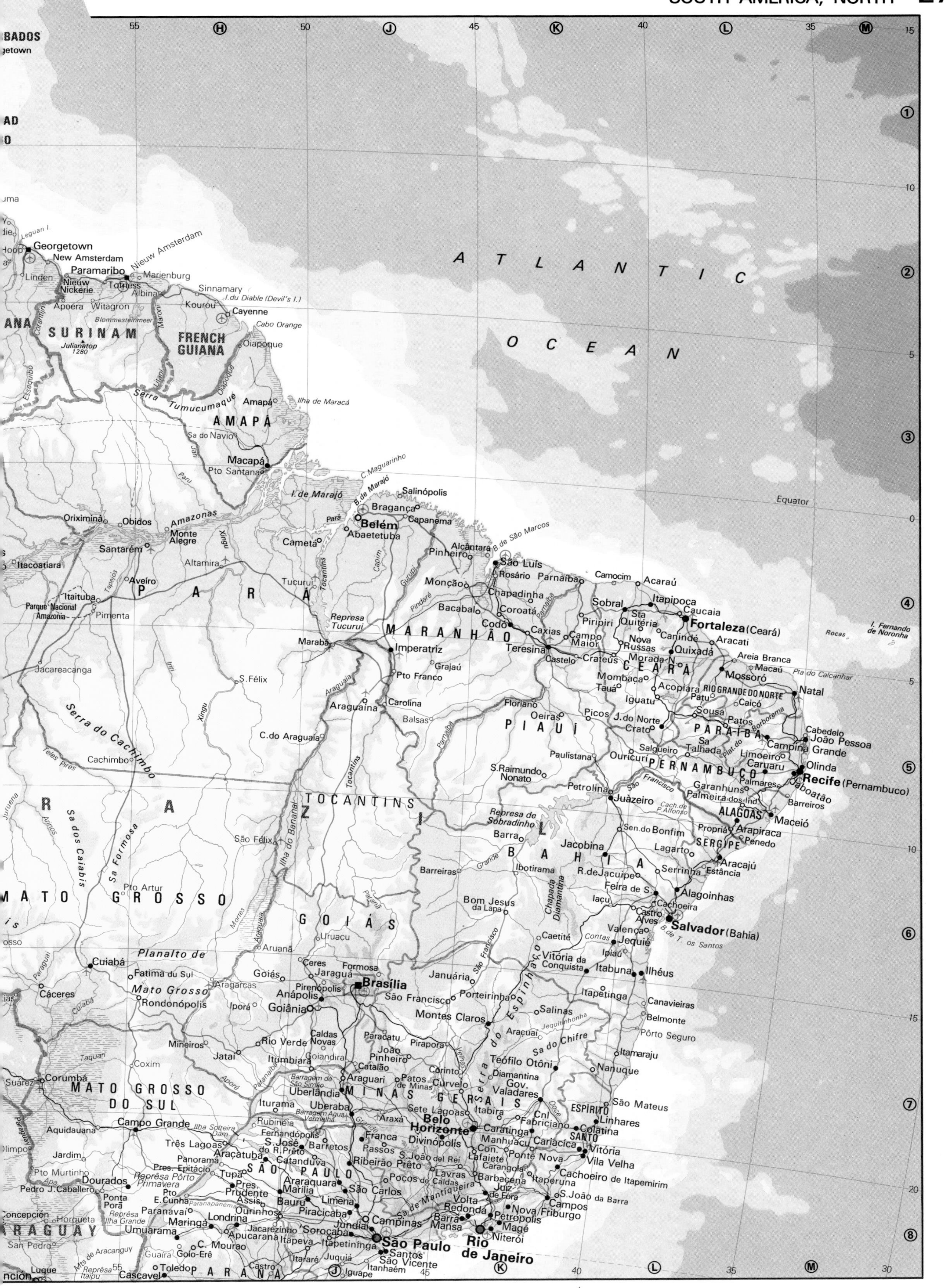
ATLANTIC
OCEAN
Equator
SURINAM
FRENCH GUIANA
AMAPÁ
PARÁ
MARANHÃO
CEARÁ
PIAUÍ
RIO GRANDE DO NORTE
PARAÍBA
PERNAMBUCO
ALAGOAS
SERGIPE
BAHIA
TOCANTINS
GOIÁS
MATO GROSSO
MATO GROSSO DO SUL
MINAS GERAIS
ESPIRITO SANTO
SÃO PAULO
PARANÁ
PARAGUAY
Georgetown
New Amsterdam
Paramaribo
Nieuw Amsterdam
Marienburg
Nieuw Nickerie
Totness
Albina
Linden
Apoera
Witagron
Sinnamary
I. du Diable (Devil's I.)
Kourou
Cayenne
Cabo Orange
Oiapoque
Julianatop 1280
Serra Tumucumaque
Amapá
Ilha de Maracá
Sa do Navio
Macapá
Pto Santana
C. Maguarinho
I. de Marajó
B. de Marajó
Salinópolis
Bragança
Capanema
Belém
Abaetetuba
Cametá
Oriximiná
Obidos
Amazonas
Monte Alegre
Santarém
Itacoatiara
Altamira
Aveíro
Tucuruí
Itaituba
Parque Nacional Amazonia
Pimenta
Represa Tucuruí
Marabá
Imperatriz
Grajaú
Pto Franco
Carolina
Araguaína
Balsas
Alcântara
B. de São Marcos
Pinheiro
São Luís
Rosário
Parnaíba
Camocim
Acaraú
Monção
Chapadinha
Bacabal
Coroatá
Codó
Caxias
Teresina
Campo Maior
Piripiri
Sobral
Itapipoca
Caucaia
Sta Quitéria
Fortaleza (Ceará)
Canindé
Aracati
Nova Russas
Quixadá
Crateús
Castelo
Morada N.
Areia Branca
Macaú
Pta do Calcanhar
Mossoró
Mombaça
Tauá
Acopiara
Iguatu
Patu
Caicó
Natal
Floriano
Oeiras
Picos
J. do Norte
Crato
Sousa
Patos
Cabedelo
João Pessoa
Campina Grande
Salgueiro
Talhada
Limoeiro
Caruaru
Olinda
Recife (Pernambuco)
Jaboatão
Palmares
Garanhuns
Palmeira dos Índ.
Barreiros
Maceió
Paulistana
Ouricurí
S. Raimundo Nonato
Petrolina
Juàzeiro
Represa de Sobradinho
Sen. do Bonfim
Propriá
Arapiraca
Penedo
Barra
Jacobina
Lagarto
Aracajú
Estância
Serrinha
Barreiras
Ibotirama
R. de Jacuípe
Feira de S.
Alagoinhas
Iaçu
Bom Jesus da Lapa
Chapada Diamantina
Cachoeira
Castro Alves
Salvador (Bahia)
Valença
B. de T. os Santos
Jequié
Ipiaú
Caetité
Vitória da Conquista
Itabuna
Ilhéus
I. Fernando de Noronha
Rocas
Jacareacanga
S. Félix
Serra do Cachimbo
Cachimbo
Teles Pires
C. do Araguaia
São Félix
Sa dos Caiabis
Sa Formosa
Pto Artur
Uruaçu
Aruanã
Planalto de Mato Grosso
Cuiabá
Fatima du Sul
Aragarças
Goiás
Ceres
Jaraguá
Formosa
Brasília
Pirenópolis
Anápolis
Goiânia
Cáceres
Rondonópolis
Iporá
Januária
São Francisco
Porteirinha
Montes Claros
Serra do Espinhaço
Itapetinga
Salinas
Canavieiras
Belmonte
Pôrto Seguro
Araçuaí
Sa do Chifre
Itamaraju
Nanuque
Teófilo Otôni
Caldas Novas
Rio Verde
Paracatu
Pirapora
João Pinheiro
Mineiros
Jataí
Itumbiara
Coxim
Catalão
Goiandira
Araguari
Patos de Minas
Curvelo
Corinto
Diamantina
Gov. Valadares
São Mateus
Linhares
Colatina
Corumbá
Uberlândia
Uberaba
Iturama
Araxá
Sete Lagoas
Itabira
Belo Horizonte
Caratinga
Cnl Fabriciano
Manhuaçu
Cariacica
Vitória
Vila Velha
Campo Grande
Aquidauana
Três Lagoas
Rubinéia
Fernandópolis
S. José do R. Prêto
Barretos
Franca
Passos
Divinópolis
Araçatuba
Catanduva
Ribeirão Prêto
S. João del Rei
Con. Lafaiete
Ponte Nova
Carangola
Cachoeiro de Itapemirim
Itaperuna
Barbacena
Juiz de Fora
Campos
S. João da Barra
Jardim
Pto Murtinho
Dourados
Represa Pôrto Primavera
Pres. Epitácio
Tupã
Pres. Prudente
Assis
Marília
Araraquara
São Carlos
Poços de Caldas
Lavras
Sa de Mantiqueira
Pedro J. Caballero
Ponta Porã
Pto E. Cunha
Bauru
Limeira
Volta Redonda
Nova Friburgo
Petrópolis
Concepción
Horqueta
Paranavaí
Ourinhos
Piracicaba
Campinas
Barra Mansa
Magé
Niterói
Rio de Janeiro
Maringá
Londrina
Jundiaí
Umuarama
Apucarana
Jacarezinho
Sorocaba
Itapeva
Itapetininga
São Paulo
Santos
São Vicente
Itanhaém
C. Mourão
Guaira
Goio-Erê
San Pedro
Luque
Toledo
Cascavel
Castro
Itararé
Juquiá
Iguape
Represa Itaipu

100   200   300 km
50   100   150 mls

BRAZIL

Passo Fundo · Novo Hamburgo · Porto Alegre · Caxias do Sul · Montenegro · S. Leopoldo · Capães

Sta Maria · S. Sepé · Cachoeira do Sul · Rio Grande · do Sul · Pelotas · Rio Grande

URUGUAY

Salto · Paysandú · Mercedes · Trinidad · Durazno · Florida · Minas · Rocha · Maldonado · Punta del Este

Montevideo · Las Piedras · Canelones

ARGENTINA

Corrientes · Resistencia · Chaco · Goya · Mercedes · Curuzú Cuatiá

Santa Fe · Paraná · Santa Fe · Rafaela · San Francisco

Córdoba · Río Cuarto · Villa María · Bell Ville

Buenos Aires · Avellaneda · La Plata · Mar del Plata · Bahía Blanca

Rosario · San Nicolás · Pergamino · Junín · Venado Tuerto · Rufino

La Rioja · Catamarca · Concepción · Santiago del Estero · La Banda

San Juan · **Mendoza** · San Rafael · Godoy Cruz · Rivadavia

La Pampa · Santa Rosa · Gral Pico

San Luis · Mercedes

Río Negro · Neuquén · Cipolletti · Gral Roca

CHILE

Santiago · Valparaíso · Viña del Mar · San Bernardo · Rancagua · San Antonio

Talca · Linares · Chillán · Concepción · Talcahuano · Los Ángeles · Temuco · Valdivia

ATLANTIC OCEAN

PACIFIC OCEAN

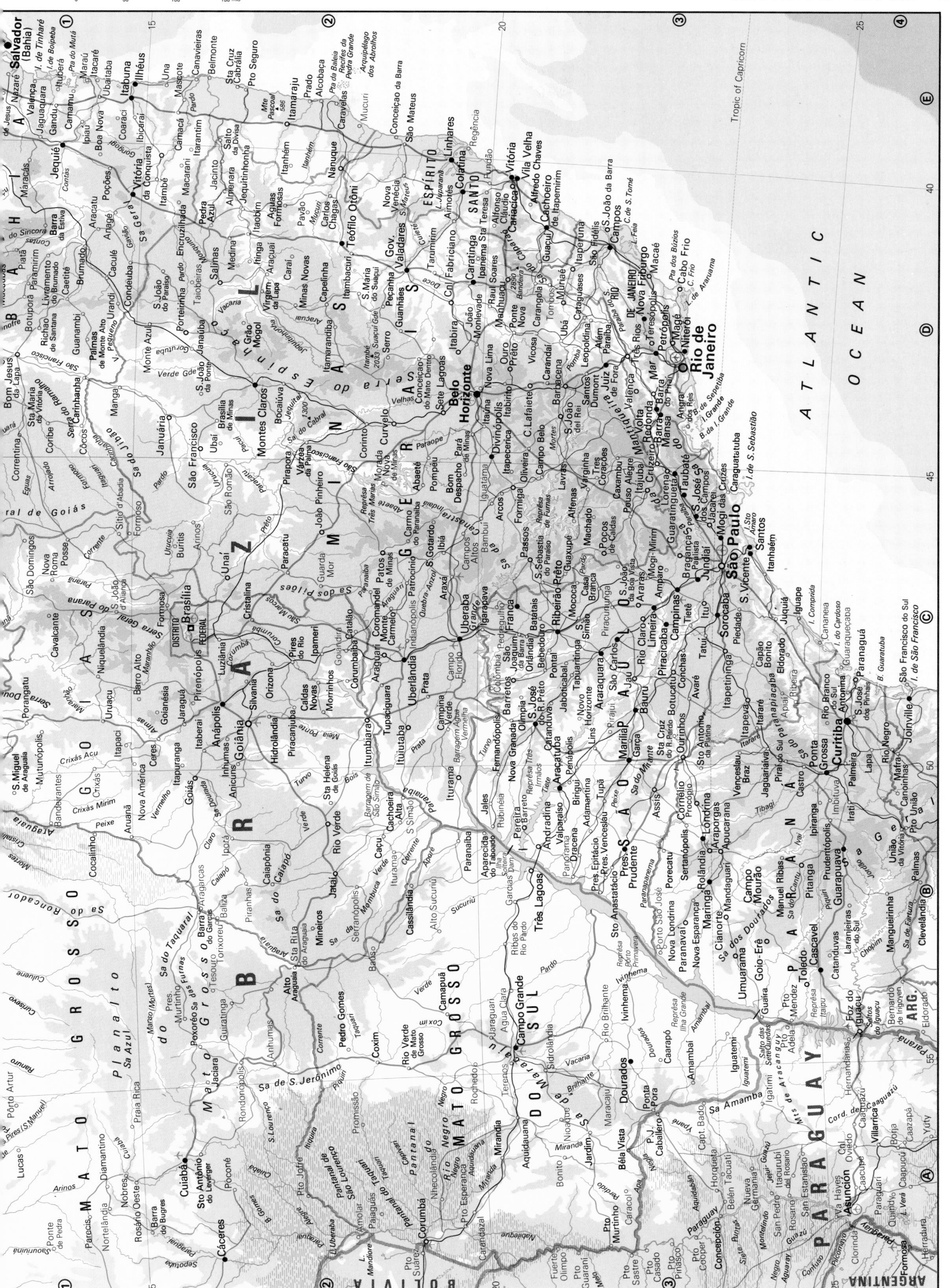
ATLANTIC
OCEAN
Tropic of Capricorn
MATO GROSSO
MATO GROSSO DO SUL
GOIÁS
MINAS GERAIS
BAHIA
ESPÍRITO SANTO
RIO DE JANEIRO
SÃO PAULO
PARANÁ
PARAGUAY
BOLIVIA
ARGENTINA
ARG.
BRAZIL
DISTRITO FEDERAL
Brasília
Rio de Janeiro
São Paulo
Belo Horizonte
Salvador (Bahia)
Vitória
Curitiba
Goiânia
Campo Grande
Cuiabá
Asunción
Campinas
Santos
Niterói
Juiz de Fora
Uberlândia
Uberaba
Ribeirão Prêto
Londrina
Maringá
Ponta Grossa
Joinville
Corumbá
Anápolis
Montes Claros
Governador Valadares
Teófilo Otôni
Vitória da Conquista
Ilhéus
Itabuna
Jequié
Campos
Petrópolis
Volta Redonda
Sorocaba
Bauru
Marília
Pres. Prudente
Dourados
Foz do Iguaçu
Cascavel
Planalto do Mato Grosso
Serra do Espinhaço
Serra Geral de Goiás
Serra da Canastra
Serra da Mantiqueira
Sa do Mar
Pantanal

1:15M

200   400   600 km
100   200   300 mls

A   40   B   ②   30   C   20   70   D   10   E   F   10   G

Greenland
(Den.)

Kap Farvel

Jan Mayen
(Nor.)

A R C T I
A R C T I

ICELAND

Reykjavik

Arctic Circle

N O R W E G I A N

Vesterålen

Lofoten

③

S E A

N O R W A Y

Trondheim

Færøerne
(Den.)

Bergen

Shetland

Stavanger

Oslo

Vänern

Stou

S

Göteborg   Jönköping

Orkney

Ålborg

50

A T L A N T I C

Aberdeen

UNITED KINGDOM
OF GREAT BRITAIN AND
NORTHERN IRELAND

Glasgow

Edinburgh

N O R T H

DENMARK

København

Malmö

Belfast

Newcastle

S E A

Bornholm

Bal

IRELAND

Liverpool

Manchester

Rostock

Dublin

Hamburg

O C E A N

Cork

Birmingham

Amsterdam

Hannover

Berlin

Pozna

Cardiff

Bristol

's-Gravenhage

Rotterdam

NETHERLANDS

Essen

G E R M A N Y

P

④

London

Bruxelles

Lille

Köln

Leipzig

Dresden

Wrocław

English Channel

BELGIUM

Bonn

Frankfurt

Le Havre

Rouen

LUXEMBOURG

Praha

CZECH

Seine

Nürnberg

REPUBLI

Paris

Strasbourg

Brno

Nantes

Stuttgart

Loire

Tours

München

Wien

S

Br

Bern

Zurich

Salzburg

Bordeaux

Clermont-
Ferrand

Genève

SWITZERLAND

LIECHTENSTEIN

AUSTRIA

Graz

Bay of
Biscay

40

F R A N C E

Lyon

Rhône

Ljubljana

SLOVENIA

La Coruña

Torino

Milano

Trieste

Zagreb

CROATI

Bilbao

Toulouse

Venezia

Porto

Valladolid

Genova

BOS

HERZE

Split

Marseille

MONACO

Firenze

P O R T U G A L

ANDORRA

Zaragoza

SAN
MARINO

A D R I A T I C

S E

Madrid

Barcelona

Corse

Bastia

I T A L Y

Lisboa

S P A I N

Toledo

Tajo

Ajaccio

Roma

⑤

Faro

Sevilla

Valencia

Is Baleares

Menorca

Sardegna

Olbia

Napoli

Ta

Murcia

Ibiza

Mallorca

TYRRHENIAN

Málaga

SEA

Madeira
(Port.)

Cagliari

Tanger

Gibraltar (U.K.)

Ceuta (Sp.)

M E D I T E R R A N E A N

Palermo

Messina

Casablanca

Rabat

Melilla
(Sp.)

Oran

Alger

Sicilia

Reggio di Calabria

Islas Canarias
(Sp.)

Marrakech

M O R O C C O

A L G E R I A

E A

N

S E

MALTA

Tunis

TUNISIA

D   E   E   F   G   10

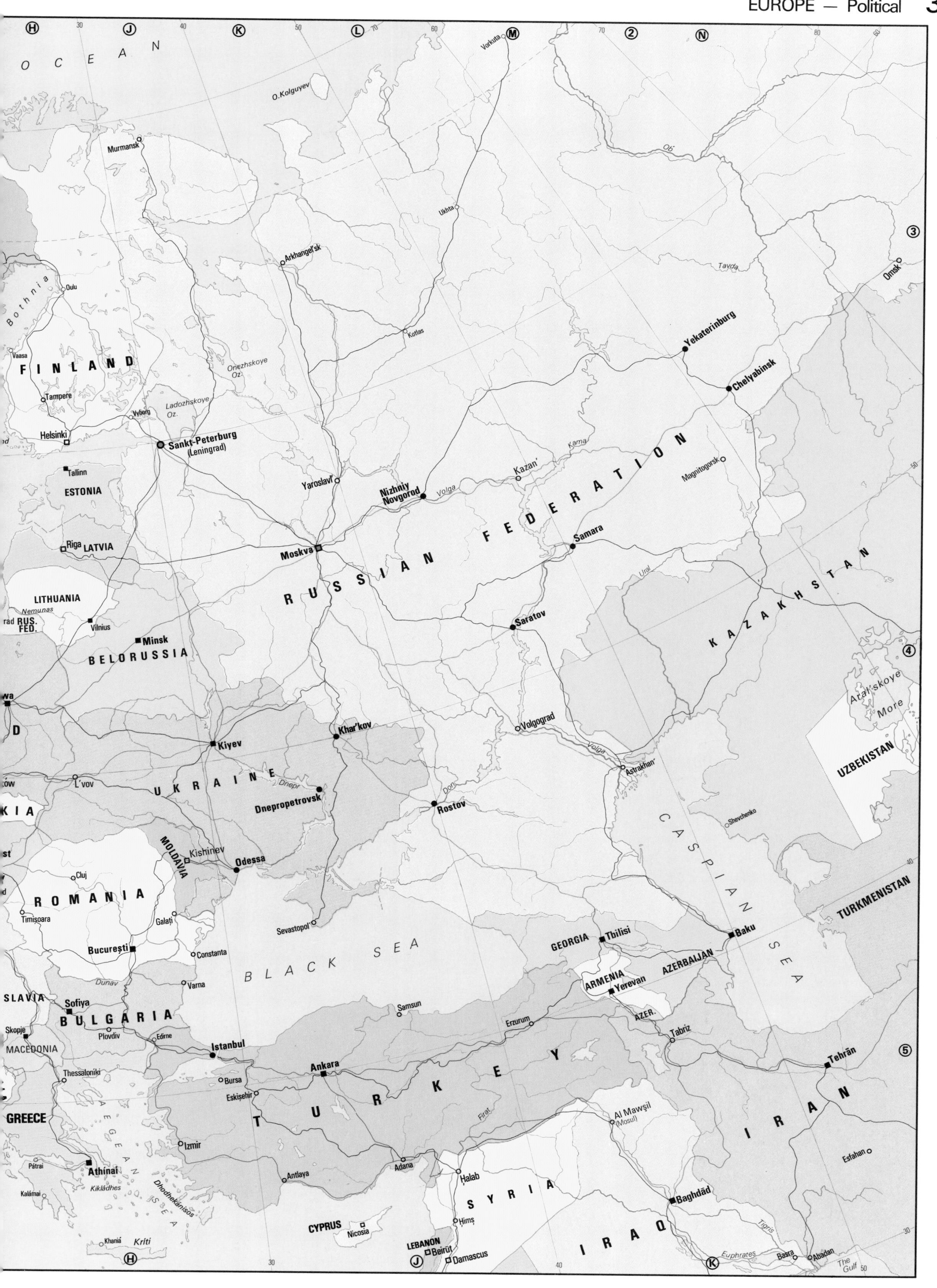
O C E A N
O.Kolguyev
Vorkuta
Murmansk
Ob'
Ukhta
Arkhangel'sk
Tavda
Omsk
Bothnia
Oulu
Kotlas
Yekaterinburg
Vaasa
FINLAND
Onezhskoye Oz.
Chelyabinsk
Tampere
Ladozhskoye Oz.
Vyborg
Helsinki
Sankt-Peterburg (Leningrad)
Kama
Tallinn
Kazan'
Magnitogorsk
ESTONIA
Yaroslavl'
Nizhniy Novgorod
Volga
RUSSIAN FEDERATION
Riga
LATVIA
Samara
Moskva
Ural
LITHUANIA
Nemunas
RUS. FED.
Vilnius
Saratov
KAZAKHSTAN
Minsk
BELORUSSIA
Aral'skoye More
Volgograd
Khar'kov
Kiyev
UZBEKISTAN
Astrakhan'
L'vov
UKRAINE
Dnepr
Don
Dnepropetrovsk
Rostov
Shevchenko
MOLDAVIA
Kishinev
Odessa
CASPIAN SEA
Cluj
ROMANIA
TURKMENISTAN
Timişoara
Galaţi
Sevastopol'
Baku
GEORGIA
Tbilisi
Bucureşti
Constanta
BLACK SEA
AZERBAIJAN
ARMENIA
Yerevan
Dunav
Varna
Sofiya
BULGARIA
Samsun
Erzurum
AZER.
Skopje
Plovdiv
Edirne
Tabriz
MACEDONIA
Istanbul
Tehrān
Thessaloniki
Ankara
Bursa
Eskişehir
TURKEY
GREECE
AEGEAN SEA
Al Mawşil (Mosul)
IRAN
Firat
Izmir
Esfahan
Pátrai
Athínai
Adana
Antalya
Ḩalab
Kalámai
Kikládhes
Dhodhekánisos
SYRIA
Baghdād
CYPRUS
Nicosia
Ḩimş
Tigris
Khaniá
Kríti
LEBANON
Beirūt
Damascus
IRAQ
Euphrates
Basra
Abādān
The Gulf

ICELAND

Reykjavik

Føroyar (Den.)
Streymoy
Vágar
Sandoy
Suduroy
Tórshavn

ARCTIC OCEAN

NORWEGIAN SEA

Arctic Circle

N O R W A Y

S W E D E N

F I N L A N D

Murmansk
Kol'skiy Poluostrov
BARENTS SEA

Tromsø
Narvik
Bodø
Kiruna
Gällivare
Rovaniemi
Oulu
Luleå
Skellefteå
Umeå
Vaasa
Östersund
Sundsvall
Trondheim
Gävle
Tampere
Helsinki (Helsingfors)
Turku
Sankt-Peterburg (Lenin...)

Bergen
Oslo
Uppsala
Stockholm
Örebro
Norrköping
Linköping

ESTONIA
Tallinn
Narva

RUSSIAN FEDERATION
Pskov

Göteborg
Jönköping
Visby
Gotland

LATVIA
Riga
Daugavpils

Kristiansand
Stavanger

Skagerrak
Kattegat

DENMARK
Århus
København
Malmö

LITHUANIA
Šiauliai
Panevėžys
Klaipėda
Vilnius

BALTIC SEA
Bornholm (Den.)

RUS. FED.
Kaliningrad
Kaunas

Minsk
BELORUSSIA

GERMANY
Hamburg
Bremen
Kiel
Lübeck
Rostock
Berlin

POLAND
Szczecin
Gdynia
Gdańsk
Bydgoszcz
Warszawa
Białystok

1:5M 0 50 100 150 200 km
0 50 100 mls

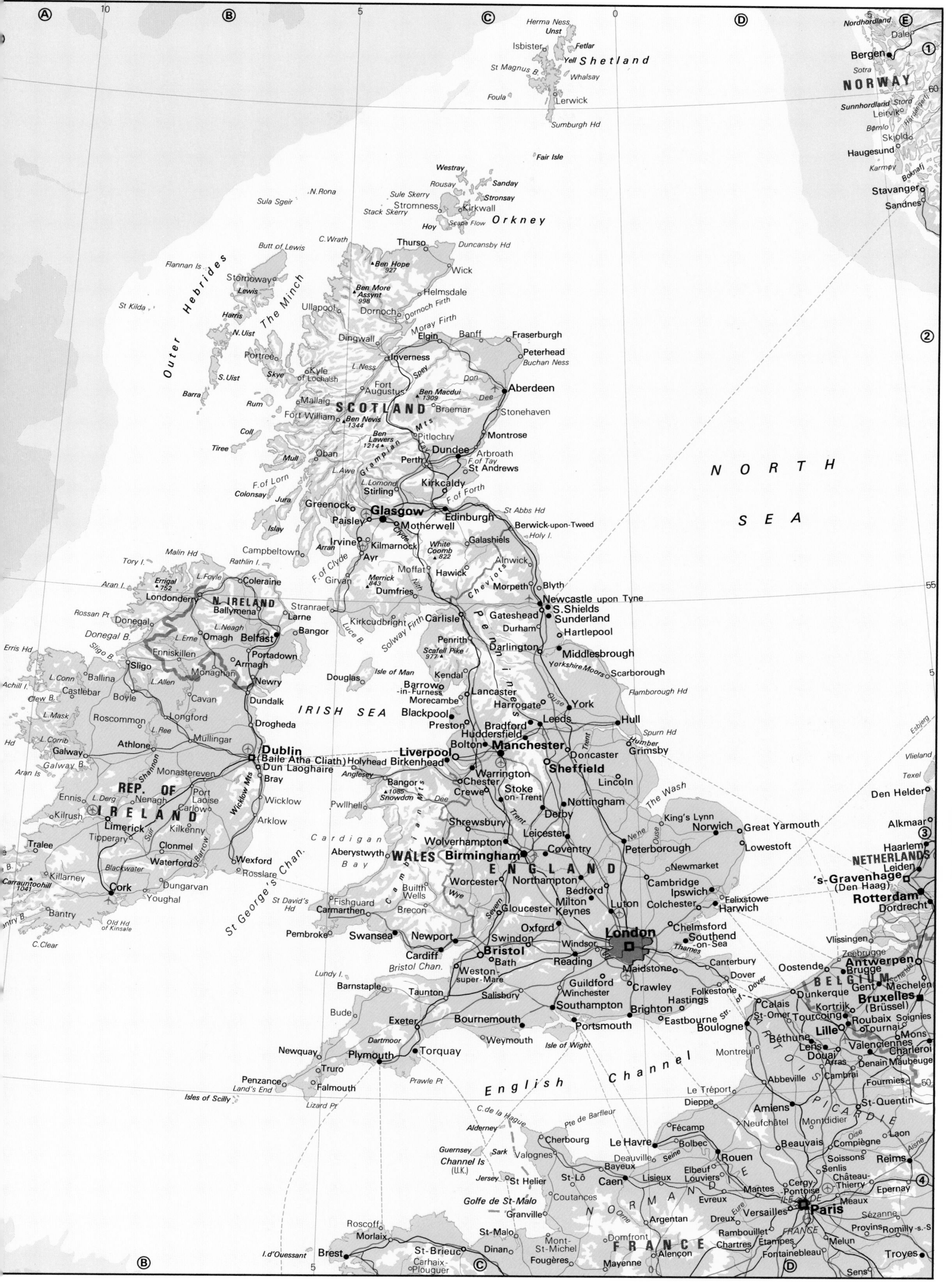
Shetland
Herma Ness
Unst
Fetlar
Yell
Whalsay
Isbister
St Magnus B.
Foula
Lerwick
Sumburgh Hd
Fair Isle
Orkney
Westray
Rousay
Sanday
Stronsay
Sule Skerry
Stromness
Kirkwall
Stack Skerry
Hoy
Scapa Flow
N.Rona
Sula Sgeir
C.Wrath
Butt of Lewis
Thurso
Duncansby Hd
Wick
Flannan Is
Ben Hope 927
Stornoway
Lewis
Ben More Assynt 998
Helmsdale
Outer Hebrides
The Minch
St Kilda
Harris
Ullapool
Dornoch
Dornoch Firth
Moray Firth
N.Uist
Dingwall
Elgin
Banff
Fraserburgh
Portree
Inverness
Peterhead
Buchan Ness
Skye
Kyle of Lochalsh
L.Ness
Spey
S.Uist
Fort Augustus
Ben Macdui 1309
Don
Aberdeen
Barra
Rum
Mallaig
SCOTLAND
Braemar
Dee
Fort William
Ben Nevis 1344
Stonehaven
Coll
Grampian Mts
Pitlochry
Montrose
Tiree
Ben Lawers 1214
Mull
Oban
Dundee
Arbroath
Perth
Tay
F.of Tay
St Andrews
L.Awe
F.of Lorn
Colonsay
Jura
L.Lomond
Stirling
Kirkcaldy
F.of Forth
NORTH SEA
Greenock
Glasgow
Edinburgh
St Abbs Hd
Paisley
Motherwell
Berwick-upon-Tweed
Islay
Holy I.
Clyde
Irvine
Arran
Kilmarnock
White Coomb 822
Galashiels
Campbeltown
Ayr
F.of Clyde
Malin Hd
Rathlin I.
Tory I.
Alnwick
Moffat
Hawick
Cheviots
Errigal 752
L.Foyle
Coleraine
Merrick 843
Girvan
Nith
Aran I.
Dumfries
Morpeth
Blyth
Londonderry
N.IRELAND
Ballymena
Stranraer
Newcastle upon Tyne
Larne
S.Shields
Rossan Pt
Donegal
L.Neagh
Kirkcudbright
Carlisle
Gateshead
Sunderland
Bangor
Solway Firth
Donegal B.
L.Erne
Omagh
Belfast
Luce B.
Durham
Pennines
Erris Hd
Sligo B.
Enniskillen
Portadown
Penrith
Hartlepool
Armagh
Darlington
Sligo
Scafell Pike 977
Middlesbrough
L.Conn
Ballina
Monaghan
Isle of Man
Yorkshire Moors
Scarborough
Achill I.
Castlebar
Newry
Douglas
Kendal
Clew B.
Boyle
L.Allen
Barrow-in-Furness
Lancaster
Flamborough Hd
Cavan
Dundalk
Morecambe
Harrogate
Ouse
York
L.Mask
Roscommon
Longford
IRISH SEA
Blackpool
Preston
Bradford
Leeds
Hull
L.Ree
Drogheda
Huddersfield
Spurn Hd
L.Corrib
Athlone
Mullingar
Bolton
Manchester
Humber
Galway
Dublin (Baile Atha Cliath)
Holyhead
Liverpool
Birkenhead
Doncaster
Grimsby
Trent
Galway B.
Shannon
Dun Laoghaire
Anglesey
Warrington
Sheffield
Aran Is
Monastereven
Bray
Chester
Lincoln
Bangor
Snowdon 1085
Crewe
Stoke-on-Trent
The Wash
REP. OF IRELAND
Port Laoise
Wicklow Mts
Ennis
L.Derg
Nenagh
Carlow
Wicklow
Pwllheli
Dee
Nottingham
Kilrush
Limerick
Arklow
Derby
King's Lynn
Kilkenny
Shrewsbury
Norwich
Great Yarmouth
Tipperary
Cardigan Bay
Leicester
Nene
Tralee
Clonmel
Barrow
Wolverhampton
Lowestoft
Aberystwyth
WALES
Birmingham
Coventry
Peterborough
Waterford
Wexford
ENGLAND
Cambrian Mts
Newmarket
Blackwater
Rosslare
Killarney
St George's Chan.
Worcester
Northampton
Cambridge
Carrauntoohill 1041
Builth Wells
Wye
Bedford
Ipswich
Felixstowe
Cork
Dungarvan
Milton Keynes
Harwich
Youghal
Fishguard
Luton
Colchester
St David's Hd
Carmarthen
Brecon
Gloucester
Severn
Bantry
Chelmsford
Oxford
Old Hd of Kinsale
Pembroke
Swansea
Newport
Swindon
London
Southend-on-Sea
C.Clear
Cardiff
Windsor
Thames
Bristol
Bath
Reading
Canterbury
Bristol Chan.
Weston-super-Mare
Maidstone
Dover
Lundy I.
Barnstaple
Taunton
Guildford
Crawley
Folkestone
Salisbury
Winchester
Hastings
Str. of Dover
Bude
Southampton
Brighton
Eastbourne
Exeter
Bournemouth
Portsmouth
Dartmoor
Weymouth
Isle of Wight
Newquay
Plymouth
Torquay
Truro
English Channel
Penzance
Land's End
Falmouth
Prawle Pt
Isles of Scilly
Lizard Pt
C.de la Hague
Pte de Barfleur
Alderney
Cherbourg
Le Havre
Fécamp
Bolbec
Guernsey
Sark
Channel Is (U.K.)
Valognes
Deauville
Seine
Rouen
Jersey
St Helier
St-Lô
Bayeux
Caen
Lisieux
Elbeuf
Louviers
Coutances
Golfe de St-Malo
Granville
NORMANDIE
Orne
Evreux
Argentan
Dreux
Eure
Roscoff
Morlaix
St-Malo
Mont-St-Michel
Dinan
Domfront
FRANCE
I.d'Ouessant
Brest
St-Brieuc
Carhaix-Plouguer
Fougères
Mayenne
Alençon
Chartres
Rambouillet
Versailles
Paris
Mantes
Cergy-Pontoise
ILE-DE-FRANCE
Étampes
Fontainebleau
Melun
Meaux
Epernay
Château-Thierry
Sézanne
Provins
Romilly-s.-S
Troyes
Sens
Senlis
Soissons
Reims
Compiègne
Oise
Aisne
Laon
Beauvais
Montdidier
Neufchâtel
Amiens
St-Quentin
PICARDIE
Dieppe
Le Tréport
Abbeville
Fourmies
Montreuil
Boulogne
Béthune
Lens
Douai
Arras
Cambrai
ARTOIS
St-Omer
Calais
Dunkerque
Lille
Roubaix
Tourcoing
Kortrijk
Tournai
Valenciennes
Mons
Charleroi
Denain
Maubeuge
Soignies
Bruxelles (Brüssel)
Mechelen
Gent
Brugge
Oostende
Zeebrugge
Antwerpen
Schelde
BELGIUM
Vlissingen
Rotterdam
Dordrecht
's-Gravenhage (Den Haag)
Leiden
Haarlem
NETHERLANDS
Alkmaar
Den Helder
Texel
Vlieland
Esbjerg
NORWAY
Nordhordland
Dale
Bergen
Sotra
Sunnhordland
Stord
Leirvik
Hardangerfj.
Bømlo
Skjold
Haugesund
Karmøy
Boknafj.
Stavanger
Sandnes

1:2.5M 0 25 50 75 100 km 0 25 50 mls

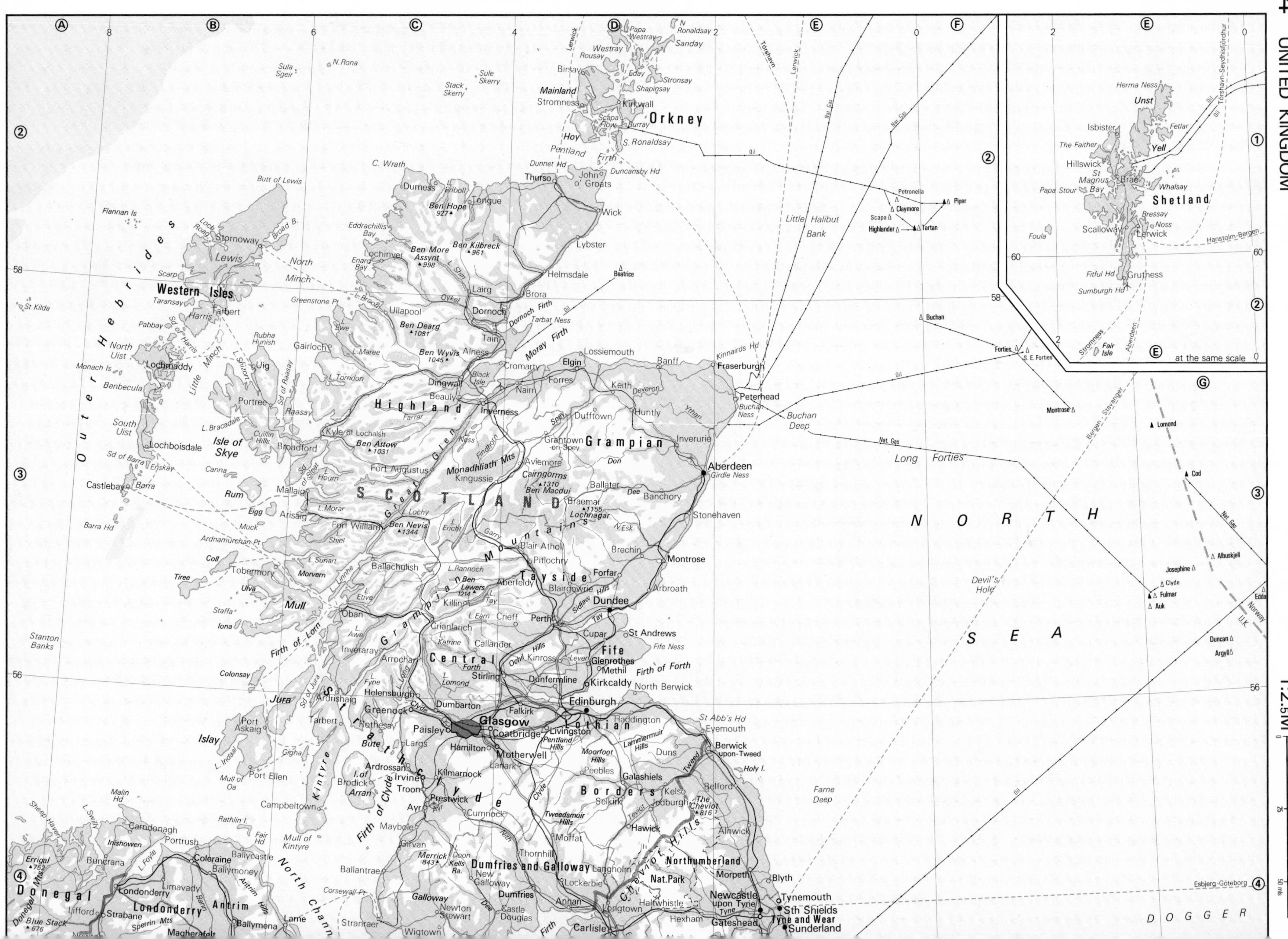
Shetland
Unst
Yell
Whalsay
Fetlar
Bressay
Noss
Lerwick
Scalloway
Hillswick
St Magnus Bay
Papa Stour
Foula
Fair Isle
Sumburgh Hd
Fitful Hd
Herma Ness
The Faither
at the same scale
Orkney
Mainland
Hoy
Stromness
Kirkwall
Westray
Sanday
Stronsay
Shapinsay
Rousay
Birsay
S. Ronaldsay
N Ronaldsay
Pentland Firth
Dunnet Hd
Duncansby Hd
John o' Groats
Wick
Thurso
Lybster
Helmsdale
Brora
Dornoch
Tain
Lairg
Tongue
Durness
C. Wrath
Ben Hope 927
Ben Kilbreck 961
Ben More Assynt 998
Lochinver
Ullapool
Ben Dearg 1081
Ben Wyvis 1045
Moray Firth
Dornoch Firth
Tarbat Ness
Cromarty
Nairn
Inverness
Black Isle
Dingwall
Beauly
Alness
Forres
Elgin
Lossiemouth
Keith
Dufftown
Huntly
Banff
Fraserburgh
Kinnairds Hd
Peterhead
Buchan Ness
Inverurie
Aberdeen
Girdle Ness
Stonehaven
Banchory
Ballater
Braemar
Lochnagar 1155
Grampian
Mountains
Cairngorms 1310
Ben Macdui
Aviemore
Grantown-on-Spey
Kingussie
Monadhliath Mts
Highland
Glen More
Fort Augustus
Fort William
Ben Nevis 1344
Loch Ness
Mallaig
Arisaig
Kyle of Lochalsh
Ben Attow 1031
Gairloch
Isle of Skye
Portree
Uig
Broadford
Cuillin Hills
Rum
Eigg
Muck
Canna
Coll
Tiree
Mull
Tobermory
Iona
Staffa
Ulva
Oban
Ballachulish
Morvern
Ardnamurchan Pt
Firth of Lorn
Colonsay
Jura
Islay
Port Askaig
Port Ellen
Mull of Oa
Kintyre
Campbeltown
Mull of Kintyre
Tarbert
Ardrishaig
Arran
Brodick
Firth of Clyde
Bute
Rothesay
Greenock
Helensburgh
Dumbarton
Inveraray
Arrochar
Glasgow
Paisley
Coatbridge
Hamilton
Motherwell
Lanark
Kilmarnock
Irvine
Ardrossan
Troon
Prestwick
Ayr
Cumnock
Maybole
Girvan
Ballantrae
Stranraer
Wigtown
Newton Stewart
New Galloway
Merrick 843
Dumfries and Galloway
Dumfries
Castle Douglas
Thornhill
Annan
Lockerbie
Moffat
Langholm
Carlisle
Borders
Peebles
Selkirk
Galashiels
Hawick
Jedburgh
Kelso
Duns
Berwick-upon-Tweed
Eyemouth
St Abb's Hd
Lothian
Edinburgh
Livingston
Haddington
North Berwick
Firth of Forth
Fife
Kirkcaldy
Glenrothes
Methil
Dunfermline
Kinross
Cupar
St Andrews
Fife Ness
Dundee
Tay
Perth
Crieff
Tayside
Forfar
Arbroath
Montrose
Brechin
Pitlochry
Blair Atholl
Aberfeldy
Killin
Crianlarich
Callander
Stirling
Falkirk
Central
Loch Lomond
Scotland
Northumberland
Nat. Park
Cheviot 816
Alnwick
Morpeth
Blyth
Newcastle upon Tyne
Gateshead
Tynemouth
Sth Shields
Tyne and Wear
Sunderland
Hexham
Haltwhistle
Outer Hebrides
Western Isles
Lewis
Harris
Stornoway
Tarbert
Butt of Lewis
North Uist
South Uist
Benbecula
Lochmaddy
Lochboisdale
Barra
Castlebay
Barra Hd
St Kilda
Flannan Is
Monach Is
North Minch
Little Minch
Sula Sgeir
N. Rona
Sule Skerry
Stack Skerry
Stanton Banks
North Channel
Antrim
Ballymena
Ballycastle
Ballymoney
Coleraine
Portrush
Londonderry
Limavady
Strabane
Sperrin Mts
Donegal
Buncrana
Inishowen
Malin Hd
Errigal 752
NORTH SEA
Long Forties
Buchan Deep
Little Halibut Bank
Devil's Hole
Farne Deep
DOGGER
Piper
Tartan
Claymore
Highlander
Scapa
Petronella
Beatrice
Buchan
Forties
Montrose
Cod
Albuskjell
Josephine
Clyde
Fulmar
Auk
Lomond
Duncan
Argyll
Nat. Gas
Oil
Norway
U.K.
Esbjerg-Göteborg
Bergen - Stavanger
Tórshavn
Lerwick

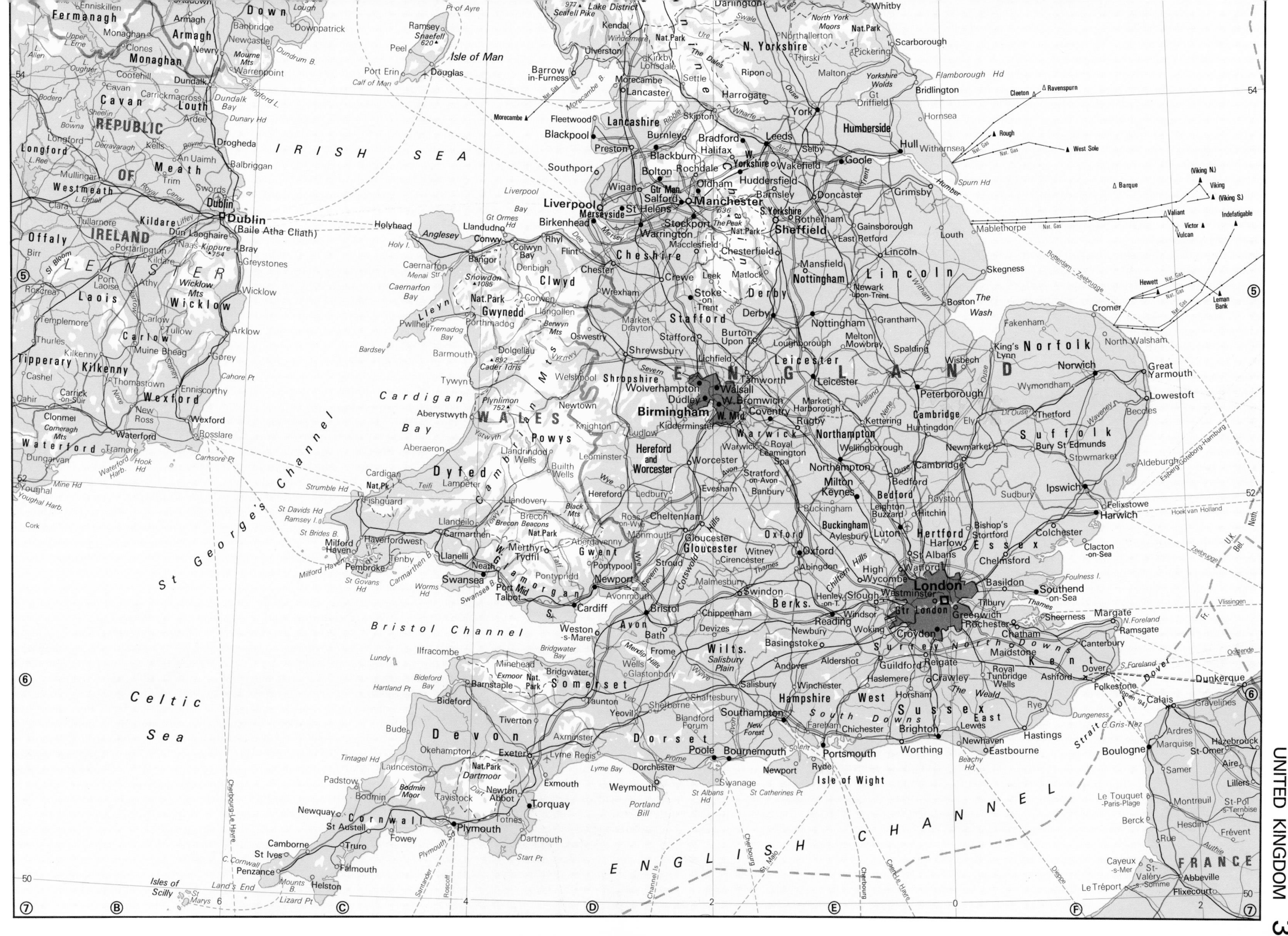
IRISH SEA
Bristol Channel
Cardigan Bay
St George's Channel
Celtic Sea
ENGLISH CHANNEL
Strait of Dover
ENGLAND
WALES
REPUBLIC OF IRELAND
FRANCE
Isle of Man
Isle of Wight
Isles of Scilly
London
Birmingham
Manchester
Liverpool
Leeds
Sheffield
Bristol
Cardiff
Swansea
Plymouth
Southampton
Portsmouth
Brighton
Dover
Norwich
Ipswich
Cambridge
Oxford
Nottingham
Leicester
Coventry
Derby
Hull
York
Dublin
Wexford
Waterford
Douglas
Calais
Boulogne
Dunkerque
Norfolk
Suffolk
Essex
Kent
Surrey
West Sussex
East Sussex
Hampshire
Dorset
Devon
Cornwall
Somerset
Avon
Wilts.
Berks.
Gloucester
Hereford and Worcester
Shropshire
Stafford
Cheshire
Lancashire
Merseyside
Gtr Man.
S. Yorkshire
N. Yorkshire
Humberside
Lincoln
Northampton
Warwick
W. Mid
Buckingham
Bedford
Hertford
Gtr London
Clwyd
Gwynedd
Powys
Dyfed
Gwent
Louth
Meath
Wicklow
Kildare
Carlow
Kilkenny
Laois
Offaly
Westmeath
Longford
Tipperary
Monaghan
Cavan
Armagh
Down
Fermanagh
LEINSTER
Snowdon 1085
Plynlimon 752
Cader Idris 892
The Wash
Humber
Thames
Severn
The Weald
North Downs
South Downs
Chiltern Hills
Cotswold Hills
Mendip Hills
Salisbury Plain
Dartmoor
Exmoor
Bodmin Moor
Land's End
Lizard Pt
Start Pt
Portland Bill
Beachy Hd
Spurn Hd
Flamborough Hd
Nat. Gas
Viking
Indefatigable
Leman Bank
West Sole
Rough
Cleeton
Ravenspurn
Morecambe
Cherbourg-Le Havre

1:2.5M 0 25 50 75 100 km
0 25 50 mls

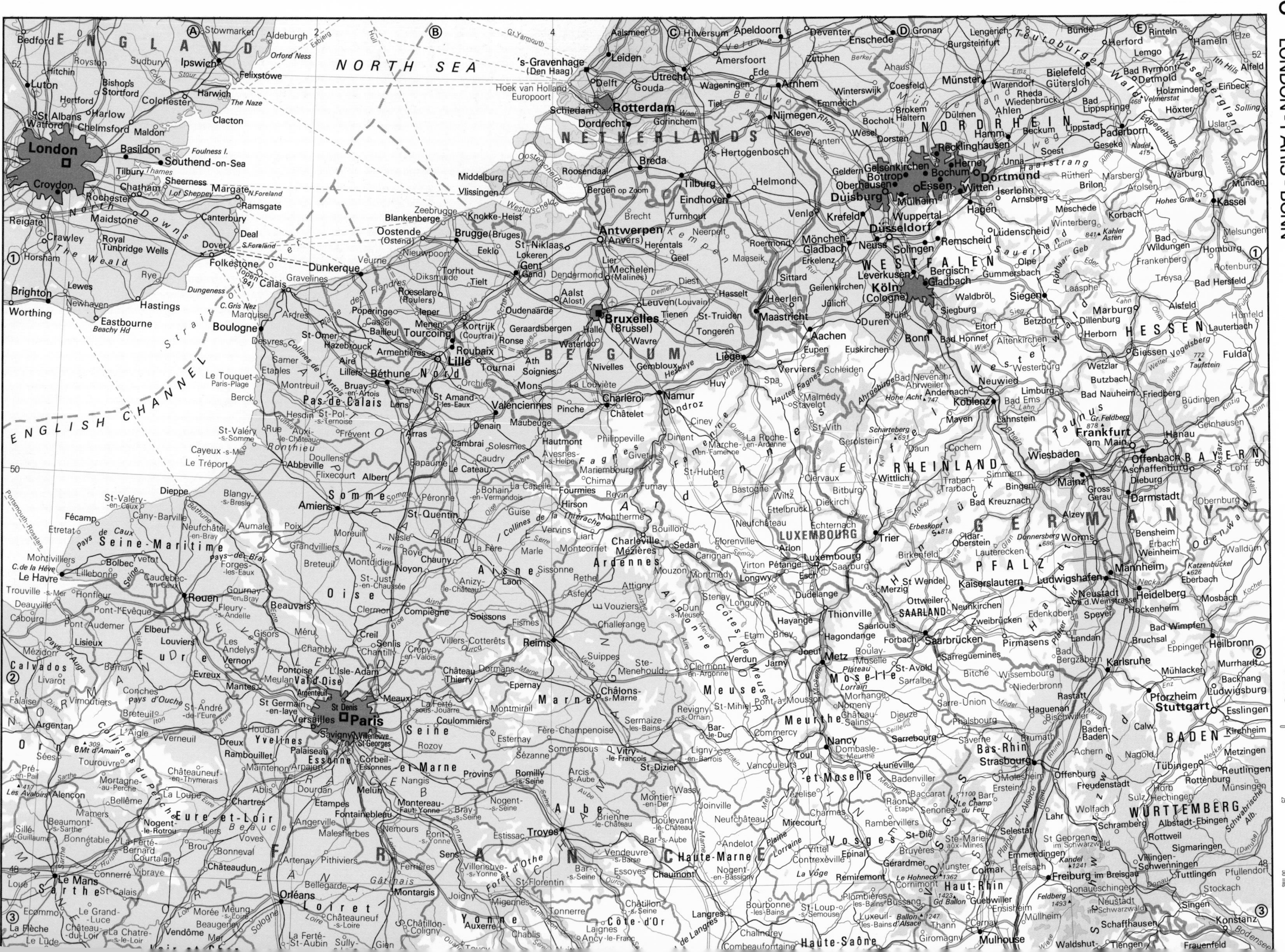
NORTH SEA
ENGLISH CHANNEL
Strait of Dover
ENGLAND
NETHERLANDS
BELGIUM
LUXEMBOURG
GERMANY
FRANCE
NORDRHEIN-WESTFALEN
HESSEN
RHEINLAND-PFALZ
SAARLAND
BADEN-WÜRTTEMBERG
BAYERN
London
Paris
Bruxelles (Brussel)
Rotterdam
's-Gravenhage (Den Haag)
Antwerpen (Anvers)
Köln (Cologne)
Bonn
Düsseldorf
Essen
Dortmund
Frankfurt am Main
Stuttgart
Luxembourg
Lille
Reims
Metz
Nancy
Strasbourg
Rouen
Le Havre
Amiens
Orléans
Le Mans
Calais
Dover
Brighton
Ipswich
Liège
Aachen
Mannheim
Karlsruhe
Kassel
Mulhouse
Troyes
Chartres

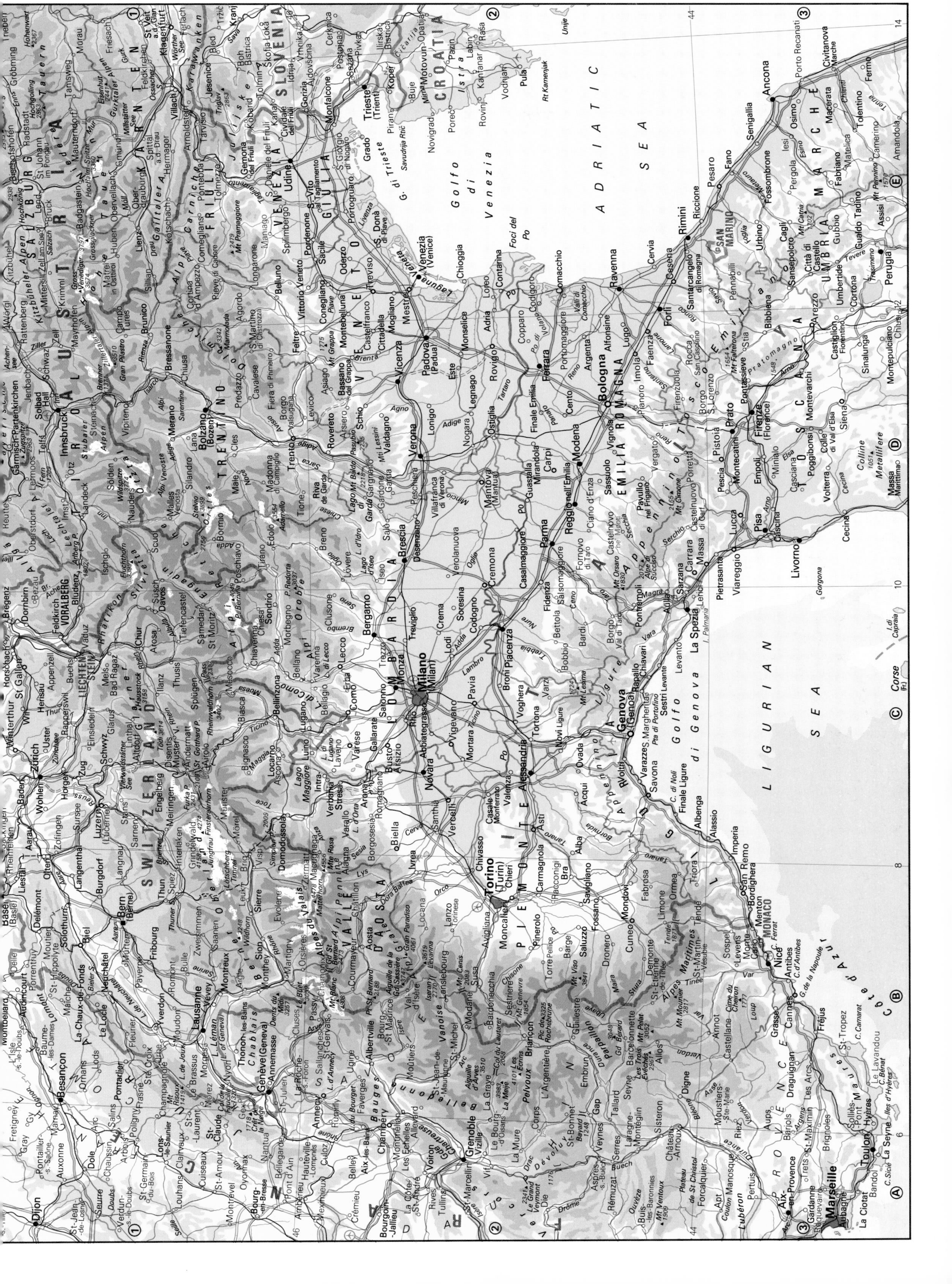

1:2.5M

0 25 50 75 100 km
0 25 50 mls

Countries/Regions: SWITZERLAND, ÖSTERREICH (AUSTRIA), TIROL, SALZBURG, KÄRNTEN, VORARLBERG, LIECHTENSTEIN, SLOVENIA, CROATIA, FRIULI, VENEZIA GIULIA, VENETO, TRENTINO, LOMBARDIA, PIEMONTE, VALLE D'AOSTA, EMILIA ROMAGNA, TOSCANA, UMBRIA, MARCHE, LIGURIA, PROVENCE, SAN MARINO, MONACO

Seas: ADRIATIC SEA, LIGURIAN SEA, Golfo di Venezia, Golfo di Genova, Golfo di Trieste

Major cities: Milano (Milan), Torino (Turin), Genova (Genoa), Bologna, Firenze (Florence), Venezia (Venice), Verona, Padova (Padua), Vicenza, Trieste (Trieste), Udine, Bolzano (Bozen), Trento, Innsbruck, Zürich, Bern (Berne), Genève (Geneva), Lausanne, Besançon, Grenoble, Marseille, Nice, Monaco, Ancona, Perugia, Ravenna, Rimini, Parma, Modena, Bergamo, Brescia, Piacenza, Cremona, Mantova (Mantua), Ferrara, Livorno, Pisa, La Spezia, Ljubljana, Klagenfurt

1:5M 0 50 100 150 200 km 0 50 100 mls

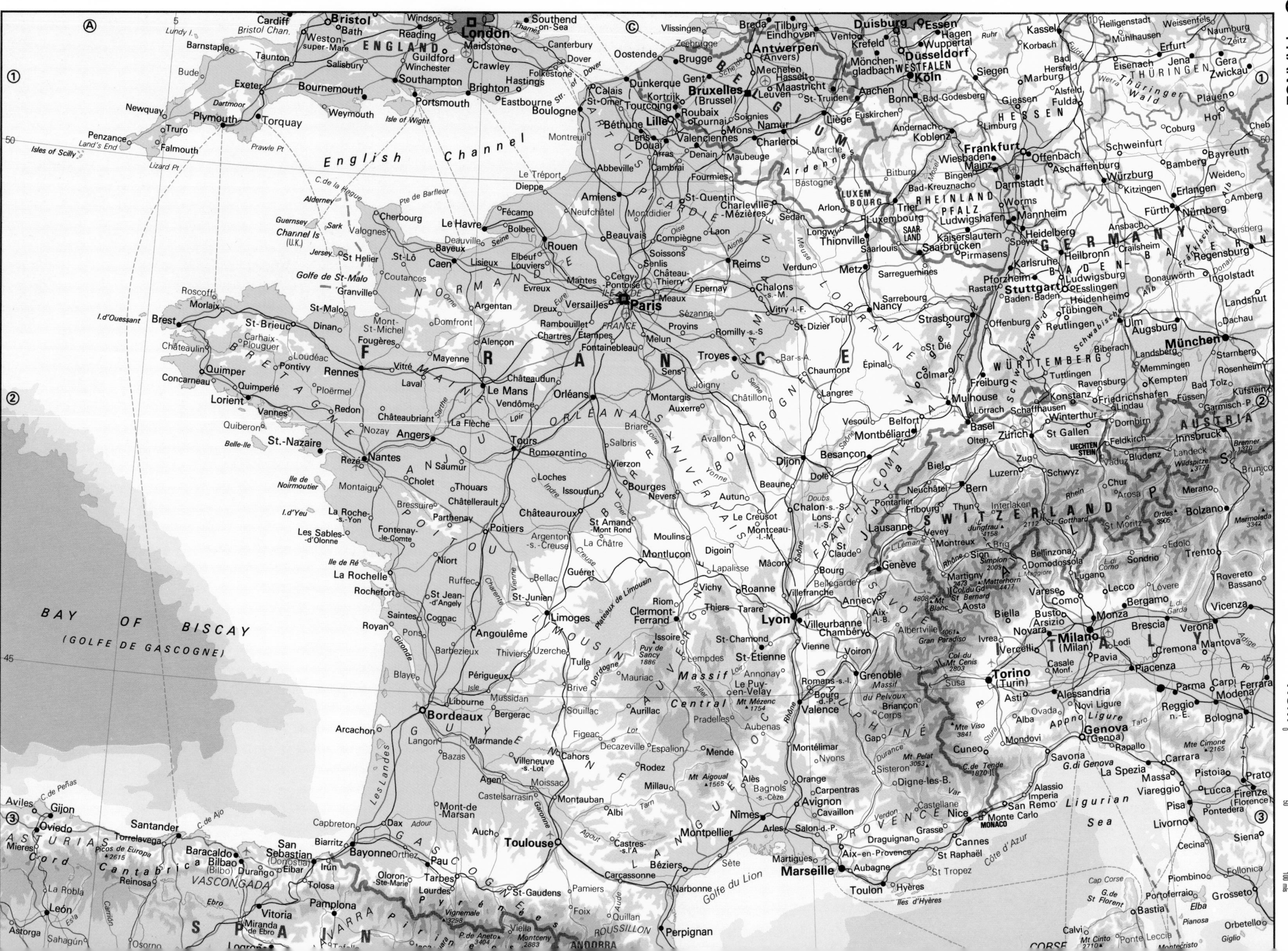
FRANCE
ENGLAND
BELGIUM
LUXEMBOURG
GERMANY
SWITZERLAND
AUSTRIA
ITALY
SPAIN
ANDORRA
MONACO
CORSE
English Channel
BAY OF BISCAY (GOLFE DE GASCOGNE)
Ligurian Sea
Golfe du Lion
Paris
London
Bruxelles (Brussel)
Lyon
Marseille
Bordeaux
Toulouse
Nantes
Milano (Milan)
Torino (Turin)
Genova (Genoa)
München
Stuttgart
Frankfurt
Köln
Strasbourg
Genève
Bern
Zürich
Lille
Rennes
Orléans
Limoges
Clermont-Ferrand
Montpellier
Nice
Grenoble
Dijon
Reims
Rouen
Le Havre
Brest
Bilbao
Santander
Oviedo
Pamplona
San Sebastian
Massif Central
Pyrénées
Les Landes

1:5M

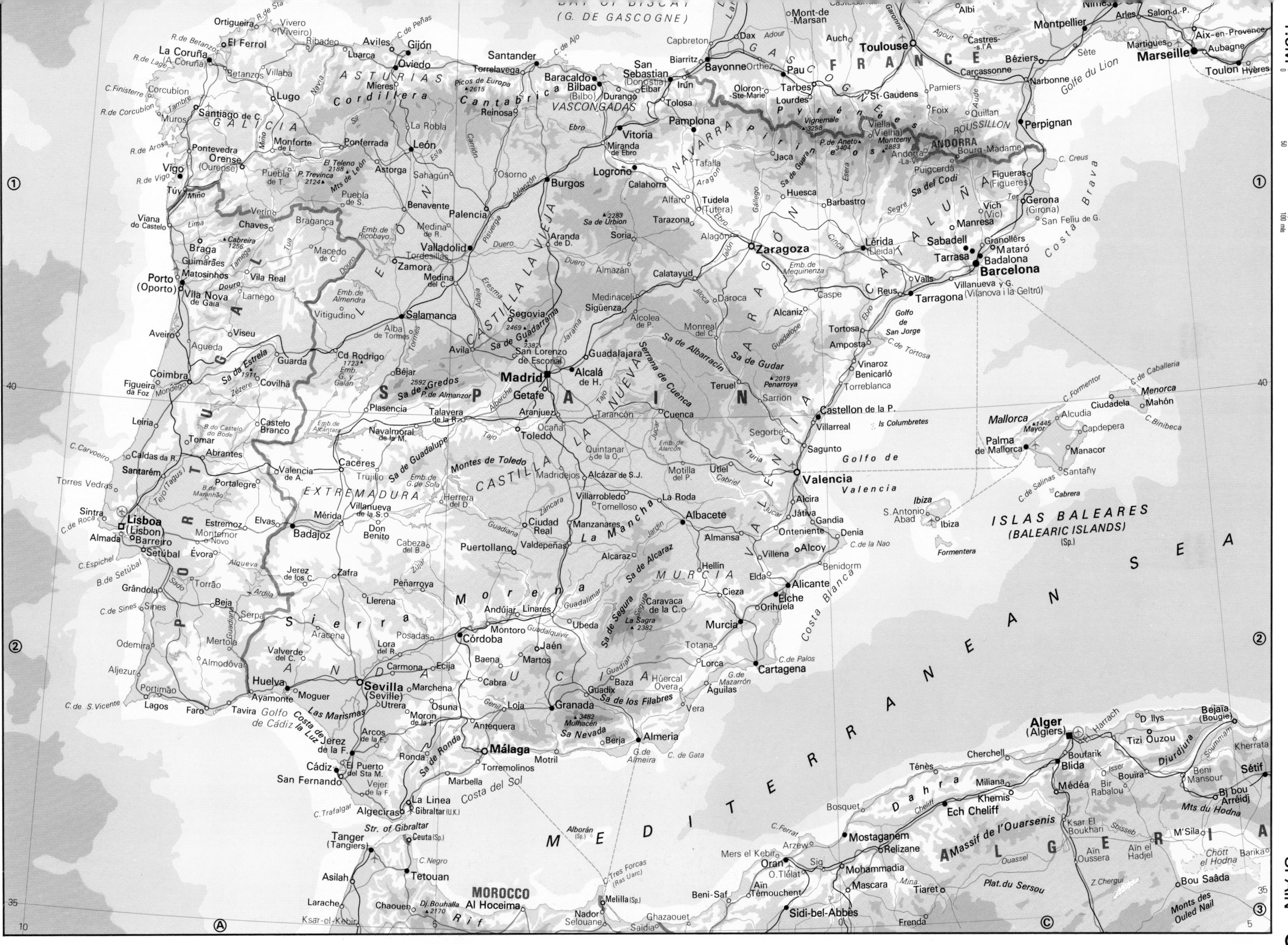

1:5M 0 50 100 150 200 km 0 50 100 mls

A B C 5 10 15

Avallon Vesoul Belfort Freiburg Mulhouse Lörrach Basel Tuttlingen Biberach Landsberg München Wels Vöcklabruck Wien Pölten Mödling Hainfeld Wr. Neustadt

Dijon Besançon Montbéliard Olten Zürich Schaffhausen Konstanz Winterthur Friedrichshafen Lindau Ravensburg Memmingen Kempten GERMANY Starnberg Rosenheim Bad Tolz Füssen Salzburg Gmunden Steyr Bad Ischl Mariazell Neunkirchen

Beaune Dole Biel St Gallen Zug LIECHTENSTEIN Dornbirn Feldkirch Garmisch-P. Kufstein Innsbruck Kitzbühel Hochkönig 2938 Dachstein 2996 Liezen Eisenerz Leoben Bruck an der Mur Sopron Szombathely

Autun Le Creusot Montceau-l.-M. Chalon-s.-S. Lons-l.-S. Digoin Neuchâtel Pontarlier Fribourg Bern Luzern Schwyz Thun Interlaken Rhein Chur Vaduz Bludenz Landeck Wildspitze 3774 Brenner 1375 AUSTRIA Grossglockner 3798 Radstadt Badgastein Judenburg Gleisdorf Graz

Mâcon FRANCHE-COMTÉ Jura Lausanne SWITZERLAND Vevey Montreux Jungfrau 4158 St Gotthard 2112 Arosa Merano Bruneck Brunico Lienz Spittal Wolfsberg Leibnitz Zalaegerszeg

Roanne Bourg St Claude Genève L. Léman Rhône Sion Brig Simplon 2009 Ortles 3905 Bolzano St Moritz Cortina d'A. Villach Tarvisio Jesenice Klagenfurt Maribor Drava Velenje Nagykanizsa

Tarare Villefranche Bellegarde Lyon Annecy Martigny 2473 Col du Gd St Bernard 4808 Mt Blanc Matterhorn 4477 Bellinzona Domodossola L. Maggiore Edolo L. di Como Sondrio Marmolada 3342 Alpi Dolomitiche Gemona Kranj Varaždin Celje

St-Chamond St-Etienne Villeurbanne Chambéry Aix-l.-B. Vienne Albertville Aosta SAVOIE Varese Lugano Como Lecco Trento Belluno Udine Ljubljana Gorizia Koprivnica Bjelovar

Annonay FRANCE Voiron Gran Paradiso 4061 Biella Busto Arsizio Monza Bergamo Lovere L. di Garda Rovereto Bassano Piave Monfalcone SLOVENIA Sava Brežice Novo Mesto Zagreb

Romans-s.-I. Grenoble Massif du Pelvoux Col du Mt Cenis 2083 Ivrea Novara Vercelli Milano (Milan) Lodi Brescia Verona Vicenza Padova Treviso Mestre Trieste Postojna Karlovac Sisak

Mt Mézenc 1754 Bourg d'Oisans Valence Rhône Briançon Corps Susa Torino (Turin) Casale Monf. Pavia Cremona Mantova Adige Venezia (Venice) G. di Venezia Chioggia Koper Poreč Rijeka (Fiume) Vrbovsko Kupa CROATIA Ogulin Una

Aubenas Montélimar Gap DAUPHINÉ Po Asti Alessandria Piacenza Parma Carpi Modena Rovigo Ferrara Istra Rovinj Pula Krk Cres Senj Velebit Bihać Banja Luka

Nyons Mte Viso 3841 Stura Cuneo Alba Ovada Novi Ligure Appno Ligure Genova (Genoa) Reggio n.-E. Bologna Reno Argenta Rab Perušić Vrtoče Gospić

Bagnols-s.-Cèze Orange Carpentras Durance Sisteron Mt Pelat 3053 Mondovi C. de Tende 1870 Rapallo Taro Appno Tosco-Emiliano Imola Faenza Forlì Ravenna Lošinj Karlobag Pag

Nîmes Avignon Cavaillon Digne-les-B. Savona G. di Genova La Spezia Carrara Mte Cimone 2165 Cesena Rimini SAN MARINO ADRIATIC SEA BOSNIA

Arles Salon-d.-P. Verdon Castellane PROVENCE Nice Alassio Imperia San Remo Monte Carlo MONACO Massa Pistoia Viareggio Prato Pesaro Fano Zadar Dugi O. DALMATIA Knin

Martigues Aix-en-Provence Draguignan Grasse Cannes Ligurian Sea Lucca Pisa Firenze (Florence) Urbino Senigallia Kornat Šibenik Cetina

Marseille Aubagne St-Raphaël Côte d'Azur Livorno Pontedera Arezzo Città di Castello Ancona Split (Spalato) Makarska

Toulon Hyères St-Tropez Îles d'Hyères Cecina Siena Fabriano Macerata Brač

Cap Corse G. de St Florent Piombino Follonica Perugia Mte Amiata 1738 Foligno Ascoli Piceno Vis Hvar Korčula

Portoferraio Bastia Elba Pianosa Grosseto L. di Bolsena Terni Teramo Lastovo

Calvi Mt Cinto 2710 Ponte Leccia C. Rosso Corte Montecristo Giglio Orbetello Viterbo Tevere (Tiber) Mte Corno 2912 Pescara Rieti L'Aquila Chieti Pianosa Palagruža (Yug.)

Ajaccio L'Incudine 2136 G. d'Ajaccio Cateraggio CORSE (CORSICA) Sartène Porto Vecchio Civitavecchia L. di Bracciano Città del Vaticano Tivoli Roma (Rome) Avezzano Sulmona Appno Abruzzese Atessa Vasto Termoli I. Tremiti Rodi Garganico Vieste

Bonifacio Strait of Bonifacio Sta Teresa di G. Lido di Ostia Ostia Frosinone Sora Isernia Campobasso S. Severo 1056 Prom. del Gargano Manfredonia

Asinara Anzio Latina Terracina Cassino Mte Miletto 2050 Formia Gaeta Foggia Cerignola Barletta

Porto Torres Olbia Sassari L. del Coghinas Alghero Siniscola I. Ponziane Caserta Benevento Appno Napoletano Ofanto Andria Altamura Le Murge

Napoli (Naples) Pozzuoli Vesuvio 1277 Ischia Torre del G. Avellino Salerno Capri Sorrento Eboli Potenza Basento Matera

Macomer Tirso Nuoro SARDEGNA (SARDINIA) L. Omodeo Mti del Gennargentu 1835 Oristano G. de Oristano Arbatax TYRRHENIAN SEA Agropoli Pta Licosa Appno Lucano Agri Metaponto

Sapri G. di Policastro Mte Pollino 2248 Castrovillari Corigliano Calabro

Sanluri Iglesias Muravera S. Pietro Carbonia Cagliari S. Antioco San Antioco G. de Cagliari C. Carbonara C. Teulada Paola Cosenza La Botte Donato 1929 Sila Crotone Nicastro Catanzaro

Stromboli Ustica Vibo Valentia Alicudi Filicudi Salina Lipari Isole Lipari Vulcano SICILIA (SICILY) Pecoraro 1423

MEDITERRANEAN SEA C. San Vito Palermo Partinico Trapani Alcamo I. Egadi Marsala Cefalù Barcellona Messina Palmi Montalto 1956 Locri Reggio di Calabria Str. de Messina C. Spartivento

Mti Nebrodi Etna 3323 Castelvetrano Mazara del Vallo Sciacca Enna Paterno Giarre Acireale Catania

La Galite C. Bougaroun Ras El Hadid C. Serrat C. Blanc Bizerte Caltanissetta Canicatti Agrigento Lentini Licata Gela Ragusa Siracusa (Syracuse) Vittoria Modica Noto Sicilian Channel Pantelleria (It.) C. I. d. Correnti

Jijel Skikda El Milia Petite Kabylie 'Annaba (Bône) El Kala Azzaba Tabarka Mateur Menzel G. de Tunis C. Bon Tunis Halq el Qued Kelibia

Constantine Guelma Mts de la Medjerda Béja Medjerda El Eulma El Kroub Souk Ahras Jendouba Téboursouk 1295 Dj Zaghouan Nabeul Hammamet Golfe de Hammamet

ALGERIA Le Kef TUNISIA Mellègue Oumel Bouaghi Aïn Beïda Enfida Malta Channel Gozo MALTA Malta Valletta

Mts de Belezma Batna Khenchela Mf de l'Aures 2328 Dj Chélia Makthar Kalaat Khasba Sousse M'saken Monastir Kairouan Moknine Tébessa Mts des Nementcha Mts de Tébessa

① ② ③ 40

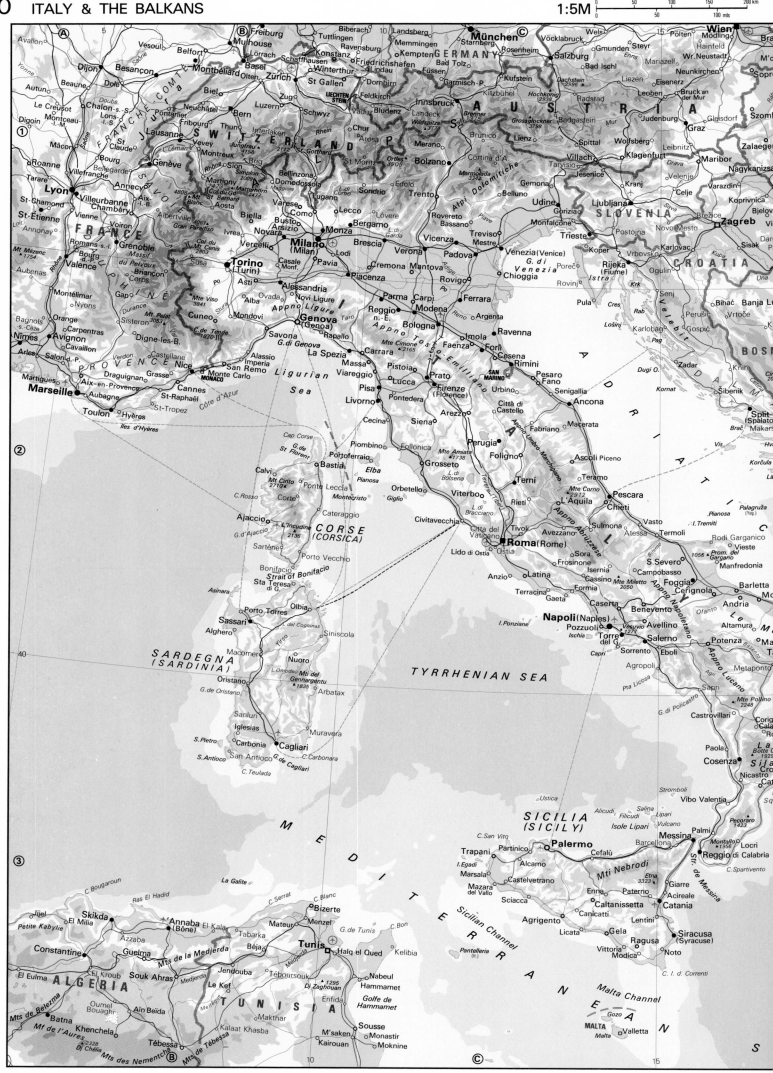

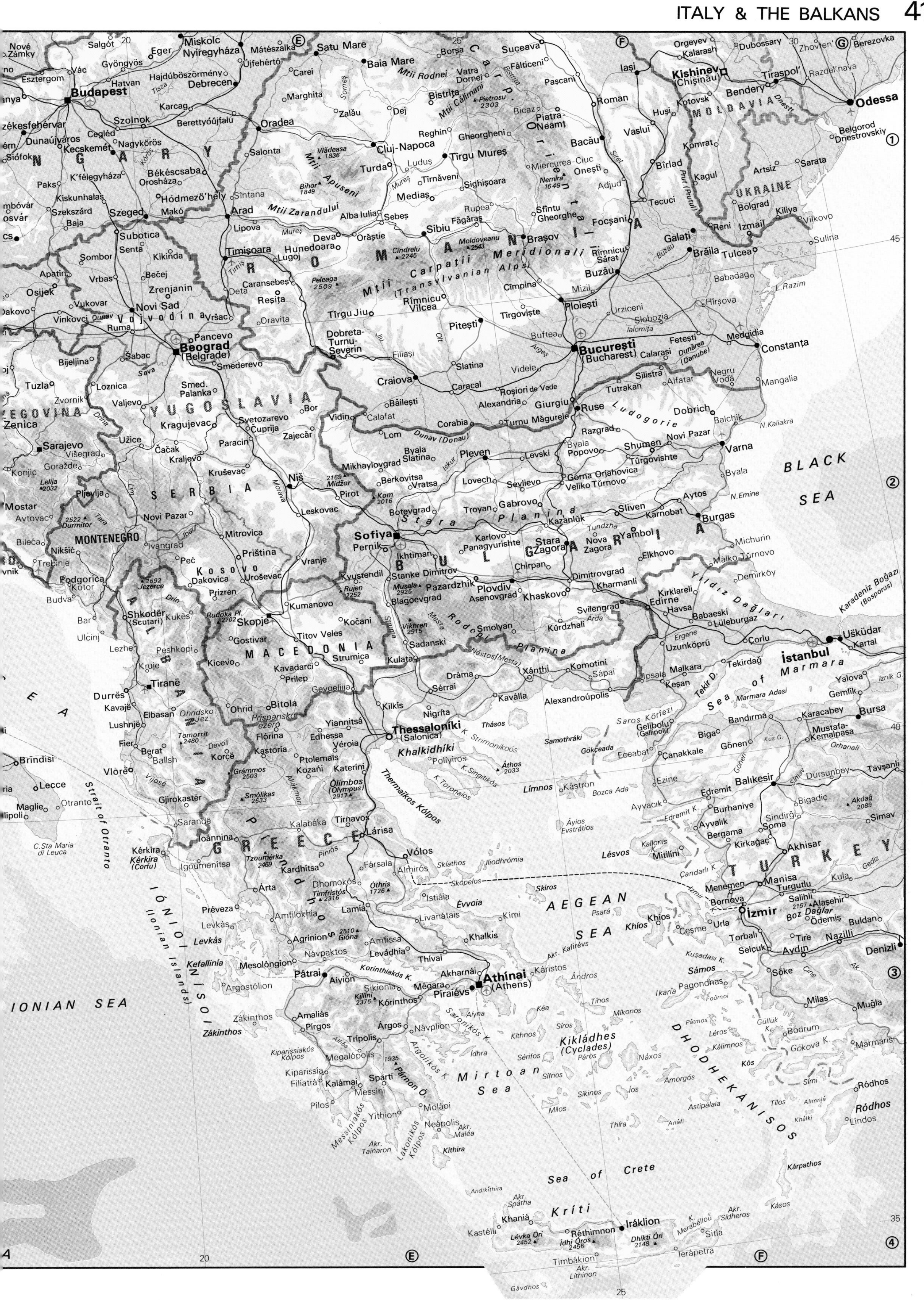
Budapest
Miskolc
Nyíregyháza
Debrecen
Satu Mare
Baia Mare
Suceava
Iaşi
Kishinev (Chişinău)
Tiraspol'
Odessa
Oradea
Cluj-Napoca
Tîrgu Mureş
Bacău
Szeged
Arad
Timişoara
Sibiu
Braşov
Galaţi
Brăila
Tulcea
Novi Sad
Beograd (Belgrade)
Ploieşti
Bucureşti (Bucharest)
Constanţa
Craiova
Ruse
Varna
Sarajevo
Niš
Sofiya
Plovdiv
Burgas
Skopje
Tiranë
Thessaloníki (Salonica)
İstanbul
Edirne
Bursa
İzmir
Lárisa
Pátrai
Athínai (Athens)
Piraiévs
Iráklion
Kríti
Ródhos
H U N G A R Y
R O M A N I A
M O L D A V I A
U K R A I N E
Y U G O S L A V I A
S E R B I A
MONTENEGRO
MACEDONIA
B U L G A R I A
A L B A N I A
G R E E C E
T U R K E Y
BLACK SEA
AEGEAN SEA
IONIAN SEA
Sea of Crete
Mirtoan Sea
Sea of Marmara
Strait of Otranto
Kikládhes (Cyclades)
Dhodhekánisos
Carpaţii Meridionali (Transylvanian Alps)
Stara Planina
Rodopi Planina
Pindhos
Dunav (Donau)
Olimbos (Olympus) 2917
Musala 2925
Moldoveanu 2543
Vojvodina
Kosovo
1
2
3
4
E
F
G
20
25
30
35
40
45

1:5M 0 50 100 150 200 km 0 50 100 mls

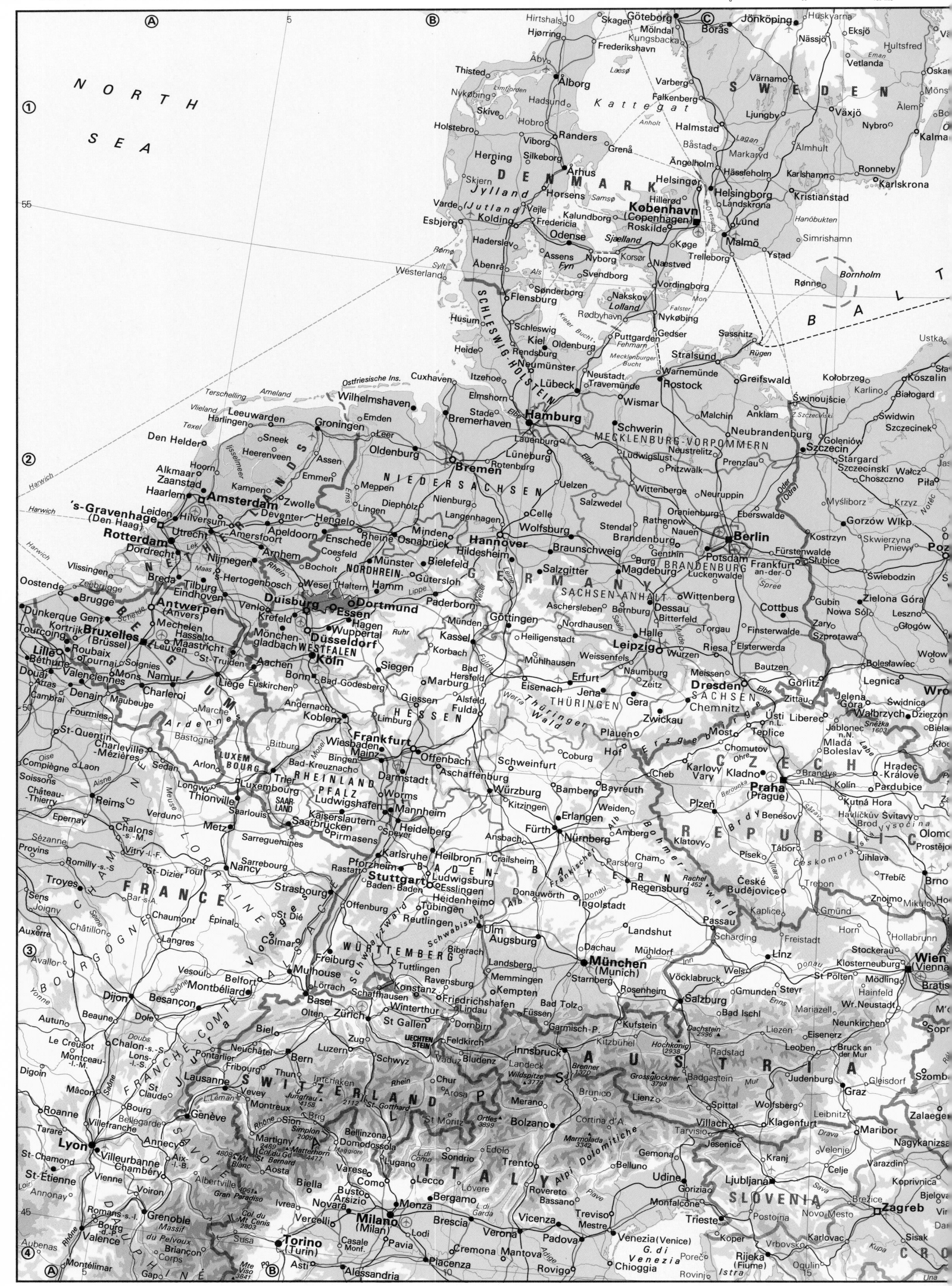
NORTH SEA
DENMARK
Jylland (Jutland)
Kattegat
SWEDEN
BALTIC
København (Copenhagen)
Göteborg
Malmö
Århus
Ålborg
Odense
Bornholm
SCHLESWIG-HOLSTEIN
MECKLENBURG-VORPOMMERN
NIEDERSACHSEN
BRANDENBURG
SACHSEN-ANHALT
NORDRHEIN-WESTFALEN
HESSEN
THÜRINGEN
SACHSEN
RHEINLAND-PFALZ
SAAR-LAND
BADEN-WÜRTTEMBERG
BAYERN
GERMANY
NETHERLANDS
BELGIUM
LUXEMBOURG
FRANCE
LORRAINE
CHAMPAGNE
BOURGOGNE
FRANCHE-COMTÉ
SAVOIE
DAUPHINÉ
CZECH REPUBLIC
AUSTRIA
SWITZERLAND
LIECHTENSTEIN
ITALY
SLOVENIA
Hamburg
Bremen
Hannover
Berlin
Leipzig
Dresden
Köln
Düsseldorf
Dortmund
Essen
Frankfurt
Stuttgart
München (Munich)
Nürnberg
Amsterdam
's-Gravenhage (Den Haag)
Rotterdam
Antwerpen (Anvers)
Bruxelles (Brüssel)
Luxembourg
Strasbourg
Praha (Prague)
Wien (Vienna)
Salzburg
Innsbruck
Zürich
Bern
Genève
Lyon
Milano (Milan)
Torino (Turin)
Venezia (Venice)
Ljubljana
Zagreb
Alps

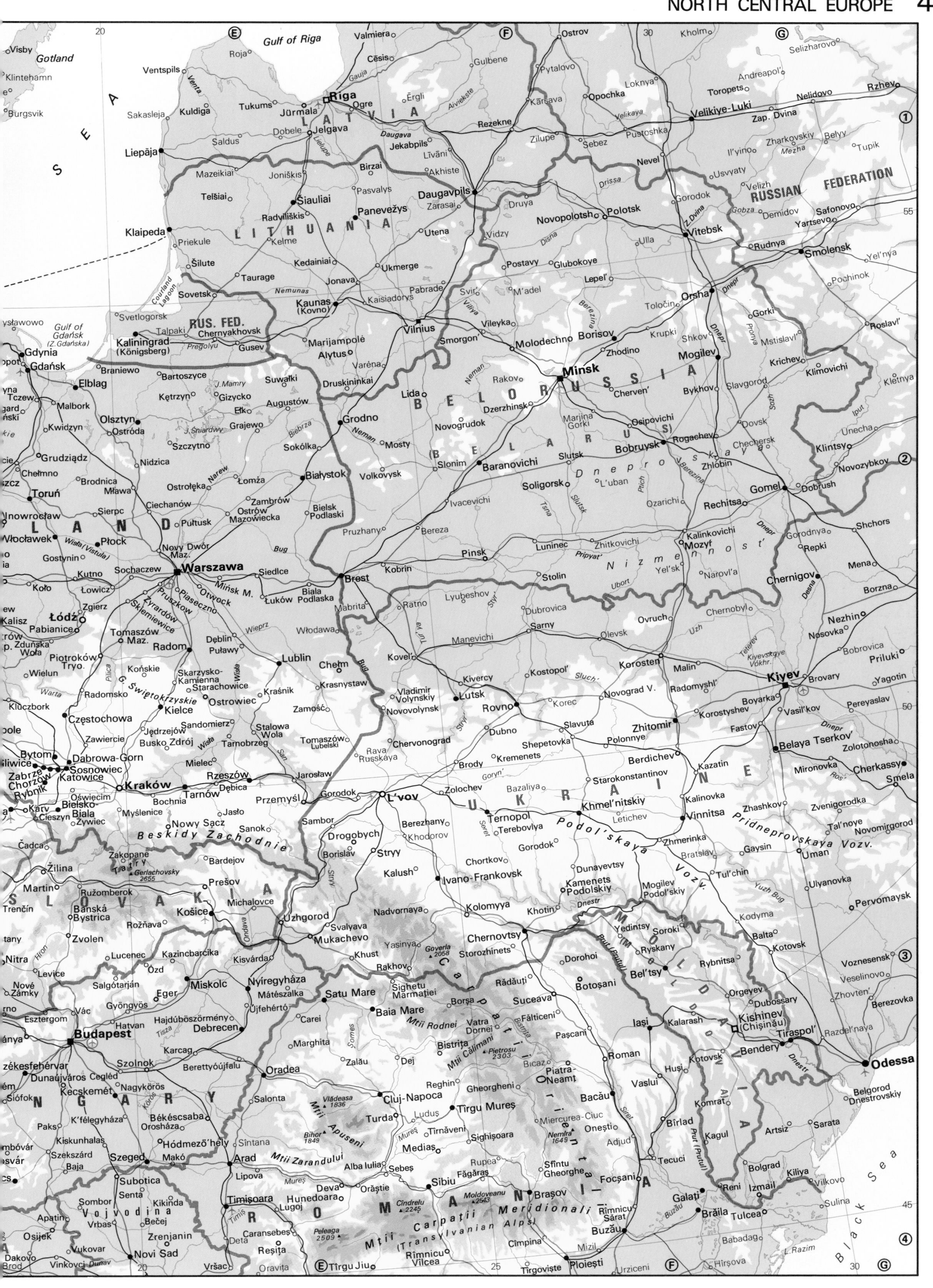
Gulf of Riga
Gotland
Visby
Klintehamn
Burgsvik
S E A
Ventspils
Roja
Venta
Riga
Jūrmala
Tukums
Ogre
Ērgli
Cēsis
Valmiera
Gauja
Gulbene
Sakasleja
Kuldiga
L A T V I A
Jelgava
Dobele
Saldus
Lielupe
Daugava
Jekabpils
Aiviekste
Rezekne
Kārsava
Ostrov
Pytalovo
Opochka
Loknya
Kholm
Selizharovo
Andreapol'
Toropets
Rzhev
Nelidovo
Velikiye-Luki
Zap. Dvina
Velikaya
Pustoshka
Zilupe
Sebez
Il'yino
Zharkovskiy
Belyy
Mezha
Tupik
Nevel'
Usvyaty
Velizh
RUSSIAN FEDERATION
Liepāja
Mazeikiai
Joniškis
Birzai
Līvāni
Akhiste
Pasvalys
Daugavpils
Zarasai
Druya
Drissa
Gorodok
Gobza
Demidov
Safonovo
Yartsevo
Telšiai
Šiauliai
Radviliškis
Panevežys
Novopolotsk
Polotsk
Z. Dvina
Vitebsk
Klaipeda
Priekule
L I T H U A N I A
Kelme
Utena
Vidzy
Disna
Ulla
Rudnya
Smolensk
Yel'nya
Šilute
Kedainiai
Ukmerge
Postavy
Glubokoye
Taurage
Jonava
Pabrade
Svir'
M'adel
Lepel'
Berezina
Orsha
Dnepr
Toločin
Gorki
Pochinok
Roslavl'
Courland Lagoon
Sovetsk
Nemunas
Kaunas (Kovno)
Kaisiadorys
Viliya
Vileyka
Krupki
Shkov
Pronya
Mstislavl'
Svetlogorsk
RUS. FED.
Chernyakhovsk
Talpaki
Kaliningrad (Königsberg)
Pregolya
Gusev
Vilnius
Smorgon'
Molodechno
Borisov
Zhodino
Mogilev
Gulf of Gdańsk (Z. Gdańska)
Gdynia
Gdańsk
Marijampolė
Alytus
Varėna
Druskininkai
Neman
Rakov
Minsk
Cherven'
Krichev
Klimovichi
Kletnya
Braniewo
Elblag
Bartoszyce
J. Mamry
Suwałki
Lida
B E L O R U S S I A
Bykhov
Slavgorod
Sozh
Iput
Tczew
Malbork
Olsztyn
Ostróda
Kętrzyn
Gizycko
Ełk
Augustów
Grodno
Dzerzhinsk
Marjina Gorki
Osipovichi
Dovsk
Unecha
Kwidzyn
J. Śniardwy
Grajewo
Biebrza
Novogrudok
Rogachev
Chechersk
Klintsy
Grudziądz
Szczytno
Sokółka
Mosty
Bobruysk
Zhlobin
Novozybkov
Chełmno
Nidzica
Narew
Slonim
Baranovichi
Slutsk
D n e p r o v s k a y a
Brodnica
Mława
Ostrołęka
Łomża
Białystok
Volkovysk
Soligorsk
L'uban
Ptich
Berezina
Gomel
Dobrush
Toruń
Ciechanów
Zambrów
Ostrów Mazowiecka
Bielsk Podlaski
Ivacevichi
Tsna
Ozarichi
Rechitsa
Inowrocław
Sierpc
Pułtusk
Pruzhany
Bereza
Kalinkovichi
Mozyr
Gorodnya
Shchors
Włocławek
Płock
Wisła (Vistula)
Nowy Dwór Maz.
Bug
Pinsk
Luninec
Zhitkovichi
Pripyat'
N i z m e n n o s t'
Repki
Gostynin
Sochaczew
Warszawa
Siedlce
Brest
Kobrin
Stolin
Yel'sk
Narovl'a
Mena
Kutno
Koło
Łowicz
Mińsk M.
Otwock
Biala Podlaska
Łuków
Lyubeshov
Ubort
Chernigov
Desna
Borzna
Zgierz
Łódź
Pabianice
Kalisz
Żyrardów
Pruszków
Piaseczno
Skierniewice
Mabrita
Ratno
Styr'
Dubrovica
Ovruch
Chernobyl'
Nezhin
Nosovka
Tomaszów Maz.
Radom
Dęblin
Puławy
Wieprz
Włodawa
Tur'ya
Sarny
Olevsk
Uzh
Teterev
Kiyevskoye Vdkhr.
Bobrovica
Priluki
Zduńska Wola
Piotrków Tryb.
Lublin
Chełm
Kovel'
Manevichi
Korosten
Malin
Kiyev
Brovary
Yagotin
Wieluń
Końskie
Skarżysko-Kamienna
Starachowice
Ostrowiec
Kraśnik
Krasnystaw
Vladimir Volynskiy
Kivercy
Lutsk
Kostopol'
Sluch'
Novograd V.
Radomyshl'
Pereyaslav
Warta
Pilica
Radomsko
G. Świętokrzyskie
Kielce
Zamość
Novovolynsk
Rovno
Korec
Korostyshev
Boyarka
Vasil'kov
Kluczbork
Częstochowa
Jędrzejów
Sandomierz
Stalowa Wola
Dubno
Slavuta
Zhitomir
Fastov
Dnepr
Zawiercie
Busko Zdrój
Tarnobrzeg
Tomaszów Lubelski
Chervonograd
Rava Russkaya
Shepetovka
Polonnye
Belaya Tserkov'
Zolotonosha
Bytom
Dabrowa-Gorn
Sosnowiec
Katowice
Zabrze
Chorzów
Rybnik
Mielec
Jarosław
Brody
Kremenets
Berdichev
Kazatin
Mironovka
Cherkassy
Smela
Kraków
Rzeszów
Dębica
Tarnów
Bochnia
Oświęcim
Przemyśl
Gorodok
L'vov
Zolochev
Goryn'
Bazaliya
Starokonstantinov
Kalinovka
Ros'
U K R A I N E
Bielsko-Biala
Cieszyn
Żywiec
Myślenice
Nowy Sącz
Jasło
Sanok
Sambor
Berezhany
Khodorov
Ternopol
Terebovlya
Seret
Khmel'nitskiy
Letichev
Vinnitsa
Zhashkov
Zvenigorodka
Tal'noye
Novomirgorod
Beskidy Zachodnie
Drogobych
Borislav
Stryy
Gorodok
Podol'skaya Vozv.
Zhmerinka
Bratslav
Gaysin
Uman
Pridneprovskaya Vozv.
Čadca
Zakopane
Tatry
Gerlachovsky 2655
Bardejov
Kalush
Ivano-Frankovsk
Chortkov
Dunayevtsy
Kamenets Podolskiy
Mogilev Podol'skiy
Tul'chin
Yuzh Bug
Ulyanovka
Pervomaysk
Žilina
Martin
Ružomberok
Prešov
S L O V A K I A
Michalovce
Trenčín
Banská Bystrica
Košice
Uzhgorod
Nadvornaya
Kolomyya
Khotin
Dnestr
Kodyma
Rožňava
Ondava
Svalyava
Mukachevo
Chernovtsy
Yedintsy
Soroki
Balta
Kotovsk
Zvolen
Hron
Kazincbarcika
Yasinya
Goverla 2058
Storozhinets
Ryskany
Rybnitsa
Voznesensk
Nitra
Lučenec
Ózd
Kisvárda
Khust
Rakhov
Dorohoi
Prut (Prutul)
Bel'tsy
M O L D A V I A
Veselinovo
Levice
Salgótarján
Miskolc
Nyíregyháza
Mátészalka
Satu Mare
Sighetu Marmației
Rădăuți
Botoșani
Orgeyev
Dubossary
Zhovten'
Berezovka
Nové Zámky
Eger
Gyöngyös
Vác
Hajdúböszörmény
Újfehértó
Baia Mare
Borșa
Suceava
Fălticeni
Kishinev (Chișinău)
Kalarash
Esztergom
Hatvan
Debrecen
Carei
Mtii Rodnei
Vatra Dornei
Bistrița
Iași
Tiraspol'
Razdel'naya
Budapest
Tisza
Karcag
Marghita
Someș
Bistrița
Mtii Călimani
Pietrosu 2303
Pașcani
Bendery
Odessa
Székesfehérvár
Szolnok
Berettyóújfalu
Oradea
Zalău
Dej
Bicaz
Piatra-Neamț
Roman
Vaslui
Huși
Kotovsk
Dnestr
Dunaújváros
Cegléd
Nagykőrös
Kecskemét
Salonta
Cluj-Napoca
Reghin
Gheorgheni
Bacău
Belgorod Dnestrovskiy
Siófok
Kőrös
Vlădeasa 1836
Mtii Apuseni
Turda
Ludus
Tirgu Mureș
Miercurea-Ciuc
Onești
Siret
Komrat
Békéscsaba
Orosháza
K'félegyháza
Paks
Bihor 1849
Mureș
Tirnăveni
Sighișoara
Nemira 1649
Adjud
Bîrlad
Kagul
Artsiz
Sarata
Kiskunhalas
Hódmezővásárhely
Sîntana
Mediaș
Prut (Prutul)
Szekszárd
Baja
Szeged
Makó
Arad
Mtii Zarandului
Alba Iulia
Sebeș
Rupea
Sfîntu Gheorghe
Tecuci
Bolgrad
Subotica
Lipova
Deva
Orăștie
Sibiu
Făgăraș
Focșani
Reni
Izmail
Kiliya
Vilkovo
Black Sea
Sombor
Senta
Kikinda
Timișoara
Hunedoara
Lugoj
Cindrelu 2245
Moldoveanu 2543
Brașov
Galați
Sulina
Vojvodina
Apatin
Vrbas
Bečej
Timiș
Mtii Carpații Meridionali
Rîmnicu Sărat
Buzău
Brăila
Tulcea
Osijek
Zrenjanin
Caransebeș
Reșița
Peleaga 2509
(Transylvanian Alps)
Cimpina
Mizil
Babadag
Vukovar
Novi Sad
Rîmnicu Vîlcea
L. Razim
Dakovo
Brod
Vinkovci
Dunav
Vršac
Oravița
Tîrgu Jiu
Tirgoviște
Ploiești
Urziceni
Hîrșova
R O M A N I A
H U N G A R Y
P O L A N D
20
25
30
45
50
55
E
F
G
1
2
3
4

1:10M

0 100 200 300 400 km

0 100 200 mls

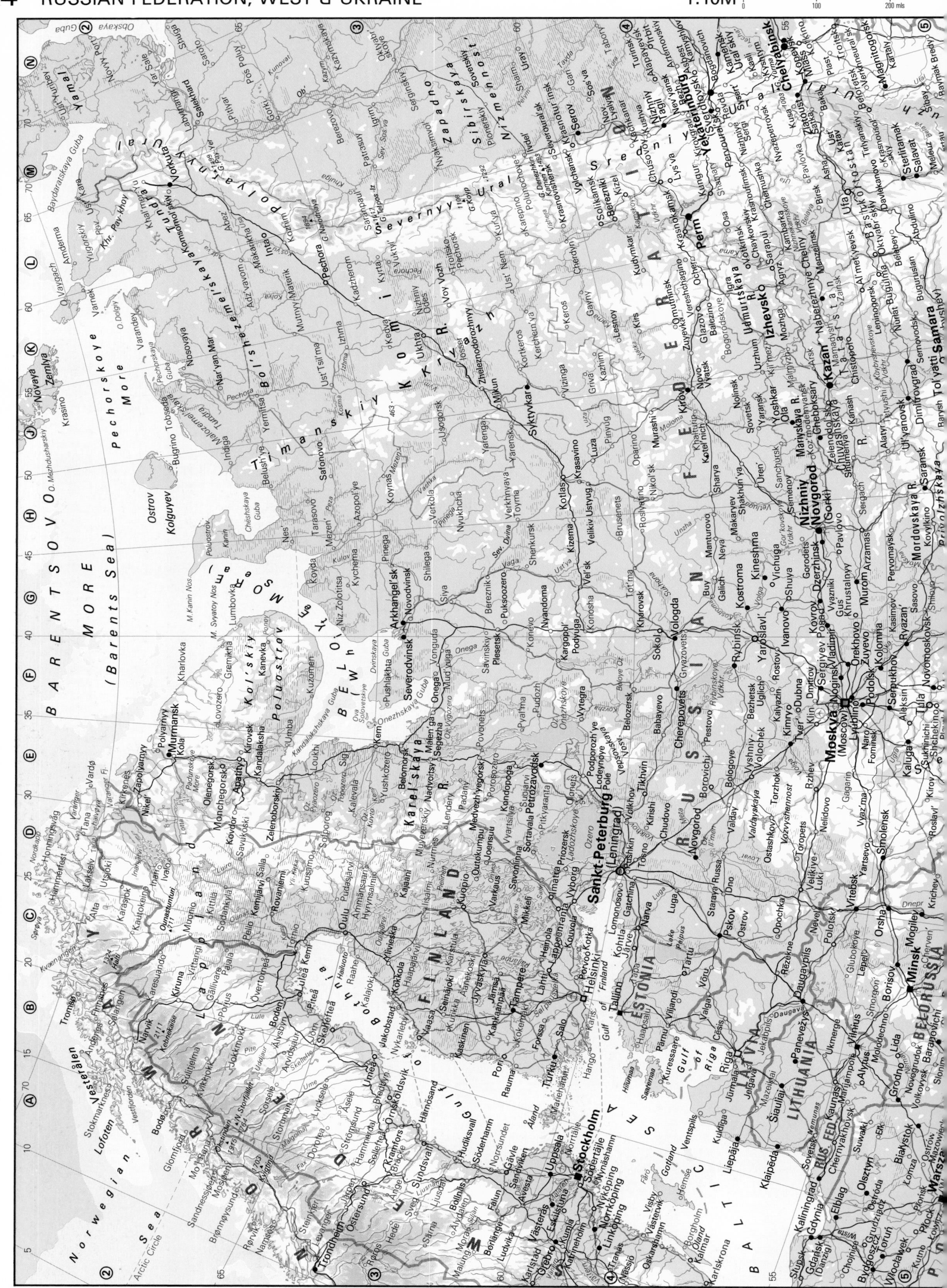
BARENTSOVO MORE (Barents Sea)
Norwegian Sea
Arctic Circle
Pechorskoye More
Beloye More (White Sea)
Gulf of Bothnia
Gulf of Finland
Gulf of Riga
BALTIC SEA
NORWAY
SWEDEN
FINLAND
ESTONIA
LATVIA
LITHUANIA
BELORUSSIA
RUS. FED.
Lappland
Kol'skiy Poluostrov
Karel'skaya
Timanskiy Kryazh
Polyarnyy Ural
Severnyy Ural
Sredniy Ural
Zapadno Sibirskaya Nizmennost'
Bol'shezemel'skaya Tundra
Novaya Zemlya
Yamal
Ostrov Kolguyev
Murmansk
Arkhangel'sk
Severodvinsk
Sankt-Peterburg (Leningrad)
Moskva (Moscow)
Nizhniy Novgorod (Gor'kiy)
Kazan'
Perm'
Yekaterinburg (Sverdlovsk)
Chelyabinsk
Samara
Izhevsk
Kirov
Syktyvkar
Ukhta
Vorkuta
Pechora
Vologda
Yaroslavl'
Petrozavodsk
Helsinki
Tallinn
Riga
Stockholm
Minsk
Vilnius
Smolensk
Novgorod
Pskov
Tampere
Turku
Oulu
Trondheim
Kaliningrad
Gdańsk
Warszawa

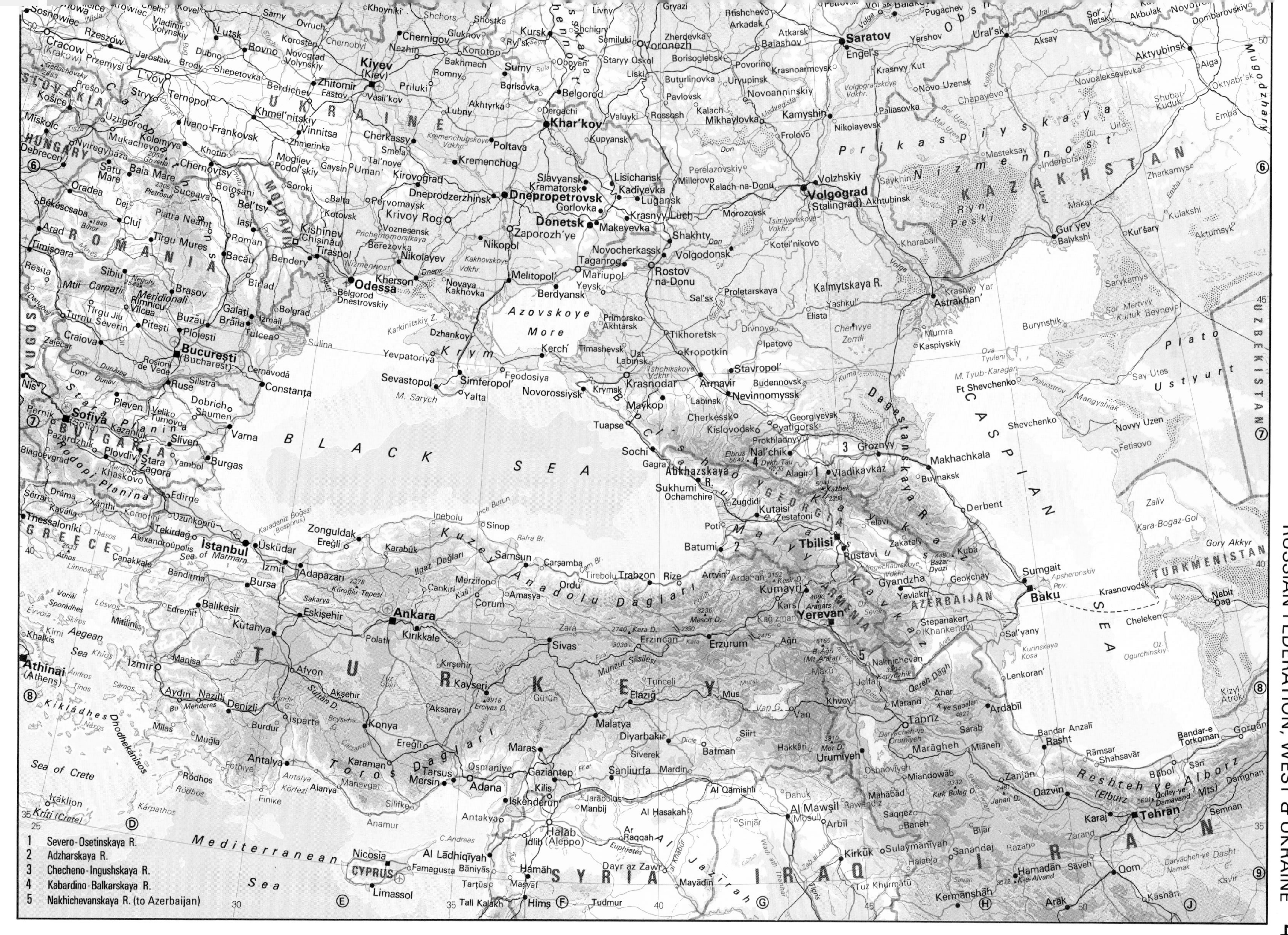

1 Severo-Osetinskaya R.
2 Checheno-Ingushskaya R.
3 Dagestanskaya R.
4 Kabardino-Balkarskaya R.
5 Nakhichevanskaya R. (to Azerbaijan)

1:40M

400 800 1200 1600 km
400 800 mils

③ ICELAND ② ① Greenland (Den.) Ⓐ ARCTIC OCEAN Ⓛ

20 Ⓑ Ⓚ

IRELAND Ⓒ Svalbard (Nor.) Zemlya Frantsa Iosifa Severnaya Ⓙ
Edinburgh Barents Zemlya
□ Dublin Ⓔ 80 Ⓕ 100 Ⓖ Ⓗ
Ⓐ London ■ Sea Novaya Zemlya 140 120
PORT. UNITED NORWAY Novosibirskiye
KINGDOM DENMARK SWEDEN Ostrova
SPAIN NETH. Oslo Murmansk Vorkuta Lena
FRANCE BEL. Helsinki FINLAND Arkhangel'sk Yakutsk
Paris ■ GERMANY København Stockholm Sankt-Peterburg
Marseille SWITZ. LUX. Warszawa Riga EST. (Leningrad)
Corse CZECH POLAND LAT. Moskva RUSSIAN FEDERATION
ITALY AUSTRIA REPUBLIC Vilnius LITH. Nizhniy
Sardegna SLOV. HUNGARY SLOVAKIA BELORUSSIA Novgorod Yekaterinburg Ⓑ
Roma CROATIA Kiyev Ob Krasnoyarsk
ALB. MAC. BOSNA. ROMANIA UKRAINE Khar'kov Samara Chelyabinsk Yenisey
Tunis YUGOSLAVIA Bucuresti MOLD. Volga Omsk Novosibirsk
GREECE BULGARIA Odessa Rostov Astrakhan' KAZAKHSTAN Irkutsk
Athinai Black Sea Aral Ulaanbaatar
Krti TURKEY Istanbul Ankara Caspian Sea Sea MONGOLIA
Ⓒ LIBYA CYPRUS Adana Tbilisi GEORGIA Baku Ürümqi INNER MONGOLIA
Alexandria Bairut ARM. AZER. Yerevan Tabriz UZBEKISTAN Taiyuan
Cairo LEB. Halab Ashkhabad TURKMENISTAN Bishkek Alma Ata SINKIANG Lanzhou Zhengzhou
ISRAEL Jerusalem Damascus SYRIA Al Mawsil TASHKENT KIRGHIZIA Xi'an
EGYPT JOR. Amman Baghdad (Mosul) Mashhad (KYRGYZSTAN) C H I N A Chengdu Wu
Aswân IRAQ IRAN Tehrān TAJIKISTAN Dushanbe TIBET Chongqing Changs
SAUDI KUWAIT Esfahān Herat Kabul Islamabad Lhasa Guiyang Chang Jiang
Basra Abadan BAHRAIN AFGHANISTAN Kashmir Lahore Guiyang
SUDAN RED Ar Riyāḍ QATAR Kermān PAKISTAN Delhi NEPAL Kunming Guang
Makkah ARABIA Abu Dhabi Kathmandu Thimphu
Khartoum ERITREA SEA U.A.E. Indus Kanpur Lucknow BHUTAN Brahmaputra Imphal Hanoi Haiphong
Asmera OMAN Muscat Patna BANGLA- Dhākā
YEMEN Ahmadābād Ganga DESH Chittagong Mandalay
Ⓔ DJIBOUTI San'a Jabalpur INDIA Calcutta BURMA Chiang Mai
Ādis Ababa Adan G. of Aden Socotra ARABIAN Karachi Hyderābād Nāgpur Godāvari (MYANMA) Vientiane Da N
ETHIOPIA (Yemen) SEA Bombay Yangon
KENYA SOMALIA Hyderabad Krishna Bay of (Rangoon) THAILAND
Muqdisho Bangalore Madras Bengal Moulmein Bangkok
Lakshadweep Andaman Is. CAMBODIA
Mombasa (Ind.) Mādurai (Ind.) Phnom
Dar es Salaam Nicobar Is. Penh Ho Chi Mi
TANZANIA SRI LANKA (Ind.) (Saigon)
SEYCHELLES Equator Colombo Kandy George MALA
Aldabra Is. MALDIVES Town
(Sey.) Kuala
INDIAN OCEAN Lumpur
MOZAMBIQUE COMOROS SINGAPORE
SUMATERA
Chagos Arch. Padang
(U.K.) Palembang
MADAGASCAR Cocos Is. Jakarta
Antananarivo (Aust.)
Arctic Circle

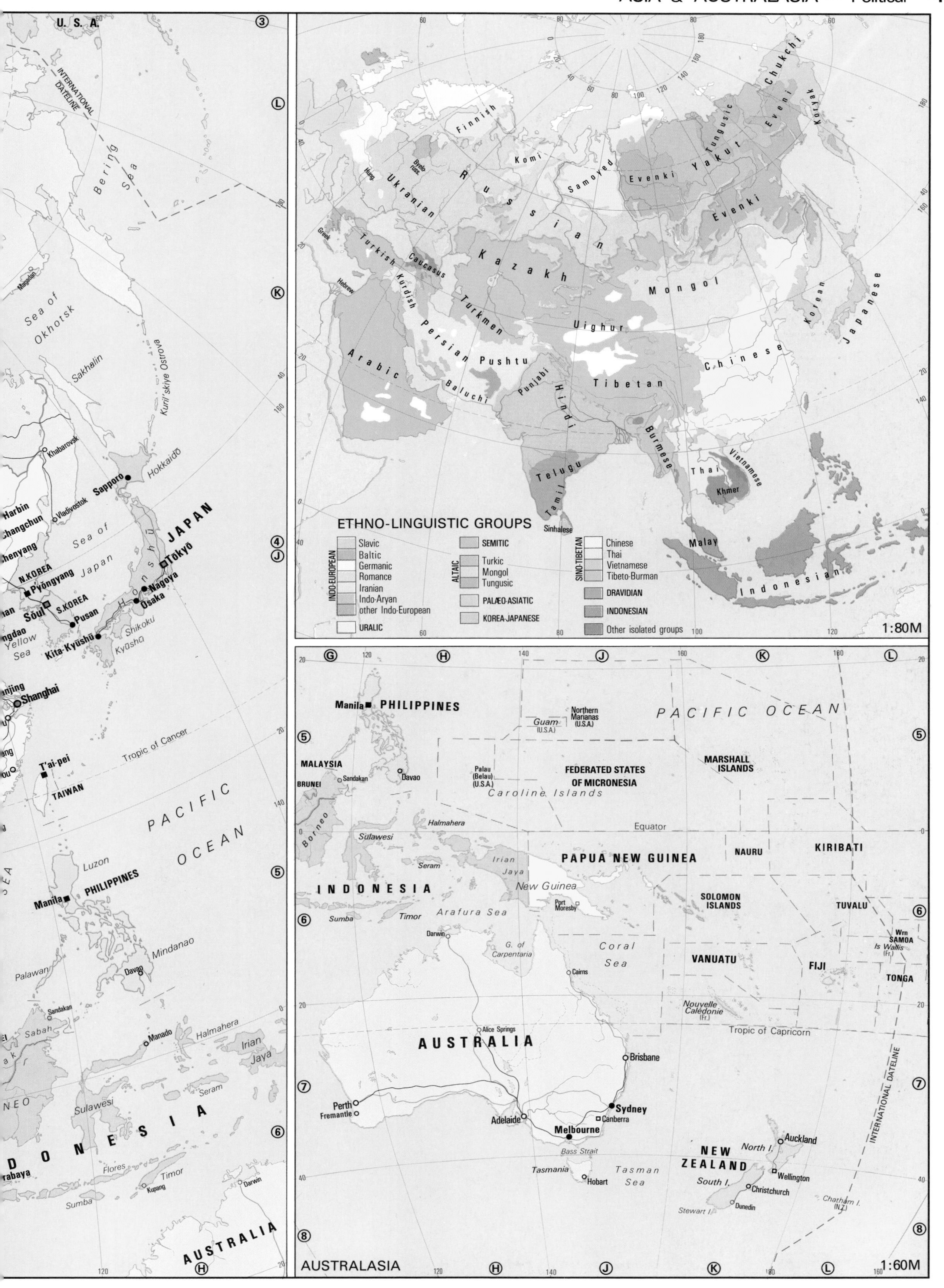
ETHNO-LINGUISTIC GROUPS
INDO-EUROPEAN
Slavic
Baltic
Germanic
Romance
Iranian
Indo-Aryan
other Indo-European
URALIC
SEMITIC
ALTAIC
Turkic
Mongol
Tungusic
PALÆO-ASIATIC
KOREA-JAPANESE
SINO-TIBETAN
Chinese
Thai
Vietnamese
Tibeto-Burman
DRAVIDIAN
INDONESIAN
Other isolated groups
1:80M
Finnish
Komi
Russian
Samoyed
Evenki
Yakut
Tungusic
Chukchi
Koryak
Ukranian
Byelo-russ.
Hung.
Greek
Turkish
Caucasus
Kazakh
Hebrew
Kurdish
Turkmen
Mongol
Korean
Japanese
Uighur
Persian
Pushtu
Arabic
Baluchi
Punjabi
Hindi
Tibetan
Chinese
Burmese
Telugu
Tamil
Sinhalese
Thai
Khmer
Vietnamese
Malay
Indonesian
U. S. A.
INTERNATIONAL DATELINE
Bering Sea
Sea of Okhotsk
Sakhalin
Kuril'skiye Ostrova
Khabarovsk
Hokkaidō
Sapporo
Harbin
Vladivostok
Sea of Japan
JAPAN
Honshū
Tōkyō
Nagoya
Ōsaka
N.KOREA
P'yŏngyang
S.KOREA
Sŏul
Pusan
Shikoku
Kyūshū
Kita-Kyūshū
Yellow Sea
Shanghai
T'ai-pei
TAIWAN
Tropic of Cancer
PACIFIC OCEAN
Luzon
Manila
PHILIPPINES
Mindanao
Davao
Palawan
Sandakan
Sabah
Manado
Halmahera
Irian Jaya
Seram
Sulawesi
INDONESIA
Flores
Timor
Kupang
Sumba
Darwin
AUSTRALIA
PHILIPPINES
MALAYSIA
BRUNEI
Sandakan
Davao
Borneo
Guam (U.S.A.)
Northern Marianas (U.S.A.)
PACIFIC OCEAN
Palau (Belau) (U.S.A.)
FEDERATED STATES OF MICRONESIA
Caroline Islands
MARSHALL ISLANDS
Halmahera
Sulawesi
Equator
PAPUA NEW GUINEA
NAURU
KIRIBATI
Seram
Irian Jaya
New Guinea
INDONESIA
Port Moresby
SOLOMON ISLANDS
TUVALU
Sumba
Timor
Arafura Sea
Darwin
G. of Carpentaria
Coral Sea
Wrn SAMOA
Is Wallis (Fr.)
Cairns
VANUATU
FIJI
TONGA
Nouvelle Calédonie (Fr.)
Tropic of Capricorn
Alice Springs
AUSTRALIA
Brisbane
Perth
Fremantle
Adelaide
Sydney
Canberra
Melbourne
Bass Strait
Tasmania
Hobart
Tasman Sea
NEW ZEALAND
North I.
Auckland
Wellington
South I.
Christchurch
Dunedin
Stewart I.
Chatham I. (N.Z.)
INTERNATIONAL DATELINE
AUSTRALASIA
1:60M

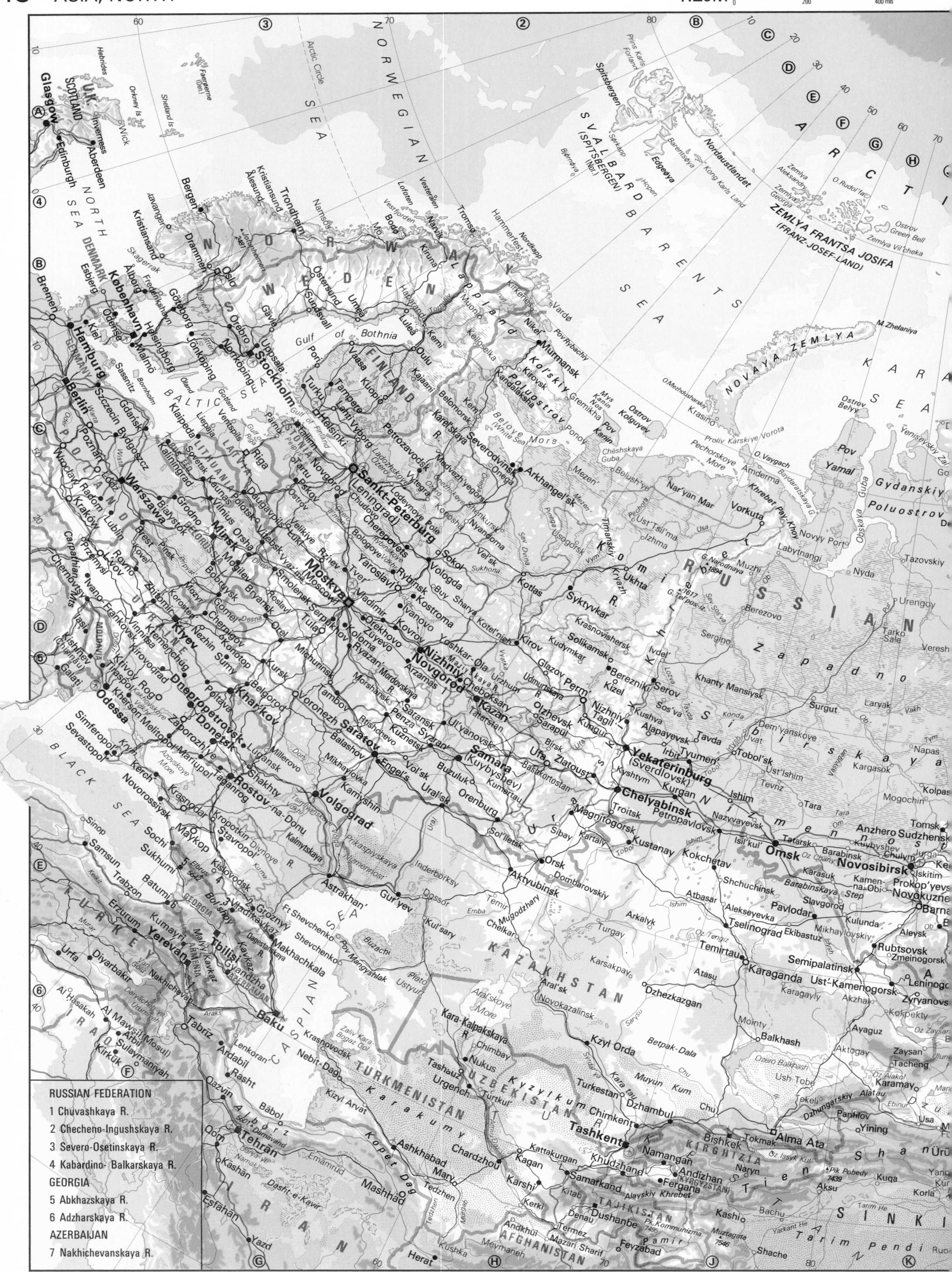

RUSSIAN FEDERATION
1 Chuvashkaya R.
2 Checheno-Ingushshkaya R.
3 Severo-Osetinskaya R.
4 Kabardino- Balkarskaya R.
GEORGIA
5 Abkhazskaya R.
6 Adzharskaya R.
AZERBAIJAN
7 Nakhichevanskaya R.

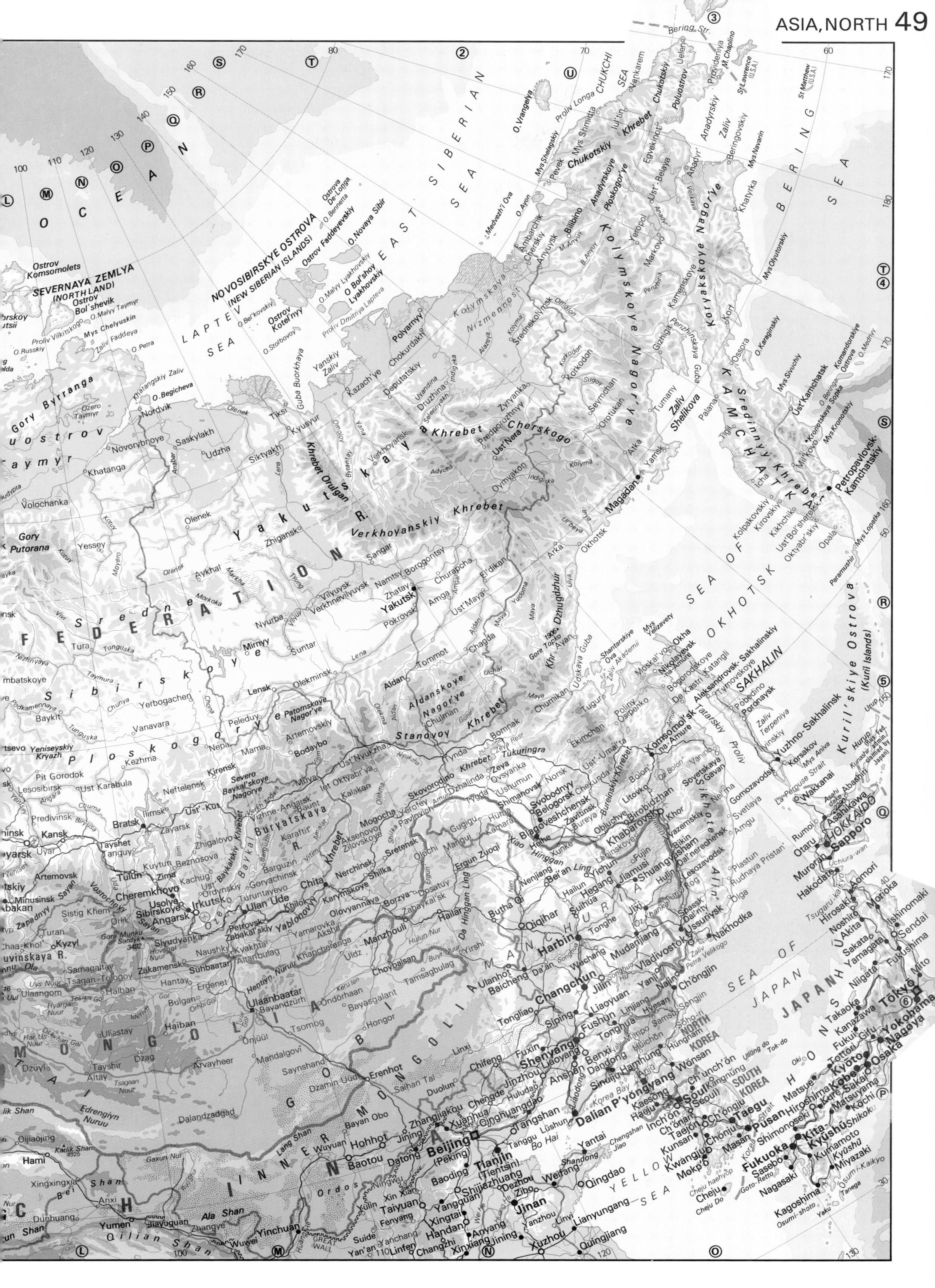
ARCTIC OCEAN
EAST SIBERIAN SEA
LAPTEV SEA
CHUKCHI SEA
BERING SEA
SEA OF OKHOTSK
SEA OF JAPAN
YELLOW SEA
SEVERNAYA ZEMLYA (NORTH LAND)
NOVOSIBIRSKYE OSTROVA (NEW SIBERIAN ISLANDS)
SAKHALIN
HOKKAIDO
HONSHU
KYUSHU
SHIKOKU
Kuril'skiye Ostrova (Kuril Islands)
MONGOLIA
MANCHURIA
INNER MONGOLIA
NORTH KOREA
SOUTH KOREA
JAPAN
Magadan
Yakutsk
Petropavlovsk-Kamchatskiy
Khabarovsk
Vladivostok
Irkutsk
Ulan Ude
Chita
Ulaanbaatar
Harbin
Changchun
Shenyang
Beijing (Peking)
Tianjin (Tientsin)
P'yŏngyang
Sŏul (Seoul)
Pusan
Tōkyō
Yokohama
Ōsaka
Nagoya
Kyōto
Sapporo

1:20M
0 200 400 600 800 km
0 200 400 mls

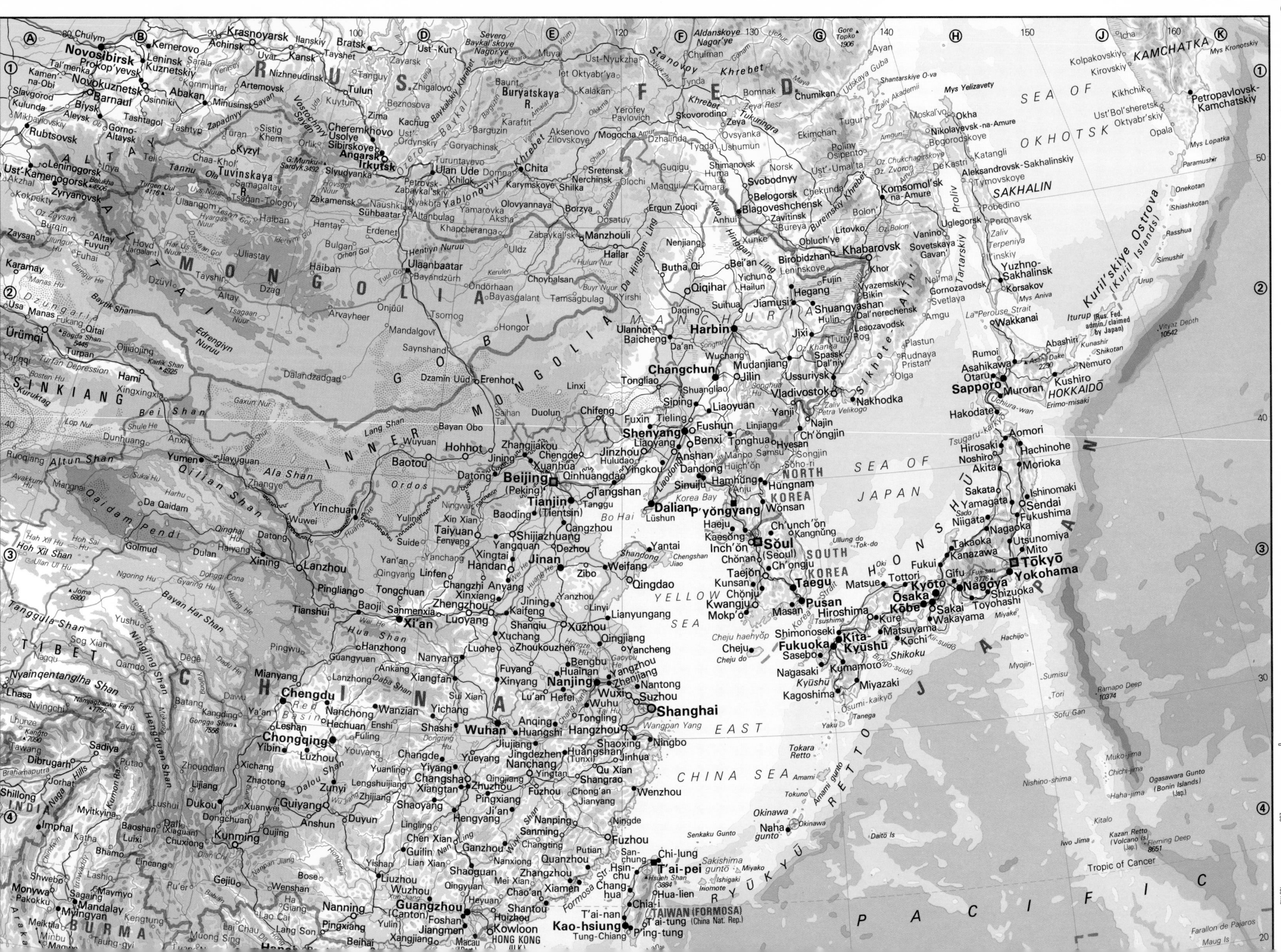
SEA OF OKHOTSK
SEA OF JAPAN
YELLOW SEA
EAST CHINA SEA
PACIFIC
MONGOLIA
MANCHURIA
INNER MONGOLIA
CHINA
TIBET
SINKIANG
KAMCHATKA
SAKHALIN
HOKKAIDŌ
HONSHŪ
NORTH KOREA
SOUTH KOREA
JAPAN
TAIWAN (FORMOSA)
BURMA
INDIA
Beijing (Peking)
Tōkyō
Shanghai
Sŏul (Seoul)
P'yŏngyang
Harbin
Vladivostok
Khabarovsk
Ulaanbaatar
Irkutsk
Novosibirsk
Chongqing
Chengdu
Wuhan
Xi'an
Lanzhou
Ürümqi
Lhasa
Kunming
Guangzhou (Canton)
Hong Kong
T'ai-pei
Ōsaka
Sapporo
Kuril'skiye Ostrova (Kuril Islands)
Tropic of Cancer

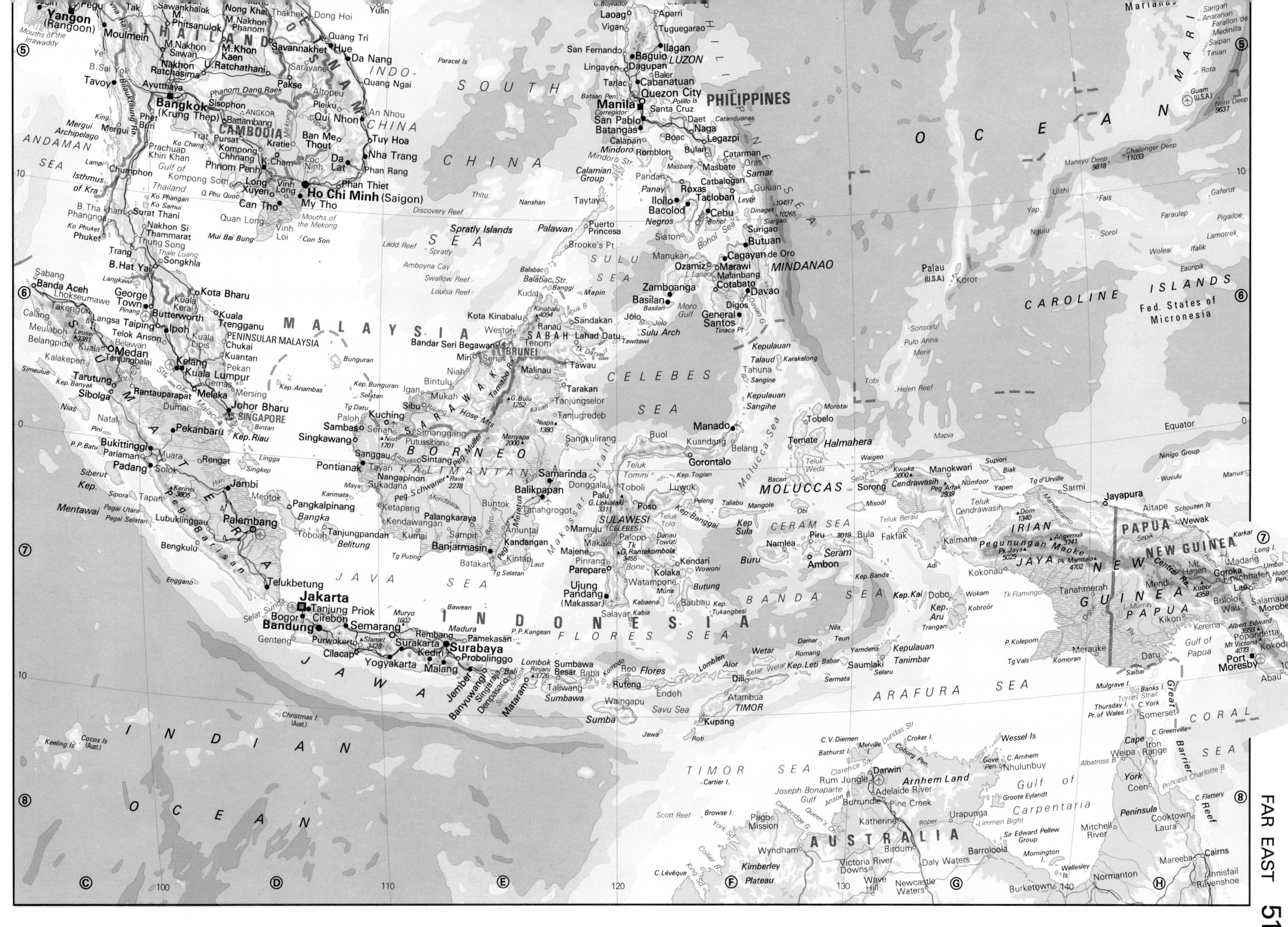
PHILIPPINES
LUZON
MINDANAO
Manila
Quezon City
Davao
Zamboanga
Cebu
SOUTH CHINA SEA
SULU SEA
CELEBES SEA
Molucca Sea
BANDA SEA
CERAM SEA
FLORES SEA
JAVA SEA
TIMOR SEA
ARAFURA SEA
CORAL SEA
INDIAN OCEAN
ANDAMAN SEA
OCEAN
CAROLINE ISLANDS
Fed. States of Micronesia
MALAYSIA
PENINSULAR MALAYSIA
BRUNEI
SINGAPORE
BORNEO
KALIMANTAN
SABAH
SARAWAK
SULAWESI (CELEBES)
MOLUCCAS
INDONESIA
IRIAN JAYA
PAPUA NEW GUINEA
NEW GUINEA
AUSTRALIA
CAMBODIA
THAILAND
Bangkok (Krung Thep)
Yangon (Rangoon)
Ho Chi Minh (Saigon)
Phnom Penh
Kuala Lumpur
Johor Bharu
Jakarta
Bandung
Surabaya
Semarang
Yogyakarta
Palembang
Medan
Padang
Jayapura
Port Moresby
Darwin
Kota Kinabalu
Bandar Seri Begawan
Ujung Pandang (Makassar)
Manado
Ambon
Dili
Kupang
JAWA
TIMOR
Halmahera
Palawan
Equator
Gulf of Carpentaria
Great Barrier Reef
Arnhem Land
Cape York Peninsula

1:10M

MONGOLIA

GOBI

NEI MONGOL

Yin Shan

GOBI

Badain Jaran Shamo

Tengger Shamo

Mu Us Shamo

Ningxia

GANSU

Qinghai

Qinghai Hu

Xining

Lanzhou

Shaanxi

Shanxi

Taiyuan

Hebei

Beijing (Peking)

Tianjin (Tientsin)

Baoding

Shijiazhuang

Jinan (Tsinan)

Shandong

BO HAI

Dalian

Qingdao (Tsingtao)

YELLOW SEA (HUANG HAI)

Shenyang

Liaoning

Jinzhou

Qinhuangdao

Tangshan

Zhengzhou

Henan

Luoyang

Xi'an (Sian)

Qin Ling

Baoji

Xianyang

CHINA

SICHUAN

Chengdu

Chongqing (Chungking)

Hubei

Wuhan

Yichang

Nanyang

Xiangfan

Jiangsu

Nanjing (Nanking)

Hefei

Anhui

Xuzhou

Lianyungang

Shanghai

Suzhou

Hangzhou

Zhejiang

Ningbo

Wenzhou

Guizhou

Guiyang

Hunan

Changsha

Jiangxi

Nanchang

Fujian

Fuzhou (Foochow)

Xiamen (Amoy)

TAIWAN (FORMOSA)

Kao-hsiung

T'ai-pei

Yunnan

Kunming

Guangxi

Nanning

Guangdong

Guangzhou (Canton)

HONG KONG (U.K.)

Macao

Shenzhen

Shantou (Swatow)

Foshan

VIETNAM

Hanoi

Haiphong

LAOS

GULF OF TONGKIN

Hainan

Haikou

SOUTH CHINA SEA

Dongsha Qundao (Prates)

1:10M

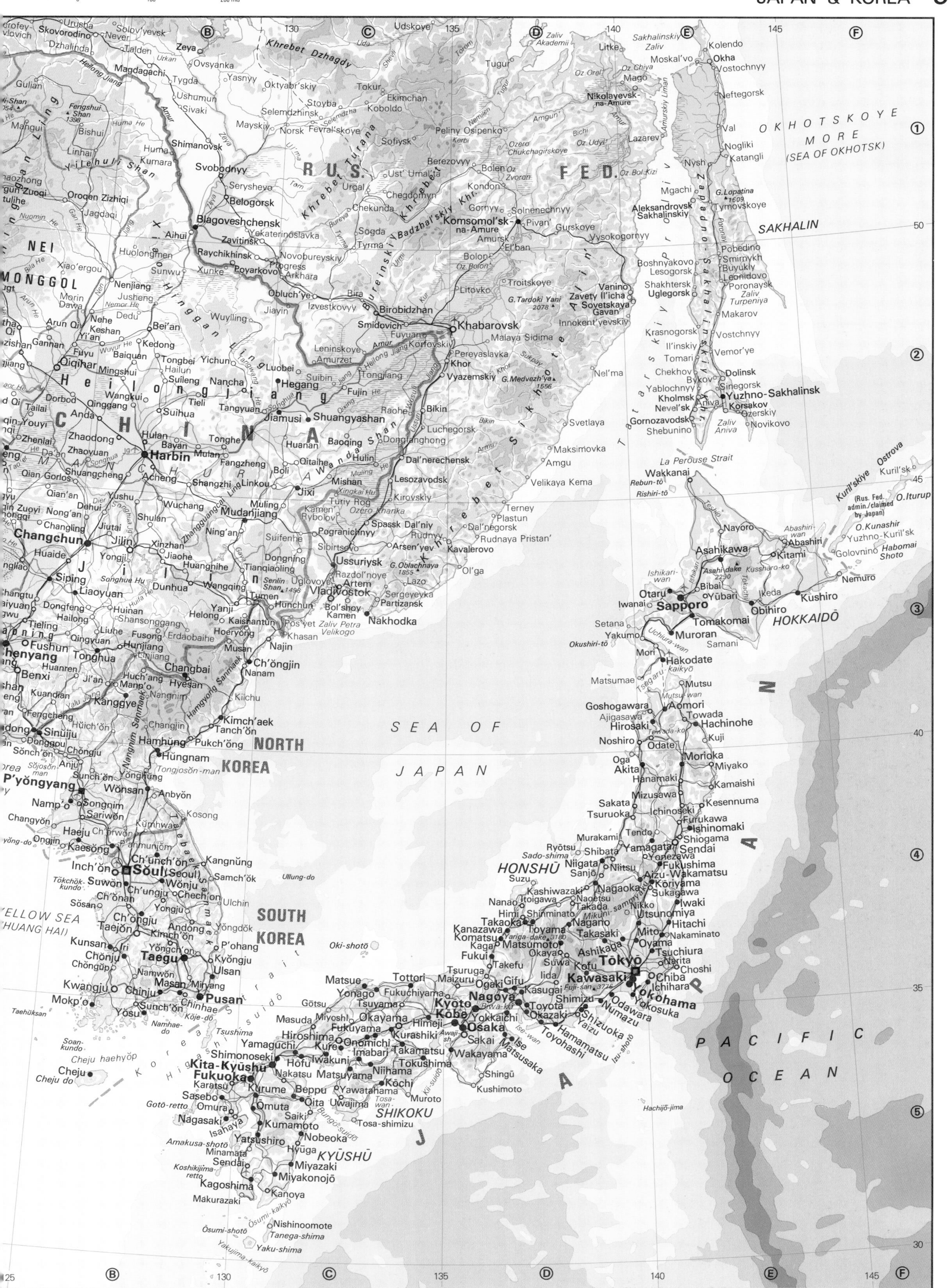

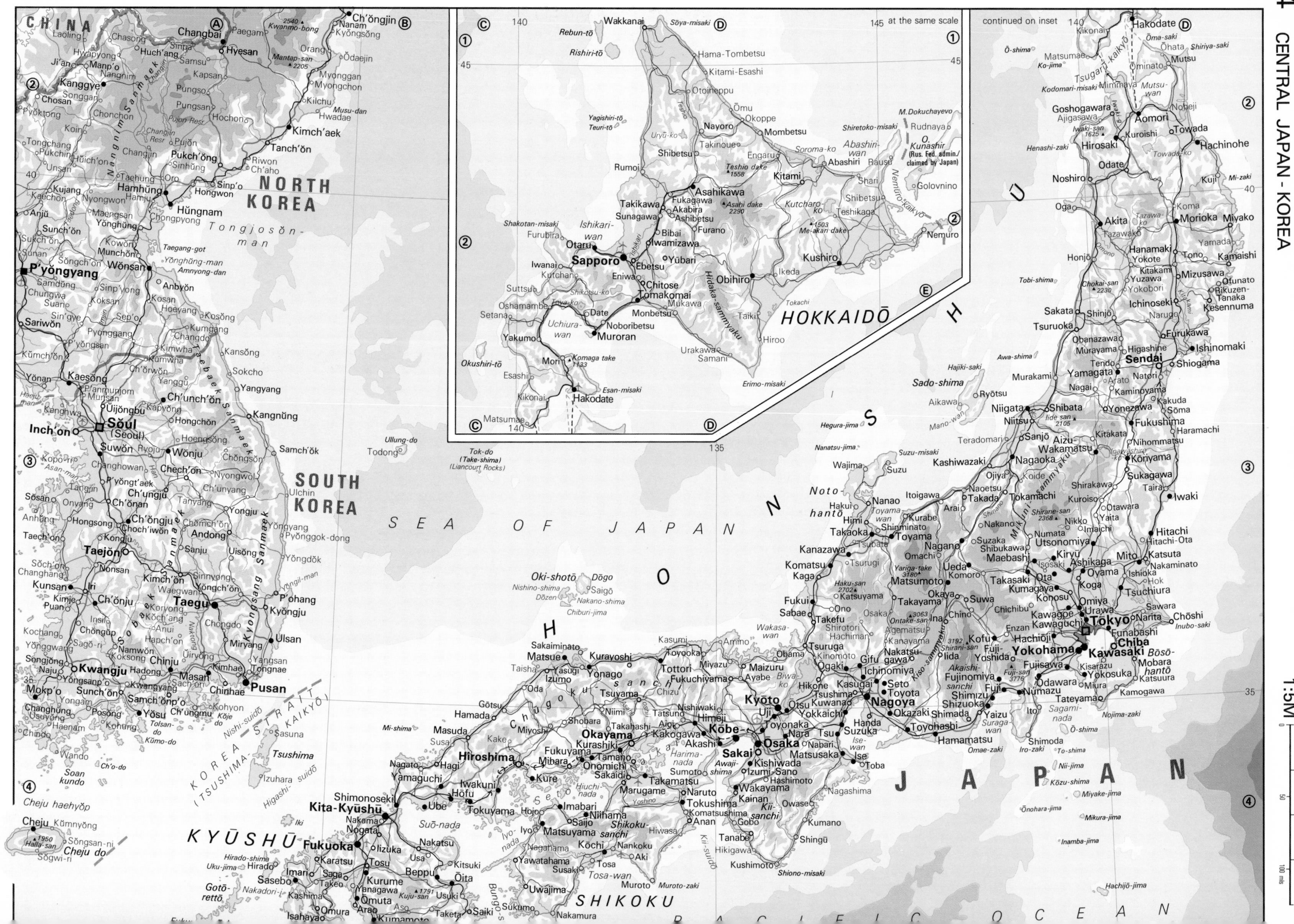

1:5M

NORTH KOREA

SOUTH KOREA

HOKKAIDŌ

Sapporo

Hakodate

Sendai

Tōkyō

Kawasaki

Yokohama

Chiba

Nagoya

Kyōto

Ōsaka

Kōbe

Sakai

Hiroshima

SHIKOKU

KYŪSHŪ

Fukuoka

Kita-Kyūshū

Sōul

Inch'ōn

P'yŏngyang

Taegu

Pusan

Taejŏn

CHINA

SEA OF JAPAN

PACIFIC OCEAN

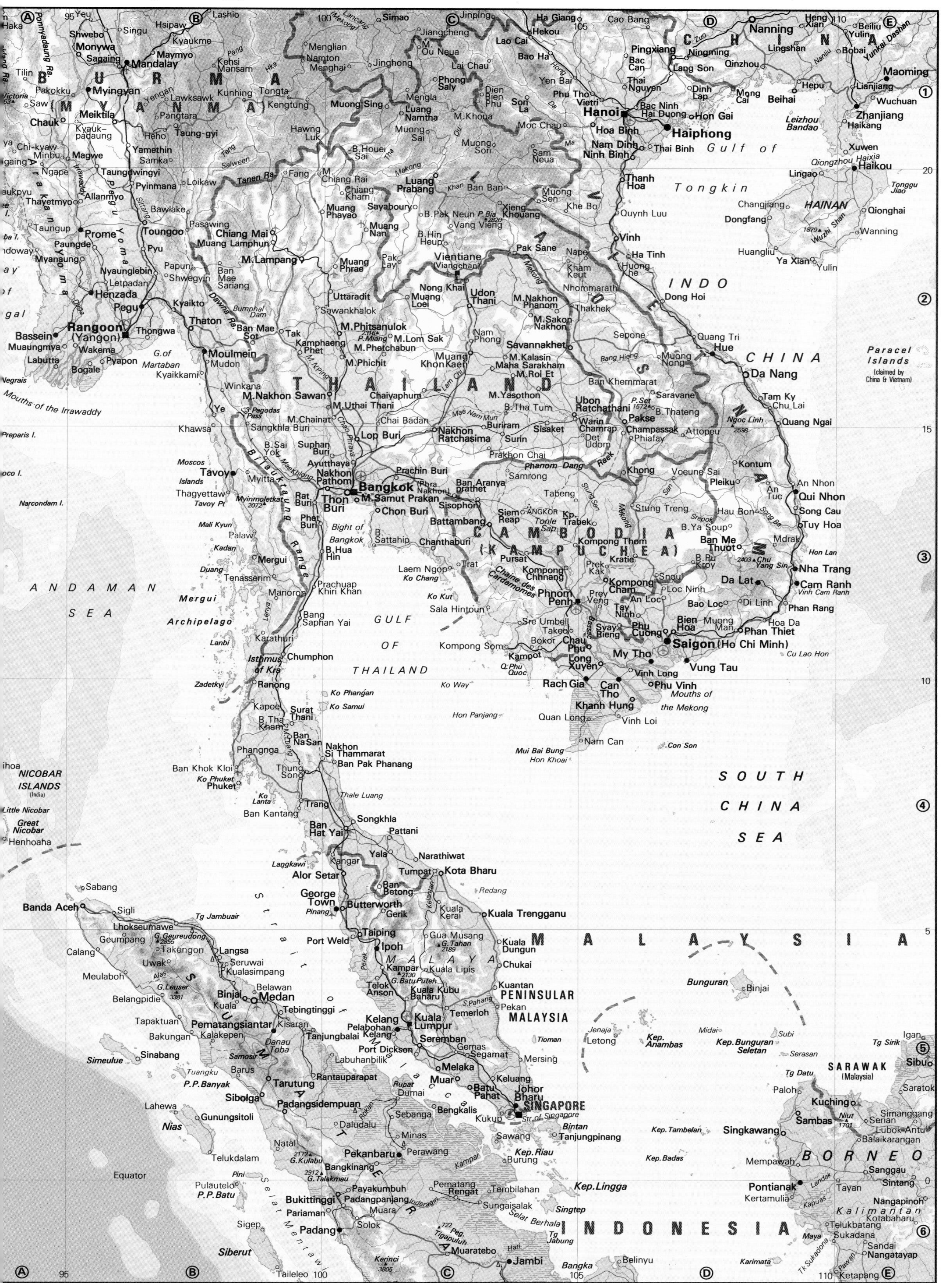

1:10M

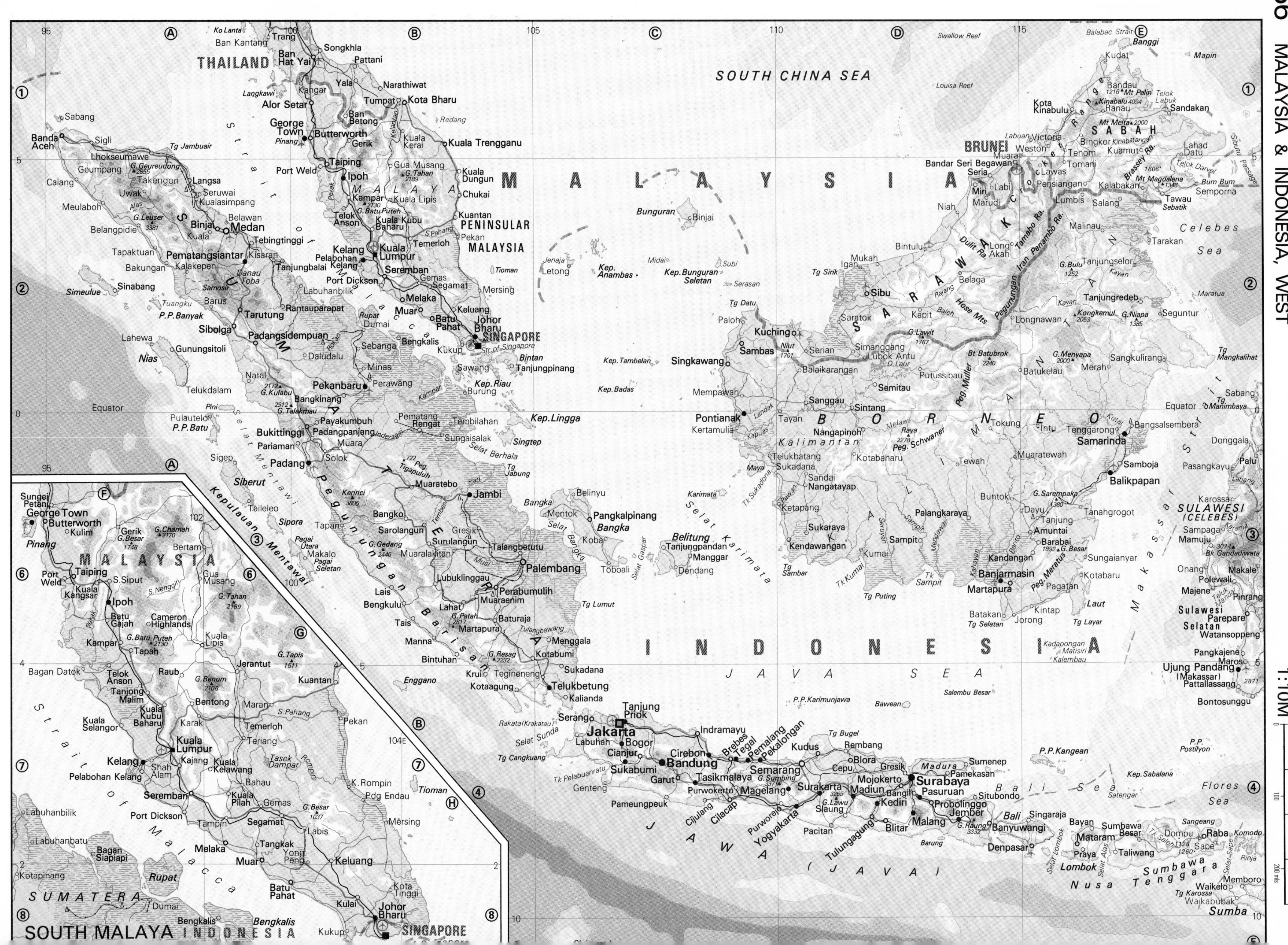

0 100 200 300 400 km
0 100 200 mls
SOUTH CHINA SEA
THAILAND
MALAYSIA
PENINSULAR MALAYSIA
SINGAPORE
BRUNEI
SABAH
SARAWAK
BORNEO
Kalimantan
INDONESIA
SULAWESI (CELEBES)
Celebes Sea
Makassar Strait
JAVA SEA
Flores Sea
Bali Sea
Nusa Tenggara
JAWA (JAVA)
Strait of Malacca
Kepulauan Mentawai
Pegunungan Barisan
Selat Karimata
Selat Sunda
Selat Bangka
Selat Gaspar
Jakarta
Kuala Lumpur
Bandar Seri Begawan
Kuching
Pontianak
Palembang
Medan
Padang
Surabaya
Bandung
Semarang
Banjarmasin
Balikpapan
Samarinda
Ujung Pandang (Makassar)
Kota Kinabalu
Sandakan
Ipoh
George Town
Johor Bharu
Pekanbaru
Jambi
Bengkulu
Telukbetung
Pangkalpinang
Banda Aceh
Nias
Siberut
Bangka
Belitung
Madura
Bali
Lombok
Sumbawa
SOUTH MALAYA

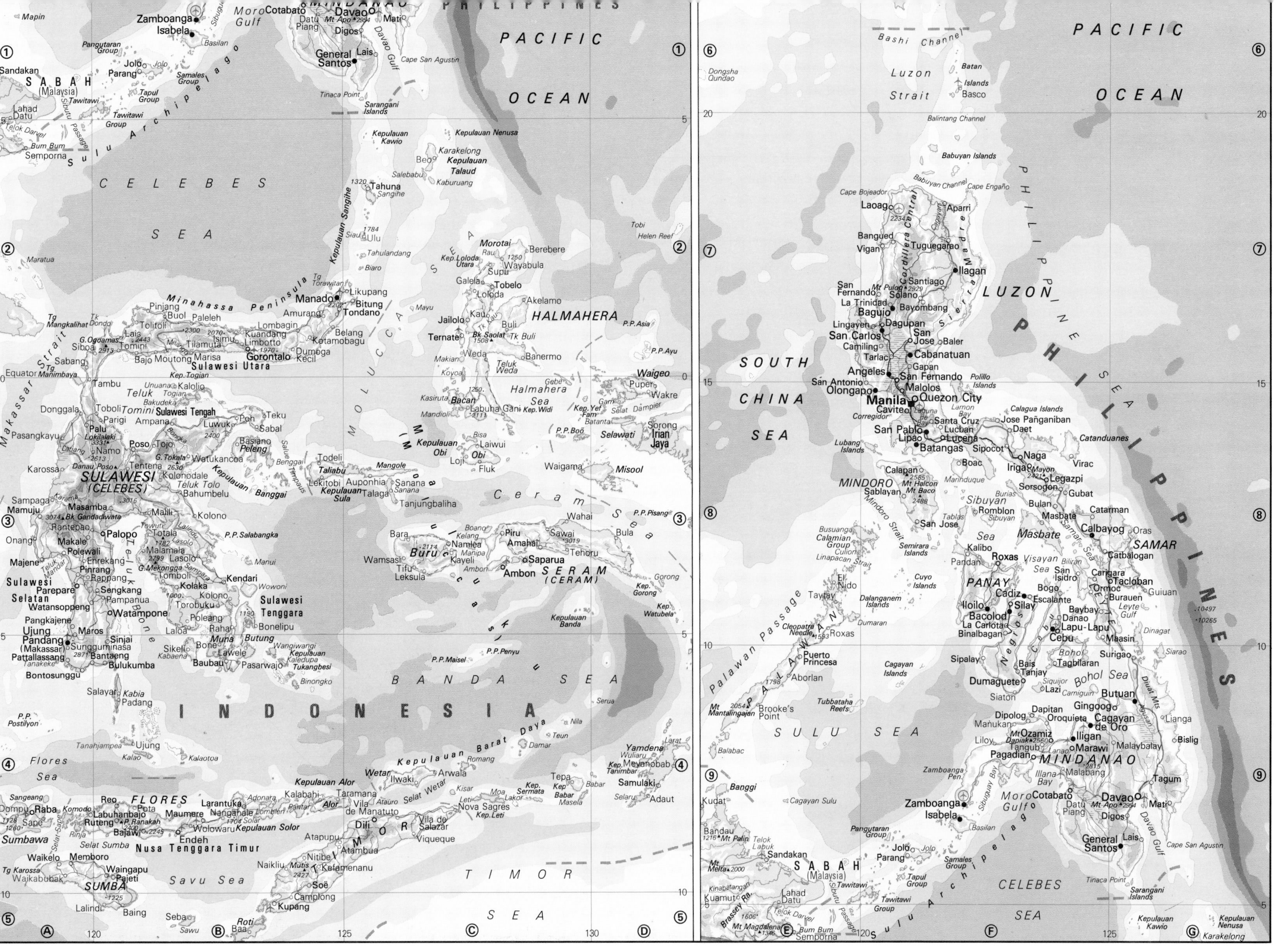
PACIFIC OCEAN
CELEBES SEA
Sulu Archipelago
SABAH (Malaysia)
MOLUCCA SEA
HALMAHERA
Halmahera Sea
Ceram Sea
SERAM (CERAM)
Buru
SULAWESI (CELEBES)
Makassar Strait
BANDA SEA
INDONESIA
Flores Sea
FLORES
Savu Sea
SUMBA
TIMOR
TIMOR SEA
PHILIPPINE SEA
PHILIPPINES
LUZON
Luzon Strait
Bashi Channel
SOUTH CHINA SEA
MINDORO
Sibuyan Sea
Visayan Sea
PANAY
Masbate
SAMAR
PALAWAN
Palawan Passage
SULU SEA
Bohol Sea
MINDANAO
Moro Gulf
Davao Gulf
Manila
Quezon City
Cebu
Davao
Zamboanga
Manado
Ambon
Kupang
Ujung Pandang (Makassar)

200 400 600 800 km
200 400 mls

Beograd
Sarajevo B.-H. Split ROMANIA Sibiu Meridionali Carpatii Galati Nikolayev Mariupol' Zaporozh'ye Donetsk Tsimlyanskoye Volgograd Temir Chelkar KAZ
Dubrovnik Nis YUGOS. Bucuresti Ploiesti Sulina Odessa Melitopol' Berdyansk Rostov-na-Donu Taganrog Shakhty Don Kropotkin RUS. Astrakhan' Gur'yev Kul'sary Aral'sk
Shkoder Skopje Sofiya BULGARIA Ruse Constanta Sevastopol' Krym Kerch Azovskoye More Krasnodar Novorossiysk Stavropol Maykop Kislovodsk Groznyy Makhachkala Novokazalinsk Kzyl-O
Tiranë MACEDONIA Plovdiv Varna Burgas Simferopol' Sochi Elbrus Vladikavkaz Dagestanskaya Plato Ustyurt Chimbay K-y-z-y-l-k-u-m
Trikkala Olimbos Thessaloniki Edirne Zonguldak Sinop Samsun Sukhumi Kutaisi Tbilisi GEORGIA Gyandzha Krasnovodsk Nukus Tashauz UZBEKISTAN
GREECE Patrai Athinai Aegean Sea Istanbul Uskudar Bursa Eskisehir Ankara Kayseri Sivas Trabzon Batumi Kumayri Yerevan AZERBAIJAN Baku Urgench Turtkul
Peloponnisos Kalamai Izmir Afyon Kuzey Anadolu Daglari Kizil Irmak Erzurum Büyük Agri Nakhichevan Zaliv Kara-Bogaz Nebit-Dag Karakumy Chardzhou Bukhara Karshi
Kriti Rodhos Denizli Toros Daglari Konya Adana Malatya Diyarbakir Van Van Golu Khvoy Tabriz Ardabil Lenkoran' Kizyl-Arvat Kopet Dag Ashkhabad Tedzhen Mary Kerki

MEDITERRANEAN SEA Antalya Gaziantep Halab Al Hasakah Al Mawsil (Mosul) Zanjan Rasht Bābol Bojnurd Koneurgench
Darnah Tobruq LIBYA Matruh Al Ladhiqiyah CYPRUS Hamah Hims SYRIA Dayr az Zawr Arbil Sulaymaniyah Qazvin Tehrān Shāhrud Sabzevar Mashhad
Nicosia Famagusta Beirut LEBANON Damascus Tudmur Kirkuk Samarra Hamadan Qom Dasht-e Kavir Herat AFGHAN
Alexandria Dumyat Port Said Haifa Tel Aviv ISRAEL Amman Dar'a Ar Ramadi Baghdad Kermanshah Arak Kāshān Esfahan Birjand
Cairo Tanta Ismailiya Jerusalem JORDAN Ar Rutbar IRAQ Ad Diwaniyah Al Amarah Khorramabad Dezful Yazd Farah Girishk
El Faiyum Suez Sinai Ma'an An Najaf Karbala Ahvaz Abadan Comishen Kandahar Zaranj Dilaram
Beni Suef Aqaba Badanah Basra Kuwait Bandar Khomeyni Shiraz Sa'idabad Kermān Zahedan Nushki
El Minya Tabuk An Nafud KUWAIT Busher Lar Kuh-e Taftan Baluchistan Turbat
EGYPT Al Jawf Hail Safaniya Bam Hāmun-e Jaz Bandar 'Abbas Chāh Bahar Gwadar Kara
Asyut Hurghada Taymā Ha'il The Gulf Str. of Hormuz Jask Makran
El Kharga Luxor Unayzah Buraydah Dhahran BAHRAIN Manamah QATAR Dubai Muscat Tropic of Cancer
Aswan L. Nasser Yanbu al Bahr Medina Shaqra Ar Riyad Al Hufuf Dukhan Doha Abu Dhabi Al Khaburah Al Hadd
Wadi Halfa Rabigh Jiddah Makkah SAUDI ARABIA As Salamiyah UNITED ARAB EMIRATES Al Liwa Nazwa Sur OMAN
Nubian Desert At Ta'if Layla Rub' al Khali Masirah Gulf of Oman
Port Sudan Al Lith Qal'at Bishah Gulf of Khali
Dongola Suakin Al Qunfidhah Abha YEMEN Salalah Ra's al Madrakah ARAB
Berber Atbara Sabya Jizan Sa'dah Tamm Hadramawt Ra's Fartak SE
Omdurman Khartoum Kassala Mits'iwa (Massawa) Al Luhayyah San'a Nisab Ash Shihr Sayhut
SUDAN Wad Medani ERITREA Ta'izz Al Hudaydah Al Mukalla
Ed Dueim El Obeid Asmera Al Mukha Adan (Aden) Gulf of Aden Socotra (Suqutra) (Yemen) Hadiboh
En Nahud Kosti Singa Gonder L. Tana ETHIOPIA Djibouti Berbera Ceerigaabo Raas Caseyr
Malakal Sennar Birhan Dese DJIBOUTI Hargeysa Raas Xaafuun
Rumbek Debre Markos Dire Dawa Harer
Adis Abeba Nazret Jima ETHIOPIA Ginir SOMALIA Carlsberg
Juba Batu Negele Shebele Hobyo Somali Basin INDI
ZAIRE Watsa Nimule L. Rudolf Dolo Odo Moyale
Bunia Pakwach KENYA Wajir
UGANDA Kampala Jinja Mt Elgon Kirinyaga (Mt Kenya) Garissa Muqdisho (Mogadishu) Marka Baraawe
RWANDA Kigali Nakuru Kismayo
BURUNDI Bujumbura Kilimanjaro Nairobi Equator
TANZANIA L. Victoria Arusha Moshi

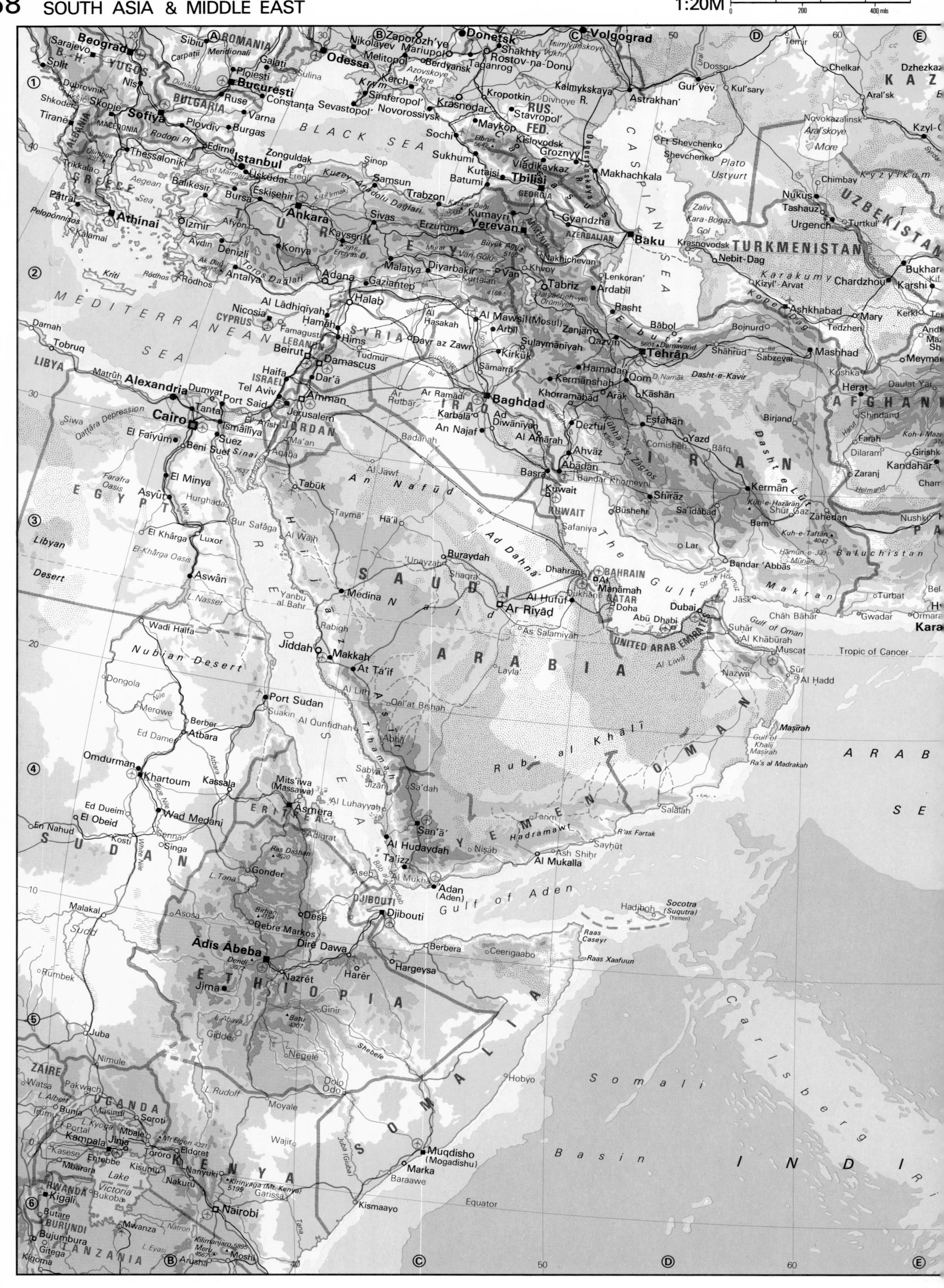

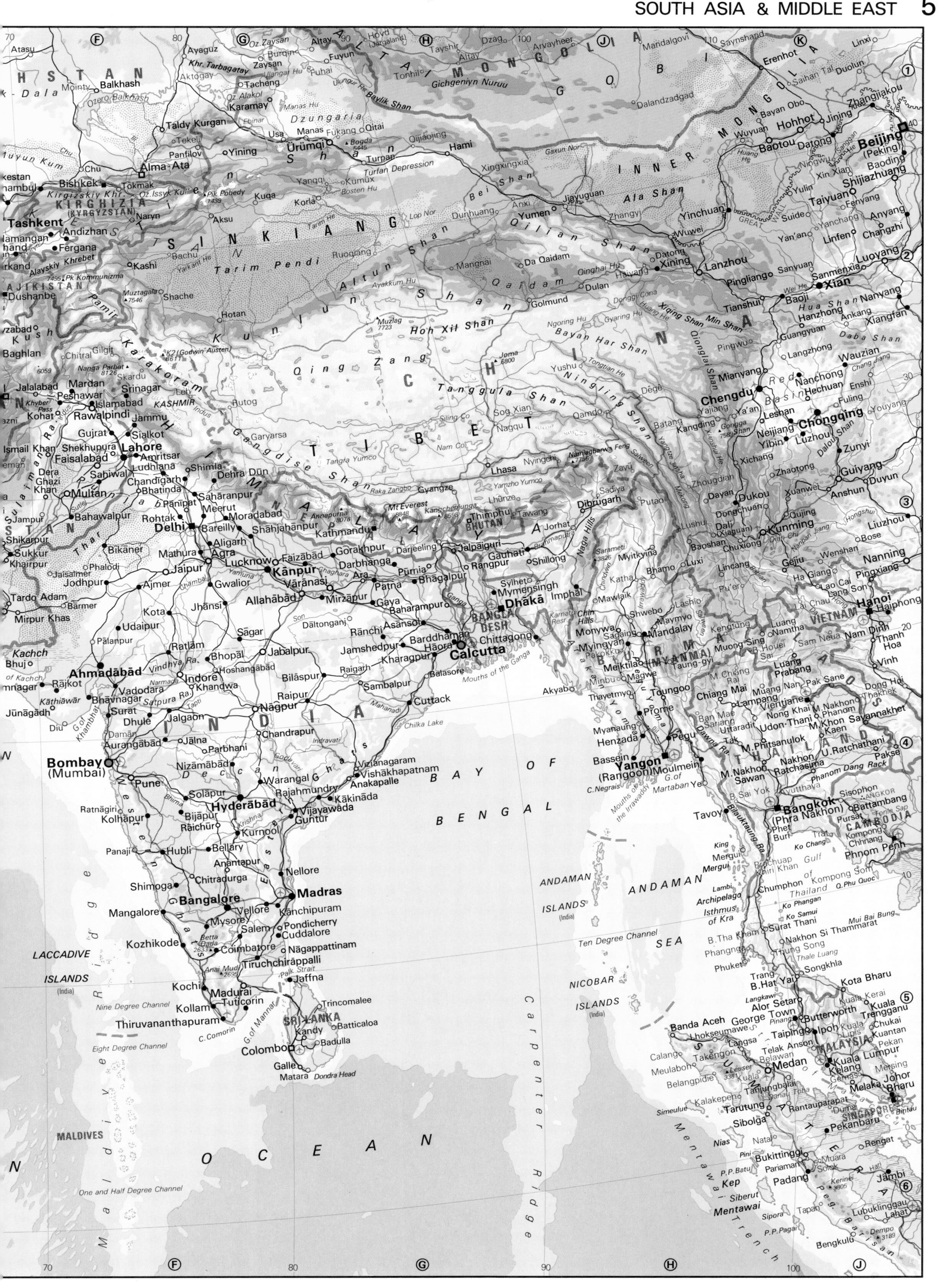

MONGOLIA
GOBI
INNER MONGOLIA
SINKIANG
TIBET
CHINA
KIRGHIZIA (KYRGYZSTAN)
TAJIKISTAN
KASHMIR
INDIA
BANGLADESH
BHUTAN
BURMA (MYANMAR)
THAILAND
LAOS
VIETNAM
CAMBODIA
MALAYSIA
SINGAPORE
SRI LANKA
MALDIVES
SUMATERA
Tarim Pendi
Dzungaria
Tien Shan
Altun Shan
Kunlun Shan
Qaidam
Qilian Shan
Bayan Har Shan
Tanggula Shan
Qing Zang
Gangdise Shan
Hoh Xil Shan
Karakoram
Hindu Kush
Pamir
Himalaya
Thar
Deccan
Western Ghats
Eastern Ghats
Red Basin
Ala Shan
Bei Shan
Turfan Depression
Altay
Gichgeniyn Nuruu
Mt Everest 8848
K2 (Godwin Austen) 8611
Nanga Parbat 8126
Kangchenjunga 8598
Annapurna 8078
Muztagata 7546
Pik Pobedy 7439
Pik Kommunizma 7495
Bay of Bengal
Andaman Sea
Indian Ocean
Andaman Islands (India)
Nicobar Islands (India)
Laccadive Islands (India)
Ten Degree Channel
Nine Degree Channel
Eight Degree Channel
One and Half Degree Channel
Carpenter Ridge
Mentawai Trench
Maldive Ridge
Gulf of Thailand
Gulf of Martaban
Gulf of Mannar
Palk Strait
Mouths of the Ganga
Mouths of the Irrawaddy
Isthmus of Kra
Mentawai
Beijing (Peking)
Tianjin
Baotou
Hohhot
Datong
Shijiazhuang
Taiyuan
Yinchuan
Lanzhou
Xining
Xian
Chengdu
Chongqing
Guiyang
Kunming
Nanning
Hanoi
Haiphong
Ürümqi
Hami
Lhasa
Kashi
Hotan
Alma-Ata
Bishkek
Tashkent
Dushanbe
Islamabad
Rawalpindi
Peshawar
Lahore
Faisalabad
Multan
Delhi
Agra
Jaipur
Lucknow
Kanpur
Varanasi
Allahabad
Patna
Kathmandu
Thimphu
Dhaka
Calcutta
Chittagong
Ahmadabad
Bombay (Mumbai)
Pune
Nagpur
Hyderabad
Bangalore
Madras
Colombo
Mandalay
Yangon (Rangoon)
Moulmein
Chiang Mai
Vientiane
Bangkok (Phra Nakhon)
Phnom Penh
Kuala Lumpur
Medan
Padang
Jambi
Pekanbaru

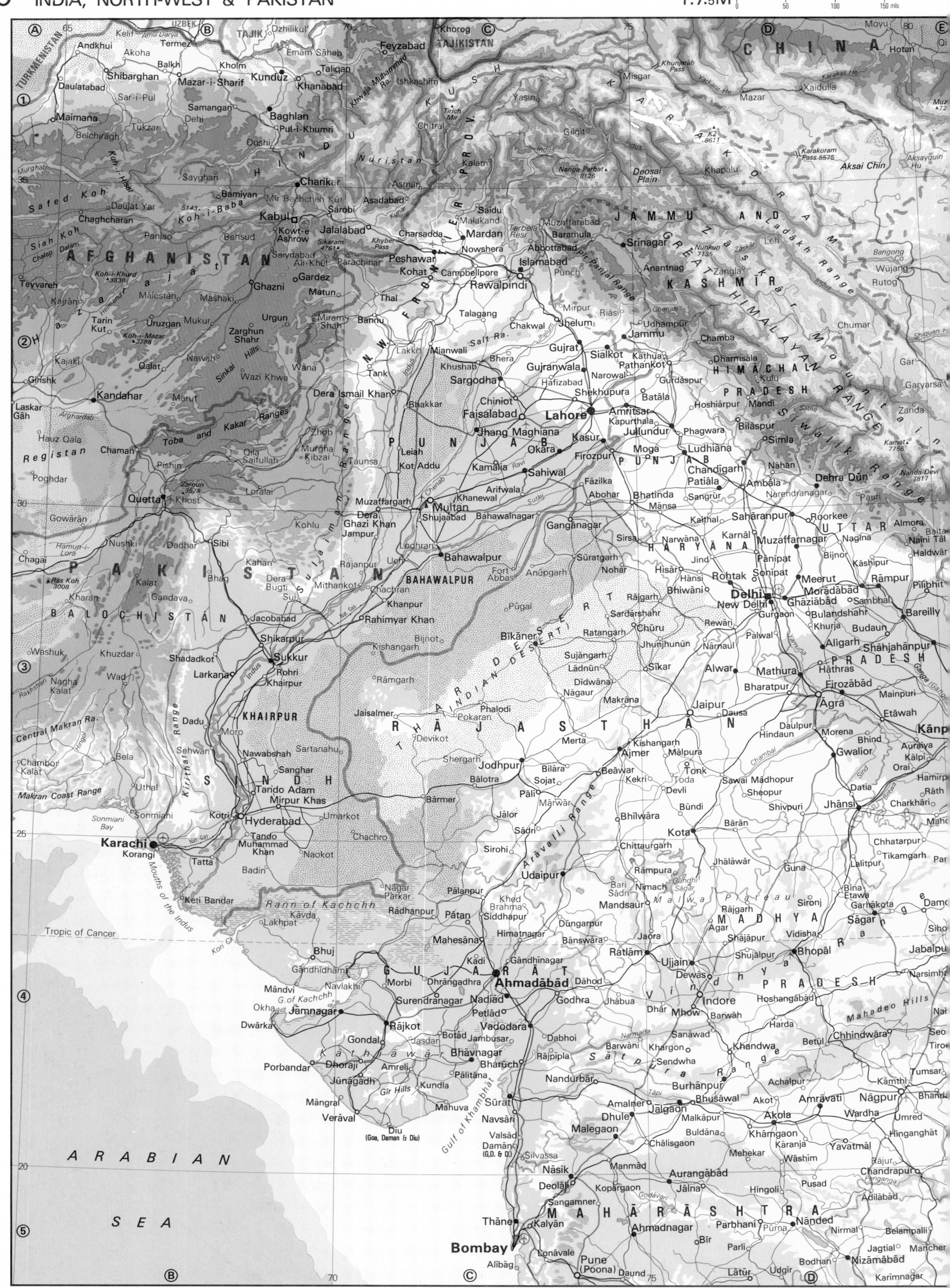
1:7.5M
0 100 200 300 km
0 50 100 150 mls
CHINA
AFGHANISTAN
PAKISTAN
TAJIKISTAN
TURKMENISTAN
UZBEK
JAMMU AND KASHMIR
HIMACHAL PRADESH
PUNJAB
HARYANA
UTTAR PRADESH
RAJASTHAN
GUJARAT
MADHYA PRADESH
MAHARASHTRA
BALOCHISTAN
SINDH
KHAIRPUR
BAHAWALPUR
N.W. FRONTIER PROV.
HINDU KUSH
KARAKORAM
GREAT HIMALAYAN RANGE
Siwalik Range
Sulaiman Range
Kirthar Range
Aravalli Range
Satpura Range
Vindhya Range
Malwa Plateau
THAR DESERT
INDIAN DESERT
Rann of Kachchh
Tropic of Cancer
ARABIAN SEA
Gulf of Khambhat
G. of Kachchh
Mouths of the Indus
Kathiawar
Registan
Safed Koh
Siah Koh
Koh-i-Baba
Toba and Kakar Ranges
Central Makran Ra.
Makran Coast Range
Hazarajat
Sinkai Hills
Salt Ra.
Deosai Plain
Aksai Chin
K2 8611
Nanga Parbat 8126
Tirich Mir
Nunkun 7135
Kamet 7756
Nanda Devi 7817
Khunjerab Pass
Karakoram Pass 5575
Khyber Pass
Kabul
Islamabad
Rawalpindi
Peshawar
Lahore
Faisalabad
Multan
Karachi
Hyderabad
Quetta
Sukkur
Kandahar
Ghazni
Jalalabad
Delhi
New Delhi
Agra
Jaipur
Jodhpur
Ajmer
Bikaner
Ahmadabad
Vadodara
Surat
Rajkot
Jamnagar
Bhavnagar
Indore
Bhopal
Ujjain
Gwalior
Jhansi
Kota
Udaipur
Amritsar
Jullundur
Ludhiana
Chandigarh
Simla
Srinagar
Jammu
Bombay
Thane
Kalyan
Pune (Poona)
Nasik
Aurangabad
Ahmadnagar
Nagpur
Amravati
Akola
Jalgaon
Dhule
Malegaon
Diu (Goa, Daman & Diu)
Daman (G.D. & D.)
Silvassa
Bahawalpur
Sargodha
Gujranwala
Sialkot
Jhelum
Mardan
Kohat
Dera Ismail Khan
Dera Ghazi Khan
Rahimyar Khan
Jacobabad
Shikarpur
Larkana
Nawabshah
Mirpur Khas
Meerut
Moradabad
Bareilly
Aligarh
Mathura
Firozabad
Saharanpur
Dehra Dun
Ambala
Patiala
Rohtak
Hisar
Ganganagar
Bhuj
Porbandar
Junagadh
Veraval
Khandwa
Burhanpur
Hotan
Kargil
Gilgit
Leh
Mazar-i-Sharif
Kunduz
Baghlan
Charikar
Feyzabad
Maimana
Shibarghan
Andkhui
Termez
Khorog
Gardez
Zhob
Sibi
Chaman
Kalat
Khuzdar
Bela
Sonmiani Bay
Korangi
Tatta
Badin
Keti Bandar
Lakhpat
Nagar Parkar
Barmer
Jaisalmer
Phalodi
Pokaran
Nagaur
Churu
Sikar
Alwar
Bharatpur
Tonk
Bundi
Bhilwara
Chittaurgarh
Mandsaur
Ratlam
Dewas
Mhow
Hoshangabad
Sagar
Vidisha
Guna
Shivpuri
Lalitpur
Tikamgarh
Chhatarpur
Chhindwara
Betul
Wardha
Chandrapur
Yavatmal
Nanded
Parbhani
Jalna
Latur
Daund
Lonavale
Alibag
Deolali
Sangamner
Kopargaon
Manmad
Chalisgaon
Buldana
Khamgaon
Hingoli
Nizamabad
Karimnagar
Bodhan
Nirmal
Mancher
Godhra
Dahod
Nadiad
Petlad
Anand
Bharuch
Navsari
Valsad
Rajpipla
Dabhoi
Nandurbar
Mahesana
Palanpur
Patan
Radhanpur
Siddhapur
Himatnagar
Gandhinagar
Surendranagar
Morbi
Dhrangadhra
Gandhidham
Mandvi
Okha
Dwarka
Gondal
Dhoraji
Amreli
Kundla
Palitana
Mahuva
Mangrol
Gir Hills
Indus
Chenab
Jhelum
Ravi
Sutlej
Narmada
Tapi
Godavari
Chambal
Yamuna
Ganga
Helmand
Hingol
Kunar
Kabul
Tarbela Resr
Ras Koh 3008
Zargun 3578
Sikaram 4761
Koh-i-Khurd 3830
Koh-i-Mazar 3788
65 70 75 80
35 30 25 20

1:7.5M

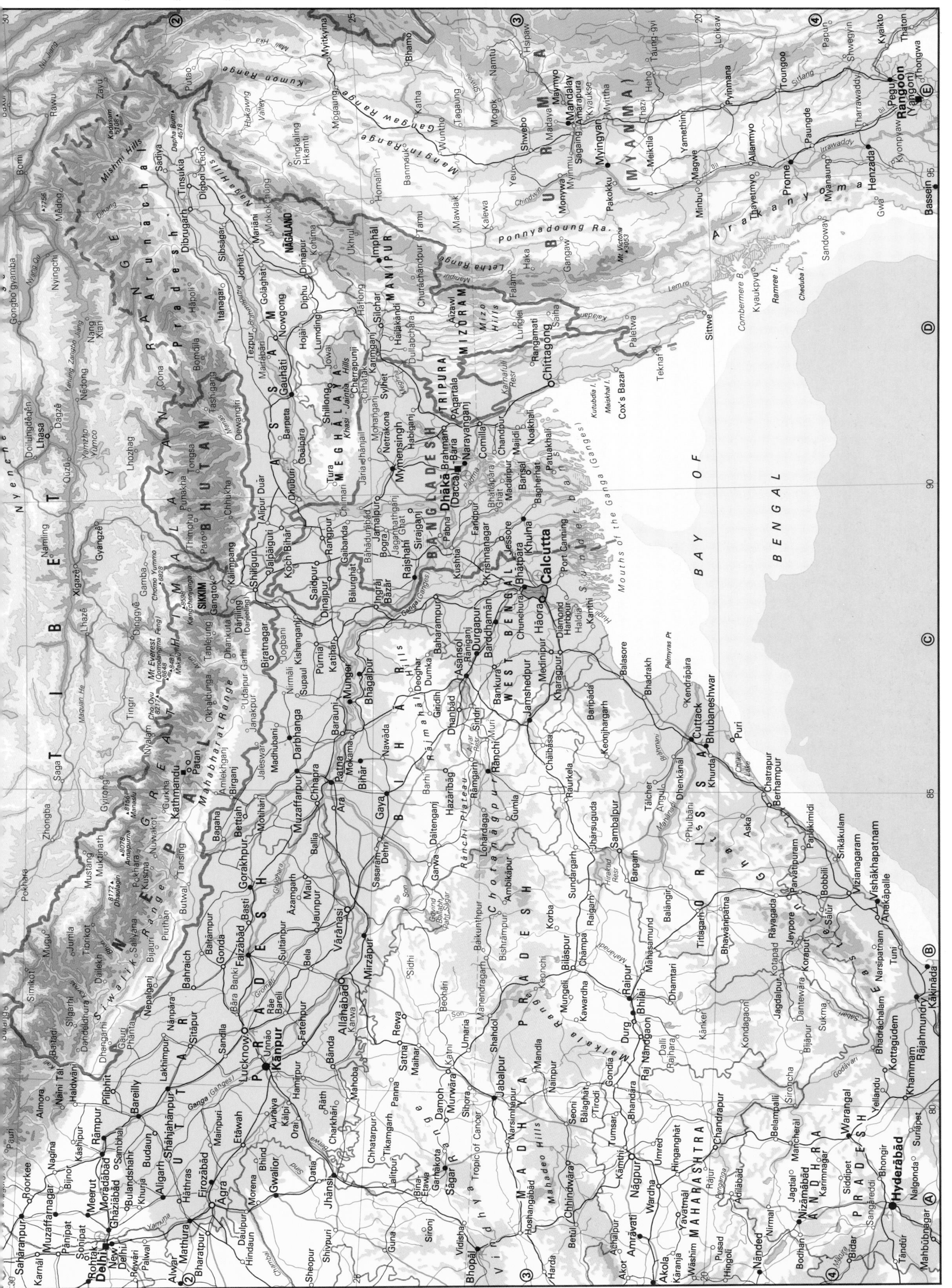

1:7.5M

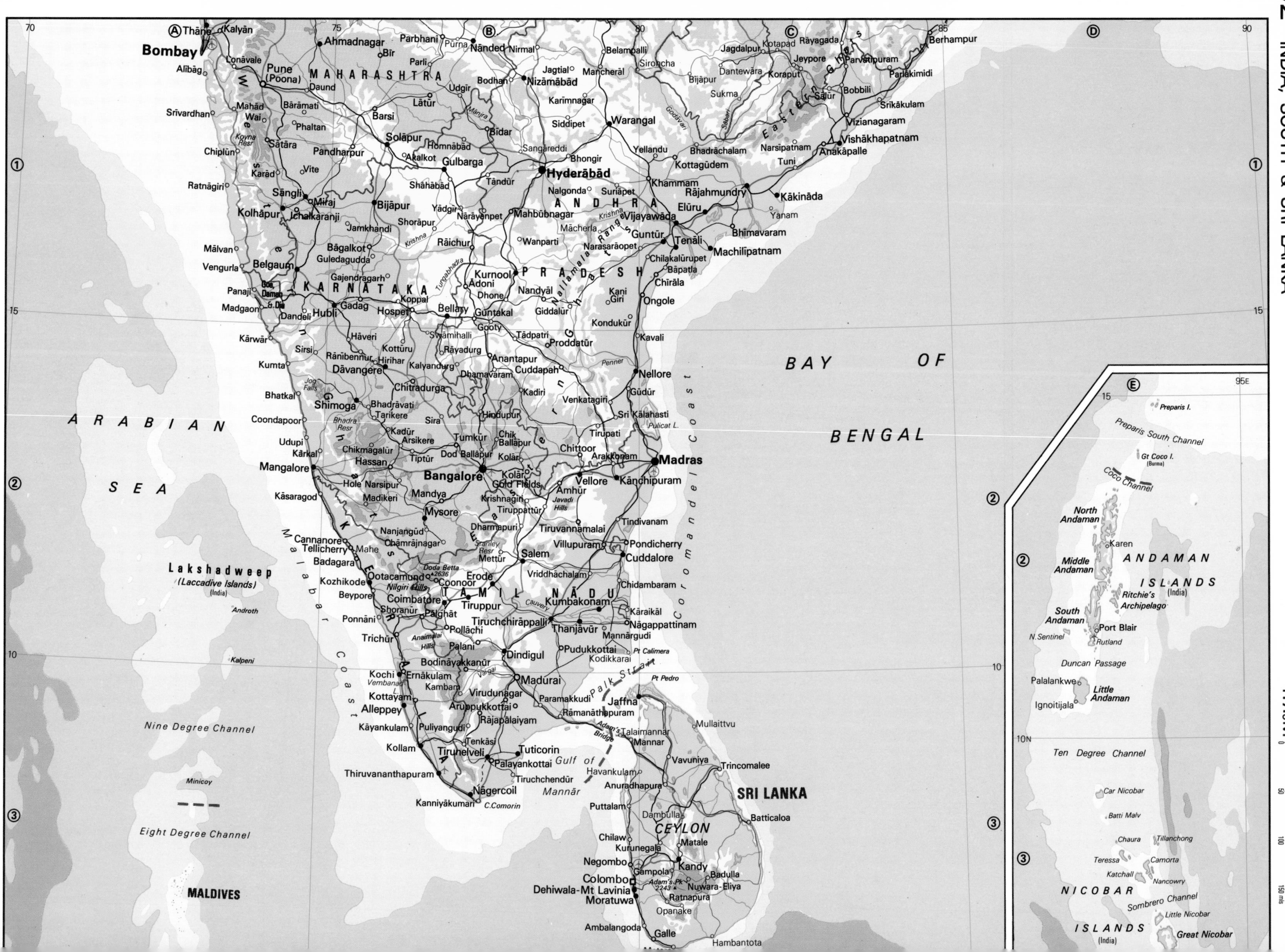
BAY OF BENGAL
ARABIAN SEA
MAHARASHTRA
KARNATAKA
ANDHRA PRADESH
TAMIL NADU
SRI LANKA
CEYLON
Bombay
Hyderābād
Madras
Bangalore
Colombo
Coromandel Coast
Malabar Coast
Palk Strait
Gulf of Mannār
Adam's Bridge
Lakshadweep
(Laccadive Islands)
(India)
Nine Degree Channel
Eight Degree Channel
MALDIVES
ANDAMAN ISLANDS
(India)
Ten Degree Channel
NICOBAR ISLANDS
(India)
Port Blair
Great Nicobar

1:7.5M

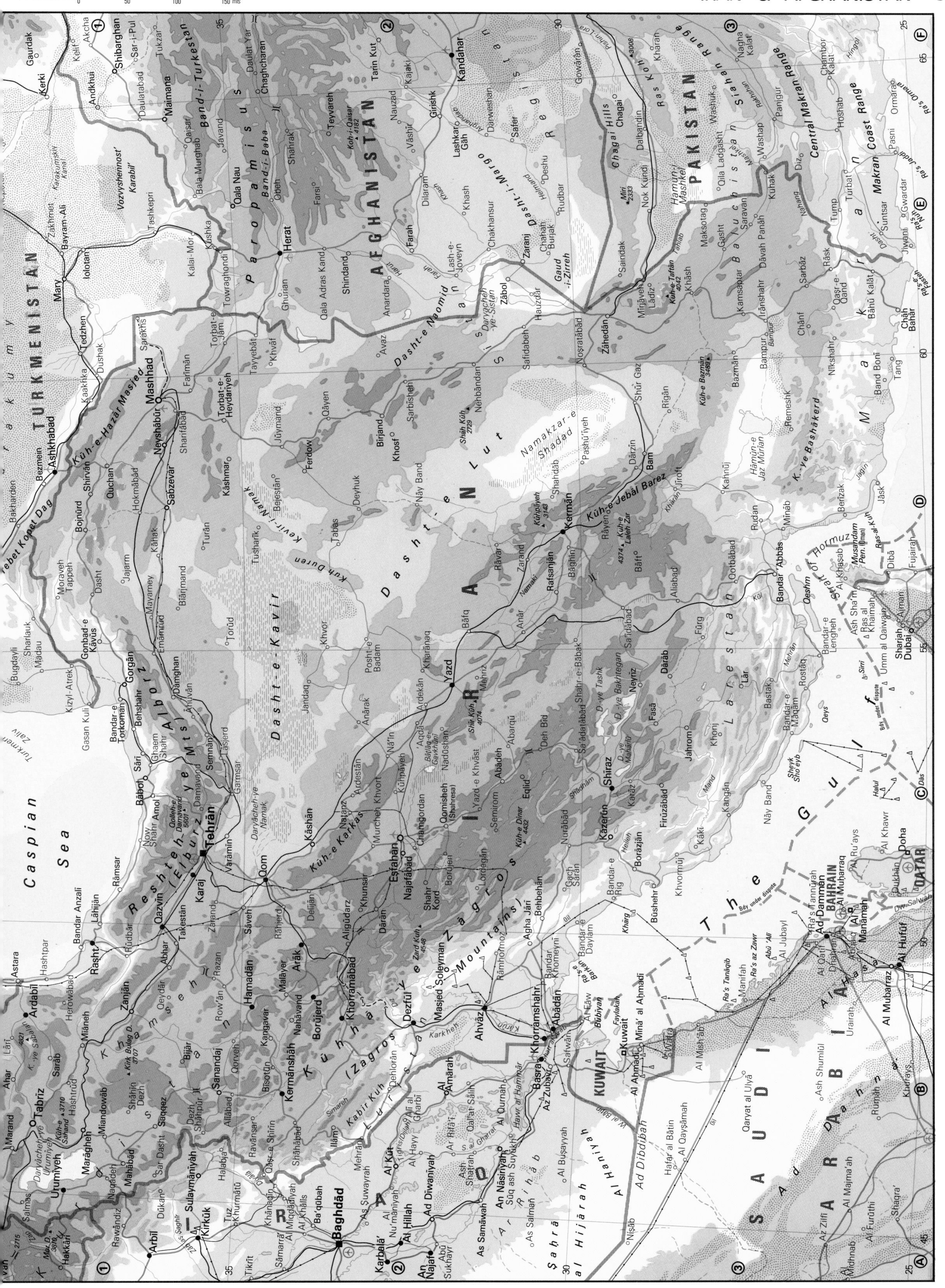

1:7.5M

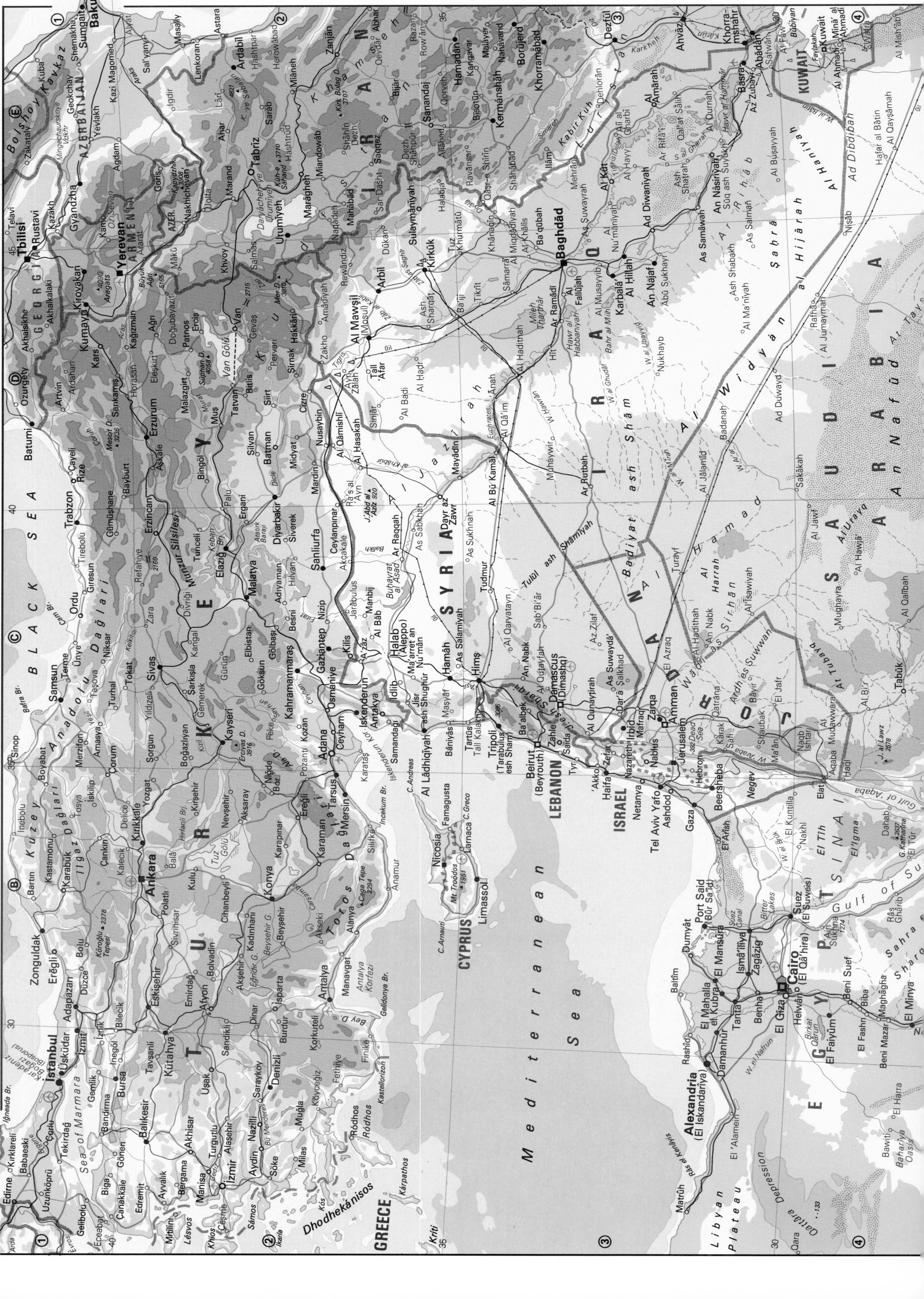

BLACK SEA
Mediterranean Sea
TURKEY
SYRIA
IRAQ
IRAN
LEBANON
ISRAEL
JORDAN
CYPRUS
GREECE
EGYPT
SAUDI ARABIA
KUWAIT
GEORGIA
ARMENIA
AZERBAIJAN
Istanbul
Ankara
Baghdād
Damascus (Dimashq)
Beirut (Beyrouth)
Amman
Jerusalem
Cairo (El Qâhira)
Alexandria (El Iskandarîya)
Tbilisi
Yerevan
Baku
Nicosia
Tabrīz
Halab (Aleppo)
Al Mawşil (Mosul)
Kuwait
Anadolu Dağlari
Toros Dağlari
Sea of Marmara
Sinai
Libyan Plateau
Qattara Depression
Badiyat ash Sham
An Nafūd
Gulf of Aqaba
Gulf of Suez

1:2.5M
0 25 50 75 100 km
0 25 50 mls

CYPRUS
C.A. Andreas
Rizokaipaso
Yialousa
Leonarisso
C. Kormakiti
Lapithos
Kyrenia
Akanthou
Morphou Bay
Kythrea
Trikomo
C. Elea
Morphou
Lefkoniko
Famagusta Bay
Khrysokhou Bay
Karavostasi
SALAMIS
C. Arnauti
Lefka
ATTILA LINE
Nicosia
Famagusta
Polis
Pedhoulas
Dhali
IDALION
Athna
Mt Olympus 1951
Troödos Range
Paleokhorio
Larnaca
Platres
Larnaca Bay
C. Greco
Lefkara
Paphos
C. Kiti
Zyyi
Episkopi
Limassol
Episkopi B.
Akrotiri Bay
C. Zevgari
C. Gata

M E D I T E R R A N E A N

S E A

SYRIA
Seraï
Jisr ash Shughūr
Al Bayluliyah
Ra's Ibn Hāni
Al Haffah
Ma'arrat an Nu'mān
Al Lādhiqīyah
(Latakia)
Şilinfah
SAHYŪN
Shathah
At Tahta'
Khān Shaykhūn
Al Qardahah
Jablah
Şuqaylibiyah
(Orontes)
Sūrān
'Arab al Mulk
Dayr Shumayyil
Bāniyās
1385
QAL'AT AL MARQAB
Al Qadmūs
Hamāh
Maşyāf
Kafr Behum
Bīrīn
Ar Rastan
Tartūs
Duraykīsh
Kafrūn Bashūr
Arwad
Şāfītā
An Nāşirah
Tall Bīsah
Qal'at al Hişn (KRAK DES CHEVALIERS)
Hims (Homs)
Hamīdīyah
Tall Kalakh
Kleiat
Kebir
Qoubayat
Shinshār
Halba
Al Quşayr
El Mīna
El Hermel
Jūsīyah
Tripoli
Zghorta
Hisyah
(Tarābulus esh Shām)
Qornet es Saouda 3086
Jabal Halimah 2464
Batroun
Amioune
Bcharre
Laboue
Deir el Ahmar
Jubail
BYBLOS
Kartaba
Dayr 'Atīyah
LEBANON
Rhazīr
2659
An Nabk
Jouniė
Bikfaya 2628
Ba'albek
Yabrūd
Baie de St Georges
Beirut
(Beyrouth)
Ba'abda
Zahle
Rayak
Jayrūd
Aley
Az Zabdānī
Al J. Ma'lūla
Damour
1910
Qutayfah
Beit ed Dīne
'Ayn al Fījah
Dumayr
Saïda
(Sidon)
Māchgharab
At Tall
Dūmā
'Adhrā'
Barada
Jezzine
Rachaya
Damascus
(Dimashq)
Qatanā
Hasbaiya
J. ash Shaykh (Mt Hermon)
Al Hijānah
A'waj
Marjayoun
Al Kiswah
Dayr 'Alī
Līţānī
Tyr
(Tyre, Sour)
Q. Shemona
Baniyas
Jouai'ya
Mas'adah
CEASE FIRE LINES 1974
Ghabāghib
Burāq
Enn Nâqoûra
Bennt Jbail
Al Qunaytirah
Mismīyah
Yesud Hama'ala
Aş Şanamayn
Khabab
Nahariya
1208 Har Meron
Ma'alot Tarshiha
Zefat (Safad)
Khushnīyah
Al Lajāh 863
Shaqqā
'Akko (Acre)
B. of Haifa
Q. Yam
Rama
Nawā
Izra'
Shahbā
Haifa (Hefa)
Shefar'am
Tiberias
L. Tiberias (Yam Kinneret) (Sea of Galilee)
Shaykh Miskīn
Jabal al 'Arab 1735
Q. Ata
Fīq
Tasīl
'Atlit
528 Mt Carmel
Nazareth
Ma'agan
Yarmūk
As Suwaydā'
Afula
Irbid
Dar'a
Zikhron Ya'aqov
MEGIDDO ARMAGEDDON
Deir Abū Sa'id
Ramtha
Buşrá ash Shām
CAESAREA
Pardes Hanna
Hadera
Jenin
Beyt Shean
Şalkhad
Tīsīyah
Husn
Netanya
Tulkarm
Qabatiya
Tubas
Ajlūn
J. Umm ed Daraj 1247
Mafraq
Sabhā
ISRAEL
ARMISTICE LINE
Jarash
Sabastiya
Fār'a
Herzliya
Kefar Sava
Nablus
Es Samrā
Yarqon
Bat Yam
Petah Tiqwa
Er Rummān
Ramat Gan
Tel Aviv
Sarida
Salt
Suweilih
Zarqa
Yafo (Jaffa)
Holon
Ba'al Hazor 1016
CEASE FIRE LINE
Karama
Marka
Amman
Rishon le Zion
Lod
Ramallah
Wadi es Sir
Rehovot
Ramla
Jericho (Arīhā)
Naur
Sahab
Ashdod
Latrun
Jerusalem (El Quds)
(Yerushalayim)
Mādabā
Jiza
Beit Jala
Bethlehem (Bayt Lahm)
Qasr el Kharana
Jebel Mudeisisat 963
Ashqelon
Qiryat Gat
Bet Guvrin
Dead Sea (Bahrat Lut)
Dab'a
Hebron (El Khalil)
Dhībān
Khan ez Zabīb
Gaza
Sederot
LACHISH
Dura
En Gedi
Gaza Strip
Yatta
Edh Dhahiriya
Mazra
Khan Yunis
MEZADA
Rafah
Beersheba (Be'er Sheva)
El Lisān
Rabba
Qatrāna
Ofaqim
Nevatim
'Arad
Qa'el Hafira
El 'Arīsh
Zeelim
Karak
HALUZA
Sedom
1253 T. el Meise
Mazār
Dimona
MAMSHIT
Manzil
Revivim
Safi
J. Ed Dabāb 1305
Yeroham
JORDAN
Qeziot
SHIVTA
Oron
Tafila
Sede Boqer
NIZANA
AVEDAT
Zin
Hāsā
1356 J. Qasred Deir
Qa'el Jinz
Hazeva
Rashādīya
Jurf ed Darāwīsh
El Quseima
N e g e v
Danā
1641 J. el Atā'ita
Jebel Ithriyat
1082
Mizpe Ramon
Ein Yahav
Shaubak
1305 Har Ramon
EDOM
Nijil
Uneisa
Har Hakippa 467
1615 Jum Suwwāna
Wādī Mūsā
G. Araif el Naqa 934
1006 Har Saggi
Beer Menuha
PETRA
J. Hārūn
Ābū el Jurdhān
El Jafr
El Jafr
Taiyiba
1727 J. Mubrak
Ma'ān
Hiyon
Esh Sharā
Zenifim
Vahel
Naqb Ishtar
Paran
El Kuntilla
Ras en Naqb
Yotvata
1242 J. Qatim
Tuwayilel Hāj 1095
El Quwetra
Mikhrot Timna
1420 Ras Um Seisabān
J. el Harad 1274
Beer Ora
J. Baqir 1592
J. Ram 1754
J. Um Ishrin 1753
Elat
Aqaba
Ram
G. of Aqaba
1216 J. Um el Hashīm

EGYPT
Râs el Barr
Masabb Dumyât
Dumyât
(Damietta)
Kafr Sa'd
Fâriskûr
Bahra el Manzala
Port Said
(Bûr Saîd)
Bûr Fu'ad
Shirbîn
El Zarqa
El Matariya
Râs Burûn
Sabkhet el Bardawîl
Mit el Nasâra
El Manzala
Khalig el Tîna
El Mansûra
Dikirnis
El Tîna
PELUSIUM
Românî
Bîr Lahfân
W. Hareidîn
Simbillâwein
DAPHNAE
Bîr el Duweidâr
W. el 'Arîsh
Abu 'Aweigila
Kafr Saqr
El Sâlhîya
El Qantara
Abu Kebir
Hihya
Fâqûs
El Firdân
G. Libni 463
Kathib el Henu 207
G. Maghâra 735
892 G. Halâl
Zagazig
El Abbâsa
Ismâ'ilîya
Talata
L. Timsâh
Abu Suweir
Minya el Qamn
Bilbeis
Khamsa
Great Bitter Lake
Bîr Gifgâfa
Bîr Hasana
1094 G. Yi'allaq
Shibîn el Qanâtir
El Khânka
Fâyid
Sabâ'a
W. el Hasana
704 G. Kharîm
W. el Qîraiya
W. el Gafra
Little Bitter Lake
Giddi Pass
W. el Brûk
Gineifa
El Shallûfa
840 G. el Giddi
Mitla Pass
520
Suez
(El Suweis)
El Kûbri
El Shatt
Cairo (El Qâ'hira)
Bîr Gindali
G. Ataqa
Bûr Taufiq
Nakhl
W. el 'Aqaba
Helwân
Uyûn Mûsa
Gulf of Suez
S I N A I
G. Sinn Bishr 622
G. Budhîya
Bîr Udeib
Bîr el 'Agramîya
'Ain Sukhna
Sudr
Râs el Sudr
G e b e l e l T î h
El Thamad
G. Sha'îra 1030
Asl
W. el Siq
1076
1018 G. Abu Rûtha
Gebel el Galâla el Baharîya
Râs Matarma
1080 Râs el Nafas
W. Abu Tarfa

32 34 36
30 32 34

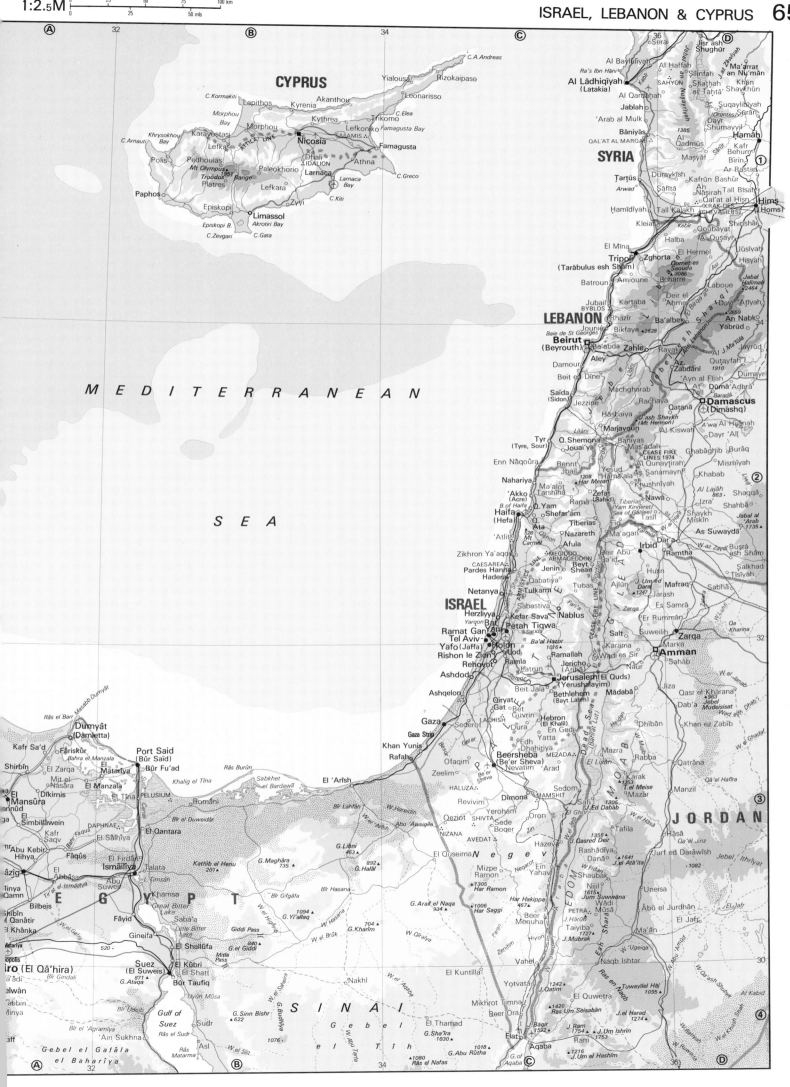

1:7.5M

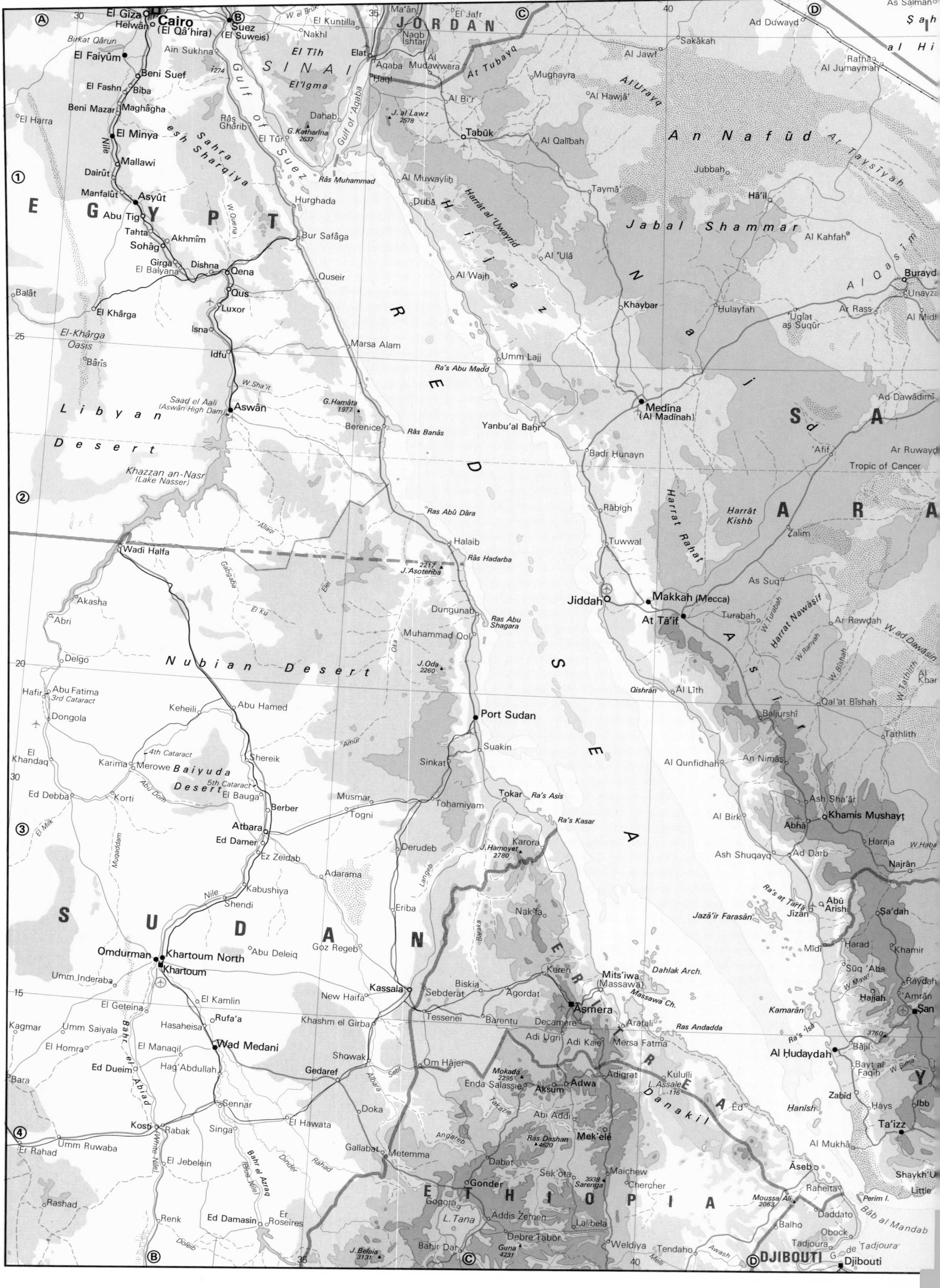

100 200 300 km
50 100 150 mls

JORDAN

EGYPT

El Giza · Cairo (El Qâ'hira) · Helwân · Suez (El Suweis)
El Faiyûm · Beni Suef · Ain Sukhna
El Fashn · Biba
Beni Mazar · Maghâgha
El Harra · El Minya
Mallawi · Dairût
Manfalût · Asyût · Abu Tig
Tahta · Akhmîm
Sohâg
Girga · Dishna · Qena
El Balyana · Qus
Balât · El Khârga · Luxor
Isna
El-Khârga Oasis · Idfu
Bârîs
Saad el Aali (Aswân High Dam) · Aswân

Birkat Qârun
esh Sharqiya
Râs Ghârib
Râs Muhammad
El Tûr
Hurghada
Bur Safâga
Quseir
Marsa Alam
G. Hamâta 1977
Berenice · Râs Banâs

El Tîh · SINAI · El 'Igma
Nakhl · El Kuntilla
Ma'ân · El Jafr
Elat · 'Aqaba · Naqb Ishtar
Haql
Dahab
G. Katharîna 2637
J. al Lawz 2578
Tabûk
Al Bi'r
Al Muwaylih
Dubâ
Al Wajh
Umm Lajj
Ra's Abu Madd
Yanbu' al Bahr

Libyan Desert

Khazzan an-Nasr (Lake Nasser)
Wadi Halfa
Akasha
Abri
Delgo
Hafir · Abu Fatima 3rd Cataract
Dongola
El Khandaq · Karima · Merowe
Ed Debba · Korti
El Milk · El Bauga 5th Cataract
Keheili · Abu Hamed
Kagmar
Bara · Er Rahad
Umm Ruwaba

Nubian Desert
Baiyuda Desert
4th Cataract

'Allâqi
El Ku
Eiei
Oka
J. Oda 2260
Dungunab
Muhammad Qol
Ras Abu Shagara
Halaib · Râs Hadarba
J. Asoteriba 2217
Amûr

SUDAN

Omdurman · Khartoum North · Khartoum
Umm Inderaba
El Geteina · El Kamlin
Umm Saiyala · Hasaheisa · Rufa'a
El Homra · El Manaqil · Wad Medani
Ed Dueim · Hag 'Abdullah
Kosti · Rabak · Singa
Rashad · Renk · Ed Damasin

Abu Deleiq
Kabushiya · Shendi
Atbara · Ed Damer · Ez Zeidab
Berber
Musmar · Togni
Derudeb
Adarama
Goz Regeb
New Haifa
Khashm el Girba
Kassala
Gedaref
Showak · Om Hâjer
Doka
Gallabat · Metemma
Gonder
L. Tana · Bahir Dar

Port Sudan
Suakin
Sinkat
Tohamiyam
Tokar · Ra's Asis
Ra's Kasar
Karora · J. Hamoyet 2780
Eriba
Langeb
Nak'fa

RED SEA

Ras Abû Dâra

ERITREA
Keren · Mits'iwa (Massawa)
Agordat · Decamere · Asmera
Biskia · Sebderat
Tessenei · Barentu
Adi Ugri · Adi Kaie
Aratali · Mersa Fatma
Adigrat · Kululli
Aksum · Adwa · L. Assale
Abi Addi
Mokadâ 2295 · Enda Salassie
Mek'ele · Maichew
Sek'ota · 3938 Sarenga
Dabat · Lalibela
Debre Tabor
Gogora
J. Belaia 3131 · Guna 4231
Addis Zemen · Bahir Dar

Dahlak Arch.
Massawa Ch.
Ras Andadda
Ra's at Tarfa
Ras 'Isa
Jazâ'ir Farasân
Kamarân

DANAKIL
Mersa Fatma
Ras Dashan 4620
Chercher
Moussa Ali 2063
Tendaho · Awash
Balho · Obock
Tadjoura · G. de Tadjoura

ETHIOPIA

DJIBOUTI · Djibouti

SAUDI ARABIA

An Nafûd
Jabal Shammar
As Salmano
Ad Duwayd
Sakâkah
Al Jawf
Mughayra · Al Hawja'
Al Qalîbah
Taymâ'
Jubbah
Hâ'il
Al Kahfah
Khaybar
Hulayfah
Medîna (Al Madînah)
Badr Hunayn
Râbigh
Tuwwal
Harrat Rahat
Harrat Kishb
Jiddah · Makkah (Mecca) · At Tâ'if
Turabah
Al Lîth
Qishrân
Al Qunfidhah
Al Birk
An Nimâs
Ash Shuqayq
Abhâ · Khamis Mushayt
Ash Sha'âr
Ad Darb · Haraja
Midi · Abû Arish · Jizân
Sa'dah · Khamir
Harad · Khamis
Sûq 'Abs · Hajjah
Al Hudaydah · Bâjil · Raydah · Amrân
Bayt al Faqih
Zabid · Hays · Ibb
Ta'izz
Al Mukhâ
Âseb
Perim I.
Bâb al Mandab

Al Jumaymah
Rafhâ
Al 'Urayq
At Taysîyah
Al Qasîm
Burayda
Unayza
Ar Rass
Al Midh
Ad Dawâdimi
'Afif
Ar Ruwaydh
Tropic of Cancer
Harrât Rahat · Zalim
As Suq
W. Turabah
Harrat Nawâsif
Ar Rawdah · W. ad Dawâsir
Baljurshi
Qal'at Bîshah
Tathlith
W. Tathlith
W. Bîshah
W. Runyah
W. Habâ

Gulf of Suez
Gulf of Aqaba

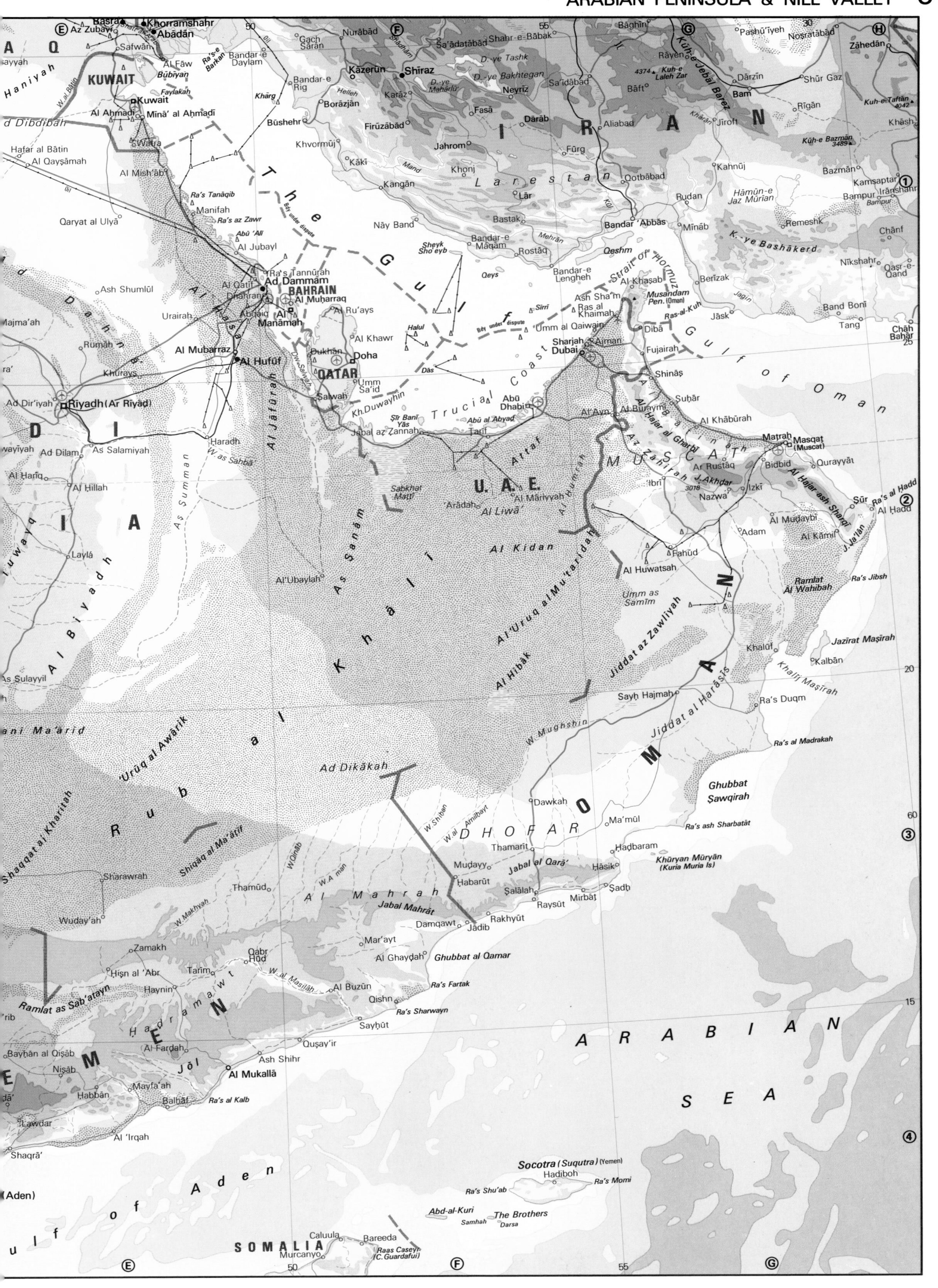
KUWAIT
Kuwait
Basra
Khorramshahr
Abādān
Az Zubayr
Safwān
Al Fāw
Būbiyān
Faylakah
Al Aḥmadī
Mīnā' al Aḥmadī
Wafra
Ḥafar al Bāṭin
Al Qayşâmah
Al Mish'āb
Ra's Tanāqib
Manifah
Ra's az Zawr
Abū 'Alī
Al Jubayl
Qaryat al Ulyā
Ra's Tannūrah
Al Qaţīf
Ad Dammām
Dhahran
Abqaiq
BAHRAIN
Al Muḥarraq
Al Manāmah
Ash Shumlūl
Urairah
Al Mubarraz
Al Hufūf
Rumāh
Khurays
Riyadh (Ar Riyāḍ)
Ad Dir'iyah
Haradh
As Salamiyah
Ad Dilam
Al Ḥarīq
Al Ḥillah
Laylā
As Sulayyil
Al Biyadh
Al Jāfūrah
As Summan
W. as Sahbā
Dukhān
Doha
QATAR
Umm Sa'id
Salwah
Ra's Rakan
Al Khawr
Ru'ays
Ḥalul
Dās
Bandar-e Deylam
Khārg
Būshehr
Bandar-e Rig
Borāzjān
Khvormūj
Kākī
Kāzerūn
Shīrāz
Fīrūzābād
Jahrom
Fasā
Neyrīz
Dārāb
Fūrg
Nūrābād
Sa'ādatābād
Shahr-e-Bābak
D. ye Tashk
D. ye Bakhtegan
Sa'īdābād
Bāghīn
Rāyen
Kuh-e Jebal Barez
Bam
Bāft
Dārzīn
Shūr Gaz
Zāhedān
Nosratābād
Pashū'īyeh
Rīgān
Kuh-e Taftān 4042
Khāsh
Kūh-e Bazmān 3489
Bazmān
Kamsaptar
Īrānshahr
Bampur
Jīroft
Aliabad
Kahnūj
Qotbābad
Rudan
Hāmūn-e Jaz Mūrīan
Remeshk
Chānf
Mīnāb
Bandar 'Abbās
K. ye Bashākerd
Nīkshahr
Qaşr-e-Qand
Larestan
Lār
Khonj
Kangān
Nāy Band
Bastak
Bandar-e Māqām
Rostāq
Sheyk Sho'eyb
Qeys
Bandar-e Lengheh
Qeshm
Strait of Hormuz
Al Khasab
Musandam Pen. (Oman)
Ras-al-Kuh
Bērizak
Jāsk
Band Bonī
Tang
Chāh Bahār
IRAN
The Gulf
Bdy under dispute
Sirri
Ash Sha'm
Ras al Khaimah
Umm al Qaiwain
Ajman
Sharjah
Dubai
Dibā
Fujairah
Shināş
Şuḥār
Trucial Coast
Abū Dhabi
Abū al Abyad
Şīr Banī Yās
Kh. Duwayhin
Jabal az Zannah
Tarīf
Sabkhat Maţţī
U. A. E.
Al Māriyyah
'Arādah
Al Liwā'
Attaf
Al 'Ayn
Al Buraymī
Al Hajar al Gharbī
Az Zahirah
MUSCAT
Al Khābūrah
Maţraḥ
Masqaţ (Muscat)
Bidbid
Ar Rustāq
Qurayyāt
'Ibrī
J. Akhḍar 3018
Nazwā
Izkī
Al Hajar ash Sharqī
Şūr
Ra's al Ḥadd
Al Ḥadd
Al Muḍaybī
Al Kāmil
J. Ja'lān
Adam
Fahūd
Al Huwatsah
Umm as Samīm
Ramlat Al Wahibah
Ra's Jibsh
Al Kidan
Al 'Ubaylah
As Şanām
Al 'Urūq al Mu'tariḍah
Al Hibāk
Jiddat az Zawlīyah
Jazīrat Maşīrah
Khalūf
Kalbān
Khalīj Maşīrah
Sayḥ Hajmah
Jiddat al Ḥarāsīs
Ra's Duqm
Ra's al Madrakah
W. Mughshin
OMAN
Rub al Khālī
'Urūq al Awārik
Ad Dikākah
Shaqqat al Kharītah
Shiqāq al Ma'āṭif
Ghubbat Şawqirah
Dawkah
Ma'mūl
DHOFAR
Ra's ash Sharbatāt
Thamarīt
Ḥaḍbaram
Khūryan Mūryān (Kuria Muria Is)
Muḍayy
Ḥabarūt
Jabal al Qarā'
Ḥāsik
Şalālah
Mirbāţ
Şadḥ
Raysūt
Rakhyūt
Jādib
Damqawt
Jabal Mahrāt
Al Mahrah
Thamūd
Sharawrah
Wuday'ah
Zamakh
Qabr Hūd
Mar'ayt
Al Ghayḍah
Ghubbat al Qamar
Ḥişn al 'Abr
Tarīm
W. al Masīlah
Al Buzūn
Ra's Fartak
Haynin
Ḥaḍramawt
Qishn
Ra's Sharwayn
Ramlat as Sab'atayn
Sayḥūt
YEMEN
Bayḥān al Qişāb
Al Fardah
Quşay'ir
Ash Shiḥr
Nişāb
Jōl
Al Mukallā
Mayfa'ah
Ḥabbān
Balḥāf
Ra's al Kalb
Lawdar
Al 'Irqah
Shaqrā'
(Aden)
Gulf of Aden
ARABIAN SEA
Socotra (Suqutra) (Yemen)
Hadiboh
Ra's Momi
Ra's Shu'ab
Abd-al-Kuri
Samhah
The Brothers
Darsa
SOMALIA
Caluula
Bareeda
Raas Caseyr (C. Guardafui)
Murcanyo
SAUDI ARABIA
E
F
G
H
50
55
30
25
20
15
60
1
2
3
4

1:40M

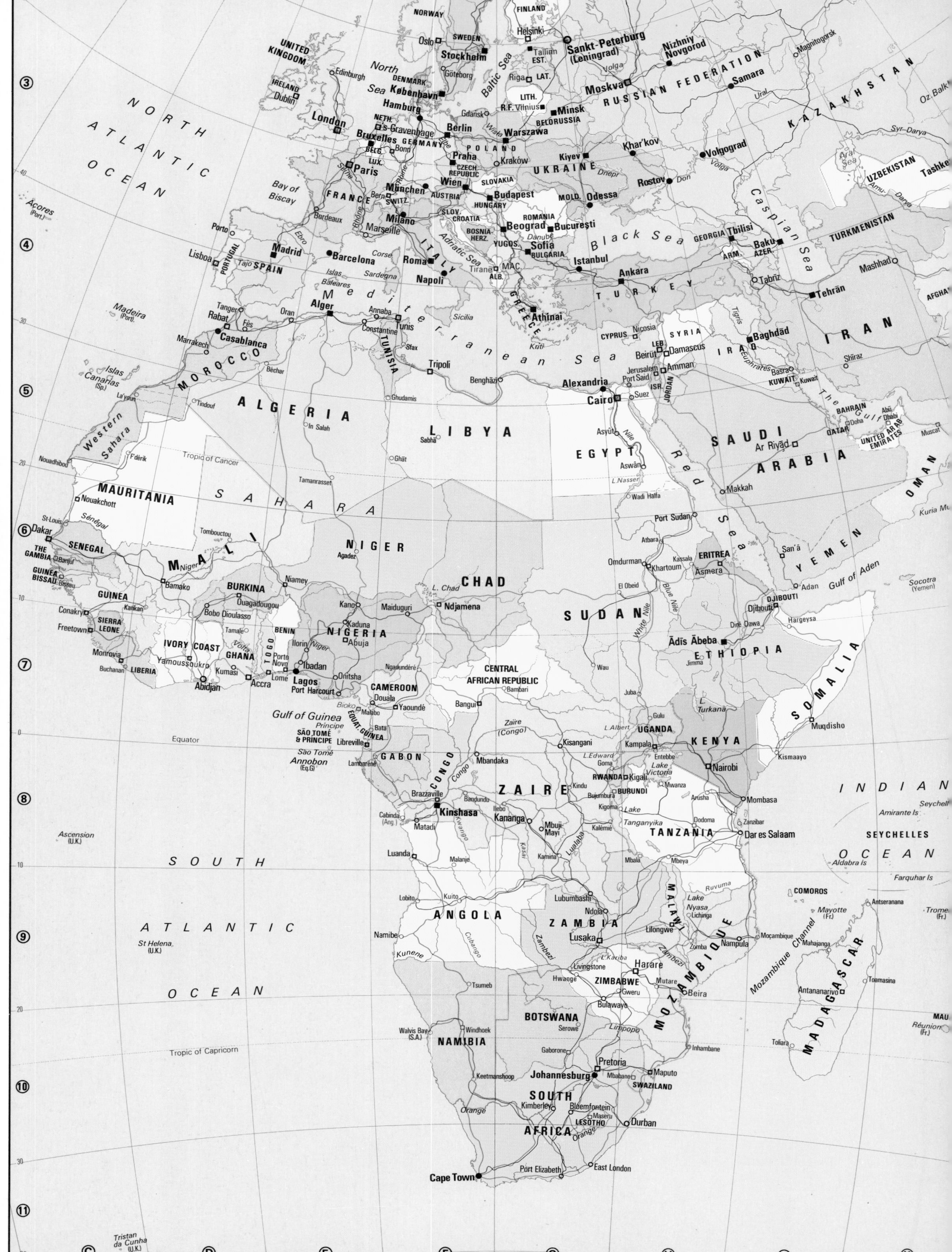

400 800 1200 1600 km
0
0 400 800 mls

A 2 30 B 20 C 10 D 0 E 10 F 20 G 30 H 40 J 50 K 60 L 70 2 M

NORWAY FINLAND

NORTH
ATLANTIC
OCEAN

UNITED
KINGDOM

SWEDEN
Oslo Stockholm Helsinki Tallinn Sankt-Peterburg (Leningrad) Nizhniy Novgorod Magnitogorsk

Edinburgh DENMARK Göteborg Baltic Sea Riga EST. Volga Moskva RUSSIAN FEDERATION Samara KAZAKHSTAN
IRELAND North Sea LAT. Ural Oz.Balk
Dublin København Gdansk LITH. Minsk Oz.Balk
London Hamburg Berlin R.F. Vilnius BELORUSSIA
's-Gravenhage NETH. Warszawa Kiev Khar'kov Volgograd Aral Sea UZBEKISTAN Tashke
Bruxelles BELG. POLAND Wisla UKRAINE Dnepr Rostov Don Syr-Darya
Bonn GERMANY Kraków Amu- Dar
Paris LUX. Praha Dnepr MOLD. Odessa Caspian Sea TURKMENISTAN
FRANCE CZECH REPUBLIC Wien SLOVAKIA Volga
München AUSTRIA Budapest ROMANIA Bucureşti GEORGIA Tbilisi Baku Mashhad
Bordeaux SLOV. HUNGARY Danube ARM. AZER. AFGH
Milano CROATIA Beograd București GEORGIA Tbilisi Baku
Bay of Biscay Marseille BOSNIA HERZ. YUGOS. Sofia BULGARIA Istanbul Ankara Tabriz Tehrān
Porto Rhône Roma Adriatic Sea Tirane MAC. Istanbul TURKEY IRAN
Madrid Barcelona Napoli ALB. GREECE Athinai Nicosia SYRIA Baghdad Shiraz
Lisboa PORTUGAL SPAIN Corse Sardegna Sicilia CYPRUS LEB. Damascus IRAQ Euphrates Basra
Tajo Ebro Islas Baleares Mediterranean Sea Kriti Beirut Jerusalem Amman Euphrates KUWAIT Kuwait
Açores (Port.) Madeira (Port.) Tanger Rabat Fès Oran Alger Annaba Tunis Port Said ISR. JORDAN BAHRAIN Abu Dhabi
Marrakech Casablanca TUNISIA Constantine Sfax Tripoli Benghāzi Alexandria Cairo Suez SAUDI Ar Riyād QATAR UNITED ARAB EMIRATES
Islas Canarias (Sp.) MOROCCO Ghudamis Asyūt Nile ARABIA Makkah Doha OMAN
La'youn Béchar ALGERIA In Salah LIBYA Sabha Ghāt EGYPT Aswān L.Nasser Red Sea San'ā Kuria Muria
Western Sahara Tindouf Tamanrasset SAHARA Wadi Halfa YEMEN Gulf of Aden Socotra (Yemen)
Nouadhibou F'dérik Tropic of Cancer Port Sudan Adan Gulf of Aden
MAURITANIA Nouakchott Atbara ERITREA DJIBOUTI Djibouti Hargeysa
St-Louis Dakar Sénégal Tombouctou NIGER Agadez L.Chad CHAD Omdurman Khartoum Asmera Dire Dawa
THE GAMBIA Banjul SENEGAL Bamako MALI Niger Niamey Kano Maiduguri Ndjamena SUDAN El Obeid Kassala Ādīs Ābeba Jimma
GUINEA BISSAU Bissau GUINEA Kankan BURKINA Ouagadougou Kaduna NIGERIA Blue Nile Wau ETHIOPIA SOMALIA
Conakry SIERRA LEONE Bobo Dioulasso BENIN Ilorin Niger Abuja Ngaoundéré CENTRAL AFRICAN REPUBLIC Juba L.Turkana Muqdisho
Freetown Tamale TOGO Ibadan Onitsha Bambari Wau Gulu KENYA
Monrovia IVORY COAST GHANA Volta Porto Novo Lagos CAMEROON Bangui Zaire (Congo) L.Albert UGANDA Kismaayo
Buchanan LIBERIA Yamoussoukro Kumasi Accra Lomé Port Harcourt Douala Yaoundé Kisangani Kampala Nairobi
Abidjan Malabo Bioko EQUAT. GUINEA Goma Lake Victoria INDIAN
Gulf of Guinea Principe SÃO TOMÉ & PRÍNCIPE Bata GABON Congo Mbandaka L.Edward RWANDA Kigali Mwanza Mombasa Seychell
Libreville São Tomé Lambaréné CONGO Brazzaville ZAIRE Kindu BURUNDI Bujumbura Arusha Zanzibar SEYCHELLES Amirante Is
Annobon (Eq.G) Cabinda (Ang.) Kinshasa Iebo Kananga Kigoma Lake Tanganyika Dodoma Dar es Salaam Aldabra Is
Ascension (U.K.) Matadi Mbuji Mayi Kalemie TANZANIA OCEAN
SOUTH Luanda Malanje Kasai Kamina Mbala Farquhar Is
ATLANTIC Lobito Kuito Lubumbashi Mbeya Lake Nyasa COMOROS Antseranana
OCEAN St Helena (U.K.) ANGOLA Ndola ZAMBIA Lilongwe MALAWI Mayotte (Fr.) Trome (Fr.)
Namibe Cubango Zambezi Lusaka Lichinga Nampula Moçambique Mahajanga
Equator Cunene L'Kariba Harare Zomba MOZAMBIQUE Mozambique Channel Antananarivo Toamasina
Tsumeb Livingstone ZIMBABWE Gweru Mutare Beira MADAGASCAR
Walvis Bay (S.A.) Windhoek BOTSWANA Hwange Bulawayo Limpopo Inhambane Toliara Réunion (Fr.) MAU
NAMIBIA Serowe Gaborone Pretoria Maputo MAU
Tropic of Capricorn Keetmanshoop Johannesburg Mbabane SWAZILAND
SOUTH AFRICA Kimberley Bloemfontein LESOTHO Maseru Durban
Orange Orange East London
Cape Town Port Elizabeth
Tristan da Cunha (U.K.)

C 20 D 0 E 40 F 20 G 40 H 40 J 50 K

1:15M

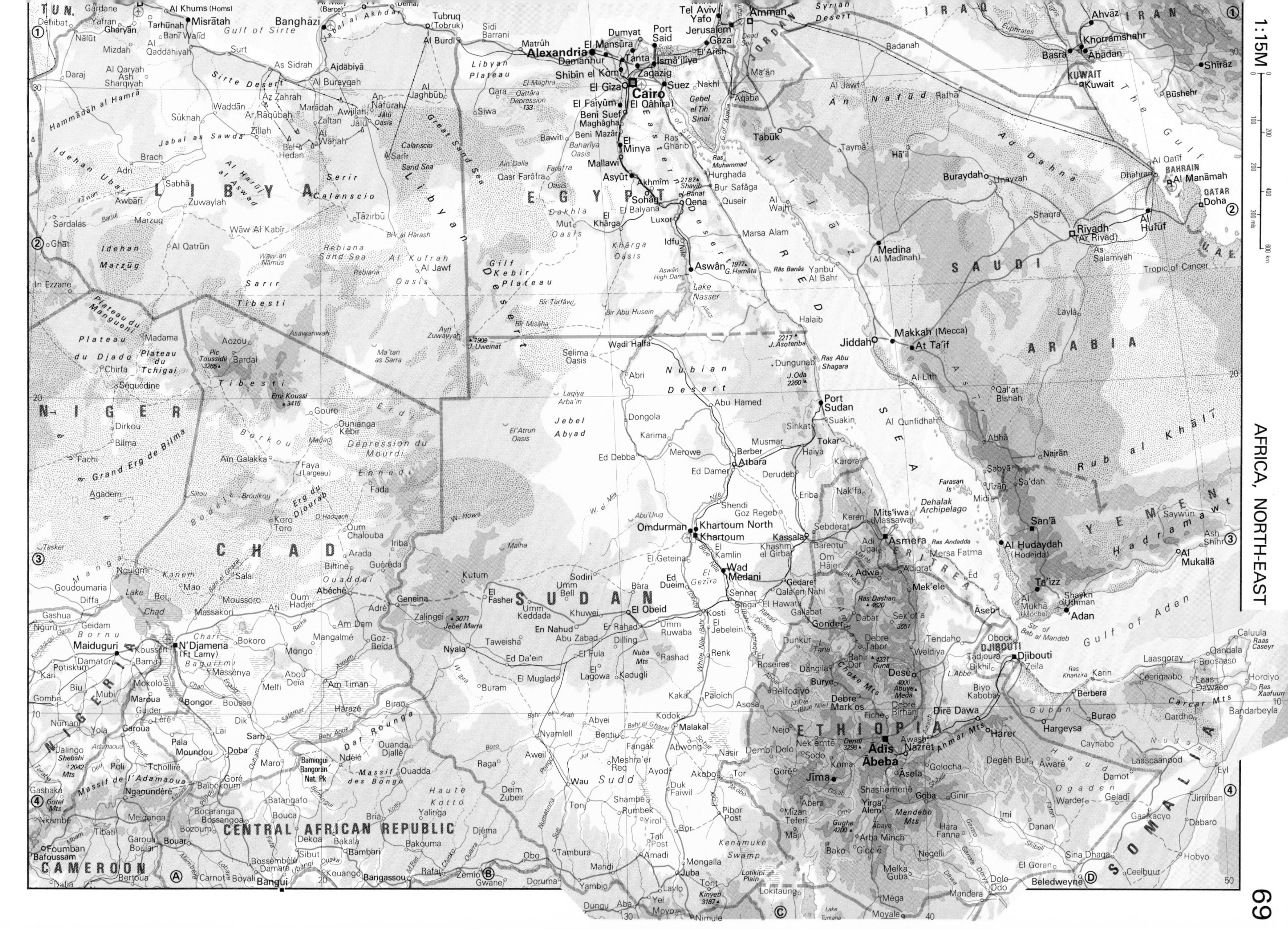

1:15M

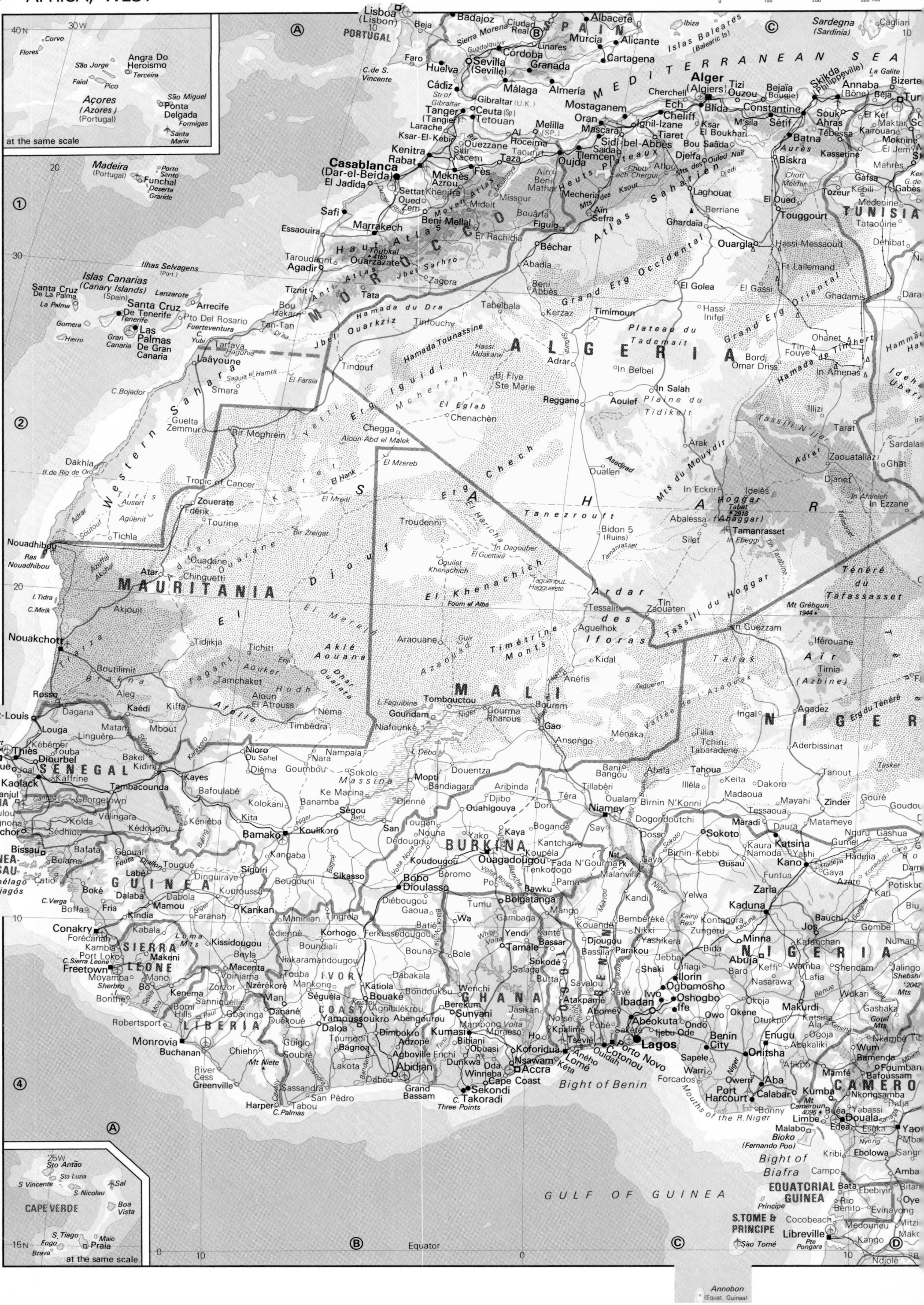

200   400   600 km
100   200   300 mils

0 200 400 600 km
0 100 200 300 mls
Açores (Azores) (Portugal)
Corvo, Flores, São Jorge, Faial, Pico, Terceira, Angra Do Heroismo, São Miguel, Ponta Delgada, Formigas, Santa Maria
at the same scale
Madeira (Portugal), Porto Santo, Funchal, Deserta Grande
Islas Canarias (Canary Islands) (Spain)
Ilhas Selvagens (Port.)
PORTUGAL, SPAIN, MOROCCO, ALGERIA, TUNISIA, Western Sahara, MAURITANIA, MALI, NIGER, SENEGAL, THE GAMBIA, GUINEA-BISSAU, GUINEA, SIERRA LEONE, LIBERIA, IVORY COAST, BURKINA, GHANA, TOGO, BENIN, NIGERIA, CAMEROON, EQUATORIAL GUINEA
MEDITERRANEAN SEA
SAHARA
GULF OF GUINEA
Bight of Benin
Bight of Biafra
Tropic of Cancer
Equator
CAPE VERDE
Sto Antão, Sta Luzia, S Vincente, S Nicolau, Sal, Boa Vista, S. Tiago, Fogo, Brava, Maio, Praia
at the same scale
S.TOME & PRINCIPE
Annobon (Equat. Guinea)

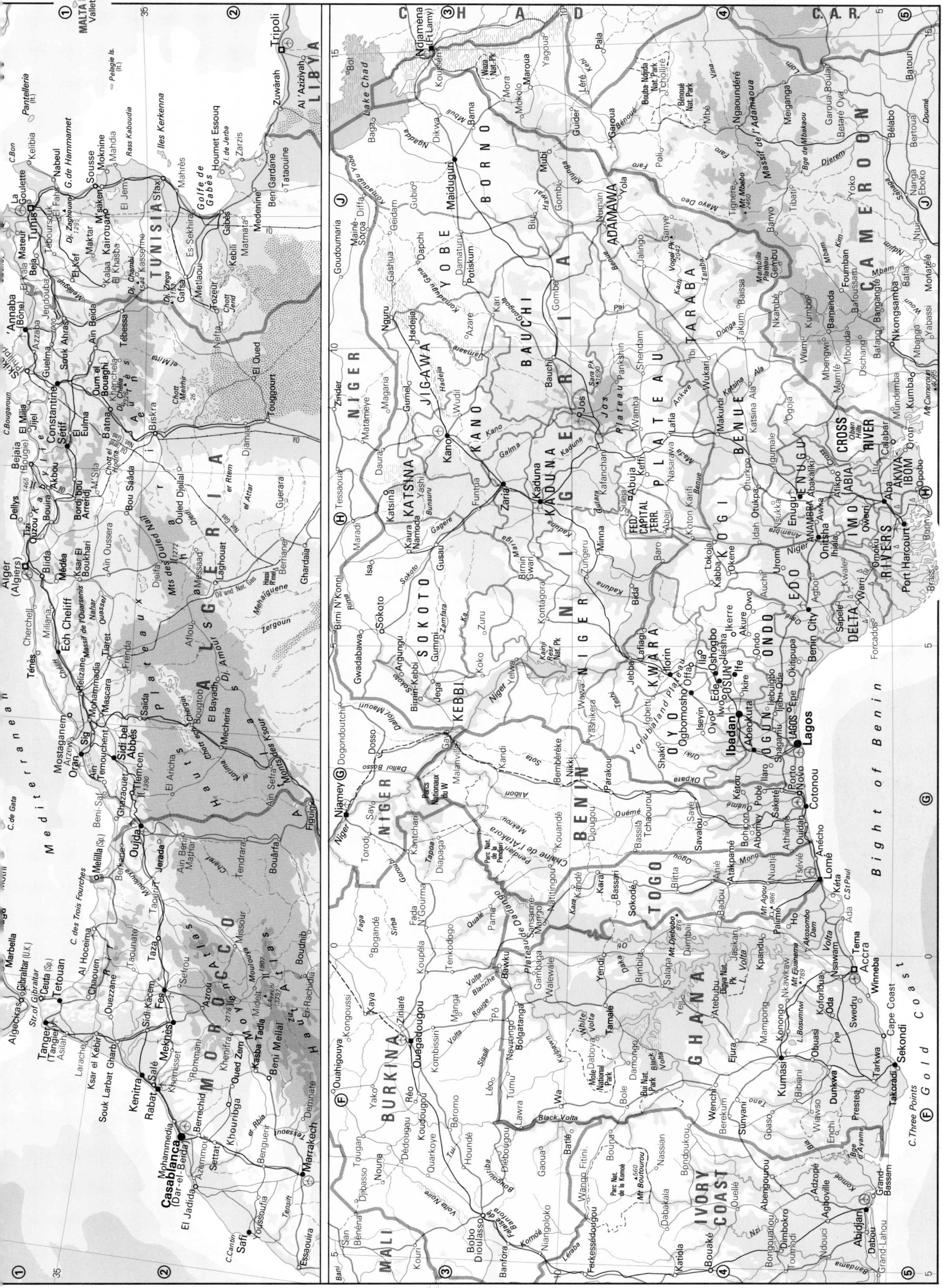

1:7.5M

100   200   300 km
50   100   150 mls

MALTA
Valletta

LIBYA

TUNISIA
Tunis
Tripoli
Zuwārah
Al 'Azīzīyah
Sousse
Sfax
Gabès
Golfe de Gabès
Kairouan
El Jem
Gafsa

ALGERIA
Annaba
Bône
Constantine
Sétif
Béjaïa
Alger (Algiers)
Blida
Médéa
Oran
Tlemcen
Sidi bel Abbès
Mostaganem
Biskra
El Oued
Touggourt
Ghardaïa
Laghouat

MOROCCO
Tanger (Tangier)
Tetouan
Oujda
Fès
Meknes
Rabat
Salé
Casablanca
(Dar-el-Beida)
Marrakech
Safi
Essaouira

Gibraltar (U.K.)
Ceuta (Sp.)
Melilla (Sp.)

Mediterranean
Str. of Gibraltar
C. de Gata

CHAD
Ndjamena (Ft. Lamy)

NIGER
Zinder
Maradi
Niamey

NIGERIA
Maiduguri
Kano
Kaduna
Zaria
Katsina
Sokoto
Abuja
FED. CAPITAL TERR.
Jos
Bauchi
Ibadan
LAGOS
Benin City
Port Harcourt
Enugu
Onitsha
Aba
Calabar

BORNO
YOBE
JIGAWA
KATSINA
KANO
BAUCHI
ADAMAWA
TARABA
PLATEAU
KADUNA
NIGER
KWARA
KEBBI
SOKOTO
OYO
OSUN
OGUN
ONDO
EDO
DELTA
RIVERS
IMO
ABIA
AKWA IBOM
CROSS RIVER
ENUGU
ANAMBRA
KOGI
BENUE

CAMEROON
Garoua
Ngaoundéré
C.A.R.

Lake Chad

BENIN
Porto Novo
Cotonou

TOGO
Lomé

GHANA
Accra
Tema
Kumasi
Takoradi
Sekondi
Cape Coast

BURKINA
Ouagadougou

IVORY COAST
Abidjan
Bouaké

MALI
Bobo Dioulasso

Bight of Benin
Gold Coast
C. Three Points

1:15M

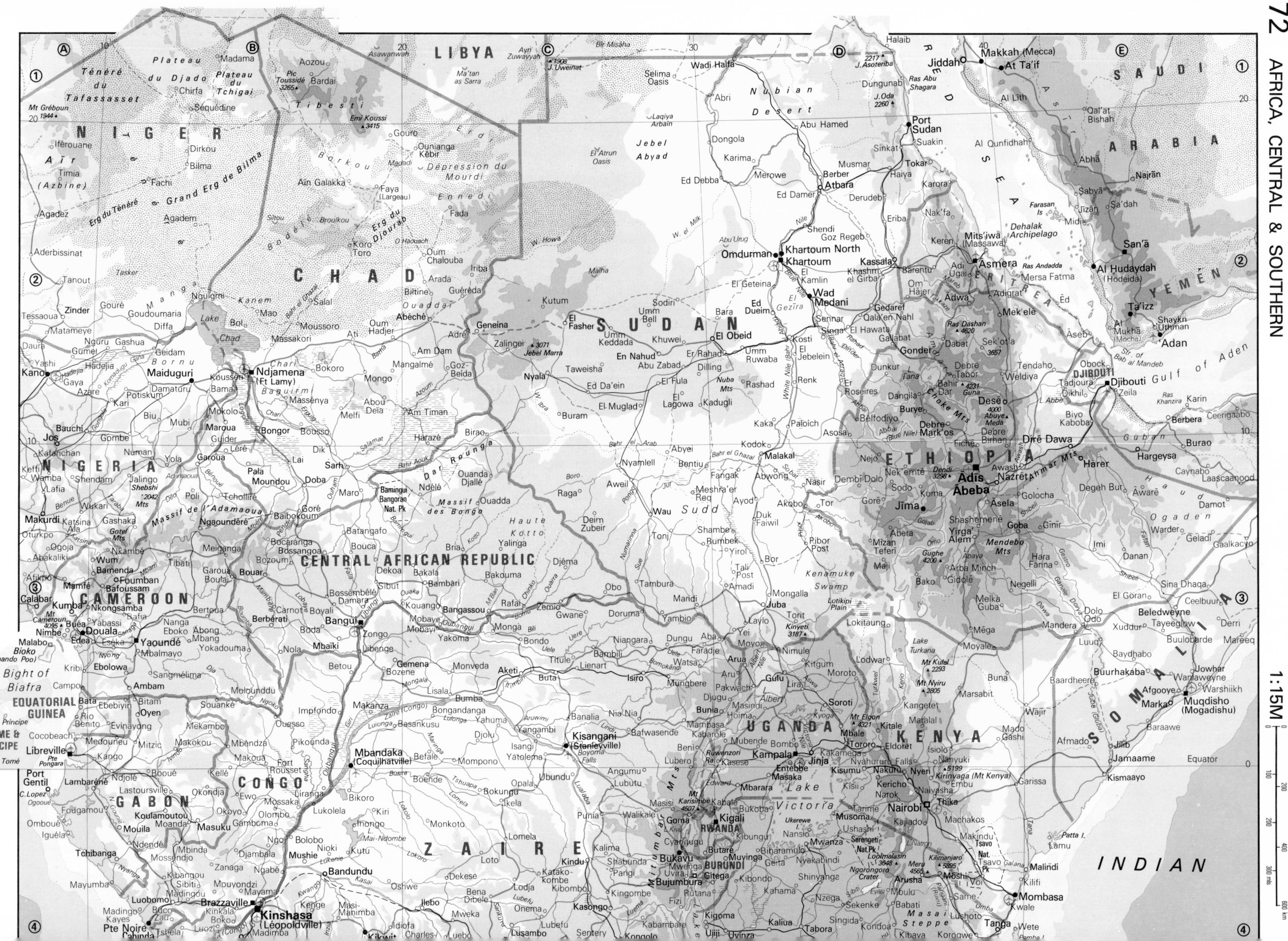
0 200 400 600 km
0 100 200 300 mls
LIBYA
NIGER
CHAD
SUDAN
SAUDI ARABIA
YEMEN
ERITREA
DJIBOUTI
ETHIOPIA
SOMALIA
KENYA
UGANDA
RWANDA
BURUNDI
ZAIRE
CONGO
GABON
CAMEROON
NIGERIA
CENTRAL AFRICAN REPUBLIC
EQUATORIAL GUINEA
S.TOME & PRINCIPE
INDIAN
RED SEA
Gulf of Aden
Nubian Desert
Lake Chad
Lake Victoria
Bight of Biafra
Tibesti
Jebel Abyad
Khartoum
Omdurman
Addis Abeba
Nairobi
Kampala
Kinshasa (Léopoldville)
Brazzaville
Ndjamena (Ft Lamy)
Bangui
Yaoundé
Libreville
Mombasa
Muqdisho (Mogadishu)
Djibouti
Asmera
San'ā
Adan
Jiddah
Makkah (Mecca)
Port Sudan
Kisangani (Stanleyville)
Mbandaka (Coquilhatville)

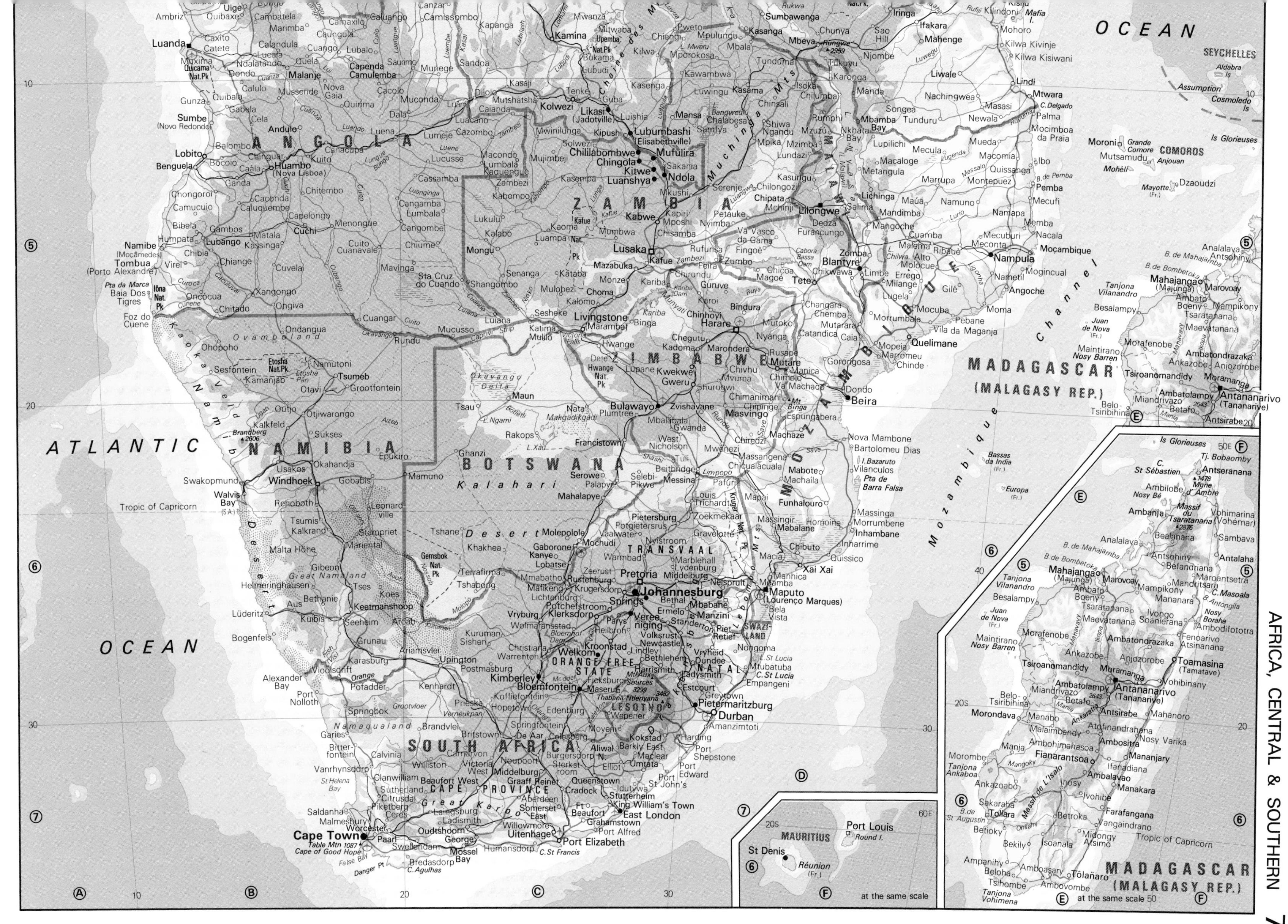
ATLANTIC
OCEAN
OCEAN
Mozambique Channel
ANGOLA
ZAMBIA
MALAWI
ZIMBABWE
MOZAMBIQUE
BOTSWANA
NAMIBIA
SOUTH AFRICA
LESOTHO
SWAZILAND
TRANSVAAL
ORANGE FREE STATE
NATAL
CAPE PROVINCE
MADAGASCAR (MALAGASY REP.)
COMOROS
SEYCHELLES
MAURITIUS
Kalahari
Desert
Namib Desert
Tropic of Capricorn
Luanda
Lobito
Benguela
Huambo (Nova Lisboa)
Lubango
Namibe (Moçâmedes)
Tombua (Porto Alexandre)
Lusaka
Ndola
Kitwe
Livingstone
Harare
Bulawayo
Blantyre
Lilongwe
Beira
Maputo (Lourenço Marques)
Nampula
Quelimane
Windhoek
Walvis Bay
Swakopmund
Lüderitz
Gaborone
Francistown
Pretoria
Johannesburg
Bloemfontein
Kimberley
Durban
Pietermaritzburg
East London
Port Elizabeth
Cape Town
Maseru
Mbabane
Antananarivo (Tananarive)
Mahajanga (Majunga)
Toamasina (Tamatave)
Port Louis
St Denis
Réunion (Fr.)
at the same scale

1:7.5M

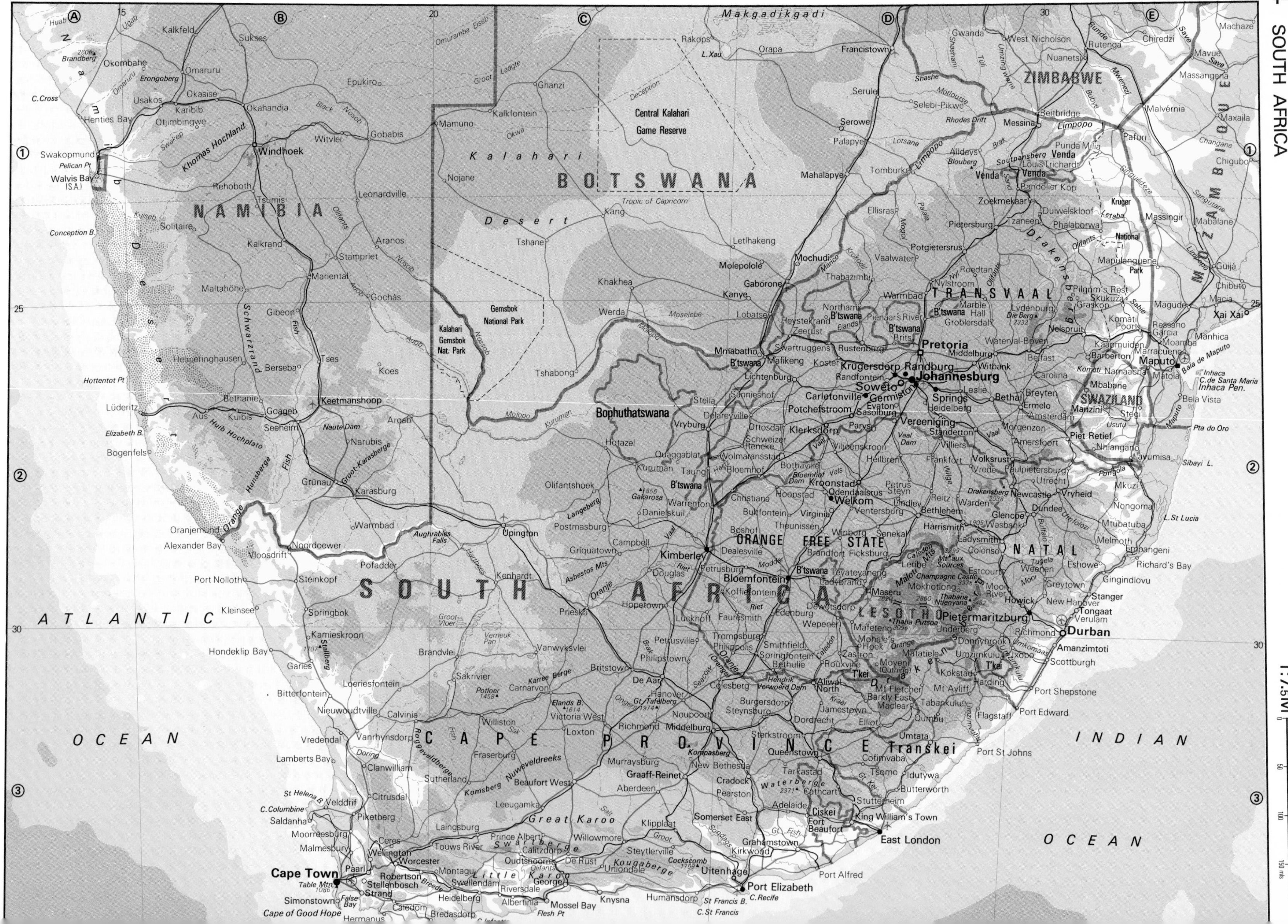

0 100 200 300 km
0 50 100 150 mls
SOUTH AFRICA
BOTSWANA
NAMIBIA
ZIMBABWE
MOZAMBIQUE
LESOTHO
SWAZILAND
TRANSVAAL
ORANGE FREE STATE
NATAL
CAPE PROVINCE
Transkei
Ciskei
Bophuthatswana
Venda
ATLANTIC OCEAN
INDIAN OCEAN
Kalahari Desert
Central Kalahari Game Reserve
Gemsbok National Park
Kalahari Gemsbok Nat. Park
Kruger National Park
Tropic of Capricorn
Drakensberg
Great Karoo
Makgadikgadi
Pretoria
Johannesburg
Soweto
Durban
Pietermaritzburg
Bloemfontein
Kimberley
Port Elizabeth
East London
Cape Town
Maputo
Maseru
Mbabane
Windhoek
Gaborone
Walvis Bay
Lüderitz
Upington
Welkom
Cape of Good Hope
Orange
Limpopo
Vaal

1:7.5M 0 100 200 300 km 0 50 100 150 mls

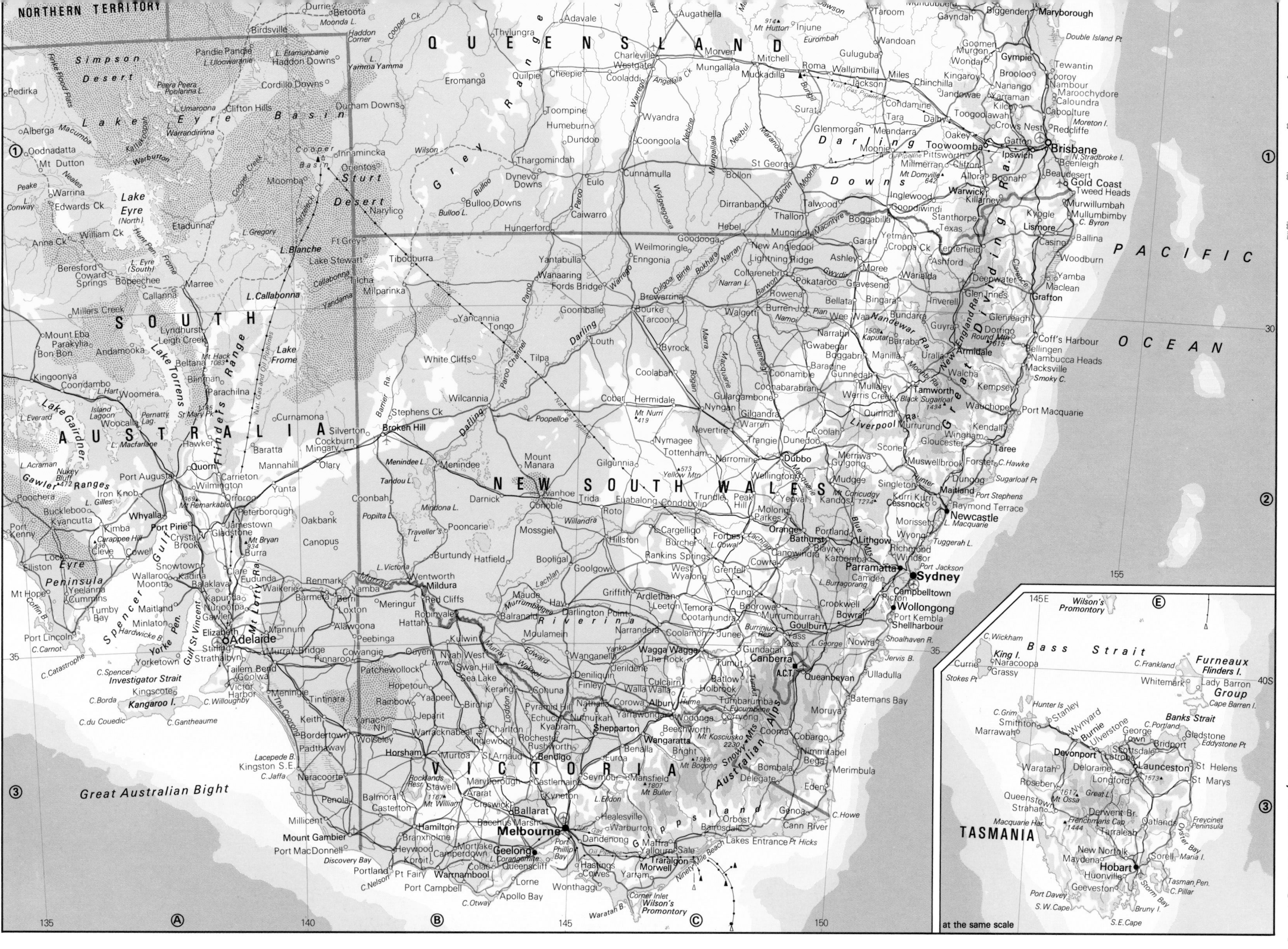
PACIFIC OCEAN
QUEENSLAND
NEW SOUTH WALES
SOUTH AUSTRALIA
VICTORIA
TASMANIA
NORTHERN TERRITORY
Great Australian Bight
Bass Strait
Banks Strait
Furneaux Group
Flinders I.
King I.
Wilson's Promontory
Kangaroo I.
Investigator Strait
Spencer Gulf
Gulf St Vincent
Yorke Pen.
Eyre Peninsula
Gawler Ranges
Lake Eyre (North)
L. Eyre (South)
Lake Torrens
Lake Gairdner
Lake Frome
L. Blanche
L. Callabonna
Flinders Range
Mt Lofty Ra.
Simpson Desert
Sturt Desert
Lake Eyre Basin
Darling Downs
Great Dividing Ra.
Australian Alps
Snowy Mts
New England Ra.
Liverpool Ra.
Blue Mts
Riverina
Gippsland
Darling
Murray
Murrumbidgee
Lachlan
Macquarie
Barwon
Warrego
Paroo
Cooper Creek
Brisbane
Gold Coast
Toowoomba
Ipswich
Maryborough
Gympie
Grafton
Lismore
Coff's Harbour
Port Macquarie
Armidale
Tamworth
Newcastle
Maitland
Cessnock
Sydney
Parramatta
Wollongong
Canberra
Goulburn
Queanbeyan
Bathurst
Orange
Lithgow
Dubbo
Wagga Wagga
Albury
Griffith
Broken Hill
Mildura
Bourke
Cobar
Wangaratta
Shepparton
Bendigo
Ballarat
Geelong
Melbourne
Morwell
Traralgon
Horsham
Hamilton
Warrnambool
Portland
Mount Gambier
Adelaide
Elizabeth
Port Pirie
Port Augusta
Whyalla
Port Lincoln
Devonport
Burnie
Launceston
Hobart
Roma
Charleville
Cunnamulla
St George
Goondiwindi
Moree
Narrabri
Walgett
Wilcannia
Menindee
Renmark
Murray Bridge
Victor Harbor
Kingscote
Woomera
Moomba
Innamincka
Birdsville
Oodnadatta
Mt Kosciusko 2230
Mt Bogong 1986
Mt Buller 1807
Mt Ossa 1617
at the same scale

1:20M

200 400 600 800 km
200 400 mls

Seas & Oceans: INDIAN OCEAN · Java Trench · Timor Sea · Arafura Sea · Banda Sea · Flores Sea · Ceram Sea · Molucca Sea · Makassar Strait · Bismarck Sea · Coral Sea · Gulf of Carpentaria · Great Australian Bight · Bass Strait · Torres Strait

Regions / States: BORNEO · SULAWESI (CELEBES) · INDONESIA · MOLUCCAS · IRIAN JAYA · NEW GUINEA · PAPUA · NEW GUINEA · Bismarck Archipelago · WESTERN AUSTRALIA · NORTHERN TERRITORY · SOUTH AUSTRALIA · QUEENSLAND · NEW SOUTH WALES · VICTORIA · TASMANIA · A.C.T. · Arnham Land · Kimberley Plateau · Nullarbor Plain · Lake Eyre Basin

Western Australia / towns: Perth · Fremantle · Bunbury · Busselton · Augusta · Albany · Manjimup · Katanning · Wagin · Narrogin · Collie · Pinjarra · Northam · Merredin · Southern Cross · Bullfinch · Bencubbin · Moora · Goomalling · Mullewa · Geraldton · Dongara · Northampton · Mt Magnet · Leonora · Laverton · Wiluna · Cue · Meekatharra · Sandstone · Carnarvon · Gascoyne · Murchison · Shark B. · Dirk Hartog I. · Houtman Abrolhos · Kalgoorlie · Coolgardie · Norseman · Esperance · Onslow · Exmouth · Roebourne · Dampier · Karratha · Port Hedland · De Grey · Shay Gap · Marble Bar · Nullagine · Wittenoom · Paraburdoo · Newman · Tom Price · Mt Bruce · Hamersley Ra. · Barlee Ra. · Lyons · Ashburton · Fortescue · Monte Bello Is. · Barrow I. · North West C. · Broome · Lagrange · Derby · Fitzroy Crossing · Hall's Creek · L. Argyle · Mt Ord · King Leopold Ra. · C. Lévêque · Collier B. · King Sound · Wyndham · Cartier I. · Scott Reef · Rowley Shoals · Gibson Desert · Great Sandy Desert · L. Disappointment · L. Carnegie · L. Wells · Great Victoria Desert

Northern Territory: Darwin · Adelaide River · Burrundie · Pine Creek · Katherine · Rum Jungle · Joseph Bonaparte Gulf · Daly · Victoria River Downs · Birdum · Daly Waters · Newcastle Waters · Wave Hill · Powell Creek · Tennant Creek · Barrow Creek · Alice Springs · Mt Zeil 1510 · Macdonnell Ranges · Musgrave Ra. · Mt Woodroffe 1440 · Mt Aloysius 987 · Tomkinson Ra. · Petermann Ra. · Van Diemen G. · Melville I. · Bathurst I. · Cobourg Pen. · Croker I. · Groote Eylandt · Limmen Bight · Sir Edward Pellew Group · Borroloola · Mornington

South Australia: Adelaide · Elizabeth · Oodnadatta · Coober Pedy · Marree · Leigh Ck · L. Eyre · L. Torrens · L. Gairdner · L. Everard · Tarcoola · Ooldea · Penong · Ceduna · Woomera · Andamooka · Marla · Port Augusta · Port Pirie · Whyalla · Port Lincoln · Wallaroo · Peterborough · Quorn · St Mary Pk 1189 · Kingston · Naracoorte · Mount Gambier · Renmark · Spencer Gulf · Eyre Pen. · Gawler Ranges · Kangaroo I. · Investigator Str. · Murray Bridge · Victor Harbour · Simpson Desert · Birdsville · Diamantina

Queensland: Cairns · Mt Bartle Frere 1611 · Innisfail · Ingham · Townsville · Ayr · Bowen · Mackay · Rockhampton · Mount Morgan · Emerald · Clermont · Blackall · Barcaldine · Longreach · Winton · Cloncurry · Mount Isa · Dajarra · Camooweal · Burketown · Normanton · Croydon · Georgetown · Forsayth · Hughenden · Richmond · Charters Towers · Ravenshoe · Cooktown · Laura · Mitchell River · Weipa · Coen · Iron Range · C. York · Somerset · Princess Charlotte B. · Cape York Peninsula · Thursday I. · Gregory Ra. · Selwyn · Flinders · Leichhardt · Barkly Tableland · Windorah · Quilpie · Charleville · Roma · St George · Cunnamulla · Goondiwindi · Warrego · Barcoo · Cooper Ck · Great Dividing Ra.

New South Wales / Victoria: Sydney · Wollongong · Canberra A.C.T. · Newcastle · Bathurst · Orange · Dubbo · Broken Hill · Wilcannia · Menindee · Ivanhoe · Hay · Cobar · Bourke · Walgett · Narrabri · Tamworth · Moree · Cootamundra · Wagga Wagga · Albury · Deniliquin · Balranald · Mildura · Griffith · Cobram · Shepparton · Bendigo · Ballarat · Geelong · Melbourne · Morwell · Sale · Bairnsdale · Horsham · Ararat · Hamilton · Portland · Port Fairy · Warrnambool · Colac · Wonthaggi · Wilson's Prom. · Murray · Darling · Lachlan · Murrumbidgee · Riverina · Australian Alps · Mt Kosciusko 2230

Tasmania: Hobart · Launceston · Devonport · Burnie · Smithton · Queenstown · St Mary's · Geeveston · Mt Ossa · King I. · Furneaux Group · Flinders I. · C. Barren · South West C. · South East C. · C. Grim

Indonesia / New Guinea: Manado · Gorontalo · Palu · Poso · Kendari · Ujung Pandang (Makassar) · Banjarmasin · Samarinda · Balikpapan · Halmahera · Ternate · Morotai · Sorong · Fakfak · Kaimana · Ambon · Buru · Ceram · Obi · Dili · Timor · Kupang · Flores · Sumba · Sumbawa · Lombok · Bali · Denpasar · Mataram · Waingapu · Ende · Ruteng · Jayapura · Wewak · Madang · Lae · Morobe · Mt Hagen · Goroka · Mendi · Mt Wilhelm · Kikori · Gulf of Papua · Port Moresby · Kupiano · Daru · Merauke · Tanahmerah · Pegunungan Maoke · Pt Jaya 5029 · Admiralty Is · Bismarck Archipelago · Kavieng · Manam · Owen Stanley Ra.

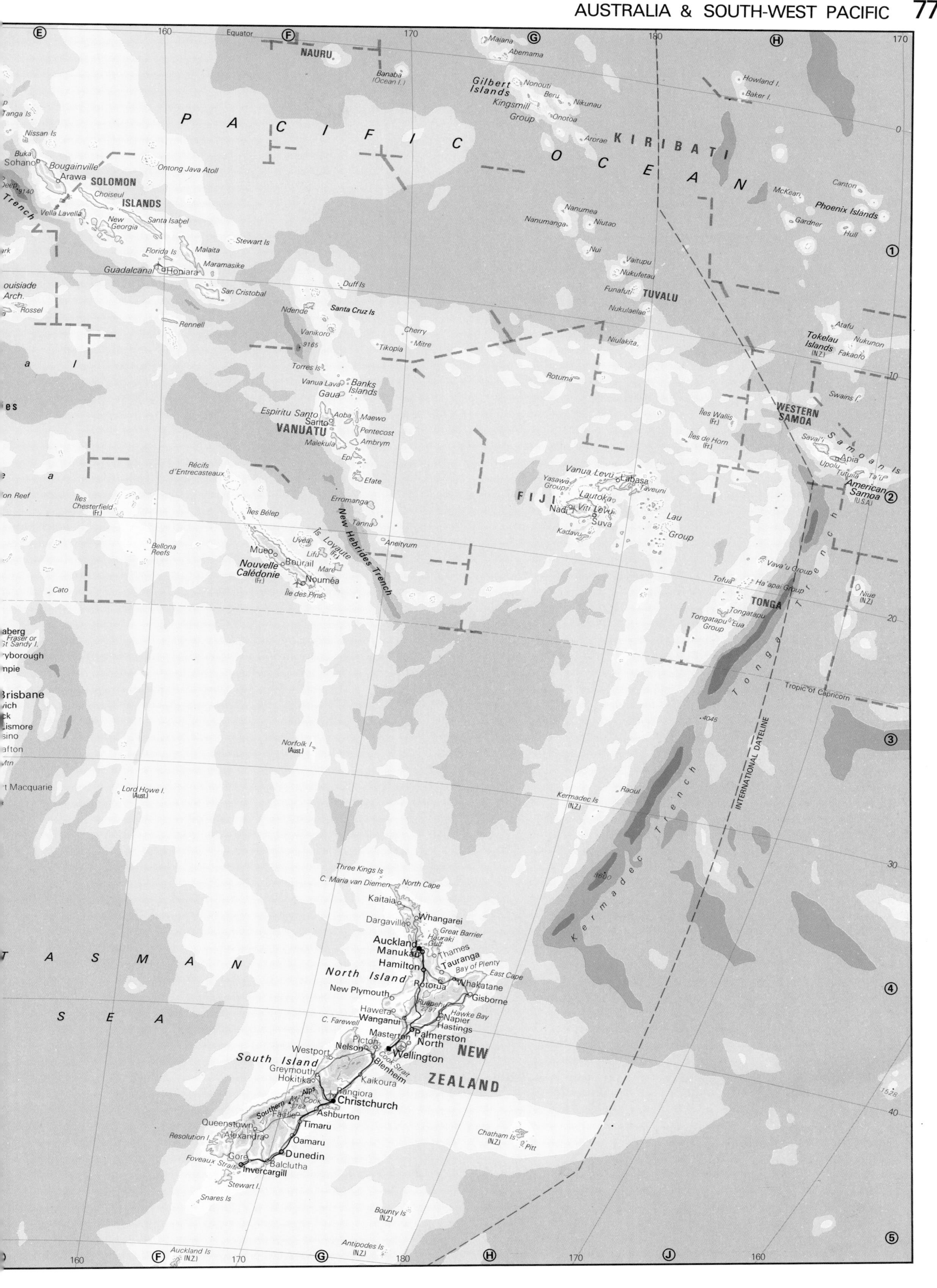
Equator
NAURU
Banaba
(Ocean I.)
Majana
Abemama
Gilbert Islands
Nonouti
Beru
Nikunau
Kingsmill Group
Onotoa
Arorae
KIRIBATI
Howland I.
Baker I.
PACIFIC OCEAN
Tanga Is
Nissan Is
Buka
Sohano
Bougainville
Arawa
Ontong Java Atoll
SOLOMON ISLANDS
Choiseul
Vella Lavella
New Georgia
Santa Isabel
Stewart Is
Florida Is
Malaita
Maramasike
Guadalcanal
Honiara
Louisiade Arch.
Rossel
San Cristobal
Duff Is
Rennell
Ndende
Santa Cruz Is
Vanikoro
9165
Cherry
Mitre
Tikopia
Torres Is
Vanua Lava
Banks Islands
Gaua
Espiritu Santo
Santo
Aoba
Maewo
VANUATU
Pentecost
Malekula
Ambrym
Epi
Efate
Récifs d'Entrecasteaux
Îles Chesterfield
(Fr.)
Îles Bélep
Erromanga
New Hebrides Trench
Tanna
Aneityum
Bellona Reefs
Uvéa
Lifu
Is Loyauté
Maré
Mueo
Bourail
Nouvelle Calédonie
(Fr.)
Nouméa
Île des Pins
Cato
Nanumea
Nanumanga
Niutao
Nui
Vaitupu
Nukufetau
Funafuti
TUVALU
Nukulaelae
Niulakita
Rotuma
McKean
Canton
Phoenix Islands
Gardner
Hull
Atafu
Tokelau Islands
(N.Z.)
Nukunon
Fakaofo
Swains I.
WESTERN SAMOA
Îles Wallis
(Fr.)
Îles de Horn
(Fr.)
Savai'i
Apia
Upolu
Samoan Is
Tutuila
Ta'u
American Samoa
(U.S.A.)
Vanua Levu
Labasa
Taveuni
Yasawa Group
Lautoka
FIJI
Nadi
Viti Levu
Suva
Kadavu
Lau Group
Vava'u Group
Tofua
Ha'apai Group
TONGA
Tongatapu
Tongatapu Group
Eua
Niue
(N.Z.)
Tonga Trench
Tropic of Capricorn
4046
INTERNATIONAL DATELINE
Bundaberg
Fraser or Gt Sandy I.
Maryborough
Gympie
Brisbane
Lismore
Grafton
Port Macquarie
Norfolk I.
(Aust.)
Lord Howe I.
(Aust.)
Kermadec Is
(N.Z.)
Raoul
Kermadec Trench
8600
Three Kings Is
C. Maria van Diemen
North Cape
Kaitaia
Dargaville
Whangarei
Great Barrier
Hauraki Gulf
Auckland
Manukau
Thames
Hamilton
Tauranga
Bay of Plenty
East Cape
North Island
Rotorua
Whakatane
New Plymouth
Gisborne
Ruapehu
2797
Hawera
Wanganui
Napier
Hawke Bay
Hastings
C. Farewell
Masterton
Palmerston North
Westport
Nelson
Picton
Wellington
NEW ZEALAND
Cook Strait
South Island
Greymouth
Blenheim
Hokitika
Kaikoura
Rangiora
Christchurch
Southern Alps
Mt Cook
3764
Fairlie
Ashburton
Queenstown
Alexandra
Timaru
Resolution I.
Oamaru
Dunedin
Gore
Foveaux Strait
Balclutha
Invercargill
Stewart I.
Snares Is
Chatham Is
(N.Z.)
Pitt
Bounty Is
(N.Z.)
Antipodes Is
(N.Z.)
Auckland Is
(N.Z.)
1528
TASMAN SEA
160
170
180
170
160
0
10
20
30
40
E
F
G
H
J
1
2
3
4
5

1:5M

50 100 150 200 km
50 100 mls

A 170 **B** 175

Three Kings Is
C. Maria van Diemen
North Cape
Rangaunu B.
Ninety Mile Beach
Doubtless B.
Ahipara B.
Tauroa Pt
Kaitaia
Bay of Islands
C.Brett
Russell
Kaikohe
Kawakawa
Hokianga Har.
Hikurangi
Whangarei
Dargaville
Bream B.
Hen & Chickens Is
Little Barrier I.
Great Barrier I.
Wellsford
Kaipara Har.
C. Colville
Hauraki Gulf
Manly
Mercury Is
Takapuna
Mercury Bay
Auckland
Coromandel Peninsula
Papatoetoe
Manukau
Papakura
Coromandel Ra.
Pukekohe
Thames
Waiuku
Paeroa
Waihi
Mayor I.
Huntly
Te Aroha
Matakana I.
White I.
C. Runaway
Hicks Bay

NORTH ISLAND

Glen Afton
Morrinsville
Tauranga Har.
Bay of Plenty
Ngaruawahia
Cambridge
Tauranga
Hamilton
Te Puke
Whakatane
Te Awamutu
Putaruru
Rotorua
Kawerau
Opotiki
Kawhia
Otorohanga
Rotorua
Waitomo
Te Kuiti
Mangakino
Murupara
Tolaga Bay
Ohura
Taumarunui
Taupo
Gisborne
N. Taranaki Bight
Mt Ngauruhoe 2291
Poverty Bay
Waitara
New Plymouth
Mt Makorako 1727
Inglewood
Mt Egmont 2518
Stratford
Mt Ruapehu 2797
Mohaka
Wairoa
C. Egmont
Waiouru
Mahia Peninsula
Opunake
Eltham
Ohakune
Eskdale
Hawera
Raetihi
Taradale
Napier
Portland I.
S. Taranaki Bight
Patea
Waiouru
Hastings
Taihape
C. Kidnappers
Havelock North
Wanganui
Marton
Waipukurau
Feilding
Dannevirke
Palmerston N.
Woodville
Foxton
Pahiatua
Levin
C.Turnagain
Herbertville
Otaki
Eketahuna
C. Farewell
Farewell Spit
Collingwood
Golden Bay
Separation Pt
C. Stephens
Masterton
Takaka
Tasman Bay
D'Urville I.
Carterton
Rocks Pt
Paraparaumu
Tasman Mts
Motueka
Porirua
Upper Hutt
The Twins 1826
Nelson
Picton
Tawa
Martinborough
Karamea
Motueka
Richmond
Wellington
Lower Hutt
Mt Ross 983
Karamea Bight
Richmond Ra.
Blenheim
Palliser Bay
Seddonville
Wairau
C. Palliser
Westport
Murchison
Awatere
C. Campbell
C. Foulwind
L. Rotoroa
L. Rotoiti
Kaikoura Ra.
Buller
Reefton
Mt Travers 2338
Tapuaenuku 2885
Runanga
Grey
Spenser Mts
Clarence
Greymouth
Kaikoura
Lewis Pass
Hanmer Springs
Kaikoura Pen.
Hokitika
Brunner
Waiau
Waiau
Ross
L. Sumner
Culverden
Arthurs Pass
Hurunui
Cheviot
Abut Hd
Waimakariri
Waiau
Franz Josef Gl.
Otira
Rangiora
Pegasus Bay
Coleridge
Kaiapoi
SOUTH ISLAND
Methven
Kaiapoi
SOUTHERN ALPS
Hornby
Christchurch
Mt Cook 3764
Lyttelton
Mt Sefton 3157
Lincoln
Banks Peninsula
Hermitage
Akaroa
Jackson Hd
L. Tekapo
Geraldine
L. Ellesmere
Cascade Pt
Ashburton
Canterbury Plains
Pollux 2542
Temuka
Canterbury Bight
Awarua Pt
L. Pukaki
Ohau
Timaru
Mt Aspiring 3027
Wanaka
L. Benmore
Milford Sd
Hawea
Omarama
Milford Sd
Wanaka
L. Aviemore
Mt Pyramid 2326
Arrowtown
Kurow
Waimate
Horner Tunnel
Dunstan Mts
George Sd
Cromwell
Oamaru
Caswell Sd
Queenstown
Clyde
Ranfurly
Secretary I.
Wakatipu
Alexandra
Hampden
Fiordland Nat. Park
Te Anau
Kingston
Roxburgh
Palmerston
Doubtful Sd
L. Te Anau
Breaksea Sd
Manapouri
Lumsden
Heriot
Waikouaiti
Resolution I.
Mt Ward
Manapouri
Riversdale
Port Chalmers
Dusky Sd
Mt Ward 1718
Tapanui
Mosgiel
Otago Peninsula
Ohai
Lawrence
Dunedin
Puysegur Pt
Cameron Mts
Winton
Gore
Milton
L. Hauroko
Te Waewae Bay
Mataura
Balclutha
Edendale
Kaitangata
Riverton
Owaka
Invercargill
Bluff
Foveaux Strait
Solander I.
Codfish I.
Stewart Island
Oban
Paterson Inlet
Mt Allen 730
Shelter Pt
Port Pegasus

TASMAN SEA

COOK STRAIT

PACIFIC OCEAN

35
40
45

1:40M

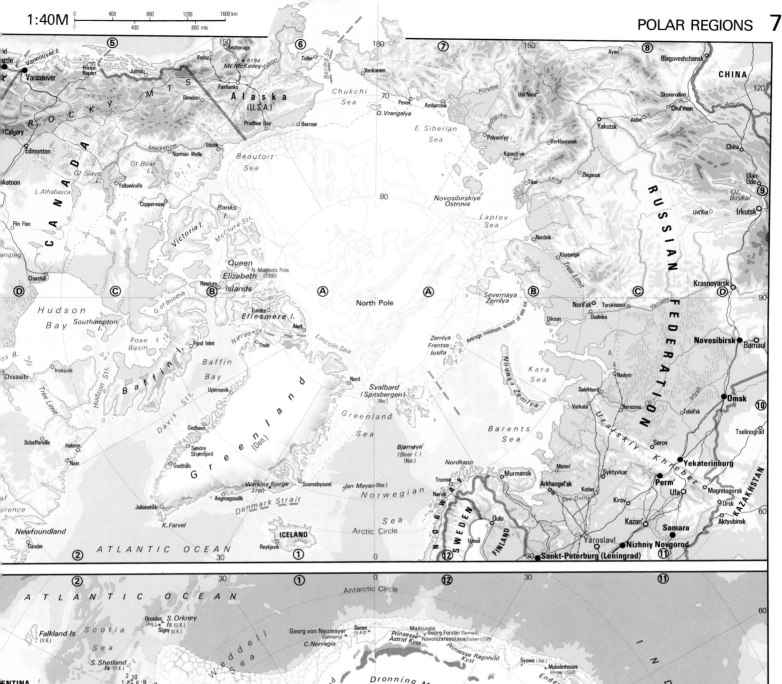

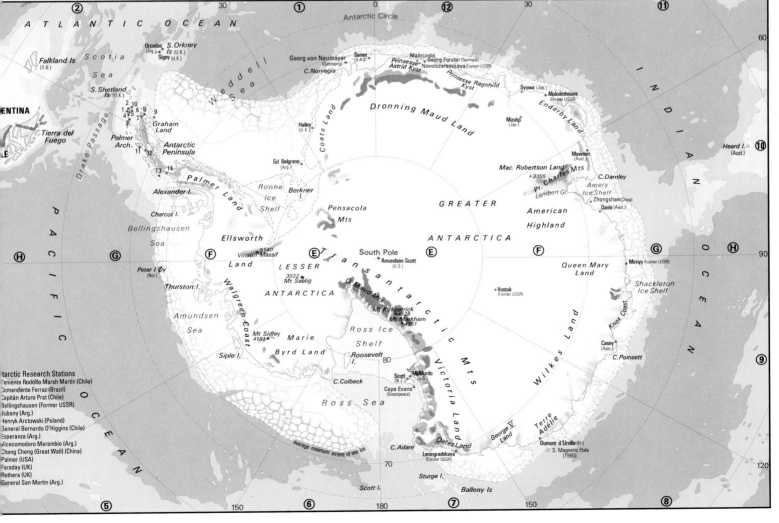

Antarctic Research Stations
Teniente Rodolfo Marsh Martin (Chile)
Comandante Ferraz (Brazil)
Capitán Arturo Prat (Chile)
Bellingshausen (Former USSR)
Jubany (Arg.)
Henryk Arctowski (Poland)
General Bernardo O'Higgins (Chile)
Esperanza (Arg.)
Vicecomodoro Marambio (Arg.)
Chang Cheng (Great Wall) (China)
Palmer (USA)
Faraday (UK)
Rothera (UK)
General San Martin (Arg.)

Abbreviations
Abbreviations used in Reference Map Section

	Full Form	English Form	Language
A			
a.d.	an der	on the	German
Akr.	Akra, Akrotirion	cape	Greek
Appno	Appennino	mountain range	Italian
Arch.	Archipelago	archipelago	English
B			
B.	1. Baai, Bahía, Baia, Baie, Bay, Bucht, Bukhta, Bugt	bay	Dutch, Spanish, Portuguese, French, English, German, Russian, Danish
	2. Ban	village	Indo-Chinese
	3. Barrage	dam	French
Bol.	Bol'sh/aya, -oy, -oye	big	Russian
Br.	1. Branch	branch	English
	2. Bridge, Brücke	bridge	English, German
	3. Burun	cape	Turkish
Brj	Baraj,-i	dam	Turkish
C			
C.	Cabo, Cap, Cape	cape	Spanish, French, English
Can.	Canal	canal	English
Cd	Ciudad	town	Spanish
Chan.	Channel	channel	English
Ck	Creek	creek	English
Cord.	Cordillera	mountain range	Spanish
D			
D.	1. Dağ, Dagh, Daği, Dağlari	mountain, range	Persian, Turkish
	2. Daryācheh	lake	Persian
Dj.	Djebel	mountain	Arabic
E			
E.	East	east	English
Emb.	Embalse	reservoir	Spanish
Escarp.	Escarpment	escarpment	English
Estr.	Estrecho	strait	Spanish
F			
F.	Firth	estuary	Gaelic
Fj.	1. Fjell	mountain	Norwegian
	2. Fjord, Fjorður	fjord	Norwegian, Icelandic
Ft	Fort	fort	English
G			
G.	1. Gebel	mountain	Arabic
	2. Göl, Gölü	lake	Turkish
	3. Golfe, Golfo, Gulf	gulf	French, Italian, Portuguese, Spanish, English
	4. Gora, -gory	mountain, range	Russian
	5. Gunung	mountain	Malay, Indonesian
Gd, Gde	Grand, Grande	grand	English, French
Geb.	Gebirge	mountain range	German
Gl.	Glacier	glacier	French, English
Grl	General	general	Spanish
Gt, Gtr	Great, Groot, -e, Greater	greater	English, Dutch
H			
Har.	Harbour	harbour	English
Hd	Head	head	English
I			
I.	Ile, Ilha, Insel, Isla, Island Isle, Isola, Isole	island	French, Portuguese, German Spanish, English, Italian
In.	1. Indre, Inner	inner	Norwegian, English
	2. Inlet	inlet	English
Is	Iles, Ilhas, Islands, Isles, Islas	islands	French, Portuguese, English, Spanish
Isth.	Isthmus	isthmus	English
J			
J.	Jabal, Jebel, Jibal	mountain	Arabic
K			
K.	1. Kaap, Kap, Kapp	cape	Dutch, German, Norwegian, Swedish
	2. Koh, Kuh, Kuhha	mountain	Persian
	3. Kolpos	gulf	Greek
Kep.	Kepulauan	islands	Indonesian
Khr.	Khrebet	mountain range	Russian
Kör.	Körfez, -i	gulf, bay	Turkish
L			
L.	1. Lac, Lago, Lagoa, Lake, Liman, Limni, Loch, Lough	lake	French, Italian, Spanish, Portuguese, English, Russian, Greek, Gaelic
Lag.	Lagoon, Laguna, -e, Lagôa	lagoon	English, Spanish, French, Portuguese
Ld	Land	land	English
Lit.	Little	little	English
M			
M.	1. Muang	town	Thai
	2. Mys	cape	Russian
m	metre, -s	metre(s)	English, French
Mal.	Mali, -o, -yy	small	Russian
Mf	Massif	mountain group	French
Mgne	Montagne(s)	mountain(s)	French
Mont	Monument	monument	English
Mt	Mont, Mount	mountain	French, English
Mte	Monte	mountain	Italian, Portuguese, Spanish
Mti	Monti	mountain, range	Italian
Mtn	Mountain	mountain	English
Mts	Monts, Mountains Montañas, Montes	mountains	French, English, Spanish, Italian, Portuguese

	Full Form	English Form	Language
N			
N.	1. Neu, Ny	new	German
	2. Nevado	snow capped mtns	Spanish
	3. Noord, Nord, Norte Nørre, North	north	Danish, French, Portuguese, Spanish, Danish, English
Nat.	National	national	English
Nat. Pk	National Park	national park	English
Ndr	Neder, Nieder	lower	Dutch, Swedish, German
N.E.	North East	north east	English
N.M.	National Monument	national monument	English
N.P.	National Park	national park	English
N.W.	North West	north west	English
O			
O.	1. Oost, Ost	east	Dutch, German
	2. Ostrov	island	Russian
Ø	Øy	island	Norwegian
Oz.	Ozero, Ozera	lake(s)	Russian
P			
P.	1. Pass, Passo	pass	English, German, Italian
	2. Pic, Pico, Pizzo	peak	French, Portuguese, Spanish, Italian
	3. Pulau	island	Malay, Indonesian
P.P.	Pulau-pulau	islands	Indonesian
Pass.	Passage	passage	English
Peg.	Pegunungan	mountains	Indonesian
Pen.	Peninsula, Peninsola	peninsula	English, Italian
Pk	1. Park	park	English
	2. Peak, Pik	peak	English, Russian
Plat.	Plateau, Planalto	plateau	English, French, Portuguese
Pov	Poluostrov	peninsula	Russian
Pr.	Prince	prince	English
Pres.	President, Presidente	president	English, Spanish, Portuguese
Promy	Promontory	promontory	English
Pt	Point	point	English
Pta	1. Ponta, Punta	point	Portuguese, Italian, Spanish
	2. Puerta	pass	Spanish
Pte	Pointe	point	French
Pto	Porto, Puerto	port	Spanish
R			
R.	1. Rio, River, Rivière,	river	Portuguese, Spanish, English, French
	2. Ría	river mouth	Spanish
Ra.	Range	range	English
Rap.	Rapids	rapids	English
Res.	Reserve, Reservation	reserve, reservation	English
Resr	Reservoir	reservoir	English
Résr	Réservoir	reservoir	French
S			
S.	1. Salar, Salina	salt marsh	Spanish
	2. San, São	saint	Spanish, Portuguese
	3. See	sea, lake	German
	4. South, Sud	south	English, French
s.	sur	on	French
Sa	Serra, Sierra	mountain range	Portuguese, Spanish
Sd	Sound, Sund	sound	English, German, Swedish
S.E.	South East	south east	English
Sev.	Sever, Severnaya	north	Russian
Sp.	Spitze	peak	German
Spr.	Spring,(s)	spring(s)	English
St	Saint	saint	English
Sta	Santa	saint	Spanish
Sta.	Station	station	English
Ste	Sainte	saint	French
Sto	Santo	saint	Portuguese, Spanish
Str.	Strait	strait	English
S.W.	South West	south west	English
T			
T.	Tall, Tel	hill, mountain	Arabic, Hebrew
Tg	Tanjong, Tandjong	cape	Malay, Indonesian
Tk	Têluk, Têlok	bay	Indonesian
Tr.	Trench, Trough	trench, trough	English
U			
U.	Uad	wadi	Arabic
Ug	Ujung	cape	Malay
Upr	Upper	upper	English
V			
V.	1. Val, Valle	valley	French, Italian, Spanish
	2. Ville	town	French
Va	Villa	town	Spanish
Vdkhr.	Vodokhranilishche	reservoir	Russian
Vol.	Volcán, Volcano	volcano	Spanish, English
Vozv.	Vozvyshennost'	upland	Russian
W			
W.	1. Wadi	wadi	Arabic
	2. Water	water	English
	3. Well	well	English
	4. West	west	English
Y			
Yuzh.	Yuzhnaya, Yuzhno, Yuzhnyy	south	Russian
Z			
Z.	Zaliv	gulf, bay	Russian
Zap.	Zapadnyy, -aya, -o, -oye	western	Russian
Zem.	Zemlya	country, land	Russian

Index

Introduction to the index

In the index, the first number refers to the page, and the following letter and number to the section of the map in which the index entry can be found. For example, 38C2 **Paris** means that Paris can be found on page 38 where column C and row 2 meet.

Abbreviations used in the index

Abbreviation	Meaning	Abbreviation	Meaning	Abbreviation	Meaning	Abbreviation	Meaning
Afghan	Afghanistan	Hung	Hungary	Phil	Philippines	Arch	Archipelago
Alb	Albania	Ind	Indonesia	Pol	Poland	B	Bay
Alg	Algeria	Irish Rep	Irish Republic	Port	Portugal	C	Cape
Ant	Antarctica	N Ire	Ireland, Northern	Rom	Romania	Chan	Channel
Arg	Argentina	Leb	Lebanon	Russian Fed	Russian Federation	Cl	Glacier
Aust	Australia	Lib	Liberia	S Arabia	Saudi Arabia	I(s)	Island(s)
Bang	Bangladesh	Liech	Liechtenstein	Scot	Scotland	Lg	Lagoon
Belg	Belgium	Lux	Luxembourg	Sen	Senegal	L	Lake
Bol	Bolivia	Madag	Madagascar	S Africa	South Africa	Mt(s)	Mountain(s)
Bulg	Bulgaria	Malay	Malaysia	Switz	Switzerland	O	Ocean
Camb	Cambodia	Maur	Mauritania	Tanz	Tanzania	P	Pass
Can	Canada	Mor	Morocco	Thai	Thailand	Pass	Passage
CAR	Central African Republic	Mozam	Mozambique	Turk	Turkey	Pen	Peninsula
Czech	Czechoslovakia	Neth	Netherlands	USA	United States of America	Plat	Plateau
Den	Denmark	NZ	New Zealand	Urug	Uruguay	Pt	Point
Dom Rep	Dominican Republic	Nic	Nicaragua	Ven	Venezuela	Res	Reservoir
El Sal	El Salvador	Nig	Nigeria	Viet	Vietnam	R	River
Eng	England	Nor	Norway	Yugos	Yugoslavia	S	Sea
Eq Guinea	Equatorial Guinea	Pak	Pakistan	Zim	Zimbabwe	Sd	Sound
Eth	Ethiopia	PNG	Papua New Guinea			Str	Strait
Fin	Finland	Par	Paraguay			V	Valley

Bosnia-Herzegovina, Czech Republic, Eritrea, Macedonia and Slovakia
Although the maps in this edition have been revised to take account of the independence of the countries listed above, the index reflects the previous political situation.

A

42B2 **Aachen** Germany
36C1 **Aalst** Belg
32K6 **Äänekoski** Fin
37C1 **Aarau** Switz
37B1 **Aare** *R* Switz
52A3 **Aba** China
71H4 **Aba** Nig
72D3 **Aba** Zaïre
63B2 **Abādān** Iran
63C2 **Abādeh** Iran
70B1 **Abadla** Alg
29C2 **Abaeté** Brazil
29C2 **Abaeté** *R* Brazil
27J4 **Abaetetuba** Brazil
52D1 **Abagnar Qi** China
71H4 **Abaji** Nig
19E3 **Abajo Mts** USA
71H4 **Abakaliki** Nig
49L4 **Abakan** Russian Fed
70C3 **Abala** Niger
70C2 **Abalessa** Alg
26D6 **Abancay** Peru
63C2 **Abarqū** Iran
53E3 **Abashiri** Japan
53E3 **Abashiri-wan** *B* Japan
22C1 **Abasolo** Mexico
51H7 **Abau** PNG
72D3 **Abaya** *L* Eth
72D2 **Abbai** *R* Eth
72E2 **Abbe** *L* Eth
38C1 **Abbeville** France
17D4 **Abbeville** Louisiana, USA
15C2 **Abbeville** S Carolina, USA
37C2 **Abbiategrasso** Italy
18B1 **Abbotsford** Can
12A2 **Abbotsford** USA
60C2 **Abbottabad** Pak
67F4 **Abd-al-Kuri** *I* Yemen
44J5 **Abdulino** Russian Fed
72C2 **Abéché** Chad
71F4 **Abengourou** Ivory Coast
32F7 **Åbenrå** Den
42B1 **Åbenra** Den
71G4 **Abeokuta** Nig
72D3 **Abera** Eth
35C5 **Aberaeron** Wales
20C2 **Aberdeen** California, USA
13D3 **Aberdeen** Maryland, USA
15B2 **Aberdeen** Mississippi, USA
74C3 **Aberdeen** S Africa
34D3 **Aberdeen** Scot
8D2 **Aberdeen** S Dakota, USA
8A2 **Aberdeen** Washington, USA
6J3 **Aberdeen L** Can
34D3 **Aberfeldy** Scot
35D6 **Abergavenny** Wales
35C5 **Aberystwyth** Wales
44L2 **Abez'** Russian Fed
66D3 **Abhā** S Arabia
63B1 **Abhar** Iran
71H4 **Abia** *State* Nigeria
66C4 **Abi Addi** Eth
71F4 **Abidjan** Ivory Coast
17C2 **Abilene** Kansas, USA
16C3 **Abilene** Texas, USA
35E6 **Abingdon** Eng
12C3 **Abingdon** USA
7K4 **Abitibi** *R* Can
7L5 **Abitibi,L** Can
45G7 **Abkhazskaya** Respublika, Georgia
36A2 **Ablis** France
60C2 **Abohar** India
71G4 **Abomey** Benin
72B3 **Abong Mbang** Cam
57E9 **Aborlan** Phil
72B2 **Abou Deïa** Chad
67E1 **Abqaiq** S Arabia
39A2 **Abrantes** Port
72D1 **'Abri** Sudan
76A3 **Abrolhos** *Is* Aust
8B2 **Absaroka Range** *Mts* USA
67F2 **Abū al Abyad** *I* UAE
67E1 **Abū 'Ali** *I* S Arabia
66D3 **Abū Arish** S Arabia
66B3 **Abu Deleiq** Sudan
67F2 **Abū Dhabi** UAE
66B3 **'Abu Dom** *Watercourse* Sudan
65C3 **Ābū el Jurdhān** Jordan
66B3 **Abu Fatima** Sudan
72D2 **Abu Hamed** Sudan
68E7 **Abuja** Nigeria
65A3 **Abu Kebir Hihya** Egypt
26E5 **Abunã** Brazil
26E6 **Abuna** *R* Bol
64D3 **Abú Sukhayr** Iraq
65B3 **Abu Suweir** Egypt
78B2 **Abut Head** *C* NZ
66B1 **Abu Tig** Egypt
72D2 **Abu'Urug** *Well* Sudan
72D2 **Abuye Meda** *Mt* Eth
72C2 **Abu Zabad** Sudan
72D3 **Abwong** Sudan
42B1 **Åby** Den
65C3 **Aby 'Aweigîla** *Well* Egypt
72C3 **Abyei** Sudan
13F2 **Acadia Nat Pk** USA
21B2 **Acambaro** Mexico
23B5 **Acandi** Colombia
21B2 **Acaponeta** Mexico
21B3 **Acapulco** Mexico
27L4 **Acaraú** Brazil
26E2 **Acarigua** Ven
22C2 **Acatlán** Mexico
22C2 **Acatzingo** Mexico
22D2 **Acayucan** Mexico
71F4 **Accra** Ghana
28E2 **Aceguá** Urug
60D4 **Achalpur** India
25B6 **Achao** Chile
53B2 **Acheng** China
37D1 **Achensee** *L* Austria
36E2 **Achern** Germany
33A3 **Achill** *I* Irish Rep
49L4 **Achinsk** Russian Fed
40D3 **Acireale** Italy
11D3 **Ackley** USA
23C2 **Acklins** *I* Caribbean
26D6 **Acobamba** Peru
25B4 **Aconcagua** *Mt* Chile
27L5 **Acopiara** Brazil
68B4 **Açores** *Is* Atlantic O
A Coruna = La Coruña
37C2 **Acqui** Italy
75A2 **Acraman,L** Aust
Acre = 'Akko
26D5 **Acre State,** Brazil
20C3 **Acton** USA
22C1 **Actopan** Mexico
71G4 **Ada** Ghana
17C3 **Ada** USA
39B1 **Adaja** *R* Spain
10C6 **Adak** *I* USA
67G2 **Adam** Oman
72D3 **Adama** Eth
29B3 **Adamantina** Brazil
72B3 **Adamaoua** Region, Nig/Cam
71J4 **Adamawa** State, Nigeria
37D1 **Adamello** *Mt* Italy
14D1 **Adams** USA
62B3 **Adam's Bridge** India/Sri Lanka
3E3 **Adams L** Can
8A2 **Adams,Mt** USA
62C3 **Adam's Peak** *Mt* Sri Lanka
67E4 **'Adan** Yemen
45F8 **Adana** Turk
45E7 **Adapazari** Turk
66B3 **Adarama** Sudan
79F7 **Adare,C** Ant
57D4 **Adaut** Indon
75B1 **Adavale** Aust
37C2 **Adda** *R* Italy
67E1 **Ad Dahna'** Region, S Arabia
66D4 **Ad Dālī'** Yemen
67F1 **Ad Damman** S Arabia
66D3 **Ad Darb** S Arabia
66D2 **Ad Dawādimī** S Arabia
67E1 **Ad Dibdibah** Region, S Arabia
67F3 **Ad Dikākah** Region, S Arabia
67E2 **Ad Dilam** S Arabia
67E2 **Ad Dir'iyah** S Arabia
66C4 **Addis Zeman** Eth
64D3 **Ad Dīwanīyah** Iraq
64D3 **Ad Duwayd** S Arabia
11D3 **Adel** USA
76C4 **Adelaide** Aust
6J3 **Adelaide Pen** Can
51G8 **Adelaide River** Aust
20D3 **Adelanto** USA
Aden = 'Adan
58C4 **Aden,G of** Yemen/Somalia
70C3 **Aderbissinat** Niger
65D2 **Adhra** Syria
51G7 **Adi** *I* Indon
40C1 **Adige** *R* Italy
72D2 **Adigrat** Eth
66C4 **Adi Kale** Eth
60D5 **Adilābād** India
18B2 **Adin** USA
13E2 **Adirondack Mts** USA
72D3 **Ādīs Ābeba** Eth
72D2 **Adi Ugai** Eth
64C2 **Adıyaman** Turk
41F1 **Adjud** Rom
10G1 **Admiralty B** USA
6E4 **Admiralty I** USA
7K2 **Admiralty Inlet** *B* Can
76D1 **Admiralty Is** PNG
57B4 **Adonara** *I* Indon
62B1 **Ādoni** India
38B3 **Adour** *R* France
70A2 **Adrar** Region, Maur
70C2 **Adrar** *Mts* Alg
70A2 **Adrar Soutouf** Region, Mor
72C2 **Adré** Chad
69A2 **Adri** Libya
37E2 **Adria** Italy
12C2 **Adrian** Michigan, USA
16B2 **Adrian** Texas, USA
40C2 **Adriatic S** Italy/Yugos
72D2 **Adwa** Eth
49P3 **Adycha** *R* Russian Fed
71F4 **Adzopé** Ivory Coast
44K2 **Adz'va** *R* Russian Fed
44K2 **Adz'vavom** Russian Fed
41E3 **Aegean** *S* Greece
58E2 **Afghanistan** Republic, Asia
72E3 **Afgooye** Somalia
66D2 **'Afif** S Arabia
71H4 **Afikpo** Nig
32G6 **Åfjord** Nor
71C2 **Aflou** Alg
72E3 **Afmado** Somalia
70A3 **Afollé** Region, Maur
14C1 **Afton** New York, USA
18D2 **Afton** Wyoming, USA
65C2 **Afula** Israel
45E8 **Afyon** Turk
65A3 **Aga** Egypt
72B2 **Agadem** Niger
70C3 **Agadez** Niger
70B1 **Agadir** Mor
60D4 **Agar** India
61D3 **Agartala** India
18B1 **Agassiz** Can
10A6 **Agattu** *I* USA
10A5 **Agattu Str** USA
71H4 **Agbor** Nig
71F4 **Agboville** Ivory Coast
64E1 **Agdam** Azerbaijan
54C3 **Agematsu** Japan
38C3 **Agen** France
63B2 **Agha Jārī** Iran
45G8 **Ağn** Turk
37D2 **Agno** *R* Italy
66C3 **Agordat** Eth
37E1 **Agordo** Italy
71G4 **Agou,Mt** Togo
38C3 **Agout** *R* France
60D3 **Āgra** India
64D2 **Ağri** Turk
40D2 **Agri** *R* Italy
40C3 **Agrigento** Italy
41E3 **Agrínion** Greece
28A3 **Agrio** *R* Chile
40C2 **Agropoli** Italy
44J4 **Agryz** Russian Fed
7N3 **Agto** Greenland
29B3 **Agua Clara** Brazil
28B4 **Aguada de Guerra** Arg
23D3 **Aguadilla** Puerto Rico

Aguado Cicilio
Al Qardāhah

28B4 **Aguado Cicilio** Arg
22B1 **Aguanava** *R* Mexico
5J3 **Aguanish** Can
5J3 **Aguanus** *R* Can
28D1 **Aguapey** *R* Arg
21B1 **Agua Prieta** Mexico
29A3 **Aguaray Guazu** Par
21B2 **Aguascalientes** Mexico
22B1 **Aguascalientes** State, Mexico
29D2 **Aguas Formosas** Brazil
25G1 **Agua Vermelha, Barragem** *Res* Brazil
39A1 **Agueda** Port
70C3 **Aguelhok** Mali
70A2 **Agüenit** *Well* Mor
39B2 **Aguilas** Spain
22B2 **Aguililla** Mexico
xxviiiC7 **Agulhas Basin** Indian O
73C7 **Agulhas,C** S Africa
xxviiiC6 **Agulhas Plat** Indian O
57G9 **Agusan** *R* Phil
Ahaggar = Hoggar
45H8 **Ahar** Iran
78B1 **Ahipara B** NZ
36D1 **Ahlen** Germany
60C4 **Ahmadābād** India
62A1 **Ahmadnagar** India
72E3 **Ahmar** *Mts* Eth
15D1 **Ahoskie** USA
36D1 **Ahr** *R* Germany
36D1 **Ahrgebirge** Region, Germany
22B1 **Ahuacatlán** Mexico
22B1 **Ahualulco** Mexico
32G7 **Åhus** Sweden
63C1 **Āhuvān** Iran
63B2 **Ahvāz** Iran
23A4 **Aiajuela** Costa Rica
37B1 **Aigle** Switz
28E2 **Aiguá** Urug
37B2 **Aiguille d'Arves** *Mt* France
37B2 **Aiguille de la Grand Sassière** *Mt* France
53B1 **Aihui** China
54C3 **Aikawa** Japan
15C2 **Aiken** USA
52A5 **Ailao Shan** *Upland* China
28B1 **Aimogasta** Arg
29D2 **Aimorés** Brazil
37A1 **Ain** *R* France
71D1 **Aïn Beïda** Alg
71B2 **Ain Beni Mathar** Mor
69B2 **Ain Dalla** *Well* Egypt
39C2 **Aïn el Hadjel** Alg
72B2 **Aïn Galakka** Chad
71C1 **Aïn Oussera** Alg
71B2 **Aïn Sefra** Alg
64B4 **'Ain Sukhna** Egypt
11C3 **Ainsworth** USA
71B1 **Aïn Temouchent** Alg
54B4 **Aioi** Japan
70B2 **Aioun Abd el Malek** *Well* Maur
70B3 **Aïoun El Atrouss** Maur
26E7 **Aiquile** Bol
70C3 **Aïr** *Desert Region* Niger
3F3 **Airdrie** Can
36B1 **Aire** France
35E5 **Aire** *R* Eng
36C2 **Aire** *R* France
7L3 **Airforce I** Can
37C1 **Airolo** Switz
6E3 **Aishihik** Can
10L3 **Aishihik L** Can
36B2 **Aisne** Department, France
38C2 **Aisne** *R* France
76D1 **Aitape** PNG
43F1 **Aiviekste** *R* Latvia
52B2 **Aixa Zuogi** China
38D3 **Aix-en-Provence** France
37A2 **Aix-les-Bains** France
61C3 **Aiyar Res** India
41E3 **Aíyion** Greece
41E3 **Aíyna** *I* Greece
61D3 **Āīzawl** India
73B6 **Aizeb** *R* Namibia
53E4 **Aizu-Wakamatsu** Japan
40B2 **Ajaccio** Corse
22C2 **Ajalpan** Mexico
69B1 **Ajdabiyak** Libya
37E2 **Ajdovščina** Slovenia, Yugos
53E3 **Ajigasawa** Japan
65C2 **Ajlūn** Jordan
67G1 **Ajman** UAE
60C3 **Ajmer** India
19D4 **Ajo** USA
41F2 **Ajtos** Bulg
22B2 **Ajuchitan** Mexico
41F3 **Ak** *R* Turk
54D2 **Akabira** Japan
54C3 **Akaishi-sanchi** *Mts* Japan
62B1 **Akalkot** India
65B1 **Akanthou** Cyprus
78B2 **Akaroa** NZ
66B2 **Akasha** Sudan
54B4 **Akashi** Japan
71C1 **Akbou** Alg
45K5 **Akbulak** Russian Fed
64C2 **Akçakale** Turk
70A2 **Akchar** *Watercourse* Maur
41F3 **Ak Dağ** *Mt* Turk
57C2 **Akelamo** Indon
72C3 **Aketi** Zaïre
64D1 **Akhalkalaki** Georgia
64D1 **Akhalsikhe** Georgia
41E3 **Akharnái** Greece
10H4 **Akhiok** USA
64A2 **Akhisar** Turk
43F1 **Akhiste** Latvia
69C2 **Akhmîm** Egypt
45H6 **Akhtubinsk** Russian Fed
45E5 **Akhtyrka** Ukraine
54B4 **Aki** Japan
7K4 **Akimiski I** Can
53E4 **Akita** Japan
70A3 **Akjoujt** Maur
65C2 **'Akko** Israel
10L2 **Aklavik** Can
70B3 **Aklé Aouana** *Desert Region* Maur
72D3 **Akobo** Sudan
72D3 **Akobo** *R* Sudan
60B1 **Akoha** Afghan
60D4 **Akola** India
71G4 **Akosombo Dam** Ghana
60D4 **Akot** India
7M3 **Akpatok I** Can
41E3 **Ákra Kafirévs** *C* Greece
41E4 **Ákra Líthinon** *C* Greece
41E3 **Ákra Maléa** *C* Greece
32A2 **Akranes** Iceland
41F3 **Ákra Sídheros** *C* Greece
41E3 **Ákra Spátha** *C* Greece
41E3 **Ákra Taínaron** *C* Greece
9E2 **Akron** USA
65B1 **Akrotiri B** Cyprus
60D1 **Aksai Chin** *Mts* China
45E8 **Aksaray** Turk
45J5 **Aksay** Kazakhstan
60D1 **Aksayquin Hu** *L* China
64B2 **Akşehir** Turk
64B2 **Akseki** Turk
49N4 **Aksenovo Zilovskoye** Russian Fed
50E1 **Aksha** Russian Fed
59G1 **Aksu** China
66C4 **Aksum** Eth
48J5 **Aktogay** Kazakhstan
45K6 **Aktumsyk** Kazakhstan
45K5 **Aktyubinsk** Kazakhstan
4F1 **Akulivik** Can
71H4 **Akure** Nig
32B1 **Akureyri** Iceland
10E5 **Akutan** USA
10E5 **Akutan** *I* USA
10E5 **Akutan Pass** USA
71H5 **Akwa Ibom** *State* Nigeria
48K5 **Akzhal** Kazakhstan
9E3 **Alabama** State, USA
15B2 **Alabama** *R* USA
15B2 **Alabaster** USA
64C2 **Ala Dağlari** *Mts* Turk
45G7 **Alagir** Russian Fed
37B2 **Alagna** Italy
27L5 **Alagoas** State, Brazil
27L6 **Alagoinhas** Brazil
39B1 **Alagón** Spain
64E4 **Al Ahmadi** Kuwait
21D3 **Alajuela** Costa Rica
10F3 **Alakanuk** USA
48K5 **Alakol, Ozero** *L* Russian Fed/Kazakhstan
32L5 **Alakurtti** Russian Fed
64E3 **Al Amārah** Iraq
19B3 **Alameda** USA
22C1 **Alamo** Mexico
19C3 **Alamo** USA
16A3 **Alamogordo** USA
16C4 **Alamo Heights** USA
16A2 **Alamosa** USA
32H6 **Åland** *I* Fin
45E8 **Alanya** Turk
15C2 **Alapaha** *R* USA
44L4 **Alapayevsk** Russian Fed
56A2 **Alas** *R* Indon
64A2 **Alaşehir** Turk
50D3 **Ala Shan** *Mts* China
6C3 **Alaska** State, USA
6D4 **Alaska,G of** USA
10G4 **Alaska Pen** USA
6C3 **Alaska Range** *Mts* USA
40B2 **Alassio** Italy
37C3 **Alássio** Region, Italy
10H2 **Alatna** *R* USA
44H5 **Alatyr'** Russian Fed
75B2 **Alawoona** Aust
67G2 **Al'Ayn** UAE
59F2 **Alayskiy Khrebet** *Mts* Tajikistan
49R3 **Alazeya** *R* Russian Fed
71E2 **Al'Azīzīyah** Libya
38D3 **Alba** Italy
64C2 **Al Bāb** Syria
39B2 **Albacete** Spain
39A1 **Alba de Tormes** Spain
64D2 **Al Badi** Iraq
41E1 **Alba Iulia** Rom
41D2 **Albania** Republic, Europe
76A4 **Albany** Aust
15C2 **Albany** Georgia, USA
12B3 **Albany** Kentucky, USA
13E2 **Albany** New York, USA
8A2 **Albany** Oregon, USA
4E3 **Albany** *R* Can
66C4 **Albara** *R* Sudan
28B2 **Albardón** Arg
67G2 **Al Batinah** Region, Oman
51H8 **Albatross B** Aust
69B1 **Al Bayḍā** Libya
67E4 **Al Baydā'** Yemen
65C1 **Al Baylūlīyah** Syria
15C1 **Albemarle** USA
15D1 **Albemarle Sd** USA
37C2 **Albenga** Region, Italy
39B1 **Alberche** *R* Spain
75A1 **Alberga** Aust
36B1 **Albert** France
6G4 **Alberta** Province, Can
51H7 **Albert Edward** *Mt* PNG
74C3 **Albertinia** S Africa
72D3 **Albert,L** Uganda/Zaïre
9D2 **Albert Lea** USA
72D3 **Albert Nile** *R* Uganda
18D1 **Alberton** USA
5J4 **Alberton** Can
38D2 **Albertville** France
38C3 **Albi** France
17D1 **Albia** USA
27H2 **Albina** Surinam
12C2 **Albion** Michigan, USA
11C3 **Albion** Nebraska, USA
13D2 **Albion** New York, USA
64C4 **Al Bi'r** S Arabia
66D3 **Al Birk** S Arabia
67E2 **Al Biyadh** Region, S Arabia
39B2 **Alborán** *I* Spain
32G7 **Ålborg** Den
36E2 **Albstadt-Ebingen** Germany
64D3 **Al Bū Kamāl** Syria
37C1 **Albula** *R* Switz
8C3 **Albuquerque** USA
67G2 **Al Buraymi** Oman
69A1 **Al Burayqah**
69B1 **Al Burdī** Libya
76D4 **Albury** Aust
64E3 **Al Buşayyah** Iraq
34G3 **Albuskjell** *Oilfield* N Sea
67F3 **Al Buzūn** Yemen
39B1 **Alcalá de Henares** Spain
40C3 **Alcamo** Italy
39B1 **Alcaniz** Spain
27K4 **Alcântara** Brazil
39B2 **Alcaraz** Spain
39B2 **Alcázar de San Juan** Spain
39B2 **Alcira** Spain
29E2 **Alcobaça** Brazil
39B1 **Alcolea de Pinar** Spain
39B2 **Alcoy** Spain
39C2 **Alcudia** Spain
68J8 **Aldabra** *Is* Indian O
16A4 **Aldama** Mexico
22C1 **Aldama** Mexico
49O4 **Aldan** Russian Fed
49P4 **Aldan** *R* Russian Fed
49O4 **Aldanskoye Nagor'ye** *Upland* Russian Fed
35F5 **Aldeburgh** Eng
38B2 **Alderney** *I* UK
35E6 **Aldershot** Eng
70A3 **Aleg** Maur
29A2 **Alegre** *R* Brazil
25E3 **Alegrete** Brazil
28C2 **Alejandro Roca** Arg
49Q4 **Aleksandrovsk Sakhalinskiy** Russian Fed
48J4 **Alekseyevka** Kazakhstan
44F5 **Aleksin** Russian Fed
42D1 **Ålem** Sweden
29D3 **Além Paraiba** Brazil
38C2 **Alençon** France
20E5 **Alenuihaha Chan** Hawaiian Is
Aleppo = Ḥalab
7M1 **Alert** Can
38C3 **Alès** France
40B2 **Alessandria** Italy
48B3 **Ålesund** Nor
10B5 **Aleutian Is** USA
10G4 **Aleutian Range** *Mts* USA
xxixL2 **Aleutian Trench** Pacific O
6E4 **Alexander Arch** USA
74B2 **Alexander Bay** S Africa
15B2 **Alexander City** USA
79G3 **Alexander I** Ant
78A3 **Alexandra** NZ
25J8 **Alexandra,C** South Georgia
7L2 **Alexandra Fjord** Can
69B1 **Alexandria** Egypt
9D3 **Alexandria** Louisiana, USA
9D2 **Alexandria** Minnesota, USA
9F3 **Alexandria** Virginia, USA
41F2 **Alexandroúpolis** Greece
5K3 **Alexis** *R* Can
3D3 **Alexis Creek** Can
65C2 **Aley** Leb
48K4 **Aleysk** Russian Fed
64D3 **Al Fallūjah** Iraq
67E4 **Al Fardah** Yemen
39B1 **Alfaro** Spain
41F2 **Alfatar** Bulg
64E3 **Al Fāw** Iraq
36E1 **Alfeld** Germany
29C3 **Alfensas** Brazil
41E3 **Alfiós** *R* Greece
37D2 **Alfonsine** Italy
29D3 **Alfonzo Cláudio** Brazil
29D3 **Alfredo Chaves** Brazil
67E1 **Al Furūthi** S Arabia
45K6 **Alga** Kazakhstan
28A1 **Algarrobal** Chile
28B3 **Algarrobo del Águila** Arg
39A2 **Algeciras** Spain
71C1 **Alger** Alg
70B2 **Algeria** Republic, Africa
67F3 **Al Ghaydah** Yemen
40B2 **Alghero** Sardegna
Algiers = Alger
11D3 **Algona** USA
13D1 **Algonquin Park** Can
4F4 **Algonquin Prov Park** Can
28D2 **Algorta** Urug
67G2 **Al Hadd** Oman
64D3 **Al Hadithah** Iraq
64C3 **Al Haḍithah** S Arabia
64D2 **Al Haḍr** Iraq
65D1 **Al Haffah** Syria
67G2 **Al Hajar al Gharbī** *Mts* Oman
67G2 **Al Hajar ash Sharqī** *Mts* Oman
64C3 **Al Hamad** *Desert Region* Jordan/S Arabia
64E4 **Al Haniyah** *Desert Region* Iraq
67E2 **Al Harīq** S Arabia
64C3 **Al Harrah** *Desert Region* S Arabia
69A2 **Al Harūj al Aswad** *Upland* Libya
67E1 **Al Hasa** Region, S Arabia
64D2 **Al Hasakah** Syria
64C4 **Al Hawjā'** S Arabia
64E3 **Al Hayy** Iraq
67F2 **Al Hibāk** Region, S Arabia
65D2 **Al Hījānah** Syria
64D3 **Al Hillah** Iraq
67E2 **Al Hillah** S Arabia
71B1 **Al Hoceima** Mor
66D4 **Al Hudaydah** Yemen
67E1 **Al Hufūf** S Arabia
67F2 **Al Humrah** Region, UAE
67G2 **Al Huwatsah** Oman
63B1 **Aliābad** Iran
63D3 **Aliabad** Iran
41E2 **Aliákmon** *R* Greece
64E3 **Alī al Gharbī** Iraq
62A1 **Alībāg** India
71B3 **Alibori** *R* Benin
39B2 **Alicante** Spain
8D4 **Alice** USA
76C3 **Alice Springs** Aust
40C3 **Alicudi** *I* Italy
60D3 **Aligarh** India
63B2 **Aligūdarz** Iran
60B2 **Ali-Khel** Afghan
41F3 **Alimniá** *I* Greece
61C2 **Alīpur Duār** India
12C2 **Aliquippa** USA
67E4 **Al'Irqah** Yemen
64C3 **Al'Īsawiyah** S Arabia
74D3 **Aliwal North** S Africa
69B2 **Al Jaghbūb** Libya
64D3 **Al Jālamīd** S Arabia
69B2 **Al Jawf** Libya
64C4 **Al Jawf** S Arabia
64C2 **Al Jazīrah** Syria
64D2 **Al Jazīrah** *Desert* Region Syria/Iraq
39A2 **Aljezur** Port
67E1 **Al Jubayl** S Arabia
65D4 **Al Kabid** *Desert* Jordan
66D1 **Al Kahfah** S Arabia
67G2 **Al Kāmil** Oman
64D2 **Al Khābūr** *R* Syria
67G2 **Al Khābūrah** Oman
64D3 **Al Khālis** Iraq
66D2 **Al Khamāsīn** S Arabia
67G1 **Al Khasab** Oman
67F1 **Al Khawr** Qatar
69A1 **Al Khums** Libya
67F2 **Al Kidan** Region, S Arabia
65D2 **Al Kiswah** Syria
42A2 **Alkmaar** Neth
69B2 **Al Kufrah Oasis** Libya
64E3 **Al Kūt** Iraq
64C2 **Al Lādhiqīyah** Syria
61B2 **Allahābād** India
65D2 **Al Lajāh** *Mt* Syria
10H2 **Allakaket** USA
55B2 **Allanmyo** Burma
66B2 **'Allaqi** *Watercourse* Egypt
15C2 **Allatoona L** USA
74D1 **Alldays** S Africa
13D2 **Allegheny** *R* USA
9F3 **Allegheny Mts** USA
14A2 **Allegheny Res** USA
15C2 **Allendale** USA
78A3 **Allen,Mt** NZ
13D2 **Allentown** USA
62B3 **Alleppey** India
38C2 **Aller** *R* France
37D1 **Allgäu** *Mts* Germany
11B3 **Alliance** USA
66D2 **Al Līth** S Arabia
67F2 **Al Liwā** Region, UAE
75D1 **Allora** Aust
37B2 **Allos** France
12C2 **Alma** Michigan, USA
16C1 **Alma** Nebraska, USA
59F1 **Alma Ata** Kazakhstan
39A2 **Almada** Port
Al Madīnah = Medina S Arabia
51H5 **Almagan** I Pacific O
67F3 **Al Mahrah** Region, Yemen
67E1 **Al Majma'ah** S Arabia
67F1 **Al Manāmah** Bahrain
64D3 **Al Ma'nīyah** Iraq
19B2 **Almanor,L** USA
39B2 **Almansa** Spain
3C2 **Alma Peak** *Mt* Can
67F2 **Al Māriyyah** UAE
5G4 **Alma** Can
69B1 **Al Marj** Libya
39B1 **Almazán** Spain
36E1 **Alme** *R* Germany
29D2 **Almenara** Brazil
39B2 **Almeria** Spain
29C2 **Almes** *R* Brazil
44J5 **Al'met'yevsk** Russian Fed
42C1 **Älmhult** Sweden
66D1 **Al Midhnab** S Arabia
64E3 **Al Miqdādīyah** Iraq
79G3 **Almirante Brown** *Base* Ant
28A1 **Almirante Latorre** Chile
41E3 **Almirós** Greece
67E1 **Al Mish'āb** A Arabia
39A2 **Almodôvar** Port
60D3 **Almora** India
67E1 **Al Mubarraz** S Arabia
64C4 **Al Mudawwara** Jordan
67G2 **Al Mudaybi** Oman
67F1 **Al Muharraq** Bahrain
67E4 **Al Mukallā** Yemen
66D4 **Al Mukhā** Yemen
64D3 **Al Musayyib** Iraq
66C1 **Al Muwaylih** S Arabia
34C3 **Alness** Scot
64E3 **Al Nu'mānīyah** Iraq
34E4 **Alnwick** Eng
4B3 **Alonsa** Can
57B4 **Alor** *I* Indon
55C4 **Alor Setar** Malay
Alost = Aalst
76E2 **Alotau** PNG
76B3 **Aloysius,Mt** Aust
28C3 **Alpachiri** Arg
37D2 **Alpe di Succiso** *Mt* Italy
12C1 **Alpena** USA
37B1 **Alpes du Valais** *Mts* Switz
37B2 **Alpes Maritimes** *Mts* France
37E1 **Alpi Carniche** *Mts* Italy
40C1 **Alpi Dolomitiche** *Mts* Italy
37B2 **Alpi Graie** *Mts* Italy
19E4 **Alpine** Arizona, USA
16B3 **Alpine** Texas, USA
18D2 **Alpine** Wyoming, USA
37C1 **Alpi Orobie** *Mts* Italy
37B2 **Alpi Penine** *Mts* Italy
37C1 **Alpi Retiche** *Mts* Switz
37D1 **Alpi Venoste** *Mts* Italy
40B1 **Alps** *Mts* Europe
69A1 **Al Qaddāhiyah** Libya
65D1 **Al Qadmūs** Syria
64D3 **Al Qā'im** Iraq
64C4 **Al Qalībah** S Arabia
64D2 **Al Qāmishlī** Syria
65D1 **Al Qardāhah** Syria

Al Qaryah Ash Sharqiyah

Arad

69A1 **Al Qaryah Ash Sharqiyah** Libya
64C3 **Al Qaryatayn** Syria
66D1 **Al Qasim** Region, S Arabia
67E1 **Al Qātif** S Arabia
69A2 **Al Qatrūn** Libya
67E1 **Al Qayşāmah** S Arabia
65D2 **Al Quatayfah** Syria
39A2 **Alquera** *Res* Port/Spain
64C3 **Al Qunaytirah** Syria
66D3 **Al Qunfidhah** S Arabia
64E3 **Al Qurnah** Iraq
65D1 **Al Quşayr** Syria
64C3 **Al Qutayfah** Syria
67E2 **Al Quwayīyah** S Arabia
42B1 **Als** *I* Den
38D2 **Alsace** Region, France
42B2 **Alsfeld** Germany
34D4 **Alston** Eng
32J5 **Alta** Nor
25D4 **Alta Gracia** Arg
23D5 **Altagracia de Orituco** Ven
50B2 **Altai** *Mts* Mongolia
15C2 **Altamaha** *R* USA
27H4 **Altamira** Brazil
22C1 **Altamira** Mexico
40D2 **Altamura** Italy
50D1 **Altanbulag** Mongolia
49M5 **Altanbulag** Russian Fed
51H7 **Altape** PNG
21B2 **Altata** Mexico
48K5 **Altay** China
49L5 **Altay** Mongolia
48K4 **Altay** *Mts* Russian Fed
37C1 **Altdorf** Switz
36D1 **Altenkirchen** Germany
28B3 **Altiplanicie del Payún** *Plat* Arg
37B1 **Altkirch** France
29B2 **Alto Araguaia** Brazil
73D5 **Alto Molócue** Mozam
12A3 **Alton** USA
13D2 **Altoona** USA
28B2 **Alto Pencoso** *Mts* Arg
29B2 **Alto Sucuriú** Brazil
22C2 **Altotonga** Mexico
22B2 **Altoyac de Alvarez** Mexico
59G2 **Altun Shan** *Mts* China
18B2 **Alturas** USA
16C3 **Altus** USA
67F2 **Al'Ubaylah** S Arabia
66C1 **Al'Ulā** S Arabia
28A3 **Aluminé** Arg
64C4 **Al Urayq** *Desert Region* S Arabia
67F2 **Al'Uruq al Mu'taridah** Region, S Arabia
16C2 **Alva** USA
22C2 **Alvarado** Mexico
17C3 **Alvarado** USA
32G6 **Älvdalen** Sweden
28D1 **Alvear** Arg
17C4 **Alvin** USA
32J5 **Alvsbyn** Sweden
69A2 **Al Wāha** Libya
66C1 **Al Wajh** S Arabia
60D3 **Alwar** India
64D3 **Al Widyān** *Desert Region* Iraq/S Arabia
52A2 **Alxa Yougi** China
64E2 **Alyat** Azerbaijan
32J8 **Alytus** Lithuania
36E2 **Alzey** Germany
22C2 **Amacuzac** *R* Mexico
72D3 **Amadi** Sudan
64D2 **Amādīyah** Iraq
7L3 **Amadjuak L** Can
57C3 **Amahai** Indon
53B5 **Amakusa-shotō** *I* Japan
32G7 **Åmål** Sweden
49N4 **Amalat** *R* Russian Fed
41E3 **Amaliás** Greece
60C4 **Amalner** India
29A3 **Amambai** Brazil
29B3 **Amambai** *R* Brazil
50F4 **Amami** *I* Japan
50F4 **Amami gunto** *Arch* Japan
27H3 **Amapá** Brazil
27H3 **Amapá** State, Brazil
4B3 **Amaranth** Can
61E3 **Amarapura** Burma
16B2 **Amarillo** USA
45F7 **Amasya** Turk
22B1 **Amatitan** Mexico
22C1 **Amaulipas** Mexico
Amazonas = Solimões
27H4 **Amazonas** Brazil
26E4 **Amazonas** State, Brazil
24D4 **Amazonas** *R* Brazil
60D2 **Ambāla** India
62C3 **Ambalangoda** Sri Lanka
73E6 **Ambalavao** Madag
72B3 **Ambam** Cam
73E5 **Ambanja** Madag
49S3 **Ambarchik** Russian Fed
26C4 **Ambato** Ecuador
73E5 **Ambato-Boeny** Madag
73E5 **Ambatolampy** Madag
73E5 **Ambatondrazaka** Madag
42C3 **Amberg** Germany
21D3 **Ambergris Cay** *I* Belize
37A2 **Ambérieu** France
61B3 **Ambikāpur** India
73E5 **Ambilobe** Madag
73E6 **Amboasary** Madag
73E5 **Ambodifototra** Madag
73E6 **Ambohimahasoa** Madag
57C3 **Ambon** Indon
57C3 **Ambon** *I* Indon
73E6 **Ambositra** Madag
73E6 **Ambovombe** Madag
73B4 **Ambriz** Angola
77F2 **Ambrym** *I* Vanuatu
10B6 **Amchitka** USA
10B6 **Amchitka** *I* USA
10C6 **Amchitka Pass** USA
72C2 **Am Dam** Chad
44L2 **Amderma** Russian Fed
21B2 **Ameca** Mexico
22A1 **Ameca** *R* Mexico
22C2 **Amecacameca** Mexico
28C2 **Ameghino** Arg
42B2 **Ameland** *I* Neth
14D2 **Amenia** USA
18D2 **American Falls** USA
18D2 **American Falls Res** USA
19D2 **American Fork** USA
79F10 **American Highland** *Upland* Ant
xxixL5 **American Samoa** *Is* Pacific O
15C2 **Americus** USA
42B2 **Amersfoort** Neth
74D2 **Amersfoort** S Africa
11D2 **Amery** USA
79G10 **Amery Ice Shelf** Ant
11D3 **Ames** USA
14E1 **Amesbury** USA
4E4 **Ameson** Can
41E3 **Amfilokhía** Greece
41E3 **Amfissa** Greece
49P3 **Amga** Russian Fed
49P3 **Amgal** *R* Russian Fed
53D2 **Amgu** Russian Fed
10C2 **Amguema** *R* Russian Fed
53D1 **Amgun'** *R* Russian Fed
72D2 **Amhara** *Region* Eth
7M5 **Amherst** Can
14D1 **Amherst** Massachusetts, USA
13D3 **Amherst** Virginia, USA
62B2 **Amhūr** India
38C2 **Amiens** France
54C3 **Amino** Japan
65C1 **Amioune** Leb
68K8 **Amirante Is** Indian O
3H3 **Amisk L** Can
16B4 **Amistad Res** Mexico
61C2 **Amlekhgan** Nepal
10D6 **Amlia** *I* USA
64C3 **Amman** Jordan
32K6 **Ämmänsaario** Fin
54A3 **Amnyong-dan** *C* N Korea
63C1 **Amol** Iran
7L5 **Amos** Can
Amoy = Xiamen
57B3 **Ampana** Indon
73E6 **Ampanihy** Madag
29C3 **Amparo** Brazil
39C1 **Amposta** Spain
5H4 **Amqui** Can
66D3 **Amrān** Yemen
60D4 **Amrāvati** India
60C4 **Amreli** India
60C2 **Amritsar** India
42A2 **Amsterdam** Neth
74E2 **Amsterdam** S Africa
13E2 **Amsterdam** USA
72C2 **Am Timan** Chad
48H5 **Amu Darya** *R* Uzbekistan
10D6 **Amukta** *I* USA
10D6 **Amukta Pass** USA
7J2 **Amund Ringnes I** Can
6F2 **Amundsen G** Can
79F4 **Amundsen S** Ant
79E **Amundsen-Scott** *Base* Ant
56E3 **Amuntai** Indon
49O4 **Amur** *R* Russian Fed
66C3 **Amur** *Watercourse* Sudan
57B2 **Amurang** Indon
53D1 **Amursk** Russian Fed
53E1 **Amurskiy Liman** *Str* Russian Fed
53C2 **Amurzet** Russian Fed
49N2 **Anabar** *R* Russian Fed
26F2 **Anaco** Ven
8B2 **Anaconda** USA
18B1 **Anacortes** USA
16C2 **Anadarko** USA
49T3 **Anadyr'** Russian Fed
49T3 **Anadyr'** *R* Russian Fed
49U3 **Anadyrskiy Zaliv** *S* Russian Fed
49T3 **Anadyrskoye Ploskogor'ye** *Plat* Russian Fed
41F3 **Anáfi** *I* Greece
29D1 **Anagé** Brazil
64D3 **'Ānah** Iraq
19C4 **Anaheim** USA
62B2 **Anaimalai Hills** India
62C1 **Anakāpalle** India
10J2 **Anaktuvuk P** USA
73E5 **Analalaya** Madag
71H4 **Anambra** *State* Nig
71H4 **Anambra** *R* Nig
12A2 **Anamosa** USA
45E8 **Anamur** Turk
54B4 **Anan** Japan
62B2 **Anantapur** India
60D2 **Anantnag** India
27J7 **Anápolis** Brazil
63D2 **Anār** Iran
63C2 **Anārak** Iran
63E2 **Anardara** Afghan
51H5 **Anatahan** *I* Pacific O
25D3 **Añatuya** Arg
53B4 **Anbyŏn** N Korea
20C4 **Ancapa Is** USA
28B1 **Ancasti** Arg
6D3 **Anchorage** USA
26E7 **Ancohuma** *Mt* Bol
26C6 **Ancón** Peru
40C2 **Ancona** Italy
14D1 **Ancram** USA
25B6 **Ancud** Chile
36C3 **Ancy-le-Franc** France
26D6 **Andabuaylas** Peru
28A3 **Andacollo** Arg
75A1 **Andado** Aust
28B1 **Andagalá** Arg
32F6 **Andalsnes** Nor
39A2 **Andalucia** Region, Spain
15B2 **Andalusia** USA
59H4 **Andaman Is** Burma
59H4 **Andaman S** Burma
75A2 **Andamooka** Aust
29D1 **Andaraí** Brazil
35B5 **Andee** Irish Rep
36C2 **Andelot** France
32H5 **Andenes** Nor
37C1 **Andermatt** Switz
42B2 **Andernach** Germany
12B2 **Anderson** Indiana, USA
17D2 **Anderson** Missouri, USA
15C2 **Anderson** S Carolina, USA
6F3 **Anderson** *R* Can
62B1 **Andhra Pradesh** State, India
41E3 **Andikíthira** *I* Greece
48J5 **Andizhan** Uzbekistan
48H6 **Andkhui** Afghan
53B4 **Andong** S Korea
39C1 **Andorra** Principality, SW Europe
39C1 **Andorra-La-Vella** Andorra
35E6 **Andover** Eng
14E1 **Andover** New Hampshire, USA
14B1 **Andover** New York, USA
29B3 **Andradina** Brazil
10F3 **Andreafsky** USA
10C6 **Andreanof Is** USA
43G1 **Andreapol'** Russian Fed
64B2 **Andreas,C** Cyprus
16B3 **Andrews** USA
40D2 **Andria** Italy
9F4 **Andros** *I* Bahamas
41E3 **Ándros** *I* Greece
62A2 **Androth** *I* India
39B2 **Andújar** Spain
73B5 **Andulo** Angola
71G4 **Anécho** Togo
70C3 **Anéfis** Mali
77F3 **Aneityum** *I* Vanuatu
28B3 **Añelo** Arg
66C4 **Angareb** *Watercourse* Eth
49M4 **Angarsk** Russian Fed
44A3 **Ånge** Sweden
21A2 **Angel de la Guarda** *I* Mexico
57F7 **Angeles** Phil
32G7 **Angelholm** Sweden
75C1 **Angellala Creek** *R* Aust
20B1 **Angels Camp** USA
51G7 **Angemuk** *Mt* Indon
38B2 **Angers** France
36B2 **Angerville** France
55C3 **Angkor** *Hist Site* Camb
33C3 **Anglesey** *I* Wales
17C4 **Angleton** USA
7P3 **Angmagssalik** Greenland
73E5 **Angoche** Mozam
25B5 **Angol** Chile
12C2 **Angola** Indiana, USA
14A1 **Angola** New York, USA
73B5 **Angola** Republic, Africa
xxxJ5 **Angola Basin** Atlantic O
10M4 **Angoon** USA
38C2 **Angoulême** France
70A1 **Angra do Heroismo** Açores
29D3 **Angra dos Reis** Brazil
28C3 **Anguil** Arg
23E3 **Anguilla** *I* Caribbean
23B2 **Anguilla Cays** *Is* Caribbean
61C3 **Angul** India
72C4 **Angumu** Zaïre
42C1 **Anholt** *I* Den
52C4 **Anhua** China
52D3 **Anhui** Province, China
29B2 **Anhumas** Brazil
54A3 **Anhŭng** S Korea
10G3 **Aniak** USA
29C2 **Anicuns** Brazil
71G4 **Anié** Togo
16A2 **Animas** *R* USA
16A3 **Animas Peak** *Mt* USA
11D3 **Anita** USA
36B2 **Anizy-le-Château** France
38B2 **Anjou** Republic, France
73E5 **Anjouan** *I* Comoros
73E5 **Anjozorobe** Madag
53B4 **Anju** N Korea
52B3 **Ankang** China
45E8 **Ankara** Turk
73E5 **Ankaratra** *Mt* Madag
73E6 **Ankazoabo** Madag
73E5 **Ankazobe** Madag
11D3 **Ankeny** USA
42C2 **Anklam** Germany
71H4 **Ankwe** *R* Nig
55D3 **An Loc** Viet
52B4 **Anlong** China
52C3 **Anlu** China
12B3 **Anna** USA
71D1 **'Annaba** Alg
64C3 **An Nabk** S Arabia
64C3 **An Nabk** Syria
75A1 **Anna Creek** Aust
69B2 **An Nāfūrah** Libya
64D3 **An Najaf** Iraq
34D4 **Annan** Scot
13D3 **Annapolis** USA
61B2 **Annapurna** *Mt* Nepal
12C2 **Ann Arbor** USA
65D1 **An Nāsirah** Syria
64E3 **An Nāsirīyah** Iraq
37B2 **Annecy** France
37B1 **Annemasse** France
3B2 **Annette I** USA
55D3 **An Nhon** Viet
66D3 **An Nimās** S Arabia
52A5 **Anning** China
15B2 **Anniston** USA
70C4 **Annobon, I** Eq Guinea
38C2 **Annonay** France
37B3 **Annot** France
23J1 **Annotto Bay** Jamaica
52D3 **Anqing** China
52B2 **Ansai** China
42C3 **Ansbach** Germany
23C3 **Anse d'Hainault** Haiti
52E1 **Anshan** China
52B4 **Anshun** China
16C1 **Ansley** USA
16C3 **Anson** USA
51F8 **Anson B** Aust
70C3 **Ansongo** Mali
12C1 **Ansonville** Can
12C3 **Ansted** USA
45F8 **Antakya** Turk
73F5 **Antalaha** Madag
45E8 **Antalya** Turk
45E8 **Antalya Körfezi** *B* Turk
73E5 **Antananarivo** Madag
79G1 **Antarctic Circle** Ant
79G3 **Antarctic Pen** Ant
39B2 **Antequera** Spain
16A3 **Anthony** USA
70B1 **Anti-Atlas** *Mts* Mor
37B3 **Antibes** France
7M5 **Anticosti, Î d'** Can
5J4 **Anticosti Prov Park** Can
12B1 **Antigo** USA
23E3 **Antigua** *I* Caribbean
Anti Lebanon = Jebel esh Sharqi
19B3 **Antioch** USA
77G5 **Antipodes Is** NZ
17C3 **Antlers** USA
25B2 **Antofagasta** Chile
29C4 **Antonina** Brazil
16A2 **Antonito** USA
34B4 **Antrim** County, N Ire
34B4 **Antrim** N Ire
14E1 **Antrim** USA
34B4 **Antrim Hills** N Ire
73E5 **Antseranana** Madag
73E5 **Antsirabe** Madag
73E5 **Antsohiny** Madag
55D3 **An Tuc** Viet
28C1 **Añtuya** Arg
36C1 **Antwerpen** Belg
35B5 **An Uaimh** Irish Rep
54A3 **Anui** S Korea
60C3 **Anupgarh** India
62C3 **Anuradhapura** Sri Lanka
Anvers = Antwerpen
6B3 **Anvik** USA
10B6 **Anvil Pk** *Mt* USA
49L5 **Anxi** China
52C2 **Anyang** China
52A3 **A'nyêmaqên Shan** *Upland* China
49S3 **Anyuysk** Russian Fed
37C2 **Anza** *R* Italy
3F2 **Anzac** Can
48K4 **Anzhero-Sudzhensk** Russian Fed
40C2 **Anzio** Italy
77F2 **Aoba** *I* Vanuatu
53E3 **Aomori** Japan
40B1 **Aosta** Italy
70B3 **Aoukar** *Desert Region* Maur
70C2 **Aoulef** Alg
72B1 **Aozou** Chad
25E2 **Apa** *R* Brazil/Par
9E4 **Apalachee B** USA
15C3 **Apalachicola** USA
15B3 **Apalachicola B** USA
22C2 **Apan** Mexico
26D3 **Apaporis** *R* Colombia
29B3 **Aparecida do Taboado** Brazil
57F7 **Aparri** Phil
41D1 **Apatin** Croatia, Yugos
44E2 **Apatity** Russian Fed
21B3 **Apatzingan** Mexico
42B2 **Apeldoorn** Neth
77H2 **Apia** Western Samoa
29C3 **Apiai** Brazil
22B1 **Apizolaya** Mexico
27G2 **Apoera** Surinam
75B3 **Apollo Bay** Aust
57G9 **Apo,Mt** Phil
15C3 **Apopka,L** USA
27H7 **Aporé** *R* Brazil
12A1 **Apostle Is** USA
22B1 **Apozol** Mexico
9E3 **Appalachian Mts** USA
37D2 **Appenino Tosco-Emiliano** *Mts* Italy
40C2 **Appennino Abruzzese** *Mts* Italy
40B2 **Appennino Ligure** *Mts* Italy
40D2 **Appennino Lucano** *Mts* Italy
40D2 **Appennino Napoletano** *Mts* Italy
40C2 **Appennino Tosco-Emilliano** *Mts* Italy
40C2 **Appennino Umbro-Marchigiano** *Mts* Italy
37C1 **Appenzell** Switz
35D4 **Appleby** Eng
11C2 **Appleton** Minnesota, USA
12B2 **Appleton** Wisconsin, USA
45J7 **Apsheronskiy Poluostrov** *Pen* Azerbaijan
4F5 **Apsley** Can
37A3 **Apt** France
25F2 **Apucarana** Brazil
22C1 **Apulco** Mexico
26E2 **Apure** *R* Ven
26D6 **Apurimac** *R* Peru
64C4 **'Aqaba** Jordan
64B4 **'Aqaba,G of** Egypt/S Arabia
63C2 **'Aqdā** Iran
27G8 **Aqidauana** Brazil
22A1 **Aqua Nueva** Mexico
29A3 **Aquidabán** *R* Par
25E2 **Aquidauana** Brazil
29A2 **Aquidauana** *R* Brazil
22B2 **Aquila** Mexico
61B2 **Ara** India
15B2 **Arab** USA
65C1 **'Arab al Mulk** Syria
58E4 **Arabian** *S* Asia/Arabian Pen
xxviiiE4 **Arabian Basin** Indian O
27L6 **Aracajú** Brazil
25E2 **Aracanguy, Mts de** *Mts* Brazil
29A3 **Aracanguy, Mts de** Par
27L4 **Aracati** Brazil
29D1 **Aracatu** Brazil
27H8 **Araçatuba** Brazil
39A2 **Aracena** Spain
27K7 **Araçuai** Brazil
65C3 **Arad** Israel
45C6 **Arad** Rom

Arada Augustine I

72C2 **Arada** Chad
67F2 **'Arādah** UAE
76C1 **Arafura S** Indon/Aust
27H7 **Aragarças** Brazil
45G7 **Aragats** *Mt* Armenia
39B1 **Aragón** Region, Spain
39B1 **Aragon** *R* Spain
29C1 **Araguaçu** Brazil
27H6 **Araguaia** *R* Brazil
27J5 **Araguaína** Brazil
27J7 **Araguari** Brazil
29C2 **Araguari** *R* Brazil
54C3 **Arai** Japan
70C2 **Arak** Alg
63B2 **Arāk** Iran
10D3 **Arakamchechen, Ostrov** *Is* Russian Fed
55A2 **Arakan Yoma** *Mts* Burma
62B2 **Arakkonam** India
64E2 **Araks** *R* Azerbaijan
48H5 **Aral'sk** Kazakhstan
48G5 **Aral'skoye More** *S* Kazakhstan/Uzbekistan
22C1 **Aramberri** Mexico
33B2 **Aran** *I* Irish Rep
39B1 **Aranda de Duero** Spain
22B1 **Arandas** Mexico
39B1 **Aranjuez** Spain
74B1 **Aranos** Namibia
17F4 **Aransas Pass** USA
54B4 **Arao** Japan
70B3 **Araouane** Mali
16C1 **Arapahoe** USA
25E4 **Arapey** *R* Urug
28D2 **Arapey Grande** *R* Urug
27L6 **Arapiraca** Brazil
29B3 **Araporgas** Brazil
25G3 **Ararangua** Brazil
27J8 **Araraquara** Brazil
29C3 **Araras** Brazil
76D4 **Ararat** Aust
64D2 **Ararat** Armenia
64D1 **Aras** *R* Turk
45H8 **Aras** *R* Azerbaijan/Iran
66C3 **Aratali** Eth
54D3 **Arato** Japan
26E2 **Arauca** *R* Ven
28A3 **Arauco** Chile
26D2 **Arauea** Colombia
60C3 **Arāvalli Range** *Mts* India
77E1 **Arawa** PNG
27J7 **Araxá** Brazil
45G8 **Araxes** *R* Iran
72D3 **Arba Minch** Eth
40B3 **Arbatax** Sardegna
45G8 **Arbīl** Iraq
37A1 **Arbois** France
4B3 **Arborg** Can
32H6 **Arbrå** Sweden
34D3 **Arbroath** Scot
37A3 **Arc** *R* France
37B2 **Arc** *R* France
38B3 **Arcachon** France
14A1 **Arcade** USA
15E4 **Arcadia** USA
18B2 **Arcata** USA
20D1 **Arc Dome, Mt** USA
22B2 **Arcelia** Mexico
14C2 **Archbald** USA
20E3 **Arches Nat Pk** USA
23B2 **Archipiélago de Camaguey** *Arch* Cuba
25B8 **Archipiélago de la Reina Adelaida** *Arch* Chile
25B6 **Archipiélago de las Chones** *Arch* Chile
26C2 **Archipiélago de las Perlas** *Arch* Panama
36C2 **Arcis-sur-Aube** France
18D2 **Arco** USA
29C3 **Arcos** Brazil
39A2 **Arcos de la Frontera** Spain
37A1 **Arc Senans** France
79C1 **Arctic Circle**
6E3 **Arctic Red** Can
6E3 **Arctic Red River** Can
6D3 **Arctic Village** USA
79G2 **Arctowski** *Base* Ant
41F2 **Arda** *R* Bulg
45H8 **Ardabīl** Iran
45G7 **Ardahan** Turk
70C2 **Ardar des Iforas** *Upland* Alg/Mali
63C2 **Ardekān** Iran
32F6 **Ardel** Nor
36C2 **Ardennes** Department, France
42B2 **Ardennes** Region, Belg
63C2 **Ardestan** Iran
64C3 **Ardh es Suwwan** *Desert Region* Jordan
39A2 **Ardila** *R* Port
75C2 **Ardlethan** Aust
8D3 **Ardmore** USA
34B3 **Ardnamurchan** *Pt* Scot
35F6 **Ardres** France
36A1 **Ardres** France
34C3 **Ardrishaig** Scot
34C4 **Ardrossan** Scot
23D3 **Arecibo** Puerto Rico
27L4 **Areia Branca** Brazil
19B3 **Arena,Pt** USA
32F7 **Arendal** Nor
26D7 **Arequipa** Peru
40C2 **Arezzo** Italy
37B3 **Argens** *R* France
40C2 **Argenta** Italy
38C2 **Argentan** France
36B2 **Argenteuil** France
5L4 **Argentia** Can
24D7 **Argentina** Republic, S America
xxxF7 **Argentine Basin** Atlantic O
38C2 **Argenton-sur-Creuse** France
41F2 **Argeşul** *R* Rom
60B2 **Arghardab** *R* Afghan
41E3 **Argolikós Kólpos** *G* Greece
36C2 **Argonne** Region, France
41E3 **Árgos** Greece
41E3 **Argostólion** Greece
20B3 **Arguello,Pt** USA
71G3 **Argungu** Nig
20D3 **Argus Range** *Mts* USA
76B2 **Argyle,L** Aust
34G3 **Argyll** *Oilfield* N Sea
42C1 **Århus** Den
73C6 **Ariamsvlei** Namibia
39B1 **Arian zón** *R* Spain
28C2 **Arias Venado** Arg
70B3 **Aribinda** Burkina
25B1 **Arica** Chile
60C2 **Arifwala** Pak
Arihā = Jericho
16B2 **Arikaree, R** USA
23L1 **Arima** Trinidad
29C2 **Arinos** Brazil
27G6 **Arinos** *R* Brazil
22B2 **Ario de Rosales** Mexico
23L1 **Aripo,Mt** Trinidad
26F5 **Aripuana** Brazil
26F5 **Aripuanã** *R* Brazil
34C3 **Arisaig** Scot
62B2 **Ariskere** India
22B1 **Arista** Mexico
22D2 **Arista** Mexico
3C3 **Aristazabal I** Can
28B3 **Arizona** Arg
8B3 **Arizona** State, USA
32G7 **Årjäng** Sweden
49O4 **Arka** Russian Fed
45G5 **Arkadak** Russian Fed
17D3 **Arkadelphia** USA
48H4 **Arkalyk** Kazakhstan
9D3 **Arkansas** State, USA
9D3 **Arkansas** *R* USA
17C2 **Arkansas City** USA
44G3 **Arkhangel'sk** Russian Fed
53C2 **Arkhara** Russian Fed
49K2 **Arkipelag Nordenshelda** *Arch* Russian Fed
33B3 **Arklow** Irish Rep
5G5 **Arkville** USA
37D1 **Arlberg P** Austria
38C3 **Arles** France
11C3 **Arlington** S Dakota, USA
17C3 **Arlington** Texas, USA
13D3 **Arlington** Virginia, USA
18B1 **Arlington** Washington, USA
12B2 **Arlington Heights** USA
42B3 **Arlon** Belg
Armageddon = Megido
35B4 **Armagh County,** N Ire
35B4 **Armagh** N Ire
41F3 **Armagós** *I* Greece
36B3 **Armançon** *R* France
45G7 **Armavir** Russian Fed
22B2 **Armena** Mexico
45G7 **Armenia** *Republic* Europe
26C3 **Armenia** Colombia
76E4 **Armidale** Aust
3E3 **Armstrong** Can
53D2 **Armu** *R* Russian Fed
7L3 **Arnaud** *R* Can
64B2 **Arnauti** *C* Cyprus
16C2 **Arnett** USA
42B2 **Arnhem** Neth
76C2 **Arnhem,C** Aust
76C2 **Arnhem Land** Aust
37D3 **Arno** *R* Italy
20B1 **Arnold** USA
37E1 **Arnoldstein** Austria
4B2 **Arnot** Can
4F4 **Arnprior** Can
36E1 **Arnsberg** Germany
74B2 **Aroab** Namibia
36E1 **Arolsen** Germany
37C2 **Arona** Italy
10F3 **Aropuk L** USA
77G1 **Arorae** *I* Kiribati
40B1 **Arosa** Switz
36B2 **Arpajon** France
29E2 **Arquipélago dos Abrolhos** *Arch* Brazil
70A3 **Arquipélago dos Bijagós** *Arch* Guinea-Bissau
29C1 **Arraias** Brazil
64D3 **Ar Ramādī** Iraq
34C4 **Arran** *I* Scot
64C2 **Ar Raqqah** Syria
69A2 **Ar Rāqūbah** Libya
38C1 **Arras** France
66D1 **Ar Rass** S Arabia
65D1 **Ar Rastan** Syria
66D2 **Ar Rawdah** S Arabia
70A2 **Arrecife** Canary Is
28C2 **Arrecifes** Arg
22B1 **Arriaga** Mexico
22D2 **Arriaga** Mexico
64E3 **Ar Rifā't** Iraq
64E3 **Ar Rihāb** *Desert Region* Iraq
Ar Rīyād = Riyadh
34C3 **Arrochar** Scot
28E2 **Arroio Grande** Brazil
29C1 **Arrojado** *R* Brazil
18C2 **Arrowrock Res** USA
78A2 **Arrowtown** NZ
20B3 **Arroyo Grande** USA
22C1 **Arroyo Seco** Mexico
67F1 **Ar Ru'ays** Qatar
67G2 **Ar Rustaq** Oman
64D3 **Ar Rutbah** Iraq
66D2 **Ar Ruwaydah** S Arabia
53C3 **Arsen'yev** Russian Fed
37D2 **Arsiero** Italy
38D2 **Arsizio** Italy
44H4 **Arsk** Russian Fed
41E3 **Árta** Greece
22B2 **Arteaga** Mexico
53C3 **Artem** Russian Fed
49L4 **Artemovsk** Russian Fed
49N4 **Artemovskiy** Russian Fed
36A2 **Artenay** France
8C3 **Artesia** USA
78B2 **Arthurs P** NZ
32G7 **Årthus** Den
7K2 **Artic Bay** Can
25E4 **Artigas** Urug
28D2 **Artigas** Urug
6H3 **Artillery L** Can
38C1 **Artois** Region, France
43F3 **Artsiz** Ukraine
79G2 **Arturo Prat** *Base* Ant
45G7 **Artvin** Turk
72D3 **Aru** Zaïre
27H6 **Aruanã** Brazil
23C4 **Aruba** *I* Caribbean
61C2 **Arun** *R* Nepal
61D2 **Arunāchal Pradesh** Union Territory, India
53A2 **Arun He** *R* China
53A2 **Arun Qi** China
62B3 **Aruppukkottai** India
72D4 **Arusha** Tanz
72C3 **Aruwimi** *R* Zaïre
16A2 **Arvada** USA
50D2 **Arvayheer** Mongolia
37B2 **Arve** *R* France
7L5 **Arvida** Can
32H5 **Arvidsjaur** Sweden
44B2 **Arvidsjaur** Sweden
32G7 **Arvika** Sweden
19C3 **Arvin** USA
65C1 **Arwad** *I* Syria
57C4 **Arwala** Indon
44G4 **Arzamas** Russian Fed
71B1 **Arzew** Alg
60C2 **Asadabad** Afghan
54B4 **Asahi** *R* Japan
53E3 **Asahi dake** *Mt* Japan
53E3 **Asahikawa** Japan
54A3 **Asan-man** *B* S Korea
61C3 **Asansol** India
69A2 **Asawanwah** *Well* Libya
44L4 **Asbest** Russian Fed
74C2 **Asbestos Mts** S Africa
13E2 **Asbury Park** USA
xxxH5 **Ascension** *I* Atlantic O
42B3 **Aschaffenburg** Germany
42C2 **Aschersleben** Germany
40C2 **Ascoli Piceno** Italy
37C1 **Ascona** Switz
72E2 **Āseb** Eth
70C2 **Asedjirad** *Upland* Alg
72D3 **Asela** Eth
32H6 **Åsele** Sweden
41E2 **Asenovgrad** Bulg
36C2 **Asfeld** France
44K4 **Asha** Russian Fed
15C2 **Ashburn** USA
77G5 **Ashburton** NZ
76A3 **Ashburton** *R* Aust
64B3 **Ashdod** Israel
17D3 **Ashdown** USA
15D1 **Asheboro** USA
4B3 **Ashern** Can
9E3 **Asheville** USA
75D1 **Ashford** Aust
35F6 **Ashford** Eng
19D3 **Ash Fork** USA
54D2 **Ashibetsu** Japan
53D4 **Ashikaga** Japan
54B4 **Ashizuri-misaki** *Pt* Japan
48G6 **Ashkhabad** Turkmenistan
16C2 **Ashland** Kansas, USA
9E3 **Ashland** Kentucky, USA
11A2 **Ashland** Montana, USA
17C1 **Ashland** Nebraska, USA
12C2 **Ashland** Ohio, USA
8A2 **Ashland** Oregon, USA
13D3 **Ashland** Virginia, USA
11D2 **Ashland** Wisconsin, USA
75C1 **Ashley** Aust
11C2 **Ashley** USA
14C2 **Ashokan Res** USA
65C3 **Ashqelon** Israel
64D3 **Ash Shabakh** Iraq
67G1 **Ash Sha'm** UAE
66D3 **Ash Sh'ār** S Arabia
64D2 **Ash Sharqāt** Iraq
64E3 **Ash Shatrah** Iraq
67E4 **Ash Shihr** Yemen
67E1 **Ash Shumlul** S Arabia
66D3 **Ash Shuqayq** S Arabia
12C2 **Ashtabula** USA
7M4 **Ashuanipi L** Can
5G4 **Ashuapmushuan Prov Park** Can
45F8 **'Āsī** *R* Syria
37D2 **Asiago** Italy
71A1 **Asilah** Mor
40B2 **Asinara** *I* Medit S
48K4 **Asino** Russian Fed
66D2 **Asir** Region, S Arabia
61B4 **Aska** India
64D2 **Aşkale** Turk
32G7 **Askersund** Sweden
65B4 **Asl** Egypt
60C1 **Asmar** Afghan
72D2 **Asmera** Eth
54B4 **Aso** Japan
72D2 **Asosa** Eth
16B3 **Aspermont** USA
78A2 **Aspiring,Mt** NZ
37A2 **Aspres-sur-Buëch** France
64C2 **As Sabkhah** Syria
67E2 **As Salamiyah** S Arabia
64C2 **As Salamīyah** Syria
66D4 **Assale,L** Eth
64D3 **As Salmān** Iraq
61D2 **Assam** State, India
64E3 **As Samāwah** Iraq
67F2 **AsŞanām** Region, S Arabia
65D2 **As Sanamayn** Syria
37B3 **Asse** *R* France
42B2 **Assen** Neth
42C1 **Assens** Den
69A1 **As Sidrah** Libya
6H5 **Assiniboia** Can
6G4 **Assiniboine,Mt** Can
4B4 **Assiniboine** *R* Can
5G3 **Assinica Prov Park** Can
37E3 **Assissi** Italy
64C3 **As Sukhnah** Syria
67E2 **As Sulayyil** S Arabia
67E2 **As Summan** Region, S Arabia
73E4 **Assumption** *I* Seychelles
66D2 **As Suq** S Arabia
64C3 **As Suwaydā'** Syria
64D3 **As Suwayrah** Iraq
64E2 **Astara** Azerbaijan
40B2 **Asti** Italy
41F3 **Astipálaia** *I* Greece
39A1 **Astorga** Spain
8A2 **Astoria** USA
45H6 **Astrakhan'** Russian Fed
39A1 **Asturias** Region, Spain
25E3 **Asunción** Par
72D3 **Aswa** *R* Uganda
66B2 **Aswân** Egypt
69C2 **Aswân High Dam** Egypt
69C2 **Asyût** Egypt
64C3 **As Zilaf** Syria
77H1 **Atafu** *I* Tokelau Is
71G4 **Atakpamé** Togo
57B5 **Atambua** Indon
7N3 **Atangmik** Greenland
57B4 **Atapupu** Indon
70A2 **Atar** Maur
20B3 **Atascadero** USA
48J5 **Atasu** Kazakhstan
57C4 **Atauro** *I* Indon
72D2 **Atbara** Sudan
48H4 **Atbasar** Kazakhstan
9D4 **Atchafalaya B** USA
9D3 **Atchison** USA
14C3 **Atco** USA
71F4 **Atebubu** Ghana
22B1 **Atenguillo** Mexico
40C2 **Atessa** Italy
36B1 **Ath** Belg
3F3 **Athabasca** Can
6G4 **Athabasca** *R* Can
6H4 **Athabasca, L** Can
Athens = Athínai
15B2 **Athens** Alabama, USA
9E3 **Athens** Georgia, USA
12C3 **Athens** Ohio, USA
14B2 **Athens** Pennsylvania, USA
15C1 **Athens** Tennessee, USA
17C3 **Athens** Texas, USA
71G4 **Athiémé** Benin
41E3 **Athínai** Greece
33B3 **Athlone** Irish Rep
65B1 **Athna** Cyprus
14D1 **Athol** USA
41E2 **Áthos** *Mt* Greece
35B5 **Athy** Irish Rep
72B2 **Ati** Chad
7J5 **Atikoken** Can
5J3 **Atikonak L** Can
49R3 **Atka** Russian Fed
10D6 **Atka** *I* USA
45G5 **Atkarsk** Russian Fed
17D2 **Atkins** USA
22C2 **Atlacomulco** Mexico
9E3 **Atlanta** Georgia, USA
12C2 **Atlanta** Michigan, USA
17C1 **Atlantic** USA
9F3 **Atlantic City** USA
14C2 **Atlantic Highlands** USA
xxxH8 **Atlantic Indian Basin** Atlantic O
xxxH7 **Atlantic Indian Ridge** Atlantic O
70C1 **Atlas Saharien** *Mts* Alg
6E4 **Atlin** Can
6E4 **Atlin L** Can
65C2 **'Atlit** Israel
22C2 **Atlixco** Mexico
9E3 **Atmore** USA
73E6 **Atofinandrahana** Madag
10H4 **Atognak I** USA
17C3 **Atoka** USA
22B1 **Atotonilco** Mexico
22C2 **Atoyac** *R* Mexico
26C2 **Atrato** *R* Colombia
67F2 **Attaf** Region, UAE
66D2 **At Tā'if** S Arabia
65D2 **At Tall** Syria
15B2 **Attalla** USA
7K4 **Attawapiskat** Can
4D3 **Attawapiskat L** Can
7K4 **Attawapiskat** *R* Can
64D3 **At Taysīyah** *Desert Region* S Arabia
12B2 **Attica** Indiana, USA
14A1 **Attica** New York, USA
36C2 **Attigny** France
5H2 **Attikamagen L** Can
65B1 **Attila Line** Cyprus
13E2 **Attleboro** Massachusetts, USA
55D3 **Attopeu** Laos
10A5 **Attu** USA
10A5 **Attu** *I* USA
64C4 **At Tubayq** *Upland* S Arabia
28B3 **Atuel** *R* Arg
32H7 **Atvidaberg** Sweden
20B2 **Atwater** USA
38D3 **Aubagne** France
36C2 **Aube** Department, France
36C2 **Aube** *R* France
38C3 **Aubenas** France
10N2 **Aubry L** Can
15B2 **Auburn** Alabama, USA
19B3 **Auburn** California, USA
12B2 **Auburn** Indiana, USA
13E2 **Auburn** Maine, USA
17C1 **Auburn** Nebraska, USA
13D2 **Auburn** New York, USA
18B1 **Auburn** Washington, USA
38C3 **Auch** France
71H4 **Auchi** Nig
77G4 **Auckland** NZ
xxixK7 **Auckland Is** NZ
38C3 **Aude** *R* France
7K4 **Auden** Can
37B1 **Audincourt** France
11D3 **Audubon** USA
75C1 **Augathella** Aust
74B2 **Aughrabies Falls** S Africa
42C3 **Augsburg** Germany
76A4 **Augusta** Aust
9E3 **Augusta** Georgia, USA
17C2 **Augusta** Kansas, USA
9G2 **Augusta** Maine, USA
18D1 **Augusta** Montana, USA
12A2 **Augusta** Wisconsin, USA
10H4 **Augustine I** USA

Augustow
Bandolier Kop

43E2 Augustow Pol
76A3 Augustus,Mt Aust
34G3 Auk *Oilfield* N Sea
37C2 Aulla Italy
36A2 Aumale France
74B1 Auob *R* Namibia
5H2 Aupalak Can
57C3 Auponhia Indon
37B3 Aups France
60D3 Auraiya India
60D5 Aurangābād India
71D1 Aurès *Mts* Alg
38C3 Aurillac France
8C3 Aurora Colorado, USA
12B2 Aurora Illinois, USA
12C3 Aurora Indiana, USA
17D2 Aurora Mississippi, USA
17C1 Aurora Nebraska, USA
74B2 Aus Namibia
12C2 Au Sable USA
70A2 Ausert *Well* Mor
9D2 Austin Minnesota, USA
19C3 Austin Nevada, USA
14A2 Austin Pennsylvania, USA
8D3 Austin Texas, USA
76D4 Australian Alps *Mts* Aust
30G4 Austria, *Fed Republic* Europe
36A1 Authie *R* France
21B3 Autlán Mexico
38C2 Autun France
38C2 Auvergne Region, France
38C2 Auxerre France
36A1 Auxi-le-Châteaux France
37A1 Auxonne France
38C2 Avallon France
20C4 Avalon USA
7N5 Avalon Pen Can
28D1 Avalos *R* Arg
29C3 Avaré Brazil
63E2 Avaz Iran
65C3 Avedat *Hist Site* Israel
27G4 Aveiro Brazil
39A1 Aveiro Port
25E4 Avellaneda Arg
40C2 Avellino Italy
20B3 Avenal USA
36B1 Avesnes-sur-Helpe France
32H6 Avesta Sweden
40C2 Avezzano Italy
34D3 Aviemore Scot
78B2 Aviemore,L NZ
37B2 Avigliana Italy
38C3 Avignon France
39B1 Avila Spain
39A1 Aviles Spain
37D1 Avisio *R* Italy
11C3 Avoca Iowa, USA
14B1 Avoca New York, USA
75B3 Avoca *R* Aust
35D6 Avon County, Eng
14B1 Avon USA
35E6 Avon *R* Dorset, Eng
35E5 Avon *R* Warwick, Eng
19D4 Avondale USA
35D6 Avonmouth Wales
15E4 Avon Park USA
36B2 Avre *R* France
41D2 Avtovac Bosnia & Herzegovina, Yugos
65D2 A'waj *R* Syria
53D5 Awaji-shima *B* Japan
72E3 Awarē Eth
78A2 Awarua Pt NZ
72E3 Awash Eth
72E3 Awash *R* Eth
54C3 Awa-shima *I* Japan
78B2 Awatere *R* NZ
69A2 Awbārī Libya
72C3 Aweil Sudan
69B2 Awjilah Libya
71H4 Awka Nig
10G2 Awuna *R* USA
7J1 Axel Heiberg I Can
35D6 Axminster Eng
54C3 Ayabe Japan
25E5 Ayacucho Arg
23C5 Ayacucho Colombia
26D6 Ayacucho Peru
48K5 Ayaguz Kazakhstan
59G2 Ayakkum Hu *L* China
39A2 Ayamonte Spain
49P4 Ayan Russian Fed
26D6 Ayauiri Peru
45D8 Aydin Turk
41F3 Áyios Evstrátios *I* Greece
49N3 Aykhal Russian Fed
35E5 Aylesbury Eng
3E3 Aylmer,Mt Can
65D2 'Ayn al Fījah Syria
64D2 Ayn Zālah Iraq
69B2 Ayn Zuwayyah *Well* Libya
72D3 Ayod Sudan
49S3 Ayon, Ostrov *I* Russian Fed
76D2 Ayr Aust
34C4 Ayr Scot
34C4 Ayr *R* Scot
35C4 Ayre,Pt of Eng
55C3 Aytthaya Thai
22B1 Ayutla Mexico
41F3 Ayvacik Turk
41F3 Ayvalik Turk
61B2 Āzamgarh India
70B3 Azaouad *Desert Region* Mali
71J3 Azare Nig
64C2 A'Zāz Syria
Azbine = Aïr
70A2 Azeffal, *Watercourse* Maur
71A2 Azemmour Mor
45H7 Azerbaijan *Republic* Europe
26C4 Azogues Ecuador
44H2 Azopol'ye Russian Fed
Azores = Açores
72C2 Azoum, R Chad
45F6 Azovskoye More *S* Russian Fed/Ukraine
71A2 Azrou Mor
16A2 Aztec USA
28D3 Azucena Arg
26B2 Azuero,Pen de Panama
25E5 Azúl Arg
71D1 Azzaba Alg
65D2 Az-Zabdānī Syria
67G2 Az Zāhirah *Mts* Oman
69A2 Az Zahrah Libya
66D1 Az Zilfi S Arabia
64E3 Az Zubayr Iraq

B

57B5 Baa Indon
65C2 Ba'abda Leb
64C3 Ba'albek Leb
65C3 Ba'al Hazor *Mt* Israel
72E3 Baardheere Somalia
41F2 Babadag Rom
64A1 Babaeski Turk
66D4 Bāb al Mandab *Str* Djibouti/Yemen
26C4 Babanoyo Ecuador
57C4 Babar *I* Indon
72D4 Babati Tanz
44F4 Babayevo Russian Fed
11D2 Babbitt USA
12C2 Baberton USA
3C2 Babine *R* Can
3C3 Babine L Can
76C1 Babo Indon
63C1 Bābol Iran
57F7 Babuyan Chan Phil
57F7 Babuyan Is Phil
27J4 Bacabal Brazil
57C3 Bacan *I* Indon
45D6 Bacău Rom
55D1 Bac Can Viet
36D2 Baccarat France
75B3 Bacchus Marsh Aust
59F2 Bachu China
6J3 Back *R* Can
10N3 Backbone Ranges *Mts* Can
36E2 Backnang Germany
55D1 Bac Ninh Viet
57F8 Bacolod Phil
57F8 Baco,Mt Phil
62B2 Badagara India
52A1 Badain Jaran Shamo *Desert* China
39A2 Badajoz Spain
39C1 Badalona Spain
64D3 Badanah S Arabia
37E1 Bad Aussee Austria
36E2 Bad Bergzabern Germany
36D1 Bad Ems Germany
38D2 Baden Region, Germany
37C1 Baden Switz
42B3 Baden-Baden Germany
36D2 Badenviller France
42B3 Baden-Württemberg State, Germany
42C3 Badgastein Austria
20C2 Badger USA
42B2 Bad-Godesberg Germany
42B2 Bad Hersfeld Germany
36D1 Bad Honnef Germany
60B4 Badin Pak
40C1 Bad Ischl Austria
64C3 Badiyat ash Sham *Desert Region* Jordan/Iraq
42B3 Bad-Kreuznach Germany
11B2 Badlands USA
36E1 Bad Lippspringe Germany
36E1 Bad Nauheim Germany
36D1 Bad Nevenahr-Ahrweiler Germany
71G4 Badou Togo
37C1 Bad Ragaz Switz
66C2 Badr Hunayn S Arabia
36E1 Bad Ryrmont Germany
42C3 Bad Tolz Germany
62C3 Badulla Sri Lanka
36E1 Bad Wildungen Germany
36E2 Bad Wimpfen Germany
53C1 Badzhal'skiy Khrebet *Mts* Russian Fed
39B2 Baena Spain
71J4 Bafang Cam
70A3 Bafatá Guinea-Bissau
7L2 Baffin B Greenland/Can
17F4 Baffin B USA
7L2 Baffin I Can
72B3 Bafia Cam
70A3 Bafing *R* Mali
70A3 Bafoulabé Mali
72B3 Bafoussam Cam
63D2 Bāfq Iran
45F7 Bafra Burun *Pt* Turk
63D3 Bāft Iran
72C3 Bafwasende Zaïre
71J3 Baga Nig
61B2 Bagaha India
62B1 Bāgalkot India
73D4 Bagamoyo Tanz
56F7 Bagan Datok Malay
56F7 Bagan Siapiapi Indon
19D4 Bagdad USA
25F4 Bagé Brazil
16A1 Baggs USA
64D3 Baghdād Iraq
61C3 Bagherhat Bang
63D2 Bāghīn Iran
60B1 Baghlan Afghan
11C2 Bagley USA
70B4 Bagnoa Ivory Coast
38C3 Bagnols-sur-Cèza France
70B3 Bagoé *R* Mali
57F7 Baguio Phil
61C2 Bāhādurābād India
9F4 Bahamas,The *Is* Caribbean
61C3 Baharampur India
64A4 Bahariya Oasis Egypt
56G7 Bahau Malay
60C3 Bahawahpur Province, Pak
60C3 Bahawalpur Pak
60C3 Bahawathagar Pak
Bahia = Salvador
27K6 Bahia State, Brazil
28C4 Bahia Anegada Arg
25D5 Bahía Blanca Arg
25D5 Bahía Blanca *B* Arg
28A3 Bahia Concepción *B* Chile
29D3 Bahia da Ilha Grande *B* Brazil
21B2 Bahia de Banderas *B* Mexico
21C2 Bahia de Campeche *B* Mexico
26B2 Bahia de Corando *B* Costa Rica
21D3 Bahia de la Ascension *B* Mexico
21B3 Bahia de Petacalco *B* Mexico
70A2 Bahia de Rio de Oro *B* Mor
29D3 Bahia de Sepetiba *B* Brazil
19C4 Bahiá de Todos Santos *B* Mexico
25C8 Bahía Grande *B* Arg
8B4 Bahia Kino Mexico
21A2 Bahia Magdalena *B* Mexico
28A1 Bahia Salada *B* Chile
28D3 Bahia Samborombon *B* Arg
21A2 Bahia Sebastia Vizcaino *B* Mexico
66C4 Bahir Dar Eth
65A3 Bahrael Manzala *L* Egypt
61B2 Bahraich India
58D3 Bahrain Sheikdom, Arabian Pen
64D3 Bahr al Milh *L* Iraq
72C3 Bahr Aouk *R* Chad/CAR
Bahrat Lut = Dead S
Bahr el Abiad = White Nile
66B4 Bahr el Abiad *R* Sudan
72C3 Bahr el Arab *Watercourse* Sudan
Bahr el Azraq = Blue Nile
66B4 Bahr el Azraq *R* Sudan
72D3 Bahr el Ghazal *R* Sudan
72B2 Bahr el Ghazal *Watercourse* Chad
65A3 Bahr Fâqûs *R* Egypt
63E3 Bāhū-Kalāt Iran
57B3 Bahumbelu Indon
5H2 Baie de Keglo *B* Can
5J4 Baie de Malbaie *B* Can
74E2 Baia de Maputo *B* Mozam
27J4 Baia de Marajó *B* Brazil
73E5 Baiá de Pemba *B* Mozam
27K4 Baia de São Marcos *B* Brazil
5H4 Baie des Chaleurs *B* Can
39A2 Baia de Setúbal *B* Port
27L6 Baia de Todos os Santos *B* Brazil
73B5 Baia dos Tigres Angola
29C4 Baiá Guaratuba Brazil
45C6 Baia Mare Rom
72B3 Baïbokoum Chad
53A2 Baicheng China
73F5 Baie Antongila *B* Madag
7M5 Baie-Comeau Can
73E5 Baie de Bombetoka *B* Madag
73E5 Baie de Mahajamba *B* Madag
73E6 Baie de St Augustin *B* Madag
65C2 Baie de St Georges *B* Leb
7L4 Baie-du-Poste Can
5F2 Baie Kogaluc *B* Can
5G4 Baie Saint Paul Can
7N5 Baie Verte Can
52B3 Baihe China
52C3 Bai He *R* China
64D3 Ba'iji Iraq
61B3 Baikunthpur India
Baile Atha Cliath = Dublin
41E2 Băileşti Rom
36B1 Bailleul France
10N1 Baillie Is Can
52A3 Baima China
15C2 Bainbridge USA
57B5 Baing Indon
53B2 Baiquan China
10F3 Baird Inlet USA
6B3 Baird Mts USA
52D1 Bairin Youqi China
52D1 Bairin Zuoqi China
76D4 Bairnsdale Aust
57F9 Bais Phil
71J4 Baissa Nig
61B2 Baitadi Nepal
66B3 Baiyuda *Desert* Sudan
41D1 Baja Hung
21A1 Baja California *Pen* Mexico
19C4 Baja California Norte Mexico
57B4 Bajawi Indon
66D4 Bājil Yemen
57B2 Bajo Indon
44K5 Bakal Russian Fed
72C3 Bakala CAR
70A3 Bakel Sen
19C3 Baker California, USA
8C2 Baker Montana, USA
8B2 Baker Oregon, USA
7J3 Baker Foreland *Pt* Can
6J3 Baker L Can
6J3 Baker Lake Can
8A2 Baker,Mt USA
8B3 Bakersfield USA
63D1 Bakharden Turkmenistan
63D1 Bakhardok Turkmenistan
45E5 Bakhmach Ukraine
32C1 Bakkaflói *B* Iceland
72D3 Bako Eth
72C3 Bakouma CAR
45H7 Baku Azerbaijan
57B3 Bakudek *I* Indon
56A2 Bakungan Indon
64B2 Balâ Turk
57E9 Balabac *I* Phil
56E1 Balabac *Str* Malay
61B3 Bālāghāt India
56D2 Balaikarangan Indon
75A2 Balaklava Aust
45H5 Balakovo Russian Fed
63E1 Bala Murghab Afghan
61B3 Balāngīr India
45G5 Balashov Russian Fed
61C3 Balasore India
66A1 Balât Egypt
41D1 Balaton *L* Hung
35B5 Balbriggan Irish Rep
25E5 Balcarce Arg
41F2 Balchik Bulg
77F5 Balclutha NZ
17D2 Bald Knob USA
4B2 Baldock L Can
15C2 Baldwin USA
4D5 Baldwin Michigan, USA
18E1 Baldy Mt USA
8C3 Baldy Peak *Mt* USA
Balearic Is = Islas Baleares
56D2 Baleh, R Malay
57F7 Baler Phil
44J4 Balezino Russian Fed
67E4 Balhāf Yemen
66D4 Balho Djibouti
76A1 Bali *I* Indon
64A2 Balıkesir Turk
64C2 Balīkh *R* Syria
56E3 Balikpapan Indon
57F7 Balintang Chan Phil
56D4 Bali S Indon
29B2 Baliza Brazil
66D3 Baljurshī S Arabia
60B1 Balkh Afghan
48J5 Balkhash Kazakhstan
48J5 Balkhash, Ozero *L* Kazakhstan
34C3 Ballachulish Scot
34C4 Ballantrae Scot
6G2 Ballantyne Str Can
62B2 Ballapur India
76D4 Ballarat Aust
34D3 Ballater Scot
79F7 Balleny Is Ant
61B2 Ballia India
75D1 Ballina Aust
33B3 Ballina Irish Rep
16C3 Ballinger USA
36D3 Ballon d'Alsace *Mt* France
41D2 Ballsh Alb
14D1 Ballston Spa USA
34B4 Ballycastle N Ire
34B4 Ballymena N Ire
34B4 Ballymoney N Ire
35A4 Ballyshannon Irish Rep
75B3 Balmoral Aust
16B3 Balmorhea USA
28C2 Balnearia Arg
60B3 Balochistān Region, Pak
73B5 Balombo Angola
75C1 Balonn *R* Aust
60C3 Balotra India
61B2 Balrāmpur India
76D4 Balranald Aust
27J5 Balsas Brazil
22C2 Balsas Mexico
21B3 Balsas *R* Mexico
45D6 Balta Ukraine
28D2 Baltasar Brum Urug
32H7 Baltic S N Europe
64B3 Baltîm Egypt
9F3 Baltimore USA
61C2 Bālurghāt India
45J6 Balykshi Kazakhstan
63D3 Bam Iran
72B2 Bama Nig
70B3 Bamako Mali
72C3 Bambari CAR
15C2 Bamberg USA
42C3 Bamberg Germany
72C3 Bambili Zaïre
29C3 Bambui Brazil
72B3 Bamenda Cam
3C4 Bamfield Can
72B3 Bamingui *R* CAR
72B3 Bamingui Bangoran National Park, CAR
60B2 Bamiyan Afghan
63E3 Bampur Iran
63E3 Bampur *R* Iran
77F1 Banaba *I* Kiribati
72C3 Banalia Zaïre
70B3 Banamba Mali
62E3 Bananga Nicobar Is
55C3 Ban Aranyaprathet Thai
55C2 Ban Ban Laos
55C4 Ban Betong Thai
35B4 Banbridge N Ire
35E5 Banbury Eng
34D3 Banchory Scot
21D3 Banco Chinchorro *Is* Mexico
4F4 Bancroft Can
61B2 Bānda India
56A1 Banda Aceh Indon
70B4 Bandama *R* Ivory Coast
63D3 Bandar Abbās Iran
45H8 Bandar Anzalī Iran
63C3 Bandar-e Daylam Iran
63C3 Bandar-e Lengheh Iran
63C3 Bandar-e Māqām Iran
63C3 Bandar-e Rig Iran
45J8 Bandar-e Torkoman Iran
63B2 Bandar Khomeynī Iran
56D2 Bandar Seri Begawan Brunei
51F7 Banda S Indon
56E1 Bandau Malay
63D3 Band Bonī Iran
29D3 Bandeira *Mt* Brazil
28C1 Bandera Arg
29B1 Banderantes Brazil
70B3 Bandiagara Mali
63E2 Band-i-Baba *Upland* Afghan
45D7 Bandirma Turk
63E1 Band-i-Turkestan *Mts* Afghan
37A3 Bandol France
74D1 Bandolier Kop S Africa

Bandundu Bei Shan

72B4 **Bandundu** Zaïre
56C4 **Bandung** Indon
45H8 **Baneh** Iran
57C2 **Banermo** Indon
21E2 **Banes** Cuba
3E3 **Banff** Can
34D3 **Banff** Scot
6G4 **Banff** *R* Can
3E3 **Banff Nat Pk** Can
71F3 **Banfora** Burkina
62B2 **Bangalore** India
71J4 **Bangangté** Cam
72C3 **Bangassou** CAR
56E1 **Banggi** *I* Malay
55D2 **Bang Hieng** *R* Laos
56C3 **Bangka** *I* Indon
56B2 **Bangkinang** Indon
56B3 **Bangko** Indon
55C3 **Bangkok** Thai
59H3 **Bangladesh** Republic, Asia
60D2 **Bangong Co** *L* China
9G2 **Bangor** Maine, USA
34B4 **Bangor** N Ire
14C2 **Bangor** Pennsylvania, USA
35C5 **Bangor** Wales
56E3 **Bangsalsembera** Indon
55B3 **Bang Saphan Yai** Thai
57F7 **Bangued** Phil
72B3 **Bangui** CAR
73D5 **Bangweulu** *L* Zambia
55C4 **Ban Hat Yai** Thai
55C2 **Ban Hin Heup** Laos
55C1 **Ban Houei Sai** Laos
55B3 **Ban Hua Hin** Thai
70B3 **Bani** *R* Mali
70C3 **Bani Bangou** Niger
67E3 **Banī Ma'arid** Region, S Arabia
69A1 **Banī Walīd** Libya
64C2 **Bāniyās** Syria
65C2 **Baniyas** Syria
40D2 **Banja Luka** Bosnia & Herzegovina, Yugos
56D3 **Banjarmasin** Indon
70A3 **Banjul** The Gambia
55B4 **Ban Kantang** Thai
55D2 **Ban Khemmarat** Laos
55B4 **Ban Khok Kloi** Thai
77F2 **Banks** *Is* Vanuatu
51H8 **Banks I** Aust
6E4 **Banks I** British Columbia, Can
6F2 **Banks I** Northwest Territories, Can
18C1 **Banks L** USA
78B2 **Banks Pen** NZ
75E3 **Banks Str** Aust
61C3 **Bankura** India
55B2 **Ban Mae Sariang** Thai
55B2 **Ban Mae Sot** Thai
61E3 **Banmauk** Burma
55D3 **Ban Me Thuot** Viet
34B4 **Bann** *R* N Ire
55B4 **Ban Na San** Thai
60C2 **Bannu** Pak
28A4 **Baños de Chihuio** Chile
28A3 **Baños Maule** Chile
55C2 **Ban Pak Neun** Laos
55C4 **Ban Pak Phanang** Thai
55D3 **Ban Ru Kroy** Camb
55B3 **Ban Sai Yok** Thai
55C3 **Ban Sattahip** Thai
43D3 **Banská Bystrica** Czech
60C4 **Bānswāra** India
57B4 **Bantaeng** Indon
55B4 **Ban Tha Kham** Thai
55D2 **Ban Thateng** Laos
55C2 **Ban Tha Tum** Thai
33B3 **Bantry** Irish Rep
33A3 **Bantry** *B* Irish Rep
55D3 **Ban Ya Soup** Viet
71J4 **Banyo** Cam
56D4 **Banyuwangi** Indon
xxviiiE7 **Banzare Seamount** Indian O
52C3 **Baofeng** China
55C1 **Bao Ha** Viet
52B3 **Baoji** China
55D3 **Bao Loc** Viet
53C2 **Baoqing** China
50C4 **Baoshan** China
52C1 **Baotou** China
62C1 **Bāpatla** India
36B1 **Bapaume** France
64D3 **Ba'Qūbah** Iraq
41D2 **Bar** Montenegro, Yugos
57C3 **Bara** Indon
72D2 **Bara** Sudan
72E3 **Baraawe** Somalia
56E3 **Barabai** Indon
61B2 **Bāra Banki** India
48J4 **Barabinsk** Russian Fed
48J4 **Barabinskaya Step** *Steppe* Kazakhstan/Russian Fed
39B1 **Baracaldo** Spain
23C2 **Baracoa** Cuba
65D2 **Baradá** *R* Syria
75C2 **Baradine** Aust
66C3 **Baraka** *Watercourse* Eth
62A1 **Bārāmati** India
60C2 **Baramula** Pak
60D3 **Bārān** India
57F8 **Barangas** Phil
6E4 **Baranof I** USA
44D5 **Baranovichi** Belorussia
75A2 **Baratta** Aust
61C2 **Barauni** India
27K8 **Barbacena** Brazil
23F4 **Barbados** *I* Caribbean
39C1 **Barbastro** Spain
74E2 **Barberton** S Africa
38B2 **Barbezieux** France
26D2 **Barbòsa** Colombia
23E3 **Barbuda** *I* Caribbean
76D3 **Barcaldine** Aust
Barce = Al Marj
40D3 **Barcellona** Italy
39C1 **Barcelona** Spain
26F1 **Barcelona** Ven
37B2 **Barcelonnette** France
76D3 **Barcoo** *R* Aust
28B3 **Barda del Medio** Arg
72B1 **Bardai** Chad
25C5 **Bardas Blancas** Arg
61C3 **Barddhamān** India
43E3 **Bardejov** Czech
37C2 **Bardi** Italy
37B2 **Bardonecchia** Italy
35C5 **Bardsey** *I* Wales
12B3 **Bardstown** USA
67F4 **Bareeda** Somalia
60D3 **Bareilly** India
44F1 **Barentsovo More** *S* Russian Fed
48D2 **Barentsøya** *I* Barents S
Barents S = Barentsovo More
72D2 **Barentu** Eth
61B3 **Bargarh** India
37B2 **Barge** Italy
49M4 **Barguzin** Russian Fed
49N4 **Barguzin** *R* Russian Fed
13F2 **Bar Harbor** USA
61C3 **Barhi** India
40D2 **Bari** Italy
39D2 **Barika** Alg
26D2 **Barinas** Ven
61C3 **Baripāda** India
66B2 **Bârîs** Egypt
60C4 **Bari Sādri** India
61D3 **Barisal** Bang
56D3 **Barito** *R* Indon
37B3 **Barjols** France
69A2 **Barjuj** *Watercourse* Libya
52A3 **Barkam** China
17E2 **Barkley,L** USA
3C4 **Barkley Sd** Can
74D3 **Barkly East** S Africa
76C2 **Barkly Tableland** *Mts* Aust
36C2 **Bar-le-Duc** France
76A3 **Barlee,L** Aust
76A3 **Barlee Range** *Mts* Aust
40D2 **Barletta** Italy
60C3 **Barmer** India
75B2 **Barmera** Aust
35C5 **Barmouth** Wales
35E4 **Barnard Castle** Eng
48K4 **Barnaul** Russian Fed
14C3 **Barnegat** USA
14C3 **Barnegat B** USA
14A2 **Barnesboro** USA
7L2 **Barnes Icecap** Can
15C2 **Barnesville** Georgia, USA
12C3 **Barnesville** Ohio, USA
16B3 **Barnhart** USA
35E5 **Barnsley** Eng
35C6 **Barnstaple** Eng
71H4 **Baro** Nig
61D2 **Barpeta** India
26E1 **Barquisimeto** Ven
35F5 **Barqe** *Oilfield* N Sea
36D2 **Barr** France
27K6 **Barra** Brazil
34B3 **Barra** *I* Scot
75D2 **Barraba** Aust
29D1 **Barra da Estiva** Brazil
22B2 **Barra de Navidad** Mexico
29D3 **Barra de Piraí** Brazil
22D2 **Barra de Tonalá** Mexico
29A2 **Barra do Bugres** Brazil
29B2 **Barra do Garças** Brazil
28D2 **Barra do Quarai** Brazil
28E2 **Barra do Ribeiro** Brazil
71F4 **Barrage d'Ayama** Ivory Coast
71J4 **Barrage de Mbakaou** *Dam* Cam
27K6 **Barragem de Sobradinho** Brazil
39A2 **Barragem do Castelo do Bode** *Res* Port
39A2 **Barragem do Maranhão** Port
34B3 **Barra Head** *Pt* Scot
27K8 **Barra Mansa** Brazil
26C6 **Barranca** Peru
26D2 **Barrancabermeja** Colombia
26F2 **Barrancas** Ven
105E3 **Barranqueras** Arg
26D1 **Barranquilla** Colombia
34B3 **Barra,Sound of** *Chan* Scot
4F4 **Barraute** Can
14D1 **Barre** USA
28B2 **Barreal** Arg
27K6 **Barreiras** Brazil
39A2 **Barreiro** Port
27L5 **Barreiros** Brazil
76D5 **Barren,C** Aust
10H4 **Barren Is** USA
27J8 **Barretos** Brazil
3F3 **Barrhead** Can
4F5 **Barrie** Can
3D3 **Barrière** Can
75B2 **Barrier Range** *Mts* Aust
3H2 **Barrington L** Can
76E4 **Barrington,Mt** Aust
29C2 **Barro Alto** Brazil
51G8 **Barroloola** Aust
12A1 **Barron** USA
23N2 **Barrouaillie** St Vincent
6C2 **Barrow** USA
35B5 **Barrow** *R* Irish Rep
76C3 **Barrow Creek** Aust
76A3 **Barrow I** Aust
35D4 **Barrow-in-Furness** Eng
6C2 **Barrow,Pt** USA
7J2 **Barrow Str** Can
13D1 **Barry's Bay** Can
14C2 **Barryville** USA
62B1 **Barsi** India
8B3 **Barstow** USA
38C2 **Bar-sur-Aube** France
36C2 **Bar-sur-Seine** France
27G2 **Bartica** Guyana
64B1 **Bartın** Turk
76D2 **Bartle Frere,Mt** Aust
8D3 **Bartlesville** USA
11C3 **Bartlett** USA
73D6 **Bartolomeu Dias** Mozam
43E2 **Bartoszyce** Pol
26B2 **Barú** Panama
56D4 **Barung** *I* Indon
56A2 **Barus** Indon
60D4 **Barwāh** India
60C4 **Barwāni** India
75C1 **Barwon** *R* Aust
44H5 **Barysh** Russian Fed
28D1 **Basail** Arg
20C1 **Basalt** USA
72B3 **Basankusu** Zaïre
28D2 **Basavilbas** Arg
57F6 **Basco** Phil
36D3 **Basel** France
40B1 **Basel** Switz
40D2 **Basento** *R* Italy
3F3 **Bashaw** Can
57F6 **Bashi Chan** Phil
44J5 **Bashkirskaya** Respublika, Russian Fed
57B3 **Basiano** Indon
57F9 **Basilan** *I* Phil
35F6 **Basildon** Eng
28E2 **Basilio** Brazil
18E2 **Basin** USA
35E6 **Basingstoke** Eng
8B2 **Basin Region** USA
64E3 **Basra** Iraq
36D2 **Bas-Rhin** Department, France
55D3 **Bassac** *R* Camb
3F3 **Bassano** Can
40C1 **Bassano** Italy
37D2 **Bassano del Grappa** Italy
71G4 **Bassari** Togo
73D6 **Bassas da India** *I* Mozam Chan
55A2 **Bassein** Burma
23E3 **Basse Terre** Guadeloupe
11C3 **Bassett** USA
71G4 **Bassila** Benin
20C2 **Bass Lake** USA
76D5 **Bass Str** Aust
32G7 **Båstad** Sweden
63C3 **Bastak** Iran
61B2 **Basti** India
40B2 **Bastia** Corse
42B3 **Bastogne** Belg
17D3 **Bastrop** Louisiana, USA
17C3 **Bastrop** Texas, USA
72A3 **Bata** Eq Guinea
56D3 **Batakan** Indon
60D2 **Batala** India
50C3 **Batang** China
72B3 **Batangafo** CAR
57F6 **Batan Is** Phil
57D3 **Batanta** *I* Indon
29C3 **Batatais** Brazil
13D2 **Batavia** USA
75D3 **Batemans Bay** Aust
15C2 **Batesburg** USA
17D2 **Batesville** Arkansas, USA
17E3 **Batesville** Mississippi, USA
5H4 **Bath** Can
35D6 **Bath** Eng
13F2 **Bath** Maine, USA
13D2 **Bath** New York, USA
72B2 **Batha** *R* Chad
12C1 **Bathawana Mt** Can
76D4 **Bathurst** Aust
7M5 **Bathurst** Can
6F2 **Bathurst,C** Can
76C2 **Bathurst I** Aust
6H2 **Bathurst I** Can
6H3 **Bathurst Inlet** *B* Can
71F4 **Batié** Burkina
63C2 **Bātlāq-e-Gavkhūnī** *Salt Flat* Iran
75C3 **Batlow** Aust
64D2 **Batman** Turk
71D1 **Batna** Alg
9D3 **Baton Rouge** USA
65C1 **Batroun** Leb
55C3 **Battambang** Camb
62C3 **Batticaloa** Sri Lanka
62E3 **Batti Malv** *I* Indian O
3G3 **Battle** *R* Can
9E2 **Battle Creek** USA
7N4 **Battle Harbour** Can
18C2 **Battle Mountain** USA
56F6 **Batu Gajah** Malay
56E2 **Batukelau** Indon
45G7 **Batumi** Georgia
55C5 **Batu Pahat** Malay
56B3 **Baturaja** Indon
65C2 **Bat Yam** Israel
76B1 **Baubau** Indon
71H3 **Bauchi** Nig
71H3 **Bauchi** State, Nig
11D2 **Baudette** USA
37B2 **Bauges** *Mts* France
7N4 **Bauld,C** Can
37B1 **Baumes-les-Dames** France
49N4 **Baunt** Russian Fed
27J8 **Bauru** Brazil
29B2 **Baus** Brazil
42C2 **Bautzen** Germany
56D4 **Baween** *I* Indon
69B2 **Bawîti** Egypt
71F3 **Bawku** Ghana
55B2 **Bawlake** Burma
75A2 **Bawlen** Aust
15C2 **Baxley** USA
61E1 **Baxoi** China
21E2 **Bayamo** Cuba
53B2 **Bayan** China
56E4 **Bayan** Indon
50D2 **Bayandzürh** Mongolia
50C3 **Bayan Har Shan** *Mts* China
52A1 **Bayan Mod** China
52B1 **Bayan Obo** China
11B3 **Bayard** Nebraska, USA
16A3 **Bayard** New Mexico, USA
37B2 **Bayard** *P* France
10N4 **Bayard,Mt** Can
49N5 **Bayasgalant** Mongolia
57F8 **Baybay** Phil
64D1 **Bayburt** Turk
9E2 **Bay City** Michigan, USA
17C4 **Bay City** Texas, USA
64B2 **Bay Dağlari** Turk
44M2 **Baydaratskaya Guba** *B* Russian Fed
72E3 **Baydhabo** Somalia
38B2 **Bayeaux** France
37D1 **Bayerische Alpen** *Mts* Germany
42C3 **Bayern** State, Germany
12A1 **Bayfield** USA
67E4 **Bayhan al Qisāb** Yemen
64C3 **Bāyir** Jordan
49M6 **Baykal, Ozero** *L* Kazakhstan
50D1 **Baykalskiy Khrebet** *Mts* Russian Fed
49L3 **Baykit** Russian Fed
49L5 **Baylik Shan** *Mts* China/Mongolia
44K5 **Baymak** Russian Fed
15B2 **Bay Minette** USA
57F7 **Bayombang** Phil
38B3 **Bayonne** France
63E1 **Bayram Ali** Turkmenistan
42C3 **Bayreuth** Germany
17E3 **Bay St Louis** USA
13E2 **Bay Shore** USA
13D1 **Bays,L of** Can
66D4 **Bayt al Faqih** Yemen
50B2 **Baytik Shan** *Mts* China
Bayt Lahm = Bethlehem
17D4 **Baytown** USA
39B2 **Baza** Spain
43F3 **Bazaliya** Ukraine
45H7 **Bazar-Dyuzi** *Mt* Azerbaijan
38B3 **Bazas** France
52B3 **Bazhong** China
63E3 **Bazmān** Iran
65D1 **Bcharre** Leb
11B2 **Beach** USA
14C3 **Beach Haven** USA
35F6 **Beachy Head** Eng
14D2 **Beacon** USA
73E5 **Bealanana** Madag
18D2 **Bear** *R* USA
12A2 **Beardstown** USA
Bear I = Bjørnøya
18D2 **Bear L** USA
4C3 **Bearskin Lake** Can
20B1 **Bear Valley** USA
8D2 **Beatrice** USA
34D2 **Beatrice** *Oilfield* N Sea
3D2 **Beatton** *R* Can
6F4 **Beatton River** Can
8B3 **Beatty** USA
4F4 **Beattyville** Can
36A2 **Beauce** Region, France
25E8 **Beauchene Is** Falkland Is
75D1 **Beaudesert** Aust
79B5 **Beaufort S** Can
74C3 **Beaufort West** S Africa
36A3 **Beaugeney** France
13E1 **Beauharnois** Can
34C3 **Beauly** Scot
19C4 **Beaumont** California, USA
9D3 **Beaumont** Texas, USA
36A2 **Beaumont-sur-Sarthe** France
38C2 **Beaune** France
4B3 **Beauséjour** Can
38C2 **Beauvais** France
3G2 **Beauval** Can
10J2 **Beaver** Alaska, USA
19D3 **Beaver** Utah, USA
4D2 **Beaver** *R* Can
3G3 **Beaver** *R* Saskatchewan, Can
3C1 **Beaver** *R* Yukon, Can
6D3 **Beaver Creek** Can
10J2 **Beaver Creek** USA
12B3 **Beaver Dam** Kentucky, USA
12B2 **Beaver Dam** Wisconsin, USA
18D1 **Beaverhead Mts** USA
3F3 **Beaverhill L** Can
12B1 **Beaver I** USA
17D2 **Beaver L** USA
3E2 **Beaverlodge** Can
60C3 **Beawar** India
28B2 **Beazley** Arg
29C3 **Bebedouro** Brazil
35F5 **Beccles** Eng
41E1 **Bečej** Serbia, Yugos
70B1 **Béchar** Alg
10G4 **Becharof L** USA
10F4 **Bechevin B** USA
9E3 **Beckley** USA
36E1 **Beckum** Germany
35E5 **Bedford** County, Eng
35E5 **Bedford** Eng
12B3 **Bedford** Indiana, USA
14A3 **Bedford** Pennsylvania, USA
23M2 **Bedford Pt** Grenada
14B2 **Beech Creek** USA
6D2 **Beechey Pt** USA
75C3 **Beechworth** Aust
75D1 **Beenleigh** Aust
65C3 **Beer Menuha** Israel
65C4 **Beer Ora** Israel
64B3 **Beersheba** Israel
Beèr Sheva = Beersheba
65C3 **Beér Sheva,** *R* Israel
8D4 **Beeville** USA
72C3 **Befale** Zaïre
73E5 **Befandriana** Madag
75C3 **Bega** Aust
49N2 **Begicheva, Ostrov** *I* Russian Fed
63C2 **Behbehān** Iran
10M4 **Behm Canal** *Sd* USA
63C1 **Behshahr** Iran
60B2 **Behsud** Afghan
53B2 **Bei'an** China
52B5 **Beihai** China
55D1 **Beihai** China
52D2 **Beijing** China
55E1 **Beiliu** China
52B4 **Beipan Jiang** *R* China
52E1 **Beipiao** China
73D5 **Beira** Mozam
64C3 **Beirut** Leb
50C2 **Bei Shan** *Mts* China

Beitbridge
Biratnagar

74E1 **Beitbridge** Zim
65C2 **Beit ed Dine** Leb
65C3 **Beit Jala** Israel
39A2 **Beja** Port
71D1 **Beja** Tunisia
71D1 **Bejaïa** Alg
39A1 **Béjar** Spain
63D2 **Bejestān** Iran
43E3 **Békéscsaba** Hung
73E6 **Bekily** Madag
61B2 **Bela** India
60B3 **Bela** Pak
56D2 **Belaga** Malay
14B3 **Bel Air** USA
62B1 **Belamoalli** India
57B2 **Belang** Indon
56A2 **Belangpidie** Indon
xxviiiH4 **Belau** *I* Pacific O
Belau = Palau
74E2 **Bela Vista** Mozam
29A3 **Béla Vista** Par/Brazil
56A2 **Belawan** Indon
44K4 **Belaya** *R* Ukraine
43G3 **Belaya Tserkov'** Russian Fed
7J2 **Belcher Chan** Can
7L4 **Belcher Is** Can
60B1 **Belchiragh** Afghan
44J5 **Belebey** Russian Fed
72E3 **Beled Weyne** Somalia
27J4 **Belém** Brazil
28B1 **Belén** Arg
26C3 **Belén** Colombia
29A3 **Belén** Par
28D2 **Belén** Urug
8C3 **Belen** USA
28B1 **Belén** *R* Arg
34B4 **Belfast** N Ire
74E2 **Belfast** S Africa
5H5 **Belfast** USA
34B4 **Belfast Lough** *Estuary* N Ire
11B2 **Belfield** USA
72D2 **Bēlfodiyo** Eth
34E4 **Belford** Eng
38D2 **Belfort** France
62A1 **Belgaum** India
42A2 **Belgium** Kingdom, N W Europe
45F5 **Belgorod** Russian Fed
45E6 **Belgorod Dnestrovskiy** Ukraine
Belgrade = Beograd
18D1 **Belgrade** USA
69A2 **Bel Hedan** Libya
56C3 **Belinyu** Indon
56C3 **Belitung** *I* Indon
21D3 **Belize** Belize
21D3 **Belize** Republic, C America
49P2 **Bel'kovskiv, Ostrov** *I* Russian Fed
38C2 **Bellac** France
6F4 **Bella Coola** Can
37C2 **Bellagio** Italy
17C4 **Bellaire** USA
37C1 **Bellano** Italy
62B1 **Bellary** India
75C1 **Bellata** Aust
28D2 **Bella Union** Urug
28D1 **Bella Vista** Arg
37B2 **Belledonne** *Mts* France
14B2 **Bellefonte** USA
8C2 **Belle Fourche** USA
11B3 **Belle Fourche** *R* USA
38D2 **Bellegarde** France
15E4 **Belle Glade** USA
7N4 **Belle I** Can
38B2 **Belle-Ile** *I* France
7N4 **Belle Isle,Str of** Can
36A2 **Bellême** France
5K4 **Belleoram** Can
7L5 **Belleville** Can
12B3 **Belleville** Illinois, USA
17C2 **Belleville** Kansas, USA
18D2 **Bellevue** Idaho, USA
12A2 **Bellevue** Iowa, USA
18B1 **Bellevue** Washington, USA
37A2 **Belley** France
75D2 **Bellingen** Aust
8A2 **Bellingham** USA
79G2 **Bellingshausen** *Base* Ant
79G3 **Bellingshausen S** Ant
40B1 **Bellinzona** Switz
26C2 **Bello** Colombia
77E3 **Bellona Reefs** Nouvelle Calédonie
20B1 **Bellota** USA
13E2 **Bellows Falls** USA
7K3 **Bell Pen** Can
40C1 **Belluno** Italy
25D4 **Bell Ville** Arg
4C5 **Belmond** USA
14B1 **Belmont** USA
27L7 **Belmonte** Brazil
21D3 **Belmopan** Belize
53B1 **Belogorsk** Russian Fed
73E6 **Beloha** Madag
27K7 **Belo Horizonte** Brazil
16C2 **Beloit** Kansas, USA
9E2 **Beloit** Wisconsin, USA
44E3 **Belomorsk** Russian Fed
44K5 **Beloretsk** Russian Fed
44D5 **Belorussia** *Republic* Europe
73E5 **Belo-Tsiribihina** Madag
44F2 **Beloye More** *S*
44F3 **Beloye Ozero** *L* Russian Fed
44F3 **Belozersk** Russian Fed
12C3 **Belpre** USA
75A2 **Beltana** Aust
17C3 **Belton** USA
43F3 **Bel'tsy** Moldavia
48K5 **Belukha** *Mt* Russian Fed
44H2 **Belush'ye** Russian Fed
12B2 **Belvidere** Illinois, USA
14C2 **Belvidere** New Jersey, USA
48J2 **Belyy, Ostrov** *I* Russian Fed
73B4 **Bembe** Angola
71G3 **Bembéréke** Benin
9D2 **Bemidji** USA
15B1 **Bemis** USA
32G6 **Bena** Nor
72C4 **Bena Dibele** Zaïre
75C3 **Benalla** Aust
34C2 **Ben Attow** *Mt* Scot
39A1 **Benavente** Spain
34B3 **Benbecula** *I* Scot
76A4 **Bencubbin** Aust
8A2 **Bend** USA
69E3 **Bendarbeyla** Somalia
34C3 **Ben Dearg** *Mt* Scot
43F3 **Bendery** Moldavia
76D4 **Bendigo** Aust
71F3 **Bénéna** Mali
42C3 **Benešov** Czech
40C2 **Benevento** Italy
59G4 **Bengal,B of** Asia
69A1 **Ben Gardane** Libya
71E2 **Ben Gardane** Tunisia
52D3 **Bengbu** China
57B3 **Benggai** *I* Indon
69B1 **Benghāzī** Libya
56B2 **Bengkalis** Indon
56B3 **Bengkulu** Indon
73B5 **Benguela** Angola
71A2 **Benguerir** Mor
64B3 **Benha** Egypt
34C2 **Ben Hope** *Mt* Scot
72C3 **Beni** Zaïre
26E6 **Béni** *R* Bol
70B1 **Beni Abbes** Alg
39C1 **Benicarló** Spain
39B2 **Benidorm** Spain
39C2 **Beni Mansour** Alg
69C2 **Beni Mazar** Egypt
71A2 **Beni Mellal** Mor
70C4 **Benin** Republic, Africa
71H4 **Benin City** Nig
71B1 **Beni-Saf** Alg
69C2 **Beni Suef** Egypt
16B2 **Benkelman** USA
34C2 **Ben Kilbreck** *Mt* Scot
33C2 **Ben Lawers** *Mt* Scot
34D3 **Ben Macdui** *Mt* Scot
34C2 **Ben More Assynt** *Mt* Scot
78B2 **Benmore,L** NZ
49R2 **Bennetta, Ostrov** *I* Russian Fed
34C3 **Ben Nevis** *Mt* Scot
13E2 **Bennington** USA
65C2 **Bennt Jbail** Leb
72B3 **Bénoué** *R* Cam
71J4 **Bénoué Nat Pk** Cam
36E2 **Bensheim** Germany
8B3 **Benson** Arizona, USA
11C2 **Benson** Minnesota, USA
72C3 **Bentiu** Sudan
29A2 **Bento Gomes** *R* Brazil
17D3 **Benton** Arkansas, USA
20C2 **Benton** California, USA
12B3 **Benton** Kentucky, USA
12B2 **Benton Harbor** USA
71H4 **Benue** State, Nig
71H4 **Benue** *R* Nig
34C3 **Ben Wyvis** *Mt* Scot
52E1 **Benxi** China
57C2 **Beo** Indon
41E2 **Beograd** Serbia, Yugos
61B3 **Beohāri** India
53C5 **Beppu** Japan
41D2 **Berat** Alb
72D2 **Berber** Sudan
72E2 **Berbera** Somalia
72B3 **Berbérati** CAR
36A1 **Berck** France
43F3 **Berdichev** Ukraine
45F6 **Berdyansk** Ukraine
12C3 **Berea** USA
57C2 **Berebere** Indon
71F4 **Berekum** Ghana
20B2 **Berenda** USA
66C2 **Berenice** Egypt
4C3 **Berens** *R* Can
6J4 **Berens River** Can
75A1 **Beresford** Aust
11C3 **Beresford** USA
43E3 **Berettyoújfalu** Hung
43E2 **Bereza** Belorussia
43E3 **Berezhany** Ukraine
43F2 **Berezina** *R* Belorussia
44G3 **Bereznik** Russian Fed
44K4 **Berezniki** Russian Fed
45E6 **Berezovka** Ukraine
44L3 **Berezovo** Russian Fed
53D1 **Berezovyy** Russian Fed
64A2 **Bergama** Turk
40B1 **Bergamo** Italy
32F6 **Bergen** Nor
14B1 **Bergen** USA
36C1 **Bergen op Zoom** Neth
38C3 **Bergerac** France
36D1 **Bergisch-Gladbach** Germany
4D4 **Bergland** USA
62C1 **Berhampur** India
49S4 **Beringa, Ostrov** *I* Russian Fed
10K3 **Bering Gl** USA
49T3 **Beringovskiy** Russian Fed
xxixK2 **Bering S** Russian Fed/USA
79C6 **Bering Str** Russian Fed/ USA
63D3 **Berīzak** Iran
39B2 **Berja** Spain
71B2 **Berkane** Mor
8A3 **Berkeley** USA
14A3 **Berkeley Spring** USA
79F2 **Berkner I** Ant
41E2 **Berkovitsa** Bulg
35E6 **Berkshire** County, Eng
14D1 **Berkshire Hills** USA
3E3 **Berland** *R* Can
42C2 **Berlin** Germany
13E2 **Berlin** New Hampshire, USA
14A3 **Berlin** Pennsylvania, USA
42C2 **Berlin** State, Germany
26F8 **Bermejo** Bol
25E3 **Bermejo** *R* Arg
2M5 **Bermuda** *I* Atlantic O
40B1 **Bern** Switz
16A2 **Bernalillo** USA
29B4 **Bernardo de Irigoyen** Arg
14C2 **Bernardsville** USA
28C3 **Bernasconi** Arg
36A2 **Bernay** France
42C2 **Bernburg** Germany
37B1 **Berner Orberland** *Mts* Switz
7K2 **Bernier B** Can
42C3 **Berounka** *R* Czech
71A2 **Berrechid** Mor
75B2 **Berri** Aust
71C2 **Berriane** Alg
38C2 **Berry** Region, France
20A1 **Berryessa,L** USA
9F4 **Berry Is** Bahamas
14B3 **Berryville** USA
74B2 **Berseba** Namibia
56F6 **Bertam** Malay
16A2 **Berthoud P** USA
72B3 **Bertoua** Cam
77G1 **Beru** *I* Kiribati
13D2 **Berwick** USA
34D4 **Berwick-upon-Tweed** Eng
35D5 **Berwyn** *Mts* Wales
73E5 **Besalampy** Madag
38D2 **Besançon** France
43E3 **Beskidy Zachodnie** *Mts* Pol
3G2 **Besnard L** Can
64C2 **Besni** Turk
65C3 **Besor** *R* Israel
15B2 **Bessemer** Alabama, USA
12B1 **Bessemer** Michigan, USA
73E5 **Betafo** Madag
39A1 **Betanzos** Spain
71J4 **Betaré Oya** Cam
65C3 **Bet Guvrin** Israel
74D2 **Bethal** S Africa
74B2 **Bethanie** Namibia
17D1 **Bethany** Missouri, USA
17C2 **Bethany** Oklahoma, USA
6B3 **Bethel** Alaska, USA
14D2 **Bethel** Connecticut, USA
12C2 **Bethel Park** USA
13D3 **Bethesda** USA
65C3 **Bethlehem** Israel
74D2 **Bethlehem** S Africa
13D2 **Bethlehem** USA
74D3 **Bethulie** S Africa
38C1 **Bethune** France
36A2 **Béthune** *R* France
73E6 **Betioky** Madag
75B1 **Betoota** Aust
72B3 **Betou** Congo
59E1 **Betpak Dala** *Steppe* Kazakhstan
73E6 **Betroka** Madag
7M5 **Betsiamites** Can
12A2 **Bettendorf** USA
61B2 **Bettiah** India
10H2 **Bettles** USA
37C2 **Bèttola** Italy
60D4 **Bētul** India
36C1 **Betuwe** Region, Neth
60D3 **Betwa** *R* India
36D1 **Betzdorf** Germany
10G4 **Beverley,L** USA
14E1 **Beverly** USA
20C3 **Beverly Hills** USA
70B4 **Beyla** Guinea
62B2 **Beypore** India
Beyrouth = Beirut
64B2 **Beyşehir** Turk
45E8 **Beyşehir Gölü** *L* Turk
65C2 **Beyt Shean** Israel
37C1 **Bezan** Austria
44F4 **Bezhetsk** Russian Fed
38C3 **Béziers** France
63D1 **Bezmein** Turkmenistan
50D1 **Beznosova** Russian Fed
61C2 **Bhadgaon** Nepal
62C1 **Bhadrāchalam** India
61C3 **Bhadrakh** India
62B2 **Bhadra Res** India
62B2 **Bhadrāvati** India
60B3 **Bhag** Pak
61C2 **Bhāgalpur** India
60C2 **Bhakkar** Pak
61E3 **Bhamo** Burma
60D4 **Bhandāra** India
60D3 **Bharatpur** India
60C4 **Bharūch** India
61C3 **Bhātiāpāra Ghat** Bang
60C2 **Bhatinda** India
62A2 **Bhatkal** India
61C3 **Bhātpāra** India
60C4 **Bhāvnagar** India
61B4 **Bhawānipatna** India
60C2 **Bhera** Pak
61B2 **Bheri** *R* Nepal
61B3 **Bhilai** India
60C3 **Bhīlwāra** India
62C1 **Bhīmavaram** India
60D3 **Bhind** India
60D3 **Bhiwāni** India
62B1 **Bhongir** India
60D4 **Bhopāl** India
61C3 **Bhubaneshwar** India
60B4 **Bhuj** India
60D4 **Bhusāwal** India
59H3 **Bhutan** Kingdom, Asia
71F4 **Bia** *R* Ghana
51G7 **Biak** *I* Indon
43E2 **Biala Podlaska** Pol
42D2 **Bialograd** Pol
43E2 **Bialystok** Pol
32A1 **Biargtangar** *C* Iceland
63D1 **Biārjmand** Iran
57C2 **Biaro** *I* Indon
38B3 **Biarritz** France
37C1 **Biasca** Switz
64B4 **Biba** Egypt
53E3 **Bibai** Japan
73B5 **Bibala** Angola
37D3 **Bibbiena** Italy
42B3 **Biberach** Germany
71F4 **Bibiani** Ghana
5H4 **Bic** Can
41F1 **Bicaz** Rom
53D1 **Bichi** *R* Russian Fed
19D3 **Bicknell** USA
71H4 **Bida** Nig
62B1 **Bīdar** India
67G2 **Bidbid** Oman
13E2 **Biddeford** USA
35C6 **Bideford** Eng
35C6 **Bideford B** Eng
70C2 **Bidon 5** Alg
43E2 **Biebrza** Pol
40B1 **Biel** Switz
42D2 **Bielawa** Pol
42B2 **Bielefeld** Germany
37B1 **Bieler See** *L* Switz
40B1 **Biella** Italy
43E2 **Bielsk Podlaski** Pol
55D3 **Bien Hoa** Viet
40C2 **Biferno** *R* Italy
64A1 **Biga** Turk
41F3 **Bigadiç** Turk
5H4 **Big Bald Mt** Can
4D3 **Big Beaver House** Can
16B4 **Big Bend Nat Pk** USA
18D1 **Big Belt Mts** USA
17E3 **Big Black** *R* USA
17C1 **Big Blue** *R* USA
15E4 **Big Cypress Swamp** USA
6D3 **Big Delta** USA
38D2 **Bigent** Germany
3G3 **Biggar** Can
75D1 **Biggenden** Aust
10L4 **Bigger,Mt** Can
18D1 **Big Hole** *R* USA
11A2 **Bighorn** *R* USA
11A2 **Bighorn L** USA
11A3 **Bighorn Mts** USA
55C3 **Bight of Bangkok** *B* Thai
70C4 **Bight of Benin** *B* W Africa
70C4 **Bight of Biafra** *B* Cam
7L3 **Big I** Can
10G4 **Big Koniuji** *I* USA
16B3 **Big Lake** USA
37C1 **Bignasco** Switz
70A3 **Bignona** Sen
19C3 **Big Pine** USA
15E4 **Big Pine Key** USA
20C3 **Big Pine Mt** USA
12B2 **Big Rapids** USA
6H4 **Big River** Can
4B2 **Big Sand L** Can
18D1 **Big Sandy** USA
3H3 **Big Sandy L** Can
11C3 **Big Sioux** *R* USA
20D1 **Big Smokey V** USA
8C3 **Big Spring** USA
16B1 **Big Springs** USA
11C2 **Big Stone City** USA
12C3 **Big Stone Gap** USA
4B3 **Bigstone L** Can
20B2 **Big Sur** USA
18E1 **Big Timber** USA
7J4 **Big Trout L** Can
4D3 **Big Trout Lake** Can
40D2 **Bihać** Bosnia & Herzegovina, Yugos
61C2 **Bihār** India
61C3 **Bihar** State, India
72D4 **Biharamulo** Tanz
45C6 **Bihor** *Mt* Rom
62B1 **Bijāpur** India
62C1 **Bījāpur** India
63B1 **Bījār** Iran
61B2 **Bijauri** Nepal
41D2 **Bijeljina** Bosnia & Herzegovina, Yugos
52B4 **Bijie** China
60D3 **Bijnor** India
60C3 **Bijnot** Pak
60C3 **Bikāner** India
65C2 **Bikfaya** Leb
53C2 **Bikin** Russian Fed
53D2 **Bikin** *R* Russian Fed
72B4 **Bikoro** Zaïre
53A2 **Bila He** *R* China
60C3 **Bilara** India
60D2 **Bilaspur** India
61B3 **Bilāspur** India
55B3 **Bilauktaung Range** *Mts* Thai
39B1 **Bilbao** Spain
65A3 **Bilbeis** Egypt
Bilbo = Bilbao
42D3 **Bílé** *R* Czech
41D2 **Bileća** Bosnia & Herzegovina, Yugos
64B1 **Bilecik** Turk
72C3 **Bili** *R* Zaïre
49S3 **Bilibino** Russian Fed
57F8 **Biliran** *I* Phil
8C2 **Billings** USA
72B2 **Bilma** Niger
9E3 **Biloxi** USA
72C2 **Biltine** Chad
71F4 **Bimbita** Ghana
60D4 **Bina-Etawa** India
57F8 **Binalbagan** Phil
73D5 **Bindura** Zim
73C5 **Binga** Zim
73D5 **Binga** *Mt* Zim
75D1 **Bingara** Aust
42B3 **Bingen** Germany
13F1 **Bingham** USA
9F2 **Binghamton** USA
56E1 **Bingkor** Malay
64D2 **Bingöl** Turk
52D3 **Binhai** China
56A2 **Binjai** Indon
56C2 **Binjai** Indon
57B4 **Binongko** *I* Indon
56B2 **Bintan** *I* Indon
56B3 **Bintuhan** Indon
56D2 **Bintulu** Malay
25B5 **Bió Bió** *R* Chile
xxxJ4 **Bioko** *I* Atlantic O
62B1 **Bīr** India
53C2 **Bira** Russian Fed
69B2 **Bîr Abu Husein** *Well* Egypt
69B2 **Bi'r al Harash** *Well* Libya
72C2 **Birao** CAR
61C2 **Biratnagar** Nepal

Birch **Bourg**

3F2 **Birch** *R* Can
10J2 **Birch Creek** USA
75B3 **Birchip** Aust
11D2 **Birch L** USA
4C3 **Birch L** Can
6G4 **Birch Mts** Can
7J4 **Bird** Can
76C3 **Birdsville** Aust
76C2 **Birdum** Aust
65A4 **Bir el 'Agramîya** *Well* Egypt
65B3 **Bir el Duweidâr** *Well* Egypt
61B2 **Birganj** Nepal
65B3 **Bîr Gifgâfa** *Well* Egypt
65A4 **Bîr Gindali** *Well* Egypt
65B3 **Bîr Hasana** *Well* Egypt
29B3 **Birigui** Brazil
65D1 **Bīrīn** Syria
63D2 **Birjand** Iran
64B4 **Birkat Qarun** *L* Egypt
36D2 **Birkenfeld** Germany
35D5 **Birkenhead** Eng
45D6 **Bîrlad** Rom
65B3 **Bir Lahfân** *Well* Egypt
35D5 **Birmingham** Eng
9E3 **Birmingham** USA
69B2 **Bîr Mîsâha** *Well* Egypt
70A2 **Bir Moghrein** Maur
71H3 **Birnin Gwari** Nig
71G3 **Birnin Kebbi** Nig
71H3 **Birni N'Konni** Nig
53C2 **Birobidzhan** Russian Fed
35B5 **Birr** Irish Rep
39C2 **Bir Rabalou** Alg
75C1 **Birrie** *R* Aust
34D2 **Birsay** Scot
44K4 **Birsk** Russian Fed
69B2 **Bîr Tarfâwi** *Well* Egypt
11B1 **Birtle** Can
65B4 **Bîr Udelb** *Well* Egypt
49L4 **Biryusa** *R* Russian Fed
32J7 **Biržai** Lithuania
70B2 **Bir Zreigat** *Well* Maur
57C3 **Bisa** *I* Indon
19E4 **Bisbee** USA
38A2 **Biscay,B of** Spain/France
15E4 **Biscayne B** USA
37E1 **Bischofshofen** Austria
36D2 **Bischwiller** France
12C1 **Biscotasi L** Can
52B4 **Bishan** China
59F1 **Bishkek** Kirgizia
8B3 **Bishop** USA
35E4 **Bishop Auckland** Eng
35F6 **Bishop's Stortford** Eng
61B3 **Bishrāmpur** India
53A1 **Bishui** China
66C3 **Biskia** Eth
71D2 **Biskra** Alg
57G9 **Bislig** Phil
8C2 **Bismarck** USA
76D1 **Bismarck Arch** PNG
76D1 **Bismarck Range** *Mts* PNG
76D1 **Bismarck S** PNG
63B2 **Bīsotūn** Iran
70A3 **Bissau** Guinea-Bissau
4B3 **Bissett** Can
6G4 **Bistcho L** Can
41F1 **Bistrita** *R* Rom
72B3 **Bitam** Gabon
3G1 **Bitau L** Can
42B3 **Bitburg** Germany
36D2 **Bitche** France
64D2 **Bitlis** Turk
41E2 **Bitola** Macedonia, Yugos
42C2 **Bitterfeld** Germany
74B3 **Bitterfontein** S Africa
64B3 **Bitter Lakes** Egypt
8B2 **Bitteroot Range** *Mts* USA
57C2 **Bitung** Indon
71J3 **Biu** Nig
53D4 **Biwa-ko** *L* Japan
72E2 **Biyo Kaboba** Eth
48K4 **Biysk** Russian Fed
71D1 **Bizerte** Tunisia
39C2 **Bj bou Arréridj** Alg
40D1 **Bjelovar** Croatia, Yugos
70B2 **Bj Flye Ste Marie** Alg
48C2 **Bjørnøya** *I* Barents S
10K2 **Black** *R* USA
17D2 **Black** *R* USA
76D3 **Blackall** Aust
12B1 **Black B** Can
3G2 **Black Birch L** Can
35D5 **Blackburn** Eng
6D3 **Blackburn,Mt** USA
19D4 **Black Canyon City** USA
3F3 **Black Diamond** Can
11D2 **Blackduck** USA
4D2 **Black Duck** *R* Can
18D1 **Black Eagle** USA
18D2 **Blackfoot** USA
18D1 **Blackfoot** *R* USA
6H5 **Black Hills** USA
34C3 **Black Isle** *Pen* Scot
3G2 **Black L** Can
3G2 **Black Lake** Can
23Q2 **Blackman's** Barbados
19D3 **Black Mts** USA
35D6 **Black Mts** Wales
74B1 **Black Nossob** *R* Namibia
35D5 **Blackpool** Eng
23H1 **Black River** Jamaica
4E5 **Black River** USA
12A2 **Black River Falls** USA
8B2 **Black Rock Desert** USA
45D7 **Black S** Europe/Asia
12C3 **Blacksburg** USA
75D2 **Black Sugarloaf** *Mt* Aust
71F4 **Black Volta** *R* Ghana
15B2 **Black Warrior** *R* USA
33B3 **Blackwater** *R* Irish Rep
10O3 **Blackwater L** Can
17C2 **Blackwell** USA
41E2 **Blagoevgrad** Bulg
49O4 **Blagoveshchensk** Russian Fed
18D1 **Blaikiston,Mt** Can
18B1 **Blaine** USA
11C3 **Blair** USA
34D3 **Blair Atholl** Scot
34D3 **Blairgowrie** Scot
15C2 **Blakely** USA
16A2 **Blanca Peak** *Mt* USA
75A1 **Blanche,L** Aust
28A2 **Blanco** *R* Arg
28B1 **Blanco** *R* Arg
22C1 **Blanco** *R* Mexico
8A2 **Blanco,C** USA
7N4 **Blanc Sablon** Can
35D6 **Blandford Forum** Eng
19E3 **Blanding** USA
36A2 **Blangy-sur-Bresle** France
36B1 **Blankenberge** Belg
28D2 **Blanquillo** Urug
73D5 **Blantyre** Malawi
38B2 **Blaye** France
75C2 **Blayney** Aust
77G5 **Blenheim** NZ
37B2 **Bléone** *R* France
71C1 **Blida** Alg
4E4 **Blind River** Can
75A2 **Blinman** Aust
56D4 **Blitar** Indon
71G4 **Blitta** Togo
13E2 **Block I** USA
14E2 **Block Island Sd** USA
74D2 **Bloemfontin** S Africa
74D2 **Bloemhof** S Africa
74D2 **Bloemhof Dam** *Res* S Africa
36A3 **Blois** France
27G3 **Blommesteinmeer** *L* Surinam
32A1 **Blonduós** Iceland
12B3 **Bloomfield** Indiana, USA
17D1 **Bloomfield** Iowa, USA
11C3 **Bloomfield** Nebraska, USA
16A2 **Bloomfield** New Mexico, USA
12B2 **Bloomington** Illinois, USA
12B3 **Bloomington** Indiana, USA
11D3 **Bloomington** Minnesota, USA
14B2 **Bloomsburg** USA
56D4 **Blora** Indon
14B2 **Blossburg** USA
7Q3 **Blosseville Kyst** *Mts* Greenland
74D1 **Blouberg** *Mt* S Africa
42B3 **Bludenz** Austria
9E3 **Bluefield** USA
26B1 **Bluefields** Nic
16C1 **Blue Hill** USA
14A2 **Blue Knob** *Mt* USA
23B3 **Blue Mountain Peak** *Mt* Jamaica
14B2 **Blue Mt** USA
75D2 **Blue Mts** Aust
23J1 **Blue Mts** Jamaica
8A2 **Blue Mts** USA
72D2 **Blue Nile, R** Sudan
6G3 **Bluenose L** Can
15C2 **Blue Ridge** USA
9E3 **Blue Ridge Mts** USA
3E3 **Blue River** Can
34A4 **Blue Stack** *Mt* Irish Rep
78A3 **Bluff** NZ
19E3 **Bluff** USA
5K3 **Bluff,C** Can
76A4 **Bluff Knoll** *Mt* Aust
25G3 **Blumenau** Brazil
38D2 **Blundez** Austria
11C3 **Blunt** USA
18B2 **Bly** USA
10J4 **Blying Sd** USA
34E4 **Blyth** Eng
8B3 **Blythe** USA
9E3 **Blytheville** USA
70A4 **Bo** Sierra Leone
57F8 **Boac** Phil
52D2 **Boading** China
57C3 **Boano** *I* Indon
29D1 **Boa Nova** Brazil
12C2 **Boardman** USA
49M5 **Boatou** China
26F3 **Boa Vista** Brazil
70A4 **Boa Vista** *I* Cape Verde
55E1 **Bobai** China
62C1 **Bobbili** India
37C2 **Bóbbio** Italy
71F3 **Bobo Dioulasso** Burkina
43G2 **Bobrovica** Ukraine
44D5 **Bobruysk** Belorussia
15E4 **Boca Chica Key** *I* USA
26E4 **Bôca do Acre** Brazil
29D2 **Bocaiúva** Brazil
22C1 **Boca Jesús Maria** Mexico
72B3 **Bocaranga** CAR
15E4 **Boca Raton** USA
43E3 **Bochnia** Pol
42B2 **Bocholt** Germany
36D1 **Bochum** Germany
73B5 **Bocoio** Angola
72B3 **Boda** CAR
49N4 **Bodaybo** Russian Fed
19B3 **Bodega Head** *Pt* USA
72B2 **Bodélé** *Desert Region* Chad
32J5 **Boden** Sweden
37C1 **Bodensee** *L* Switz/Germany
62B1 **Bodhan** India
62B2 **Bodināyakkanūr** India
35C6 **Bodmin** Eng
35C6 **Bodmin Moor** *Upland* Eng
32G5 **Bodø** Nor
41F3 **Bodrum** Turk
72C4 **Boende** Zaïre
70A3 **Boffa** Guinea
55B2 **Bogale** Burma
17E3 **Bogalusa** USA
75C2 **Bogan** *R* Aust
71F3 **Bogandé** Burkina
64C2 **Boğazlıyan** Turk
44L4 **Bogdanovich** Russian Fed
50B2 **Bogda Shan** *Mt* China
74B2 **Bogenfels** Namibia
75D1 **Boggabilla** Aust
75C2 **Boggabri** Aust
57F8 **Bogo** Phil
75C3 **Bogong,Mt** Aust
56C4 **Bogor** Indon
44J4 **Bogorodskoye** Russian Fed
26D3 **Bogotá** Colombia
49K4 **Bogotol** Russian Fed
61C3 **Bogra** Bang
52D2 **Bo Hai** *B* China
36B2 **Bohain-en-Vermandois** France
52D2 **Bohai Wan** *B* China
37E1 **Boh Bistrica** Slovenia, Yugos
71G4 **Bohicon** Benin
42C3 **Bohmer-wald** *Upland* Germany
57F9 **Bohol** *I* Phil
57F9 **Bohol S** Phil
29B2 **Bois** *R* Brazil
12C1 **Bois Blanc I** USA
8B2 **Boise** USA
16B2 **Boise City** USA
11B2 **Boissevain** Can
70A2 **Bojador,C** Mor
57F7 **Bojeador,C** Phil
63D1 **Bojnūrd** Iran
70A3 **Boké** Guinea
75C1 **Bokhara** *R* Aust
32F7 **Boknafjord** *Inlet* Nor
72B4 **Boko** Congo
55C3 **Bokor** Camb
72B2 **Bokoro** Chad
72C4 **Bokungu** Zaïre
72B2 **Bol** Chad
22B1 **Bolaãnos** Mexico
70A3 **Bolama** Guinea-Bissau
22B1 **Bolanos** *R* Mexico
38C2 **Bolbec** France
71F4 **Bole** Ghana
53D1 **Bolen** Russian Fed
42D2 **Boleslawiec** Pol
71F3 **Bolgatanga** Ghana
45D6 **Bolgrad** Ukraine
53C2 **Boli** China
28C3 **Bolívar** Arg
17D2 **Bolivar** Missouri, USA
17E2 **Bolivar** Tennessee, USA
26E7 **Bolivia** Republic, S America
32H6 **Bollnas** Sweden
75C1 **Bollon** Aust
26D2 **Bollvar** *Mt* Ven
72B4 **Bolobo** Zaire
40C2 **Bologna** Italy
44E4 **Bologoye** Russian Fed
53D2 **Bolon'** Russian Fed
53D2 **Bolon', Ozero** *L* Russian Fed
49M2 **Bol'shevik, Ostrov** *I* Russian Fed
44J2 **Bol'shezemel'skaya Tundra** *Plain* Russian Fed
49S3 **Bol'shoy Anyuy** *R* Russian Fed
53E1 **Bol'shoye Kizi, Ozero** *L* Russian Fed
45H5 **Bol'shoy Irgiz** *R* Russian Fed
53C3 **Bol'shoy Kamen** Russian Fed
45F5 **Bol'shoy Kavkaz** *Mts* Georgia
49Q2 **Bol'shoy Lyakhovskiy, Ostrov** *I* Russian Fed
45H6 **Bol'shoy Uzen** *R* Kazakhstan
8C4 **Bolson de Mapimi** *Desert* Mexico
35D5 **Bolton** Eng
4B3 **Bolton L** Can
64B1 **Bolu** Turk
32A1 **Bolugarvik** Iceland
64B2 **Bolvadin** Turk
40C1 **Bolzano** Italy
72B4 **Boma** Zaïre
76D4 **Bombala** Aust
62A1 **Bombay** India
72D3 **Bombo** Uganda
61D2 **Bomdila** India
61E2 **Bomi** China
70A4 **Bomi Hills** Lib
27K6 **Bom Jesus da Lapa** Brazil
49O4 **Bomnak** Russian Fed
72C3 **Bomokandi** *R* Zaïre
72C3 **Bomu** *R* CAR/Zaïre
13D3 **Bon Air** USA
23D4 **Bonaire** *I* Caribbean
10K3 **Bona,Mt** USA
21D3 **Bonanza** Nic
7N5 **Bonavista** Can
5L4 **Bonavista B** Can
5L4 **Bonavista,C** Can
75A2 **Bon Bon** Aust
29C2 **Bon Despacho** Brazil
72C3 **Bondo** Zaïre
71F4 **Bondoukou** Ivory Coast
Bône = 'Annaba
57B4 **Bone** Indon
57B3 **Bonelipu** Indon
11C3 **Bonesteel** USA
27G3 **Bonfim** Guyana
72C3 **Bongandanga** Zaïre
57B3 **Bongka** *R* Indon
72B2 **Bongor** Chad
71F4 **Bongouanou** Ivory Coast
17C3 **Bonham** USA
40B2 **Bonifacio** Corse
40B2 **Bonifacio,Str of** *Chan* Medit S
Bonin Is = Ogasawara Gunto
15E4 **Bonita Springs** USA
29A3 **Bonito** Brazil
42B2 **Bonn** Germany
18C1 **Bonners Ferry** USA
36A2 **Bonnétable** France
10M2 **Bonnet Plume** *R* Can
36A2 **Bonneval** France
3F3 **Bonnyville** Can
76A1 **Bonthain** Indon
70A4 **Bonthe** Sierra Leone
57A4 **Bontosunggu** Indon
69D3 **Booaaso** Somalia
75B2 **Booligal** Aust
75D1 **Boonah** Aust
16B2 **Boone** Colorado, USA
11D3 **Boone** Iowa, USA
15C1 **Boone** North Carolina, USA
13D2 **Boonville** USA
75C2 **Boorowa** Aust
7J2 **Boothia,G of** Can
7J2 **Boothia Pen** Can
72B4 **Booué** Gabon
75A1 **Bopeechee** Aust
74C2 **Bophuthatswana** Self governing homeland, S Africa
16B4 **Boquillas** Mexico
72D3 **Bor** Sudan
64B2 **Bor** Turk
41E2 **Bor** Serbia, Yugos
8B2 **Borah Peak** *Mt* USA
32G7 **Borås** Sweden
63C3 **Borāzjān** Iran
75A3 **Borda,C** Aust
38B3 **Bordeaux** France
6G2 **Borden I** Can
7K2 **Borden Pen** Can
14C2 **Bordentown** USA
34D4 **Borders** Region, Scot
75B3 **Bordertown** Aust
37B3 **Bordighera** Italy
70C2 **Bordi Omar Dris** Alg
71C1 **Bordj bou Arreridj** Alg
32K6 **Borgå** Fin
32A2 **Borgarnes** Iceland
8C3 **Borger** USA
32H7 **Borgholm** Sweden
37D3 **Borgo San Lorenzo** Italy
37C2 **Borgosia** Italy
37C2 **Borgo Val di Taro** Italy
37D1 **Borgo Valsugana** Italy
43E3 **Borislav** Ukraine
45G5 **Borisoglebsk** Russian Fed
44D5 **Borisov** Belorussia
45F5 **Borisovka** Russian Fed
29A4 **Borja** Par
72B2 **Borkou** *Desert Region* Chad
32H6 **Borlänge** Sweden
37C2 **Bormida** Italy
37D1 **Bormio** Italy
32H7 **Bornholm** *I* Den
71J3 **Borno** State, Nig
41F3 **Bornova** Turk
72C3 **Boro** *R* Sudan
49P3 **Borogontsy** Russian Fed
71F3 **Boromo** Burkina
20D3 **Boron** USA
44E4 **Borovichi** Russian Fed
76C2 **Borroloola** Aust
41E1 **Borsa** Rom
63B2 **Borūjed** Iran
63C2 **Borūjen** Iran
42D2 **Bory Tucholskie** Region, Pol
43G2 **Borzna** Ukraine
49N4 **Borzya** Russian Fed
52B5 **Bose** China
53E2 **Boshnyakovo** Russian Fed
74D2 **Boshof** S Africa
41D2 **Bosna** *R* Bosnia & Herzegovina, Yugos
40D2 **Bosnia and Herzegovina** *Republic* Yugos
54D3 **Bōsō-hantō** *B* Japan
Bosporus = Karadeniz Boğazi
39C2 **Bosquet** Alg
72B3 **Bossangoa** CAR
72B3 **Bossèmbélé** CAR
17D3 **Bossier City** USA
48K5 **Bosten Hu** *L* China
35E5 **Boston** Eng
9F2 **Boston** USA
9D3 **Boston Mts** USA
71F4 **Bosumtwi,L** Ghana
60C4 **Botād** India
41E2 **Botevgrad** Bulg
74D2 **Bothaville** S Africa
44B3 **Bothnia,G of** Sweden/Fin
73C6 **Botletli** *R* Botswana
45D6 **Botosani** Rom
73C6 **Botswana** Republic, Africa
40D3 **Botte Donato** *Mt* Italy
11B2 **Bottineau** USA
36D1 **Bottrop** Germany
29C3 **Botucatu** Brazil
29D1 **Botupora** Brazil
7N5 **Botwood** Can
70B4 **Bouaflé** Ivory Coast
68D7 **Bouaké** Ivory Coast
72B3 **Bouar** CAR
71B2 **Bouârfa** Mor
71J4 **Bouba Ndjia Nat Pk** Cam
72B3 **Bouca** CAR
71B2 **Boudnib** Mor
39C2 **Boufarik** Alg
77E1 **Bougainville** *I* PNG
Bougie = Bejaïa
70B3 **Bougouni** Mali
71F3 **Bougouriba** *R* Burkina
71C2 **Bougtob** Alg
36C2 **Bouillon** France
71C1 **Bouira** Alg
70B2 **Bou Izakarn** Mor
36D2 **Boulay-Moselle** France
8C2 **Boulder** Colorado, USA
18D1 **Boulder** Montana, USA
8B3 **Boulder City** USA
20A2 **Boulder Creek** USA
38C1 **Boulogne** France
72B3 **Boumba** *R* CAR
71F4 **Bouna** Ivory Coast
8B3 **Boundary Peak** *Mt* USA
70B4 **Boundiali** Ivory Coast
18D2 **Bountiful** USA
77G5 **Bounty Is** NZ
77F3 **Bourail** Nouvelle Calédonie
36C3 **Bourbonne-les-Bains** France
70B3 **Bourem** Mali
38D2 **Bourg** France

Bourg de Péage

Burundi

38D2 Bourg de Péage France
37A1 Bourg-en-Bresse France
38C2 Bourges France
38C3 Bourg-Madame France
38C2 Bourgogne Region, France
37A2 Bourgoin-Jallieu France
37B2 Bourg-St-Maurice France
75C2 Bourke Aust
35E6 Bournemouth Eng
71C1 Bou Saâda Alg
72B2 Bousso Chad
70A3 Boutilmit Maur
71F4 Boutourou,Mt Ivory Coast
xxxJ7 Bouvet I Atlantic O
28D2 Bovril Arg
3F3 Bow R Can
11B2 Bowbells USA
76D2 Bowen Aust
19E4 Bowie Arizona, USA
17C3 Bowie Texas, USA
3F4 Bow Island Can
9E3 Bowling Green Kentucky, USA
17D2 Bowling Green Missouri, USA
12C2 Bowling Green Ohio, USA
13D3 Bowling Green Virginia, USA
11B2 Bowman USA
13D2 Bowmanville Can
75D2 Bowral Aust
3D3 Bowron R Can
52D3 Bo Xian China
52D2 Boxing China
64B1 Boyabat Turk
72B3 Boyali CAR
43G2 Boyarka Ukraine
6J4 Boyd Can
14C2 Boyertown USA
3F3 Boyle Can
33B3 Boyle Irish Rep
35B5 Boyne R Irish Rep
15E4 Boynoton Beach USA
72C3 Boyoma Falls Zaïre
18E2 Boysen Res USA
41F3 Bozcaada I Turk
41F3 Boz Dağlari Mts Turk
8B2 Bozeman USA
Bozen = Bolzano
72B3 Bozene Zaïre
72B3 Bozoum CAR
37B2 Bra Italy
40D2 Brač I Croatia, Yugos
4F4 Bracebridge Can
69A2 Brach Libya
32H6 Bräcke Sweden
16B4 Brackettville USA
15E4 Bradenton USA
35E5 Bradford Eng
14A2 Bradford USA
20B3 Bradley USA
16C3 Brady USA
34E1 Brae Scot
34D3 Braemar Scot
39A1 Braga Port
28C3 Bragado Arg
39A1 Bragana Port
27J4 Bragança Brazil
29C3 Bragança Paulista Brazil
61D3 Brahman-Baria Bang
61C3 Brähmani R India
61D2 Brahmaputra R India
45D6 Brăila Rom
9D2 Brainerd USA
74C3 Brak R S Africa
74D1 Brak R S Africa
70A3 Brakna Region, Maur
6F4 Bralorne Can
4F5 Brampton Can
26F3 Branco R Brazil
73B6 Brandberg Mt Namibia
42C2 Brandenburg Germany
42C2 Brandenburg State, Germany
74D2 Brandfort S Africa
8D2 Brandon Can
11C3 Brandon USA
74C3 Brandvlei S Africa
42C2 Brandys nad Lebem Czech
43D2 Braniewo Pol
9E2 Brantford Can
75B3 Branxholme Aust
7M5 Bras d'Or L Can
29D2 Brasila de Minas Brazil
26E6 Brasiléia Brazil
27J7 Brasilia Brazil
41F1 Brasov Rom
56E2 Brassay Range Mts Malay
42D3 Bratislava Czech
49M4 Bratsk Russian Fed
43F3 Bratslav Ukraine
13E2 Brattleboro USA
42C2 Braunschweig Germany
70A4 Brava I Cape Verde
8B3 Brawley USA
35B5 Bray Irish Rep
7L3 Bray I Can
36B2 Bray-sur-Seine France
3E3 Brazeau R Can
3E3 Brazeau,Mt Can
24E5 Brazil Republic, S America
xxxG5 Brazil Basin Atlantic O
8D3 Brazos R USA
72B4 Brazzaville Congo
42C3 Brdy Upland Czech
78A3 Breaksea Sd NZ
78B1 Bream B NZ
56C4 Brebes Indon
34D3 Brechin Scot
36C1 Brecht Belg
11C2 Breckenridge Minnesota, USA
16C3 Breckenridge Texas, USA
42D3 Břeclav Czech
35D6 Brecon Wales
35D6 Brecon Beacons Mts Wales
35C5 Brecon Beacons Nat Pk Wales
42A2 Breda Neth
74C3 Bredasdorp S Africa
32H6 Bredby Sweden
44B3 Bredbyn Sweden
44K5 Bredy Russian Fed
74B3 Breede R S Africa
13D2 Breezewood USA
37C1 Bregenz Austria
37C1 Bregenzer Ache R Austria
32A1 Breiðafjörður B Iceland
36D2 Breisach Germany
37C2 Brembo Italy
37C2 Brembo R Italy
15B2 Bremen USA
42B2 Bremen Germany
42B2 Bremerhaven Germany
18B1 Bremerton USA
19E3 Brendel USA
17C3 Brenham USA
38E2 Brenner Mt Austria
42C3 Brenner P Austria/Italy
37D2 Breno Italy
4F4 Brent Can
37D2 Brenta R Italy
20B2 Brentwood USA
40C1 Brescia Italy
Breslau = Wrocław
37D1 Bressanone Italy
34E1 Bressay I Scot
38B2 Bressuire France
38B2 Brest France
43E2 Brest Belorussia
38B2 Bretagne Region, France
36B2 Breteuil France
36A2 Bretevil France
15B3 Breton Sd USA
14C2 Breton Woods USA
78B1 Brett,C NZ
15C1 Brevard USA
75C1 Brewarrina Aust
13F2 Brewer USA
14D2 Brewster New York, USA
18C1 Brewster Washington, USA
15B2 Brewton USA
74D2 Breyten S Africa
40D1 Brežice Slovenia, Yugos
72C3 Bria CAR
38D3 Briancon France
38C2 Briare France
15B2 Bridgeport Alabama, USA
19C3 Bridgeport California, USA
13E2 Bridgeport Connecticut, USA
11B3 Bridgeport Nebraska, USA
17C3 Bridgeport Texas, USA
20C1 Bridgeport Res USA
18E1 Bridger USA
16A1 Bridger Peak USA
14C3 Bridgeton USA
23F4 Bridgetown Barbados
5H5 Bridgetown Can
7M5 Bridgewater Can
14E2 Bridgewater USA
35D6 Bridgwater Eng
35D6 Bridgwater B Eng
35E4 Bridlington Eng
75E3 Bridport Aust
36C2 Brienne-le-Château France
37B1 Brienzer See L Switz
36C2 Briey France
40B1 Brig Switz
8B2 Brigham City USA
75C3 Bright Aust
35E6 Brighton Eng
37B3 Brignoles France
29A3 Brilhante R Brazil
36E1 Brilon Germany
41D2 Brindisi Italy
17D3 Brinkley USA
77E3 Brisbane Aust
13E2 Bristol Connecticut, USA
35D6 Bristol Eng
13E2 Bristol Pennsylvania, USA
14E2 Bristol Rhode Island, USA
9E3 Bristol Tennessee, USA
10F4 Bristol B USA
35C6 Bristol Chan Eng/Wales
6F4 British Columbia Province, Can
7K1 British Empire Range Mts Can
10K2 British Mts USA/Can
74D2 Brits S Africa
74C3 Britstown S Africa
4E4 Britt Can
11C2 Britton USA
38C2 Brive France
42D3 Brno Czech
15C2 Broad R USA
14C1 Broadalbin USA
7L4 Broadback R Can
34B2 Broad Bay Inlet Scot
34C3 Broadford Scot
11A2 Broadus USA
11B1 Broadview Can
11B3 Broadwater USA
6H4 Brochet Can
6G2 Brock I Can
13D2 Brockport USA
14E1 Brockton USA
4F5 Brockville Can
14A2 Brockway USA
7K2 Brodeur Pen Can
34C4 Brodick Scot
43D2 Brodnica Pol
45D5 Brody Ukraine
36D1 Brokem Haltern Germany
16C1 Broken Bow Nebraska, USA
17D3 Broken Bow Oklahoma, USA
17D3 Broken Bow L USA
76D4 Broken Hill Aust
37C2 Broni Italy
32G5 Brønnøysund Nor
14D2 Bronx Borough New York, USA
57E9 Brooke's Point Phil
17D2 Brookfield Missouri, USA
12B2 Brookfield Wisconsin, USA
9D3 Brookhaven USA
18B2 Brookings Oregon, USA
8D2 Brookings South Dakota, USA
14E1 Brookline USA
11D3 Brooklyn USA
14D2 Brooklyn Borough New York, USA
11D2 Brooklyn Center USA
6G4 Brooks Can
10G4 Brooks,L USA
10E2 Brooks Mt USA
6C3 Brooks Range Mts USA
15C3 Brooksville USA
13E2 Brookton USA
75D1 Brooloo Aust
76B2 Broome Aust
34D2 Brora Scot
18B2 Brothers USA
67F4 Brothers,The Is Yemen
36A2 Brou France
72B2 Broulkou Well Chad
43G2 Brovary Ukraine
11D2 Browerville USA
16B3 Brownfield USA
3F4 Browning USA
8D4 Brownsville USA
8D3 Brownwood USA
51F8 Browse I Aust
36B1 Bruay-en-Artois France
76A3 Bruce,Mt Aust
4E5 Bruce Pen Can
36E2 Bruchsal Germany
37E1 Bruck Austria
42D3 Bruck an der Mur Austria
Bruges = Brugge
36B1 Brugge Belg
36D1 Brühl Germany
29D1 Brumado Brazil
36D2 Brumath France
18C2 Bruneau USA
18C2 Bruneau R USA
56D2 Brunei Sultanate, S E Asia
40C1 Brunico Italy
78B2 Brunner,L NZ
9E3 Brunswick Georgia, USA
13F2 Brunswick Maine, USA
17D2 Brunswick Mississippi, USA
25B8 Brunswick,Pen de Chile
75E3 Bruny I Aust
44G3 Brusenets Russian Fed
16B1 Brush USA
23A3 Brus Laguna Honduras
Brussel = Bruxelles
42A2 Bruxelles Belg
36D2 Bruyères France
8D3 Bryan USA
75A2 Bryan,Mt Aust
44E5 Bryansk Russian Fed
17D3 Bryant USA
20D3 Bryce Canyon Nat Pk USA
42D2 Brzeg Pol
64E4 Būbīyan I Kuwait/Iraq
72D4 Bubu R Tanz
74E1 Bubye R Zim
26D2 Bucaramanga Colombia
34E3 Buchan Oilfield N Sea
70A4 Buchanan Lib
16C3 Buchanan,L USA
34E3 Buchan Deep N Sea
7L2 Buchan G Can
33C2 Buchan Ness Pen Scot
7N5 Buchans Can
28C2 Buchardo Arg
Bucharest = Bucureşti
20B3 Buchon, Pt USA
37C1 Buchs Switz
19D4 Buckeye USA
35E5 Buckingham Eng
10F2 Buckland USA
10F2 Buckland R USA
75A2 Buckleboo Aust
13F2 Bucksport USA
72B4 Buco Zau Congo
5J4 Buctouche Can
41F2 Bucureşti Rom
43D3 Budapest Hung
60D3 Budaun India
35C6 Bude Eng
17D3 Bude USA
45G7 Budennovsk Russian Fed
36E1 Büdingen Germany
41D2 Budva Montenegro, Yugos
72A3 Buéa Cam
37A2 Buech R France
20B3 Buellton USA
28B2 Buena Esperanza Arg
26C3 Buenaventura Colombia
16A4 Buenaventura Mexico
16A2 Buena Vista Colorado, USA
22B2 Buenavista Mexico
13D3 Buena Vista Virginia, USA
20C3 Buena Vista L USA
28A4 Bueno R Chile
25E4 Buenos Aires Arg
25E5 Buenos Aires State, Arg
17D2 Buffalo Mississipi, USA
9F2 Buffalo New York, USA
11B2 Buffalo South Dakota, USA
17C3 Buffalo Texas, USA
8C2 Buffalo Wyoming, USA
74E2 Buffalo R S Africa
3E2 Buffalo Head Hills Mts Can
18C1 Buffalo Hump USA
3F3 Buffalo L Alberta, Can
3E1 Buffalo L Northwest Territories, Can
6H4 Buffalo Narrows Can
15C2 Buford USA
41F2 Buftea Rom
43E2 Bug R Pol/Ukraine
26C3 Buga Colombia
63C1 Bugdayli Turkmenistan
44H2 Bugrino Russian Fed
53A2 Bugt China
44J5 Bugulma Russian Fed
44J5 Buguruslan Russian Fed
64C2 Buhayrat al Asad Res Syria
18D2 Buhl Idaho, USA
11D2 Buhl Minnesota, USA
71F4 Bui Dam Ghana
35D5 Builth Wells Wales
28A2 Buin Chile
37A2 Buis-les-Baronnies France
37E2 Buje Croatia, Yugos
72C4 Bujumbura Burundi
77E1 Buka I PNG
73C4 Bukama Zaïre
72C4 Bukavu Zaïre
58E2 Bukhara Uzbekistan
56D2 Bukit Batubrok Mt Indon
56B3 Bukittinggi Indon
72D4 Bukoba Tanz
57B3 Buku Gandadiwata Mt Indon
57C2 Buku Saolat Mt Indon
51G7 Bula Indon
57F8 Bulan Phil
60D3 Bulandshahr India
73C6 Bulawayo Zim
41F3 Buldan Turk
60D4 Buldāna India
10B6 Buldir I USA
50D2 Bulgan Mongolia
41E2 Bulgaria Republic, Europe
57C2 Buli Indon
37B1 Bulle Switz
78B2 Buller R NZ
75C3 Buller,Mt Aust
76A4 Bullfinch Aust
75B1 Bulloo R Aust
75B1 Bulloo Downs Aust
75B1 Bulloo L Aust
17D2 Bull Shoals Res USA
28A3 Bulnes Chile
76D1 Bulolo PNG
74D2 Bultfontein S Africa
57B4 Bulukumba Indon
72C3 Bumba Zaïre
56E2 Bum Bum I Malay
45D8 Bu Menderes R Turk
55B2 Bumphal Dam Thai
72D3 Buna Kenya
76A4 Bunbury Aust
34B4 Buncrana Irish Rep
77E3 Bundaberg Aust
75D2 Bundarra Aust
60D3 Būndi India
75C1 Bungil R Aust
73B4 Bungo Angola
54B4 Bungo-suidō Str Japan
56C2 Bunguran I Indon
72D3 Bunia Zaïre
17D2 Bunker USA
17D3 Bunkie USA
15C3 Bunnell USA
71H3 Bunsuru R Nig
56D3 Buntok Indon
57B2 Buol Indon
65D2 Burāg Syria
72C2 Buram Sudan
61B1 Burang China
72E3 Burao Somalia
57G8 Burauen Phil
66D1 Buraydah S Arabia
19C4 Burbank USA
75C2 Burcher Aust
63E1 Burdalyk Turkmenistan
45E8 Burdur Turk
53C1 Bureinskiy Khrebet Mts Russian Fed
50F2 Bureya Russian Fed
53C1 Bureya R Russian Fed
65B3 Bûr Fu'ad Egypt
42C2 Burg Germany
41F2 Burgas Bulg
15D2 Burgaw USA
37B1 Burgdorf Switz
5K4 Burgeo Can
74D3 Burgersdorp S Africa
48K5 Burgin China
22C1 Burgos Mexico
39B1 Burgos Spain
43D1 Burgsvik Sweden
41F3 Burhaniye Turk
60D4 Burhānpur India
57F8 Burias I Phil
5K4 Burin Pen Can
55C2 Buriram Thai
29C2 Buritis Brazil
3C3 Burke Chan Can
76C2 Burketown Aust
70B3 Burkina Republic, Africa
13D1 Burk's Falls Can
8B2 Burley USA
4F5 Burlington Can
16B2 Burlington Colorado, USA
9D2 Burlington Iowa, USA
14C2 Burlington New Jersey, USA
15D1 Burlington North Carolina, USA
9F2 Burlington Vermont, USA
18B1 Burlington Washington, USA
4D5 Burlington Wisconsin, USA
59H3 Burma Republic, Asia
16C3 Burnet USA
18B2 Burney USA
14B2 Burnham USA
76D5 Burnie Aust
35D5 Burnley Eng
18C2 Burns USA
6F4 Burns Lake Can
59G1 Burqin China
75A2 Burra Aust
75D2 Burragorang,L Aust
34D2 Burray I Scot
75C2 Burren Junction Aust
75C2 Burrinjuck Res Aust
51G8 Burrundie Aust
45D7 Bursa Turk
66B1 Bur Safâga Egypt
Bûr Sa'îd = Port Said
65B4 Bûr Taufiq Egypt
12C2 Burton USA
35E5 Burton upon Trent Eng
32J6 Burtrask Sweden
75B2 Burtundy Aust
57C3 Buru Indon
72C4 Burundi Republic, Africa

Burung **Cap-Haitien**

56B2 **Burung** Indon
11C3 **Burwell** USA
49N4 **Buryatskaya** Respublika, Russian Fed
72D2 **Burye** Eth
45J6 **Burynshik** Kazakhstan
35F5 **Bury St Edmunds** Eng
63C3 **Būshehr** Iran
72B4 **Busira** *R* Zaïre
43E2 **Buskozdroj** Pol
65D2 **Busrā ash Shām** Syria
36D3 **Bussang** France
76A4 **Busselton** Aust
38D2 **Busto** Italy
40B1 **Busto Arsizio** Italy
57E8 **Busuanga** *I* Phil
72C3 **Buta** Zaïre
28B3 **Buta Ranquil** Arg
72C4 **Butare** Rwanda
34C4 **Bute** *I* Scot
53A2 **Butha Qi** China
13D2 **Butler** USA
8B2 **Butte** USA
55C4 **Butterworth** Malay
74D3 **Butterworth** S Africa
33B2 **Butt of Lewis** *C* Scot
7M3 **Button Is** Can
20C3 **Buttonwillow** USA
57G9 **Butuan** Phil
57B4 **Butung** *I* Indon
45G5 **Buturlinovka** Russian Fed
61B2 **Butwal** Nepal
36E1 **Butzbach** Germany
72E3 **Buulobarde** Somalia
72E3 **Buurhaakaba** Somalia
44G4 **Buy** Russian Fed
52B1 **Buyant Ovvo** Mongolia
45H7 **Buynaksk** Russian Fed
49N5 **Buyr Nuur** *L* Mongolia
45G8 **Büyük Ağri Daği** *Mt* Turk
53E2 **Buyukly** Russian Fed
64A2 **Büyük Menderes** *R* Turk
41F1 **Buzău** Rom
41F1 **Buzău** *R* Rom
44J5 **Buzuluk** Russian Fed
14E2 **Buzzards B** USA
41F2 **Byala** Bulg
41E2 **Byala Slatina** Bulg
6H2 **Byam Martin Chan** Can
6H2 **Byam Martin I** Can
65C1 **Byblos** *Hist. Site* Leb
43D2 **Bydgoszcz** Pol
16B2 **Byers** USA
32F7 **Bygland** Nor
43G2 **Bykhov** Belorussia
53E2 **Bykov** Russian Fed
7K2 **Bylot I** Can
75C2 **Byrock** Aust
20B2 **Byron** USA
75D1 **Byron,C** Aust
49P3 **Bytantay** *R* Russian Fed
43D2 **Bytom** Pol

C

25E3 **Caacupé** Par
29A4 **Caaguazú** Par
73B5 **Caála** Angola
3C3 **Caamano Sd** Can
29A4 **Caapucú** Par
29B3 **Caarapó** Brazil
25E3 **Caazapá** Par
16A3 **Caballo Res** USA
57F7 **Cabanatuan** Phil
13F1 **Cabano** Can
27M5 **Cabedelo** Brazil
39A2 **Cabeza del Buey** Spain
28C3 **Cabildo** Arg
28A2 **Cabildo** Chile
26D1 **Cabimas** Ven
72B4 **Cabinda** Angola
72B4 **Cabinda** Province, Angola
18C1 **Cabinet Mts** USA
23C3 **Cabo Beata** Dom Rep
39C2 **Cabo Binibeca** *C* Spain
71A2 **Cabo Cantin** *C* Mor
40B3 **Cabo Carbonara** *C* Sardegna
28A3 **Cabo Carranza** *C* Chile
39A2 **Cabo Carvoeiro** *C* Port
8B3 **Cabo Colnett** *C* Mexico
28D3 **Cabo Corrientes** *C* Arg
26C2 **Cabo Corrientes** *C* Colombia
21B2 **Cabo Corrientes** *C* Mexico
23B3 **Cabo Cruz** *C* Cuba
39B1 **Cabo de Ajo** *C* Spain
39C1 **Cabo de Caballeria** *C* Spain
39C1 **Cabo de Creus** *C* Spain
25C9 **Cabo de Hornos** *C* Chile
39C2 **Cabo de la Nao** *C* Spain
39A1 **Cabo de Peñas** *C* Spain
39A2 **Cabo de Roca** *C* Port
39C2 **Cabo de Salinas** *C* Spain
74E2 **Cabo de Santa Maria** *C* Mozam
29D3 **Cabo de São Tomé** *C* Brazil
39A2 **Cabo de São Vicente** *C* Port
39B2 **Cabo de Sata** *C* Spain
39A2 **Cabo de Sines** *C* Port
39C1 **Cabo de Tortosa** *C* Spain
25C6 **Cabo Dos Bahias** *C* Arg
39A2 **Cabo Espichel** *C* Port
8B4 **Cabo Falso** *C* Mexico
39B2 **Cabo Ferrat** *C* Alg
39A1 **Cabo Finisterre** *C* Spain
39C1 **Cabo Formentor** *C* Spain
29D3 **Cabo Frio** Brazil
29D3 **Cabo Frio** *C* Brazil
23A4 **Cabo Gracias à Dios** Honduras
28A1 **Cabo Leones** *C* Chile
27J4 **Cabo Maguarinho** *C* Brazil
39A2 **Cabo Negro** *C* Mor
75D1 **Caboolture** Aust
27H3 **Cabo Orange** *C* Brazil
19C4 **Cabo Punta Banda** *C* Mexico
73D5 **Cabora Bassa Dam** Mozam
21A1 **Caborca** Mexico
21C2 **Cabo Rojo** *C* Mexico
22C1 **Cabos** Mexico
28D3 **Cabo San Antonio** *C* Arg
23A2 **Cabo San Antonio** *C* Cuba
25C8 **Cabo San Diego** *C* Arg
26B4 **Cabo San Lorenzo** *C* Ecuador
40B3 **Cabo Teulada** *C* Sardegna
39A2 **Cabo Trafalgar** *C* Spain
39B2 **Cabo Tres Forcas** *C* Mor
25C7 **Cabo Tres Puntas** *C* Arg
7M5 **Cabot Str** Can
39B2 **Cabra** Spain
39A1 **Cabreira** *Mt* Port
39C2 **Cabrera** *I* Spain
28A3 **Cabrero** Chile
39B2 **Cabriel** *R* Spain
22C2 **Cacahuamilpa** Mexico
41E2 **Čačak** Serbia, Yugos
28E2 **Cacapava do Sul** Brazil
14A3 **Cacapon** *R* USA
22C2 **C A Carillo** Mexico
28E1 **Caceoul** Brazil
27G7 **Cáceres** Brazil
39A2 **Caceres** Spain
17D2 **Cache** *R* USA
3D3 **Cache Creek** Can
20A1 **Cache Creek, R** USA
18D2 **Cache Peak** *Mt* USA
25C3 **Cachi** Arg
27G5 **Cachimbo** Brazil
27L6 **Cachoeira** Brazil
29B2 **Cachoeira Alta** Brazil
27L5 **Cachoeira de Paulo Afonso** *Waterfall* Brazil
25F4 **Cachoeira do Sul** Brazil
27K8 **Cachoeiro de Itapemirim** Brazil
20C3 **Cachuma, L** USA
73B5 **Cacolo** Angola
73B5 **Caconda** Angola
16B2 **Cactus** USA
29B2 **Caçu** Brazil
29D1 **Caculé** Brazil
73B5 **Caculuvar** *R* Angola
43D3 **Čadca** Czech
35D5 **Cader Idris** *Mts* Wales
11A2 **Cadillac** Can
9E2 **Cadillac** USA
57F8 **Cadiz** Phil
39A2 **Cadiz** Spain
27K6 **Caeité** Brazil
38B2 **Caen** France
35C5 **Caernarfon** Wales
35C5 **Caernarfon B** Wales
65C2 **Caesarea** *Hist Site* Israel
29D1 **Caetité** Brazil
25C3 **Cafayate** Arg
64B2 **Caga Tepe** Turk
57F7 **Cagayan** *R* Phil
57F9 **Cagayan de Oro** Phil
57F9 **Cagayan Is** Phil
37E3 **Cagli** Italy
40B3 **Cagliari** Sardegna
23D3 **Caguas** Puerto Rico
15B2 **Cahaba** *R* USA
35B5 **Cahir** Irish Rep
35B5 **Cahone Pt** Irish Rep
38C3 **Cahors** France
73D5 **Caia** Mozam
73C5 **Caianda** Angola
29B2 **Caiapó** *R* Brazil
29B2 **Caiapônia** Brazil
27L5 **Caicó** Brazil
23C2 **Caicos Is** Caribbean
9F4 **Caicos Pass** Bahamas
10G3 **Cairn Mt** USA
76D2 **Cairns** Aust
64B3 **Cairo** Egypt
9E3 **Cairo** USA
75B1 **Caiwarro** Aust
26C5 **Cajabamba** Peru
26C5 **Cajamarca** Peru
23D5 **Calabozo** Ven
41E2 **Calafat** Rom
25B8 **Calafate** Arg
57F8 **Calagua Is** Phil
39B1 **Calahorra** Spain
38C1 **Calais** France
13F1 **Calais** USA
25C2 **Calama** Chile
26D3 **Calamar** Colombia
57E8 **Calamian Group** *Is* Phil
73B4 **Calandula** Angola
56A2 **Calang** Indon
69B2 **Calanscio Sand Sea** Libya
57F8 **Calapan** Phil
41F2 **Calarasi** Rom
39B1 **Calatayud** Spain
20B2 **Calaveras Res** USA
57F8 **Calbayog** Phil
17D4 **Calcasieu L** USA
61C3 **Calcutta** India
39A2 **Caldas da Rainha** Port
27J7 **Caldas Novas** Brazil
25B3 **Caldera** Chile
8B2 **Caldwell** USA
74B3 **Caledon** S Africa
74D3 **Caledon** *R* S Africa
12A2 **Caledonia** Minnesota, USA
14B1 **Caledonia** New York, USA
5H4 **Caledonia Hills** Can
22B1 **Calera** Mexico
25C7 **Caleta Olivia** Arg
8B3 **Calexico** USA
6G4 **Calgary** Can
15C2 **Calhoun** USA
15C2 **Calhoun Falls** USA
26C3 **Cali** Colombia
20C3 **Caliente** California, USA
8B3 **Caliente** Nevada, USA
16A2 **Caliente** New Mexico, USA
20C3 **California Aqueduct** USA
8A3 **California** State, USA
62B2 **Calimera,Pt** India
28B2 **Calingasta** Arg
19C4 **Calipatria** USA
74C3 **Calitzdorp** S Africa
75B1 **Callabonna** *R* Aust
75A1 **Callabonna,L** Aust
13D1 **Callander** Can
34C3 **Callander** Scot
75A1 **Callanna** Aust
26C6 **Callao** Peru
22C1 **Calles** Mexico
14C2 **Callicoon** USA
3F2 **Calling L** Can
22C1 **Calnali** Mexico
15E4 **Caloosahatchee** *R* USA
75D1 **Caloundra** Aust
22C2 **Calpulalpan** Mexico
40C3 **Caltanissetta** Italy
73B4 **Caluango** Angola
73B5 **Calulo** Angola
73B5 **Caluquembe** Angola
67E4 **Caluula** Somalia
3C3 **Calvert I** Can
40B2 **Calvi** Corse
22B1 **Calvillo** Mexico
74B3 **Calvinia** S Africa
36E2 **Calw** Germany
29E1 **Camacari** Brazil
22B1 **Camacho** Mexico
28E2 **Camaguã** Brazil
28E2 **Camaguã** *R* Brazil
21E2 **Camagüey** Cuba
21E2 **Camagüey,Arch de** *Is* Cuba
29E1 **Camamu** Brazil
26D7 **Camaná** Peru
10N5 **Camania** *I* Can
29B2 **Camapuã** Brazil
26E8 **Camargo** Bol
20C3 **Camarillo** USA
25C6 **Camarones** Arg
18B1 **Camas** USA
73B4 **Camaxilo** Angola
73B4 **Cambatela** Angola
55C3 **Cambodia** Republic, S E Asia
35C6 **Camborne** Eng
38C1 **Cambrai** France
20B3 **Cambria** USA
35D5 **Cambrian Mts** Wales
12C2 **Cambridge** Can
35E5 **Cambridge** County, Eng
35F5 **Cambridge** Eng
23H1 **Cambridge** Jamaica
13D3 **Cambridge** Maryland, USA
13E2 **Cambridge** Massachussets, USA
11D2 **Cambridge** Minnesota, USA
78C1 **Cambridge** NZ
12C2 **Cambridge** Ohio, USA
6H3 **Cambridge Bay** Can
51F8 **Cambridge G** Aust
45F7 **Cam Burun** *Pt* Turk
9D3 **Camden** Arkansas, USA
75D2 **Camden** Aust
13E3 **Camden** New Jersey, USA
14C1 **Camden** New York, USA
15C2 **Camden** South Carolina, USA
10J1 **Camden B** USA
37E3 **Camerino** Italy
17D2 **Cameron** Missouri, USA
17C3 **Cameron** Texas, USA
56F6 **Cameron Highlands** Malay
6H2 **Cameron I** Can
78A3 **Cameron Mts** NZ
72B3 **Cameroon** Federal Republic, Africa
72A3 **Cameroun** *Mt* Cam
27J4 **Cametá** Brazil
57F9 **Camiguin** *I* Phil
57F7 **Camiling** Phil
15C2 **Camilla** USA
20B1 **Camino** USA
26F8 **Camiri** Bol
73C4 **Camissombo** Angola
27K4 **Camocim** Brazil
76C2 **Camooweal** Aust
62E3 **Camorta** *I* Indian O
28D2 **Campana** Arg
25A7 **Campana** *I* Chile
3C3 **Campania I** Can
74C2 **Campbell** S Africa
78B2 **Campbell,C** NZ
3C3 **Campbell I** Can
xxixN7 **Campbell I** NZ
10M2 **Campbell L** Can
6E3 **Campbell,Mt** Can
60C2 **Campbellpore** Pak
6F5 **Campbell River** Can
12B3 **Campbellsville** USA
7M5 **Campbellton** Can
75D2 **Campbelltown** Aust
34C4 **Campbeltown** Scot
21C3 **Campeche** Mexico
75B3 **Camperdown** Aust
27L5 **Campina Grande** Brazil
27J8 **Campinas** Brazil
29C2 **Campina Verde** Brazil
57B5 **Camplong** Indon
20C2 **Camp Nelson** USA
72A3 **Campo** Cam
40C2 **Campobasso** Italy
29C3 **Campo Belo** Brazil
28C1 **Campo del Cielo** Arg
29C2 **Campo Florido** Brazil
25D3 **Campo Gallo** Arg
25F2 **Campo Grande** Brazil
27K4 **Campo Maior** Brazil
25F2 **Campo Mourão** Brazil
28E1 **Campo Novo** Brazil
29D3 **Campos** Brazil
29C2 **Campos Altos** Brazil
37D1 **Campo Tures** Italy
19D4 **Camp Verde** USA
55D3 **Cam Ranh** Viet
6G4 **Camrose** Can
73B5 **Camucuio** Angola
23K1 **Canaan** Tobago
14D1 **Canaan** USA
73B5 **Canacupa** Angola
2F3 **Canada** Dominion, N America
25D4 **Cañada de Gomez** Arg
14C2 **Canadensis** USA
16B2 **Canadian** USA
8C3 **Canadian** *R* USA
45D7 **Canakkale** Turk
28B3 **Canalejas** Arg
3E3 **Canal Flats** Can
14B1 **Canandaigua** USA
14B1 **Canandaigua L** USA
21A1 **Cananea** Mexico
29C4 **Cananeia** Brazil
xxxG3 **Canary Basin** Atlantic O
Canary Is = Islas Canarias
22B2 **Canas** Mexico
21B2 **Canatlán** Mexico
9E4 **Canaveral,C** USA
27L7 **Canavieiras** Brazil
76D4 **Canberra** Aust
18B2 **Canby** California, USA
11C3 **Canby** Minnesota, USA
41F3 **Çandarli Körfezi** *B* Turk
3G3 **Candle L** Can
14D2 **Candlewood,L** USA
11C2 **Cando** USA
14B1 **Candor** USA
25E4 **Canelones** Urug
17C2 **Caney** USA
73C5 **Cangamba** Angola
73C5 **Cangombe** Angola
28E2 **Canguçu** Brazil
52D2 **Cangzhou** China
7M4 **Caniapiscau** *R* Can
7M4 **Caniapiscau, Réservoir** *Res* Can
40C3 **Canicatti** Italy
27L4 **Canindé** Brazil
14B1 **Canisteo** USA
14B1 **Canisteo** *R* USA
22B1 **Canitas de Felipe Pescador** Mexico
16A2 **Canjilon** USA
64B1 **Çankırı** Turk
3E3 **Canmore** Can
34B3 **Canna** *I* Scot
62B2 **Cannanore** India
38D3 **Cannes** France
11B2 **Cannonball** *R* USA
75C3 **Cann River** Aust
25F3 **Canõas** Brazil
3G2 **Canoe L** Can
29B4 **Canoinhas** Brazil
16A2 **Canon City** USA
75B2 **Canopus** Aust
6H4 **Canora** Can
75C2 **Canowindra** Aust
5J4 **Canso** Can
35B5 **Cansore Pt** Irish Rep
35F6 **Canterbury** Eng
78B2 **Canterbury Bight** *B* NZ
78B2 **Canterbury Plains** NZ
55D4 **Can Tho** Viet
20D3 **Cantil** USA
28A1 **Canto de Augua** Chile
Canton = Guangzhou
17E3 **Canton** Mississippi, USA
12A2 **Canton** Missouri, USA
9E2 **Canton** Ohio, USA
14B2 **Canton** Pensylvania, USA
11C3 **Canton** S Dakota, USA
77H1 **Canton** *I* Phoeniz Is
10J3 **Cantwell** USA
36A2 **Cany-Barville** France
16B3 **Canyon** USA
18C2 **Canyon City** USA
18D1 **Canyon Ferry L** USA
19D3 **Canyonlands Nat Pk** USA
10N3 **Canyon Range** *Mts* Can
18B2 **Canyonville** USA
73C4 **Canzar** Angola
55D1 **Cao Bang** Viet
27J4 **Capanema** Brazil
29C3 **Capão Bonito** Brazil
37B3 **Cap Bénat** *C* France
71D1 **Cap Blanc** *C* Tunisia
71E1 **Cap Bon** *C* Tunisia
71D1 **Cap Bougaron** *C* Alg
38B3 **Capbreton** France
37B3 **Cap Camarat** *C* France
5H4 **Cap Chat** Can
22A1 **Cap Corrientes** *C* Mexico
40B2 **Cap Corse** *C* Corse
73E5 **Cap d'Ambre** *C* Madag
37B3 **Cap d'Antibes** *C* France
5J4 **Cap de Gaspé** *C* Can
38B2 **Cap de la Hague** *C* France
5G4 **Cap-de-la-Madeleine** Can
7L3 **Cap de Nouvelle-France** *C* Can
39C2 **Capdepera** Spain
22B2 **Cap de Tancitiario** *C* Mexico
71B1 **Cap des Trois Fourches** *C* Mor
75E3 **Cape Barren I** Aust
xxxJ6 **Cape Basin** Atlantic O
7N5 **Cape Breton I** Can
71F4 **Cape Coast** Ghana
13E2 **Cape Cod B** USA
7M3 **Cape Dyer** Can
79F7 **Cape Evans** *Base* Ant.
15D2 **Cape Fear** *R* USA
17E2 **Cape Girardeau** USA
Cape Horn = Cabo de Hornos
xxviiiH4 **Cape Johnston Depth** Pacific O
29D2 **Capelinha** Brazil
10E2 **Cape Lisburne** USA
73B5 **Capelongo** Angola
13E3 **Cape May** USA
73B4 **Capenda Camulemba** Angola
6F2 **Cape Parry** Can
74C3 **Cape Province** S Africa
74B3 **Cape Town** S Africa
xxxG4 **Cape Verde** *Is* Atlantic O
xxxG4 **Cape Verde Basin** Atlantic O
10K4 **Cape Yakataga** USA
76D2 **Cape York Pen** Aust
37B3 **Cap Ferrat** *C* France
36A1 **Cap Gris Nez** *C* France
23C3 **Cap-Haitien** Haiti

Capim **Champa**

27J4 **Capim** *R* Brazil
29A3 **Capitán Bado** Par
20D3 **Capitol Reef Nat Pk** USA
29A2 **Capivari** *R* Brazil
5K3 **Cap Mécatina** *C* Can
23P2 **Cap Moule à Chique** *C* St Lucia
37C2 **Capo di Noli** *C* Italy
40D3 **Capo Isola de Correnti** *C* Italy
40D3 **Capo Rizzuto** *C* Italy
41D3 **Capo Santa Maria di Leuca** *C* Italy
40C3 **Capo San Vito** Italy
40D3 **Capo Spartivento** *C* Italy
23P2 **Cap Pt** St Lucia
40C2 **Capri** *I* Italy
73C5 **Caprivi Strip** Region, Namibia
40B2 **Cap Rosso** *C* Corse
71D1 **Cap Serrat** *C* Tunisia
37A3 **Cap Sicié** *C* France
70A3 **Cap Vert** *C* Sen
26D4 **Caquetá** *R* Colombia
41E2 **Caracal** Rom
26F3 **Caracaraí** Brazil
26E1 **Caracas** Ven
29A3 **Caracol** Brazil
29C3 **Caraguatatuba** Brazil
25B5 **Carahue** Chile
29D2 **Caraí** Brazil
29D3 **Carandaí** Brazil
29A2 **Carandazal** Brazil
27K8 **Carangola** Brazil
41E1 **Caransebeş** Rom
75A2 **Carappee Hill** *Mt* Aust
23A3 **Caratasca** Honduras
29D2 **Caratinga** Brazil
39B2 **Caravaca** Spain
29E2 **Caravelas** Brazil
28E1 **Carazinho** Brazil
12B3 **Carbondale** Illinois, USA
14C2 **Carbondale** Pennsylvania, USA
7N5 **Carbonear** Can
40B3 **Carbonia** Sardegna
6G4 **Carcajou** Can
69D3 **Carcar Mts** Somalia
38C3 **Carcassonne** France
6E3 **Carcross** Can
22C2 **Cardel** Mexico
21D2 **Cardenas** Cuba
22C1 **Cárdenas** Mexico
22D2 **Cárdenas** Mexico
35D6 **Cardiff** Wales
35C5 **Cardigan** Wales
35C5 **Cardigan B** Wales
28D2 **Cardóna** Urug
3F4 **Cardston** Can
3G2 **Careen L** Can
41E1 **Carei** Rom
27G4 **Careiro** Brazil
28A2 **Carén** Chile
12C2 **Carey** USA
38B2 **Carhaix-Plouguer** France
25D5 **Carhué** Arg
27K8 **Cariacica** Brazil
24C2 **Caribbean S** C America
4B2 **Caribou** Can
13F1 **Caribou** USA
10N3 **Caribou** *R* Can
6G4 **Caribou Mts** Alberta, Can
6F4 **Caribou Mts** British Columbia, Can
57F8 **Carigara** Phil
36C2 **Carignan** France
36B1 **Carin** France
29D1 **Carinhanha** Brazil
29D1 **Carinhanha** *R* Brazil
26F1 **Caripito** Ven
4F4 **Carleton Place** Can
74D2 **Carletonville** S Africa
18C2 **Carlin** USA
12B3 **Carlinville** USA
34D4 **Carlisle** Eng
13D2 **Carlisle** USA
10D5 **Carlisle** *I* USA
28C3 **Carlos** Arg
29D2 **Carlos Chagas** Brazil
35B5 **Carlow** County, Irish Rep
35B5 **Carlow** Irish Rep
19C4 **Carlsbad** California, USA
8C3 **Carlsbad** New Mexico, USA
16B3 **Carlsbad Caverns Nat Pk** USA
xxviiiE4 **Carlsberg Ridge** Indian O
6H5 **Carlyle** Can
10L3 **Carmacks** Can
37B2 **Carmagnola** Italy
35C6 **Carmarthen** Wales
35C6 **Carmarthen B** Wales
20B2 **Carmel** California, USA
14D2 **Carmel** New York, USA
65C2 **Carmel,Mt** Israel
28D2 **Carmelo** Urug
20B2 **Carmel Valley** USA
8B4 **Carmen** *I* Mexico
25D6 **Carmen de Patagones** Arg
12B3 **Carmi** USA
19B3 **Carmichael** USA
29C2 **Carmo do Paranaiba** Brazil
39A2 **Carmona** Spain
76A3 **Carnarvon** Aust
74C3 **Carnarvon** S Africa
29E2 **Carncacá** Brazil
34B4 **Carndonagh** Irish Rep
76B3 **Carnegi,L** Aust
34D3 **Carngorms** *Mts* Scot
62E3 **Car Nicobar** *I* Indian O
72B3 **Carnot** CAR
75A2 **Carnot,C** Aust
10N2 **Carnwath** *R* Can
15E4 **Carol City** USA
27J5 **Carolina** Brazil
74E2 **Carolina** S Africa
15D2 **Carolina Beach** USA
xxviiiJ4 **Caroline Is** Pacific O
45C6 **Carpathians** *Mts* E Europe
43F3 **Carpatii Orientali** *Mts* Rom
76C2 **Carpentaria,G of** Aust
59H5 **Carpenter Ridge** Indian O
38D3 **Carpentras** France
40C2 **Carpi** Italy
20C3 **Carpinteria** USA
15C3 **Carrabelle** USA
40C2 **Carrara** Italy
33B3 **Carrauntoohill** *Mt* Irish Rep
35B5 **Carrickmacross** Irish Rep
35B5 **Carrick-on-Suir** Irish Rep
75A2 **Carrieton** Aust
8D2 **Carrington** USA
39B1 **Carrión** *R* Spain
28A1 **Carrizal Bajo** Chile
17F4 **Carrizo Spring** USA
16A3 **Carrizozo** USA
9D2 **Carroll** USA
15B2 **Carrollton** Georgia, USA
12B3 **Carrollton** Kentucky, USA
17D2 **Carrollton** Missouri, USA
3H3 **Carrot** *R* Can
17E2 **Carruthersville** USA
45F7 **Carsamba** Turk
45E8 **Carsamba** *R* Turk
8B3 **Carson City** USA
12C2 **Carsonville** USA
23B4 **Cartagena** Colombia
39B2 **Cartagena** Spain
26C3 **Cartago** Colombia
21D4 **Cartago** Costa Rica
20C2 **Cartago** USA
26D1 **Cartegena** Colombia
78C2 **Carterton** NZ
17D2 **Carthage** Missouri, USA
13D2 **Carthage** New York, USA
17D3 **Carthage** Texas, USA
76B2 **Cartier I** Timor S
7N4 **Cartwright** Can
27L5 **Caruaru** Brazil
26F1 **Carúpano** Ven
15D1 **Cary** USA
28A2 **Casablanca** Chile
71A2 **Casablanca** Mor
29C3 **Casa Branca** Brazil
8B3 **Casa Grande** USA
40B1 **Casale Monferrato** Italy
37D2 **Casalmaggiore** Italy
28C3 **Casares** Arg
22C1 **Casas** Mexico
28E1 **Casca** Brazil
18D1 **Cascade** USA
3D4 **Cascade Mts** Can/USA
78A2 **Cascade Pt** NZ
8A2 **Cascade Range** *Mts* USA
18C2 **Cascade Res** USA
25F2 **Cascavel** Brazil
37D3 **Casciana** Italy
37D3 **Cascina** Italy
40C2 **Caserta** Italy
79G9 **Casey** *Base* Ant
35B5 **Cashel** Irish Rep
28C2 **Casilda** Arg
77E3 **Casino** Aust
26C5 **Casma** Peru
20B3 **Casmalia** USA
39C1 **Caspe** Spain
8C2 **Casper** USA
45H7 **Caspian S** Asia/Europe
13D3 **Cass** USA
73C5 **Cassamba** Angola
36B1 **Cassel** France
11C2 **Casselton** USA
3C2 **Cassiar** Can
6E3 **Cassiar Mts** Can
29B2 **Cassilândia** Brazil
40C2 **Cassino** Italy
11D2 **Cass Lake** USA
20C3 **Castaic** USA
28B2 **Castaño** *R* Arg
37D2 **Castelfranco** Italy
38D3 **Castellane** France
28D3 **Castelli** Arg
39C1 **Castellon de la Plana** Spain
37D2 **Castelnovo ne'Monti** Italy
37D2 **Castelnuovo di Garfagnana** Italy
27K5 **Castelo** Brazil
39A2 **Castelo Branco** Port
38C3 **Castelsarrasin** France
40C3 **Castelvetrano** Italy
75B3 **Casterton** Aust
37D3 **Castiglion Fiorentino** Italy
28A1 **Castilla** Chile
39B2 **Castilla La Nueva** Region, Spain
39B1 **Castilla La Vieja** Region, Spain
28E2 **Castillos** Urug
33B3 **Castlebar** Irish Rep
34B3 **Castlebay** Scot
19D3 **Castle Dale** USA
34D4 **Castle Douglas** Scot
18C1 **Castlegar** Can
75B3 **Castlemain** Aust
20B3 **Castle,Mt** USA
18D2 **Castle Peak** USA
75C2 **Castlereagh** Aust
16B2 **Castle Rock** USA
38C3 **Castres-sur-l'Agout** France
23E4 **Castries** St Lucia
25B6 **Castro** Arg
25F2 **Castro** Brazil
27L6 **Castro Alves** Brazil
40D3 **Castrovillari** Italy
20B2 **Castroville** USA
28D2 **Casupa** Urug
78A2 **Caswell Sd** NZ
21E2 **Cat** *I* Bahamas
57F8 **Catabalogan** Phil
26B5 **Catacaos** Peru
29D3 **Cataguases** Brazil
17D3 **Catahoula L** USA
29C2 **Catalão** Brazil
39C1 **Cataluña** Region, Spain
25C3 **Catamarca** Arg
25C3 **Catamarca** State, Arg
73D5 **Catandica** Mozam
57F8 **Catanduanes** *I* Phil
25G2 **Catanduva** Brazil
29B4 **Catanduvas** Brazil
40D3 **Catania** Italy
28A3 **Catan-Lil** Arg
40D3 **Catanzaro** Italy
17F4 **Catarina** USA
57F8 **Catarman** Phil
75A2 **Catastrophe,C** Aust
23C5 **Catatumbo** *R* Ven
14B2 **Catawissa** USA
22C2 **Catemaco** Mexico
38D3 **Cater** Corse
40B2 **Cateraggio** Corse
73B4 **Catete** Angola
74D3 **Cathcart** S Africa
28B1 **Catinzaco** Arg
70A3 **Catio** Guinea-Bissau
4C3 **Cat L** Can
4C3 **Cat Lake** Can
77E3 **Cato** *I* Aust
21D2 **Catoche,C** Mexico
14B3 **Catoctin Mt** USA
13D3 **Catonsville** USA
28C3 **Catrilo** Arg
13E2 **Catskill** USA
13E2 **Catskill Mts** USA
5J2 **Caubvick,Mt** Can
26D2 **Cauca** *R* Colombia
27L4 **Caucaia** Brazil
26C2 **Caucasia** Colombia
45G7 **Caucasus** *Mts* Georgia
36A2 **Caudebec-en-Caux** France
36B1 **Caudry** France
73B4 **Caungula** Angola
25B5 **Cauquenes** Chile
13F1 **Causapscal** Can
62B2 **Cauvery** *R* India
38D3 **Cavaillon** France
29C1 **Cavalcanta** Brazil
37D1 **Cavalese** italy
11C2 **Cavalier** USA
70B4 **Cavally** *R* Lib
35B5 **Cavan** County, Irish Rep
35B5 **Cavan** Irish Rep
57F8 **Cavite** Phil
26D4 **Caxias** Brazil
27K4 **Caxias** Brazil
25F3 **Caxias do Sul** Brazil
73B4 **Caxito** Angola
15C2 **Cayce** USA
64D1 **Çayeli** Turk
27H3 **Cayenne** French Guiana
36A1 **Cayeux-sur-Mer** France
21E3 **Cayman Brac** *I* Caribbean
23A3 **Cayman Is** Caribbean
23A3 **Cayman Trench** Caribbean
72E3 **Caynabo** Somalia
20B3 **Cayncos** USA
21E2 **Cayo Romana** *I* Cuba
21D3 **Cayos Mistikos** *Is* Nic
23A2 **Cay Sal** *I* Caribbean
14B1 **Cayuga L** USA
14C1 **Cazenovia** USA
73C5 **Cazombo** Angola
5J4 **C Breton Highlands** Can
Ceará = Fortaleza
27K5 **Ceara State**, Brazil
28B1 **Cebollar** Arg
28E2 **Cebollati** Urug
57F8 **Cebu** Phil
57F8 **Cebu** *I* Phil
14C3 **Cecilton** USA
40C2 **Cecina** Italy
37D3 **Cecina** *R* Italy
11D3 **Cedar** *R* USA
8B3 **Cedar City** USA
17C3 **Cedar Creek Res** USA
11D3 **Cedar Falls** USA
6H4 **Cedar L** Can
20D1 **Cedar Mts** USA
9D2 **Cedar Rapids** USA
15B2 **Cedartown** USA
22B1 **Cedral** Mexico
21A2 **Cedros** *I* Mexico
76C4 **Ceduna** Aust
72E3 **Ceelbuur** Somalia
69D3 **Ceerigaabo** Somalia
40C3 **Cefalù** Italy
43D3 **Cegléd** Hung
73B5 **Cela** Angola
21B2 **Celaya** Mexico
Celebes = Sulawesi
51F6 **Celebes S** S E Asia
12C2 **Celina** USA
40D1 **Celje** Slovenia, Yugos
42C2 **Celle** Germany
35B6 **Celtic S** UK
51G7 **Cendrawasih** *Pen* Indon
37C2 **Ceno** *R* Italy
17D3 **Center** USA
15B1 **Center Hill L** USA
14D2 **Center Moriches** USA
37D2 **Cento** Italy
34C3 **Central** Region, Scot
16A3 **Central** USA
72B3 **Central African Republic** Africa
17C1 **Central City** Nebraska, USA
14A2 **Central City** Pennsylvania, USA
12B3 **Centralia** Illinois, USA
8A2 **Centralia** Washington, USA
74C1 **Central Kalahari Game Res** Botswana
63E3 **Central Makran Range** *Mts* Pak
18B2 **Central Point** USA
51H7 **Central Range** *Mts* PNG
14B1 **Central Square** USA
15B2 **Centre Point** USA
15B2 **Centreville** Alabama, USA
14B3 **Centreville** Maryland, USA
56D4 **Cepu** Indon
Ceram = Seram
51F7 **Ceram Sea** Indonesia
28C3 **Cereales** Arg
28C1 **Ceres** Arg
27J7 **Ceres** Brazil
74B3 **Ceres** S Africa
20B2 **Ceres** USA
38C2 **Cergy-Pontoise** France
40D2 **Cerignola** Italy
45D7 **Cernavodă** Rom
36D3 **Cernay** France
8C4 **Cerralvo** *I* Mexico
22B1 **Cerritos** Mexico
28B2 **Cerro Aconcagua** *Mt* Arg
22C1 **Cerro Azul** Mexico
28B1 **Cerro Boneta** *Mt* Arg
28A3 **Cerro Campanario** *Mt* Chile
28C2 **Cerro Champaqui** *Mt* Arg
28D2 **Cerro Chatto** Urug
22B2 **Cerro Cuachaia** *Mt* Mexico
22C1 **Cerro de Astillero** Mexico
28B1 **Cerro del Potro** *Mt* Chile/Arg
22C1 **Cerro del Tigre** *Mt* Mexico
28B1 **Cerro del Toro** *Mt* Chile/Arg
28B2 **Cerro de Olivares** *Mt* Arg
26C6 **Cerro de Pasco** Peru
23D3 **Cerro de Punta** *Mt* Puerto Rico
22B2 **Cerro El Cantado** *Mt* Mexico
28B3 **Cerro El Nevado** Arg
28B1 **Cerro General M Belgrano** *Mt* Arg
22B2 **Cerro Grande** *Mts* Mexico
22A1 **Cerro Huehueto** *Mt* Mexico
28A2 **Cerro Juncal** *Mt* Arg/Chile
22B1 **Cerro la Ardilla** *Mts* Mexico
28A1 **Cerro las Tortolas** *Mt* Chile
22B2 **Cerro Laurel** *Mt* Mexico
28A2 **Cerro Mercedario** *Mt* Arg
28A3 **Cerro Mora** *Mt* Chile
23C4 **Cerron** *Mt* Ven
28B3 **Cerro Payún** *Mt* Arg
22C1 **Cerro Peña Nevada** *Mt* Mexico
22C2 **Cerro Penón del Rosario** *Mt* Mexico
28B2 **Cerro Sosneado** *Mt* Arg
22B2 **Cerro Teotepec** *Mt* Mexico
28B2 **Cerro Tupungato** *Mt* Arg
22C2 **Cerro Yucuyacau** *Mt* Mexico
37E2 **Cervia** Italy
37C2 **Cervo** *R* Italy
40C2 **Cesena** Italy
44D4 **Cēsis** Latvia
42C3 **České Budějovice** Czech
42C3 **České Zemé** Region, Czech
42D3 **Českomoravská Vysočina** *Mts* Czech
41F3 **Çeşme** Turk
76E4 **Cessnock** Aust
40D2 **Cetina** *R* Croatia, Yugos
71A1 **Ceuta** N W Africa
64C2 **Ceyham** Turk
64C2 **Ceyhan** *R* Turk
64C2 **Ceylanpınar** Turk
Ceylon = Sri Lanka
49L4 **Chaa-Khol** Russian Fed
38C2 **Chaâteaudun** France
37B1 **Chablis** Region, France
36B3 **Chablis** France
28C2 **Chacabuco** Arg
26C5 **Chachapoyas** Peru
28B3 **Chacharramendi** Arg
60C3 **Chachran** Pak
25D3 **Chaco** State, Arg
72B2 **Chad** Republic, Africa
72B2 **Chad** *L* C Africa
28B3 **Chadileuvu** *R* Arg
8C2 **Chadron** USA
17E2 **Chaffee** USA
60A3 **Chagai** Pak
63E3 **Chagai Hills** Pak
49P4 **Chagda** Russian Fed
60B2 **Chaghcharan** Afghan
xxviiiE5 **Chagos Arch** Indian O
23L1 **Chaguanas** Trinidad
63E2 **Chahah Burjak** Afghan
63E3 **Chāh Bahār** Iran
54A2 **Ch'aho** N Korea
55C2 **Chai Badan** Thai
61C3 **Chāībāsa** India
71G3 **Chaîne de l'Atakor** *Mts* Benin
55C3 **Chaine des Cardamomes** *Mts* Camb
73C4 **Chaine des Mitumba** *Mts* Zaïre
55C2 **Chaiyaphum** Thai
28D2 **Chajari** Arg
63E2 **Chakhansur** Afghan
60C2 **Chakwal** Pak
26D7 **Chala** Peru
73D5 **Chalabesa** Zambia
60A2 **Chalap Dalam** *Mts* Afghan
36C3 **Chalindrey** France
52C4 **Chaling** China
60D4 **Chālisgaon** India
10K2 **Chalkyitsik** USA
36C2 **Challerange** France
18D2 **Challis** USA
36C2 **Châlons sur Marne** France
38C2 **Chalon sur Saône** France
42C3 **Cham** Germany
16A2 **Chama** USA
60B2 **Chaman** Pak
60D2 **Chamba** India
60D3 **Chambal** *R* India
11C3 **Chamberlain** USA
10J2 **Chamberlin,Mt** USA
13D3 **Chambersburg** USA
38D2 **Chambéry** France
36B2 **Chambly** France
13E1 **Chambord** Can
60A3 **Chambor Kalat** Pak
22A2 **Chamela** Mexico
63C2 **Chamgordan** Iran
28B2 **Chamical** Arg
37B2 **Chamonix** France
61B3 **Champa** India

12

Chukotskiy Khrebet — Contreras

49T3 **Chukotskiy Khrebet** *Mts* Russian Fed
49U3 **Chukotskiy Poluostrov** *Pen* Russian Fed
55D2 **Chu Lai** Viet
19C4 **Chula Vista** USA
10J3 **Chulitna** USA
50F1 **Chulman** Russian Fed
26B5 **Chulucanas** Peru
26E7 **Chulumani** Bol
48K4 **Chulym** Russian Fed
49K4 **Chulym** *R* Russian Fed
49L4 **Chuma** *R* Russian Fed
60D2 **Chumar** India
28B1 **Chumbicha** Arg
49P4 **Chumikan** Russian Fed
55B3 **Chumphon** Thai
53B4 **Ch'unch'ŏn** S Korea
61C3 **Chunchura** India
53B4 **Ch'ungju** S Korea
Chungking = Chongqing
54A4 **Ch'ungmu** S Korea
54A3 **Chungwa** N Korea
73D4 **Chunya** Tanz
49M3 **Chunya** *R* Russian Fed
54A3 **Ch'unyang** S Korea
23L1 **Chupara Pt** Trinidad
25C2 **Chuquicamata** Chile
40B1 **Chur** Switz
61D3 **Churāchāndpur** India
49P3 **Churapcha** Russian Fed
7J4 **Churchill** Can
7M4 **Churchill** *R* Labrador, Can
7J4 **Churchill** *R* Manitoba, Can
7J4 **Churchill,C** Can
7M4 **Churchill Falls** Can
6H4 **Churchill L** Can
60C3 **Chūru** India
22B2 **Churumuco** Mexico
44K4 **Chusovoy** Russian Fed
44H4 **Chuvashkaya** Respublika, Russian Fed
50C4 **Chuxiong** China
55D3 **Chu Yang Sin** *Mt* Viet
56C4 **Cianjur** Indon
37D2 **Ciano d'Enza** Italy
29B3 **Cianorte** Brazil
43E2 **Ciechanow** Pol
22B2 **Ciedad Altamirano** Mexico
26D1 **Ciedad Ojeda** Ven
21E2 **Ciego de Avila** Cuba
26D1 **Ciénaga** Colombia
21D2 **Cienfuegos** Cuba
43D3 **Cieszyn** Pol
39B2 **Cieza** Spain
64B2 **Cihanbeyli** Turk
22B2 **Cihuatlán** Mexico
56C4 **Cijulang** Indon
56C4 **Cilacap** Indon
16B2 **Cimarron** USA
16C2 **Cimarron** *R* USA
37B3 **Cime du Cheiron** *Mt* France
41F1 **Cîmpina** Rom
39C1 **Cinca** *R* Spain
40D2 **Činčer** *Mt* Bosnia & Herzegovina, Yugos
9E3 **Cincinnati** USA
41E1 **Cindrelu** *Mt* Rom
41F3 **Cine** *R* Turk
36C1 **Ciney** Belg
22D2 **Cintalapa** Mexico
28B3 **Cipolletti** Arg
6D3 **Circle** Alaska, USA
11A2 **Circle** Montana, USA
12C3 **Circleville** USA
56C4 **Cirebon** Indon
35E6 **Cirencester** Eng
16C3 **Cisco** USA
37D2 **Citadella** Italy
21C3 **Citlaltepetl** *Mt* Mexico
74B3 **Citrusdal** S Africa
40C2 **Citta del Vaticano** Italy
40C2 **Città di Castello** Italy
21B2 **Ciudad Acuña** Mexico
26F2 **Ciudad Bolivar** Ven
21B2 **Ciudad Camargo** Mexico
21C3 **Ciudad del Carmen** Mexico
39C2 **Ciudadela** Spain
26F2 **Ciudad Guayana** Ven
21B3 **Ciudad Guzman** Mexico
22B2 **Ciudad Hidalgo** Mexico
21B1 **Ciudad Juárez** Mexico
8C4 **Ciudad Lerdo** Mexico
21C2 **Ciudad Madero** Mexico
22C2 **Ciudad Mendoza** Mexico
21B2 **Ciudad Obregon** Mexico
23C4 **Ciudad Ojeda** Ven
26F2 **Ciudad Piar** Ven
39B2 **Ciudad Real** Spain
39A1 **Ciudad Rodrigo** Spain
21C2 **Ciudad Valles** Mexico
21C2 **Ciudad Victoria** Mexico
37E1 **Cividale del Friuli** Italy
37E3 **Civitanova Marche** Italy
40C2 **Civitavecchia** Italy
64D2 **Cizre** Turk
35F6 **Clacton-on-Sea** Eng
6G4 **Claire,L** Can
13D2 **Clairton** USA
37A1 **Clairvaux** France
15B2 **Clanton** USA
74B3 **Clanwilliam** S Africa
35B5 **Clara** Irish Rep
28D3 **Claraz** Arg
12C2 **Clare** USA
13E2 **Claremont** USA
17C2 **Claremore** USA
75D1 **Clarence** *R* Aust
78B2 **Clarence** *R* NZ
76C2 **Clarence Str** Aust
10M4 **Clarence Str** USA
17D3 **Clarendon** USA
5L4 **Clarenville** Can
7N5 **Clarenville** Can
6G4 **Claresholm** Can
17C1 **Clarinda** USA
11D3 **Clarion** Iowa, USA
13D2 **Clarion** Pennsylvania, USA
21A3 **Clarión** *I* Mexico
13D2 **Clarion** *R* USA
xxixM4 **Clarion Fracture Zone** Pacific O
9E3 **Clark Hill Res** USA
10O3 **Clark,Mt** Can
19C3 **Clark Mt** USA
12C2 **Clark,Pt** Can
12C3 **Clarksburg** USA
9D3 **Clarksdale** USA
10G4 **Clarks Point** USA
18C1 **Clarkston** USA
17D2 **Clarksville** Arkansas, USA
15B1 **Clarksville** Tennessee, USA
29B2 **Claro** *R* Brazil
25E5 **Claromecó** Arg
17C2 **Clay Center** USA
34E2 **Claymore** *Oilfield* N Sea
3C4 **Clayoquot Sd** Can
8C3 **Clayton** New Mexico, USA
13D2 **Clayton** New York, USA
33B3 **Clear** *C* Irish Rep
10J4 **Cleare,C** USA
14A2 **Clearfield** Pennsylvania, USA
18D2 **Clearfield** Utah, USA
3E2 **Clear Hills** *Mts* Can
19B3 **Clear L** USA
11D3 **Clear Lake** USA
18B2 **Clear Lake Res** USA
11A3 **Clearmont** USA
3D3 **Clearwater** Can
9E4 **Clearwater** USA
3F2 **Clearwater** *R* Can
3D3 **Clearwater L** Can
18C1 **Clearwater Mts** USA
8D3 **Cleburne** USA
35F4 **Cleeton** *Oilfield* N Sea
20B1 **Clements** USA
57E8 **Cleopatra Needle** *Mt* Phil
76D3 **Clermont** Aust
36B2 **Clermont** France
36C2 **Clermont-en-Argonne** France
38C2 **Clermont-Ferrand** France
36D1 **Clervaux** Germany
37D1 **Cles** Italy
75A2 **Cleve** Aust
35E4 **Cleveland** County, Eng
17D3 **Cleveland** Mississippi, USA
9E2 **Cleveland** Ohio, USA
15C1 **Cleveland** Tennessee, USA
17C3 **Cleveland** Texas, USA
29B4 **Clevelândia** Brazil
18D1 **Cleveland,Mt** USA
33B3 **Clew** *B* Irish Rep
19E4 **Clifton** Arizona, USA
75D1 **Clifton** Aust
14C2 **Clifton** New Jersey, USA
75A1 **Clifton Hills** Aust
3J2 **Clifton L** Can
3G4 **Climax** Can
15C1 **Clinch** *R* USA
15C1 **Clinch Mts** USA
17D2 **Clinton** Arkansas, USA
6F4 **Clinton** Can
14D2 **Clinton** Connecticut, USA
12A2 **Clinton** Iowa, USA
14E1 **Clinton** Massachusetts, USA
17D3 **Clinton** Mississippi, USA
17D2 **Clinton** Missouri, USA
15D2 **Clinton** N Carolina, USA
14C2 **Clinton** New Jersey, USA
16C2 **Clinton** Oklahoma, USA
6H3 **Clinton-Colden L** Can
21B3 **Clipperton I** Pacific O
26E7 **Cliza** Bol
28C1 **Clodomira** Arg
76D3 **Cloncurry** Aust
35B4 **Clones** Irish Rep
35B5 **Clonmel** Irish Rep
9D2 **Cloquet** USA
29A4 **Clorinda** Arg
11A3 **Cloud Peak** *Mt* USA
10G3 **Cloudy Mt** USA
20A1 **Cloverdale** USA
20C2 **Clovis** California, USA
8C3 **Clovis** New Mexico, USA
45C6 **Cluj** Rom
41E1 **Cluj-Napoca** Rom
37B1 **Cluses** France
37C2 **Clusone** Italy
78A3 **Clutha** *R* NZ
35D5 **Clwyd** County, Wales
7M2 **Clyde** Can
78A3 **Clyde** NZ
14B1 **Clyde** USA
34C4 **Clyde** *R* Scot
19C4 **Coachella** USA
22B2 **Coahuayana** Mexico
16B4 **Coahuila** State, Mexico
10N3 **Coal** *R* Can
22B2 **Coalcomán** Mexico
3F4 **Coaldale** Can
19C3 **Coaldale** USA
19B3 **Coalinga** USA
18D2 **Coalville** USA
29E1 **Coaraci** Brazil
26F5 **Coari** *R* Brazil
15B2 **Coastal Plain** USA
6E4 **Coast Mts** Can
8A2 **Coast Ranges** *Mts* USA
34C4 **Coatbridge** Scot
22C2 **Coatepec** Mexico
14C3 **Coatesville** USA
13E1 **Coaticook** Can
7K3 **Coats I** Can
79F1 **Coats Land** Region, Ant
21C3 **Coatzacoalcas** Mexico
22D2 **Coatzacoalcos** *R* Mexico
7L5 **Cobalt** Can
21C3 **Cobán** Guatemala
76D4 **Cobar** Aust
75C3 **Cobargo** Aust
4C3 **Cobham** *R* Can
26E6 **Cobija** Bol
14C1 **Cobleskill** USA
39B2 **Cobo de Palos** *C* Spain
7L5 **Cobourg** Can
76C2 **Cobourg Pen** Aust
42C2 **Coburg** Germany
26C4 **Coca** Ecuador
15C3 **Coca** USA
29B1 **Cocalinho** Brazil
26E7 **Cochabamba** Bol
36D1 **Cochem** Germany
3F3 **Cochrane** Alberta, Can
7K5 **Cochrane** Ontario, Can
3H2 **Cochrane** *R* Can
75B2 **Cockburn** Aust
14B3 **Cockeysville** USA
23H1 **Cockpit Country,The** Jamaica
74C3 **Cockscomb** *Mt* S Africa
21D3 **Coco** *R* Honduras/Nic
72A3 **Cocobeach** Gabon
62E2 **Coco Channel** Andaman Is
29D1 **Côcos** Brazil
23L1 **Cocos B** Trinidad
xxviiiF5 **Cocos Is** Indian O
xxixP4 **Cocos Ridge** Pacific O
22B1 **Cocula** Mexico
34G3 **Cod** *Oilfield* N Sea
9F2 **Cod,C** USA
78A3 **Codfish I** NZ
7M4 **Cod I** Can
37E2 **Codigoro** Italy
27K4 **Codó** Brazil
37C2 **Codogno** Italy
8C2 **Cody** USA
51H8 **Coen** Aust
42B2 **Coesfeld** Germany
3E4 **Coeur d'Alene** USA
8D3 **Coffeyville** USA
75A2 **Coffin B** Aust
75D2 **Coff's Harbour** Aust
74D3 **Cofimvaba** S Africa
22C2 **Cofre de Perote** *Mt* Mexico
38B2 **Cognac** France
14B1 **Cohocton** USA
14B1 **Cohocton** *R* USA
13E2 **Cohoes** USA
75B3 **Cohuna** Aust
25B7 **Coihaique** Chile
62B2 **Coimbatore** India
39A1 **Coimbra** Port
26B3 **Cojimies** Ecuador
18D2 **Cokeville** USA
76D4 **Colac** Aust
27K7 **Colatina** Brazil
79F6 **Colbeck,C** Ant
16B2 **Colby** USA
35F6 **Colchester** Eng
14D2 **Colchester** USA
37B1 **Col de la Faucille** France
3F3 **Cold L** Can
40B1 **Col du Grand St Bernard** *P* Switz/Italy
37B2 **Col du Lautaret** *P* France
40B1 **Col du Mont Cenis** *P* Italy/France
38D2 **Col du Mt Cenis** *P* Italy
12C2 **Coldwater** USA
4D4 **Coldwell** Can
10K2 **Coleen** *R* USA
18D1 **Coleman** Can
12C2 **Coleman** Michigan, USA
16C3 **Coleman** Texas, USA
74D2 **Colenso** S Africa
34B4 **Coleraine** N Ire
78B2 **Coleridge,L** NZ
74D3 **Colesberg** S Africa
20C1 **Coleville** USA
19B3 **Colfax** California, USA
17D3 **Colfax** Louisiana, USA
18C1 **Colfax** Washington, USA
21B3 **Colima** Mexico
22B2 **Colima** State, Mexico
28A2 **Colina** Chile
34B3 **Coll** *I* Scot
75C1 **Collarenebri** Aust
40B2 **Colle de Tende** *P* Italy/France
37D3 **Colle di Val d'Elsa** Italy
10J3 **College** USA
15C2 **College Park** Georgia, USA
14B3 **College Park** Washington, USA
17C3 **College Station** USA
76A4 **Collie** Aust
76B2 **Collier B** Aust
37D3 **Colline Metallifere** *Mts* Italy
36A1 **Collines de L'Artois** *Mts* France
36B2 **Collines De Thiérache** France
36A2 **Collines du Perche** *Mts* France
4E5 **Collingwood** Can
78B2 **Collingwood** NZ
17E3 **Collins** Mississippi, USA
14A1 **Collins** New York, USA
6H2 **Collinson Pen** Can
76D3 **Collinsville** Aust
12B3 **Collinsville** Illinois, USA
17C2 **Collinsville** Oklahoma, USA
28A3 **Collipulli** Chile
38D2 **Colmar** France
28C1 **Colmena** Arg
36A1 **Colne** *R* Eng
Cologne = Köln
29C3 **Colômbia** Brazil
26D3 **Colombia** Republic, S America
13D3 **Colombia** USA
62B3 **Colombo** Sri Lanka
25E4 **Colón** Arg
21D2 **Colon** Cuba
26C2 **Colón** Panama
25E4 **Colonia** Urug
28D2 **Colonia del Sacramento** Urug
28B3 **Colonia 25 de Mayo** Arg
28C1 **Colonia Dora** Arg
28B3 **Colonia Josefa** Arg
25C7 **Colonia Las Heras** Arg
13D3 **Colonial Heights** USA
34B3 **Colonsay** *I* Scot
23E5 **Coloradito** Ven
8C3 **Colorado** State, USA
8B3 **Colorado** *R* Arizona, USA
25D5 **Colorado** *R* Buenos Aires, Arg
28B1 **Colorado** *R* La Rioja, Arg
8D3 **Colorado** *R* Texas, USA
16B3 **Colorado City** USA
8B3 **Colorado Plat** USA
8C3 **Colorado Springs** USA
22B1 **Colptlán** Mexico
14B3 **Columbia** Maryland, USA
17E3 **Columbia** Mississippi, USA
9D3 **Columbia** Missouri, USA
13D2 **Columbia** Pennsylvania, USA
9E3 **Columbia** S Carolina, USA
9E3 **Columbia** Tennessee, USA
3E3 **Columbia** *R* Can
8A2 **Columbia** *R* USA
18D1 **Columbia Falls** USA
6G4 **Columbia,Mt** Can
18C1 **Columbia Plat** USA
74B3 **Columbine,C** S Africa
9E3 **Columbus** Georgia, USA
12B3 **Columbus** Indiana, USA
9E3 **Columbus** Mississippi, USA
18E1 **Columbus** Montana, USA
8D2 **Columbus** Nebraska, USA
16A3 **Columbus** New Mexico, USA
9E2 **Columbus** Ohio, USA
17C4 **Columbus** Texas, USA
12B2 **Columbus** Wisconsin, USA
18C1 **Colville** USA
6C3 **Colville** *R* USA
78C1 **Colville,C** NZ
6F3 **Colville L** Can
35D5 **Colwyn Bay** Wales
37E2 **Comacchio** Italy
22D2 **Comalcalco** Mexico
16C3 **Comanche** USA
20B1 **Comanche Res** USA
21D3 **Comayagua** Honduras
28A2 **Combarbalá** Chile
35C4 **Comber** N Ire
61D4 **Combermere B** Burma
36C3 **Combeufontaine** France
37E1 **Comeglians** Italy
35B5 **Comeragh** *Mts* Irish Rep
16C3 **Comfort** USA
61D3 **Comilla** Bang
21C3 **Comitán** Mexico
36C2 **Commercy** France
7K3 **Committee B** Can
40B1 **Como** Italy
25C7 **Comodoro Rivadavia** Arg
22B1 **Comonfort** Mexico
62B3 **Comorin,C** India
73E5 **Comoros** *Is* Indian O
38C2 **Compiègne** France
22B1 **Compostela** Mexico
28B2 **Comte Salas** Arg
61D2 **Cona** China
70A4 **Conakry** Guinea
28A1 **Conay** Chile
28B2 **Concarán** Arg
38B2 **Concarneau** France
29E2 **Conceiçao da Barra** Brazil
27J5 **Conceição do Araguaia** Brazil
29D2 **Conceiçao do Mato Dentro** Brazil
28B1 **Concepción** Arg
29A3 **Concepción** Brazil/Par
25B5 **Concepción** Chile
25E2 **Concepción** Par
25E4 **Concepción** *R* Arg
21B2 **Concepcion del Oro** Mexico
28D2 **Concepcion del Uruguay** Arg
74A1 **Conception B** Namibia
8A3 **Conception,Pt** USA
29C3 **Conchas** Brazil
16B2 **Conchas** *L* USA
36A2 **Conches** France
8C4 **Conchos** *R* Mexico
19B3 **Concord** California, USA
9F2 **Concord** New Hampshire, USA
15C1 **Concord** North Carolina, USA
25E4 **Concordia** Arg
22A1 **Concordia** Mexico
8D3 **Concordia** USA
18B1 **Concrete** USA
75D1 **Condamine** Aust
29D1 **Condeuba** Brazil
76D4 **Condobolin** Aust
18B1 **Condon** USA
36C1 **Condroz, Mts** Belg
27H8 **Condrina** Brazil
15B2 **Conecuh** *R* USA
37E2 **Conegliano** Italy
14B1 **Conesus L** USA
29A3 **Confuso** *R* Par
68F8 **Congo** Republic, Africa
68F8 **Congo** *R* Congo
Congo,R = Zaïre,R
12C1 **Coniston** Can
12C2 **Conneaut** USA
9F2 **Connecticut** State, USA
13E2 **Connecticut** *R* USA
13D2 **Connellsville** USA
36A2 **Connerré** France
12B3 **Connersville** USA
75B2 **Conoble** Aust
18D1 **Conrad** USA
17C3 **Conroe** USA
29D3 **Conselheiro Lafaiete** Brazil
55D4 **Con Son** *Is* Viet
Constance,L = Bodensee
45D7 **Constanta** Rom
71D1 **Constantine** Alg
10G4 **Constantine,C** USA
25B5 **Constitución** Chile
28D2 **Constitución** Urug
3G4 **Consul** Can
18D2 **Contact** USA
37E2 **Contarina** Italy
27K6 **Contas** *R* Brazil
22C2 **Contreras** Mexico

Dalay **Dibrugarh**

52A1 **Dalay** Mongolia
63E3 **Dalbandin** Pak
76E3 **Dalby** Aust
15B1 **Dale Hollow L** USA
32F7 **Dalen** Nor
35D4 **Dales,The** *Upland* Eng
15B2 **Daleville** USA
8C3 **Dalhart** USA
5H4 **Dalhousie** Can
6E2 **Dalhousie,C** Can
52E2 **Dalian** China
65B1 **Dalion** *Hist Site* Cyprus
8D3 **Dallas** USA
18B1 **Dalles,The** USA
10M5 **Dall I** USA
61B3 **Dalli Rajhara** India
70C3 **Dallol** *R* Niger
71G3 **Dallol Bosso** *R* Niger
71G3 **Dallol Maouri** *R* Niger
40D2 **Dalmatia** *Region* Bosnia & Herzegovina, Yugos
53D3 **Dal'negorsk** Russian Fed
53C2 **Dal'nerechensk** Russian Fed
70B4 **Daloa** Ivory Coast
52B4 **Dalou Shan** *Mts* China
61B3 **Dāltenganj** India
4E4 **Dalton** Can
15C2 **Dalton** Georgia, USA
14D1 **Dalton** Massachusetts, USA
56B2 **Daludalu** Indon
76C2 **Daly** *R* Aust
19B3 **Daly City** USA
76C2 **Daly Waters** Aust
57F9 **Damaguete** Phil
60C4 **Damān** India
64B3 **Damanhûr** Egypt
76B1 **Damar** *I* Indon
72B3 **Damara** CAR
64C3 **Damascus** Syria
14B3 **Damascus** USA
71J3 **Damaturu** Nig
63C1 **Damavand** Iran
73B4 **Damba** Angola
62C3 **Dambulla** Sri Lanka
63C1 **Damghan** Iran
Damietta = Dumyât
60D4 **Damoh** India
71F4 **Damongo** Ghana
72E3 **Damot** Eth
65C2 **Damour** Leb
76A3 **Dampier** Aust
67F3 **Damqawt** Yemen
65C3 **Danā** Jordan
66D4 **Danakil** Region, Eth
20C2 **Dana,Mt** USA
70B4 **Danané** Lib
55D2 **Da Nang** Viet
57F8 **Danao** Phil
57B3 **Danau Poso** *Mt* Indon
56A2 **Danau Tobu** *L* Indon
57B3 **Danau Tuwuti** *L* Indon
52A3 **Danbu** China
13E2 **Danbury** USA
14D1 **Danby** USA
61B2 **Dandeldhura** Nepal
62A1 **Dandeli** India
75C3 **Dandenong** Aust
53A3 **Dandong** China
74B3 **Danger Pt** S Africa
72D2 **Dangila** Eth
18D2 **Daniel** USA
7N4 **Daniel's Harbour** Can
74C2 **Danielskuil** S Africa
7P3 **Dannebrogs Øy** *I* Greenland
78C2 **Dannevirke** NZ
14B1 **Dansville** USA
62C1 **Dantewāra** India
Danube = Dunărea
Danube = Donau
45G8 **Danuk** Iraq
9E2 **Danville** Illinois, USA
9E3 **Danville** Kentucky, USA
14B2 **Danville** Pennsylvania, USA
9F3 **Danville** Virginia, USA
Danzig = Gdańsk
52C4 **Dao Xian** China
52B4 **Daozhen** China
71J3 **Dapchi** Nig
61E2 **Dapha Bum** *Mt* India
65B3 **Daphnae** *Hist Site* Egypt
57F9 **Dapiak,Mt** Phil
57F9 **Dapitan** Phil
50C3 **Da Qaidam** China
53B2 **Daqing** China
65D2 **Dar'a** Syria
63C3 **Dārāb** Iran
69A1 **Daraj** Libya
63C2 **Dārān** Iran
64C3 **Dar'ā Salkhad** Syria
61C2 **Darbhanga** India
20C1 **Dardanelle** USA
17D2 **Dardanelle,L** USA
Dar-el-Beida = Casablanca Mor
73D4 **Dar Es Salaam** Tanz
78B1 **Dargaville** NZ
15C2 **Darien** USA
Darjeeling = Dārjiling
61C2 **Dārjiling** India
76D4 **Darling** *R* Aust
75C1 **Darling Downs** Aust
7L1 **Darling Pen** Can
75B2 **Darlington** Aust
35E4 **Darlington** Eng
15D2 **Darlington** USA
42B3 **Darmstadt** Germany
69B1 **Darnah** Libya
75B2 **Darnick** Aust
6F3 **Darnley B** Can
79G10 **Darnley,C** Ant
39B1 **Daroca** Spain
72C3 **Dar Rounga** Region, CAR
67F4 **Darsa** *I* Yemen
35D6 **Dart** *R* Eng
33C3 **Dartmoor** *Moorland* Eng
35D6 **Dartmoor Nat Pk** Eng
7M5 **Dartmouth** Can
35D6 **Dartmouth** Eng
76D1 **Daru** PNG
40D1 **Daruvar** Croatia, Yugos
63E2 **Darweshan** Afghan
76C2 **Darwin** Aust
63C3 **Daryacheh-ye Bakhtegan** *L* Iran
63C3 **Daryacheh-ye Mahārlū** *L* Iran
63C2 **Daryācheh-ye Namak** *Salt Flat* Iran
63E2 **Daryacheh-ye-Sistan** *Salt Lake* Iran/Afghan
63C3 **Daryacheh-ye Tashk** *L* Iran
45H8 **Daryācheh-ye Urumīyeh** *L* Iran
63D3 **Dārzīn** Iran
67F1 **Das** *I* UAE
52C3 **Dashennonglia** *Mt* China
63D1 **Dasht** Iran
63E3 **Dasht** *R* Pak
63C2 **Dasht-e-Kavir** *Salt Desert* Iran
63D2 **Dasht-e Lut** *Salt Desert* Iran
63E2 **Dasht-e Naomid** *Desert Region* Iran
63E2 **Dasht-i-Margo** *Desert* Afghan
54D2 **Date** Japan
60D3 **Datia** India
52A2 **Datong** China
52C1 **Datong** China
52A2 **Datong He** *R* China
57F9 **Datu Piang** Phil
44D4 **Daugava** *R* Latvia
44D4 **Daugavpils** Latvia
38D2 **Daughiné** Region, France
7M1 **Dauguard Jensen Land** Greenland
60A1 **Daulatabad** Afghan
60D3 **Daulpur** India
36D1 **Daun** Germany
62A1 **Daund** India
6H4 **Dauphin** Can
14B2 **Dauphin** USA
15B2 **Dauphin I** USA
4B3 **Dauphin L** Can
70C3 **Daura** Nig
60D3 **Dausa** India
63E3 **Dāvah Panāh** Iran
62B2 **Dāvangere** India
57G9 **Davao** Phil
57G9 **Davao G** Phil
20A2 **Davenport** California, USA
9D2 **Davenport** Iowa, USA
26B2 **David** Panama
3G3 **Davidson** Can
6D3 **Davidson Mts** USA
3H2 **Davin L** Can
19B3 **Davis** USA
79G10 **Davis** *Base* Ant
7M4 **Davis Inlet** Can
7N3 **Davis Str** Greenland/Can
44K5 **Davlekanovo** Russian Fed
37C1 **Davos** Switz
3G2 **Davy L** Can
72E3 **Dawa** *R* Eth
52A4 **Dawan** China
60B2 **Dawat Yar** Afghan
67F1 **Dawḩat Salwah** *B* Qatar/S Arabia
67F3 **Dawkah** Oman
55B2 **Dawna Range** *Mts* Burma
6E3 **Dawson** Can
15C2 **Dawson** Georgia, USA
11C2 **Dawson** N Dakota, USA
76D3 **Dawson** *R* Aust
6F4 **Dawson Creek** Can
3F1 **Dawson Landing** Can
3E3 **Dawson,Mt** Can
10L3 **Dawson Range** *Mts* Can
52A3 **Dawu** China
52C3 **Dawu** China
38B3 **Dax** France
52B3 **Daxian** China
52B5 **Daxin** China
52A3 **Daxue Shan** *Mts* China
28D2 **Dayman** *R* Urug
52C4 **Dayong** China
65D2 **Dayr'Ali** Syria
65D1 **Dayr'Atīyah** Syria
64D2 **Dayr az Zawr** Syria
65D1 **Dayr Shumayyil** Syria
9E3 **Dayton** Ohio, USA
15B1 **Dayton** Tennessee, USA
17D4 **Dayton** Texas, USA
18C1 **Dayton** Washington, USA
9E4 **Daytona Beach** USA
52C4 **Dayu** China
56E3 **Dayu** Indon
52D2 **Da Yunhe** China
52D2 **Da Yunhe** *R* China
18C2 **Dayville** USA
52B3 **Dazhu** China
74C3 **De Aar** S Africa
23C2 **Deadman's Cay** Bahamas
64C3 **Dead S** Israel/Jordan
11B3 **Deadwood** USA
36A1 **Deal** Eng
74D2 **Dealesville** S Africa
3C3 **Dean** *R* Can
3C3 **Dean Chan** Can
28C2 **Deán Funes** Arg
12C2 **Dearborn** USA
3B2 **Dease Lake** Can
3C2 **Dease** *R* Can
6F3 **Dease Arm** *B* Can
8B3 **Death V** USA
20D2 **Death Valley Nat Mon** USA
38C2 **Deauville** France
71F4 **Debakala** Ivory Coast
10F3 **Debauch Mt** USA
3G3 **Debden** Can
23L1 **Débé** Trinidad
43E2 **Debica** Pol
43E2 **Deblin** Pol
70B3 **Débo,L** Mali
72D3 **Debre Birhan** Eth
43E3 **Debrecen** Hung
72D2 **Debre Mark'os** Eth
72D2 **Debre Tabor** Eth
66C3 **Decamere** Eth
9E3 **Decatur** Alabama, USA
15C2 **Decatur** Georgia, USA
9E3 **Decatur** Illinois, USA
12C2 **Decatur** Indiana, USA
38C3 **Decazeville** France
74C1 **Deception** *R* Botswana
52A4 **Dechang** China
11D3 **Decorah** USA
71F3 **Dedougou** Burkina
53B2 **Dedu** China
73D5 **Dedza** Malawi
34C4 **Dee** *R* Dumfries and Galloway, Scot
35D5 **Dee** *R* Eng/Wales
34D3 **Dee** *R* Grampian, Scot
4F4 **Deep River** Can
14D2 **Deep River** USA
20D2 **Deep Springs** USA
75D1 **Deepwater** Aust
10F5 **Deer I** USA
7N5 **Deer Lake** Can
8B2 **Deer Lodge** USA
26E7 **Deésaguadero** *R* Bol
18C2 **Deeth** USA
28D3 **Defferrari** Arg
4E5 **Defiance** USA
15B2 **De Funiak Springs** USA
50C3 **Dêgê** China
76A3 **De Grey** *R* Aust
66D3 **Dehalak** *Arch* Eth
63C2 **Deh Bīd** Iran
60B1 **Dehi** Afghan
70D1 **Dehibat** Tunisia
62B3 **Dehiwala-Mt Lavinia** Sri Lanka
63B2 **Dehlorān** Iran
60D2 **Dehra Dūn** India
61B3 **Dehri** India
53B3 **Dehui** China
72C3 **Deim Zubeir** Sudan
65C2 **Deir Abu Sa'id** Jordan
65D1 **Deir el Ahmar** Leb
45C6 **Dej** Rom
12B2 **De Kalb** Illinois, USA
17D3 **De Kalb** Texas, USA
49Q4 **De Kastri** Russian Fed
72C4 **Dekese** Zaïre
72B3 **Dekoa** CAR
8B3 **Delano** USA
19D3 **Delano Peal** *Mt* USA
74D2 **Delareyville** S Africa
10C6 **Delarof Is** USA
9F3 **Delaware** State, USA
12C2 **Delaware** USA
13D2 **Delaware** *R* USA
9F3 **Delaware B** USA
75C3 **Delegate** Aust
37B1 **Delemont** Switz
73E5 **Delgado** *C* Mozam
66B2 **Delgo** Sudan
16B2 **Delhi** Colorado, USA
60D3 **Delhi** India
13E2 **Delhi** New York, USA
64B1 **Delice** Turk
21B2 **Delicias** Mexico
63C2 **Delījān** Iran
37B1 **Delle** France
11C3 **Dell Rapids** USA
71C1 **Dellys** Alg
20D4 **Del Mar** USA
32F8 **Delmenhorst** Germany
10F2 **De Long Mts** USA
49R2 **De-Longa, Ostrov** *I* Russian Fed
75E3 **Deloraine** Aust
6H5 **Deloraine** Can
15E4 **Delray Beach** USA
8C4 **Del Rio** USA
8B3 **Delta** USA
10J3 **Delta** *R* USA
71H4 **Delta** *State* Nigeria
10J3 **Delta Junction** USA
14C1 **Delta Res** USA
72D3 **Dembī Dolo** Eth
36C1 **Demer** *R* Belg
43G1 **Demidov** Russian Fed
16A3 **Deming** USA
41F2 **Demirköy** Turk
71A2 **Demnate** Mor
37B2 **Demonte** Italy
15B2 **Demopolis** USA
48H4 **Demyanskoya** Russian Fed
38C1 **Denain** France
59E2 **Denau** Uzbekistan
35D5 **Denbigh** Wales
10F3 **Denbigh,C** USA
56C3 **Dendang** Indon
36C1 **Dendermond** Belg
72D3 **Dendi** *Mt* Eth
36B1 **Dèndre** *R* Belg
52B1 **Dengkou** China
52C3 **Deng Xian** China
Den Haag = 's-Gravenhage
23H1 **Denham,Mt** Jamaica
42A2 **Den Helder** Neth
39C2 **Denia** Spain
76D4 **Deniliquin** Aust
18C2 **Denio** USA
11C3 **Denison** Iowa, USA
8D3 **Denison** Texas, USA
10H4 **Denison,Mt** USA
45D8 **Denizli** Turk
32F7 **Denmark** Kingdom, Europe
79C1 **Denmark Str** Greenland/ Iceland
23P2 **Dennery** St Lucia
56E4 **Denpasar** Indon
14C3 **Denton** Maryland, USA
8D3 **Denton** Texas, USA
76E1 **D'Entrecasteaux Is** PNG
37B1 **Dents du Midi** *Mt* Switz
8C3 **Denver** USA
4F2 **Denys** *R* Can
72B3 **Déo** *R* Cam
61C3 **Deoghar** India
60C5 **Deolāli** India
60D1 **Deosai Plain** India
14A1 **Depew** USA
14C1 **Deposit** USA
72C2 **Dépression du Mourdi** *Desert Region* Chad
49P3 **Deputatskiy** Russian Fed
17D3 **De Queen** USA
60C3 **Dera** Pak
60B3 **Dera Bugti** Pak
60B2 **Dera Ismail Khan** Pak
45H7 **Derbent** Russian Fed
76B2 **Derby** Aust
14D2 **Derby** Connecticut, USA
35E5 **Derby** County, Eng
35E5 **Derby** Eng
17C2 **Derby** Kansas, USA
45F5 **Dergachi** Ukraine
17D3 **De Ridder** USA
69B1 **Derna** Libya
72E3 **Derri** Somalia
14E1 **Derry** USA
72D2 **Derudeb** Sudan
74C3 **De Rust** S Africa
14C1 **De Ruyter** USA
75E3 **Derwent Bridge** Aust
28B2 **Desaguadero** Arg
28B2 **Desaguadero** *R* Arg
19C4 **Descanso** Mexico
3H3 **Deschambault L** Can
18B2 **Deschutes** *R* USA
72D2 **Desē** Eth
25C7 **Deseado** Arg
25C7 **Deseado** *R* Arg
37D2 **Desenzano** Italy
70A1 **Deserta Grande** *I* Medeira
19C4 **Desert Centre** USA
19D2 **Desert Peak** *Mt* USA
63E2 **Deshu** Afghan
25C2 **Desierto de Atacama** *Desert* Chile
17D2 **Desloge** USA
9D2 **Des Moines** Iowa, USA
16B2 **Des Moines** New Mexico, USA
11D3 **Des Moines** *R* USA
45E5 **Desna** *R* Russian Fed
25B8 **Desolación** *I* Chile
12B2 **Des Plaines** USA
42C2 **Dessau** Germany
10L3 **Destruction Bay** Can
36A1 **Desvres** France
41E1 **Deta** Rom
73C5 **Dete** Zim
36E1 **Detmold** Germany
9E2 **Detroit** USA
5J4 **Détroit d'Honguedo** *Str* Can
5J3 **Détroit de Jacques Cartier** *Str* Can
11C2 **Detroit Lakes** USA
55D3 **Det Udom** Thai
41E1 **Deva** Rom
42B2 **Deventer** Neth
34D3 **Deveron** *R* Scot
60C3 **Devikot** India
20C2 **Devil Postpile Nat Mon** USA
20C3 **Devils Den** USA
20C1 **Devils Gate** *P* USA
34F3 **Devil's Hole** *Region* N Sea
Devil's Island = Isla du Diable
11C2 **Devils L** N Dakota, USA
16B4 **Devils L** Texas, USA
8D2 **Devils Lake** USA
10M4 **Devils Paw** *Mt* Can
35E6 **Devizes** Eng
60D3 **Devli** India
41E2 **Devoll** *R* Alb
37A2 **Dévoluy** *Mts* France
35C6 **Devon** County, Eng
7J2 **Devon I** Can
76D5 **Devonport** Aust
61D2 **Dewangiri** Bhutan
60D4 **Dewās** India
74D2 **Dewetsdorp** S Africa
9E3 **Dewey Res** USA
17D3 **De Witt** USA
17E2 **Dexter** Missouri, USA
16B3 **Dexter** New Mexico, USA
52A3 **Deyang** China
63D2 **Deyhuk** Iran
63B2 **Dezfūl** Iran
52D2 **Dezhou** China
63B1 **Dezh Shāhpūr** Iran
67F1 **Dhahran** S Arabia
61D3 **Dhākā** Bang
65B1 **Dhali** Cyprus
66D4 **Dhamār** Yemen
62B2 **Dhamavaram** India
61B3 **Dhamtari** India
61C3 **Dhanbād** India
61B2 **Dhangarhi** Nepal
61C2 **Dhankuta** Nepal
60D4 **Dhār** India
62B2 **Dharmapuri** India
60D2 **Dharmsāla** India
70B3 **Dhar Oualata** *Desert Region* Maur
61B2 **Dhaulagiri** *Mt* Nepal
61C3 **Dhenkānāi** India
65C3 **Dhibah** Jordan
41F3 **Dhíkti Óri** *Mt* Greece
67F3 **Dhofar** Region, Oman
41E3 **Dhomokós** Greece
62B1 **Dhone** India
60C4 **Dhoraji** India
60C4 **Dhrāngadhra** India
61C2 **Dhuburi** India
60C4 **Dhule** India
20B2 **Diablo,Mt** USA
19B3 **Diablo Range** *Mts* USA
28C2 **Diamante** Arg
28B2 **Diamante** *R* Arg
27K7 **Diamantina** Brazil
76D3 **Diamantina** *R* Aust
29A1 **Diamantino** Brazil
61C3 **Diamond Harbours** India
20B1 **Diamond Springs** USA
18D2 **Diamondville** USA
71G3 **Diapaga** Burkina
67G1 **Dibā** UAE
73C4 **Dibaya** Zaïre
61D2 **Dibrugarh** India

Durham

Embarras Portage

9F3 **Durham** N Carolina, USA
14E1 **Durham** New Hampshire, USA
75B1 **Durham Downs** Aust
41D2 **Durmitor** *Mt* Montenegro, Yugos
34C2 **Durness** Scot
41D2 **Durrës** Alb
75B1 **Durrie** Aust
41F3 **Dursunbey** Turk
78B2 **D'Urville I** NZ
63E1 **Dushak** Turkmenistan
52B4 **Dushan** China
59E2 **Dushanbe** Tajikistan
14B2 **Dushore** USA
78A3 **Dusky Sd** NZ
42B2 **Düsseldorf** Germany
10E5 **Dutch Harbor** USA
19D3 **Dutton,Mt** USA
52B4 **Duyun** China
64B1 **Düzce** Turk
44F2 **Dvinskaya Guba** *B* Russian Fed
60B4 **Dwärka** India
18C1 **Dworshak Res** USA
9E3 **Dyersburg** USA
35C5 **Dyfed** County, Wales
45G7 **Dykh Tau** *Mt* Russian Fed
75B1 **Dynevor Downs** Aust
50C2 **Dzag** Mongolia
50D2 **Dzamïn Uüd** Mongolia
73E5 **Dzaoudzi** Mayotte
50C2 **Dzavhan Gol** *R* Mongolia
44G4 **Dzerzhinsk** Russian Fed
49O4 **Dzhalinda** Russian Fed
48J5 **Dzhambul** Kazakhstan
45E6 **Dzhankoy** Ukraine
48H5 **Dzhezkazgan** Kazakhstan
60B1 **Dzhilikul'** Tajikistan
48J5 **Dzhungarskiy Alatau** *Mts* Kazakhstan
42D2 **Dzierzoniow** Pol
59G1 **Dzungaria** Basin, China
49L5 **Dzüyl** Mongolia

E

7K4 **Eabamet L** Can
10K3 **Eagle** Alaska, USA
16A2 **Eagle** Colorado, USA
5K3 **Eagle** *R* Can
11B2 **Eagle Butte** USA
18B2 **Eagle L** California, USA
11D2 **Eagle L** Can
13F1 **Eagle L** Maine, USA
13F1 **Eagle Lake** USA
17C3 **Eagle Mountain L** USA
8C4 **Eagle Pass** USA
16A3 **Eagle Peak** *Mt* USA
6E3 **Eagle Plain** Can
10J3 **Eagle River** USA
11D1 **Ear Falls** Can
19C3 **Earlimart** USA
19D4 **Earp** USA
16B3 **Earth** USA
15C2 **Easley** USA
13D2 **East Aurora** USA
15B3 **East B** USA
35F6 **Eastbourne** Eng
14C1 **East Branch Delaware** *R* USA
77G4 **East,C** NZ
10B6 **East C** USA
12B2 **East Chicago** USA
50F3 **East China Sea** China/ Japan
61B4 **Eastern Ghats** *Mts* India
4B3 **Easterville** Can
25E8 **East Falkland** *I* Falkland Is
10J2 **East Fork** *R* USA
19C3 **Eastgate** USA
11C2 **East Grand Forks** USA
14D1 **Easthampton** USA
14D2 **East Hampton** USA
12B2 **East Lake** USA
12C2 **East Liverpool** USA
74D3 **East London** S Africa
7L4 **Eastmain** Can
7L4 **Eastmain** *R* Can
15C2 **Eastman** USA
12A2 **East Moline** USA
13D3 **Easton** Maryland, USA
13D2 **Easton** Pennsylvania, USA
14C2 **East Orange** USA
xxixO5 **East Pacific Ridge** Pacific O
xxixO4 **East Pacific Rise** Pacific O
15C2 **East Point** USA
13F2 **Eastport** USA
35E5 **East Retford** Eng
15B1 **East Ridge** USA
9D3 **East St Louis** USA
49R2 **East Siberian S** Russian Fed
35F6 **East Sussex** County, Eng
13D3 **Eastville** USA
20C1 **East Walker** USA
15C2 **Eatonton** USA
11D3 **Eau Claire** USA
51H6 **Eauripik** *I* Pacific O
22C1 **Ebano** Mexico
72B3 **Ebebiyin** Eq Guinea
14A2 **Ebensburg** USA
36E2 **Eberbach** Germany
42C2 **Eberswalde** Germany
54D2 **Ebetsu** Japan
52A4 **Ebian** China
48K5 **Ebinur** *L* China
40D2 **Eboli** Italy
72B3 **Ebolowa** Cam
39B1 **Ebro** *R* Spain
64A1 **Eceabat** Turk
71C1 **Ech Cheliff** Alg
52D2 **Eching** China
18C1 **Echo** USA
Echo Bay = Port Radium
6G3 **Echo Bay** Can
36D2 **Echternach** Lux
75B3 **Echuca** Aust
39A2 **Ecija** Spain
7K2 **Eclipse Sd** Can
36A3 **Ecommoy** France
26C4 **Ecuador** Republic, S America
34D2 **Eday** *I* Scot
72E2 **Ed** Eth
34G3 **Edda** *Oilfield* N Sea
72C2 **Ed Da'ein** Sudan
66B4 **Ed Damasin** Sudan
72D2 **Ed Damer** Sudan
72D2 **Ed Debba** Sudan
34C2 **Eddrachillis** *B* Scot
72D2 **Ed Dueim** Sudan
75E3 **Eddystone Pt** Aust
71G4 **Ede** Nig
72A3 **Edea** Cam
75C3 **Eden** Aust
16C3 **Eden** Texas, USA
18E2 **Eden** Wyoming, USA
34D4 **Eden** *R* Eng
74D2 **Edenburg** S Africa
78A3 **Edendale** NZ
36D2 **Edenkoben** Germany
36E1 **Eder** *R* Germany
11C2 **Edgeley** USA
7M3 **Edgell I** Can
11B3 **Edgemont** USA
48D2 **Edgeøya** *I* Barents S
14B3 **Edgewood** USA
65C3 **Edh Dhahiriya** Israel
41E2 **Edhessa** Greece
17F4 **Edinburg** USA
34D3 **Edinburgh** Scot
45D7 **Edirne** Turk
20C3 **Edison** USA
15C2 **Edisto** *R* USA
18B1 **Edmonds** USA
6G4 **Edmonton** Can
11C2 **Edmore** USA
7M5 **Edmundston** Can
17C4 **Edna** USA
10M4 **Edna Bay** USA
71H4 **Edo** *State* Nigeria
40C1 **Edolo** Italy
65C3 **Edom** Region, Jordan
45D8 **Edremit** Turk
41F3 **Edremit Körfezi** *B* Turk
50C2 **Edrengiyn Nuruu** *Mts* Mongolia
6G4 **Edson** Can
28C3 **Eduardo Castex** Arg
10N3 **Eduni,Mt** Can
75B3 **Edward** *R* Aust
72C4 **Edward,L** Zaïre/Uganda
20D3 **Edwards** USA
75A1 **Edwards Creek** Aust
8C3 **Edwards Plat** USA
12B3 **Edwardsville** USA
3B2 **Edziza,Mt** Can
10F3 **Eek** USA
36B1 **Eeklo** Belg
77F2 **Efate** *I* Vanuatu
9E3 **Effingham** USA
19D3 **Egan Range** *Mts* USA
7N3 **Egedesminde** Greenland
10G4 **Egegik** USA
3H2 **Egenolf L** Can
43E3 **Eger** Hung
32F7 **Egersund** Nor
36E1 **Eggegebirge** Region, Germany
14C3 **Egg Harbor City** USA
6G2 **Eglinton I** Can
78B1 **Egmont,C** NZ
78B1 **Egmont,Mt** NZ
64B2 **Eğridir Gölü** *L* Turk
29C1 **Eguas** *R* Brazil
49U3 **Egvekinot** Russian Fed
69B2 **Egypt** Republic, Africa
32K6 **Ehsenvaara** Fin
39B1 **Eibar** Spain
38C2 **Eibeuf** France
75D1 **Eidsvolo** Aust
36D1 **Eifel** Region, Germany
34B3 **Eigg** *I* Scot
59F5 **Eight Degree Chan** Indian O
76B2 **Eighty Mile Beach** Aust
75C3 **Eildon,L** Aust
36E1 **Einbeck** Germany
42B2 **Eindhoven** Neth
37C1 **Einsiedeln** Switz
65C3 **Ein Yahav** Israel
42C2 **Eisenach** Germany
42C3 **Eisenerz** Austria
37E1 **Eisenhut** *Mt* Austria
36D1 **Eitorf** Germany
52A1 **Ejin qi** China
71F4 **Ejuanema,Mt** Ghana
71F4 **Ejura** Ghana
22C2 **Ejutla** Mexico
11B2 **Ekalaka** USA
78C2 **Eketahuna** NZ
48J4 **Ekibastuz** Kazakhstan
49P4 **Ekimchan** Russian Fed
64B3 **Ek Mahalla el Kubra** Egypt
32H7 **Eksjo** Sweden
4D3 **Ekwan** *R* Can
65A3 **El Abbâsa** Egypt
64A3 **El'Alamein** Egypt
74D2 **Elands** *R* S Africa
74C3 **Elands Berg** S Africa
22B1 **El Arenal** Mexico
71B2 **El Aricha** Alg
64B3 **El'Arîsh** Egypt
64B4 **Elat** Israel
72C2 **El' Atrun Oasis** Sudan
71C2 **el Attar** *R* Alg
45F8 **Elazig** Turk
64C3 **El Azraq** Jordan
40C2 **Elba** *I* Italy
69C2 **El Balyana** Egypt
53D1 **El'ban** Russian Fed
26D2 **El Banco** Colombia
41E2 **Elbasan** Alb
66B3 **El Bauga** Sudan
23D5 **El Baúl** Ven
71C2 **El Bayadh** Alg
42C2 **Elbe** *R* Germany
65D1 **El Bega'a** *R* Leb
12B2 **Elberta** USA
8C3 **Elbert,Mt** USA
15C2 **Elberton** USA
36A2 **Elbeuf** France
64C2 **Elbistan** Turk
43D2 **Elblag** Pol
25B6 **El Bolson** Arg
11C2 **Elbow Lake** USA
22B1 **El Bozal** Mexico
45G7 **Elbrus** *Mt* Russian Fed
Elburz Mts = Reshteh-ye Alborz
19C4 **El Cajon** USA
17C4 **El Campo** USA
19C4 **El Centro** USA
39B2 **Elche** Spain
4D4 **Elcho** USA
28B3 **El Cuy** Arg
39B2 **Elda** Spain
49P3 **El'dikan** Russian Fed
26C3 **El Diviso** Colombia
70B2 **El Djouf** *Desert* Region Maur
17D2 **Eldon** USA
29B4 **Eldorado** Arg
9D3 **El Dorado** Arkansas, USA
29C3 **Eldorado** Brazil
3G2 **Eldorado** Can
8D3 **El Dorado** Kansas, USA
21B2 **El Dorado** Mexico
16B3 **Eldorado** Texas, USA
26F2 **El Dorado** Ven
72D3 **Eldoret** Kenya
14A2 **Eldred** USA
65C1 **Elea,C** Cyprus
18D2 **Electric Peak** *Mt* USA
70B2 **El Eglab** Region, Alg
66B2 **Elel** *Watercourse* Egypt
16A3 **Elephant Butte Res** USA
39B1 **El Escorial** Spain
64D2 **Eleşkirt** Turk
71D1 **El Eulma** Alg
9F4 **Eleuthera** *I* Bahamas
71D1 **El Fahs** Tunisia
64B4 **El Faiyûm** Egypt
70B2 **El Farsia** *Well* Mor
72C2 **El Fasher** Sudan
64B4 **El Fashn** Egypt
39A1 **El Ferrol del Caudillo** Spain
65B3 **El Firdân** Egypt
72C2 **El Fula** Sudan
70C1 **El Gassi** Alg
72D2 **El Geteina** Sudan
72D2 **El Gezîra** Region, Sudan
65C3 **El Ghor** *V* Israel/Jordan
9E2 **Elgin** Illinois, USA
11B2 **Elgin** N Dakota, USA
34D3 **Elgin** Scot
64B3 **El Gîza** Egypt
70C1 **El Golea** Alg
19D4 **El Golfo de Santa Clara** Mexico
72D3 **Elgon,Mt** Uganda/Kenya
72E3 **El Goran** Eth
22B2 **El Grullo** Mexico
70B2 **El Guettara** *Well* Mali
70B2 **El Haricha** *Desert Region* Mali
64A4 **El Harra** Egypt
39C2 **El Harrach** Alg
66B4 **El Hawata** Sudan
22C1 **El Hig** Mexico
66B4 **El Homra** Sudan
28A3 **El Huecu** Arg
64B4 **El'Igma** *Desert Region* Egypt
10F3 **Elim** USA
Elisabethville = Lubumbashi
32K6 **Elisenvaara** Russian Fed
El Iskandarîya = Alexandria Egypt
45G6 **Elista** Russian Fed
76C4 **Elizabeth** Aust
13E2 **Elizabeth** USA
74B2 **Elizabeth B** Namibia
9F3 **Elizabeth City** USA
14E2 **Elizabeth Is** USA
15C1 **Elizabethton** Tennessee, USA
12B3 **Elizabethtown** Kentucky, USA
15D2 **Elizabethtown** N Carolina, USA
14B2 **Elizabethtown** Pennsylvania, USA
71A2 **El Jadida** Mor
64C3 **El Jafr** Jordan
65D3 **El Jafr** *L* Jordan
72D2 **El Jebelein** Sudan
71E1 **El Jem** Tunisia
43E2 **Elk** Pol
14C3 **Elk** *R* Maryland, USA
12C3 **Elk** *R* W Virginia, USA
11D3 **Elkader** USA
71D1 **El Kala** Alg
72D2 **El Kamlin** Sudan
71D1 **El Kef** Tunisia
20B1 **Elk Grove** USA
El Khalil = Hebron Israel
66B3 **El Khandaq** Sudan
65A3 **El Khânka** Egypt
66B1 **El Khârga** Egypt
66B1 **El-Khârga Oasis** Egypt
12B2 **Elkhart** USA
70B2 **El Khenachich** *Desert* Region Mali
11C3 **Elkhorn** *R* USA
41F2 **Elkhovo** Bulg
13D3 **Elkins** USA
14B2 **Elkland** USA
11A3 **Elk Mt** USA
18C1 **Elko** Can
8B2 **Elko** USA
71B2 **el Korima** *R* Alg
14C3 **Elkton** USA
66B2 **El Ku** *Watercourse* Egypt
65B3 **El Kûbri** Egypt
64B3 **El Kuntilla** Egypt
72C2 **El Lagowa** Sudan
6H2 **Ellef Ringnes I** Can
11C2 **Ellendale** USA
19D3 **Ellen,Mt** USA
8A2 **Ellensburg** USA
14C2 **Ellenville** USA
7K2 **Ellesmere I** Can
78B2 **Ellesmere,L** NZ
14B3 **Ellicott City** USA
74D3 **Elliot** S Africa
7K5 **Elliot Lake** Can
18D2 **Ellis** USA
65C3 **El Lisan** *Pen* Jordan
74D1 **Ellisras** S Africa
13F2 **Ellsworth** USA
79F3 **Ellsworth Land** *Region* Ant
65A4 **El Ma'âdi** Egypt
69B1 **El Maghra** *L* Egypt
66B4 **El Manaqil** Sudan
64B3 **El Mansûra** Egypt
65A3 **El Manzala** Egypt
65A3 **El Matarîya** Egypt
65B3 **El Matarîya** Egypt
14C3 **Elmer** USA
70B3 **El Mereié** *Desert Region* Maur
28B2 **El Milagro** Arg
71D1 **El Milia** Alg
66B3 **El Milk** *Watercourse* Sudan
65C1 **El Mîna** Leb
64B4 **El Minya** Egypt
20B1 **Elmira** California, USA
9F2 **Elmira** New York, USA
19D4 **El Mirage** USA
71D2 **el Mitta** *R* Alg
17F4 **El Moral** Mexico
70B2 **El Mreitl** *Well* Maur
42B2 **Elmsborn** Germany
72C2 **El Muglad** Sudan
70B2 **El Mzereb** *Well* Mali
57E8 **El Nido** Phil
72D2 **El Obeid** Sudan
22B2 **El Oro** Mexico
22A1 **Elota** Mexico
71D2 **El Oued** Alg
19D4 **Eloy** USA
8C3 **El Paso** USA
19B3 **El Porta** USA
20C2 **El Portal** USA
16A3 **El Porvenir** Mexico
22B1 **El Potosí** Mexico
39A2 **El Puerto del Sta Maria** Spain
El Qâhira = Cairo
65B3 **El Qantara** Egypt
El Quds = Jerusalem
22A1 **El Quelite** Mexico
65C3 **El Quseima** Egypt
65C4 **El Quwetra** Jordan
8D3 **El Reno** USA
6E3 **Elsa** Can
37D3 **Elsa** *R* Italy
65A4 **El Saff** Egypt
65B3 **El Sâlhîya** Egypt
22A1 **El Salto** Mexico
21D3 **El Salvador** Republic, C America
4E4 **Elsas** Can
19C4 **El Sauzal** Mexico
65B3 **El Shallûfa** Egypt
65B4 **El Shatt** Egypt
65A3 **El Simbillâwein** Egypt
20D4 **Elsinore L** USA
28B3 **El Sosneade** Arg
42C2 **Elsterwerde** Germany
16A4 **El Sueco** Mexico
El Suweis = Suez
65A4 **El Tabbin** Egypt
39A1 **El Teleno** *Mt* Spain
78B1 **Eltham** NZ
65C4 **El Thamad** Egypt
26F2 **El Tigre** Ven
64B4 **El Tîh** *Desert Region* Egypt
65B3 **El Tîna** Egypt
28C2 **El Tio** Arg
18C1 **Eltopia** USA
28A1 **El Toro** Chile
28A1 **El Transito** Chile
22A1 **El Tuito** Mexico
64B4 **El Tûr** Egypt
62C1 **Elūru** India
39A2 **Elvas** Port
26D5 **Elvira** Brazil
6H2 **Elvira,C** Can
28A2 **El Volcán** Chile
12B2 **Elwood** USA
35F5 **Ely** Eng
9D2 **Ely** Minnesota, USA
8B3 **Ely** Nevada, USA
12C2 **Elyria** USA
65A3 **El Zarqa** Egypt
63D1 **Emāmrūd** Iran
60B1 **Emām Sāheb** Afghan
42D1 **Eman** *R* Sweden
45K6 **Emba** Kazakhstan
45K6 **Emba** *R* Kazakhstan
25C5 **Embalse Cerros Colorados** *L* Arg
39B2 **Embalse de Alarcón** *Res* Spain
39A2 **Embalse de Alcántarà** *Res* Spain
39A1 **Embalse de Almendra** *Res* Spain
39A2 **Embalse de Garcia de Sola** *Res* Spain
26F2 **Embalse de Guri** *L* Ven
39B1 **Embalse de Mequinenza** *Res* Spain
39A1 **Embalse de Ricobayo** *Res* Spain
25E4 **Embalse de Rio Negro** *Res* Urug
28B3 **Embalse El Choc1on** *Res* Arg
25C5 **Embalse Ezequil Ramos Mexia** *L* Arg
25C6 **Embalse Florentine Ameghino** *L* Arg
39A1 **Embalse Gabriel y Galan** *Res* Spain
28B1 **Embalse Rio Hondo** *Res* Arg
25D2 **Embarcación** Arg
6G4 **Embarras Portage** Can

37B2 **Embrun** France
72D4 **Embu** Kenya
42B2 **Emden** Germany
52A4 **Emei** China
76D3 **Emerald** Aust
7M4 **Emeril** Can
6J5 **Emerson** Can
18C2 **Emigrant P** USA
72B1 **Emi Koussi** *Mt* Chad
28B3 **Emilo Mitre** Arg
64B2 **Emirdağ** Turk
14C2 **Emmaus** USA
42B2 **Emmen** Neth
36D2 **Emmendingen** Germany
36D1 **Emmerich** Germany
18C2 **Emmett** USA
14B3 **Emmitsburg** USA
10F3 **Emmonak** USA
8C4 **Emory Peak** *Mt* USA
21A2 **Empalme** Mexico
74E2 **Empangeni** S Africa
25E3 **Empedrado** Arg
xxixK2 **Emperor Seamount Chain** Pacific O
37D3 **Empoli** Italy
17C2 **Emporia** Kansas, USA
13D3 **Emporia** Virginia, USA
14A2 **Emporium** USA
42B2 **Ems** *R* Germany
4F4 **Emsdale** Can
34C2 **Enard** *B* Scot
22B1 **Encarnacion** Mexico
25E3 **Encarnación** Par
71F4 **Enchi** Ghana
17F4 **Encinal** USA
20D4 **Encinitas** USA
29D2 **Encruzilhada** Brazil
28E2 **Encruzilhada do Sul** Brazil
66C4 **Enda Salassie** Eth
76B1 **Endeh** Indon
3E3 **Enderby** Can
79G11 **Enderby Land** Region, Ant
11C2 **Enderlin** USA
13D2 **Endicott** USA
10H2 **Endicott Mts** USA
15D1 **Enfield** USA
37D1 **Engadin** *Mts* Switz
57F7 **Engaño,C** Phil
54D2 **Engaru** Japan
65C3 **En Gedi** Israel
37C1 **Engelberg** Switz
45H5 **Engel's** Russian Fed
56B4 **Enggano** *I* Indon
33C3 **England** Country, UK
7N4 **Englee** Can
15D1 **Englehard** USA
13D1 **Englehart** Can
16B2 **Englewood** USA
11D1 **English** *R* Can
33C3 **English Channel** Eng/ France
4C4 **English River** Can
17C2 **Enid** USA
54D2 **Eniwa** Japan
70B3 **Enji** *Well* Maur
32H7 **Enkoping** Sweden
40C3 **Enna** Italy
72C2 **En Nahud** Sudan
72C2 **Ennedi** *Desert Region* Chad
10C2 **Ennelen** Russian Fed
75C1 **Enngonia** Aust
11B3 **Enning** USA
33B3 **Ennis** Irish Rep
18D1 **Ennis** Montana, USA
17C3 **Ennis** Texas, USA
35B5 **Enniscorthy** Irish Rep
35B4 **Enniskillen** N Ire
65C2 **Enn Nâqoûra** Leb
42C3 **Enns** *R* Austria
57A3 **Enrekang** Indon
32F8 **Enschede** Neth
21A1 **Ensenada** Mexico
52B3 **Enshi** China
36D3 **Ensisheim** France
72D4 **Entebbe** Uganda
15B2 **Enterprise** Alabama, USA
3E1 **Enterprise** Can
18C1 **Enterprise** Oregon, USA
71H4 **Enugu** Nig
71H4 **Enugu** *State* Nig
10D2 **Enurmino** Russian Fed
36E2 **Enz** *R* w Germ
54C3 **Enzan** Japan
71G4 **Epe** Nig
38C2 **Epernay** France
19D3 **Ephraim** USA
14B2 **Ephrata** Pennsylvania, USA
18C1 **Ephrata** Washington, USA
77F2 **Epi** *I* Vanuatu
38D2 **Épinal** France
65B1 **Episkopi** Cyprus
65B1 **Episkopi B** Cyprus
36E2 **Eppingen** Germany
36A2 **Epte** *R* France
74B1 **Epukiro** Namibia
28C3 **Epu pel** Arg
63C2 **Eqlid** Iran
68D7 **Equator**
72A3 **Equatorial Guinea** Republic, Africa
14D1 **Equinox Mt** USA
14C2 **Equinunk** USA
37C2 **Erba** Italy
36E2 **Erbach** Germany
36D2 **Erbeskopf** *Mt* Germany
28A3 **Ercilla** Chile
64D2 **Erciş** Turk
45F8 **Erciyas Daglari** *Mt* Turk
53B3 **Erdaobaihe** China
52C1 **Erdene** Mongolia
50D2 **Erdenet** Mongolia
72C2 **Erdi** *Desert Region* Chad
25F3 **Erechim** Brazil
64B1 **Ereğli** Turk
64B2 **Ereğli** Turk
50E2 **Erenhot** China
39B1 **Eresma** *R* Spain
36D1 **Erft** *R* Germany
42C2 **Erfurt** Germany
64C2 **Ergani** Turk
70B2 **Erg Chech** *Desert Region* Alg
72B2 **Erg du Djourab** *Desert Region* Chad
70D3 **Erg Du Ténéré** *Desert Region* Niger
64A1 **Ergene** *R* Turk
70B2 **Erg Iguidi** *Region* Alg
43F1 **Ērgli** Latvia
72B2 **Erguig** *R* Chad
50E1 **Ergun** *R* China/Russian Fed
49O4 **Ergun Zuoqi** China
10C2 **Erguveyem** *R* Russian Fed
72D2 **Eriba** Sudan
9F2 **Erie** USA
9E2 **Erie,L** USA/Can
4B3 **Eriksdale** Can
54D2 **Erimo-misaki** *C* Japan
35C4 **Erin Port** Eng
34B3 **Eriskay** *I* Scot
66C3 **Eritrea** Region, Eth
36D1 **Erkelenz** Germany
42C3 **Erlangen** Germany
17D3 **Erling,L** USA
74D2 **Ermelo** S Africa
62B3 **Ernākulam** India
62B2 **Erode** India
75B1 **Eromanga** Aust
74B1 **Erongoberg** *Mt* Namibia
71B2 **Er Rachidia** Mor
72D2 **Er Rahad** Sudan
73D5 **Errego** Mozam
33B2 **Errigal** *Mt* Irish Rep
33A3 **Erris Head** *Pt* Irish Rep
77F2 **Erromanga** *I* Vanuatu
72D2 **Er Roseires** Sudan
71C2 **er Rtem** *R* Alg
65C2 **Er Rummān** Jordan
11C2 **Erskine** USA
36D2 **Erstein** France
28E2 **Erval** Brazil
42C2 **Erzgebirge** *Upland* Germany
45F8 **Erzincan** Turk
45G8 **Erzurum** Turk
54D2 **Esan-misaki** *C* Japan
38C3 **Esara** *R* Spain
54D2 **Esashi** Japan
42B1 **Esbjerg** Den
19D3 **Escalante** USA
8C4 **Escalón** Mexico
9E2 **Escanaba** USA
21C3 **Escárcega** Mexico
36C2 **Esch** Luxembourg
19C4 **Escondido** USA
21B2 **Escuinapa** Mexico
21C3 **Escuintla** Guatemala
72B3 **Eséka** Cam
39C1 **Esera** *R* Spain
63C2 **Eşfahān** Iran
74E2 **Eshowe** S Africa
65C3 **Esh Sharā** *Upland* Jordan
37E3 **Esino** Italy
78C1 **Eskdale** NZ
32C1 **Eskifjörður** Iceland
32H7 **Eskilstuna** Sweden
6E3 **Eskimo L** Can
7J3 **Eskimo Point** Can
45E8 **Eskisehir** Turk
39A1 **Esla** *R* Spain
26C3 **Esmeraldas** Ecuador
23B2 **Esmerelda** Cuba
25A7 **Esmerelda** *I* Chile
38C3 **Espalion** France
4E4 **Espanola** Can
16A2 **Espanola** USA
76B4 **Esperance** Aust
28C2 **Esperanza** Arg
79G2 **Esperanza** *Base* Ant
29D2 **Espírito Santo** State, Brazil
77F2 **Espiritu Santo** *I* Vanuatu
73D6 **Espungabera** Mozam
25B6 **Esquel** Arg
18B1 **Esquimalt** Can
28D2 **Esquina** Arg
65D2 **Es Samra** Jordan
71A2 **Essaourira** Mor
71E2 **Es-Sekhira** Tunisia
42B2 **Essen** Germany
27G3 **Essequibo** Guyana
35F6 **Essex** County, Eng
12C2 **Essexville** USA
42B3 **Esslingen** Germany
36B2 **Essonne** France
36C2 **Essoyes** France
27L6 **Estância** Brazil
74D2 **Estcourt** S Africa
37D2 **Este** Italy
26A1 **Esteli** Nic
36B2 **Esternay** France
20B3 **Estero B** USA
22C1 **Esteros** Mexico
25D2 **Esteros** Par
28D1 **Esteros del Iberá** *Swamp* Arg
16A1 **Estes Park** USA
6H5 **Estevan** Can
11D3 **Estherville** USA
15C2 **Estill** USA
36B2 **Estissac** France
44C4 **Estonia** *Republic* Europe
25B8 **Estrecho de Magallanes** *Str* Chile
20B3 **Estrella** *R* USA
39A2 **Estremoz** Port
43D3 **Esztergom** Hung
75A1 **Etadunna** Aust
7L2 **Etah** Can
36C2 **Etam** France
5K3 **Etamamiou** Can
38C2 **Etampes** France
75A1 **Etamunbanie,L** Aust
36A1 **Etaples** France
60D3 **Etāwah** India
72D3 **Ethiopia** Republic, Africa
22C2 **Etla** Mexico
40C3 **Etna** *Mt* Italy
10M4 **Etolin I** USA
10E3 **Etolin Str** USA
73B5 **Etosha Nat Pk** Namibia
73B5 **Etosha Pan** *Salt L* Namibia
15C2 **Etowah** *R* USA
36A2 **Etretat** France
3D2 **Etsha Plateau** Can
36C2 **Ettelbruck** Lux
77H3 **Eua** *I* Tonga
75C2 **Euabalong** Aust
12C2 **Euclid** USA
75C3 **Eucumbene,L** Aust
75A2 **Eudunda** Aust
17C2 **Eufala L** USA
15B2 **Eufaula** USA
8A2 **Eugene** USA
75C1 **Eulo** Aust
17D3 **Eunice** Louisiana, USA
16B3 **Eunice** New Mexico, USA
36D1 **Eupen** Germany
64D3 **Euphrates** *R* Iraq
17E3 **Eupora** USA
36A2 **Eure** Department, France
38C2 **Eure** *R* France
36A2 **Eure-et-Loir** Department, France
18B2 **Eureka** California, USA
7K1 **Eureka** Can
18C1 **Eureka** Montana, USA
8B3 **Eureka** Nevada, USA
11C2 **Eureka** S Dakota, USA
19D3 **Eureka** Utah, USA
7K2 **Eureka Sound** Can
20D2 **Eureka V** USA
75C3 **Euroa** Aust
75C1 **Eurombah** *R* Aust
73E6 **Europa** *I* Mozam Chan
36C1 **Europort** Neth
42B2 **Euskirchen** Germany
15B2 **Eutaw** USA
3C3 **Eutsuk L** Can
3F3 **Evansburg** Can
7K1 **Evans,C** Can
7L4 **Evans,L** Can
16A2 **Evans,Mt** Colorado, USA
18D1 **Evans,Mt** Montana, USA
7K3 **Evans Str** Can
12B2 **Evanston** Illinois, USA
8B2 **Evanston** Wyoming, USA
9E3 **Evansville** Indiana, USA
11A3 **Evansville** Wyoming, USA
74D2 **Evaton** S Africa
76C4 **Everard,L** Aust
59G3 **Everest,Mt** Nepal/China
14A2 **Everett** Pennsylvania, USA
8A2 **Everett** Washington, USA
14D1 **Everett,Mt** USA
9E4 **Everglades,The** *Swamp* USA
15B2 **Evergreen** USA
35E5 **Evesham** Eng
72B3 **Evinayong** Eq Guinea
32F7 **Evje** Nor
37B1 **Evolène** Switz
39A2 **Évora** Port
38C2 **Evreux** France
41E3 **Évvoia** *I* Greece
72B4 **Ewo** Congo
20C1 **Excelisor Mt** USA
20C1 **Excelisor Mts** USA
17D2 **Excelsior Springs** USA
19C3 **Exeter** California, USA
35D6 **Exeter** Eng
13E2 **Exeter** New Hampshire, USA
35D6 **Exmoor Nat Pk** Eng
35D6 **Exmouth** Eng
39A2 **Extremadura** Region, Spain
21E2 **Exuma Sd** Bahamas
72D4 **Eyasi** *L* Tanz
34D4 **Eyemouth** Scot
69D4 **Eyl** Somalia
76B4 **Eyre** Aust
76C3 **Eyre Creek** *R* Aust
76C3 **Eyre,L** Aust
76C4 **Eyre Pen** Aust
3H2 **Eyrie L** Can
57F8 **Eyte** *I* Phil
22B1 **Ezatlan** Mexico
41F3 **Ezine** Turk
66B3 **Ez Zeidab** Sudan

F

4G3 **Faber L** Can
32F7 **Fåborg** Den
40C2 **Fabriano** Italy
37B2 **Fabrosa** Italy
73B2 **Fachi** Niger
72C2 **Fada** Chad
71G3 **Fada N'Gourma** Burkina
49Q2 **Faddeyevskiy, Ostrov** *I* Russian Fed
40C2 **Faenza** Italy
7N3 **Faeringehavn** Greenland
30E2 **Faeroerne** Is, N Atlantic
72B3 **Fafa** *R* CAR
72E3 **Fafan** *R* Eth
71G3 **Faga** *R* Burkina
41E1 **Făgăraş** Rom
36C1 **Fagnes** Region, Belg
70B3 **Faguibine,L** Mali
67G2 **Fahud** Oman
70A1 **Faiol** *I* Açores
16A3 **Fairacres** USA
6D3 **Fairbanks** USA
12C3 **Fairborn** USA
8D2 **Fairbury** USA
14B3 **Fairfax** USA
19B3 **Fairfield** California, USA
14D2 **Fairfield** Connecticut, USA
18D2 **Fairfield** Idaho, USA
18D1 **Fairfield** Montana, USA
12C3 **Fairfield** Ohio, USA
34B4 **Fair Head** *Pt* N Ire
33C2 **Fair Isle** *I* Scot
78B2 **Fairlie** NZ
11D3 **Fairmont** Minnesota, USA
12C3 **Fairmont** W Virginia, USA
14B1 **Fairport** USA
3E2 **Fairview** Can
16C2 **Fairview** USA
6E4 **Fairweather,Mt** USA
51H6 **Fais** *I* Pacific O
60C2 **Faisalabad** Pak
11B2 **Faith** USA
34E1 **Faither,The** *Pen* Scot
61B2 **Faizābād** India
77H1 **Fakaofo** *I* Tokeau Is
35F5 **Fakenham** Eng
76C1 **Fakfak** Indon
32G7 **Faköping** Sweden
71F3 **Falaise de Banfora** Burkina
61D3 **Falam** Burma
28B4 **Falckner** Arg
21C2 **Falcon Res** USA/Mexico
70A3 **Falémé** *R* Mali/Sen
17F4 **Falfurrias** USA
3E2 **Falher** Can
32G7 **Falkenberg** Sweden
34D4 **Falkirk** Scot
25D8 **Falkland Is** Dependency, S Atlantic
25E8 **Falkland Sd** Falkland Is
20D4 **Fallbrook** USA
8B3 **Fallon** USA
13E2 **Fall River** USA
16A1 **Fall River P** USA
17C1 **Falls City** USA
35C6 **Falmouth** Eng
23H1 **Falmouth** Jamaica
13E2 **Falmouth** Maine, USA
14E2 **Falmouth** Massachusetts, USA
74B3 **False B** S Africa
21A2 **Falso,C** Mexico
42C2 **Falster** *I* Den
41F1 **Fălticeni** Rom
32H6 **Falun** Sweden
64B2 **Famagusta** Cyprus
65B1 **Famagusta B** Cyprus
28B1 **Famatina** Arg
36C1 **Famenne** Region, Belg
4B3 **Family L** Can
20C3 **Famoso** USA
55B2 **Fang** Thai
72D3 **Fangak** Sudan
52E5 **Fang liao** Taiwan
53B2 **Fangzheng** China
40C2 **Fano** Italy
65A3 **Fâqûs** Egypt
79G3 **Faraday** *Base* Ant
72C3 **Faradje** Zaïre
73E6 **Farafangana** Madag
69B2 **Farafra Oasis** Egypt
63E2 **Farah** Afghan
63E2 **Farah** *R* Afghan
51H5 **Farallon de Medinilla** *I* Pacific O
70A3 **Faranah** Guinea
51H6 **Faraulep** *I* Pacific O
35E6 **Fareham** Eng
Farewell,C = Kap Farvel
77G5 **Farewell,C** NZ
78B2 **Farewell Spit** *Pt* NZ
8D2 **Fargo** USA
65C2 **Fari'a** *R* Israel
9D2 **Faribault** USA
61C3 **Faridpur** Bang
63D1 **Farīmān** Iran
65A3 **Fâriskûr** Egypt
13E2 **Farmington** Maine, USA
17D2 **Farmington** Missouri, USA
14E1 **Farmington** New Hampshire, USA
8C3 **Farmington** New Mexico, USA
18D2 **Farmington** Utah, USA
20B2 **Farmington Res** USA
34E4 **Farne Deep** N Sea
3E3 **Farnham,Mt** Can
10M3 **Faro** Can
39A2 **Faro** Port
32H7 **Fåro** *I* Sweden
71J4 **Faro** *R* Cam
68K8 **Farquhar** *Is* Indian O
34C3 **Farrar** *R* Scot
12C2 **Farrell** USA
41E3 **Fársala** Greece
63E2 **Farsi** Afghan
16B3 **Farwell** USA
63C3 **Fasā** Iran
45D5 **Fastov** Ukraine
61B2 **Fatehpur** India
27H7 **Fatima du Sul** Brazil
18C1 **Fauquier** Can
74D2 **Fauresmith** S Africa
37B2 **Faverges** France
4C3 **Fawcett L** Can
7K4 **Fawn** *R* Can
32H6 **Fax** *R* Sweden
32A2 **Faxaflóri** *B* Iceland
72B2 **Faya** Chad
15B2 **Fayette** USA
9D3 **Fayetteville** Arkansas, USA
9F3 **Fayetteville** N Carolina, USA
15B1 **Fayetteville** Tennessee, USA
65B3 **Fâyid** Egypt
64E4 **Faylakah** *I* Kuwait
60C2 **Fāzilka** India
70A2 **Fdérik** Maur
9F3 **Fear,C** USA
19B3 **Feather Middle Fork** *R* USA
36A2 **Fécamp** France
28D2 **Federación** Arg
28D2 **Federal** Arg
71H4 **Federal Capital Territory** Nig
51H6 **Federated States of Micronesia** *Is* Pacific O
42C2 **Fehmarn** *I* Germany
26D5 **Feijó** Brazil
52C5 **Feilai Xai Bei Jiang** *R* China
78C2 **Feilding** NZ
73D5 **Feira** Zambia
27L6 **Feira de Santan** Brazil
64C2 **Feke** Turk
36D3 **Feldberg** *Mt* Germany
42B3 **Feldkirch** Austria
28D2 **Feliciano** *R* Arg
33D3 **Felixstowe** Eng
37D1 **Feltre** Italy
32G6 **Femund** *L* Nor

Fengcheng Funafuti

53A3 Fengcheng China
52B4 Fengdu China
52D1 Fenging China
52B3 Fengjie China
53A1 Fengshui Shan *Mt* China
52B3 Feng Xian China
52C1 Fengzhen China
52C2 Fen He *R* China
10C6 Fenimore Pass USA
73E5 Fenoarivo Atsinanana Madag
45F7 Feodosiya Ukraine
63D2 Ferdow Iran
36B2 Fère France
36B2 Fère-Champenoise France
59F2 Fergana Uzbekistan
3J2 Fergus *R* Can
11C2 Fergus Falls USA
35B4 Fermanagh County, N Ire
37E3 Fermo Italy
37D1 Fern *Mt* Austria
28C1 Fernandez Arg
15C2 Fernandina Beach USA
xxxG5 Fernando de Noronha *I* Atlantic O
29B3 Fernandópolis Brazil
70C4 Fernando Poo *I* Eq Guinea
18B1 Ferndale USA
18C1 Fernie Can
19C3 Fernley USA
40C2 Ferrara Italy
26C5 Ferreñafe Peru
17D3 Ferriday USA
36B2 Ferriéres France
71A2 Fès Mor
5G4 Festubert Can
17D2 Festus USA
41F2 Feteşti Rom
64A2 Fethiye Turk
45J7 Fetisovo Kazakhstan
34E1 Fetlar *I* Scot
53C1 Fevral'skoye Russian Fed
48J6 Feyzabad Afghan
28B1 Fiambalá Arg
73E6 Fianarantsoa Madag
72D3 Fichē Eth
74D2 Ficksburg S Africa
37D2 Fidenza Italy
41D2 Fier Alb
37D1 Fiera Di Primeiro Italy
34D3 Fife Region, Scot
34D3 Fife Ness *Pen* Scot
38C3 Figeac France
39A1 Figueira da Foz Port
39C1 Figueras Spain
Figueres = Figueras
71B2 Figuig Mor
77G2 Fiji *Is* Pacific O
27G8 Filadelpia Par
41E2 Filiaşi Rom
41E3 Filiatrá Greece
40C3 Filicudi *I* Italy
19C4 Fillmore California, USA
19D3 Fillmore Utah, USA
37C2 Finale Ligure Italy
34C3 Findhorn *R* Scot
9E2 Findlay USA
3E3 Findlay,Mt Can
13D2 Finger Lakes USA
73D5 Fingoè Mozam
45E8 Finike Turk
76C3 Finke *R* Aust
75A1 Finke Flood Flats Aust
44C3 Finland Republic, N Europe
32J7 Finland,G of N Europe
6F4 Finlay *R* Can
6F4 Finlay Forks Can
75C3 Finley Aust
32H5 Finnsnes Nor
51H7 Finschhafen PNG
37C1 Finsteraarhorn *Mt* Switz
42C2 Finsterwalde Germany
35B4 Fintona N Ire
78A3 Fiordland Nat Pk NZ
65C2 Fiq Syria
45F8 Firat *R* Turk
3F2 Firebag *R* Can
20B2 Firebaugh USA
40C2 Firenze Italy
37D2 Firenzuola Italy
3C2 Fireside Can
28C2 Firmat Arg
60D3 Firozābād India
60C2 Firozpur India
32H7 Firspång Sweden
34C4 Firth of Clyde *Estuary* Scot
34D3 Firth of Forth *Estuary* Scot
34B3 Firth of Lorn *Estuary* Scot
33C2 Firth of Tay *Estuary* Scot
63C3 Firūzābād Iran
74B2 Fish *R* Namibia
74C3 Fish *R* S Africa
20C2 Fish Camp USA
14D2 Fishers I USA
7K3 Fisher Str Can
35C6 Fishguard Wales
10O3 Fish L Can
7N3 Fiskenaesset Greenland
36B2 Fismes France
13E2 Fitchburg USA
34E2 Fitful Head *Pt* Scot
15C2 Fitzgerald USA
3F2 Fitzgerald Can
76B2 Fitzroy *R* Aust
76B2 Fitzroy Crossing Aust
12C1 Fitzwilliam I Can
Fiume = Rijeka
72C4 Fizi Zaïre
74D3 Flagstaff S Africa
8B3 Flagstaff USA
13E1 Flagstaff L USA
35E4 Flamborough Head *C* Eng
8C2 Flaming Gorge Res USA
34B2 Flannan Isles *Is* Scot
10N3 Flat *R* Can
3F4 Flathead *R* USA
8B2 Flathead L USA
17D2 Flat River USA
51H8 Flattery,C Aust
8A2 Flattery,C USA
35D5 Fleetwood Eng
32F7 Flekkefjord *Inlet* Nor
50H4 Fleming Deep Pacific Oc
14C2 Flemington USA
42B2 Flensburg Germany
5K3 Fleur-de-Lys Can
37B1 Fleurier Switz
36A2 Fleury-sur-Andelle France
76C4 Flinders I Aust
76D5 Flinders *I* Aust
76C4 Flinders Range *Mts* Aust
6H4 Flin Flon Can
9E2 Flint USA
35D5 Flint Wales
9E3 Flint *R* USA
36B1 Flixecourt France
12A1 Floodwood USA
15B2 Florala USA
Florence = Firenze
9E3 Florence Alabama, USA
19D4 Florence Arizona, USA
16A2 Florence Colorado, USA
17C2 Florence Kansas, USA
18B2 Florence Oregon, USA
9F3 Florence S Carolina, USA
20C2 Florence,L USA
26C3 Florencia Colombia
36C2 Florenville Belg
21D3 Flores Guatemala
70A1 Flores *I* Açores
76B1 Flores *I* Indon
28D3 Flores *R* Arg
51E7 Flores S Indon
27K5 Floriano Brazil
25G3 Florianópolis Brazil
21D2 Florida State, USA
25E4 Florida Urug
15E4 Florida B USA
15E4 Florida City USA
77E1 Florida Is Solomon Is
9E4 Florida Keys *Is* USA
9E4 Florida,Strs of USA
41E2 Flórina Greece
32F6 Florø Nor
16B3 Floydada USA
37D1 Fluchthorn *Mt* Austria
57C3 Fluk Indon
76D1 Fly *R* PNG
37E2 Foci del Po *Delta* Italy
41F1 Focşani Rom
40D2 Foggia Italy
37E3 Foglia *R* Italy
5L4 Fogo Can
5L4 Fogo I Can
70A4 Fogo *I* Cape Verde
38C3 Foix France
4E4 Foleyet Can
7L3 Foley I Can
40C2 Foligno Italy
35F6 Folkestone Eng
15C2 Folkston USA
40C2 Follonica Italy
20B1 Folsom USA
14C1 Fonda USA
6H4 Fond-du-Lac Can
9E2 Fond du Lac USA
38C2 Fontainebleau France
3D2 Fontas *R* Can
17D2 Fontenac USA
38B2 Fontenay-le-Comte France
41D1 Fonyód Hung
Foochow = Fuzhou
10H3 Foraker,Mt USA
36D2 Forbach France
75C2 Forbes Aust
71H4 Forcados Nig
37A3 Forcalquier France
20C3 Ford City USA
32F6 Forde Nor
75C1 Fords Bridge Aust
17D3 Fordyce USA
70A4 Forécariah Guinea
7P3 Forel,Mt Greenland
18D1 Foremost Can
12C2 Forest Can
15B2 Forest USA
11D3 Forest City Iowa, USA
14C2 Forest City Pennsylvania, USA
15C2 Forest Park USA
20A1 Forestville USA
36B2 Forêt d'Othe France
34D3 Forfar Scot
16B2 Forgan USA
36A2 Forges-les-Eaux France
18B1 Forks USA
40C2 Forlì Italy
39C2 Formentera *I* Spain
40C2 Formia Italy
70A1 Formigas *I* Açores
Formosa = Taiwan
25E3 Formosa Arg
27J7 Formosa Brazil
25D2 Formosa State, Arg
52D5 Formosa Str Taiwan/China
29C1 Formoso Brazil
29C1 Formoso *R* Brazil
37D2 Fornovo di Taro Italy
34D3 Forres Scot
76B4 Forrest Aust
9D3 Forrest City USA
3G2 Forrest L Can
76D2 Forsayth Aust
32J6 Forssa Fin
75D2 Forster Aust
17D2 Forsyth Missouri, USA
11A2 Forsyth Montana, USA
60C3 Fort Abbas Pak
7K4 Fort Albany Can
27L4 Fortaleza Brazil
34C3 Fort Augustus Scot
74D3 Fort Beaufort S Africa
18D1 Fort Benton USA
19B3 Fort Bragg USA
3F2 Fort Chipewyan Can
16C2 Fort Cobb Res USA
8C2 Fort Collins USA
4F4 Fort Coulonge Can
16B3 Fort Davis USA
23E4 Fort de France Martinique
15B2 Fort Deposit USA
9D2 Fort Dodge USA
76A3 Fortescue *R* Aust
7J5 Fort Frances Can
6F3 Fort Franklin Can
6F3 Fort Good Hope Can
75B1 Fort Grey Aust
34C3 Forth *R* Scot
16A3 Fort Hancock USA
7K4 Fort Hope Can
34F3 Forties *Oilfield* N Sea
28B3 Fortin Uno Arg
13F1 Fort Kent USA
70C1 Fort Lallemand Alg
Fort Lamy = Ndjamena
11B3 Fort Laramie USA
9E4 Fort Lauderdale USA
3D1 Fort Liard Can
6G4 Fort Mackay Can
6G5 Fort Macleod Can
6G4 Fort McMurray Can
6E3 Fort McPherson Can
12A2 Fort Madison USA
8C2 Fort Morgan USA
9E4 Fort Myers USA
6F4 Fort Nelson Can
3D2 Fort Nelson *R* Can
6F3 Fort Norman Can
15B2 Fort Payne USA
11A2 Fort Peck USA
8C2 Fort Peck Res USA
9E4 Fort Pierce USA
11B3 Fort Pierre USA
14C1 Fort Plain USA
6G3 Fort Providence Can
3H3 Fort Qu'Appelle Can
10F4 Fort Randall USA
6G3 Fort Resolution Can
72B4 Fort Rousset Congo
6F4 Fort St James Can
3D2 Fort St John Can
3F3 Fort Saskatchewan Can
17D2 Fort Scott USA
6E3 Fort Selkirk Can
7K4 Fort Severn Can
45J7 Fort Shevchenko Kazakhstan
6F3 Fort Simpson Can
6G3 Fort Smith Can
9D3 Fort Smith USA
6F3 Fort Smith Region, Can
8C3 Fort Stockton USA
16B3 Fort Sumner USA
16C2 Fort Supply USA
18B2 Fortuna California, USA
11B2 Fortuna N Dakota, USA
5K4 Fortune B Can
6G4 Fort Vermilion Can
15B2 Fort Walton Beach USA
9E2 Fort Wayne USA
34C3 Fort William Scot
16A2 Fort Wingate USA
8D3 Fort Worth USA
10K3 Fortymile *R* USA
10J2 Fort Yukon USA
52C5 Foshan China
7K2 Fosheim *Pen* Can
37B2 Fossano Italy
37E3 Fossombrone Italy
11C2 Fosston USA
3G2 Foster L Can
10L4 Foster,Mt USA
72B4 Fougamou Gabon
38B2 Fougères France
34D1 Foula *I* Scot
35F6 Foulness I Eng
78B2 Foulwind,C NZ
72B3 Foumban Cam
38C1 Fourmies France
10E5 Four Mountains,Is of USA
41F3 Foúrnoi *I* Greece
70A3 Fouta Djallon *Mts* Guinea
77F5 Foveaux Str NZ
35C6 Fowey Eng
16B2 Fowler USA
12B2 Fox *R* USA
3E3 Fox Creek Can
7K3 Foxe Basin *G* Can
7K3 Foxe Chan Can
7L3 Foxe Pen Can
10E5 Fox Is USA
3F2 Fox Lake Can
16A1 Foxpark USA
78C2 Foxton NZ
3G3 Fox Valley Can
73B5 Foz do Cuene Angola
25F3 Foz do Iquaçu Brazil
22B1 Fracisco I Madero Mexico
14B2 Frackville USA
28B2 Fraga Arg
14E1 Framingham USA
27J8 Franca Brazil
38C2 France Republic, Europe
10N3 Frances *R* Can
4D5 Francesville USA
38D2 Franche Comté Region, France
74D1 Francistown Botswana
3C3 Francois L Can
18E2 Francs Peak *Mt* USA
36E1 Frankenberg Germany
12B2 Frankfort Indiana, USA
9E3 Frankfort Kentucky, USA
14C1 Frankfort New York, USA
42B2 Frankfurt Germany
74D2 Frankfurt S Africa
36E1 Frankfurt am Main Germany
42C2 Frankfurt-an-der-Oder Germany
42C3 Fränkischer Alb *Upland* Germany
18D2 Franklin Idaho, USA
12B3 Franklin Indiana, USA
17D4 Franklin Louisiana, USA
14E1 Franklin Massachusetts, USA
15C1 Franklin N Carolina, USA
14E1 Franklin New Hampshire, USA
14C2 Franklin New Jersey, USA
13D2 Franklin Pennsylvania, USA
15B1 Franklin Tennessee, USA
13D3 Franklin Virginia, USA
6F2 Franklin B Can
18C1 Franklin D Roosevelt *L* USA
6F3 Franklin Mts Can
10G1 Franklin,Pt USA
6J2 Franklin Str Can
14A1 Franklinville USA
4E4 Franz Can
78B2 Franz Josef Glacier NZ
Franz-Joseph-Land = Zemlya Franza Josifa
4F5 Fraser *R* Can
74C3 Fraserburg S Africa
34D3 Fraserburgh Scot
75D1 Fraser I Aust
3C3 Fraser Lake Can
5J2 Fraser *R* Can
37B1 Frasne France
37C1 Frauenfield Switz
28D2 Fray Bentos Urug
33C2 Frazerburgh Scot
14C3 Frederica USA
42B1 Fredericia Den
13D3 Frederick Maryland, USA
16C3 Frederick Oklahoma, USA
16C3 Fredericksburg Texas, USA
13D3 Fredericksburg Virginia, USA
10M4 Frederick Sd USA
17D2 Fredericktown USA
7M5 Fredericton Can
7N3 Frederikshåb Greenland
32G7 Frederikshavn Den
13D2 Fredonia USA
32G7 Fredrikstad Nor
14C2 Freehold USA
20C1 Freel Peak *Mt* USA
5L4 Freels,C Can
11C3 Freeman USA
23B1 Freeport Bahamas
5H5 Freeport Can
12B2 Freeport Illinois, USA
17C4 Freeport Texas, USA
17F4 Freer USA
70A4 Freetown Sierra Leone
42B3 Freiburg Germany
36D2 Freiburg im Breisgau Germany
28A1 Freirina Chile
42C3 Freistadt Austria
37B3 Fréjus France
76A4 Fremantle Aust
20B2 Fremont California, USA
17C1 Fremont Nebraska, USA
12C2 Fremont Ohio, USA
27H3 French Guiana Dependency, S America
11A2 Frenchman *R* USA
75E3 Frenchmans Cap *Mt* Aust
xxixM5 French Polynesia *Is* Pacific O
71C1 Frenda Alg
21B2 Fresnillo Mexico
8B3 Fresno USA
20C2 Fresno *R* USA
18D1 Fresno Res USA
37A1 Fretigney France
36E2 Freudenstadt Germany
36B1 Frévent France
75E3 Freycinet Pen Aust
70A3 Fria Guinea
20C2 Friant USA
20C2 Friant Dam USA
28B1 Frías Arg
40B1 Fribourg Switz
36E1 Friedberg Germany
42B3 Friedrichshafen Germany
16C4 Frio *R* USA
16B3 Friona USA
37E1 Friuli Region, Italy
7M3 Frobisher B Can
7M3 Frobisher Bay Can
6H4 Frobisher L Can
45G6 Frolovo Russian Fed
35D6 Frome Eng
75A1 Frome *R* Aust
35D6 Frome *R* Eng
76C4 Frome,L Aust
21C3 Frontera Mexico
13D3 Front Royal USA
40C2 Frosinone Italy
14A3 Frostburg USA
16A2 Fruita USA
52C5 Fuchuan China
52E4 Fuding China
21B2 Fuerte *R* Mexico
29A3 Fuerte Olimpo Brazil
25E2 Fuerte Olimpo Par
70A2 Fuerteventura *I* Canary Is
52C2 Fugu China
50B2 Fuhai China
67G1 Fujairah UAE
54C3 Fuji Japan
52D4 Fujian Province, China
53C2 Fujin China
54C3 Fujinomiya Japan
53D4 Fuji-san *Mt* Japan
54C3 Fujisawa Japan
54C3 Fuji-Yoshida Japan
54D2 Fukagawa Japan
48K5 Fukang China
53C4 Fukuchiyima Japan
54A4 Fukue Japan
54A4 Fukue *I* Japan
53D4 Fukui Japan
53C5 Fukuoka Japan
53E4 Fukushima Japan
53C5 Fukuyama Japan
11C3 Fulda USA
42B2 Fulda Germany
42B2 Fulda *R* Germany
52B4 Fuling China
23L1 Fullarton Trinidad
20D4 Fullerton USA
12A2 Fulton Illinois, USA
12B3 Fulton Kentucky, USA
13D2 Fulton New York, USA
36C1 Fumay France
54D3 Funabashi Japan
77G1 Funafuti *I* Tuvalu

Funchal Glama

70A1 Funchal Medeira
29D2 Fundão Brazil
7M5 Fundy,B of Can
73D6 Funhalouro Mozam
52B5 Funing China
52D3 Funing China
71H3 Funtua Nig
52D4 Fuqing China
73D5 Furancungo Mozam
54D2 Furano Japan
63D3 Fürg Iran
37C1 Furka *P* Switz
76D5 Furneaux Group *Is* Aust
42C2 Fürstenwalde Germany
42C3 Fürth Germany
54D2 Furubira Japan
53D4 Furukawa Japan
7K3 Fury and Hecla Str Can
53A3 Fushun Liaoning, China
52A4 Fushun Sichuan, China
53B3 Fusong China
42C3 Füssen Germany
52E2 Fu Xian China
52E1 Fuxin China
52D3 Fuyang China
53A2 Fuyu China
53C2 Fuyuan Heilongjiang, China
52E1 Fuyuan Liaoning, China
52A4 Fuyuan Yunnan, China
50B2 Fuyun China
52D4 Fuzhou China
42C1 Fyn *I* Den

G

72E3 Gaalkacyo Somalia
19C3 Gabbs USA
20C1 Gabbs Valley Range *Mts* USA
73B5 Gabela Angola
71E2 Gabe's Tunisia
66B2 Gabgaba *Watercourse* Egypt
20B2 Gabilan Range *Mts* USA
72B4 Gabon Republic, Africa
74D1 Gaborone Botswana
41F2 Gabrovo Bulg
63C2 Gach Sārān Iran
15B2 Gadsden Alabama, USA
19D4 Gadsden Arizona, USA
40C2 Gaeta Italy
51H6 Gaferut *I* Pacific O
15C1 Gaffney USA
71D2 Gafsa Tunisia
44E4 Gagarin Russian Fed
71H3 Gagere *R* Nig
7M4 Gagnon Can
45G7 Gagra Georgia
61C2 Gaibanda India
37E1 Gailtaler Alpen *Mts* Austria
25C6 Gaimán Arg
15C3 Gainesville Florida, USA
15C2 Gainesville Georgia, USA
17C3 Gainesville Texas, USA
35E5 Gainsborough Eng
75A2 Gairdner,L Aust
34C3 Gairloch Scot
14B3 Gaithersburg USA
62B1 Gajendragarh India
52D4 Ga Jiang *R* China
74C2 Gakarosa *Mt* S Africa
72D4 Galana *R* Kenya
xxxD4 Galapagos Is Pacific O
34D4 Galashiels Scot
41F1 Galaţi Rom
12C3 Galax USA
16A3 Galeana Mexico
57C2 Galela Indon
6C3 Galena Alaska, USA
12A2 Galena Illinois, USA
17D2 Galena Kansas, USA
23L1 Galeota Pt Trinidad
23L1 Galera Pt Trinidad
12A2 Galesburg USA
14B2 Galeton USA
44G4 Galich Russian Fed
39A1 Galicia Region, Spain
Galilee,S of = Tiberias,L
23J1 Galina Pt Jamaica
66C4 Gallabat Sudan
37C2 Gallarate Italy
15B1 Gallatin USA
18D1 Gallatin *R* USA
62C3 Galle Sri Lanka
16A4 Gallego Mexico
39B1 Gállego *R* Spain
Gallipoli = Gelibolu
41D2 Gallipoli Italy
44C2 Gällivare Sweden
34C4 Galloway District
35C4 Galloway,Mull of *C* Scot
16A2 Gallup USA
71H3 Galma *R* Nig
21C2 Galveston USA
9D4 Galveston B USA
28C2 Galvez Arg
38D3 Galvi Corse
33B3 Galway Irish Rep
33B3 Galway *B* Irish Rep
57D3 Gam *I* Indon
61C2 Gamba China
71F3 Gambaga Ghana
10D3 Gambell USA
70A3 Gambia *R* The Gambia/Sen
70A3 Gambia,The Republic, Africa
5L4 Gambo Can
72B4 Gamboma Congo
73B5 Gambos Angola
62C3 Gampola Sri Lanka
19E3 Ganado USA
72E3 Ganale Dorya *R* Eth
4F5 Gananoque Can
Gand = Gent
73B5 Ganda Angola
73C4 Gandajika Zaïre
60B3 Gandava Pak
7N5 Gander Can
60B4 Gāndhīdhām India
60C4 Gāndhīnagar India
60D4 Gāndhi Sāgar *L* India
39B2 Gandia Spain
29E1 Gandu Brazil
61C3 Ganga *R* India
60C3 Ganganar India
61D3 Gangaw Burma
61E3 Gangaw Range *Mts* Burma
52A2 Gangca China
59G2 Gangdise Shan *Mts* China
Ganges = Ganga
61C2 Gangtok India
52B3 Gangu China
53A1 Gan He *R* China
57C3 Gani Indon
53A2 Gannan China
18E2 Gannett Peak *Mt* USA
52B2 Ganquan China
75A3 Gantheaume *C* Aust
32K8 Gantsevichi Belorussia
71J4 Ganye Nig
52D4 Ganzhou China
70C3 Gao Mali
52A2 Gaolan China
52C2 Gaoping China
71F3 Gaoua Burkina
70A3 Gaoual Guinea
52D3 Gaoyou Hu *L* China
52C5 Gaozhou China
38D3 Gap France
57F7 Gapan Phil
60D2 Gar China
75C1 Garah Aust
27L5 Garanhuns Brazil
19B2 Garberville USA
29C3 Garça Brazil
29B3 Garcias Brazil
37D2 Garda Italy
37A3 Gardanne France
16B2 Garden City USA
12B1 Garden Pen USA
28D3 Gardey Arg
60B2 Gardez Afghan
18D1 Gardiner USA
14D2 Gardiners I USA
14E1 Gardner USA
77H1 Gardner *I* Phoenix Is
20C1 Gardnerville USA
37D2 Gardone Italy
10C6 Gareloi *I* USA
37D2 Gargano Italy
60D4 Garhākota India
44L4 Gari Russian Fed
74B3 Garies S Africa
72D4 Garissa Kenya
17C3 Garland USA
42C3 Garmisch-Partenkirchen Germany
63C1 Garmsar Iran
17C2 Garnett USA
8B2 Garnett Peak *Mt* USA
38C3 Garonne *R* France
71J4 Garoua Cam
71J4 Garoua Boulai Cam
11B2 Garrison USA
34C3 Garry *R* Scot
6H3 Garry L Can
56C4 Garut Indon
61B3 Garwa India
12B2 Gary USA
59G2 Garyarsa China
6H3 Gary L Can
28C1 Garza Arg
17C3 Garza-Little Elm *Res* USA
63C1 Gasan Kuli Turkmenistan
38B3 Gascogne Region, France
17D2 Gasconade *R* USA
76A3 Gascoyne *R* Aust
72B3 Gashaka Nig
63E3 Gasht Iran
71J3 Gashua Nig
5J4 Gaspé Can
5H4 Gaspésie Prov Park Can
15C1 Gastonia USA
15D1 Gaston,L USA
65B1 Gata,C Cyprus
44D4 Gatchina Russian Fed
34D4 Gateshead Eng
17C3 Gatesville USA
36B2 Gâtinais Region, France
4F4 Gatineau Can
4F4 Gatineau *R* Can
15C1 Gatlinburg USA
75D1 Gatton Aust
77F2 Gaua *I* Vanuatu
63E2 Gaud-i-Zirreh *Salt Desert* Afghan
4B2 Gauer L Can
61D2 Gauháti India
43E1 Gauja *R* Latvia
63F1 Gaurdak Turkmenistan
61B2 Gauri Phanta India
41E4 Gavdhos *I* Greece
29D1 Gavião *R* Brazil
20B3 Gaviota USA
32H6 Gävle Sweden
75A2 Gawler Ranges *Mts* Aust
52A1 Gaxun Nur *L* China
61B3 Gaya India
71G3 Gaya Niger
53B3 Gaya *R* China
12C1 Gaylord USA
75D1 Gayndah Aust
44J3 Gayny Russian Fed
43F3 Gaysin Ukraine
64B3 Gaza Israel
64C2 Gaziantep Turk
70B4 Gbaringa Lib
43D2 Gdańsk Pol
43D2 Gdańsk,G of Pol
32K7 Gdov Russian Fed
43D2 Gdynia Pol
57C3 Gebe *I* Indon
65C4 Gebel Abu Rûtha *Mt* Egypt
65C3 Gebel Araif el Naqa *Mt* Egypt
65B4 Gebel Ataqa *Mt* Egypt
65B4 Gebel Budhiya Egypt
65A4 Gebel el Galâla Baharîya *Desert* Egypt
65B3 Gebel El Giddi *Mt* Egypt
65B4 Gebel El Tîh *Upland* Egypt
65B3 Gebel Halâl *Mt* Egypt
66C2 Gebel Hamata *Mt* Egypt
64B4 Gebel Katherina *Mt* Egypt
65B4 Gebel Kharim *Mt* Egypt
65B3 Gebel Libni *Mt* Egypt
65B3 Gebel Maghâra *Mt* Egypt
65C4 Gebel Sha'îra *Mt* Egypt
65B4 Gebel Sinn Bishr *Mt* Egypt
65B3 Gebel Yi'allaq *Mt* Egypt
71E2 Gebés Tunisia
22C1 Gedad del Maiz Mexico
66C4 Gedaref Sudan
41F3 Gediz *R* Turk
42C2 Gedser Den
36C1 Geel Belg
75B3 Geelong Aust
75E3 Geeveston Aust
71J3 Geidam Nig
3H2 Geikie *R* Can
36D1 Geilenkirchen Germany
72D4 Geita Tanz
52A5 Gejiu China
40C3 Gela Italy
72E3 Geladi Eth
36D1 Geldern Germany
41F2 Gelibolu Turk
64B2 Gelidonya Burun Turk
22B1 Gelleana Mexico
36E1 Gelnhausen Germany
36D1 Gelsenkirchen Germany
32F8 Gelting Germany
55C5 Gemas Malay
36C1 Gembloux Belg
71J4 Gembut Nig
72B3 Gemena Zaïre
64C2 Gemerek Turk
64A1 Gemlik Turk
40C1 Gemona Italy
37E1 Gemona del Friuli Italy
74C2 Gemsbok Nat Pk Botswana
72C2 Geneina Sudan
28C3 General Acha Arg
28C3 General Alvear Buenos Aires, Arg
28B2 General Alvear Mendoza, Arg
28C2 General Arenales Arg
28D3 General Belgrano Arg
79F2 General Belgrano *Base* Ant
79G2 General Bernardo O'Higgins *Base* Ant
28C1 General Capdevia Arg
28D3 General Conesa Buenos Aires, Arg
28C4 General Conesa Rio Negro, Arg
26F8 General Eugenio A Garay Par
20C2 General Grant Grove Section *Region* USA
28D3 General Guido Arg
28C3 General La Madrid Arg
28D3 General Lavalle Arg
28C2 General Levalle Arg
28D3 General Madariaga Arg
25C3 General Manuel Belgrano *Mt* Arg
28D3 General Paz Buenos Aires, Arg
28D1 General Paz Corrientes, Arg
28C3 General Pico Arg
28C2 General Pinto Arg
28D3 General Pirán Arg
25C5 General Roca Arg
22B1 General San Bolivar Mexico
57G9 General Santos Phil
28C3 General Viamonte Arg
28C3 General Villegas Arg
13D2 Genesee *R* USA
13D2 Geneseo USA
Geneva = Genève
17C10 Geneva Nebraska, USA
14B1 Geneva New York, USA
Geneva,L of = Lac Léman
40B1 Genève Switz
39B2 Genil *R* Spain
Genoa = Genova
75C3 Genoa Aust
40B2 Genova Italy
36B1 Gent Belg
56C4 Genteng Indon
42C2 Genthin Germany
45H7 Geokchay Azerbaijan
74C3 George S Africa
7M4 George *R* Can
5J4 George B Can
75C2 George,L Aust
15C3 George,L Florida, USA
13E2 George,L New York, USA
5K3 George's Cove Can
78A2 George Sd NZ
75E3 George Town Aust
5J4 Georgetown Can
20B1 Georgetown California, USA
13D3 Georgetown Delaware, USA
27G2 Georgetown Guyana
12C3 Georgetown Kentucky, USA
55C4 George Town Malay
23N2 Georgetown St Vincent
15D2 Georgetown S Carolina, USA
17C3 Georgetown Texas, USA
70A3 Georgetown The Gambia
79G8 George V Land Region, Ant
17F4 George West USA
79F12 Georg Forster *Base* Ant
45G7 Georgia *Republic* Europe
15C2 Georgia State, USA
4E3 Georgian B Can
3D4 Georgia,Str of Can
76C3 Georgina *R* Aust
45G7 Georgiyevsk Russian Fed
42C2 Gera Germany
36B1 Geraardsbergen Belg
78B2 Geraldine NZ
76A3 Geraldton Aust
4D4 Geraldton Can
65C3 Gerar *R* Israel
36D2 Gérardmer France
6C3 Gerdine,Mt USA
10J3 Gerdova Peak *Mt* USA
55C4 Gerik Malay
11B3 Gering USA
45C6 Gerlachovsky *Mt* Pol
3D2 Germanson Lodge Can
42B2 Germany Republic
74D2 Germiston S Africa
36D1 Gerolstein Germany
39C1 Gerona Spain
36E1 Geseke Germany
72E3 Gestro *R* Eth
39B1 Getafe Spain
5J3 Gethsémani Can
14B3 Gettysburg Pennsylvania, USA
11C2 Gettysburg S Dakota, USA
28E1 Getúlio Vargas Brazil
56A2 Geumpang Indon
64D2 Gevaş Turk
41E2 Gevgeliija Macedonia, Yugos
37B1 Gex France
65D2 Ghabāghib Syria
70C1 Ghadamis Libya
63C1 Ghaem Shahr Iran
61B2 Ghāghara *R* India
70B4 Ghana Republic, Africa
74C1 Ghanzi Botswana
71C2 Ghardaïa Alg
69A1 Gharyan Libya
69A2 Ghāt Libya
71B1 Ghazaouet Alg
60D3 Ghāziābād India
60C3 Ghazi Khan Pak
60B2 Ghazni Afghan
41F1 Gheorgheni Rom
67F3 Ghubbat al Qamar *B* Yemen
67G3 Ghubbat Sawqirah *B* Oman
68E4 Ghudamis Alg
63E2 Ghurian Afghan
40D3 Giarre Italy
16C1 Gibbon USA
74B2 Gibeon Namibia
39A2 Gibraltar Colony, SW Europe
39A2 Gibraltar,Str of Spain/Africa
76B3 Gibson Desert Aust
18B1 Gibsons Can
62B1 Giddalūr India
65B3 Giddi P Egypt
72D3 Gīdolē Eth
36B3 Gien France
42B2 Giessen Germany
15C3 Gifford USA
53D4 Gifu Japan
34C4 Gigha *I* Scot
40C2 Giglio *I* Italy
39A1 Gijon Spain
19D4 Gila *R* USA
19D4 Gila Bend USA
19D4 Gila Bend Mts USA
76D2 Gilbert *R* Aust
77G1 Gilbert Is Pacific O
3D3 Gilbert,Mt Can
18D1 Gildford USA
73D5 Gilé Mozam
65C2 Gilead Region, Jordan
69B2 Gilf Kebir Plat Egypt
75C2 Gilgandra Aust
60C1 Gilgit Pak
60C1 Gilgit *R* Pak
75C2 Gilgunnia Aust
7J4 Gillam Can
75A2 Gilles *L* Aust
11A3 Gillette USA
3C3 Gill I Can
12B1 Gills Rock USA
12B2 Gilman USA
4F5 Gilmour Can
20B2 Gilroy USA
4B3 Gimli Can
65B3 Gineifa Egypt
74E2 Gingindlovu S Africa
57G9 Gingoog Phil
72E3 Gīnīr Eth
41E3 Gióna *Mt* Greece
75C3 Gippsland *Mts* Aust
12C2 Girard USA
26D3 Girardot Colombia
34D3 Girdle Ness *Pen* Scot
64C1 Giresun Turk
66B1 Girga Egypt
60C4 Gir Hills India
72B3 Giri *R* Zaïre
61C3 Girīdīh India
60A2 Girishk Afghan
36D3 Giromagny France
Girona = Gerona
38B2 Gironde *R* France
34C4 Girvan Scot
78C2 Gisborne NZ
36A2 Gisors France
72C4 Gitega Burundi
Giuba,R = Juba,R
37E2 Giulia Region, Italy
41F2 Giurgiu Rom
36C1 Givet Belg
49S3 Gizhiga Russian Fed
43E2 Gizycko Pol
41E2 Gjirokastër Alb
6J3 Gjoatlaven Can
32G6 Gjøvik Nor
7M5 Glace Bay Can
3C2 Glacial Mt Can
3A2 Glacier B USA
10L4 Glacier Bay Nat Mon USA
3F4 Glacier Nat Pk USA
18B1 Glacier Peak *Mt* USA
7K2 Glacier Str Can
76E3 Gladstone Queensland, Aust
75A2 Gladstone S Aust, Aust
75E3 Gladstone Tasmania, Aust
12B1 Gladstone USA
32A1 Glama *Mt* Iceland

Glåma Great Slave L

32G6 **Glåma** *R* Nor
36D2 **Glan** *R* Germany
37C1 **Glarner** *Mts* Switz
37C1 **Glarus** Switz
17C2 **Glasco** USA
12B3 **Glasgow** Kentucky, USA
11A2 **Glasgow** Montana, USA
34C4 **Glasgow** Scot
14C3 **Glassboro** USA
20C2 **Glass Mt** USA
35D6 **Glastonbury** Eng
44J4 **Glazov** Russian Fed
42D3 **Gleisdorf** Austria
78C1 **Glen Afton** NZ
14B3 **Glen Burnie** USA
74E2 **Glencoe** S Africa
19D4 **Glendale** Arizona, USA
20C3 **Glendale** California, USA
11B2 **Glendive** USA
11B3 **Glendo Res** USA
10J3 **Glenhallen** USA
75D1 **Glen Innes** Aust
75C1 **Glenmorgan** Aust
75D2 **Glenreagh** Aust
14B3 **Glen Rock** USA
17C3 **Glen Rose** USA
14D1 **Glens Falls** USA
17D3 **Glenwood** Arkansas, USA
11C2 **Glenwood** Minnesota, USA
16A3 **Glenwood** New Mexico, USA
16A2 **Glenwood Springs** USA
12A1 **Glidden** USA
32F6 **Glittertind** *Mt* Nor
43D2 **Gliwice** Pol
19D4 **Globe** USA
42D2 **Głogów** Pol
32G5 **Glomfjord** Nor
75D2 **Gloucester** Aust
35D6 **Gloucester** Eng
14E1 **Gloucester** USA
14C1 **Gloversville** USA
43F1 **Glubokoye** Belorussia
45E5 **Glukhov** Russian Fed
42D3 **Gmünd** Austria
42C3 **Gmunden** Austria
43D2 **Gniezno** Pol
74B2 **Goabeg** Namibia
62A1 **Goa, Daman and Diu** Union Territory, India
61D2 **Goālpāra** India
71F4 **Goaso** Ghana
72D3 **Goba** Eth
74B1 **Gobabis** Namibia
28C2 **Gobernador Crespo** Arg
28B3 **Gobernador Duval** Arg
52B1 **Gobi** *Desert* China/ Mongolia
54C4 **Gobo** Japan
43G1 **Gobza** *R* Russian Fed
74B1 **Gochas** Namibia
62B1 **Godag** India
62C1 **Godāvari** *R* India
5H4 **Godbout** Can
20C2 **Goddard,Mt** USA
4E5 **Goderich** Can
7N3 **Godhavn** Greenland
60C4 **Godhra** India
28B2 **Godoy Cruz** Arg
4C2 **Gods** *R* Can
7J4 **Gods L** Can
7N3 **Godthåb** Greenland
Godwin Austen = K2
14E1 **Goffstown** USA
4E4 **Gogama** Can
66C4 **Gogora** Eth
29C2 **Goiandira** Brazil
29C2 **Goianésia** Brazil
29C2 **Goiânia** Brazil
29B2 **Goiás** Brazil
27J6 **Goiás** State, Brazil
29B3 **Goio-Erê** Brazil
72D3 **Gojab** *R* Eth
41F2 **Gökçeada** *I* Turk
45F8 **Goksu** *R* Turk
64C2 **Göksun** Turk
49M5 **Gol** *R* Mongolia
61D2 **Golāghāt** India
64C2 **Gölbaşi** Turk
48K2 **Gol'chikha** Russian Fed
18C2 **Golconda** USA
14B2 **Gold** USA
18B2 **Gold Beach** USA
75D1 **Gold Coast** Aust
3E3 **Golden** Can
78B2 **Golden B** NZ
18B1 **Goldendale** USA
20A2 **Golden Gate** *Chan* USA
17D4 **Golden Meadow** USA
19C3 **Goldfield** USA
4C3 **Goldpines** Can
20D2 **Gold Point** USA
4A2 **Goldsand L** Can
16C3 **Goldthwaite** USA
42C2 **Goleniów** Pol
20C3 **Goleta** USA
40B2 **Golfe d'Ajaccio** *G* Corse
71E2 **Golfe de Gabes** *G* Tunisia
Golfe de Gascogne = Biscay,Bay of
71E1 **Golfe de Hammamet** *G* Tunisia
37B3 **Golfe de la Napoule** *G* France
40B2 **Golfe de St Florent** *G* Corse
38B2 **Golfe de St-Malo** *B* France
38C3 **Golfe du Lion** *G* France
25B6 **Golfo Corcovado** *G* Chile
39B2 **Golfo de Almeira** *G* Spain
25B6 **Golfo de Ancud** *G* Chile
21D2 **Golfo de Batabano** *G* Cuba
23A2 **Golfo de Batano** *G* Cuba
39A2 **Golfo de Cadiz** *G* Spain
40B3 **Golfo de Cagliari** *G* Sardegna
21A1 **Golfo de California** *G* Mexico
21D4 **Golfo de Chiriqui** *G* Panama
21D3 **Golfo de Fonseca** Honduras
23B2 **Golfo de Guacanayabo** *G* Cuba
26B4 **Golfo de Guayaquil** *G* Ecuador
23B5 **Golfo del Darien** *G* Colombia/Panama
26B2 **Golfo de los Mosquitos** *G* Panama
26A1 **Golfo del Papagaya** *G* Nic
39B2 **Golfo de Mazarrón** *G* Spain
26A2 **Golfo de Nicoya** *G* Costa Rica
40B3 **Golfo de Oristano** *G* Sardegna
21E4 **Golfo de Panamá** *G* Panama
21D3 **Golfo de Papagayo** *G* Costa Rica
23E4 **Golfo de Paria** *G* Ven
26F1 **Golfo de Paris** *G* Ven
25B7 **Golfo de Penas** *G* Chile
38D3 **Golfo de St Florent** Corse
39C1 **Golfo de San Jorge** *G* Spain
21C3 **Golfo de Tehuantepec** *G* Mexico
26C3 **Golfo de Torugas** *G* Colombia
26C2 **Golfo de Uraba** *G* Colombia
39C2 **Golfo de Valencia** *G* Spain
37E2 **Golfo de Venezia** *G* Italy
23C4 **Golfo de Venezuela** *G* Ven
40B2 **Golfo di Genova** *G* Italy
40D3 **Golfo di Policastro** *G* Italy
40D3 **Golfo di Squillace** *G* Italy
40D2 **Golfo di Taranto** *G* Italy
37E2 **Golfo di Trieste** *G* Italy
40C1 **Golfo di Venezia** *G* Italy
21D4 **Golfo Dulce** *G* Costa Rica
25C7 **Golfo San Jorge** *G* Arg
25D6 **Golfo San Matías** *G* Arg
50C3 **Golmud** China
72E3 **Golocha** Eth
10F3 **Golovin B** USA
53F3 **Golovnino** Russian Fed
72C4 **Goma** Zaïre
71J3 **Gombe** Nig
71J3 **Gombi** Nig
43G2 **Gomel** Belorussia
70A2 **Gomera** *I* Canary Is
21B2 **Gómez Palacio** Mexico
49O4 **Gonam** *R* Russian Fed
63D1 **Gonbad-e Kāvūs** Iran
61B2 **Gonda** India
60C4 **Gondal** India
72D2 **Gonder** Eth
61B3 **Gondia** India
64A1 **Gönen** Turk
41F3 **Gonen** *R* Turk
35B5 **Goney** Irish Rep
61D1 **Gongbo'gyamba** China
52A4 **Gongga Shan** *Mt* China
52A2 **Gonghe** China
29D1 **Gongogi** *R* Brazil
71J3 **Gongola** *R* Nig
20B2 **Gonzales** California, USA
17C4 **Gonzales** Texas, USA
22C1 **Gonzalez** Mexico
28C3 **Gonzalez Chaves** Arg
74B3 **Good Hope,C of** S Africa
3D3 **Good Hope Mt** Can
18D2 **Gooding** USA
16B2 **Goodland** USA
10F4 **Goodnews Bay** USA
75C1 **Goodooga** *R* Aust
35E5 **Goole** Eng
75C2 **Goolgowi** Aust
75A3 **Goolwa** Aust
76A4 **Goomalling** Aust
75C2 **Goombalie** Aust
75D1 **Goomer** Aust
75D1 **Goomeri** Aust
75D1 **Goondiwindi** Aust
7N4 **Goose Bay** Can
15D2 **Goose Creek** USA
5J3 **Goose** *R* Can
18B2 **Goose L** USA
62B1 **Gooty** India
76D1 **Goraka** PNG
44K3 **Gora Koyp** *Mt* Russian Fed
49M4 **Gora Munku Sardyk** *Mt* Mongolia/Russian Fed
44K3 **Gora Narodnaya** *Mt* Russian Fed
44L2 **Gora Pay-Yer** *Mt* Russian Fed
44K3 **Gora Telpos-Iz** *Mt* Russian Fed
41D2 **Goražde** Bosnia & Herzegovina, Yugos
10K2 **Gordon** USA
3F2 **Gordon L** Can
13D3 **Gordonsville** USA
72B3 **Goré** Chad
72D3 **Gorē** Eth
78A3 **Gore** NZ
49P4 **Gore Topko** *Mt* Russian Fed
63C1 **Gorgān** Iran
37C3 **Gorgona** *I* Italy
36C1 **Gorinchem** Neth
64E2 **Goris** Armenia
40C1 **Gorizia** Italy
43G2 **Gorki** Belorussia
44M2 **Gorki** Russian Fed
44G4 **Gor'kovskoye Vodokhranilishche** *Res* Russian Fed
42C2 **Gorlitz** Germany
45F6 **Gorlovka** Ukraine
20C3 **Gorman** USA
41F2 **Gorna Orjahovica** Bulg
50B1 **Gorno-Altaysk** Russian Fed
53E1 **Gorno Lopatina** *Mt* Russian Fed
53D2 **Gorno Medvezh'ya** *Mt* Russian Fed
53C3 **Gorno Oblachnaya** *Mt* Russian Fed
53D2 **Gorno Tardoki Yani** *Mt* Russian Fed
53E2 **Gornozavodsk** Russian Fed
53D1 **Gornyy** Russian Fed
44K3 **Goro Denezhkin Kamen'** *Mt* Russian Fed
44G4 **Gorodets** Russian Fed
43G2 **Gorodnya** Ukraine
43F1 **Gorodok** Belorussia
43E3 **Gorodok** Ukraine
43F3 **Gorodok** Ukraine
51H7 **Goroka** PNG
61B2 **Gorokhpur** India
57D3 **Gorong** *I* Indon
73D5 **Gorongosa** Mozam
57B2 **Gorontalo** Indon
71G3 **Goroubi** *R* Burkina
44L4 **Goro Yurma** *Mt* Russian Fed
29D2 **Gorutuba** *R* Brazil
49M4 **Goryachinsk** Russian Fed
45J7 **Gory Akkyr** *Upland* Turkmenistan
49L2 **Gory Byrranga** *Mts* Russian Fed
43F3 **Goryn'** *R* Ukraine
49L3 **Gory Putorana** *Mts* Russian Fed
43E2 **Góry Świetokrzyskie** *Upland* Pol
32H8 **Gorzow Wielkopolski** Pol
20C2 **Goshen** USA
53E3 **Goshogawara** Japan
45F8 **Gosku** *R* Turk
40D2 **Gospić** Croatia, Yugos
41E2 **Gostivar** Macedonia, Yugos
43D2 **Gostynin** Pol
32G7 **Göteborg** Sweden
72B3 **Gotel** *Mts* Nig
16B1 **Gothenburg** USA
32H7 **Gotland** *I* Sweden
53B5 **Gotō-retto** *I* Japan
32H7 **Gotska Sandön** *I* Sweden
53C4 **Gōtsu** Japan
43D3 **Gottwaldov** Czech
36C1 **Gouda** Neth
72B2 **Goudoumaria** Niger
xxxH7 **Gough I** Atlantic O
75C2 **Goulburn** Aust
70B3 **Goumbou** Mali
70B3 **Goundam** Mali
72B2 **Gouré** Niger
70B3 **Gourma Rharous** Mali
36A2 **Gournay-en-Bray** France
72B2 **Gouro** Chad
18E1 **Govenlock** Can
51G8 **Gove Pen** Aust
45C6 **Goverla** *Mt* Ukraine
29D2 **Governador Valadares** Brazil
28D1 **Governador Virasoro** Arg
61B3 **Govind Ballabh Paht Sāgar** *L* India
14A1 **Gowanda** USA
60B3 **Gowārān** Afghan
28D1 **Goya** Arg
72C2 **Goz-Beïda** Chad
40C3 **Gozo** *I* Medit S
66C3 **Goz Regeb** Sudan
74C3 **Graaff-Reinet** S Africa
13D1 **Gracefield** Can
37E2 **Grado** Italy
75D1 **Grafton** Aust
11C2 **Grafton** N Dakota, USA
12C3 **Grafton** W Virginia, USA
3D2 **Graham** *R* Can
3B3 **Graham I** Can
3F2 **Graham L** Can
19E4 **Graham,Mt** USA
74D3 **Grahamstown** S Africa
27J5 **Grajaú** Brazil
43E2 **Grajewo** Pol
41E2 **Grámmos** *Mt* Greece/Alb
34D3 **Grampian** Region, Scot
34C3 **Grampian** *Mts* Scot
26D3 **Granada** Colombia
26A1 **Granada** Nic
39B2 **Granada** Spain
5G4 **Granby** Can
16A1 **Granby** USA
70A2 **Gran Canaria** *I* Canary Is
25D3 **Gran Chaco** *Region* Arg
12B2 **Grand** *R* Michigan, USA
17D1 **Grand** *R* Missouri, USA
23Q2 **Grand B** Dominica
9F4 **Grand Bahama** *I* Bahamas
36D3 **Grand Ballon** *Mt* France
7N5 **Grand Bank** Can
xxxF1 **Grand Banks** Atlantic O
71F4 **Grand Bassam** Ivory Coast
37B2 **Grand Bérard** *Mt* France
19D3 **Grand Canyon** USA
19D3 **Grand Canyon Nat Pk** USA
23A3 **Grand Cayman** *I* Caribbean
3F3 **Grand Centre** Can
18C1 **Grand Coulee** USA
28B3 **Grande** *R* Arg
27K6 **Grande** *R* Bahia, Brazil
29C2 **Grande** *R* Minas Gerais/ São Paulo, Brazil
3E3 **Grande Cache** Can
5H4 **Grande Cascapédia** Can
37A2 **Grande Chartreuse** Region, France
73E5 **Grande Comore** *I* Comoros
3E2 **Grande Prairie** Can
17C3 **Grande Prairie** USA
72B2 **Grand Erg de Bilma** *Desert Region* Niger
70B2 **Grand erg Occidental** *Mts* Alg
70C2 **Grand erg Oriental** *Mts* Alg
5J4 **Grande Rivière** Can
7L4 **Grande Rivière de la Baleine** *R* Can
18C1 **Grande Ronde** *R* USA
19D4 **Gran Desierto** USA
5H4 **Grande Vallée** Can
7M5 **Grand Falls** New Brunswick, Can
7N5 **Grand Falls** Newfoundland, Can
18C1 **Grand Forks** Can
11C2 **Grand Forks** USA
14C1 **Grand Gorge** USA
12B2 **Grand Haven** USA
16C1 **Grand Island** USA
17E3 **Grand Isle** USA
16A2 **Grand Junction** USA
5K4 **Grand L** Can
17D4 **Grand L** USA
5H5 **Grand Manan I** Can
12A1 **Grand Marais** USA
5G4 **Grand Mère** Can
5K3 **Grandois** Can
39A2 **Grândola** Port
6J4 **Grand Rapids** Can
12B2 **Grand Rapids** Michigan, USA
12A1 **Grand Rapids** Minnesota, USA
37B2 **Grand St Bernard** *P* Italy/ Switz
8B2 **Grand Teton** *Mt* USA
18D2 **Grand Teton Nat Pk** USA
16A2 **Grand Valley** USA
36A2 **Grandvilliers** France
21D1 **Grangeburg** USA
18C1 **Grangeville** USA
4B5 **Granite Falls** USA
18E1 **Granite Peak** *Mt* Montana, USA
19D2 **Granite Peak** *Mt* Utah, USA
39C1 **Granollérs** Spain
40B1 **Gran Paradiso** *Mt* Italy
37D1 **Gran Pilastro** *Mt* Austria/ Italy
35E5 **Grantham** Eng
20C1 **Grant,Mt** USA
34D3 **Grantown-on-Spey** Scot
16A2 **Grants** USA
18B2 **Grants Pass** USA
38B2 **Granville** France
14D1 **Granville** USA
6H4 **Granville L** Can
29D2 **Grão Mogol** Brazil
20C3 **Grapevine** USA
20D2 **Grapevine Mts** USA
74E1 **Graskop** S Africa
38D3 **Grasse** France
18E1 **Grassrange** USA
19B3 **Grass Valley** USA
5L4 **Grates Pt** Can
25F4 **Gravatai** Brazil
6H5 **Gravelbourg** Can
36B1 **Gravelines** France
73D6 **Gravelotte** S Africa
4F5 **Gravenhurst** Can
18D1 **Grave Peak** *Mt* USA
75D1 **Gravesend** Aust
10M4 **Gravina I** USA
37A1 **Gray** France
10F3 **Grayling** USA
4E5 **Grayling** Michigan, USA
18B1 **Grays Harbor** *B* USA
18D2 **Grays L** USA
12C3 **Grayson** USA
12B3 **Grayville** USA
42D3 **Graz** Austria
23H1 **Great** *R* Jamaica
9F4 **Great Abaco** *I* Bahamas
76B4 **Great Australian Bight** *G* Aust
14E1 **Great B** New Hampshire, USA
14C3 **Great B** New Jersey, USA
21E2 **Great Bahama Bank** Bahamas
78C1 **Great Barrier I** NZ
76D2 **Great Barrier Reef** *Is* Aust
14D1 **Great Barrington** USA
19C2 **Great Basin** USA
10O2 **Great Bear** *R* Can
6F3 **Great Bear L** Can
16C2 **Great Bend** USA
65B3 **Great Bitter L** Egypt
14A3 **Great Cacapon** USA
62E2 **Great Coco I** Burma
76D3 **Great Dividing Range** *Mts* Aust
35E4 **Great Driffield** Eng
14C3 **Great Egg Harbor** *B* USA
79F10 **Greater Antarctic** Region, Ant
23B2 **Greater Antilles** *Is* Caribbean
35E6 **Greater London** County, Eng
35D5 **Greater Manchester** County, Eng
21E2 **Great Exuma** *I* Bahamas
18D1 **Great Falls** USA
74D3 **Great Fish** *R* S Africa
34C3 **Great Glen** *V* Scot
61C2 **Great Himalayan Range** *Mts* Asia
9F4 **Great Inagua** *I* Bahamas
74C3 **Great Karroo** *Mts* S Africa
74D3 **Great Kei** *R* S Africa
75E3 **Great L** Aust
73B6 **Great Namaland** Region, Namibia
62E3 **Great Nicobar** *I* Indian O
35D5 **Great Ormes Head** *C* Wales
14E2 **Great Pt** USA
9F4 **Great Ragged** *I* Bahamas
73D4 **Great Ruaha** *R* Tanz
13E2 **Great Sacandaga L** USA
18D2 **Great Salt L** USA
18D2 **Great Salt Lake Desert** USA
69B2 **Great Sand Sea** Libya/ Egypt
76B3 **Great Sandy Desert** Aust
8A2 **Great Sandy Desert** USA
Great Sandy I = Fraser I
10C6 **Great Sitkin,** I USA
6G3 **Great Slave L** Can

Iaçu **Isle of Wight**

I

27K6 **Iaçu** Brazil
41F2 **Ialomiţa** *R* Rom
32G6 **Iärpen** Sweden
41F1 **Iaşi** Rom
71G4 **Ibadan** Nig
26C3 **Ibagué** Colombia
41E2 **Ibar** *R* Montenegro/Serbia
26C3 **Ibarra** Ecuador
66D4 **Ibb** Yemen
71H4 **Ibi** Nig
29C2 **Ibiá** Brazil
29E1 **Ibicaraí** Brazil
28D1 **Ibicui** *R* Brazil
28D2 **Ibicuy** Arg
28E1 **Ibirubá** Brazil
39C2 **Ibiza** Spain
39C2 **Ibiza** *I* Spain
73E5 **Ibo** Mozam
27K6 **Ibotirama** Brazil
67G2 **'Ibrī** Oman
26C6 **Ica** Peru
26E4 **Icá** *R* Brazil
26E3 **Icana** Brazil
32A1 **Iceland** Republic, N Atlantic O
3D3 **Ice Mt** Can
49R4 **Icha** Russian Fed
62A1 **Ichalkaranji** India
53E4 **Ichihara** Japan
54C3 **Ichinomiya** Japan
53E4 **Ichinoseki** Japan
10K4 **Icy B** USA
10F1 **Icy C** USA
3A2 **Icy Str** USA
17D3 **Idabell** USA
11C3 **Ida Grove** USA
71H4 **Idah** Nig
18D2 **Idaho** State, USA
18C2 **Idaho City** USA
18D2 **Idaho Falls** USA
16A2 **Idaho Springs** USA
18B2 **Idanha** USA
36D2 **Idar Oberstein** Germany
69A2 **Idehan Marzūg** *Desert* Libya
69A2 **Idehan Ubari** *Desert* Libya
70C2 **Idelés** Alg
50C2 **Iderlym Gol** *R* Mongolia
66B2 **Idfu** Egypt
41E3 **Ídhi Óros** *Mt* Greece
41E3 **Ídhra** *I* Greece
72B4 **Idiofa** Zaïre
10G3 **Iditarod** *R* USA
64C2 **Idlib** Syria
37E2 **Idrija** Slovenia, Yugos
32K7 **Idritsa** Russian Fed
74D3 **Idutywa** S Africa
36B1 **Ieper** Belg
41F3 **Ierápetra** Greece
37E3 **Iesi** Italy
73D4 **Ifakara** Tanz
51H6 **Ifalik** *I* Pacific
73E6 **Ifanadiana** Madag
71G4 **Ife** Nig
70C3 **Iférouane** Niger
56D2 **Igan** Malay
29C3 **Igaranava** Brazil
48K3 **Igarka** Russian Fed
29A3 **Igatimi** Par
71G4 **Igbetti** Nig
64E2 **Igdir** Iran
32H6 **Iggesund** Sweden
28B2 **Iglesia** Arg
40B3 **Iglesias** Sardegna
7K3 **Igloolik** Can
4C4 **Ignace** Can
64A1 **Iğneada Burun** *Pt* Turk
62E2 **Ignoitijala** Andaman Is
41E3 **Igoumenítsa** Greece
44J4 **Igra** Russian Fed
44L3 **Igrim** Russian Fed
22C2 **Iguala** Mexico
25G2 **Iguape** Brazil
29C3 **Iguatama** Brazil
29B3 **Iguatemi** Brazil
29A3 **Iguatemi** *R* Brazil
27L5 **Iguatu** Brazil
72A4 **Iguéla** Gabon
71H4 **Igumale** Nig
71H4 **Ihiala** Nig
73E6 **Ihosy** Madag
53D4 **Iida** Japan
54C3 **Iide-san** *Mt* Japan
32K6 **Iisalmi** Fin
54B4 **Iizuka** Japan
71G4 **Ijebulgbo** Nig
71G4 **Ijebu Ode** Nig
42B2 **Ijsselmeer** *S* Neth
28E1 **Ijuí** Brazil
28D1 **Ijuí** *R* Brazil
41F3 **Ikaría** *I* Greece
53E3 **Ikeda** Japan
72C4 **Ikela** Zaïre
71H4 **Ikerre** Nig
41E2 **Ikhtiman** Bulg
54A4 **Iki** *I* Japan
71G4 **Ikire** Nig
10H4 **Ikolik,C** USA
73E5 **Ikopa** *R* Madag
71G4 **Ila** Nig
57F7 **Ilagan** Phil
63B2 **Ilām** Iran
50C1 **Ilanskiy** Russian Fed
37C1 **Ilanz** Switz
71G4 **Ilaro** Nig
3G2 **Île à la Crosse** Can
3G2 **Île à la Crosse,L** Can
68G8 **Ilebo** Zaïre
36B2 **Île De France** Region, France
71E2 **Île de Jerba** *I* Tunisia
38B2 **Ile de Noirmoutier** *I* France
38B2 **Ile de Ré** *I* France
77F3 **Île des Pins** *I* Nouvelle Calédonie
13E1 **Ile d'Orleans** Can
38A2 **Ile d'Ouessant** *I* France
38B2 **Ile d'Yeu** *I* France
45K5 **Ilek** *R* Russian Fed
22A1 **Ile Maria Cleofas** *I* Mexico
22A1 **Ile María Madre** *I* Mexico
22A1 **Ile María Magdalena** Mexico
22A1 **Ile San Juanico** *I* Mexico
77F2 **Îles Bélèp** Nouvelle Calédonie
77E2 **Îles Chesterfield** Nouvelle Calédonie
77H2 **Îles de Horn** *Is* Pacific O
38D3 **Iles d'Hylères** *Is* France
71G4 **Ilesha** Nig
71E2 **Iles Kerkenna** *Is* Tunisia
4B2 **Ilford** Can
35C6 **Ilfracombe** Eng
64B1 **Ilgaz Dağları** *Mts* Turk
73D6 **Ilha Bazaruto** *I* Mozam
29C3 **Ilha Comprida** *I* Brazil
29E1 **Ilha de Boipeba** *I* Brazil
27H3 **Ilha De Maracá** *I* Brazil
27H4 **Ilha de Marajó** *I* Brazil
29C4 **Ilha de São Francisco** *I* Brazil
29C3 **Ilha de São Sebastião** *I* Brazil
29E1 **Ilha de Tinharé** *I* Brazil
27H6 **Ilha do Bananal** *Region* Brazil
29C4 **Ilha do Cardoso** *I* Brazil
25F2 **Ilha Grande, Reprêsa** *Res* Brazil
29D3 **Ilha Grande** *I* Brazil
29B3 **Ilha Grande ou Sete Quedas** *I* Brazil
29C3 **Ilha Santo Amaro** *I* Brazil
29B3 **Ilha Solteira Dam** Brazil
70A2 **Ilhas Selvegens** *I* Atlantic O
27L6 **Ilhéus** Brazil
48J5 **Ili** *R* Kazakhstan
10G4 **Iliamna L** USA
10H3 **Iliamna V** USA
36A2 **Iliers** France
57F9 **Iligan** Phil
49M4 **Ilim** *R* Russian Fed
49M4 **Ilimsk** Russian Fed
53E2 **Il'inskiy** Russian Fed
41E3 **Iliodhrómia** *I* Greece
14C1 **Ilion** USA
57F9 **Illana B** Phil
28A2 **Illapel** Chile
28A2 **Illapel** *R* Chile
70C3 **Illéla** Niger
37D1 **Iller** *R* Germany
22B1 **Illescas** Mexico
77H2 **Îlles Wallis** *Is* Pacific O
12B2 **Illinois** State, USA
12A3 **Illinois** *R* USA
70C2 **Illizi** Alg
44E4 **Il'men, Ozero** *L* Russian Fed
26D7 **Ilo** Peru
57F8 **Iloilo** Phil
32L6 **Ilomantsi** Fin
71G4 **Ilorin** Nig
57C4 **Ilwaki** Indon
43G1 **Il'yino** Russian Fed
54B4 **Imabari** Japan
54C3 **Imalchi** Japan
32L5 **Imandra, Ozero** *L* Russian Fed
54A4 **Imari** Japan
44D3 **Imatra** Fin
25G3 **Imbituba** Brazil
29B4 **Imbitura** Brazil
72E3 **Imi** Eth
54A3 **Imjin** *R* N Korea
18C2 **Imlay** USA
37D1 **Immenstadt** Germany
71H4 **Imo** State, Nig
40C2 **Imola** Italy
27J5 **Imperatriz** Brazil
40B2 **Imperia** Italy
16B1 **Imperial** USA
19C4 **Imperial V** USA
72B3 **Impfondo** Congo
61D3 **Imphāl** India
37D1 **Imst** Austria
10F2 **Imuruk L** USA
54C3 **Ina** Japan
70C2 **In Afahleleh** *Well* Alg
54C4 **Inamba-jima** *I* Japan
70C2 **In Amenas** Alg
32K5 **Inari** Fin
32K5 **Inarijärvi** *L* Fin
54D3 **Inawashiro-ko** *L* Japan
70C2 **In Belbel** Alg
45F7 **Ince Burun** *Pt* Turk
64B2 **Incekum Burun** *Pt* Turk
53B4 **Inch'ŏn** S Korea
70B2 **In Dagouber** *Well* Mali
29C2 **Indais** *R* Brazil
32H6 **Indals** *R* Sweden
35G5 **Indefatigable** *Gasfield* N Sea
20C2 **Independence** California, USA
11D3 **Independence** Iowa, USA
17C2 **Independence** Kansas, USA
17D2 **Independence** Missouri, USA
18C2 **Independence Mts** USA
56B3 **Inderagiri** *R* Indon
45J6 **Inderborskiy** Kazakhstan
59F4 **India** Federal Republic, Asia
12B2 **Indiana** State, USA
13D2 **Indiana** USA
xxviiiF7 **Indian-Antarctic Basin** Indian O
xxviiiF7 **Indian-Antarctic Ridge** Indian O
12B3 **Indianapolis** USA
Indian Desert = Thar Desert
7N4 **Indian Harbour** Can
3H3 **Indian Head** Can
xxviiiE5 **Indian O**
17D1 **Indianola** Iowa, USA
17D3 **Indianola** Mississippi, USA
29C2 **Indianópolis** Brazil
19C3 **Indian Springs** USA
44H2 **Indiga** Russian Fed
49Q3 **Indigirka** *R* Russian Fed
55D2 **Indo China** Region, S E Asia
51F7 **Indonesia** Republic, S E Asia
60D4 **Indore** India
56C4 **Indramayu** Indon
38C2 **Indre** *R* France
60B3 **Indus** *R* Pak
45E7 **Inebdu** Turk
70C2 **In Ebeggi** *Well* Alg
64B1 **Inebolu** Turk
70C2 **In Ecker** Alg
64A1 **Inegöl** Turk
70D2 **In Ezzane** Alg
74C3 **Infante,C** S Africa
70C3 **Ingal** Niger
12C2 **Ingersoll** Can
76D2 **Ingham** Aust
7M2 **Inglefield Land** *Region* Greenland
78B1 **Inglewood** NZ
75D1 **Inglewood** Queensland, Aust
20C4 **Inglewood** USA
75B3 **Inglewood** Victoria, Aust
32B2 **Ingólfshöfôi** *I* Iceland
42C3 **Ingolstadt** Germany
61C3 **Ingrāj Bāzār** India
70C3 **In-Guezzam** *Well* Alg
74E2 **Inhaca** *I* Mozam
74E2 **Inhaca Pen** Mozam
73D6 **Inhambane** Mozam
73D6 **Inharrime** Mozam
29C2 **Inhumas** Brazil
26E3 **Inirida** *R* Colombia
34B4 **Inishowen** District, Irish Rep
75C1 **Injune** Aust
3B2 **Inklin** Can
10M4 **Inklin** *R* Can
10G2 **Inland L** USA
37D1 **Inn** *R* Austria
75B1 **Innamincka** Aust
50D2 **Inner Mongolia** Autonomous Region, China
76D2 **Innisfail** Aust
53E2 **Innokent'yevskiy** Russian Fed
10G3 **Innoko** *R* USA
42C3 **Innsbruck** Austria
72B4 **Inongo** Zaïre
43D2 **Inowrocław** Pol
70C2 **In Salah** Alg
54A3 **Insil** S Korea
44L2 **Inta** Russian Fed
37B1 **Interlaken** Switz
77H3 **International Date Line**
11D2 **International Falls** USA
28C1 **Intiyaco** Arg
37C2 **Intra** Italy
56E3 **Intu** Indon
54D3 **Inubo-saki** *C* Japan
7L4 **Inukjuak** Can
6E3 **Inuvik** Can
6E3 **Inuvik** Region, Can
34C3 **Inveraray** Scot
78A3 **Invercargill** NZ
75D1 **Inverell** Aust
3E3 **Invermere** Can
34C2 **Inverness** Scot
34D3 **Inverurie** Scot
75A3 **Investigator Str** Aust
50B1 **Inya** Russian Fed
49Q3 **Inya** *R* Russian Fed
73D5 **Inyanga** Zim
20D3 **Inyokern** USA
20C2 **Inyo Mts** USA
72B4 **Inzia** *R* Zaïre
41E3 **Ioánnina** Greece
17C2 **Iola** USA
63E1 **Iolotan** Turkmenistan
34B3 **Iona** *I* Scot
73B5 **Iôna Nat Pk** Angola
18C1 **Ione** USA
Ionian Is = Ioníoi Nísoi
41D3 **Ionian S** Italy/Greece
41E3 **Ioníoi Nísoi** *Is* Greece
10D2 **Ioniveyem** *R* Russian Fed
41F3 **Íos** *I* Greece
44J3 **Iosser** Russian Fed
11D3 **Iowa** State, USA
11D3 **Iowa** *R* USA
12A2 **Iowa City** USA
11D3 **Iowa Falls** USA
29C2 **Ipameri** Brazil
29D2 **Ipanema** Brazil
45G6 **Ipatovo** Russian Fed
26C3 **Ipiales** Colombia
29E1 **Ipiaú** Brazil
29B4 **Ipiranga** Brazil
55C5 **Ipoh** Malay
27H7 **Iporá** Brazil
41F2 **Ipsala** Turk
75D1 **Ipswich** Aust
35F5 **Ipswich** Eng
14E1 **Ipswich** USA
43G2 **Iput** *R* Russian Fed
29C3 **Iquape** Brazil
25B2 **Iquique** Chile
26D4 **Iquitos** Peru
28E1 **Irai** Brazil
41F3 **Iráklion** Greece
58D2 **Iran** Republic, S W Asia
63E3 **Irānshahr** Iran
22B1 **Irapuato** Mexico
64D3 **Iraq** Republic, S W Asia
29B4 **Irati** Brazil
69A2 **Irā Wan** *Watercourse* Libya
65C2 **Irbid** Jordan
44L4 **Irbit** Russian Fed
27G3 **Ireng** *R* Guyana
53B4 **Iri** S Korea
51G7 **Irian Jaya** Province, Indon
72C2 **Iriba** Chad
57F8 **Iriga** Phil
73D4 **Iringa** Tanz
50F4 **Iriomote** *I* Japan
23A3 **Iriona** Honduras
27H5 **Iriri** *R* Brazil
35C5 **Irish S** Eng/Irish Rep
10H2 **Irkillik** *R* USA
49M4 **Irkutsk** Russian Fed
75A2 **Iron Knob** Aust
12B1 **Iron Mountain** USA
76D2 **Iron Range** Aust
12B1 **Iron River** USA
12C3 **Irontown** USA
12A1 **Ironwood** USA
4E4 **Iroquois Falls** Can
54C4 **Iro-zaki** *C* Japan
61E4 **Irrawaddy** *R* Burma
55A2 **Irrawaddy,Mouths of the** Burma
48H4 **Irtysh** *R* Russian Fed
39B1 **Irun** Spain
34C4 **Irvine** Scot
17C3 **Irving** USA
71H3 **Isa** Nig
57F9 **Isabela** Phil
20C3 **Isabella Res** USA
6H2 **Isachsen** Can
6H2 **Isachsen,C** Can
7Q3 **Ísafjörður** Iceland
53C5 **Isahaya** Japan
72C3 **Isangi** Zaïre
37D1 **Isar** *R* Germany
37D1 **Isarco** *R* Italy
34E1 **Isbister** Scot
37D1 **Ischgl** Austria
40C2 **Ischia** *I* Italy
54C4 **Ise** Japan
37D2 **Iseo** Italy
37A2 **Isère** *R* France
36D1 **Iserlohn** Germany
40C2 **Isernia** Italy
54C4 **Ise-wan** *B* Japan
71G4 **Iseyin** Nig
50F4 **Ishigaki** *I* Japan
53E3 **Ishikari** *R* Japan
53E3 **Ishikari-wan** *B* Japan
48H4 **Ishim** Russian Fed
48H4 **Ishim** *R* Kazakhstan
53E4 **Ishinomaki** Japan
54D3 **Ishioka** Japan
60C1 **Ishkashim** Afghan
12B1 **Ishpeming** USA
48J4 **Isil'kul'** Russian Fed
57B2 **Isimu** Indon
72D3 **Isiolo** Kenya
72C3 **Isiro** Zaïre
64C2 **Iskenderun** Turk
64C2 **Iskenferun Körfezi** *B* Turk
64B1 **İskilip** Turk
48K4 **Iskitim** Russian Fed
41E2 **Iskur** *R* Bulg
10M4 **Iskut** *R* Can/USA
22C2 **Isla** Mexico
28D1 **Isla Apipe Grande** Arg
23C3 **Isla Beata** Dom Rep
28C3 **Isla Bermejo** *I* Arg
23E4 **Isla Blanquilla** Ven
26B2 **Isla Coiba** *I* Panama
8B4 **Isla de Cedros** *I* Mexico
25B6 **Isla de Chiloé** *I* Chile
21D2 **Isla de Cozumel** *I* Mexico
23C3 **Isla de la Gonâve** Cuba
23A2 **Isla de la Juventud** *I* Cuba
28D2 **Isla de las Lechiguanas** *I* Arg
2K8 **Isla del Coco** *I* Costa Rica
21D3 **Isla del Maiz** *I* Caribbean
22C1 **Isla de Lobos** *I* Mexico
25D8 **Isla de los Estados** *I* Arg
24F4 **Isla de Marajó** *I* Brazil
xxixO6 **Isla de Pascua** *I* Pacific O
23A4 **Isla de Providencia** *I* Caribbean
23A4 **Isla de San Andres** *I* Caribbean
25G3 **Isla de Santa Catarina** *I* Brazil
27H2 **Isla du Diable** *I* French Guiana
27M4 **Isla Fernando de Noronha** *I* Brazil
25C8 **Isla Grande de Tierra del Fuego** *I* Arg/Chile
23D4 **Isla la Tortuga** *I* Ven
60C2 **Islamabad** Pak
21A2 **Isla Magdalena** *I* Mexico
23E4 **Isla Margarita** Ven
28A3 **Isla Mocha** Chile
15E4 **Islamorada** USA
4C3 **Island L** Can
75A2 **Island Lg** Aust
18D2 **Island Park** USA
5K4 **Islands,B of** Can
78B1 **Islands,B of** NZ
26B1 **Isla Providencia** *I* Colombia
26B4 **Isla Puná** *I* Ecuador
xxxD6 **Isla San Ambrosia** *I* Pacific O
xxxD6 **Isla San Felix** *I* Pacific O
21A2 **Isla Santa Margarita** *I* Mexico
28A3 **Isla Santa Maria** *I* Chile
39C2 **Islas Baleares** *Is* Spain
70A2 **Islas Canarias** *Is* Atlantic O
39C2 **Islas Columbretes** *Is* Spain
21D3 **Islas de la Bahia** *Is* Honduras
23A4 **Islas del Maiz** *Is* Caribbean
26F1 **Islas de Margarita** *Is* Ven
25C9 **Islas Diego Ramírez** *Is* Chile
26N0 **Islas Galapagos** *Is* Pacific O
26Q0 **Islas Juan Fernandez** *Is* Pacific O
26E1 **Islas los Roques** *Is* Ven
Islas Malvinas = Falkland Is
xxixO4 **Islas Revilla Gigedo** *Is* Pacific O
25C9 **Islas Wollaston** *Is* Chile
70A3 **Isla Tidra** *I* Maur
25B7 **Isla Wellington** *I* Chile
34B4 **Islay** *I* Scot
38C2 **Isle** *R* France
xxviiiE6 **Isle Amsterdam** *I* Indian O
13F2 **Isle au Haut** *I* USA
35E6 **Isle of Wight** *I* Eng

Isle Royale **Jiquilpan**

12B1 **Isle Royale** *I* USA
12B1 **Isle Royale Nat Pk** USA
xxviiiE6 **Isle St Paul** *I* Indian O
xxviiiD7 **Îsles Crozet** *I* Indian O
xxixM5 **Îsles de la Société** Pacific O
xxixN6 **Îsles Gambier** *Is* Pacific O
73E5 **Îsles Glorieuses** *Is* Madag
xxviiiE7 **Îsles Kerguelen** *Is* Indian O
77F3 **Îsles Loyauté** *Is* Nouvelle Calédonie
xxixN5 **Îsles Marquises** *Is* Pacific O
xxixM5 **Îsles Tuamotu** *Is* Pacific O
xxixM6 **Îsles Tubai** *Is* Pacific O
20B1 **Isleton** USA
64B3 **Ismâ'ilîya** Egypt
66B1 **Isna** Egypt
73E6 **Isoanala** Madag
73D5 **Isoka** Zambia
37C3 **Isola di Capraia** *I* Italy
40C3 **Isola Egadi** *I* Italy
40C2 **Isola Ponziane** *I* Italy
40C3 **Isole Lipari** *Is* Italy
40D2 **Isoles Tremiti** *Is* Italy
54C3 **Isosaki** Japan
64B2 **Isparta** Turk
65C2 **Israel** Republic, S W Asia
39C2 **Isser** *R* Alg
38C2 **Issoire** France
38C2 **Issoudun** France
37A1 **Is-sur-Tille** France
59F1 **Issyk Kul, Ozero** *I* Kirgizia
64A1 **Istanbul** Turk
41E3 **Istiáia** Greece
22D2 **Istmo de Tehuantepec** *Isthmus* Mexico
15E4 **Istokpoga,L** USA
40C1 **Istra** *Pen* Croatia, Yugos
41F2 **Istranca Dağlari** *Upland* Turk
29C2 **Itaberai** Brazil
29D2 **Itabira** Brazil
29D3 **Itabirito** Brazil
29E1 **Itabuna** Brazil
29E1 **Itacaré** Brazil
27G4 **Itacoatiara** Brazil
29A3 **Itacurubi del Rosario** Par
26C2 **Itagui** Colombia
25F2 **Itaipu, Reprêsa** *Res* Brazil
27G4 **Itaituba** Brazil
25G3 **Itajaí** Brazil
29C3 **Itajuba** Brazil
40C2 **Italy** Repubic, Europe
29E2 **Itamaraju** Brazil
29D2 **Itamarandiba** Brazil
29D2 **Itambacuri** Brazil
29D2 **Itambe** Brazil
29D2 **Itambé** *Mt* Brazil
61D2 **Itānagar** India
29C3 **Itanhaém** Brazil
29D2 **Itanhém** Brazil
29D2 **Itanhém** *R* Brazil
29D2 **Itaobím** Brazil
29C1 **Itapaci** Brazil
29C3 **Itapecerica** Brazil
29D3 **Itaperuna** Brazil
27K7 **Itapetinga** Brazil
29C3 **Itapetininga** Brazil
29C3 **Itapeva** Brazil
27L4 **Itapipoca** Brazil
29C2 **Itapuranga** Brazil
29C1 **Itaquari** *R* Brazil
28D1 **Itaqui** Brazil
29D2 **Itarantim** Brazil
29C3 **Itararé** Brazil
29C3 **Itararé** *R* Brazil
29D3 **Itaúna** Brazil
26F6 **Iténez** *R* Brazil/Bol
13D2 **Ithaca** USA
36E1 **Ith Hills** *Mts* Germany
72C3 **Itimbiri** *R* Zaïre
29C2 **Itinga** Brazil
29A2 **Itiquira** *R* Brazil
7N3 **Itivdleq** Greenland
32G6 **Itjørdal** Nor
54C4 **Ito** Japan
53D4 **Itoigawa** Japan
36A2 **Iton** *R* France
26F6 **Itonomas** *R* Bol
29C3 **Itu** Brazil
71H4 **Itu** Nig
29E1 **Ituberá** Brazil
29C2 **Itumbiara** Brazil
29B2 **Iturama** Brazil
25C2 **Iturbe** Arg
22C1 **Iturbide** Mexico
53F3 **Iturup, Ostrov** *I* Russian Fed
29C2 **Iturutaba** Brazil
28D1 **Ituzzaingó** Arg
42B2 **Itzehoe** Germany
49U3 **Iul'tin** Russian Fed
43F2 **Ivacevichi** Belorussia
29B3 **Ivai** *R* Brazil
32K5 **Ivalo** Fin
41D2 **Ivangrad** Montenegro, Yugos
75B2 **Ivanhoe** Aust
43E3 **Ivano-Frankovsk** Ukraine
44G4 **Ivanovo** Russian Fed
44L3 **Ivdel'** Russian Fed
72B3 **Ivindo** *R* Gabon
29B3 **Ivinhema** Brazil
29B3 **Ivinhema** *R* Brazil
73E6 **Ivohibe** Madag
73E5 **Ivongo Soanierana** Madag
70B4 **Ivory Coast** Republic, Africa
40B1 **Ivrea** Italy
7L3 **Ivujivik** Can
53E4 **Iwaki** Japan
54D2 **Iwaki** *R* Japan
54D2 **Iwaki-san** *Mt* Japan
53C5 **Iwakuni** Japan
54D2 **Iwamizawa** Japan
53E3 **Iwanai** Japan
71G4 **Iwo** Nig
50H4 **Iwo Jima** *I* Japan
22B1 **Ixcuintla** Mexico
22C1 **Ixmiquilpa** Mexico
22B2 **Ixtapa** Mexico
22C2 **Ixtepec** Mexico
22B1 **Ixtlán** Mexico
54B4 **Iyo** Japan
54B4 **Iyo-nada** *B* Japan
44J4 **Izhevsk** Russian Fed
44J2 **Izhma** Russian Fed
44J2 **Izhma** *R* Russian Fed
10E5 **Izigan,C** USA
67G2 **Izkī** Oman
43F3 **Izmail** Ukraine
64A2 **İzmir** Turk
41F3 **İzmir Körfezi** *B* Turk
64A1 **İzmit** Turk
64A1 **İznik** Turk
41F2 **İznik Golü** *L* Turk
65D2 **Izra'** Syria
22C2 **Izúcar de Matamoros** Mexico
54A4 **Izuhara** Japan
54C4 **Izumi-sano** Japan
54B3 **Izumo** Japan
53D5 **Izu-shotō** *Is* Japan
53C2 **Izvestkovyy** Russian Fed

J

69B1 **Jabal al Akhdar** *Mts* Libya
65D2 **Jabal al 'Arab** Syria
67F3 **Jabal al Qara'** *Mts* Oman
65D1 **Jabal an Nuşayrīyah** *Mts* Syria
69A2 **Jabal as Sawdā** *Mts* Libya
67F2 **Jabal az̧Z̧annah** UAE
65D1 **Jabal Halīmah** *Mt* Syria/ Leb
67F3 **Jabal Mahrāt** *Mts* Yemen
61B3 **Jabalpur** India
66D1 **Jabal Shammar** Region, S Arabia
67E2 **Jabal Tuwayq** *Mts* S Arabia
65C1 **Jablah** Syria
42D2 **Jablonec nad Nisou** Czech
27L5 **Jaboatão** Brazil
39B1 **Jaca** Spain
22C1 **Jacala** Mexico
27G5 **Jacareacanga** Brazil
27H8 **Jacarezinho** Brazil
29C3 **Jacarie** Brazil
25C4 **Jáchal** Arg
29B2 **Jaciara** Brazil
29D2 **Jacinto** Brazil
3G3 **Jackfish L** Can
13E1 **Jackman Station** USA
16C3 **Jacksboro** USA
14B2 **Jacks Mt** USA
15B2 **Jackson** Alabama, USA
75C1 **Jackson** Aust
20B1 **Jackson** California, USA
12C2 **Jackson** Michigan, USA
11D3 **Jackson** Minnesota, USA
17D3 **Jackson** Mississippi, USA
12B3 **Jackson** Missouri, USA
12C3 **Jackson** Ohio, USA
15B1 **Jackson** Tennessee, USA
18D2 **Jackson** Wyoming, USA
78B2 **Jackson,C** NZ
78A2 **Jackson Head** *Pt* NZ
18D2 **Jackson L** USA
17D3 **Jacksonville** Arkansas, USA
15C2 **Jacksonville** Florida, USA
12A3 **Jacksonville** Illinois, USA
15D2 **Jacksonville** N Carolina, USA
17C3 **Jacksonville** Texas, USA
15C2 **Jacksonville Beach** USA
23C3 **Jacmel** Haiti
60B3 **Jacobabad** Pak
27K6 **Jacobina** Brazil
22B2 **Jacona** Mexico
28E1 **Jacui** *R* Brazil
67F3 **Jādib** Yemen
Jadotville = Likasi
26C5 **Jaén** Peru
39B2 **Jaén** Spain
Jaffa = Tel Aviv Yafo
75A3 **Jaffa** *C* Aust
62B3 **Jaffna** Sri Lanka
14D1 **Jaffrey** USA
61C3 **Jagannathganj Ghat** Bang
62C1 **Jagdalpur** India
53A1 **Jagdaqi** China
63D3 **Jagin** *R* Iran
62B1 **Jagtial** India
29E1 **Jaguaquara** Brazil
28E2 **Jaguarão** Brazil
28E2 **Jaguarão** *R* Brazil
29C3 **Jaguarialva** Brazil
28B1 **Jagüé** Arg
28B1 **Jagüé** *R* Arg
45H8 **Jahan Dāgh** *Mt* Iran
63C3 **Jahrom** Iran
57C2 **Jailolo** Indon
60D5 **Jāina** India
52A2 **Jainca** China
60D3 **Jaipur** India
60C3 **Jaisalmer** India
63D1 **Jajarm** Iran
40D2 **Jajce** Bosnia & Herzegovina, Yugos
56C4 **Jakarta** Indon
3B1 **Jakes Corner** Can
7N3 **Jakobshavn** Greenland
32J6 **Jakobstad** Fin
16B3 **Jal** USA
22C2 **Jalaca** Mexico
53A2 **Jalaid Qi** China
60C2 **Jalalabad** Afghan
22C2 **Jalapa** Mexico
29B3 **Jales** Brazil
61C2 **Jaleswar** Nepal
60D4 **Jalgaon** India
71J4 **Jalingo** Nig
22A2 **Jalisco** State, Mexico
39B1 **Jalón** *R* Spain
60C3 **Jālor** India
22B1 **Jalostotitlan** Mexico
61C2 **Jalpāiguri** India
22C1 **Jalpan** Mexico
69B2 **Jālū** Libya
69B2 **Jālū Oasis** Libya
26B4 **Jama** Ecuador
72E3 **Jamaame** Somalia
71H3 **Jamaaré** *R* Nig
23B3 **Jamaica** *I* Caribbean
23B3 **Jamaica Chan** Caribbean
61C3 **Jamalpur** Bang
56B3 **Jambi** Indon
60C4 **Jambussar** India
11C2 **James** *R* N Dakota, USA
13D3 **James** *R* Virginia, USA
7K4 **James B** Can
75A2 **Jamestown** Aust
11C2 **Jamestown** N Dakota, USA
13D2 **Jamestown** New York, USA
14E2 **Jamestown** Rhode Island, USA
74D3 **Jamestown** S Africa
22C2 **Jamiltepec** Mexico
62B1 **Jamkhandi** India
60C2 **Jammu** India
60D2 **Jammu and Kashmir** State, India
60B4 **Jamnagar** India
60C3 **Jampur** Pak
44C3 **Jämsä** Fin
61C3 **Jamshedpur** India
61C2 **Janakpur** Nepal
29D2 **Janaúba** Brazil
63C2 **Jandaq** Iran
75D1 **Jandowae** Aust
12B2 **Janesville** USA
79B1 **Jan Mayen** *I* Norwegian S
29D2 **Januária** Brazil
60D4 **Jaora** India
53 **Japan** Empire, E Asia
53C4 **Japan,S of** S E Asia
xxviiiJ3 **Japan Trench** Pacific O
26E4 **Japurá** *R* Brazil
64C2 **Jarābulus** Syria
29C2 **Jaraguá** Brazil
29B3 **Jaraguari** Brazil
39B1 **Jarama** *R* Spain
65C2 **Jarash** Jordan
29A3 **Jardim** Brazil
39B2 **Jardin** *R* Spain
23B2 **Jardines de la Reina** *Is* Cuba
Jargalant = Hovd
27H3 **Jari** *R* Brazil
61D2 **Jaria Jhānjail** Bang
36C2 **Jarny** France
42D2 **Jarocin** Pol
43E2 **Jaroslaw** Pol
44A3 **Järpen** Sweden
52B2 **Jartai** China
60C4 **Jasdan** India
71G4 **Jasikan** Ghana
63D3 **Jāsk** Iran
43E3 **Jaslo** Pol
25D8 **Jason Is** Falkland Is
15B2 **Jasper** Alabama, USA
17D2 **Jasper** Arkansas, USA
3E3 **Jasper** Can
15C2 **Jasper** Florida, USA
12B3 **Jasper** Indiana, USA
17D3 **Jasper** Texas, USA
3E3 **Jasper Nat Pk** Can
42D2 **Jastrowie** Pol
29B2 **Jatai** Brazil
39B2 **Játiva** Spain
29C3 **Jau** Brazil
26C6 **Jauja** Peru
22C1 **Jaumave** Mexico
61B2 **Jaunpur** India
Java = Jawa
62B2 **Javadi Hills** India
63E1 **Javand** Afghan
Javari = Yavari
51D7 **Java S** Indon
76A2 **Java Trench** Indon
56C4 **Jawa** *I* Indon
51H7 **Jayapura** Indon
65D2 **Jayrūd** Syria
66D3 **Jazā'ir Farasān** *Is* S Arabia
67G2 **Jazīrat Maşīrah** *I* Oman
22B1 **Jazminal** Mexico
71B2 **Jbel Ayachi** *Mt* Mor
70B2 **Jbel Ouarkziz** *Mts* Mor
70B1 **Jbel Sarhro** *Mt* Mor
17D4 **Jeanerette** USA
71G4 **Jebba** Nig
64D2 **Jebel 'Abd al 'Azīz** *Mt* Syria
72C2 **Jebel Abyad** *Desert Region* Sudan
67G2 **Jebel Akhdar** *Mt* Oman
64C4 **Jebel al Lawz** *Mt* S Arabia
65C2 **Jebel ash Shaykh** *Mt* Syria
72D1 **Jebel Asoteriba** *Mt* Sudan
65D1 **Jebel az Zāwīyah** *Upland* Syria
65C4 **Jebel Bāqir** *Mt* Jordan
66C4 **Jebel Belaia** *Mt* Eth
65C3 **Jebel Ed Dabab** *Mt* Jordan
65C3 **Jebel el Ata'ita** *Mt* Jordan
65C4 **Jebel el Harad** *Mt* Jordan
64C3 **Jebel esh Sharqi** *Mts* Leb/ Syria
66C3 **Jebel Hamoyet** *Mt* Sudan
65C3 **Jebel Hārūn** *Mt* Jordan
65D3 **Jebel Ithrīyat** *Mt* Jordan
67G2 **Jebel Ja'lan** *Mt* Oman
65C2 **Jebel Liban** *Mts* Leb
65D2 **Jebel Ma'lūlā** *Mt* Syria
72C2 **Jebel Marra** *Mt* Sudan
65C3 **Jebel Mubrak** *Mt* Jordan
65D3 **Jebel Mudeisisat** *Mt* Jordan
66C2 **Jebel Oda** *Mt* Sudan
65C3 **Jebel Qasr ed Deir** *Mt* Jordan
65C4 **Jebel Qatim** *Mt* Jordan
65C4 **Jebel Ram** Jordan
65C2 **Jebel Um ed Daraj** *Mt* Jordan
65C4 **Jebel Um el Hashim** *Mt* Jordan
65C4 **Jebel Um Ishrīn** *Mt* Jordan
72C1 **Jebel Uweinat** *Mt* Sudan
34D4 **Jedburgh** Scot
Jedda = Jiddah
43E2 **Jedrzejów** Pol
11D3 **Jefferson** Iowa, USA
17D3 **Jefferson** Texas, USA
18D1 **Jefferson** *R* USA
9D3 **Jefferson City** USA
8B3 **Jefferson,Mt** USA
12B3 **Jeffersonville** USA
71G3 **Jega** Nig
29A3 **Jejui-Guazú** *R* Par
44D4 **Jekabpils** Latvia
42D2 **Jelena Gora** Pol
44C4 **Jelgava** Latvia
56D4 **Jember** Indon
16A2 **Jemez Pueblo** USA
42C2 **Jena** Germany
56C2 **Jenaja** *I* Indon
37D1 **Jenbach** Austria
71D1 **Jendouba** Tunisia
65C2 **Jenin** Israel
17D3 **Jennings** USA
3B2 **Jennings** *R* Can
42D2 **Jenseniky** *Upland* Czech
7O3 **Jensen Nunatakker** *Mt* Greenland
7K3 **Jens Munk I** Can
75B3 **Jeparit** Aust
27L6 **Jequié** Brazil
29D2 **Jequital** *R* Brazil
29D2 **Jequitinhonha** Brazil
27K7 **Jequitinhonha** *R* Brazil
71B2 **Jerada** Mor
56G7 **Jerantut** Malay
22B1 **Jerez** Mexico
39A2 **Jerez de la Frontera** Spain
39A2 **Jerez de los Caballeros** Spain
65C3 **Jericho** Israel
75C3 **Jerilderie** Aust
18D2 **Jerome** USA
38B2 **Jersey** *I* UK
9F2 **Jersey City** USA
13D2 **Jersey Shore** USA
12A3 **Jerseyville** USA
64C3 **Jerusalem** Israel
75D3 **Jervis B** Aust
3D3 **Jervis Inlet** *Sd* Can
40C1 **Jesenice** Slovenia, Yugos
61C3 **Jessore** Bang
9E3 **Jesup** USA
22D2 **Jesus Carranza** Mexico
28C2 **Jesus Maria** Arg
16C2 **Jetmore** USA
14E2 **Jewett City** USA
62C1 **Jeypore** India
41D2 **Jezerce** *Mt* Alb
43E2 **Jezioro Mamry** *L* Pol
43E2 **Jezioro80Sniardwy** *L* Pol
65C2 **Jezzine** Leb
60C4 **Jhābua** India
60D4 **Jhālāwār** India
60C2 **Jhang Maghiana** Pak
60D3 **Jhānsi** India
61B3 **Jhārsuguda** India
60C2 **Jhelum** Pak
60C2 **Jhelum** *R* Pak
9F3 **J H Kerr L** USA
60D3 **Jhunjhunūn** India
53C2 **Jiamusi** China
52C4 **Ji'an** Jiangxi, China
53B3 **Ji'an** Jilin, China
52D4 **Jiande** China
52B4 **Jiang'an** China
52D4 **Jiangbiancun** China
52A5 **Jiangcheng** China
52B3 **Jiang Jiang** *R* China
52B4 **Jiangjin** China
52C5 **Jiangmen** China
52D3 **Jiangsu** Province, China
52C4 **Jiangxi** Province, China
52A3 **Jiangyou** China
52D1 **Jianping** China
52A5 **Jianshui** China
52D4 **Jian Xi** *R* China
52D4 **Jianyang** China
53B3 **Jiaohe** China
52E2 **Jiaonan** China
52E2 **Jiao Xian** China
52E2 **Jiaozhou Wan** *B* China
52C2 **Jiaozuo** China
52E3 **Jiaxiang** China
53C2 **Jiayin** China
50C3 **Jiayuguan** China
66C2 **Jiddah** S Arabia
67G3 **Jiddat Al Harāsīs** Region, Oman
67G2 **Jiddat az Zawlīyah** Region, Oman
52D3 **Jieshou** China
52C2 **Jiexiu** China
71H3 **Jigawa** *State* Nig
52A3 **Jigzhi** China
42D3 **Jihlava** Czech
71D1 **Jijel** Alg
72E3 **Jilib** Somalia
53B3 **Jilin** China
53B3 **Jilin** Province, China
53A1 **Jiliu He** *R* China
39B1 **Jiloca** *R* Spain
72D3 **Jima** Eth
16B4 **Jiménez** Coahuila, Mexico
22C1 **Jiménez** Tamaulipas, Mexico
52D2 **Jinan** China
60D3 **Jind** India
52B2 **Jingbian** China
52D4 **Jingdezhen** China
55C1 **Jinghong** China
52C3 **Jingmen** China
52B2 **Jingning** China
52B4 **Jing Xiang** China
52D4 **Jinhua** China
52C1 **Jining** Nei Monggol, China
52D2 **Jining** Shandong, China
72D3 **Jinja** Uganda
55C1 **Jinping** China
52A4 **Jinsha Jiang** *R* China
52C4 **Jinshi** China
52E1 **Jinxi** China
52E2 **Jin Xian** China
52E1 **Jinzhou** China
26F5 **Jiparaná** *R* Brazil
26B4 **Jipijapa** Ecuador
22B2 **Jiquilpan** Mexico

Karachi

Khanka, Ozero

60B4 **Karachi** Pak
62A1 **Karād** India
45F7 **Kara Daglari** *Mt* Turk
45D7 **Karadeniz Boğazi** *Sd* Turk
50E1 **Karaftit** Russian Fed
48J5 **Karaganda** Kazakhstan
48J5 **Karagayly** Kazakhstan
49S4 **Karaginskiy, Ostrov** *I* Russian Fed
62B2 **Kāraikāl** India
63C1 **Karaj** Iran
64C3 **Karak** Jordan
56F7 **Karak** Malay
48G5 **Kara Kalpakskaya** Respublika, Uzbekistan
60D1 **Karakax He** *R* China
57C2 **Karakelong** *I* Indon
60D1 **Karakoram** *Mts* India
60D1 **Karakoram** *P* India/China
70A3 **Karakoro** *R* Maur/Sen
63E1 **Karakumskiy Kanal** Turkmenistan
48G6 **Karakumy** *Desert* Russian Fed
65C3 **Karama** Jordan
57A3 **Karama** *R* Indon
45E8 **Karaman** Turk
48K5 **Karamay** China
78B2 **Karamea** NZ
78B2 **Karamea Bight** *B* NZ
45E8 **Karanhk** *R* Turk
60D4 **Kāranja** India
64B2 **Karapınar** Turk
48J2 **Kara S** Russian Fed
74B2 **Karasburg** Namibia
32K5 **Karasjok** Nor
48J4 **Karasuk** Russian Fed
64C2 **Karataş** Turk
48H5 **Kara Tau** *Mts* Kazakhstan
55B3 **Karathuri** Burma
53B5 **Karatsu** Japan
48K2 **Karaul** Russian Fed
65B1 **Karavostasi** Cyprus
37E1 **Karawanken** *Mts* Austria
63C3 **Karāz** Iran
64D3 **Karbalā'** Iraq
43E3 **Karcag** Hung
41E3 **Kardhítsa** Greece
44E3 **Karel'skaya** Respublika, Russian Fed
62E2 **Karen** Andaman Is
44K3 **Karepino** Russian Fed
32J5 **Karesvando** Sweden
70B2 **Karet** *Desert Region* Maur
48K4 **Kargasok** Russian Fed
44F3 **Kargopol'** Russian Fed
45G8 **Karh** *R* Turk
71J3 **Kari** Nig
73C5 **Kariba** Zim
73C5 **Kariba** *L* Zim/Zambia
73C5 **Kariba Dam** Zim/Zambia
74B1 **Karibib** Namibia
72D2 **Karima** Sudan
56C3 **Karimata** *I* Indon
61D3 **Karimganj** Bang
62B1 **Karīmnagar** India
72E2 **Karin** Somalia
32J6 **Karis** Fin
72C4 **Karishimbe** *Mt* Zaïre
41E3 **Káristos** Greece
62A2 **Kārkal** India
51H7 **Karkar** *I* PNG
63B2 **Karkheh** *R* Iran
45E6 **Karkinitskiy Zaliv** *B* Ukraine
49L5 **Karlik Shan** *Mt* China
42D2 **Karlino** Pol
40D2 **Karlobag** Croatia, Yugos
40D1 **Karlovac** Croatia, Yugos
41E2 **Karlovo** Bulg
42C2 **Karlovy Vary** Czech
32G7 **Karlshamn** Sweden
32G7 **Karlskoga** Sweden
32H7 **Karlskrona** Sweden
42B3 **Karlsruhe** Germany
32G7 **Karlstad** Sweden
11C2 **Karlstad** USA
10H4 **Karluk** USA
61D3 **Karnafuli Res** Bang
60D3 **Karnal** India
62A1 **Karnataka** State, India
41F2 **Karnobat** Bulg
37E1 **Kärnten** Province, Austria
73C5 **Karoi** Zim
73D4 **Karonga** Malawi
72D2 **Karora** Sudan
57A3 **Karossa** Indon
41F3 **Kárpathos** *I* Greece
7N2 **Karrats Fjord** Greenland
74C3 **Karree Berge** S Africa
45G7 **Kars** Turk
48H5 **Karsakpay** Kazakhstan
43F1 **Kārsava** Latvia
58E2 **Karshi** Uzbekistan
32J6 **Karstula** Fin
65C1 **Kartaba** Leb
41F2 **Kartal** Turk
44L5 **Kartaly** Russian Fed
14A2 **Karthaus** USA
63B2 **Kārūn** *R* Iran
61B2 **Karwa** India
62A2 **Kārwār** India
50E1 **Karymskoye** Russian Fed
72B4 **Kasai** *R* Zaïre
73C5 **Kasaji** Zaïre
73D5 **Kasama** Zambia
73D4 **Kasanga** Tanz
62A2 **Kāsaragod** India
6H3 **Kasba L** Can
71A2 **Kasba Tadla** Mor
10F1 **Kasegaluk Lg** USA
73C5 **Kasempa** Zambia
73C5 **Kasenga** Zaïre
72D3 **Kasese** Uganda
63C2 **Kāshān** Iran
10G3 **Kashegelok** USA
59F2 **Kashi** China
54B4 **Kashima** Japan
60D3 **Kāshipur** India
53D4 **Kashiwazaki** Japan
63D1 **Kashmar** Iran
46E4 **Kashmir** State, India
44G5 **Kasimov** Russian Fed
57C3 **Kasiruta** *I* Indon
12B3 **Kaskaskia** *R* USA
4C2 **Kaskattama** *R* Can
32J6 **Kasko** Fin
44L4 **Kasli** Russian Fed
6G5 **Kaslo** Can
3H2 **Kasmere L** Can
72C4 **Kasonga** Zaïre
73B4 **Kasongo-Lunda** Zaïre
41F3 **Kásos** *I* Greece
45H6 **Kaspiyskiy** Russian Fed
72D2 **Kassala** Sudan
42B2 **Kassel** Germany
71D1 **Kasserine** Tunisia
73B5 **Kassinga** Angola
64B1 **Kastamonou** Turk
41E3 **Kastélli** Greece
64A2 **Kastellorizon** *I* Greece
41E2 **Kastoría** Greece
41F3 **Kástron** Greece
53D4 **Kasugai** Japan
54B3 **Kasumi** Japan
73D5 **Kasungu** Malawi
60C2 **Kasur** Pak
73C5 **Kataba** Zambia
13F1 **Katahdin,Mt** USA
72C4 **Katako-kombe** Zaïre
6D3 **Katalla** USA
49Q4 **Katangli** Russian Fed
76A4 **Katanning** Aust
62E3 **Katchall** *I* Indian O
41E2 **Kateríni** Greece
6E4 **Kates Needle** *Mt* Can/USA
61E3 **Katha** Burma
76C2 **Katherine** Aust
60C4 **Kāthiāwār** *Pen* India
65B3 **Kathib El Henu** Egypt
61C2 **Kathmandu** Nepal
60D2 **Kathua** India
61C2 **Katihār** India
73C5 **Katima Mulilo** Namibia
6C4 **Katmai,Mt** USA
10H4 **Katmai Nat Mon** USA
61B3 **Katni** India
75D2 **Katoomba** Aust
43D2 **Katowice** Pol
32H7 **Katrineholm** Sweden
71H3 **Katsina** Nig
71H3 **Katsina** *Region* Nig
71H3 **Katsina** *State* Nig
71H4 **Katsina Ala** Nig
54D3 **Katsuta** Japan
54D3 **Katsuura** Japan
54C3 **Katsuy** Japan
48H6 **Kattakurgan** Uzbekistan
32G7 **Kattegat** *Str* Denmark/Sweden
36E2 **Katzenbuckel** *Mt* Germany
57C2 **Kau** Indon
20E5 **Kauai** *I* Hawaiian Is
20E5 **Kauai Chan** Hawaiian Is
20E5 **Kaulakahi Chan** Hawaiian Is
20E5 **Kaunakaki** Hawaiian Is
44C5 **Kaunas** Lithuania
71H3 **Kaura Namoda** Nig
32J5 **Kautokeino** Nor
41E2 **Kavadarci** Macedonia, Yugos
41D2 **Kavajë** Alb
53D3 **Kavalerovo** Russian Fed
62B2 **Kavali** India
41E2 **Kavála** Greece
60B4 **Kāvda** India
76E1 **Kavieng** PNG
54C3 **Kawagoe** Japan
54C3 **Kawaguchi** Japan
20E5 **Kawaihae** Hawaiian Is
78B1 **Kawakawa** NZ
73C4 **Kawambwa** Zambia
61B3 **Kawardha** India
13D2 **Kawartha Lakes** Can
53D4 **Kawasaki** Japan
20C2 **Kaweah** *R* USA
78C1 **Kawerau** NZ
78B1 **Kawhia** NZ
71F3 **Kaya** Burkina
10K4 **Kayak I** USA
56E2 **Kayan** *R* Indon
62B3 **Kāyankulam** India
11A3 **Kaycee** USA
57C3 **Kayeli** Indon
19D3 **Kayenta** USA
70A3 **Kayes** Mali
45F8 **Kayseri** Turk
49P2 **Kazach'ye** Russian Fed
64E1 **Kazakh** Azerbaijan
48G5 **Kazakhstan** *Republic* Europe
44H4 **Kazan'** Russian Fed
41F2 **Kazanlük** Bulg
50H4 **Kazan Retto** *Is* Japan
43F3 **Kazatin** Ukraine
45G7 **Kazbek** *Mt* Georgia
63C3 **Kāzerūn** Iran
44J3 **Kazhim** Russian Fed
64E1 **Kazi Magomed** Azerbaijan
43E3 **Kazincbarcika** Hung
44M3 **Kazym** *R* Russian Fed
44M3 **Kazymskaya** Russian Fed
41E3 **Kéa** *I* Greece
20E5 **Kealaikahiki Chan** Hawaiian Is
8D2 **Kearney** USA
19D4 **Kearny** USA
64C2 **Keban Baraji** *Res* Turk
71G3 **Kebbi** *State* Nig
70A3 **Kébémer** Sen
71J4 **Kebi** *R* Chad
71D2 **Kebili** Tunisia
65D1 **Kebīr** *R* Syria/Leb
32H5 **Kebrekaise** *Mt* Sweden
3C2 **Kechika** *R* Can
43D3 **Kecskemet** Hung
43E1 **Kedainiai** Lithuania
5H4 **Kedgwick** Can
53B2 **Kedong** China
70A3 **Kédougou** Sen
44J3 **Kedva** Russian Fed
10N4 **Keechiga** *R* Can
10N3 **Keele** *R* Can
10M3 **Keele Pk** *Mt* Can
19C3 **Keeler** USA
20C3 **Keene** California, USA
13E2 **Keene** New Hampshire, USA
74B2 **Keetmanshoop** Namibia
12B2 **Keewanee** USA
4C4 **Keewatin** Can
12A1 **Keewatin** USA
6J3 **Keewatin** *Region* Can
41E3 **Kefallinia** *I* Greece
57B4 **Kefamenanu** Indon
65C2 **Kefar Sava** Israel
71H4 **Keffi** Nig
32A2 **Keflavik** Iceland
6G4 **Keg River** Can
66B3 **Keheili** Sudan
55B1 **Kehsi Mansam** Burma
75B3 **Keith** Aust
34D3 **Keith** Scot
6F3 **Keith Arm** *B* Can
7M3 **Kekertuk** Can
60D3 **Kekri** India
55C5 **Kelang** Malay
57C3 **Kelang** *I* Indon
55C4 **Kelantan** *R* Malay
71E1 **Kelibia** Tunisia
60B1 **Kelif** Turkmenistan
64C1 **Kelkit** *R* Turk
72B4 **Kellé** Congo
10O3 **Keller L** Can
6F2 **Kellet,C** Can
18C1 **Kellogg** USA
48D3 **Kelloselka** Fin
35B5 **Kells** Irish Rep
34C4 **Kells Range** *Hills* Scot
43E1 **Kelme** Lithuania
6G5 **Kelowna** Can
6F4 **Kelsey Bay** Can
34D4 **Kelso** Scot
18B1 **Kelso** USA
3H3 **Kelvington** Can
44E3 **Kem'** Russian Fed
44E3 **Kem'** *R* Russian Fed
70B3 **Ke Macina** Mali
3C3 **Kemano** Can
48K4 **Kemerovo** Russian Fed
32J5 **Kemi** Fin
32K5 **Kemi** *R* Fin
32K5 **Kemijärvi** Fin
18D2 **Kemmerer** USA
36C1 **Kempen** Region, Belg
16C3 **Kemp,L** USA
23B2 **Kemps Bay** Bahamas
75D2 **Kempsey** Aust
42C3 **Kempten** Germany
10H3 **Kenai** USA
10H4 **Kenai Mts** USA
10H3 **Kenai Pen** USA
72D3 **Kenamuke Swamp** Sudan
35D4 **Kendal** Eng
75D2 **Kendall** Aust
76B1 **Kendari** Indon
56D3 **Kendawangan** Indon
61C3 **Kendrāpāra** India
18C1 **Kendrick** USA
17F4 **Kenedy** USA
70A4 **Kenema** Sierra Leone
72B4 **Kenge** Zaïre
55B1 **Kengtung** Burma
74C2 **Kenhardt** S Africa
70A3 **Kéniéba** Mali
71A2 **Kenitra** Mor
11B2 **Kenmare** USA
16B3 **Kenna** USA
13F1 **Kennebec** *R* USA
14E1 **Kennebunk** USA
14A1 **Kennedy** USA
17D4 **Kenner** USA
17E2 **Kennett** USA
14C3 **Kennett Square** USA
18C1 **Kennewick** USA
6F4 **Kenny Dam** Can
4D3 **Kenogami** *R* Can
7J5 **Kenora** Can
9E2 **Kenosha** USA
35F6 **Kent** County, Eng
16B3 **Kent** Texas, USA
18B1 **Kent** Washington, USA
12B2 **Kentland** USA
12C2 **Kenton** USA
6H3 **Kent Pen** Can
9E3 **Kentucky** State, USA
12C3 **Kentucky** *R* USA
9E3 **Kentucky L** USA
5J4 **Kentville** Can
17D3 **Kentwood** Louisiana, USA
12B2 **Kentwood** Michigan, USA
72D3 **Kenya** Republic, Africa
72D4 **Kenya,Mt** Kenya
12A2 **Keokuk** USA
61B3 **Keonchi** India
61C3 **Keonjhargarh** India
51G7 **Kepaluan Tanimbar** *Arch* Indon
43D2 **Kepno** Pol
57C3 **Kepualuan Wīdi** *Arch* Indon
57B4 **Kepulauan Alor** *Arch* Indon
56C2 **Kepulauan Anambas** *Arch* Indon
51G7 **Kepulauan Aru** *Arch* Indon
76B1 **Kepulauan Babar** *I* Indon
56C2 **Kepulauan Badas** *Is* Indon
51G7 **Kepulauan Banda** *Arch* Indon
76B1 **Kepulauan Banggai** *I* Indon
76B1 **Kepulauan Barat Daya** *Is* Indon
56C2 **Kepulauan Bunguran Seletan** *Arch* Indon
57D3 **Kepulauan Gorong** *Arch* Indon
51G7 **Kepulauan Kai** *Arch* Indon
57C2 **Kepulauan Kawio** *Arch* Indon
76B1 **Kepulauan Leti** *I* Indon
56B3 **Kepulauan Lingga** *Is* Indon
57C2 **Kepulauan Loloda** *Arch* Indon
56A3 **Kepulauan Mentawi** *Arch* Indon
57C2 **Kepulauan Nenusa** *Arch* Indon
57C3 **Kepulauan Obi** *Arch* Indon
56B2 **Kepulauan Riau** *Arch* Indon
56E4 **Kepulauan Sabalana** *Arch* Indon
57C2 **Kepulauan Sangihe** *Arch* Indon
76B1 **Kepulauan Sermata** *I* Indon
76B1 **Kepulauan Sula** *I* Indon
57C2 **Kepulauan Talaud** *Arch* Indon
56C2 **Kepulauan Tambelan** *Is* Indon
76C1 **Kepulauan Tanimbar** *I* Indon
76B1 **Kepulauan Togian** *I* Indon
76B1 **Kepulauan Tukangbesi** *Is* Indon
57D3 **Kepulauan Watubela** *Arch* Indon
57C3 **Kepulauan Yef Fam** *Arch* Indon
57B4 **Kepulaun Solor** *Arch* Indon
62B2 **Kerala** State, India
75B3 **Kerang** Aust
32J6 **Kerava** Fin
53D1 **Kerbi** *R* Russian Fed
45F6 **Kerch'** Ukraine
44J3 **Kerchem'ya** Russian Fed
76D1 **Kerema** PNG
18C1 **Keremeps** Can
72D2 **Keren** Eth
xxviiiE7 **Kerguelen Ridge** Indian O
72D4 **Kericho** Kenya
56B3 **Kerinci** *Mt* Indon
72D3 **Kerio** *R* Kenya
58E2 **Kerki** Turkmenistan
41D3 **Kérkira** Greece
41D3 **Kérkira** *I* Greece
77H3 **Kermadec Is** NZ
77H4 **Kermadec Trench** Pacific O
63D2 **Kerman** Iran
20B2 **Kerman** USA
63B2 **Kermānshāh** Iran
41F3 **Kerme Körfezi** *B* Turk
16B3 **Kermit** USA
19C3 **Kern** *R* USA
20C3 **Kernville** USA
44J3 **Keros** Russian Fed
3G3 **Kerrobert** Can
16C3 **Kerrville** USA
15C2 **Kershaw** USA
56C3 **Kertamulia** Indon
49N5 **Kerulen** *R* Mongolia
70B2 **Kerzaz** Alg
4F3 **Kesagami L** Can
41F2 **Keşan** Turk
53E4 **Kesennuma** Japan
53B2 **Keshan** China
45G7 **Kesir Daglari** *Mt* Turk
32L5 **Kesten'ga** Russian Fed
35D4 **Keswick** Eng
71G4 **Kéta** Ghana
56D3 **Ketapang** Indon
6E4 **Ketchikan** USA
70C3 **Ketia** Niger
60B4 **Keti Bandar** Pak
71G4 **Kétou** Benin
43E2 **Ketrzyn** Pol
35E5 **Kettering** Eng
12C3 **Kettering** USA
4D2 **Kettle** *R* Manitoba, Can
18C1 **Kettle** *R* British Columbia, Can
20C2 **Kettleman City** USA
18C1 **Kettle River Range** *Mts* USA
7L3 **Kettlestone B** Can
14B1 **Keuka L** USA
63D2 **Kevir-i Namak** *Salt Flat* Iran
12B2 **Kewaunee** USA
12B1 **Keweenaw B** USA
12B1 **Keweenaw Pen** USA
4E4 **Key Harbour** Can
15E4 **Key Largo** USA
14A3 **Keyser** USA
9E4 **Key West** USA
49M4 **Kezhma** Russian Fed
41D1 **K'félegháza** Hung
10F3 **Kgun L** USA
65D2 **Khabab** Syria
53D2 **Khabarovsk** Russian Fed
45G8 **Khabur** *R* Syria
60B3 **Khairpur** Pak
60B3 **Khairpur** Region, Pak
74C1 **Khakhea** Botswana
65B3 **Khalig El Tina** *B* Egypt
67G2 **Khalīj Maşīrah** *B* Oman
41F3 **Khálki** *I* Greece
41E2 **Khalkidhíki** *Pen* Greece
41E3 **Khalkís** Greece
44L2 **Khal'mer-Yu** Russian Fed
44H4 **Khalturin** Russian Fed
67G2 **Khalūf** Oman
60C4 **Khambhāt,G of** India
60D4 **Khāmgaon** India
66D3 **Khamir** Yemen
66D3 **Khamis Mushayt** S Arabia
55C2 **Kham Keut** Laos
62C1 **Khammam** India
65B3 **Khamsa** Egypt
63B1 **Khamseh** *Mts* Iran
55C2 **Khan** *R* Laos
60B1 **Khanabad** Afghan
64E3 **Khānaqīn** Iraq
60D4 **Khandwa** India
60C2 **Khanewal** Pak
65D3 **Khan ez Zabib** Jordan
55D4 **Khanh Hung** Viet
41E3 **Khaniá** Greece
53C3 **Khanka, Ozero** *L* China

Khankendy Koma

Khankendy = Stepanakert
60C3 Khanpur Pak
65D1 Khān Shaykhūn Syria
48H3 Khanty-Mansiysk Russian Fed
65C3 Khan Yunis Egypt
60D1 Khapalu India
50E2 Khapcheranga Russian Fed
45H6 Kharabali Russian Fed
61C3 Kharagpur India
63D3 Khārān Iran
60B3 Kharan Pak
63C2 Kharānaq Iran
63C3 Khārg Is Iran
69C2 Khārga Oasis Egypt
60D4 Khargon India
45F6 Khar'kov Ukraine
44F2 Kharlovka Russian Fed
41F2 Kharmanli Bulg
44G4 Kharovsk Russian Fed
72D2 Khartoum Sudan
72D2 Khartoum North Sudan
53C3 Khasan Russian Fed
63E2 Khash Afghan
63E3 Khāsh Iran
63E2 Khash R Afghan
72D2 Khashm el Girba Sudan
61D2 Khasi-Jaintia Hills India
41F2 Khaskovo Bulg
49M2 Khatanga Russian Fed
49N2 Khatangskiy Zaliv Estuary Russian Fed
49T3 Khatyrka Russian Fed
55B3 Khawsa Burma
66C1 Khaybar S Arabia
66B2 Khazzan an-Nasr L Egypt
55C2 Khe Bo Viet
60C4 Khed Brahma India
39C2 Khemis Alg
71A2 Khemisset Mor
71D1 Khenchela Alg
71A2 Khenifra Mor
39D2 Kherrata Alg
45E6 Kherson Ukraine
49N4 Khilok Russian Fed
41F3 Khíos Greece
41F3 Khíos I Greece
45D6 Khmel'nitskiy Ukraine
43E3 Khodorov Ukraine
59E1 Khodzhent Taji
60B1 Kholm Afghan
43G1 Kholm Russian Fed
53E2 Kholmsk Russian Fed
74B1 Khomas Hochland, Mts Namibia
55D3 Khong Laos
63C3 Khonj Iran
53C2 Khor Russian Fed
53D2 Khor R Russian Fed
63B2 Khoramshahr Iran
67F2 Khōr Duwayhin B UAE
60C1 Khorog Tajikistan
63B2 Khorramābad Iran
63D2 Khosf Iran
60B2 Khost Pak
45D6 Khotin Ukraine
10G3 Khotol Mt USA
71A2 Khouribga Mor
45D5 Khoyniki Belorussia
49Q3 Khrebet Cherskogo Mts Russian Fed
53B1 Khrebet Dzhagdy Mts Russian Fed
49P4 Khrebet Dzhugdzhur Mts Russian Fed
10C2 Khrebet Iskamen Mts Russian Fed
49O3 Khrebet Orulgan Mts Russian Fed
44L2 Khrebet Pay-khoy Mts Russian Fed
53D2 Khrebet Sikhote Alin' Mts Russian Fed
59G1 Khrebet Tarbagatay Mts Kazakhstan
49O4 Khrebet Tukuringra Mts Russian Fed
53C1 Khrebet Turana Upland Russian Fed
65B1 Khrysokhou B Cyprus
44L3 Khulga R Russian Fed
61C3 Khulna Bang
60D1 Khunjerab P China/India
63C2 Khunsar Iran
67E1 Khurays S Arabia
61C3 Khurda India
60D3 Khurja India
67G3 Khūryan Mūryān Is Oman
60C2 Khushab Pak
65C2 Khushnīyah Syria
43E3 Khust Ukraine
72C2 Khuwei Sudan
60B3 Khuzdar Pak
63E2 Khvāf Iran
45H5 Khvalynsk Russian Fed
63D2 Khvor Iran
63C3 Khvormūj Iran
45G8 Khvoy Iran
60C1 Khwaja Muhammad Mts Afghan
60C2 Khyber P Afghan/Pak
73C4 Kiambi Zaïre
17C3 Kiamichi R USA
10F2 Kiana USA
72B4 Kibangou Congo
72D4 Kibaya Tanz
72C4 Kibombo Zaïre
72D4 Kibondo Tanz
72D4 Kibungu Rwanda
41E2 Kičevo Macedonia, Yugos
6G4 Kicking Horse P Can
70C3 Kidal Mali
35D5 Kidderminster Eng
70A3 Kidira Sen
78C1 Kidnappers,C NZ
42C2 Kiel Germany
43E2 Kielce Pol
42C2 Kieler Bucht B Germany
Kiev = Kiyev
58E2 Kifab Uzbekistan
70A3 Kiffa Maur
68H8 Kigali Rwanda
5J2 Kiglapatt,C Can
10E3 Kigluaik Mts USA
72C4 Kigoma Tanz
20E5 Kiholo Hawaiian Is
54C4 Kii-sanchi Mts Japan
53C5 Kii-suido B Japan
49R4 Kikhchik Russian Fed
41E1 Kikinda Serbia, Yugos
41E3 Kikládhes Is Greece
76D1 Kikon PNG
54D2 Kikonai Japan
51H7 Kikori PNG
72B4 Kikwit Zaïre
20E5 Kilauea Crater Mt Hawaiian Is
6C3 Kilbuck Mts USA
53B3 Kilchu N Korea
75D1 Kilcoy Aust
35B5 Kildane County, Irish Rep
35B5 Kildare Irish Rep
17D3 Kilgore USA
72E4 Kilifi Kenya
72D4 Kilimanjaro Mt Tanz
73D4 Kilindoni Tanz
64C2 Kilis Turk
43F3 Kiliya Ukraine
35B5 Kilkenny County, Irish Rep
35B5 Kilkenny Irish Rep
41E2 Kilkís Greece
75D1 Killarney Aust
33B3 Killarney Irish Rep
17C3 Killeen USA
10H2 Killik R USA
34C3 Killin Scot
5J1 Killinek I Can
41E3 Killini Mt Greece
34C4 Kilmarnock Scot
44J4 Kil'mez Russian Fed
73D4 Kilosa Tanz
33B3 Kilrush Irish Rep
71J4 Kilunga R Nig
73C4 Kilwa Zaïre
73D4 Kilwa Kisiwani Tanz
73D4 Kilwa Kivinje Tanz
71J4 Kim R Cam
75A2 Kimba Aust
16B1 Kimball USA
10K3 Kimball,Mt USA
3E4 Kimberley Can
74C2 Kimberley S Africa
76B2 Kimberley Plat Aust
53B3 Kimch'aek N Korea
53B4 Kimch'ŏn S Korea
54A3 Kimhae S Korea
41E3 Kími Greece
54A3 Kimje S Korea
44F4 Kimry Russian Fed
54A3 Kimwha N Korea
56E1 Kinabalu Mt Malay
56E1 Kinabatangan R Malay
4E5 Kincardine Can
3C2 Kincolith Can
17D3 Kinder USA
3G3 Kindersley Can
70A3 Kindia Guinea
72C4 Kindu Zaïre
44J5 Kinel' Russian Fed
44G4 Kineshma Russian Fed
75D1 Kingaroy Aust
19B3 King City USA
6F4 Kingcome Inlet Can
10F4 King Cove USA
17C2 Kingfisher USA
7L4 King George Is Can
76D5 King I Aust
3C3 King I Can
76B2 King Leopold Range Mts Aust
8B3 Kingman USA
72C4 Kingombe Zaïre
75A2 Kingoonya Aust
20C2 Kingsburg USA
19C3 Kings Canyon Nat Pk USA
75A3 Kingscote Aust
76B2 King Sd Aust
12B1 Kingsford USA
15C2 Kingsland USA
35F5 King's Lynn Eng
77G1 Kingsmill Group Is Kiribati
14D2 Kings Park USA
8B2 Kings Peak Mt USA
15C1 Kingsport USA
76C4 Kingston Aust
7L5 Kingston Can
21E3 Kingston Jamaica
13E2 Kingston New York, USA
78A3 Kingston NZ
14C2 Kingston Pennsylvania, USA
23E4 Kingstown St Vincent
8D4 Kingsville USA
5J2 Kingurutik R Can
34C3 Kingussie Scot
6J3 King William I Can
74D3 King William's Town S Africa
72B4 Kinkala Congo
32G7 Kinna Sweden
34D3 Kinnairds Head Pt Scot
54C3 Kinomoto Japan
34D3 Kinross Scot
72B4 Kinshasa Zaïre
16C2 Kinsley USA
15D1 Kinston USA
56E3 Kintap Indon
34C4 Kintyre Pen Scot
3E2 Kinuso Can
72D3 Kinyeti Mt Sudan
36E1 Kinzig R Germany
3H2 Kipahigan L Can
41E3 Kiparissía Greece
41E3 Kiparissiakós Kólpos G Greece
13D1 Kipawa,L Can
73D4 Kipili Tanz
10F4 Kipnuk USA
35B5 Kippure Mt Irish Rep
73C5 Kipushi Zaïre
36E2 Kirchheim Germany
49M4 Kirensk Russian Fed
48J5 Kirgizia Republic Europe
59F1 Kirgizskiy Khrebet Mts Kirgizia
72B4 Kiri Zaïre
77G1 Kiribati Is Pacific O
64B2 Kırıkkale Turk
44E4 Kirishi Russian Fed
60B3 Kirithar Range Mts Pak
41F3 Kirkağaç Turk
45H8 Kirk Bulāg Dāgh Mt Iran
35D4 Kirkby Eng
34D3 Kirkcaldy Scot
34C4 Kirkcudbright Scot
32K5 Kirkenes Nor
7K5 Kirkland Lake Can
64A1 Kırklareli Turk
79E Kirkpatrick,Mt Ant
9D2 Kirksville USA
64D2 Kirkūk Iraq
34D2 Kirkwall Scot
17D2 Kirkwood USA
74D3 Kirkwood R S Africa
44E5 Kirov Russian Fed
44H4 Kirov Russian Fed
64D1 Kirovakan Armenia
44K4 Kirovgrad Russian Fed
45E6 Kirovograd Ukraine
44E2 Kirovsk Russian Fed
49R4 Kirovskiy Kamchatka, Russian Fed
53C2 Kirovskiy Primorskiykray, Russian Fed
44J4 Kirs Russian Fed
64B2 Kirşehir Turk
42C2 Kiruna Sweden
54C3 Kiryū Japan
72C3 Kisangani Zaïre
57C4 Kisar I Indon
56A2 Kisaran Indon
54C3 Kisarazu Japan
61C2 Kishanganj India
60C3 Kishangarh India
43F3 Kishinev Moldavia
54C4 Kishiwada Japan
72D4 Kisii Kenya
73D4 Kisiju Tanz
10B6 Kiska I USA
4B3 Kiskitto L Can
43D3 Kiskunhalas Hung
45G7 Kislovodsk Russian Fed
72E4 Kismaayo Somalia
54C3 Kiso-sammyaku Mts Japan
70B4 Kissidougou Guinea
15C3 Kissimmee,L USA
3H2 Kississing L Can
72D4 Kisumu Kenya
43E3 Kisvárda Hung
70B3 Kita Mali
48H6 Kitab Uzbekistan
54D3 Kitakami Japan
54D3 Kitakami R Japan
54D3 Kitakata Japan
53C5 Kita-Kyūshū Japan
72D3 Kitale Kenya
50H4 Kitalo I Japan
53E3 Kitami Japan
54D2 Kitami-Esashi Japan
16B2 Kit Carson USA
7K5 Kitchener Can
4F3 Kitchigama R Can
72D3 Kitgum Uganda
41E3 Kíthira I Greece
41E3 Kíthnos I Greece
65B1 Kiti,C Cyprus
6G2 Kitikmeot Region, Can
6F4 Kitimat Can
32K5 Kitnen R Fin
54B4 Kitsuki Japan
13D2 Kittanning USA
13E2 Kittery USA
32J5 Kittilä Fin
15D1 Kitty Hawk USA
73D4 Kitunda Tanz
10N4 Kitwanga Can
73C5 Kitwe Zambia
42C3 Kitzbühel Austria
37E1 Kitzbühler Alpen Mts Austria
42C3 Kitzingen Germany
72C4 Kiumbi Zaïre
10F2 Kivalina USA
43F2 Kivercy Ukraine
72C4 Kivu,L Zaïre/Rwanda
6B3 Kiwalik USA
45E5 Kiyev Ukraine
43G2 Kiyevskoye Vodokhranilishche Res Ukraine
44K4 Kizel Russian Fed
44G3 Kizema Russian Fed
64C2 Kizil R Turk
58D2 Kizyl-Arvat Turkmenistan
45J8 Kizyl-Atrek Turkmenistan
42C2 Kladno Czech
42C3 Klagenfurt Austria
44C4 Klaipēda Lithuania
18B2 Klamath USA
8A2 Klamath R USA
8A2 Klamath Falls USA
18B2 Klamath Mts USA
3C2 Klappan R Can
42C3 Klatovy Czech
10M4 Klawak USA
65C1 Kleiat Leb
74B2 Kleinsee S Africa
74D2 Klerksdorp S Africa
43G2 Kletnya Russian Fed
36D1 Kleve Germany
43G2 Klimovichi Belorussia
44F4 Klin Russian Fed
43D1 Klintehamn Sweden
45E5 Klintsy Russian Fed
74C3 Klipplaat S Africa
40D2 Ključ Bosnia & Herzegovina, Yugos
42D2 Kłodzko Pol
10L3 Klondike R USA/Can
6D3 Klondike Plat USA/Can
42D3 Klosterneuburg Austria
10L3 Kluane R Can
10L3 Kluane L Can
10L3 Kluane Nat Pk Can
43D2 Kluczbork Pol
10L4 Klukwan USA
10J3 Klutina L USA
10J3 Knight I USA
35D5 Knighton Wales
40D2 Knin Croatia, Yugos
76A4 Knob,C Aust
36B1 Knokke-Heist Belg
10M5 Knox,C Can
79G9 Knox Coast Ant
11D3 Knoxville Iowa, USA
9E3 Knoxville Tennessee, USA
7Q3 Knud Ramsussens Land Region Greenland
74C3 Knysna S Africa
56C3 Koba Indon
7O3 Kobberminebugt B Greenland
53D5 Kobe Japan
42C1 København Den
37E1 Kobiard Slovenia, Yugos
42B2 Koblenz Germany
53C1 Koboldo Russian Fed
44C5 Kobrin Russian Fed
51G7 Kobroör I Indon
10G2 Kobuk R USA
41E2 Kočani Macedonia, Yugos
54A3 Kŏch'ang S Korea
55C3 Ko Chang I Thai
61C2 Koch Bihār India
37D1 Kochel Germany
36E2 Kocher R Germany
7L3 Koch I Can
62B3 Kochi India
53C5 Kōchi Japan
10H4 Kodiak USA
10H4 Kodiak I USA
62B2 Kodikkarai India
72D3 Kodok Sudan
54D2 Kodomari-misaki C Japan
43F3 Kodyma Ukraine
20D3 Koehn L USA
74B2 Koes Namibia
74D2 Koffiefontein S Africa
71F4 Koforidua Ghana
53D4 Kōfu Japan
54C3 Koga Japan
5J2 Kogaluk R Can
32G7 Køge Den
71H4 Kogi State Nig
60C2 Kohat Pak
60B2 Koh-i-Baba Mts Afghan
60B1 Koh-i-Hisar Mts Afghan
60B2 Koh-i-Khurd Mt Afghan
61D2 Kohīma India
60B1 Koh-i-Mazar Mt Afghan
63E2 Koh-i-Qaisar Mt Afghan
60B3 Kohlu Pak
44D4 Kohtla Järve Estonia
54A4 Kohung S Korea
54A4 Kohyon S Korea
54C3 Koide Japan
10K3 Koidern Can
55A4 Koihoa Is Nicobar Is
54A2 Koin N Korea
53B5 Kŏje-do I S Korea
54C2 Ko-jima I Japan
48H4 Kokchetav Kazakhstan
32J6 Kokemaki L Fin
32J6 Kokkola Fin
71G3 Koko Nig
76D1 Kokoda PNG
12B2 Kokomo USA
51G7 Kokonau Indon
50B2 Kokpekty Kazakhstan
54A3 Koksan N Korea
7M4 Koksoak R Can
54A3 Koksŏng S Korea
74D3 Kokstad S Africa
55C3 Ko Kut I Thai
44E2 Kola Russian Fed
57B3 Kolaka Indon
55B4 Ko Lanta I Thai
62B2 Kolār India
62B2 Kolār Gold Fields India
70A3 Kolda Sen
32F7 Kolding Den
53E1 Kolendo Russian Fed
44H2 Kolguyev, Ostrov I Russian Fed
62A1 Kolhāpur India
10G4 Koliganek USA
42D2 Kolín Czech
62B3 Kollam India
42B2 Köln Germany
43D2 Kolo Pol
20E5 Koloa Hawaiian Is
42D2 Kolobrzeg Pol
70B3 Kolokani Mali
44F4 Kolomna Russian Fed
45D6 Kolomyya Ukraine
57B3 Kolono Indon
57B3 Kolonodale Indon
49R4 Kolpakovskiy Russian Fed
48K4 Kolpashevo Russian Fed
41F3 Kólpos Merabéllou B Greece
41E2 Kólpos Singitikós G Greece
41E2 Kólpos Strimonikós G Greece
41E2 Kólpos Toronaíos G Greece
44F2 Kol'skiy Poluostrov Pen Russian Fed
44K2 Kolva R Russian Fed
32G6 Kolvereid Nor
73C5 Kolwezi Zaïre
49R3 Kolyma R Russian Fed
49R3 Kolymskaya Nizmennost Lowland Russian Fed
49S3 Kolymskoye Nagor'ye Mts Russian Fed
10D2 Kolyuchinskaya Guba B Russian Fed
41E2 Kom Mt Bulg/Serbia
72D3 Koma Eth

Koma Kyaukpyu

54D3 Koma Japan
71J3 Komaduga Gana R Nig
71J3 Komadugu Yobé R Nig
54D2 Komaga take Mt Japan
49S4 Komandorskiye Ostrova I Russian Fed
43D3 Komárno Czech
74E2 Komati,R S Africa
74E2 Komati Poort S Africa
53D4 Komatsu Japan
54B4 Komatsushima Japan
71F3 Kombissiri Burkina
44J3 Komi Respublika, Russian Fed
50B1 Kommunar Russian Fed
57A4 Komodo I Indon
71F4 Komoé R Ivory Coast
51G7 Komoran I Indon
54C3 Komoro Japan
41F2 Komotiní Greece
74C3 Kompasberg Mt S Africa
55D3 Kompong Cham Camb
55C3 Kompong Chhnang Mts Camb
55C3 Kompong Som Camb
55D3 Kompong Thom Camb
55D3 Kompong Trabek Camb
43F3 Komrat Moldavia
74C3 Komsberg Mts S Africa
49Li Komsomolets, Ostrov I Russian Fed
44L2 Komsomol'skiy Russian Fed
49P4 Komsomol'sk na Amure Russian Fed
48H4 Konda R Russian Fed
61B4 Kondagaon India
72D4 Kondoa Tanz
53D1 Kondon Russian Fed
44E3 Kondopoga Russian Fed
62B1 Kondukūr India
10C2 Konergino Russian Fed
44F3 Konevo Russian Fed
7P3 Kong Christian IX Land Region Greenland
7O3 Kong Frederik VI Kyst Region Greenland
54A3 Kongju S Korea
48D2 Kong Karls Land Is Barents S
56E2 Kongkemul Mt Indon
72C4 Kongolo Zaïre
71F3 Kongoussi Burkina
32F7 Kongsberg Den
32G6 Kongsvinger Nor
Königsberg = Kaliningrad
37E1 Königsee, L Germany
43D2 Konin Pol
41D2 Konjic Bosnia & Herzegovina, Yugos
71F4 Konongo Ghana
44G3 Konosha Russian Fed
54C3 Konosu Japan
45E5 Konotop Ukraine
43E2 Końskie Pol
36E3 Konstanz Germany
71H3 Kontagora Nig
55D3 Kontum Viet
10B2 Konus Mt Russian Fed
45E8 Konya Turk
18C1 Kootenay L Can
3E4 Kootenay R Can
60C5 Kopargaon India
7R3 Kópasker Iceland
32A2 Kópavogur Iceland
40C1 Koper Slovenia, Yugos
58D2 Kopet Dag Mts Iran/ Turkmenistan
44L4 Kopeysk Russian Fed
55C4 Ko Phangan I Thai
55B4 Ko Phuket I Thai
32H7 Köping Sweden
54A3 Kopo-ri S Korea
62B1 Koppal India
40D1 Koprivnica Croatia, Yugos
60B4 Korangi Pak
62C1 Koraput India
61B3 Korba India
42B2 Korbach Germany
41E2 Korçë Alb
40D2 Korčula I Croatia, Yugos
52E2 Korea B China/Korea
53B5 Korea Str S Korea/Japan
43F2 Korec Ukraine
49S3 Korf Russian Fed
64B1 Körğlu Tepesi Mt Turk
70B4 Korhogo Ivory Coast
60B4 Kori Creek India
41E3 Korinthiakós Kólpos G Greece
41E3 Kórinthos Greece
53E4 Kōriyama Japan
44L5 Korkino Russian Fed
49R3 Korkodon Russian Fed
49R3 Korkodon R Russian Fed
64B2 Korkuteli Turk
59G1 Korla China
65B1 Kormakiti,C Cyprus
40D2 Kornat I Croatia, Yugos
45E7 Köroğlu Tepesi Mt Turk
72D4 Korogwe Tanz
75B3 Koroit Aust
51G6 Koror Palau Is, Pacific O
43E3 Körös R Hung
45D5 Korosten Ukraine
43F2 Korostyshev Ukraine
72B2 Koro Toro Chad
10F4 Korovin I USA
53E2 Korsakov Russian Fed
32G7 Korsør Den
66B3 Korti Sudan
44J3 Kortkeroz Russian Fed
42A2 Kortrijk Belg
49S3 Koryakskoye Nagor'ye Mts Russian Fed
54A3 Koryong S Korea
41F3 Kós I Greece
10D2 Kosa Belyaka B Russian Fed
55C4 Ko Samui I Thai
54A3 Kosan N Korea
43D2 Koscierzyna Pol
15B2 Kosciusko USA
76D4 Kosciusko Mt Aust
10M4 Kosciusko I USA
53B5 Koshikijima-retto I Japan
43E3 Košiče Czech
44J2 Kosma R Russian Fed
53B4 Kosong N Korea
41E2 Kosovo Aut Republic Serbia, Yugos
70B4 Kossou L Ivory Coast
74D2 Koster S Africa
72D2 Kosti Sudan
43F2 Kostopol' Ukraine
44G4 Kostroma Russian Fed
42C2 Kostrzyn Pol
44K2 Kos'yu R Russian Fed
32H8 Koszalin Pol
60D3 Kota India
56B4 Kotaagung Indon
56D3 Kotabaharu Indon
56E3 Kotabaru Indon
55C4 Kota Bharu Malay
56C3 Kotabum Indon
60C2 Kot Addu Pak
56E1 Kota Kinabulu Malay
57B2 Kotamobagu Indon
62C1 Kotapad India
56F7 Kotapinang I Indon
56G8 Kota Tinggi Malay
44H4 Kotel'nich Russian Fed
45G6 Kotel'nikovo Russian Fed
49P2 Kotel'nyy, Ostrov I Russian Fed
32K6 Kotka Fin
44H3 Kotlas Russian Fed
10F3 Kotlik USA
71H4 Koton Karifi Nig
41D2 Kotor Montenegro, Yugos
45D6 Kotovsk Ukraine
60B3 Kotri Pak
37E1 Kötschach Austria
62C1 Kottagūdem India
62B3 Kottayam India
72C3 Kotto R CAR
62B2 Kottūru India
49L3 Kotuy R Russian Fed
10F2 Kotzebue USA
6B3 Kotzebue Sd USA
71G3 Kouande Benin
72C3 Kouango CAR
71F3 Koudougou Burkina
74C3 Kougaberge Mts S Africa
72B4 Koulamoutou Gabon
70B3 Koulikoro Mali
71F3 Koupéla Burkina
71F3 Kouri Mali
27H2 Kourou French Guiana
70B3 Kouroussa Guinea
72B2 Kousséri Cam
32K6 Kouvola Fin
32L5 Kovdor Russian Fed
32L5 Kovdozero, Ozero L Russian Fed
43E2 Kovel' Ukraine
Kovno = Kaunas
44G4 Kovrov Russian Fed
44G5 Kovylkino Russian Fed
44F3 Kovzha R Russian Fed
55C4 Ko Way I Thai
52C5 Kowloon Hong Kong
54A3 Kowŏn N Korea
60B2 Kowt-e-Ashrow Afghan
64A2 Köyceğiz Turk
44G2 Koyda Russian Fed
62A1 Koyna Res India
44H3 Koynas Russian Fed
57C2 Koyoa I Indon
10F3 Koyuk USA
10F2 Koyuk R USA
10G3 Koyukuk USA
10G2 Koyukuk R USA
64C2 Kozan Turk
41E2 Kozańi Greece
62B2 Kozhikode India
44K2 Kozhim Russian Fed
44H4 Koz'modemyansk Russian Fed
54C4 Kōzu-shima I Japan
71G4 Kpandu Ghana
74D3 Kraai R S Africa
32F7 Kragerø Nor
41E2 Kragujevac Serbia, Yugos
55B3 Kra,Isthmus of Burma/ Malay
Krakatau = Rakata
65D1 Krak des Chevaliers Hist Site Syria
Kraków = Cracow Pol
41E2 Kraljevo Serbia, Yugos
45F6 Kramatorsk Ukraine
32H6 Kramfors Sweden
40C1 Kranj Slovenia, Yugos
44H3 Krasavino Russian Fed
44J1 Krasino Russian Fed
43E2 Kraśnik Pol
45H5 Krasnoarmeysk Russian Fed
45F6 Krasnodar Russian Fed
53E2 Krasnogorsk Russian Fed
44K4 Krasnokamsk Russian Fed
44L4 Krasnotur'insk Russian Fed
44K4 Krasnoufimsk Russian Fed
44K5 Krasnousol'-skiy Russian Fed
44K3 Krasnovishersk Russian Fed
45J7 Krasnovodsk Turkmenistan
49L4 Krasnoyarsk Russian Fed
43E2 Krasnystaw Pol
45H5 Krasnyy Kut Russian Fed
45F6 Krasnyy Luch Ukraine
45H6 Krasnyy Yar Russian Fed
55D3 Kratie Camb
7N2 Kraulshavn Greenland
42B2 Krefeld Germany
45E6 Kremenchug Ukraine
45E6 Kremenchugskoye Vodokhranilische Res Ukraine
43F2 Kremenets Ukraine
16A1 Kremming USA
10E5 Krenitzin Is USA
72A3 Kribi Cam
44E5 Krichev Belorussia
37E1 Krimml Austria
32J6 Krinstinestad Fin
62B1 Krishna R India
62B2 Krishnagiri India
61C3 Krishnangar India
32F7 Kristiansand Nor
32G7 Kristianstad Sweden
48B3 Kristiansund Nor
32G7 Kristineham Sweden
41E3 Kríti I Greece
45E6 Krivoy Rog Ukraine
40C1 Krk I Croatia, Yugos
74D1 Krokodil R S Africa
49S4 Kronotskaya Sopka Mt Russian Fed
7P3 Kronpris Frederik Bjerge Mts Greenland
32K7 Kronshtadt Russian Fed
74D2 Kroonstad S Africa
45G6 Kropotkin Russian Fed
74E1 Kruger Nat Pk S Africa
74D2 Krugersdorp S Africa
56B4 Krui Indon
41D2 Kruje Alb
43F2 Krupki Belorussia
10F2 Krusenstern,C USA
41E2 Kruzevac Serbia, Yugos
32K7 Krustpils Latvia
10L4 Kruzof I USA
45E6 Krym Pen Ukraine
45F7 Krymsk Russian Fed
42D2 Krzyz Pol
71C1 Ksar El Boukhari Alg
71A2 Ksar el Kebir Mor
56A2 Kuala Indon
55C5 Kuala Dungun Malay
56F6 Kuala Kangsar Malay
56G7 Kuala Kelawang Malay
55C4 Kuala Kerai Malay
55C5 Kuala Kubu Baharu Malay
55C5 Kuala Lipis Malay
55C5 Kuala Lumpur Malay
56G7 Kuala Pilah Malay
56F7 Kuala Selangor Malay
56A2 Kualasimpang Indon
55C4 Kuala Trengganu Malay
56E1 Kuamut Malay
53A3 Kuandian China
55C5 Kuantan Malay
45H7 Kuba Azerbaijan
51H7 Kubar PNG
56D2 Kuching Malay
56E1 Kudat Malay
56D4 Kudus Indon
44J4 Kudymkar Russian Fed
42C3 Kufstein Austria
10M2 Kugaluk R Can
10M2 Kugmallit B Can
63E3 Kuhak Iran
63D2 Kuh Duren Upland Iran
63D3 Kūh e Bazmān Mt Iran
63C2 Kūh-e Dinar Mt Iran
63D1 Kūh-e-Hazār Masjed Mts Iran
63D3 Kūh-e Jebāl Barez Mts Iran
63C2 Kūh-e Karkas Mts Iran
63D3 Kuh-e Laleh Zar Mt Iran
63B1 Kūh-e Sahand Mt Iran
63E3 Kuh e Taftān Mt Iran
45H9 Kūhhaye Alvand Mts Iran
45H8 Kūhhaye Sabalan Mts Iran
63B2 Kūhhā-ye Zāgros Mts Iran
32K6 Kuhmo Fin
63C2 Kūhpāyeh Iran
63D2 Kūhpāyeh Mt Iran
63D3 Kūh ye Bashākerd Mts Iran
63B1 Kūh ye Sabalan Mt Iran
74B2 Kuibis Namibia
74B1 Kuiseb R Namibia
73B5 Kuito Angola
10M4 Kuiu I USA
54A3 Kujang N Korea
53E3 Kuji Japan
54B4 Kuju-san Mt Japan
10G4 Kukaklek L USA
41E2 Kukës Alb
10F2 Kukpowruk R USA
55C5 Kukup Malay
63D3 Kūl R Iran
41F3 Kula Turk
56G8 Kulai Malay
45K6 Kulakshi Kazakhstan
72D3 Kulal,Mt Kenya
41E2 Kulata Bulg
44C4 Kuldīga Latvia
56F6 Kulim Malay
44G2 Kulov R Russian Fed
71F3 Kulpawn R Ghana
45J6 Kul'sary Kazakhstan
60D2 Kulu India
64B2 Kulu Turk
66D4 Kululli Eth
48J4 Kulunda Russian Fed
75B2 Kulwin Aust
45H7 Kuma R Russian Fed
54C3 Kumagaya Japan
56D3 Kumai Indon
45L5 Kumak Russian Fed
53C5 Kumamoto Japan
54C4 Kumano Japan
41E2 Kumanovo Macedonia, Yugos
53B1 Kumara China
71F4 Kumasi Ghana
72A3 Kumba Cam
62B2 Kumbakonam India
71J4 Kumbo Cam
54A3 Kūmch'ŏn N Korea
67E2 Kumdah S Arabia
44K5 Kumertau Russian Fed
54A3 Kumgang N Korea
53B4 Kūmhwa S Korea
32H7 Kumla Sweden
54A4 Kūmnyŏng S Korea
54A4 Kūmo-do I S Korea
61E2 Kumon Range Mts Burma
62A2 Kumta India
59G1 Kūmüx China
60C2 Kunar R Afghan
53F3 Kunashir, Ostrov I Russian Fed
32K7 Kunda Estonia
60C4 Kundla India
60B1 Kunduz Afghan
68F9 Kunene R Angola
10M5 Kunghit I Can
32G7 Kungsbacka Sweden
44K4 Kungur Russian Fed
55B1 Kunhing Burma
59G2 Kunlun Shan Mts China
52A4 Kunming China
44M3 Kunovat R Russian Fed
53B4 Kunsan S Korea
32K6 Kuopio Fin
40D1 Kupa R Croatia/Bosnia & Herzegovina, Yugos
76B2 Kupang Indon
76D2 Kupiano PNG
10M4 Kupreanof I USA
10G4 Kupreanof Pt USA
45F6 Kupyansk Ukraine
59G1 Kuqa China
53C2 Kur R Russian Fed
45H8 Kura R Azerbaijan
54C3 Kurabe Japan
53C5 Kurashiki Japan
54B3 Kurayoshi Japan
63B1 Kurdistan Region, Iran
41F2 Kŭrdzhali Bulg
53C5 Kure Japan
44C4 Kuressaare Estonia
49L3 Kureyka R Russian Fed
48H4 Kurgan Russian Fed
Kuria Muria Is = Khūryan Mūryān
32J6 Kurikka Fin
Kuril Is = Kuril'skiye Ostrova
53F2 Kuril'sk Russian Fed
49Q5 Kuril'skiye Ostrova Is Russian Fed
xxviiiJ2 Kuril Trench Pacific O
45H8 Kurinskaya Kosa Sand Spit Azerbaijan
62B1 Kurnool India
54D2 Kuroishi Japan
54D3 Kuroiso Japan
78B2 Kurow NZ
75D2 Kurri Kurri Aust
45F5 Kursk Russian Fed
50B2 Kuruktag R China
74C2 Kuruman S Africa
74C2 Kuruman R S Africa
53C5 Kurume Japan
62C3 Kurunegala Sri Lanka
48K5 Kurunktag R China
44K3 Kur'ya Russian Fed
44K4 Kusa Russian Fed
41F3 Kuşadasi Körfezi B Turk
41F2 Kus Golü L Turk
53D5 Kushimoto Japan
53E3 Kushiro Japan
63E1 Kushka Afghan
61C3 Kushtia Bang
45J5 Kushum R Kazakhstan
44K4 Kushva Russian Fed
10F3 Kuskokwim R USA
10F4 Kuskokwim B USA
10G3 Kuskokwim Mts USA
61B2 Kusma Nepal
53E3 Kussharo-ko L Japan
48H4 Kustanay Kazakhstan
45D8 Kütahya Turk
56E3 Kutai R Indon
45G7 Kutaisi Georgia
54D2 Kutchan Japan
42D3 Kutná Hora Czech
43D2 Kutno Pol
72B4 Kutu Zaïre
61D3 Kutubdia I Bang
72C2 Kutum Sudan
7M4 Kuujjuaq Can
7L4 Kuujjuarapik Can
32K5 Kuusamo Fin
45K5 Kuvandyk Russian Fed
64E4 Kuwait Kuwait
58C3 Kuwait Sheikdom, S W Asia
54C3 Kuwana Japan
48J4 Kuybyshev Russian Fed
44H5 Kuybyshevskoye Vodokhranilishche Res Russian Fed
44E2 Kuyto, Ozero L Russian Fed
49M4 Kuytun Russian Fed
45F7 Kuzey Anadolu Daglari Mts Turk
44H5 Kuznetsk Russian Fed
44F2 Kuzomen Russian Fed
44C2 Kvaenangen Sd Nor
10G4 Kvichak USA
10G4 Kvichak R USA
10G4 Kvichak B USA
32G5 Kvigtind Mt Nor
44B2 Kvikkjokk Sweden
72D4 Kwale Kenya
71H4 Kwale Nig
53B4 Kwangju S Korea
72B4 Kwango R Zaïre
54A3 Kwangyang S Korea
54A2 Kwanmo-bong Mt N Korea
71H4 Kwara State, Nig
73C5 Kwekwe Zim
10F3 Kwethluk USA
10F3 Kwethluk R USA
43D2 Kwidzyn Pol
6B4 Kwigillingok USA
51G7 Kwoka Mt Indon
75C3 Kyabram Aust
55B2 Kyaikkami Burma
55B2 Kyaikto Burma
50D1 Kyakhta Russian Fed
75A2 Kyancutta Aust
55B1 Kyaukme Burma
55B1 Kyauk-padaung Burma
55A2 Kyaukpyu Burma

Kyaukse **Laoise Port**

61E3 **Kyaukse** Burma
44G2 **Kychema** Russian Fed
3G3 **Kyle** Can
33B2 **Kyle of Lochalsh** Scot
36D1 **Kyll** *R* Germany
75B3 **Kyneton** Aust
72D3 **Kyoga** *L* Uganda
75D1 **Kyogle** Aust
53B4 **Kyŏngju** S Korea
54A3 **Kyongsang Sanmaek** *Mts* S Korea
54A2 **Kyŏngsŏng** N Korea
61E4 **Kyonpyaw** Burma
53D4 **Kyoto** Japan
65B1 **Kyrenia** Cyprus
44K3 **Kyrta** Russian Fed
44L4 **Kyshtym** Russian Fed
65B1 **Kythrea** Cyprus
53C5 **Kyūshū** *I* Japan
xxviiiH4 **Kyushu-Palau Ridge** Pacific O
41E2 **Kyustendil** Bulg
49O2 **Kyusyur** Russian Fed
50C1 **Kyzyl** Russian Fed
48H5 **Kyzylkum** *Desert* Uzbekistan
48H5 **Kzyl Orda** Kazakhstan

L

72E3 **Laascaanood** Somalia
22C1 **La Ascension** Mexico
69D3 **Laas Dawaco** Somalia
36E1 **Laasphe** Germany
69D3 **Laasqoray** Somalia
26F1 **La Asunción** Ven
70A2 **Laâyoune** Mor
28C1 **La Banda** Arg
22B1 **La Barca** Mexico
18D2 **La Barge** USA
77G2 **Labasa** Fiji
70A3 **Labé** Guinea
42D2 **Labe** *R* Czech
13E1 **Labelle** Can
15E4 **La Belle** USA
10L3 **Laberge,L** Can
56D2 **Labi** Brunei
45G7 **Labinsk** Russian Fed
56G7 **Labis** Malay
65D1 **Laboué** Leb
28C2 **Laboulaye** Arg
7M4 **Labrador** *Region* Can
7M4 **Labrador City** Can
7N4 **Labrador S** Greenland/Can
26F5 **Lábrea** Brazil
56E1 **Labuan** *I* Malay
57C3 **Labuha** Indon
56C4 **Labuhan** Indon
57B4 **Labuhanbajo** Indon
56F7 **Labuhanbatu** Indon
56B2 **Labuhanbilik** Indon
55A2 **Labutta** Burma
44M2 **Labytnangi** Russian Fed
7L4 **Lac à l'Eau Claire** Can
4F2 **Lac Anuc** *L* Can
36B1 **La Capelle** France
28C2 **La Carlota** Arg
57F8 **La Carlota** Phil
4F4 **Lac au Goéland** *L* Can
5G2 **Lac aux Feuilles** *L* Can
5J2 **Lac aux Goélands** *L* Can
5G2 **Lac Bacquerville** *L* Can
5G2 **Lac Bécard** *L* Can
10N2 **Lac Belot** *L* Can
7L4 **Lac Bienville** *L* Can
3H2 **Lac Brochet** Can
5J3 **Lac Brûlé** *R* Can
4F4 **Lac Bryson** *L* Can
Laccadive Is = **Lakshadweep**
59F4 **Laccadive Is** India
5J2 **Lac Champdoré** *L* Can
5G2 **Lac Châteauguay** *L* Can
5F2 **Lac Chavigny** *L* Can
5H3 **Lac Clairambault** *L* Can
4F1 **Lac Couture** *L* Can
5G3 **Lac Dalmas** *L* Can
37B2 **Lac d'Annecy** *L* France
6G3 **Lac de Gras** *L* Can
37B1 **Lac de Joux** *L* Switz
5G3 **Lac Delorme** *L* Can
37B1 **Lac de Neuchâtel** *L* Switz
22B2 **Lac de Patzcuaro** *L* Mexico
22B2 **Lac de Sayula** *L* Mexico
6F3 **Lac des Bois** *L* Can
4C4 **Lac des Mille Lacs** *L* Can
4F4 **Lac Doda** *L* Can
11C1 **Lac du Bonnet** Can
37A2 **Lac du Bourget** *L* France
21D3 **La Ceiba** Honduras
75A3 **Lacepede B** Aust
5G2 **Lac Faribault** *L* Can
4F3 **Lac Grasset** *L* Can
5J2 **Lac Gruéard** *L* Can
4F2 **Lac Guillaume-Delisle** *L* Can
38C2 **La Châtre** France
36A3 **La Châtre-sur-le-Loir** France
37B1 **La-Chaux-de-Fonds** Switz
65C3 **Lachish** *Hist Site* Israel
76D4 **Lachlan** *R* Aust
5G3 **Lac Holmer** *L* Can
26C2 **La Chorrera** Panama
13E1 **Lachute** Can
37A3 **La Ciotat** France
22A1 **La Ciudad** Mexico
7M4 **Lac Joseph** *L* Can
13D2 **Lackawanna** USA
5G4 **Lac Kempt** *L* Can
4F4 **Lac Kipawa** *L* Can
5G1 **Lac Klotz** *L* Can
3F3 **Lac la Biche** Can
6F3 **Lac la Martre** *L* Can
5H3 **Lac Lapointe** *L* Can
5G2 **Lac La Potherie** *L* Can
6H4 **Lac la Ronge** *L* Can
40B1 **Lac Léman** *L* Switz/France
5F2 **Lac Le Roy** *L* Can
5G2 **Lac Mannessier** *L* Can
7L4 **Lac Manouane** Can
4F4 **Lac Matagami** *L* Can
10N2 **Lac Maunoir** *L* Can
7L4 **Lac Mistassini** *L* Can
4F4 **Lac Muskoka** *L* Can
5G3 **Lac Naococane** *L* Can
5G3 **Lac Néret** *L* Can
5H3 **Lac Nouveau** *L* Can
28B1 **La Cocha** Arg
3F3 **Lacombe** Can
13E2 **Laconia** USA
5H3 **Lac Opiscotéo** *L* Can
39A1 **La Coruña** Spain
37A2 **La Côte-St-André** France
4F4 **Lac Parent** *L* Can
5F2 **Lac Qilalugalik** *L* Can
5H3 **Lac Rambau** *L* Can
5J2 **Lac Ramusio** *L* Can
9D2 **La Crosse** USA
28D1 **La Cruz** Arg
22A1 **La Cruz** Mexico
5G4 **Lac Saint Jean** *L* Can
4F3 **Lac Sakami** *L* Can
7J4 **Lac Seul** *L* Can
4F4 **Lac Simard** *L* Can
5G3 **Lac Sureau** *L* Can
5G3 **Lac Taffanel** *L* Can
5G2 **Lac Tassialouc** *L* Can
17D2 **La Cygne** USA
60D2 **Ladākh Range** India
63E3 **Lādīz** Iran
60C3 **Lādnūn** India
52B5 **Ladong** China
44E3 **Ladozhskoye Ozero** *L* Ukraine
7K2 **Lady Ann Str** Can
75E3 **Lady Barron** Aust
74D2 **Ladybrand** S Africa
3D4 **Ladysmith** Can
74D2 **Ladysmith** S Africa
12A1 **Ladysmith** USA
76D1 **Lae** PNG
55C3 **Laem Ngop** Thai
42C1 **Laesø** *I* Den
16A2 **Lafayette** Colorado, USA
9E2 **Lafayette** Indiana, USA
9D3 **Lafayette** Louisiana, USA
36B2 **La Fène** France
36A2 **La-Ferté-Barnard** France
36B2 **La Ferté-St-Aubin** France
36B2 **La-Ferté-sous-Jouarre** France
71H4 **Lafia** Nig
71H4 **Lafiagi** Nig
38B2 **La Flèche** France
4E4 **Laforest** Can
71D1 **La Galite** *I* Tunisia
42C1 **Lagan** *R* Sweden
27L6 **Lagarto** Brazil
71C2 **Laghouat** Alg
29D3 **Lagoa de Araruama** Brazil
28E2 **Lagoa de Castillos** *L* Urug
28E2 **Lagoa de Rocha** Urug
25F4 **Lagoa dos Patos** *Lg* Brazil
29D3 **Lagoa Feia** Brazil
26C4 **Lago Agrio** Ecuador
29D2 **Lagoa Juparanã** *L* Brazil
29A2 **Lagoa Mandiore** *L* Brazil
28E2 **Lagoa Mangueira** *L* Brazil
25D4 **Lagoa mar Chiguita** *L* Arg
25F4 **Lagoa Mirim** *L* Urug/Brazil
28E2 **Lagoa Negra** *L* Urug
25B8 **Lago Argentino** *L* Arg
29A2 **Lagoa Uberaba** *L* Brazil
28E1 **Lagoa Vermelha** Brazil
25B7 **Lago Buenos Aries** *L* Arg
25B7 **Lago Cochrane** *L* Chile/Arg
25C7 **Lago Colhué Huapi** *L* Arg
21B2 **Lago de Chapala** *L* Mexico
26B2 **Lago de Chiriqui** *L* Panama
22B2 **Lago de Cuitzeo** *L* Mexico
25B5 **Lago de la Laja** *L* Chile
40B2 **Lago del Coghinas** *L* Sardegna
26D2 **Lago de Maracaibo** *L* Ven
26A1 **Lago de Nicaragua** *L* Nic
26B1 **Lago de Perlas** *L* Nic
22B1 **Lago de Santiaguillo** *L* Mexico
40C2 **Lago di Bolsena** *L* Italy
40C2 **Lago di Bracciano** *L* Italy
40B1 **Lago di Como** *L* Italy
37D2 **Lago d'Idro** *L* Italy
40C1 **Lago di Garda** *L* Italy
37C2 **Lago di Lecco** *L* Italy
37C2 **Lago di Lugano** *L* Italy
37D2 **Lago d'Iseo** *L* Italy
37C2 **Lago d'Orta** *L* Italy
25B7 **Lago General Carrera** *L* Chile
40B1 **Lago Maggiore** *L* Italy
25C7 **Lago Musters** *L* Arg
38B3 **Lagon** France
25B6 **Lago Nahuel Haupi** *L* Arg
25B7 **Lago O'Higgins** *L* Chile
40B2 **Lago Omodeo** *L* Sardegna
26E7 **Lago Poopó** *L* Bol
25B6 **Lago Ranco** *L* Chile
26E6 **Lago Rogaguado** *L* Bol
71G4 **Lagos** Nig
39A2 **Lagos** Port
71G4 **Lagos** State, Nig
25B7 **Lago San Martin** *L* Chile/Arg
21B2 **Lagos de Moreno** Mexico
26E7 **Lago Titicaca** Bol/Peru
37E3 **Lago Trasimeno** *L* Italy
71E1 **La Goulette** Tunisia
25B7 **Lago Viedma** *L* Arg
8B2 **La Grande** USA
4F3 **La Grande Réservoir 2** *Res* Can
5G3 **La Grande Réservoir 3** *Res* Can
5G3 **La Grande Réservoir 4** *Res* Can
76B2 **Lagrange** Aust
9E3 **La Grange** Georgia, USA
12B3 **La Grange** Kentucky, USA
15D1 **La Grange** N Carolina, USA
17C4 **La Grange** Texas, USA
26F2 **La Gran Sabana** *Mts* Ven
37B2 **La Grave** France
38B3 **Lagronño** Spain
16A3 **Laguna** USA
22A1 **Laguna Agua Brava** Mexico
28A3 **Laguna Aluminé** *L* Arg
19C4 **Laguna Beach** USA
28C3 **Laguna Colorada Grande** *L* Arg
57F8 **Laguna de Bay** *Lg* Phil
21D3 **Laguna de Caratasca** *Lg* Honduras
21D4 **Laguna de Chiriqui** *L* Panama
16A3 **Laguna de Guzmán** *L* Mexico
28C4 **Laguna del Abra** *L* Arg
22A1 **Laguna del Caimanero** *L* Mexico
21D3 **Laguna de Managua** *L* Nicaragua
21D3 **Laguna de Nicaragua** *L* Nicaragua
23A4 **Laguna de Perlas** *Lg* Nic
22C1 **Laguna de Pueblo Viejo** *L* Mexico
16A3 **Laguna de Santa Maria** *L* Mexico
21C2 **Laguna de Tamiahua** *Lg* Mexico
21C3 **Laguna de Términos** *Lg* Mexico
22B1 **Laguna de Yuriria** *L* Mexico
28D1 **Laguna Iberá** Arg
28D1 **Laguna Itati** *L* Arg
22C1 **Laguna le Altamira** Mexico
21C2 **Laguna Madre** *Lg* Mexico
17F4 **Laguna Madre** *Lg* USA
28C2 **Laguna Mar Chiquita** *L* Arg
28A4 **Laguna Nahuel Huapi** *L* Arg
10C2 **Laguna Nutauge** *Lg* Russian Fed
28C2 **Laguna Paiva** Arg
28A3 **Laguna Panguipulli** *L* Chile
28A4 **Laguna Puyehue** *L* Chile
28A4 **Laguna Ranco** Chile
28A4 **Laguna Repanco** *L* Chile
19C4 **Laguna Salada** *L* Mexico
8C4 **Laguna Seca** Mexico
22C2 **Laguna Superior** *L* Mexico
10C2 **Laguna Tenkergynpil'gyn** *Lg* Russian Fed
22C1 **Laguna Tortugas** *L* Mexico
28A4 **Laguna Traful** *L* Arg
28D1 **Laguna Trin** *L* Arg
10C2 **Laguna Vankarem** *Lg* Russian Fed
37E2 **Laguna Veneta** *Lg* Italy
28A3 **Laguna Villarrica** *L* Chile
22B1 **Lagund Seca** Mexico
56E1 **Lahad Datu** Malay
56B3 **Lahat** Indon
56A2 **Lahewa** Indon
32J6 **Lahia** Fin
66D4 **Lahij** Yemen
63C1 **Lāhījān** Iran
36D1 **Lahn** *R* Germany
36D1 **Lahnstein** Germany
60C2 **Lahore** Pak
36D2 **Lahr** France
32K6 **Lahti** Fin
22B2 **La Huerta** Mexico
72B3 **Lai** Chad
52B5 **Laibin** China
55C1 **Lai Chau** Viet
36A2 **L'Aigle** France
74C3 **Laingsburg** S Africa
34C2 **Lairg** Scot
56B3 **Lais** Indon
57G9 **Lais** Phil
57C3 **Laiwui** Indon
52E2 **Laiyang** China
52D2 **Laizhou Wan** *B* China
28A3 **Laja** *R* Chile
28E1 **Lajeado** Brazil
25F3 **Lajes** Brazil
20D4 **La Jolla** USA
8C3 **La Junta** USA
11C3 **Lake Andes** USA
75C2 **Lake Cargelligo** Aust
9D3 **Lake Charles** USA
15C2 **Lake City** Florida, USA
11D3 **Lake City** Minnesota, USA
15D2 **Lake City** S Carolina, USA
35D4 **Lake District** *Region* Eng
20D4 **Lake Elsinore** USA
76C3 **Lake Eyre Basin** Aust
13D2 **Lakefield** Can
12B2 **Lake Geneva** USA
14D1 **Lake George** USA
7M3 **Lake Harbour** Can
19D4 **Lake Havasu City** USA
20C3 **Lake Hughes** USA
14C2 **Lakehurst** USA
20C3 **Lake Isabella** USA
17C4 **Lake Jackson** USA
3F3 **Lake la Biche** Can
15C3 **Lakeland** USA
7J5 **Lake of the Woods** Can
18B1 **Lake Oswego** USA
5G5 **Lake Placid** USA
19B3 **Lakeport** USA
17D3 **Lake Providence** USA
78B2 **Lake Pukaki** NZ
4E3 **Lake River** Can
75C3 **Lakes Entrance** Aust
20C2 **Lakeshore** USA
75B1 **Lake Stewart** Aust
4E4 **Lake Superior Prov Park** Can
13D1 **Lake Traverse** Can
8A2 **Lakeview** USA
18B1 **Lakeview Mt** Can
17D3 **Lake Village** USA
15C3 **Lake Wales** USA
20C4 **Lakewood** California, USA
16A2 **Lakewood** Colorado, USA
14C2 **Lakewood** New Jersey, USA
12C2 **Lakewood** Ohio, USA
15E4 **Lake Worth** USA
61B2 **Lakhimpur** India
60B4 **Lakhpat** India
16B2 **Lakin** USA
60C2 **Lakki** Pak
41E3 **Lakonikós Kólpos** *G* Greece
57C4 **Lakor** *I* Indon
70B4 **Lakota** Ivory Coast
32K4 **Laksefjord** *Inlet* Nor
32K4 **Lakselv** Nor
62A2 **Lakshadweep** *Is* India
28C2 **La Laguna** Arg
66C4 **Lalibela** Eth
26B4 **La Libertad** Ecuador
28A2 **La Ligua** Chile
57B5 **Lalindi** Indon
57B3 **Lalindu** *R* Indon
39A2 **La Linea** Spain
60D4 **Lalitpur** India
57B3 **Laloa** Indon
6H4 **La Loche** Can
3G2 **La Loche,L** Can
36A2 **La Loupe** France
36C1 **La Louvière** Belg
23A4 **La Luz** Nic
28B1 **La Madrid** Arg
7L5 **La Malbaie** Can
22C2 **La Malinche** *Mt* Mexico
22B1 **La Mancha** Mexico
39B2 **La Mancha** Region, Spain
8C3 **Lamar** Colorado, USA
17D2 **Lamar** Missouri, USA
28B3 **Lamarque** Arg
17C4 **La Marque** USA
72B4 **Lambaréné** Gabon
26B5 **Lambayeque** Peru
79F10 **Lambert Gl** Ant
74B3 **Lamberts Bay** S Africa
14C2 **Lambertville** USA
37C2 **Lambro** *R* Italy
6F2 **Lambton,C** Can
55C2 **Lam Chi** *R* Thai
39A1 **Lamego** Port
37B2 **La Meije** *Mt* France
28B1 **La Merced** Arg
26C6 **La Merced** Peru
16B3 **Lamesa** USA
19C4 **La Mesa** USA
41E3 **Lamía** Greece
34D4 **Lammermuir Hills** Scot
32G7 **Lammhult** Sweden
57F8 **Lamon B** Phil
37D2 **Lamone** *R* Italy
17D1 **Lamoni** USA
20C3 **Lamont** California, USA
11A3 **Lamont** Wyoming, USA
51H6 **Lamotrek** *I* Pacific O
36B3 **Lamotte Beuvron** France
11C2 **La Moure** USA
16C3 **Lampasas** USA
35C5 **Lampeter** Wales
72E4 **Lamu** Kenya
37A2 **La Mure** France
37D1 **Lana** Italy
20E5 **Lanai** *I* Hawaiian Is
20E5 **Lanai City** Hawaiian Is
34D4 **Lanark** Scot
55B3 **Lanbi** *I* Burma
55C1 **Lancang** *R* China
35D5 **Lancashire** County, Eng
19C4 **Lancaster** California, USA
35D4 **Lancaster** Eng
17D1 **Lancaster** Mississippi, USA
13E2 **Lancaster** New Hampshire, USA
14A1 **Lancaster** New York, USA
12C3 **Lancaster** Ohio, USA
9F3 **Lancaster** Pennsylvania, USA
15C2 **Lancaster** S Carolina, USA
7K2 **Lancaster Sd** Can
56C3 **Landak** *R* Indon
36E2 **Landan** Germany
42C3 **Landeck** Austria
8C2 **Lander** USA
28C2 **Landeta** Arg
15C1 **Landrum** USA
42C3 **Landsberg** Germany
6F2 **Lands End** *C* Can
35C6 **Land's End** *Pt* Eng
42C3 **Landshut** Germany
32G7 **Lāndskrona** Sweden
15B2 **Lanett** USA
61B1 **La'nga Co** *L* China
11C2 **Langdon** USA
66C3 **Langeb** *Watercourse* Sudan
74C2 **Langeberg** *Mt* S Africa
3H3 **Langenburg** Can
42B2 **Langenhagen** Germany
37B1 **Langenthal** Switz
34D4 **Langholm** Scot
32A2 **Langjökull** *Mts* Iceland
55B4 **Langkawi** *I* Malay
4F4 **Langlade** Can
3D4 **Langley** Can
75C1 **Langlo** *R* Aust
37B1 **Langnau** Switz
38D2 **Langres** France
56A2 **Langsa** Indon
50D2 **Lang Shan** *Mts* China
55D1 **Lang Son** Viet
16B4 **Langtry** USA
38C3 **Languedoc** Region, France
3G3 **Lanigan** Can
25B5 **Lanin** *Mt* Arg
57F9 **Lanoa,L** Phil
14C2 **Lansdale** USA
4D3 **Lansdowne House** Can
5K3 **L'Anse au Loup** Can
14C2 **Lansford** USA
9E2 **Lansing** USA
37B2 **Lanslebourg** France
70A2 **Lanzarote** *I* Canary Is
52A2 **Lanzhou** China
37B2 **Lanzo Torinese** Italy
57F7 **Laoag** Phil
55C1 **Lao Cai** Viet
52D1 **Laoha He** *R* China
35B5 **Laois** County, Irish Rep
35B5 **Laoise Port** Irish Rep

Laoling Lima Res

54A2 **Laoling** China
36B2 **Laon** France
4D4 **Laona** USA
26C6 **La Orova** Peru
55C2 **Laos** Republic, S E Asia
29C4 **Lapa** Brazil
38C2 **Lapalisse** France
70A2 **La Palma** *I* Canary Is
26C2 **La Palmas** Panama
28E2 **La Paloma** Urug
28B3 **La Pampa** State, Arg
20B3 **La Panza Range** *Mts* USA
26F2 **La Paragua** Ven
25E4 **La Paz** Arg
28B2 **La Paz** Arg
26E7 **La Paz** Bol
21A2 **La Paz** Mexico
53E2 **La Perouse Str** Russian Fed/Japan
22C1 **La Pesca** Mexico
22B1 **La Piedad** Mexico
18B2 **La Pine** USA
65B1 **Lapithos** Cyprus
17D3 **Laplace** USA
22B2 **La Placita** Mexico
11B2 **La Plant** USA
25E4 **La Plata** Arg
3G2 **La Plonge,L** Can
12B2 **La Porte** USA
14B2 **Laporte** USA
32K6 **Lappeenranta** Fin
32H5 **Lappland** *Region* Sweden/Fin
28C3 **Laprida** Arg
17F4 **La Pryor** USA
49O2 **Laptev S** Russian Fed
32J6 **Lapua** Fin
28B1 **La Puerta** Arg
57F8 **Lapu-Lapu** Phil
28C1 **La Punta** Arg
8B4 **La Purísima** Mexico
72C1 **Laqiya Arbain** *Well* Sudan
25C2 **La Quiaca** Arg
40C2 **L'Aquila** Italy
63C3 **Lār** Iran
71A1 **Larache** Mor
37A2 **Laragne** France
8C2 **Laramie** USA
11A3 **Laramie Mts** USA
8C2 **Laramie Range** *Mts* USA
29B4 **Laranjeiras do Sul** Brazil
57B4 **Larantuka** Indon
57D4 **Larat** *I* Indon
39B2 **Larca** Spain
8D4 **Laredo** USA
63C3 **Larestan** Region, Iran
Largeau = Faya
37B2 **L'Argentière** France
15C3 **Largo** USA
34C4 **Largs** Scot
63B1 **Lārī** Iran
57A3 **Lariang** *R* Indon
25C3 **La Rioja** Arg
25C3 **La Rioja** State, Arg
41E3 **Lárisa** Greece
60B3 **Larkana** Pak
64B3 **Larnaca** Cyprus
65B1 **Larnaca B** Cyprus
34B4 **Larne** N Ire
16C2 **Larned** USA
39A1 **La Robla** Spain
36C1 **La Roche-en-Ardenne** Belg
38B2 **La Rochelle** France
37B1 **La Roche-sur-Foron** France
38B2 **La Roche-sur-Yon** France
39B2 **La Roda** Spain
23D3 **La Romana** Dom Rep
6H4 **La Ronge** Can
32F7 **Larvik** Nor
48J3 **Laryak** Russian Fed
28D1 **La Sabana** Arg
39B2 **La Sagra** *Mt* Spain
13E1 **La Salle** Can
12B2 **La Salle** USA
16B2 **Las Animas** USA
7L5 **La Sarre** Can
28C1 **Las Avispas** Arg
28A2 **Las Cabras** Chile
28E2 **Lascano** Urug
16A3 **Las Cruces** USA
23C3 **La Selle** *Mt* Haiti
52B2 **Lasengmia** China
25B3 **La Serena** Chile
37A3 **La Seyne** France
25E5 **Las Flores** Arg
63E2 **Lash-e-Joveyn** Afghan
55B1 **Lashio** Burma
40D3 **La Sila** *Mts* Italy
63C1 **Lāsjerd** Iran
60A2 **Laskar Grah** Afghan
28A3 **Las Lajas** Chile
39A2 **Las Marismas** *Marshland* Spain
22B1 **La Soledad** Mexico
57B3 **Lasolo** Indon
57B3 **Lasolo** *R* Indon
70A2 **Las Palmas de Gran Canaria** Canary Is
40B2 **La Spezia** Italy
8C3 **Las Cruces** USA
28D2 **Las Piedras** Urug
25C6 **Las Plumas** Arg
28C2 **Las Rosas** Arg
18B2 **Lassen Peak** *Mt* USA
18B2 **Lassen Volcanic Nat Pk** USA
28C1 **Las Termas** Arg
22C2 **Las Tinaja** Mexico
28C1 **Las Tinajos** Arg
3G3 **Last Mountain L** Can
28D1 **Las Toscas** Arg
72B4 **Lastoursville** Gabon
40D2 **Lastovo** *I* Croatia, Yugos
21B2 **Las Tres Marias** *Is* Mexico
22A1 **Las Varas** Mexico
28C2 **Las Varillas** Arg
8C3 **Las Vegas** New Mexico, USA
8B3 **Las Vegas** Nevada, USA
Latakia = Al Lādhiqīyah
40C2 **Latina** Italy
28B2 **La Toma** Arg
26E1 **La Tortuga** *I* Ven
57F7 **La Trinidad** Phil
75E3 **Latrobe** Aust
28B1 **La Troya** *R* Arg
65C3 **Latrun** Israel
7L5 **La Tuque** Can
62B1 **Lātūr** India
44C4 **Latvia** *Republic* Europe
35B4 **Laugh Allen** *L* Irish Rep
35B5 **Laugh Boderg** *L* Irish Rep
35B5 **Laugh Bouna** *L* Irish Rep
35B4 **Laugh Carlingford** *L* N Ire
35B5 **Laugh Derravaragh** *L* Irish Rep
35B4 **Laugh Erne** *L* N Ire
35B4 **Laugh Oughter** *L* Irish Rep
35B5 **Laugh Ree** *L* Irish Rep
35B5 **Laugh Sheelin** *L* Irish Rep
77H2 **Lau Group** *Is* Fiji
76D5 **Launceston** Aust
35C6 **Launceston** Eng
25B6 **La Unión** Chile
21D3 **La Union** El Salvador
22B2 **La Union** Mexico
26C5 **La Unión** Peru
76D2 **Laura** Aust
13D3 **Laurel** Delaware, USA
14B3 **Laurel** Maryland, USA
9E3 **Laurel** Mississippi, USA
18E1 **Laurel** Montana, USA
15C2 **Laurens** USA
5G4 **Laurentides Prov Park** Can
3H2 **Laurie L** Can
15D2 **Laurinburg** USA
40B1 **Lausanne** Switz
56E3 **Laut** *I* Indon
25B7 **Lautaro** Chile
36E1 **Lauterbach** Germany
36D2 **Lauterecken** Germany
77G2 **Lautoka** *I* Fiji
5G4 **Laval** Can
38B2 **Laval** France
20B2 **Laveaga Peak** *Mt* USA
37C2 **Laveno** Italy
22B1 **La Ventura** Mexico
29A4 **La Verá** Par
4F4 **La Verendrye Prov Park** Can
18E1 **Lavina** USA
36C2 **La Vôge** Region, France
27K8 **Lavras** Brazil
28E2 **Lavras do Sul** Brazil
10D2 **Lavrentiya** Russian Fed
74E2 **Lavumisa** Swaziland
56E2 **Lawas** Malay
67E4 **Lawdar** Yemen
57B4 **Lawele** Indon
55B1 **Lawksawk** Burma
71F3 **Lawra** Ghana
17C2 **Lawrence** Kansas, USA
13E2 **Lawrence** Massachusetts, USA
78A3 **Lawrence** NZ
15B1 **Lawrenceburg** USA
12B3 **Lawrenceville** Illinois, USA
14B2 **Lawrenceville** Pennsylvania, USA
8D3 **Lawton** USA
67E2 **Layla** S Arabia
72D3 **Laylo** Sudan
53E1 **Lazarev** Russian Fed
22B2 **Lázaro Cárdenas** Mexico
57F9 **Lazi** Phil
53C3 **Lazo** Russian Fed
8C2 **Lead** USA
3G3 **Leader** Can
16A2 **Leadville** USA
15B2 **Leaf** *R* USA
16C4 **Leakey** USA
28D1 **Leandro N Alem** Arg
17C2 **Leavenworth** USA
43D2 **Leba** Pol
16C2 **Lebanon** Kansas, USA
17D2 **Lebanon** Missouri, USA
18B2 **Lebanon** Oregon, USA
13D2 **Lebanon** Pennsylvania, USA
64C3 **Lebanon** Republic, S W Asia
12B3 **Lebanon** Tennessee, USA
20C3 **Lebec** USA
73D6 **Lebombo** *Mts* Mozam/S Africa/Swaziland
43D2 **Lebork** Pol
37B2 **Le Bourg-d'Oisans** France
37B1 **Le Brassus** Switz
25B5 **Lebu** Chile
37B1 **Le Buet** *Mt* France
36B1 **Le Cateau** France
41D2 **Lecce** Italy
40B1 **Lecco** Italy
37D1 **Lech** *R* Austria
36D2 **Le Champ de Feu** *Mt* France
37D1 **Lechtaler Alpen** *Mts* Austria
38C2 **Le Creusot** France
35D5 **Ledbury** Eng
61E2 **Ledo** India
3F3 **Leduc** Can
14D1 **Lee** USA
11D2 **Leech L** USA
33C3 **Leeds** Eng
35D5 **Leek** Eng
42B2 **Leer** Germany
15C3 **Leesburg** Florida, USA
14B3 **Leesburg** Virginia, USA
17D3 **Leesville** USA
75C2 **Leeton** Aust
74C3 **Leeugamka** S Africa
42B2 **Leeuwarden** Neth
76A4 **Leeuwin,C** Aust
20C2 **Lee Vining** USA
23E3 **Leeward Is** Caribbean
65B1 **Lefka** Cyprus
65B1 **Lefkara** Cyprus
65B1 **Lefkoniko** Cyprus
57F8 **Legazpi** Phil
37D2 **Legnago** Italy
42D2 **Legnica** Pol
36A3 **Le Grand-Luce** France
37A2 **Le Grand Veymont** *Mt* France
26D4 **Legulzamo** Colombia
27G2 **Legvan Inlet** Guyana
60D2 **Leh** India
38C2 **Le Havre** France
19D2 **Lehi** USA
14C2 **Lehigh** *R* USA
14C2 **Lehighton** USA
36D2 **Le Hohneck** *Mt* France
60C2 **Leiah** Pak
42D3 **Leibnitz** Austria
35E5 **Leicester** County, Eng
35E5 **Leicester** Eng
76C2 **Leichhardt** *R* Aust
42A2 **Leiden** Neth
36B1 **Leie** *R* Belg
76C4 **Leigh Creek** Aust
35E6 **Leighton Buzzard** Eng
42B2 **Leine** *R* Germany
35B5 **Leinster** Region, Irish Rep
42C2 **Leipzig** Germany
39A2 **Leiria** Port
32F7 **Leirvik** Nor
52C4 **Leiyang** China
52B5 **Leizhou Bandao** *Pen* China
52C5 **Leizhou Wan** *B* China
42A2 **Lek** *R* Neth
57B3 **Lekitobi** Indon
57C3 **Leksula** Indon
17D3 **Leland** USA
37B3 **Le Lavendou** France
41D2 **Lelija** *Mt* Bosnia & Herzegovina, Yugos
37B1 **Le Locle** France
36A3 **Le Lude** France
22B1 **Lema** *R* Mexico
38C2 **Le Mans** France
11C3 **Le Mars** USA
18D2 **Lemhi Range** *Mts* USA
7M3 **Lemieux Is** Can
8C2 **Lemmon** USA
19D4 **Lemmon,Mt** USA
35G5 **Lemon Bank** *Oilfield* N Sea
19C3 **Lemoore** USA
38C2 **Lempdes** France
61D3 **Lemro** *R* Burma
40D2 **Le Murge** Region, Italy
49O3 **Lena** *R* Russian Fed
37E1 **Lend** Austria
44E3 **Lendery** Russian Fed
52C4 **Lengshujiang** China
45G7 **Leninakan** Armenia
Leningrad = Sankt Peterburg
79F7 **Leningradskaya** *Base* Ant
44J5 **Leninogorsk** Tatar ASSR, Russian Fed
50B1 **Leninogorsk** Kazakhstan
48K4 **Leninsk-Kuznetskiy** Russian Fed
53C2 **Leninskoye** Russian Fed
45H8 **Lenkoran'** Azerbaijan
36E1 **Lenne** *R* Germany
15C1 **Lenoir** USA
14D1 **Lenox** USA
36B1 **Lens** France
49N3 **Lensk** Russian Fed
40C3 **Lentini** Italy
55B3 **Lenya** *R* Burma
71F3 **Léo** Burkina
40C1 **Leoben** Austria
35D5 **Leominster** Eng
14E1 **Leominster** USA
21B2 **Leon** Mexico
26A1 **León** Nic
39A1 **Leon** Region, Spain
39A1 **León** Spain
22C1 **León** State, Mexico
74B1 **Leonardville** Namibia
65C1 **Leonarisso** Cyprus
53E2 **Leonidovo** Russian Fed
76B3 **Leonora** Aust
29D3 **Leopoldina** Brazil
Léopoldville = Kinshasa
44D5 **Lepel** Belorussia
36B1 **Leper** Belg
52D4 **Leping** China
38C2 **Le Puy** France
71F4 **Léraba** *R* Ivory Coast
72B3 **Léré** Chad
74D2 **Leribe** Lesotho
37C2 **Lerici** Italy
39C1 **Lérida** Spain
37D1 **Lermoos** Austria
41F3 **Léros** *I* Greece
14B1 **Le Roy** USA
33C1 **Lerwick** Scot
36A2 **Les Andelys** France
37B3 **Les Arcs** France
23C3 **Les Cayes** Haiti
37A2 **Les Echelles** France
37B2 **Les Ecrins** *Mt* France
5H4 **Les Escoumins** Can
52A4 **Leshan** China
41E2 **Leskovac** Serbia, Yugos
38B3 **Les Landes** Region, France
74D2 **Leslie** S Africa
44J4 **Lesnoy** Russian Fed
53E2 **Lesogorsk** Russian Fed
49L4 **Lesosibirsk** Russian Fed
74D2 **Lesotho** Kingdom, S Africa
53C2 **Lesozavodsk** Russian Fed
38B2 **Les Sables-d'Olonne** France
79E **Lesser Antarctica** Region, Ant
23D4 **Lesser Antilles** *Is* Caribbean
3F2 **Lesser Slave L** Can
37B2 **Les Trois Evêchés** *Mt* France
41F3 **Lésvos** *I* Greece
42D2 **Leszno** Pol
74E1 **Letaba** *R* S Africa
74D1 **Lethakeng** Botswana
61D3 **Letha Range** *Mts* Burma
6G5 **Lethbridge** Can
27G3 **Lethem** Guyana
57C4 **Leti** *I* Indon
43F3 **Letichev** Ukraine
56C2 **Letong** Indon
35F6 **le Touquet-Paris-Plage** France
55B2 **Letpadan** Burma
38C1 **Le Tréport** France
37B1 **Leuk** Switz
42A2 **Leuven** Belg
41E3 **Levádhia** Greece
32G6 **Levanger** Nor
37B2 **Levanna** *Mt* Italy
37C2 **Levanto** Italy
16B3 **Levelland** USA
37B3 **Levens** France
76B2 **Lévêque,C** Aust
36D1 **Leverkusen** Germany
43D3 **Levice** Czech
37D2 **Levico** Italy
78C2 **Levin** NZ
7L5 **Lévis** Can
13E2 **Levittown** USA
41E3 **Lévka Óri** *Mt* Greece
41E3 **Levkás** Greece
41E3 **Levkás** *I* Greece
41F2 **Levski** Bulg
35F6 **Lewes** Eng
16C2 **Lewis** USA
33B2 **Lewis** *I* Scot
14B2 **Lewisburg** USA
78B2 **Lewis P** NZ
5K4 **Lewisporte** Can
8B2 **Lewis Range** *Mts* USA
15B2 **Lewis Smith,L** USA
8B2 **Lewiston** Idaho, USA
9F2 **Lewiston** Maine, USA
8C2 **Lewistown** Montana, USA
13D2 **Lewistown** Pennsylvania, USA
17D3 **Lewisville** USA
9E3 **Lexington** Kentucky, USA
17D2 **Lexington** Missouri, USA
15C1 **Lexington** N Carolina, USA
16C1 **Lexington** Nebraska, USA
13D3 **Lexington** Virginia, USA
13D3 **Lexington Park** USA
57G8 **Leyte G** Phil
41D2 **Lezhe** Alb
59H2 **Lhasa** China
61C2 **Lhazê** China
56A1 **Lhokseumawe** Indon
61D2 **Lhozhag** China
50C4 **Lhunze** China
Liancourt Rocks = Tok-do
57G9 **Lianga** Phil
52B3 **Liangdang** China
52C5 **Lianjiang** China
52C5 **Lianping** China
52C5 **Lian Xian** China
52D3 **Lianyungang** China
52E1 **Liaoding Bandao** *Pen* China
52E1 **Liaodong Wan** *B* China
52E1 **Liao He** *R* China
52E1 **Liaoning** Province, China
52E1 **Liaoyang** China
52E1 **Liaoyuan** China
6F3 **Liard** *R* Can
6F4 **Liard River** Can
36C2 **Liart** France
18C1 **Libby** USA
72B3 **Libenge** Zaïre
8C3 **Liberal** USA
42C2 **Liberec** Czech
70A4 **Liberia** Republic, Africa
17D2 **Liberty** Missouri, USA
13E2 **Liberty** New York, USA
14B2 **Liberty** Pennsylvania, USA
17D3 **Liberty** Texas, USA
38B3 **Libourne** France
22C2 **Libres** Mexico
72A3 **Libreville** Gabon
69A2 **Libya** Republic, Africa
69B2 **Libyan Desert** Libya
69B1 **Libyan Plat** Egypt
40C3 **Licata** Italy
35E5 **Lichfield** Eng
73D5 **Lichinga** Mozam
74D2 **Lichtenburg** S Africa
12C3 **Licking** *R* USA
20B2 **Lick Observatory** USA
44D5 **Lida** Belorussia
20D2 **Lida** USA
32G7 **LidKöping** Sweden
40C2 **Lido di Ostia** Italy
40B1 **Liechtenstein** Principality, Europe
42B2 **Liège** Belg
43E1 **Lielupe** *R* Latvia
72C3 **Lienart** Zaïre
42C3 **Lienz** Austria
32J7 **Liepāja** Latvia
36C1 **Lier** Belg
37B1 **Liestal** Switz
42C3 **Liezen** Austria
35B5 **Liffey** *R* Irish Rep
34B4 **Lifford** Irish Rep
77F3 **Lifu** *I* Nouvelle Calédonie
75C1 **Lightning Ridge** Aust
36C2 **Ligny-en-Barrois** France
73D5 **Ligonha** *R* Mozam
37C2 **Liguria** Region, Italy
40B2 **Ligurian** *S* Italy
77E1 **Lihir Group** *Is* PNG
20E5 **Lihue** Hawaiian Is
73C5 **Likasi** Zaïre
57C2 **Likupang** Indon
38C1 **Lille** France
36A2 **Lillebonne** France
32G6 **Lillehammer** Nor
36B1 **Lillers** France
32G6 **Lillestøm** Nor
3D3 **Lillooet** Can
3D3 **Lillooet** *R* Can
73D5 **Lilongwe** Malawi
57F9 **Liloy** Phil
41D2 **Lim** *R* Montenegro/Serbia, Yugos
26C6 **Lima** Peru
39A1 **Lima** Spain
9E2 **Lima** USA
18D2 **Lima Res** USA

Limassol **Lubefu**

64B3 **Limassol** Cyprus
34B4 **Limavady** N Ire
28B3 **Limay** *R* Arg
28B3 **Limay Mahuida** Arg
73D5 **Limbe** Malawi
57B2 **Limbotto** Indon
42B2 **Limburg** W Gem
27J8 **Limeira** Brazil
33B3 **Limerick** Irish Rep
42B1 **Limfjorden** *L* Den
76C2 **Limmen Bight** *B* Aust
41F3 **Limnos** *I* Greece
27L5 **Limoeiro** Brazil
38C2 **Limoges** France
21D4 **Limón** Costa Rica
8C3 **Limon** USA
37B2 **Limone** Italy
38C2 **Limousin** Region, France
74E1 **Limpopo** *R* Mozam
22C1 **Linanes** Mexico
57E8 **Linapacan Str** Phil
25B5 **Linares** Chile
8D4 **Linares** Mexico
39B2 **Linares** Spain
50C4 **Lincang** China
25D4 **Lincoln** Arg
17C1 **Lincoln** California, USA
35E5 **Lincoln** County, Eng
35E5 **Lincoln** Eng
12B2 **Lincoln** Illinois, USA
13F1 **Lincoln** Maine, USA
8D2 **Lincoln** Nebraska, USA
13E2 **Lincoln** New Hampshire, USA
78B2 **Lincoln** NZ
79A **Lincoln** *S* Greenland
18B2 **Lincoln City** USA
12C2 **Lincoln Park** USA
40B2 **L'Incudina** *Mt* Corse
42B3 **Lindau** Germany
27G2 **Linden** Guyana
32F7 **Lindesnes** *C* Nor
73D4 **Lindi** Tanz
72C3 **Lindi** *R* Zaïre
74D2 **Lindley** S Africa
41F3 **Lindos** Greece
4F5 **Lindsay** Can
20C2 **Lindsay** California, USA
11A2 **Lindsay** Montana, USA
xxixM4 **Line Is** Pacific O
52C2 **Linfen** China
55D2 **Lingao** China
57F7 **Lingayen** Phil
42B2 **Lingen** Germany
11B3 **Lingle** USA
52C4 **Lingling** China
52B5 **Lingshan** China
52C2 **Lingshi** China
70A3 **Linguère** Sen
53A1 **Linhai** Heilongjiang, China
52E4 **Linhai** Rhejiang, China
27L7 **Linhares** Brazil
52B1 **Linhe** China
53B3 **Linjiang** China
32H7 **Linköping** Sweden
53C2 **Linkou** China
52D2 **Linqing** China
29C3 **Lins** Brazil
52A2 **Lintao** China
37C1 **Linthal** Switz
11B2 **Linton** USA
50E2 **Linxi** China
52A2 **Linxia** China
42C3 **Linz** Austria
57F8 **Lipa** Phil
40C3 **Lipari** *I* Italy
45F5 **Lipetsk** Russian Fed
41E1 **Lipova** Rom
42B2 **Lippe** *R* Germany
36E1 **Lippstadt** Germany
72D3 **Lira** Uganda
72B4 **Liranga** Congo
72C3 **Lisala** Zaïre
39A2 **Lisboa** Port
Lisbon = Lisboa
11C2 **Lisbon** USA
35B4 **Lisburn** N Ire
10E2 **Lisburne,C** USA
52D4 **Lishui** China
52C4 **Li Shui** *R* China
45F6 **Lisichansk** Ukraine
38C2 **Lisieux** France
45F5 **Liski** Russian Fed
36B2 **L'Isle-Adam** France
37B1 **L'Isle-sur-le-Doubs** France
77E3 **Lismore** Aust
52B5 **Litang** China
65C2 **Lītanī** *R* Leb
27H3 **Litani** *R* Surinam
12B3 **Litchfield** Illinois, USA
11D2 **Litchfield** Minnesota, USA
76E4 **Lithgow** Aust
44C4 **Lithuania** *Republic* Europe
14B2 **Lititz** USA
53E1 **Litke** Russian Fed
53D2 **Litovko** Russian Fed
17C3 **Little** *R* USA
9F4 **Little Abaco** *I* Bahamas
66D4 **Little Aden** Yemen
62E2 **Little Andaman** *I* Andaman Is
78C1 **Little Barrier I** NZ
18D1 **Little Belt Mts** USA
65B3 **Little Bitter L** Egypt
3F3 **Little Bow** *R* Can
21D3 **Little Cayman** *I* Caribbean
4D3 **Little Current** Can
4E4 **Little Current** Can
14C3 **Little Egg Harbor** *B* USA
11D2 **Little Falls** Minnesota, USA
14C1 **Little Falls** New York, USA
16B3 **Littlefield** USA
11D2 **Littlefork** USA
11D2 **Little Fork** *R* USA
4B3 **Little Grand Rapids** Can
34E2 **Little Halibut Bank** *Sand-bank* Scot
23C2 **Little Inagua** *I* Caribbean
74C3 **Little Karroo** *R* S Africa
10G4 **Little Koniuji** *I* USA
20D3 **Little Lake** USA
11B2 **Little Missouri** *R* USA
55A4 **Little Nicobar** *I* Nicobar Is
9D3 **Little Rock** USA
20D3 **Littlerock** USA
10B6 **Little Sitkin** *I* USA
3E3 **Little Smoky** Can
3E3 **Little Smoky** *R* Can
14B3 **Littlestown** USA
10C6 **Little Tanaga** *I* USA
16A2 **Littleton** Colorado, USA
13E2 **Littleton** New Hampshire, USA
53B3 **Liuhe** China
52B5 **Liuzhou** China
41E3 **Livanátais** Greece
43F1 **Līvāni** Latvia
36A2 **Livarot** France
10J2 **Livengood** USA
37E2 **Livenza** *R* Italy
15C2 **Live Oak** USA
19B3 **Livermore** USA
16B3 **Livermore,Mt** USA
7M5 **Liverpool** Can
35D5 **Liverpool** Eng
6E2 **Liverpool B** Can
35D5 **Liverpool B** Eng
7L2 **Liverpool,C** Can
75D2 **Liverpool Range** *Mts* Aust
8B2 **Livingston** Montana, USA
15B1 **Livingston** Tennessee, USA
17D3 **Livingston** Texas, USA
73C5 **Livingstone** Zambia
17C3 **Livingston,L** USA
40D2 **Livno** Bosnia & Herzegovina, Yugos
45F5 **Livny** Russian Fed
12C2 **Livonia** USA
40C2 **Livorno** Italy
29D1 **Livramento do Brumado** Brazil
73D4 **Liwale** Tanz
35C7 **Lizard Pt** Eng
40C1 **Ljubljana** Slovenia, Yugos
32G6 **Ljungan** *R* Sweden
32G7 **Ljungby** Sweden
32H6 **Ljusdal** Sweden
44B3 **Ljusnan** *R* Sweden
35D6 **Llandeilo** Wales
35D6 **Llandovery** Wales
35D5 **Llandrindod Wells** Wales
35D5 **Llandudno** Wales
35C6 **Llanelli** Wales
35D5 **Llangollen** Wales
16C3 **Llano** USA
16C3 **Llano** *R* USA
8C3 **Llano Estacado** *Plat* USA
Z4D2 **Llanos** Region, Colombia/Ven
26F7 **Llanos de Chiquitos** Region, Bol
Lleida = Lérida
22C1 **Llera** Mexico
39A2 **Llerena** Spain
35C5 **Lleyn** *Pen* Wales
68E7 **Llorin** Nigeria
3C2 **Lloyd George,Mt** Can
3G2 **Lloyd L** Can
6H4 **Lloydminster** Can
25C2 **Llullaillaco** *Mt* Chile/Arg
25C2 **Loa** *R* Chile
38C2 **Loan** France
72B4 **Loange** *R* Zaïre
74D2 **Lobatse** Botswana
72B3 **Lobaye** *R* CAR
28D3 **Loberia** Arg
73B5 **Lobito** Angola
28D3 **Lobos** Arg
37B2 **Locano** Italy
37C1 **Locarno** Switz
34C3 **Loch Awe** *L* Scot
34B3 **Lochboisdale** Scot
34B3 **Loch Bracadale** *Inlet* Scot
34C3 **Loch Broom** *Estuary* Scot
34C4 **Loch Doon** *L* Scot
34C3 **Loch Earn** *L* Scot
34C2 **Loch Eriboll** *Inlet* Scot
34C3 **Loch Ericht** *L* Scot
38C2 **Loches** France
34C3 **Loch Etive** *Inlet* Scot
34C3 **Loch Ewe** *Inlet* Scot
34C3 **Loch Fyne** *Inlet* Scot
34C3 **Loch Hourn** *Inlet* Scot
34B4 **Loch Indaal** *Inlet* Scot
34C2 **Lochinver** Scot
34C3 **Loch Katrine** *L* Scot
34D3 **Loch Leven** *L* Scot
34C3 **Loch Linnhe** *Inlet* Scot
34C3 **Loch Lochy** *L* Scot
34C3 **Loch Lomond** *L* Scot
34C3 **Loch Long** *Inlet* Scot
34B3 **Lochmaddy** Scot
34C3 **Loch Maree** *L* Scot
34C3 **Loch Morar** *L* Scot
34D3 **Lochnagar** *Mt* Scot
34C3 **Loch Ness** *L* Scot
34C3 **Loch Rannoch** *L* Scot
34B2 **Loch Roag** *Inlet* Scot
18C1 **Lochsa** *R* USA
34C3 **Loch Sheil** *L* Scot
34C2 **Loch Shin** *L* Scot
34B3 **Loch Snizort** *Inlet* Scot
34C3 **Loch Sunart** *Inlet* Scot
34C3 **Loch Tay** *L* Scot
34C3 **Loch Torridon** *Inlet* Scot
75A2 **Lock** Aust
5H5 **Lockeport** Can
34D4 **Lockerbie** Scot
13D2 **Lock Haven** USA
13D2 **Lockport** USA
55D3 **Loc Ninh** Viet
40D3 **Locri** Italy
65C3 **Lod** Israel
75B3 **Loddon** *R* Aust
44E3 **Lodeynoye Pole** Russian Fed
18E1 **Lodge Grass** USA
60C3 **Lodhran** Pak
40B1 **Lodi** Italy
19B3 **Lodi** USA
72C4 **Lodja** Zaïre
37B1 **Lods** France
72D3 **Lodwar** Kenya
43D2 **Łódź** Pol
74B3 **Loeriesfontein** S Africa
37E1 **Lofer** Austria
32G5 **Lofoten** *Is* Nor
16B2 **Logan** New Mexico, USA
8B2 **Logan** Utah, USA
6D3 **Logan,Mt** Can
10N3 **Logan Mts** Can
12B2 **Logansport** Indiana, USA
17D3 **Logansport** Louisiana, USA
14B2 **Loganton** USA
39B1 **Logroño** Spain
61B3 **Lohārdaga** India
32J6 **Lohja** Fin
36E2 **Lohr** Germany
55B2 **Loikaw** Burma
32J6 **Loimaa** Fin
36B2 **Loing** *R* France
38C2 **Loir** *R* France
36A3 **Loir et Cher** Department, France
38C2 **Loire** *R* France
36B3 **Loiret** Department, France
26C4 **Loja** Ecuador
39B2 **Loja** Spain
57C3 **Loji** Indon
32K5 **Lokan Tekojärvi** *Res* Fin
36B1 **Lokeren** Belg
72D3 **Lokitaung** Kenya
43F1 **Loknya** Russian Fed
71H4 **Lokoja** Nig
72C4 **Lokolo** *R* Zaïre
72C4 **Lokoro** *R* Zaïre
7M3 **Loks Land** *I* Can
42C2 **Lolland** *I* Den
57C2 **Loloda** Indon
18D1 **Lolo P** USA
41E2 **Lom** Bulg
71J4 **Lom** *R* Cam
73C4 **Lomami** *R* Zaïre
70A4 **Loma Mts** Sierra Leone/Guinea
57B2 **Lombagin** Indon
37C2 **Lombardia** Region, Italy
57B4 **Lomblen** *I* Indon
56E4 **Lombok** *I* Indon
71G4 **Lomé** Togo
72C4 **Lomela** Zaïre
72C4 **Lomela** *R* Zaïre
34G3 **Lomond** *Oilfield* N Sea
44D4 **Lomonosov** Russian Fed
37B1 **Lomont** Region, France
19B4 **Lompoc** USA
43E2 **Łomza** Pol
62A1 **Lonāvale** India
25B5 **Loncoche** Chile
7K5 **London** Can
35E6 **London** Eng
12C3 **London** USA
34B4 **Londonderry** County, N Ire
34B4 **Londonderry** N Ire
25B9 **Londonderry** *I* Chile
76B2 **Londonderry,C** Aust
25C3 **Londres** Arg
25F2 **Londrina** Brazil
20D1 **Lone Mt** USA
20C2 **Lone Pine** USA
9F4 **Long** *I* Bahamas
51H7 **Long** *I* PNG
56D2 **Long Akah** Malay
37E1 **Longarone** Italy
28A3 **Longavi** *Mt* Chile
23H2 **Long B** Jamaica
15D2 **Long B** USA
8B3 **Long Beach** California, USA
13E2 **Long Beach** New York, USA
13E2 **Long Branch** USA
52D5 **Longchuan** China
18C2 **Long Creek** USA
75E3 **Longford** Aust
35B5 **Longford** County, Irish Rep
35B5 **Longford** Irish Rep
34E3 **Long Forties** *Region* N Sea
52D1 **Longhua** China
7L4 **Long I** Can
76D1 **Long I** PNG
9F2 **Long I** USA
14D2 **Long Island Sd** USA
53A2 **Longjiang** China
4D4 **Long L** Can
11B2 **Long L** USA
7K5 **Longlac** Can
52B5 **Longlin** China
8C2 **Longmont** USA
56E2 **Longnawan** Indon
36C2 **Longny** France
11D2 **Long Prairie** USA
25B5 **Longquimay** Chile
5K4 **Long Range Mts** Can
76D3 **Longreach** Aust
52A2 **Longshou Shan** *Upland* China
16A1 **Longs Peak** *Mt* USA
34D4 **Longtown** Eng
13E1 **Longueuil** Can
28A3 **Longuimay** Chile
36C2 **Longuyon** France
9D3 **Longview** Texas, USA
8A2 **Longview** Washington, USA
38D2 **Longwy** France
52A3 **Longxi** China
55D3 **Long Xuyen** Viet
52D4 **Longyan** China
52B5 **Longzhou** China
37D2 **Lonigo** Italy
38D2 **Lons-le-Saunier** France
9F3 **Lookout,C** USA
72D4 **Loolmalasin** *Mt* Tanz
3E2 **Loon** *R* Can
55C3 **Lop Buri** Thai
72A4 **Lopez** *C* Gabon
50C2 **Lop Nur** *L* China
39A2 **Lora del Rio** Spain
9E2 **Lorain** USA
60B2 **Loralai** Pak
63C2 **Lordegān** Iran
77E4 **Lord Howe** *I* Aust
xxixK5 **Lord Howe Rise** Pacific O
7J3 **Lord Mayor B** Can
8C3 **Lordsburg** USA
29C3 **Lorena** Brazil
37E2 **Loreo** Italy
22B1 **Loreto** Mexico
38B2 **Lorient** France
75B3 **Lorne** Aust
42B3 **Lörrach** Germany
38D2 **Lorraine** *Region* France
8C3 **Los Alamos** USA
28A2 **Los Andes** Chile
25B5 **Los Angeles** Chile
8B3 **Los Angeles** USA
20C3 **Los Angeles Aqueduct** USA
19B3 **Los Banos** USA
28B2 **Los Cerrillos** Arg
22A1 **Los Corchos** Mexico
19B3 **Los Gatos** USA
40C2 **Lozinj** *I* Croatia, Yugos
28C1 **Los Juries** Arg
28A3 **Los Lagos** Chile
22C1 **Los Laiaderoz** Mexico
28A1 **Los Loros** Chile
16A3 **Los Luncas** USA
28B4 **Los Menucos** Arg
21B2 **Los Mochis** Mexico
20B3 **Los Olivos** USA
28A3 **Los Sauces** Chile
34D3 **Lossiemouth** Scot
28C1 **Los Telares** Arg
23E4 **Los Testigos** *Is* Ven
20C3 **Lost Hills** USA
18D1 **Lost Trail P** USA
25B4 **Los Vilos** Chile
38C3 **Lot** *R* France
28A3 **Lota** Chile
34D4 **Lothian** Region, Scot
72D3 **Lotikipi Plain** Sudan/Kenya
72C4 **Loto** Zaïre
74D1 **Lotsane** *R* Botswana
37B1 **Lötschberg Tunnel** Switz
32K5 **Lotta** *R* Fin/Russian Fed
38B2 **Loudéac** France
70A3 **Louga** Sen
33B3 **Lough Allen** *L* Irish Rep
35E5 **Loughborough** Eng
33B3 **Lough Conn** *L* Irish Rep
33B3 **Lough Corrib** *L* Irish Rep
33B3 **Lough Derg** *L* Irish Rep
6H2 **Lougheed I** Can
35B5 **Lough Ennell** *L* Irish Rep
33B3 **Lough Erne** *L* N Ire
33B2 **Lough Foyle** *Estuary* N Ire/Irish Rep
33B3 **Lough Neagh** *L* N Ire
33B3 **Lough Ree** *L* Irish Rep
35C4 **Lough Strangford** *L* Irish Rep
34B4 **Lough Swilly** *Estuary* Irish Rep
37A1 **Louhans** France
12C3 **Louisa** USA
56D1 **Louisa Reef** *I* S E Asia
10M5 **Louise** *I* Can
10J3 **Louise,L** USA
77E2 **Louisiade Arch** Solomon Is
9D3 **Louisiana** State, USA
74D1 **Louis Trichardt** S Africa
15C2 **Louisville** Georgia, USA
9E3 **Louisville** Kentucky, USA
15B2 **Louisville** Mississippi, USA
44E2 **Loukhi** Russian Fed
11D1 **Lount L** Can
37B3 **Loup** *R* France
16C1 **Loup** *R* USA
38B3 **Lourdes** France
75C2 **Louth** Aust
35B5 **Louth** County, Irish Rep
35E5 **Louth** Eng
Louvain = Leuven
38C2 **Louviers** France
44E4 **Lovat** *R* Russian Fed
41E2 **Lovech** Bulg
16A1 **Loveland** USA
16A2 **Loveland P** USA
18E2 **Lovell** USA
19C2 **Lovelock** USA
40C1 **Lóvere** Italy
16B3 **Lovington** USA
44F2 **Lovozero** Russian Fed
7K3 **Low,C** Can
9F2 **Lowell** Massachusetts, USA
18B2 **Lowell** Oregon, USA
14E1 **Lowell** USA
18C1 **Lower Arrow L** Can
78B2 **Lower Hutt** NZ
20A1 **Lower Lake** USA
10N4 **Lower Post** Can
11C2 **Lower Red L** USA
35F5 **Lowestoft** Eng
43D2 **Łowicz** Pol
75B2 **Loxton** Aust
74C3 **Loxton** S Africa
14B2 **Loyalsock Creek** *R* USA
41D2 **Loznica** Serbia, Yugos
22B2 **loz Reyes** Mexico
48H3 **Lozva** *R* Russian Fed
73C5 **Luacano** Angola
73C4 **Luachimo** Angola
72C4 **Lualaba** *R* Zaïre
73C5 **Luampa** Zambia
73C5 **Luân** Angola
52D3 **Lu'an** China
73B4 **Luanda** Angola
73B5 **Luando** *R* Angola
73C5 **Luanginga** *R* Angola
55C1 **Luang Namtha** Laos
55C2 **Luang Prabang** Laos
73B4 **Luangue** *R* Angola
73D5 **Luangwa** *R* Zambia
52D1 **Luan He** *R* China
52D1 **Luanping** China
73C5 **Luanshya** Zambia
73C5 **Luapula** *R* Zaïre
39A1 **Luarca** Spain
73B4 **Lubalo** Angola
43F2 **L'uban** Belorussia
57F8 **Lubang Is** Phil
73B5 **Lubango** Angola
8C3 **Lubbock** USA
42C2 **Lübeck** Germany
72C4 **Lubefu** Zaïre

Lubefu **Makumbi**

72C4 **Lubefu** *R* Zaïre
72C3 **Lubero** Zaïre
37A3 **Lubéron** *R* France
73C4 **Lubilash** *R* Zaïre
43E2 **Lublin** Pol
45E5 **Lubny** Ukraine
56D2 **Lubok Antu** Malay
73C4 **Lubudi** Zaïre
73C4 **Lubudi** *R* Zaïre
56B3 **Lubuklinggau** Indon
73C5 **Lubumbashi** Zaïre
72C4 **Lubutu** Zaïre
29A1 **Lucas** Brazil
57F8 **Lucban** Phil
40C2 **Lucca** Italy
34C4 **Luce** *B* Scot
17E3 **Lucedale** USA
57F8 **Lucena** Phil
43D3 **Lucenec** Czech
Lucerne = Luzern
16A3 **Lucero** Mexico
53C2 **Luchegorsk** Russian Fed
52C5 **Luchuan** China
20B2 **Lucia** USA
42C2 **Luckenwalde** Germany
74C2 **Luckhoff** S Africa
61B2 **Lucknow** India
73C5 **Lucusse** Angola
50E2 **Lüda** China
36D1 **Lüdenscheid** Germany
74B2 **Lüderitz** Namibia
60D2 **Ludhiana** India
12B2 **Ludington** USA
19C4 **Ludlow** California, USA
35D5 **Ludlow** Eng
14D1 **Ludlow** Vermont, USA
41F2 **Ludogorie** *Upland* Bulg
15C2 **Ludowici** USA
41E1 **Luduş** Rom
32H6 **Ludvika** Sweden
42B3 **Ludwigsburg** Germany
42B3 **Ludwigshafen** Germany
42C2 **Ludwigslust** Germany
72C4 **Luebo** Zaïre
72C4 **Luema** *R* Zaïre
73C4 **Luembe** *R* Angola
73B5 **Luena** Angola
73C5 **Luene** *R* Angola
52B3 **Lüeyang** China
52D5 **Lufeng** China
9D3 **Lufkin** USA
44D4 **Luga** Russian Fed
44D4 **Luga** *R* Russian Fed
40B1 **Lugano** Switz
45F6 **Lugansk** Ukraine
73D5 **Lugela** Mozam
73D5 **Lugenda** *R* Mozam
37D2 **Lugo** Italy
39A1 **Lugo** Spain
41E1 **Lugoj** Rom
52A3 **Luhuo** China
73B4 **Lui** *R* Angola
73C5 **Luiana** Angola
73C5 **Luiana** *R* Angola
Luichow Peninsula = Leizhou Bandao
37C2 **Luino** Italy
72B3 **Luionga** *R* Zaïre
52B2 **Luipan Shan** *Upland* China
44D2 **Luiro** *R* Fin
73C5 **Luishia** Zaïre
50C4 **Luixi** China
73C4 **Luiza** Zaïre
28B2 **Luján** Arg
28D2 **Luján** Arg
52D3 **Lujiang** China
72B4 **Lukenie** *R* Zaïre
19D4 **Lukeville** USA
72B4 **Lukolela** Zaïre
43E2 **Luków** Pol
72C4 **Lukuga** *R* Zaïre
73C5 **Lukulu** Zambia
44C2 **Lule** *R* Sweden
32J5 **Luleå** Sweden
41F2 **Lüleburgaz** Turk
52C2 **Lüliang Shan** *Mts* China
17C4 **Luling** USA
26E8 **Lullaillaco** *Mt* Chile
72C3 **Lulonga** *R* Zaïre
Luluabourg = Kananga
73C5 **Lumbala Kaquengue** Angola
9F3 **Lumberton** USA
56E2 **Lumbis** Indon
44G2 **Lumbovka** Russian Fed
61D2 **Lumding** India
73C5 **Lumeje** Angola
78A3 **Lumsden** NZ
32G7 **Lund** Sweden
11C1 **Lundar** Can
73D5 **Lundazi** Zambia
73D6 **Lundi** *R* Zim
35C6 **Lundy** *I* Eng
42C2 **Lüneburg** Germany
36D2 **Lunéville** France
73C5 **Lunga** *R* Zambia
61D3 **Lunglei** India
73B5 **Lungue Bungo** *R* Angola
43F2 **Luninec** Belorussia
20C1 **Luning** USA
53C2 **Luobei** China
72B4 **Luobomo** Congo
52B5 **Luocheng** China
52C5 **Luoding** China
52C3 **Luohe** China
52C3 **Luo He** *R* Henan, China
52B2 **Luo He** *R* Shaanxi, China
52C4 **Luoxiao Shan** *Hills* China
52C3 **Luoyang** China
72B4 **Luozi** Zaïre
73C5 **Lupane** Zim
73D5 **Lupilichi** Mozam
Lu Qu = Tao He
25E3 **Luque** Par
36D3 **Lure** France
35B4 **Lurgan** N Ire
73D5 **Lurio** *R* Mozam
63B2 **Luristan** Region, Iran
73C5 **Lusaka** Zambia
72C4 **Lusambo** Zaïre
41D2 **Lushnjë** Alb
72D4 **Lushoto** Tanz
50C4 **Lushui** China
52E2 **Lüshun** China
11B3 **Lusk** USA
35E6 **Luton** Eng
45D5 **Lutsk** Ukraine
72E3 **Luuq** Somalia
11C3 **Luverne** USA
73C4 **Luvua** *R* Zaïre
73D4 **Luwegu** *R* Tanz
73D5 **Luwingu** Zambia
57B3 **Luwuk** Indon
36D2 **Luxembourg** Grand Duchy, N W Europe
38D2 **Luxembourg** Lux
36D3 **Luxeuil-les-Bains** France
52A5 **Luxi** China
69C2 **Luxor** Egypt
44H3 **Luza** Russian Fed
44H3 **Luza** *R* Russian Fed
40B1 **Luzern** Switz
14D1 **Luzerne** USA
52B5 **Luzhai** China
52B4 **Luzhi** China
52B4 **Luzhou** China
29C2 **Luziânia** Brazil
57F7 **Luzon** *I* Phil
57F6 **Luzon Str** Phil
43E3 **L'vov** Ukraine
34D2 **Lybster** Scot
32H6 **Lycksele** Sweden
73C6 **Lydenburg** S Africa
3B3 **Lyell I** Can
8B3 **Lyell,Mt** USA
14B2 **Lykens** USA
18D2 **Lyman** USA
35D6 **Lyme B** Eng
35D6 **Lyme Regis** Eng
9F3 **Lynchburg** USA
75A2 **Lyndhurst** Aust
13E2 **Lynn** USA
3A2 **Lynn Canal** *Sd* USA
15B2 **Lynn Haven** USA
3H2 **Lynn Lake** Can
4D3 **Lynx** Can
6H3 **Lynx L** Can
38C2 **Lyon** France
10L4 **Lyon Canal** *Sd* USA
15C2 **Lyons** Georgia, USA
14B1 **Lyons** New York, USA
76A3 **Lyons** *R* Aust
37B2 **Lys** *R* Italy
44K4 **Lys'va** Russian Fed
78B2 **Lyttelton** NZ
3D3 **Lytton** Can
20A1 **Lytton** USA
43F2 **Lyubeshov** Ukraine
44F4 **Lyublino** Russian Fed

M

55C1 **Ma** *R* Viet
65C2 **Ma'agan** Jordan
65C2 **Ma'alot Tarshīha** Israel
64C3 **Ma'an** Jordan
52D3 **Ma'anshan** China
65D1 **Ma'arrat an Nu'mān** Syria
36C1 **Maas** *R* Neth
36C1 **Maaseik** Belg
57F8 **Maasin** Phil
42B2 **Maastricht** Belg
74E1 **Mabalane** Mozam
27G2 **Mabaruma** Guyana
35F5 **Mablethorpe** Eng
73D6 **Mabote** Mozam
43E2 **Mabrita** Belorussia
43F2 **M'adel** Belorussia
29D3 **Macaé** Brazil
8D3 **McAlester** USA
8D4 **McAllen** USA
73D5 **Macaloge** Mozam
52C5 **Macao** Dependency, China
27H3 **Macapá** Brazil
29D2 **Macarani** Brazil
26C4 **Macas** Ecuador
27L5 **Macaú** Brazil
29D1 **Macaúbas** Brazil
72C3 **M'Bari** *R* CAR
3D3 **McBride** Can
18C2 **McCall** USA
16B3 **McCamey** USA
18D2 **McCammon** USA
10K3 **McCarthy** USA
3B3 **McCauley I** Can
35D5 **Macclesfield** Eng
7K1 **McClintock B** Can
6H2 **McClintock Chan** Can
14B2 **McClure** USA
20B2 **McClure,L** USA
6G2 **McClure Str** Can
17D3 **McComb** USA
16B1 **McConaughy,L** USA
14B3 **McConnellsburg** USA
8C2 **McCook** USA
7L2 **Macculloch,C** Can
3D2 **McCusker,Mt** Can
6F4 **McDame** Can
18C2 **McDermitt** USA
4D4 **Macdiarmid** Can
18D1 **Mcdonald Peak** *Mt* USA
76C3 **Macdonnell Ranges** *Mts* Aust
39A1 **Macedo de Cavaleiros** Port
41E2 **Macedonia** *Republic* Serbia, Yugos
27L5 **Maceió** Brazil
70B4 **Macenta** Guinea
40C2 **Macerata** Italy
3G2 **Macfarlane** *R* Can
75A2 **Macfarlane,L** Aust
17D3 **McGehee** USA
19D3 **McGill** USA
6C3 **McGrath** USA
18D1 **McGuire,Mt** USA
29C3 **Machado** Brazil
73D6 **Machaila** Mozam
72D4 **Machakos** Kenya
26C4 **Machala** Ecuador
73D6 **Machaze** Mozam
62B1 **Mācherla** India
65C2 **Machgharab** Leb
13F2 **Machias** USA
4C2 **Machichi** *R* Can
62C1 **Machilīpatnam** India
26D1 **Machiques** Ven
26D6 **Machu-Picchu** *Hist Site* Peru
73D6 **Macia** Mozam
Macias Nguema = Fernando Poo
11B2 **McIntosh** USA
75C1 **MacIntyre** *R* Aust
16A2 **Mack** USA
76D3 **Mackay** Aust
18D2 **Mackay** USA
76B3 **Mackay,L** Aust
77H1 **McKean** *I* Phoenix Is
13D2 **McKeesport** USA
3D2 **Mackenzie** Can
6F3 **Mackenzie** *R* Can
6E3 **Mackenzie B** Can
6G2 **Mackenzie King I** Can
6E3 **Mackenzie Mts** Can
12C1 **Mackinac,Str of** USA
12C1 **Mackinaw City** USA
10H3 **McKinley,Mt** USA
17C3 **McKinney** USA
7L2 **Mackinson Inlet** *B* Can
20C3 **McKittrick** USA
75D2 **Macksville** Aust
18B2 **Mclaoughlin,Mt** USA
11B2 **McLaughlin** USA
75D1 **Maclean** Aust
74D3 **Maclear** S Africa
6G4 **McLennan** Can
3E3 **McLeod** *R* Can
6G3 **McLeod B** Can
76A3 **McLeod,L** Aust
3D2 **McLeod Lake** Can
6E3 **Macmillan** *R* Can
16B3 **McMillan,L** USA
10M3 **Macmillan P** Can
18B1 **McMinnville** Oregon, USA
15B1 **McMinnville** Tennessee, USA
79F7 **McMurdo** *Base* Ant
3C2 **McNamara,Mt** Can
19E4 **McNary** USA
3E3 **McNaughton L** Can
12A2 **Macomb** USA
40B2 **Macomer** Sardegna
73D5 **Macomia** Mozam
38C2 **Mâcon** France
9E3 **Macon** Georgia, USA
17D2 **Macon** Missouri, USA
73C5 **Macondo** Angola
3H2 **Macoun L** Can
17C2 **McPherson** USA
xxviiiJ7 **Macquarie** *Is* Aust
75C2 **Macquarie** *R* Aust
75E3 **Macquarie Harbour** *B* Aust
75D2 **Macquarie,L** Aust
15C2 **McRae** USA
79F11 **Mac Robertson Land** Region, Ant
71E1 **M'saken** Tunisia
71C1 **M'Sila** Alg
6G3 **McTavish Arm** *B* Can
75A1 **Macumba** *R* Aust
37C2 **Macunaga** Italy
6F3 **McVicar Arm** *B* Can
42D3 **M'yaróvár** Hung
71H4 **Mada** *R* Nig
65C3 **Mādabā** Jordan
72C2 **Madadi** *Well* Chad
68J9 **Madagascar** *I* Indian O
xxviiiD6 **Madagascar Basin** Indian O
72B1 **Madama** Niger
76D1 **Madang** PNG
70C3 **Madaoua** Niger
61D3 **Madaripur** Bang
63C1 **Madau** Turkmenistan
5H4 **Madawaska** USA
13D1 **Madawaska** *R* Can
61E3 **Madaya** Burma
70A1 **Madeira** *I* Atlantic O
26F5 **Madeira** *R* Brazil
7M5 **Madeleine, Îles de la** Can
11D3 **Madelia** USA
21B2 **Madera** Mexico
19B3 **Madera** USA
62A1 **Madgaon** India
61C2 **Madhubani** India
61B3 **Madhya Pradesh** State, India
62B2 **Madikeri** India
72B4 **Madimba** Zaïre
72B4 **Madingo Kayes** Congo
72B4 **Madingou** Congo
9E3 **Madison** Indiana, USA
11C2 **Madison** Minnesota, USA
11C3 **Madison** Nebraska, USA
11C3 **Madison** S Dakota, USA
9E2 **Madison** Wisconsin, USA
18D1 **Madison** *R* USA
12B3 **Madisonville** Kentucky, USA
17C3 **Madisonville** Texas, USA
56D4 **Madiun** Indon
4F5 **Madoc** Can
72D3 **Mado Gashi** Kenya
37D1 **Madonna Di Campiglio** Italy
62C2 **Madras** India
18B2 **Madras** USA
25A8 **Madre de Dios** *I* Chile
26E6 **Madre de Dios** *R* Bol
39B1 **Madrid** Spain
39B2 **Madridejos** Spain
56D4 **Madura** *I* Indon
62B3 **Madurai** India
54C3 **Maebashi** Japan
55B3 **Mae Khlong** *R* Thai
55B4 **Mae Nam Lunang** *R* Thai
55C2 **Mae Nam Mun** *R* Thai
55B2 **Mae Nam Ping** *R* Thai
54A3 **Maengsan** N Korea
73E5 **Maevatanana** Madag
77F2 **Maewo** *I* Vanuatu
74D2 **Mafeking** S Africa
74D2 **Mafeteng** Lesotho
75C3 **Maffra** Aust
73D4 **Mafia** *I* Tanz
25G3 **Mafra** Brazil
64C3 **Mafraq** Jordan
49R4 **Magadan** Russian Fed
26D2 **Magargué** Colombia
71H3 **Magaria** Niger
53B1 **Magdagachi** Russian Fed
28D3 **Magdalena** Arg
8B3 **Magdalena** Mexico
16A3 **Magdalena** USA
23C4 **Magdalena** *R* Colombia
56E2 **Magdalena,Mt** Malay
42C2 **Magdeburg** Germany
26D2 **Magdelena** *R* Colombia
27K8 **Magé** Brazil
56D4 **Magelang** Indon
37C1 **Maggia** *R* Switz
64B4 **Maghâgha** Egypt
34B4 **Magherafelt** N Ire
41D2 **Maglie** Italy
44K5 **Magnitogorsk** Russian Fed
17D3 **Magnolia** USA
53E1 **Mago** Russian Fed
13E1 **Magog** Can
22C1 **Magosal** Mexico
5J3 **Magpie** *R* Can
37C2 **Magra** *R* Italy
3F3 **Magrath** Can
20D2 **Magruder Mt** USA
74E2 **Magude** Mozam
7J3 **Maguse River** Can
55B1 **Magwe** Burma
45H8 **Mahābād** Iran
61C2 **Mahabharat Range** *Mts* Nepal
62A1 **Mahād** India
60D4 **Mahadeo Hills** India
14A2 **Mahaffey** USA
73E5 **Mahajanga** Madag
74D1 **Mahalapye** Botswana
61B3 **Mahānadi** *R* India
73E5 **Mahanoro** Madag
14B2 **Mahanoy City** USA
62A1 **Maharashtra** State, India
61B3 **Māhāsamund** India
55C2 **Maha Sarakham** Thai
73E5 **Mahavavy** *R* Madag
62B1 **Mahbūbnagar** India
71E1 **Mahdia** Tunisia
62B2 **Mahe** India
60D4 **Mahekar** India
61B3 **Mahendragarh** India
73D4 **Mahenge** Tanz
60C4 **Mahesāna** India
78C1 **Mahia Pen** NZ
11C2 **Mahnomen** USA
60D3 **Mahoba** India
39C2 **Mahón** Spain
5J5 **Mahone B** Can
10N2 **Mahony L** Can
71E2 **Mahrés** Tunisia
60C4 **Mahuva** India
26D1 **Maicao** Colombia
37B1 **Maîche** France
66C4 **Maichew** Eth
35F6 **Maidstone** Eng
72B2 **Maiduguri** Nig
44B3 **Maigomaj** *R* Sweden
61B3 **Maihar** India
61D3 **Maijdi** Bang
55B3 **Mail Kyun** *I* Burma
60A1 **Maimana** Afghan
36E2 **Main** *R* Germany
4E4 **Main Chan** Can
72B4 **Mai-Ndombe** *L* Zaïre
9G2 **Maine** State, USA
36A3 **Maine** *Region* France
71J3 **Maïné-Soroa** Niger
34D2 **Mainland** *I* Scot
60D3 **Mainpuri** India
36A2 **Maintenon** France
73E5 **Maintirano** Madag
42B2 **Mainz** Germany
70A4 **Maio** *I* Cape Verde
25C4 **Maipó** *Mt* Arg/Chile
28D3 **Maipú** Arg
26E1 **Maiquetía** Ven
37B2 **Maira** *R* Italy
61D2 **Mairābāri** India
61D3 **Maiskhal I** Bang
76E4 **Maitland** New South Wales, Aust
75A2 **Maitland** S Australia, Aust
79F12 **Maitri** *Base* Ant
38D1 **Maiz** Germany
53D4 **Maizuru** Japan
76A1 **Majene** Indon
26D7 **Majes** *R* Peru
72D3 **Maji** Eth
52D2 **Majia He** *R* China
Majunga = Mahajanga
72D2 **Makale** Eth
57A3 **Makale** Indon
56B3 **Makalo** Indon
61C2 **Makalu** *Mt* China/Nepal
44K2 **Makarikha** Russian Fed
53E2 **Makarov** Russian Fed
40D2 **Makarska** Croatia, Yugos
44G4 **Makaryev** Russian Fed
Makassar Ujung Pandang
56E3 **Makassar Str** Indon
45J6 **Makat** Kazakhstan
70A4 **Makeni** Sierra Leone
45F6 **Makeyevka** Ukraine
73C6 **Makgadikgadi** *Salt* Pan Botswana
45H7 **Makhachkala** Russian Fed
64D1 **Makharadze** Georgia
57C2 **Makian** *I* Indon
72D4 **Makindu** Kenya
Makkah = Mecca S Arabia
7N4 **Makkovik** Can
43E3 **Makó** Hung
72B3 **Makokou** Gabon
78C1 **Makorako,Mt** NZ
72B3 **Makoua** Congo
60C3 **Makrāna** India
60A3 **Makran Coast Range** *Mts* Pak
53D2 **Maksimovka** Russian Fed
63E3 **Maksotag** Iran
71D1 **Maktar** Tunisia
45G8 **Mākū** Iran
72C4 **Makumbi** Zaïre

Maryborough **Metlakatla**

75B3 **Maryborough** Victoria, Aust
6F4 **Mary Henry,Mt** Can
9F3 **Maryland** State, USA
34D4 **Maryport** Eng
5K3 **Mary's Harbour** Can
5K4 **Marystown** Can
19B3 **Marysville** California, USA
17C2 **Marysville** Kansas, USA
18B1 **Marysville** Washington, USA
17D1 **Maryville** Missouri, USA
15C1 **Maryville** Tennessee, USA
69A2 **Marzuq** Libya
65A3 **Masabb Dumyât** *C* Egypt
Masada = Mezada
65C2 **Mas'adah** Syria
72D4 **Masai Steppe** *Upland* Tanz
72D4 **Masaka** Uganda
64E2 **Masally** Azerbaijan
57B3 **Masamba** Indon
53B4 **Masan** S Korea
73D5 **Masasi** Tanz
21D3 **Masaya** Nic
57F8 **Masbate** Phil
57F8 **Masbate** *I* Phil
71C1 **Mascara** Alg
xxviiiD5 **Mascarene Ridge** Indian O
22B1 **Mascota** Mexico
29E2 **Mascote** Brazil
57C4 **Masela** *I* Indon
74D2 **Maseru** Lesotho
60B2 **Mashaki** Afghan
63D1 **Mashhad** Iran
63E3 **Mashkel** *R* Pak
72B4 **Masi-Manimba** Zaïre
72D3 **Masindi** Uganda
72C4 **Masisi** Zaïre
63B2 **Masjed Soleyman** Iran
73F5 **Masoala** *C* Madag
20C1 **Mason** Nevada, USA
16C3 **Mason** Texas, USA
9D2 **Mason City** USA
67G2 **Masqat** Oman
42B2 **Mass** *R* Neth
40C2 **Massa** Italy
9F2 **Massachusetts** State, USA
13E2 **Massachusetts B** USA
72B2 **Massakori** Chad
37D3 **Massa Marittima** Italy
73D6 **Massangena** Mozam
Massawa = Mits'iwa
66C3 **Massawa Chan** Eth
13E2 **Massena** USA
72B2 **Massénya** Chad
3B3 **Masset** Can
12C1 **Massey** Can
38C2 **Massif Central** *Mts* France
71C1 **Massif de l'Ouarsenis** *Mts* Alg
72B3 **Massif de l'Adamaoua** *Mts* Cam
23C3 **Massif de la Hotte** *Mts* Haiti
73E6 **Massif de l'Isalo** *Upland* Madag
72C3 **Massif des Bongo** *Upland* CAR
38D2 **Massif du Pelvoux** *Mts* France
73E5 **Massif du Tsaratanana** *Mt* Madag
12C2 **Massillon** USA
70B3 **Massina** Region, Mali
73D6 **Massinga** Mozam
74E1 **Massingir** Mozam
45J6 **Masteksay** Kazakhstan
77G5 **Masterton** NZ
53C5 **Masuda** Japan
72B4 **Masuku** Gabon
64C2 **Maşyāf** Syria
4E4 **Matachewan** Can
16A4 **Matachie** Mexico
72B4 **Matadi** Zaïre
26A1 **Matagalpa** Nic
7L5 **Matagami** Can
8D4 **Matagorda B** USA
17F4 **Matagorda I** USA
78C1 **Matakana I** NZ
73B5 **Matala** Angola
62C3 **Matale** Sri Lanka
70A3 **Matam** Sen
70C3 **Matameye** Niger
21C2 **Matamoros** Mexico
69B2 **Ma'tan as Sarra** *Well* Libya
7M5 **Matane** Can
21D2 **Matanzas** Cuba
13F1 **Matapédia** *R* Can
28A2 **Mataquito** *R* Chile
62C3 **Matara** Sri Lanka
76A1 **Mataram** Indon
26D7 **Matarani** Peru
29E1 **Mataripe** Brazil
39C1 **Mataró** Spain
74D3 **Matatiele** S Africa
78A3 **Mataura** NZ
21B2 **Matehuala** Mexico
37E3 **Matelica** Italy
23L1 **Matelot** Trinidad
40D2 **Matera** Italy
43E3 **Mátészalka** Hung
71D1 **Mateur** Tunisia
20C2 **Mather** USA
12C1 **Matheson** Can
17F4 **Mathis** USA
60D3 **Mathura** India
57G9 **Mati** Phil
22C2 **Matías Romero** Mexico
56E3 **Matisiri** *I* Indon
35E5 **Matlock** Eng
71D2 **Matmatma** Tunisia
27G6 **Mato Grosso** Brazil
27G6 **Mato Grosso** State, Brazil
27G7 **Mato Grosso do Sul** State, Brazil
74E2 **Matola** Mozam
67G2 **Matrah** Oman
37E1 **Matrel im Osttirol** Austria
64A3 **Matrûh** Egypt
53C4 **Matsue** Japan
53E3 **Matsumae** Japan
53D4 **Matsumoto** Japan
53D5 **Matsusaka** Japan
53C5 **Matsuyama** Japan
7K5 **Mattagami** *R* Can
4F4 **Mattawa** Can
5H4 **Mattawamkeag** USA
40B1 **Matterhorn** *Mt* Switz/Italy
18C2 **Matterhorn** *Mt* USA
23C2 **Matthew Town** Bahamas
4E4 **Mattice** Can
14D2 **Mattituck** USA
12B3 **Mattoon** USA
60B2 **Matun** Afghan
23L1 **Matura B** Trinidad
26F2 **Maturin** Ven
61B2 **Mau** India
73D5 **Maúa** Mozam
38C1 **Maubeuge** France
75B2 **Maude** Aust
xxxJ8 **Maud Seamount** Atlantic O
20E5 **Maui** *I* Hawaiian Is
28A3 **Maule** *R* Chile
12C2 **Maumee** USA
12C2 **Maumee** *R* USA
57B4 **Maumere** Indon
73C5 **Maun** Botswana
20E5 **Mauna Kea** *Mt* Hawaiian Is
20E5 **Mauna Loa** *Mt* Hawaiian Is
6F3 **Maunoir,L** Can
37B3 **Maures** *Mts* France
38C2 **Mauriac** France
70A2 **Mauritania** Republic, Africa
68K10 **Mauritius** *I* Indian O
12A2 **Mauston** USA
37E1 **Mauterndorf** Austria
73C5 **Mavinga** Angola
74E1 **Mavue** Mozam
61D3 **Mawlaik** Burma
79G10 **Mawson** *Base* Ant
11B2 **Max** USA
74E1 **Maxaila** Mozam
22C1 **Maxcaltzin** Mexico
56C3 **Maya** *I* Indon
49P4 **Maya** *R* Russian Fed
64D2 **Mayādīn** Syria
9F4 **Mayaguana** *I* Bahamas
23D3 **Mayagüez** Puerto Rico
70C3 **Mayahi** Niger
72B4 **Mayama** Congo
63D1 **Mayamey** Iran
57D4 **Mayanobab** Indon
34C4 **Maybole** Scot
9F3 **May,C** USA
75E3 **Maydena** Aust
36D1 **Mayen** Germany
38B2 **Mayenne** France
19D4 **Mayer** USA
3E3 **Mayerthorpe** Can
67E4 **Mayfa'ah** Yemen
12B3 **Mayfield** USA
16A3 **Mayhill** USA
45G7 **Maykop** Russian Fed
48H6 **Maymaneh** Afghan
55B1 **Maymyo** Burma
6E3 **Mayo** Can
14B3 **Mayo** USA
71J4 **Mayo Deo** *R* Cam
57F8 **Mayon** *Mt* Phil
39C2 **Mayor** *Mt* Spain
28C3 **Mayor Buratovich** Arg
78C1 **Mayor I** NZ
25D1 **Mayor P Lagerenza** Par
73E5 **Mayotte** *I* Indian O
23H2 **May Pen** Jamaica
14C3 **May Point,C** USA
37D1 **Mayrhofen** Austria
53B1 **Mayskiy** Russian Fed
14C3 **Mays Landing** USA
3G2 **Mayson L** Can
12C3 **Maysville** USA
72B4 **Mayumba** Gabon
11C2 **Mayville** USA
16B1 **Maywood** USA
73C5 **Mazabuka** Zambia
22B1 **Mazapil** Mexico
60D1 **Mazar** China
65C3 **Mazār** Jordan
40C3 **Mazara del Vallo** Italy
60B1 **Mazar-i-Sharif** Afghan
21B2 **Mazatlán** Mexico
44C4 **Mazeikiai** Lithuania
65C3 **Mazra** Jordan
73D6 **Mbabane** Swaziland
71J4 **Mbabo,Mt** Cam
72B3 **Mbaïki** CAR
73D4 **Mbala** Zambia
73C6 **Mbalabala** Zim
72D3 **Mbale** Uganda
72B3 **Mbalmayo** Cam
72B3 **Mbam** *R* Cam
73D5 **Mbamba Bay** Tanz
72B3 **Mbandaka** Zaïre
72B4 **Mbanza Congo** Angola
72B4 **Mbanza-Ngungu** Zaïre
72D4 **Mbarara** Uganda
71J4 **Mbé** Cam
71J4 **Mbengwi** Cam
72B3 **Mbènza** Congo
72B3 **Mbére** *R* Cam
73D4 **Mbeya** Tanz
72B4 **Mbinda** Congo
71J4 **Mbouda** Cam
70A3 **Mbout** Maur
72C4 **Mbuji-Mayi** Zaïre
71J3 **Mbuli** *R* Nig
72D4 **Mbulu** Tanz
28D1 **Mburucuyá** Arg
70B2 **Mcherrah** Region, Alg
73D5 **Mchinji** Malawi
4C2 **M'Clintock** Can
55D3 **Mdrak** Viet
16B2 **Meade** USA
10G1 **Meade** *R* USA
8B3 **Mead,L** USA
6H4 **Meadow Lake** Can
12C2 **Meadville** USA
54D2 **Me-akan dake** *Mt* Japan
7N4 **Mealy Mts** Can
75C1 **Meandarra** Aust
6G4 **Meander River** Can
35B5 **Meath** Irish Rep
38C2 **Meaux** France
66C2 **Mecca** S Arabia
19C4 **Mecca** USA
14D1 **Mechanicville** USA
48G2 **Mechdusharskiy, Ostrov** *I* Russian Fed
42A2 **Mechelen** Belg
71B2 **Mecheria** Alg
42C2 **Mecklenburger Bucht** *B* Germany
42C2 **Mecklenburg-Vorpommern** State, Germany
73D5 **Meconta** Mozam
73D5 **Mecuburi** Mozam
73E5 **Mecufi** Mozam
73D5 **Mecula** Mozam
56A2 **Medan** Indon
28C3 **Medanos** Arg
28D2 **Médanos** Arg
71C1 **Médéa** Alg
26C2 **Medellin** Colombia
71E2 **Medenine** Tunisia
8A2 **Medford** USA
41F2 **Medgidia** Rom
28B2 **Media Agua** Arg
41E1 **Mediaş** Rom
18C1 **Medical Lake** USA
11A3 **Medicine Bow** USA
16A1 **Medicine Bow Mts** USA
11A3 **Medicine Bow Peak** *Mt* USA
6G5 **Medicine Hat** Can
16C2 **Medicine Lodge** USA
29D2 **Medina** Brazil
11C2 **Medina** N Dakota, USA
14A1 **Medina** New York, USA
66C2 **Medina** S Arabia
39B1 **Medinaceli** Spain
39A1 **Medina del Campo** Spain
39A1 **Medina de Rio Seco** Spain
16C4 **Medina L** USA
61C3 **Medinīpur** India
68E4 **Mediterranean S** Europe
3F3 **Medley** Can
45K5 **Mednogorsk** Russian Fed
49S4 **Mednyy, Ostrov** *I* Russian Fed
61E2 **Mêdog** China
72B3 **Medouneu** Gabon
45G5 **Medvedista** *R* Russian Fed
49S2 **Medvezh'i Ova** *I* Russian Fed
44E3 **Medvezh'yegorsk** Russian Fed
76A3 **Meekatharra** Aust
16A1 **Meeker** USA
60D3 **Meerut** India
18E2 **Meeteetse** USA
72D3 **Mēga** Eth
41E3 **Megalópolis** Greece
41E3 **Mégara** Greece
61D2 **Meghālaya** State, India
61D3 **Meghna** *R* Bang
65C2 **Megido** *Hist Site* Israel
4F4 **Mégiscane** *R* Can
71C2 **Mehaïguene** *R* Alg
10E3 **Mehoryuk** USA
63C3 **Mehran** *R* Iran
63C2 **Mehriz** Iran
29C2 **Meia Ponte** *R* Brazil
72B3 **Meiganga** Cam
55B1 **Meiktila** Burma
37C1 **Meiringen** Switz
52A4 **Meishan** China
42C2 **Meissen** Germany
52D5 **Mei Xian** China
52D5 **Meizhou** China
26D8 **Mejillones** Chile
72B3 **Mekambo** Gabon
4E4 **Mekatina** Can
71C4 **Mek'elē** Eth
71A2 **Meknès** Mor
Mekong = Lancang
55D3 **Mekong, R** Camb
71G3 **Mekrou** *R* Benin
55C5 **Melaka** Malay
xxviiiJ5 **Melanesia** *Region* Pacific O
56D3 **Melawi** *R* Indon
76D4 **Melbourne** Aust
9E4 **Melbourne** USA
8C4 **Melchor Muźguiz** Mexico
44K5 **Meleuz** Russian Fed
72B2 **Melfi** Chad
6H4 **Melfort** Can
71B1 **Melilla** N W Africa
25B6 **Melimoyu** *Mt* Chile
28C2 **Melincué** Arg
28A2 **Melipilla** Chile
11B2 **Melita** Can
45F6 **Melitopol'** Ukraine
7M2 **Meliville Bugt** *B* Greenland
72D3 **Melka Guba** Eth
71D1 **Mellègue** *R* Tunisia
66D4 **Melli** *R* Eth
74E2 **Melmoth** S Africa
28C2 **Melo** Arg
25F4 **Melo** Urug
29A3 **Melo** *R* Brazil
20B2 **Melones Res** USA
10H2 **Melozitna** *R* USA
11D2 **Melrose** USA
37C1 **Mels** Switz
36E1 **Melsungen** Germany
56E1 **Melta,Mt** Malay
35E5 **Melton Mowbray** Eng
38C2 **Melun** France
6H4 **Melville** Can
23Q2 **Melville,C** Dominica
6F3 **Melville Hills** *Mts* Can
76C2 **Melville I** Aust
6G2 **Melville I** Can
7N4 **Melville,L** Can
7K3 **Melville Pen** Can
73E5 **Memba** Mozam
76A1 **Memboro** Indon
42C3 **Memmingen** Germany
56C2 **Mempawan** Indon
9E3 **Memphis** Tennessee, USA
16B3 **Memphis** Texas, USA
17D3 **Mena** USA
43G2 **Mena** Ukraine
35C5 **Menai Str** Wales
70C3 **Ménaka** Mali
12B2 **Menasha** USA
28B4 **Mencué** Arg
56D3 **Mendawai** *R* Indon
38C3 **Mende** France
72D3 **Mendebo** *Mts* Eth
10E4 **Mendenhall,C** USA
76D1 **Mendi** PNG
35D6 **Mendip Hills** *Upland* Eng
18B2 **Mendocino,C** USA
xxixM3 **Mendocino Seascarp** Pacific O
20B2 **Mendota** California, USA
12B2 **Mendota** Illinois, USA
25C4 **Mendoza** Arg
25C5 **Mendoza** State, Arg
41F3 **Menemen** Turk
36B1 **Menen** Belg
52D3 **Mengcheng** China
56C3 **Menggala** Indon
55B1 **Menghai** China
52A5 **Mengla** China
55B1 **Menglian** China
52A5 **Mengzi** China
5H3 **Menihek Lakes** Can
76D4 **Menindee** Aust
75B2 **Menindee L** Aust
75A3 **Meningie** Aust
12B1 **Menominee** USA
12B2 **Menomonee Falls** USA
12A2 **Menomonie** USA
73B5 **Menongue** Angola
39C1 **Menorca** *I* Spain
10K3 **Mentasta Mts** USA
16A2 **Mentmore** USA
56C3 **Mentok** Indon
37B3 **Menton** France
12C2 **Mentor** USA
36B2 **Ménu** France
52A2 **Menyuan** China
44J4 **Menzelinsk** Russian Fed
42B2 **Meppen** Germany
36A3 **Mer** France
56E2 **Merah** Indon
17D2 **Meramec** *R* USA
40C1 **Merano** Italy
76D1 **Merauke** Indon
8A3 **Merced** USA
20B2 **Merced** *R* USA
25B4 **Mercedario** *Mt* Chile
25C4 **Mercedes** Arg
25E4 **Mercedes** Buenos Aires, Arg
25E3 **Mercedes** Corrientes, Arg
25E4 **Mercedes** Urug
78C1 **Mercury B** NZ
78C1 **Mercury Is** NZ
6F2 **Mercy B** Can
7M3 **Mercy,C** Can
16B2 **Meredith,L** *L* USA
55B3 **Mergui** Burma
55B3 **Mergui Arch** Burma
21D2 **Mérida** Mexico
39A2 **Mérida** Spain
26D2 **Mérida** Ven
9E3 **Meridian** USA
75C3 **Merimbula** Aust
75B2 **Meringur** Aust
16B3 **Merkel** USA
72D2 **Merowe** Sudan
76A4 **Merredin** Aust
34C4 **Merrick** *Mt* Scot
12B1 **Merrill** USA
12B2 **Merrillville** USA
14E1 **Merrimack** *R* USA
11B3 **Merriman** USA
3D3 **Merritt** Can
15C3 **Merritt Island** USA
75D2 **Merriwa** Aust
66D4 **Mersa Fatma** Eth
39B2 **Mers el Kebir** Alg
35D5 **Mersey** *R* Eng
35D5 **Merseyside** County, Eng
45E8 **Mersin** Turk
55C5 **Mersing** Malay
60C3 **Merta** India
35D6 **Merthyr Tydfil** Wales
39A2 **Mertola** Port
72D4 **Meru** *Mt* Tanz
45F7 **Merzifon** Turk
36D2 **Merzig** Germany
8B3 **Mesa** USA
16A2 **Mesa Verde Nat Pk** USA
36E1 **Meschede** Germany
64D1 **Mescit Dağ** *Mt* Turk
10G4 **Meshik** USA
72C3 **Meshra'er Req** Sudan
37C1 **Mesocco** Switz
41E3 **Mesolóngion** Greece
19D3 **Mesquite** Nevada, USA
17C3 **Mesquite** Texas, USA
71C2 **Messaad** Alg
73D5 **Messalo** *R* Mozam
40D3 **Messina** Italy
74D1 **Messina** S Africa
41E3 **Messíni** Greece
41E3 **Messiniakós Kólpos** *G* Greece
Mesta = Néstos
41E2 **Mesta, R** Bulg
40C1 **Mestre** Italy
26D3 **Meta** *R* Colombia
44E4 **Meta** *R* Russian Fed
26E2 **Meta** *R* Ven
7L3 **Meta Incognita Pen** Can
17D4 **Metairie** USA
18C1 **Metaline Falls** USA
25D3 **Metán** Arg
73D5 **Metangula** Mozam
40D2 **Metaponto** Italy
37E3 **Metauro** *R* Italy
66C4 **Metemma** Eth
34D3 **Methil** Scot
14E1 **Methuen** USA
78B2 **Methven** NZ
10M4 **Metlakatla** USA

Metlaoui Monett

71D2 **Metlaoui** Tunisia
12B3 **Metropolis** USA
62B2 **Mettūr** India
38D2 **Metz** France
36E2 **Metzingen** Germany
56A2 **Meulaboh** Indon
36A2 **Meulan** France
36A3 **Meung-sur-Loire** France
36D2 **Meurthe** *R* France
36D2 **Meurthe-et-Moselle** Department, France
36C2 **Meuse** Department, France
36C1 **Meuse** *R* Belg
38D2 **Meuse** *R* France
17C3 **Mexia** USA
21A1 **Mexicali** Mexico
19E3 **Mexican Hat** USA
21B2 **Mexico** Federal Republic, Central America
21C3 **México** Mexico
22B2 **México** State, Mexico
17D2 **Mexico** USA
21C2 **Mexico,G of** C America
37A2 **Meximieux** France
65C3 **Mezada** *Hist Site* Israel
22C2 **Mezcala** Mexico
22D2 **Mezcalapa** *R* Mexico
44G2 **Mezen'** Russian Fed
44H3 **Mezen'** *R* Russian Fed
43G1 **Mezha** *R* Russian Fed
44J1 **Mezhdusharskiy, Ostrov** *I* Russian Fed
22B1 **Mezquital** Mexico
22B1 **Mezquital** *R* Mexico
53E1 **Mgachi** Russian Fed
60D4 **Mhow** India
22C2 **Miahuatlán** Mexico
19D4 **Miami** Arizona, USA
9E4 **Miami** Florida, USA
17D2 **Miami** Oklahoma, USA
9E4 **Miami Beach** USA
45H8 **Miandowāb** Iran
73E5 **Miandrivazo** Madag
45H8 **Mīāneh** Iran
60C2 **Mianwali** Pak
52A3 **Mianyang** Sichuan, China
52C3 **Mianyang** Hubei, China
52A3 **Mianzhu** China
52E2 **Miaodao Qundao** *Arch* China
52B4 **Miao Ling** *Upland* China
44L5 **Miass** Russian Fed
43E3 **Michalovce** Czech
18D1 **Michel** Can
23D3 **Miches** Dom Rep
9E2 **Michigan** State, USA
12B2 **Michigan City** USA
9E2 **Michigan,L** USA
12C1 **Michipicoten** Can
7K5 **Michipicoten I** Can
22B2 **Michoacan** State, Mexico
41F2 **Michurin** Bulg
45G5 **Michurinsk** Russian Fed
xxviiiJ4 **Micronesia** *Region* Pacific O
56C2 **Midai** *I* Indon
xxxF4 **Mid Atlantic Ridge** Atlantic O
36B1 **Middelburg** Neth
18B2 **Middle Alkali L** USA
xxixO4 **Middle America Trench** Pacific O
62E2 **Middle Andaman** *I* Indian O
14E2 **Middleboro** USA
74C3 **Middleburg** Cape Province, S Africa
14B2 **Middleburg** Pennsylvania, USA
74D2 **Middleburg** Transvaal, S Africa
14B3 **Middleburg** Virginia, USA
14C1 **Middleburgh** USA
13E2 **Middlebury** USA
9E3 **Middlesboro** USA
35E4 **Middlesbrough** Eng
5H5 **Middleton** Can
14D2 **Middletown** Connecticut, USA
14C3 **Middletown** Delaware, USA
13E2 **Middletown** New York, USA
12C3 **Middletown** Ohio, USA
14B2 **Middletown** Pennsylvania, USA
14C1 **Middleville** USA
71B2 **Midelt** Mor
35D6 **Mid Glamorgan** County, Wales
66D3 **Mīdī** Yemen
xxviiiE5 **Mid Indian Basin** Indian O
xxviiiE5 **Mid Indian Ridge** Indian O
7L5 **Midland** Can
12C2 **Midland** Michigan, USA
8C3 **Midland** Texas, USA
73E6 **Midongy Atsimo** Madag
xxixK4 **Mid Pacific Mts** Pacific O
18C2 **Midvale** USA
xxixL3 **Midway Is** Pacific O
11A3 **Midwest** USA
17C2 **Midwest City** USA
64D2 **Midyat** Turk
41E2 **Midžor** *Mt* Serbia, Yugos
43E2 **Mielec** Pol
41F1 **Miercurea-Ciuc** Rom
39A1 **Mieres** Spain
14B2 **Mifflintown** USA
22B1 **Miguel Auza** Mexico
22C1 **Miguihuana** Mexico
54B4 **Mihara** Japan
52D1 **Mijun Shuiku** *Res* China
41E2 **Mikhaylovgrad** Bulg
45G5 **Mikhaylovka** Russian Fed
48J4 **Mikhaylovskiy** Russian Fed
65C4 **Mikhrot Timna** Israel
32K6 **Mikkeli** Fin
3F2 **Mikkwa** *R* Can
41F3 **Mikonos** *I* Greece
42D3 **Mikulov** Czech
73D4 **Mikumi** Tanz
44J3 **Mikun** Russian Fed
53D4 **Mikuni-sammyaku** *Mts* Japan
54C4 **Mikura-jima** *I* Japan
11D2 **Milaca** USA
26C4 **Milagro** Ecuador
Milan = Milano
15B1 **Milan** USA
39C2 **Milana** Alg
73D5 **Milange** Mozam
57B2 **Milango** *R* Indon
40B1 **Milano** Italy
45D8 **Milas** Turk
11C2 **Milbank** USA
76D4 **Mildura** Aust
52A5 **Mile** China
64D3 **Mileh Tharthār** *L* Iraq
76E3 **Miles** Aust
8C2 **Miles City** USA
14D2 **Milford** Connecticut, USA
13D3 **Milford** Delaware, USA
13E2 **Milford** Massachusetts, USA
17C1 **Milford** Nebraska, USA
14E1 **Milford** New Hampshire, USA
14C2 **Milford** Pennsylvania, USA
19D3 **Milford** Utah, USA
35C6 **Milford Haven** Wales
35C6 **Milford Haven** *Sd* Wales
17C2 **Milford L** USA
78A2 **Milford Sd** NZ
71C1 **Miliana** Alg
11A2 **Milk** *R* USA
49R4 **Mil'kovo** Russian Fed
3F4 **Milk River** Can
38C3 **Millau** France
14D2 **Millbrook** USA
15C2 **Milledgeville** USA
11D2 **Mille Lacs L** USA
11C3 **Miller** USA
10K3 **Miller,Mt** USA
45G6 **Millerovo** Russian Fed
14B2 **Millersburg** USA
75A1 **Millers Creek** Aust
14D1 **Millers Falls** USA
14D2 **Millerton** USA
20C2 **Millerton L** USA
75B3 **Millicent** Aust
15B1 **Millington** USA
13F1 **Millinocket** USA
75D1 **Millmerran** Aust
37E1 **Millstätter See** *L* Austria
13F1 **Milltown** Can
18D1 **Milltown** USA
20A2 **Mill Valley** USA
13E3 **Millville** USA
7Q2 **Milne Land** *I* Greenland
20E5 **Milolii** Hawaiian Is
41E3 **Milos** *I* Greece
76D3 **Milparinka** Aust
14B2 **Milroy** USA
15B2 **Milton** Florida, USA
78A3 **Milton** NZ
14B2 **Milton** Pennsylvania, USA
9E2 **Milwaukee** USA
4D3 **Miminiska L** Can
54D2 **Mimmaya** Japan
20C1 **Mina** USA
39C2 **Mina** *R* Alg
64E4 **Mīnā' al Ahmadī** Kuwait
63D3 **Mīnāb** Iran
57B2 **Minahassa Pen** Indon
4C4 **Minaki** Can
53C5 **Minamata** Japan
56B2 **Minas** Indon
25E4 **Minas** Urug
5J4 **Minas Basin** Can
5J4 **Minas Chan** Can
27J7 **Minas Gerais** State, Brazil
29D2 **Minas Novas** Brazil
21C3 **Minatitlan** Mexico
55A1 **Minbu** Burma
55A1 **Minbya** Burma
28A2 **Mincha** Chile
34B3 **Minch,Little** *Sd* Scot
34B2 **Minch,North** *Sd* Scot
33B2 **Minch,The** *Sd* Scot
10H3 **Minchumina,L** USA
37D2 **Mincio** *R* Italy
57F9 **Mindanao** *I* Phil
17D3 **Minden** Louisiana, USA
20C1 **Minden** Nevada, USA
42B2 **Minden** Germany
75B2 **Mindona L** Aust
57F8 **Mindoro** *I* Phil
57F8 **Mindoro Str** Phil
35D6 **Minehead** Eng
27H7 **Mineiros** Brazil
17C3 **Mineola** USA
22C1 **Mineral de Monte** Mexico
16C3 **Mineral Wells** USA
14B2 **Minersville** USA
5J3 **Mingan** Can
75B2 **Mingary** Aust
45H7 **Mingechaurskoye Vodokhranilische** *Res* Azerbaijan
53B2 **Mingshui** China
52A2 **Minhe** China
37D3 **Minialo** Italy
62A3 **Minicoy** *I* India
52D4 **Min Jiang** *R* Fujian, China
52A4 **Min Jiang** *R* Sichuan, China
20C2 **Minkler** USA
75A2 **Minlaton** Aust
52A2 **Minle** China
71H4 **Minna** Nig
9D2 **Minneapolis** USA
6J4 **Minnedosa** Can
9D2 **Minnesota** State, USA
11C3 **Minnesota** *R* USA
4C4 **Minnitaki L** Can
39A1 **Miño** *R* Spain
8C2 **Minot** USA
52A2 **Minqin** China
52A3 **Min Shan** *Upland* China
44D5 **Minsk** Belorussia
43E2 **Minsk Mazowiecki** Pol
10J3 **Minto** USA
6G2 **Minto Inlet** *B* Can
7L4 **Minto,L** Can
16A2 **Minturn** USA
50C1 **Minusinsk** Russian Fed
52A3 **Min Xian** China
65A3 **Minyael Qamn** Egypt
4F4 **Miquelon** Can
7N5 **Miquelon** *I* France
20D3 **Mirage L** USA
62A1 **Miraj** India
25E5 **Miramar** Arg
5J4 **Miramichi B** Can
60B2 **Miram Shah** Pak
29A2 **Miranda** *R* Brazil
39B1 **Miranda de Ebro** Spain
29A3 **Mirandia** Brazil
37D2 **Mirandola** Italy
60B2 **Mir Bachchen Kūt** Afghan
67F3 **Mirbāt** Oman
37A1 **Mirebeau** France
36C2 **Mirecourt** France
56D2 **Miri** Malay
63E3 **Miri** *Mt* Pak
70A3 **Mirik,C** Maur
28D1 **Mirinay** *R* Arg
63E3 **Mīrjāveh** Iran
37E2 **Mirna** *R* Croatia, Yugos
49K3 **Mirnoye** Russian Fed
49N3 **Mirnyy** Russian Fed
79G9 **Mirnyy** *Base* Ant
3H2 **Miron L** Can
43G3 **Mironovka** Ukraine
60C2 **Mirpur** Pak
60B3 **Mirpur Khas** Pak
41E3 **Mirtoan S** Greece
53B4 **Miryang** S Korea
61B2 **Mirzāpur** India
22C2 **Misantla** Mexico
5J4 **Miscou I** Can
60C1 **Misgar** Pak
53C2 **Mishan** China
12B2 **Mishawaka** USA
10F2 **Misheguk Mt** USA
54B4 **Mi-shima** *I* Japan
61E2 **Mishmi Hills** India
77E2 **Misima** *I* Solomon Is
25F3 **Misiones** State, Arg
43E3 **Miskolc** Hung
65D2 **Mismīyah** Syria
51G7 **Misoöl** *I* Indon
3H2 **Misow L** Can
69A1 **Misrātah** Libya
7K5 **Missinaibi** *R* Can
12C1 **Missinaibi L** Can
3H2 **Missinipe** Can
11B3 **Mission** S Dakota, USA
17F4 **Mission** Texas, USA
18B1 **Mission City** Can
13D2 **Mississauga** Can
9D3 **Mississippi** State, USA
9D3 **Mississippi** *R* USA
17E3 **Mississippi Delta** USA
8B2 **Missoula** USA
71B2 **Missour** Mor
9D3 **Missouri** State, USA
9D3 **Missouri** *R* USA
11C3 **Missouri Valley** USA
5G4 **Mistassini** Can
5G4 **Mistassini** *R* Can
5G3 **Mistassini Provincial Park** Can
5J2 **Mistastin L** Can
26D7 **Misti** *Mt* Peru
5J2 **Mistinibi L** Can
75C1 **Mitchell** Aust
8D2 **Mitchell** USA
76D2 **Mitchell** *R* Aust
9E3 **Mitchell,Mt** USA
51H8 **Mitchell River** Aust
65A3 **Mit el Nasâra** Egypt
65A3 **Mit Ghamr** Egypt
60B3 **Mithankot** Pak
41F3 **Mitilíni** Greece
22C2 **Mitla** Mexico
65B3 **Mitla P** Egypt
77G2 **Mitre** *I* Solomon Is
10G4 **Mitrofania I** USA
72D2 **Mits'iwa** Eth
37E1 **Mittersill** Austria
26D3 **Mitu** Colombia
72C4 **Mitumbar** *Mts* Zaïre
73C4 **Mitwaba** Zaïre
72B3 **Mitzic** Gabon
54C3 **Miura** Japan
52C3 **Mi Xian** China
50G3 **Miyake** *I* Japan
54C4 **Miyake-jima** *I* Japan
50F4 **Miyako** *I* Japan
53C5 **Miyakonojō** Japan
53C5 **Miyazaki** Japan
54C3 **Miyazu** Japan
53C5 **Miyoshi** Japan
52D1 **Miyun** China
54D2 **Mi-zaki** *Pt* Japan
72D3 **Mīzan Teferī** Eth
69A1 **Mizdah** Libya
41F1 **Mizil** Rom
61D3 **Mizo Hills** India
61D3 **Mizoram** Union Territory, India
65C3 **Mizpe Ramon** Israel
79F11 **Mizuho** *Base* Ant
53E4 **Mizusawa** Japan
32H7 **Mjolby** Sweden
73C5 **Mkushi** Zambia
74E2 **Mkuzi** S Africa
42C2 **Mladá Boleslav** Czech
43E2 **Mława** Pol
41D2 **Mljet** *I* Croatia, Yugos
74D2 **Mmabatho** S Africa
60D2 **Mnadi** India
57C4 **Moa** *I* Indon
70A4 **Moa** *R* Sierra Leone
65C3 **Moab** Region, Jordan
8C3 **Moab** USA
74E2 **Moamba** Mozam
72B4 **Moanda** Congo
72B4 **Moanda** Gabon
73C4 **Moba** Zaïre
54D3 **Mobara** Japan
72C3 **Mobaye** CAR
72C3 **Mobayi** Zaire
9D3 **Moberly** USA
9E3 **Mobile** USA
9E3 **Mobile B** USA
15B2 **Mobile Pt** USA
8C2 **Mobridge** USA
73E5 **Moçambique** Mozam
Moçâmedes = Namibe
55C1 **Moc Chau** Viet
74D1 **Mochudi** Botswana
73E5 **Mocimboa da Praia** Mozam
26C3 **Mocoa** Colombia
29C3 **Mococa** Brazil
28D2 **Mocoreta** *R* Arg
22C1 **Moctezulma** *R* Mexico
22B1 **Moctezuma** Mexico
73D5 **Mocuba** Mozam
37B2 **Modane** France
74D2 **Modder** *R* S Africa
40C2 **Modena** Italy
36D2 **Moder** *R* France
8A3 **Modesto** USA
20B2 **Modesto Res** USA
40C3 **Modica** Italy
42D3 **Mödling** Austria
76D4 **Moe** Aust
37C1 **Moesa** *R* Switz
34D4 **Moffat** Scot
60D2 **Moga** India
68J7 **Mogadiscio** Somalia
61E2 **Mogaung** Burma
29C3 **Mogi das Cruzes** Brazil
43G2 **Mogilev** Belorussia
45D6 **Mogilev Podol'skiy** Ukraine
29C3 **Mogi-Mirim** Brazil
73E5 **Mogincual** Mozam
37E2 **Mogliano** Italy
28B2 **Mogna** Arg
50E1 **Mogocha** Russian Fed
48K4 **Mogochin** Russian Fed
61E3 **Mogok** Burma
74D1 **Mogol** *R* S Africa
39A2 **Moguer** Spain
78C1 **Mohaka** *R* NZ
74D3 **Mohale's Hoek** Lesotho
11B2 **Mohall** USA
71C1 **Mohammadia** Alg
71A2 **Mohammedia** Mor
61D3 **Mohanganj** Bang
19D3 **Mohave,L** USA
14C1 **Mohawk** USA
13E2 **Mohawk** *R* USA
73E5 **Mohéli,I** Comoros
10E3 **Mohican,C** USA
73D4 **Mohoro** Tanz
48J5 **Mointy** Kazakhstan
32G5 **Mo i Rana** Nor
5H3 **Moisie** *R* Can
38C3 **Moissac** France
19C3 **Mojave** USA
20D3 **Mojave** *R* USA
8B3 **Mojave Desert** USA
56D4 **Mojokerto** Indon
66C4 **Mokada** *Mt* Eth
61C2 **Mokama** India
78B1 **Mokau** *R* NZ
20B1 **Mokelumne Aqueduct** USA
20B1 **Mokelumne Hill** USA
20B1 **Mokelumne North Fork** *R* USA
74D2 **Mokhotlong** Lesotho
71E1 **Moknine** Tunisia
61D2 **Mokokchūng** India
72B2 **Mokolo** Cam
53B5 **Mokp'o** S Korea
44G5 **Moksha** *R* Russian Fed
22C1 **Molango** Mexico
41E3 **Moláoi** Greece
45D6 **Moldavia** *Republic* Europe
32F6 **Molde** Nor
41E1 **Moldoveanu** *Mt* Rom
71F4 **Mole Nat Pk** Ghana
74D1 **Molepolole** Botswana
36D2 **Molesheim** France
40D2 **Molfetta** Italy
28A3 **Molina** Chile
37E1 **Möll** *R* Austria
26D7 **Mollendo** Peru
44D5 **Molodechno** Belorussia
79G11 **Molodezhnaya** *Base* Ant
20E5 **Molokai** *I* Hawaiian Is
44H4 **Moloma** *R* Russian Fed
75C2 **Molong** Aust
74C2 **Molopo** *R* S Africa/ Botswana
72B3 **Molounddu** Cam
4B3 **Molson L** Can
76B1 **Molucca S** Indon
51F7 **Moluccas** *Is* Indon
73D5 **Moma** Mozam
27K5 **Mombaca** Brazil
72D4 **Mombasa** Kenya
54D2 **Mombetsu** Japan
72C3 **Mompono** Zaïre
42C2 **Mon** *I* Den
34B3 **Monach** *Is* Scot
38D3 **Monaco** Principality, Europe
34C3 **Monadhliath** *Mts* Scot
35B4 **Monaghan** County, Irish Rep
35B4 **Monaghan** Irish Rep
16B3 **Monahans** USA
23D3 **Mona Pass** Caribbean
3C3 **Monarch Mt** Can
16A2 **Monarch P** USA
6G4 **Monashee Mts** Can
33B3 **Monastereven** Irish Rep
54D2 **Monbetsu** Japan
37B2 **Moncalieri** Italy
27J4 **Monção** Brazil
32L5 **Monchegorsk** Russian Fed
42B2 **Mönchen-gladbach** Germany
21B2 **Monclova** Mexico
7M5 **Moncton** Can
39A1 **Mondego** *R* Port
40B2 **Mondovi** Italy
23H1 **Moneague** Jamaica
13D2 **Monessen** USA
4F4 **Monet** Can
17D2 **Monett** USA

Narowal **Nipomo**

60C2 **Narowal** Pak
76D4 **Narrabri** Aust
75C1 **Narran** *L* Aust
75C1 **Narran** *R* Aust
75C2 **Narrandera** Aust
76A4 **Narrogin** Aust
75C2 **Narromine** Aust
12C3 **Narrows** USA
14C2 **Narrowsburg** USA
60D4 **Narsimhapur** India
62C1 **Narsipatnam** India
7O3 **Narssalik** Greenland
7O3 **Narssaq** Greenland
7O3 **Narssarssuaq** Greenland
74B2 **Narubis** Namibia
54D3 **Narugo** Japan
54B4 **Naruto** Japan
44D4 **Narva** Russian Fed
32H5 **Narvik** Nor
60D3 **Narwāna** India
44J2 **Nar'yan Mar** Russian Fed
75B1 **Narylico** Aust
48J5 **Naryn** Kazakhstan
71H4 **Nasarawa** Nig
xxxD5 **Nasca Ridge** Pacific O
14E1 **Nashua** USA
17D3 **Nashville** Arkansas, USA
15B1 **Nashville** Tennessee, USA
41D1 **Našice** Croatia, Yugos
60C4 **Nāsik** India
72D3 **Nasir** Sudan
5J3 **Naskaupi** *R* Can
3C2 **Nass** *R* Can
23B1 **Nassau** Bahamas
14D1 **Nassau** USA
69C2 **Nasser,L** Egypt
71F4 **Nassian** Ivory Coast
32G7 **Nässjö** Sweden
7L4 **Nastapoka Is** Can
4F2 **Nastapoca** *R* Can
73C6 **Nata** Botswana
27L5 **Natal** Brazil
56A2 **Natal** Indon
74E2 **Natal** Province, S Africa
xxviiiC6 **Natal Basin** Indian O
63C2 **Natanz** Iran
7M4 **Natashquan** Can
7M4 **Natashquan** *R* Can
17D3 **Natchez** USA
17D3 **Natchitoches** USA
75C3 **Nathalia** Aust
7Q2 **Nathorsts Land** *Region* Greenland
3D2 **Nation** *R* Can
19C4 **National City** USA
National Republic of China = Taiwan
71G3 **Natitingou** Benin
54D3 **Natori** Japan
72D4 **Natron** *L* Tanz
76A4 **Naturaliste,C** Aust
4D4 **Naubinway** USA
37D1 **Nauders** Austria
42C2 **Nauen** Germany
14D2 **Naugatuck** USA
42C2 **Naumburg** Germany
65C3 **Naur** Jordan
77F1 **Nauru** *I* Pacific O
49M4 **Naushki** Russian Fed
74B2 **Naute Dam** *Res* Namibia
22C1 **Nautla** Mexico
63E2 **Nauzad** Afghan
8C3 **Navajo Res** USA
39A2 **Navalmoral de la Mata** Spain
25C9 **Navarino** *I* Chile
39B1 **Navarra** Province, Spain
28D3 **Navarro** Arg
17C3 **Navasota** USA
17C3 **Navasota** *R* USA
39A1 **Navia** *R* Spain
28A2 **Navidad** Chile
60C4 **Navlakhi** India
45E5 **Navlya** Russian Fed
21B2 **Navojoa** Mexico
41E3 **Návpaktos** Greece
41E3 **Návplion** Greece
71F3 **Navrongo** Ghana
60C4 **Navsāri** India
65D2 **Nawá** Syria
61C3 **Nawāda** India
60B2 **Nawah** Afghan
60B3 **Nawrabshah** Pak
52B4 **Naxi** China
41F3 **Náxos** *I* Greece
22B1 **Nayar** Mexico
22A1 **Nayarit** State, Mexico
63C3 **Nāy Band** Iran
63D2 **Nāy Band** Iran
53E3 **Nayoro** Japan
29E1 **Nazaré** Brazil
65C2 **Nazareth** Israel
38B2 **Nazay** France
26D6 **Nazca** Peru
64A2 **Nazilli** Turk
49L4 **Nazimovo** Russian Fed
3D3 **Nazko** *R* Can
58B5 **Nazrēt** Eth
67G2 **Nazwa** Oman
48J4 **Nazyvayevsk** Russian Fed
73B4 **Ndalatando** Angola
72C3 **Ndélé** CAR
72B4 **Ndendé** Gabon
77F2 **Ndende** *I* Solomon Is
72B2 **Ndjamena** Chad
72B4 **Ndjolé** Gabon
73C5 **Ndola** Zambia
71F4 **Ndouci** Ivory Coast
75C1 **Neabul** Aust
75A1 **Neales** *R* Aust
41E3 **Neápolis** Greece
10A6 **Near Is** USA
35D6 **Neath** Wales
75C1 **Nebine** *R* Aust
48G6 **Nebit Dag** Turkmenistan
8C2 **Nebraska** State, USA
17C1 **Nebraska City** USA
3D3 **Nechako** *R* Can
17C3 **Neches** *R* USA
36E2 **Neckar** *R* Germany
28D3 **Necochea** Arg
61D2 **Nêdong** China
19D4 **Needles** USA
12B2 **Neenah** USA
6J4 **Neepawa** Can
36C1 **Neerpelt** Belg
71D2 **Nefta** Tunisia
53E1 **Neftegorsk** Russian Fed
49M4 **Neftelensk** Russian Fed
72D3 **Negelli** Eth
65C3 **Negev** *Desert* Israel
29A3 **Negla** *R* Par
45C6 **Negolu** *Mt* Rom
62B3 **Negombo** Sri Lanka
55A2 **Negrais,C** Burma
26B4 **Negritos** Peru
26F4 **Negro** *R* Amazonas, Brazil
28C4 **Negro** *R* Arg
29A2 **Negro** *R* Mato Grosso de Sul, Brazil
29A3 **Negro** *R* Par
28D2 **Negro** *R* Urug
57F8 **Negros** *I* Phil
41F2 **Negru Voda** Rom
63E2 **Nehbāndan** Iran
53A2 **Nehe** China
52B4 **Neijiang** China
12A2 **Neillsville** USA
52B1 **Nei Monggol** Autonomous Region, China
26C3 **Neira** Colombia
72D3 **Nejo** Eth
72D3 **Nek'emte** Eth
44E4 **Nelidovo** Russian Fed
11C3 **Neligh** USA
62B2 **Nellore** India
53D2 **Nel'ma** Russian Fed
3E4 **Nelson** Can
78B2 **Nelson** NZ
6J4 **Nelson** *R* Can
75B3 **Nelson,C** Aust
10F3 **Nelson I** USA
74E2 **Nelspruit** S Africa
70B3 **Néma** Maur
52A1 **Nemagt Uul** *Mt* Mongolia
53D1 **Nemilen** *R* Russian Fed
41F1 **Nemira** *Mt* Rom
53B2 **Nemor He** *R* China
36B2 **Nemours** France
43E1 **Nemunas** *R* Lithuania
53F3 **Nemuro** Japan
49O5 **Nen** *R* China
33B3 **Nenagh** Irish Rep
10J3 **Nenana** USA
10J3 **Nenana** *R* USA
35E5 **Nene** *R* Eng
56F6 **Nenggiri** *R* Malay
53B2 **Nenjiang** China
17C2 **Neodesha** USA
17D2 **Neosho** USA
49M4 **Nepa** Russian Fed
59G3 **Nepal** Kingdom, Asia
61B2 **Nepalganj** Nepal
19D3 **Nephi** USA
65C3 **Neqarot** *R* Israel
28A3 **Nequén** State, Arg
50E1 **Nerchinsk** Russian Fed
41D2 **Neretva** *R* Bosnia & Herzegovina/Croatia, Yugos
51H5 **Nero Deep** Pacific O
44G2 **Nes'** Russian Fed
32C1 **Neskaupstaður** Iceland
36B2 **Nesle** France
16C2 **Ness City** USA
3B2 **Nesselrode,Mt** Can/USA
5G3 **Nestaocano** *R* Can
41E2 **Néstos** *R* Greece
65C2 **Netanya** Israel
14C2 **Netcong** USA
42B2 **Netherlands** Kingdom, Europe
2M7 **Netherlands Antilles** *Is* Caribbean
49N4 **Net Oktyobr'ya** Russian Fed
61D3 **Netrakona** Bang
7L3 **Nettilling L** Can
42C2 **Neubrandenburg** Germany
37B1 **Neuchâtel** Switz
36C2 **Neufchâteau** Belg
36C2 **Neufchâteau** France
38C2 **Neufchâtel** France
36A2 **Neufchâtel-en-Bray** France
42B2 **Neumünster** Germany
40D1 **Neunkirchen** Austria
36D2 **Neunkirchen** Germany
28B3 **Neuquén** Arg
25B6 **Neuquén** State, Arg
28B3 **Neuquén** *R* Arg
42C2 **Neuruppin** Germany
15D1 **Neuse** *R* USA
36D1 **Neuss** Germany
42C2 **Neustadt** Germany
36E2 **Neustadt an der Weinstrasse** Germany
36E3 **Neustadt im Schwarzwald** Germany
42C2 **Neustrelitz** Germany
36D1 **Neuwied** Germany
8B3 **Nevada** State, USA
17D2 **Nevada** USA
28A3 **Nevada de Chillán** *Mts* Chile/Arg
22B2 **Nevada de Collima** Mexico
22C2 **Nevada de Toluca** *Mt* Mexico
65C3 **Nevatim** Israel
44D4 **Nevel'** Russian Fed
53E2 **Nevel'sk** Russian Fed
53A1 **Never** Russian Fed
38C2 **Nevers** France
75C2 **Nevertire** Aust
64B2 **Nevşehir** Turk
44L4 **Nev'yansk** Russian Fed
12C3 **New** *R* USA
73D5 **Newala** Tanz
12B3 **New Albany** Indiana, USA
17E3 **New Albany** Mississippi, USA
27G2 **New Amsterdam** Guyana
75C1 **New Angledool** Aust
13D3 **Newark** Delaware, USA
9F2 **Newark** New Jersey, USA
14B1 **Newark** New York, USA
12C2 **Newark** Ohio, USA
35E5 **Newark-upon-Trent** Eng
13E2 **New Bedford** USA
3C3 **New Bella Bella** Can
18B1 **Newberg** USA
15D1 **New Bern** USA
15C2 **Newberry** USA
74C3 **New Bethesda** S Africa
23B2 **New Bight** Bahamas
12C3 **New Boston** USA
16C4 **New Braunfels** USA
14D2 **New Britain** USA
76E1 **New Britain** *I* PNG
76E1 **New Britain Trench** PNG
7M5 **New Brunswick** Province, Can
14C2 **New Brunswick** USA
14C2 **Newburgh** USA
35E6 **Newbury** Eng
14E1 **Newburyport** USA
14D2 **New Canaan** USA
75D2 **Newcastle** Aust
5H4 **Newcastle** Can
12B3 **New Castle** Indiana, USA
35C4 **Newcastle** N Ire
12C2 **New Castle** Pennsylvania, USA
74D2 **Newcastle** S Africa
11B3 **Newcastle** Wyoming, USA
34E4 **Newcastle upon Tyne** Eng
76C2 **Newcastle Waters** Aust
20C3 **New Cuyama** USA
60D3 **New Delhi** India
75D2 **New England Range** *Mts* Aust
10F4 **Newenham,C** USA
14A1 **Newfane** USA
35E6 **New Forest,The** Eng
7M4 **Newfoundland** Province, Can
7N5 **Newfoundland** *I* Can
xxxF2 **Newfoundland Basin** Atlantic O
17D2 **New Franklin** USA
34C4 **New Galloway** Scot
77E1 **New Georgia** *I* Solomon Is
7M5 **New Glasgow** Can
76D1 **New Guinea** *I* S E Asia
66C3 **New Haifa** Sudan
10H4 **Newhalen** USA
20C3 **Newhall** USA
9F2 **New Hampshire** State, USA
11D3 **New Hampton** USA
74E2 **New Hanover** S Africa
76E1 **New Hanover** *I* PNG
35F6 **Newhaven** Eng
13E2 **New Haven** USA
3C2 **New Hazelton** Can
77F3 **New Hebrides Trench** Pacific O
17D3 **New Iberia** USA
76E1 **New Ireland** *I* PNG
9F2 **New Jersey** State, USA
16B3 **Newkirk** USA
7L5 **New Liskeard** Can
14D2 **New London** USA
76A3 **Newman** Aust
20B2 **Newman** USA
35F5 **Newmarket** Eng
13D3 **New Market** USA
18C2 **New Meadows** USA
8C3 **New Mexico** State, USA
14D2 **New Milford** Connecticut, USA
14C2 **New Milford** Pennsylvania, USA
15C2 **Newnan** USA
75E3 **New Norfolk** Aust
9D3 **New Orleans** USA
14C2 **New Paltz** USA
12C2 **New Philadelphia** USA
78B1 **New Plymouth** NZ
17D2 **Newport** Arkansas, USA
35E6 **Newport** Eng
12C3 **Newport** Kentucky, USA
14D1 **Newport** New Hampshire, USA
18B2 **Newport** Oregon, USA
14B2 **Newport** Pennsylvania, USA
13E2 **Newport** Rhode Island, USA
13E2 **Newport** Vermont, USA
35D6 **Newport** Wales
18C1 **Newport** Washington, USA
20D4 **Newport Beach** USA
9F3 **Newport News** USA
23B1 **New Providence** *I* Caribbean
35C6 **Newquay** Eng
7L3 **New Quebec Crater** Can
35B5 **New Ross** Irish Rep
35B4 **Newry** N Ire
New Siberian Is = Novosibirskye Ostrova
15C3 **New Smyrna Beach** USA
76D4 **New South Wales** State, Aust
10G4 **New Stuyahok** USA
11D3 **Newton** Iowa, USA
17C2 **Newton** Kansas, USA
14E1 **Newton** Massachusetts, USA
17E3 **Newton** Mississippi, USA
14C2 **Newton** New Jersey, USA
35D6 **Newton Abbot** Eng
34B4 **Newton Stewart** N Ire
34C4 **Newton Stewart** Scot
11B2 **New Town** USA
35D5 **Newtown** Wales
35C4 **Newtownards** N Ire
11D3 **New Ulm** USA
14B2 **Newville** USA
5J4 **New Waterford** Can
6F5 **New Westminster** Can
9F2 **New York** State, USA
9F2 **New York** USA
77G5 **New Zealand** Dominion, SW Pacific O
xxixK7 **New Zealand Plat** Pacific O
44G4 **Neya** Russian Fed
63C3 **Neyrīz** Iran
63D1 **Neyshābūr** Iran
45E5 **Nezhin** Ukraine
72B4 **Ngabé** Congo
71J3 **Ngadda** Nig
73C6 **Ngami** *L* Botswana
71J4 **N'Gaoundéré** Cam
78C1 **Ngaruawahia** NZ
78C1 **Ngaruroro** *R* NZ
78C1 **Ngauruhoe,Mt** NZ
72B4 **Ngo** Congo
55D2 **Ngoc Linh** *Mt* Viet
72B3 **Ngoko** *R* Cam
50C3 **Ngoring Hu** *L* China
72D4 **Ngorongoro Crater** Tanz
72B4 **N'Gounié** *R* Gabon
72B2 **Nguigmi** Niger
51G6 **Ngulu** *I* Pacific O
71J3 **Nguru** Nig
55D3 **Nha Trang** Viet
29A2 **Nhecolandia** Brazil
75B3 **Nhill** Aust
74E2 **Nhlangano** Swaziland
55D2 **Nhommarath** Laos
76C2 **Nhulunbuy** Aust
70B3 **Niafounké** Mali
12B1 **Niagara** USA
13D2 **Niagara Falls** Can
13D2 **Niagara Falls** USA
56D2 **Niah** Malay
70B4 **Niakaramandougou** Ivory Coast
70C3 **Niamey** Niger
72C3 **Niangara** Zaïre
71F3 **Niangoloko** Burkina
72C3 **Nia Nia** Zaïre
53A2 **Nianzishan** China
56A2 **Nias** *I* Indon
21D3 **Nicaragua** Republic, C America
40D3 **Nicastro** Italy
38D3 **Nice** France
23B1 **Nicholl's Town** Bahamas
14C2 **Nicholson** USA
59H5 **Nicobar Is** Indian O
65B1 **Nicosia** Cyprus
21D3 **Nicoya,Pen de** Costa Rica
36E1 **Nidda** *R* Germany
43E2 **Nidzica** Pol
36D2 **Niederbronn** France
37E1 **Niedere Tauern** *Mts* Austria
42B2 **Niedersachsen** State, Germany
72C4 **Niemba** Zaïre
42B2 **Nienburg** Germany
36D1 **Niers** *R* Germany
70B4 **Niete,Mt** Lib
27G2 **Nieuw Amsterdam** Surinam
27G2 **Nieuw Nickeire** Surinam
74B3 **Nieuwoudtville** S Africa
36B1 **Nieuwpoort** Belg
22B1 **Nieves** Mexico
64B2 **Niğde** Turk
70C3 **Niger** Republic, Africa
71H4 **Niger** State, Nig
71H4 **Niger** *R* Nig
70C4 **Nigeria** Federal Republic, Africa
12C1 **Nighthawk L** Can
41E2 **Nigríta** Greece
54D3 **Nihommatsu** Japan
53D4 **Niigata** Japan
53C5 **Niihama** Japan
54C4 **Nii-jima** *I* Japan
54B4 **Niimi** Japan
53D4 **Niitsu** Japan
65C3 **Nijil** Jordan
42B2 **Nijmegen** Neth
44E2 **Nikel'** Russian Fed
71G3 **Nikki** Benin
53D4 **Nikko** Japan
45E6 **Nikolayev** Ukraine
45H6 **Nikolayevsk** Russian Fed
49Q4 **Nikolayevsk-na-Amure** Russian Fed
44H5 **Nikol'sk** Penza, Russian Fed
44H4 **Nikol'sk** Russian Fed
10E5 **Nikolski** USA
45E6 **Nikopol** Ukraine
64C1 **Niksar** Turk
63E3 **Nikshahr** Iran
41D2 **Nikšić** Montenegro, Yugos
77G1 **Nikunau** *I* Kiribati
57C4 **Nila** *I* Indon
58B3 **Nile** *R* N E Africa
12B2 **Niles** USA
62B2 **Nilgiri Hills** India
22D2 **Niltepec** Mexico
60C4 **Nimach** India
38C3 **Nîmes** France
75C3 **Nimmitabel** Aust
72D3 **Nimule** Sudan
59F5 **Nine Degree Chan** Indian O
xxviiiF5 **Ninety-East Ridge** Indian O
75C3 **Ninety Mile Beach** Aust
53B3 **Ning'an** China
52D4 **Ningde** China
52D4 **Ningdu** China
50C3 **Ningjing Shan** *Mts* China
55D1 **Ningming** China
52A4 **Ningnan** China
52B2 **Ningxia** Province, China
52B2 **Ning Xian** China
52B5 **Ninh Binh** Vietnam
76D1 **Ninigo Is** PNG
10H3 **Ninilchik** USA
29A3 **Nioaque** Brazil
11B3 **Niobrara** *R* USA
72B4 **Nioki** Zaïre
70B3 **Nioro du Sahel** Mali
38B2 **Niort** France
6H4 **Nipawin** Can
7K5 **Nipigon** Can
4D4 **Nipigon B.** Can
7K5 **Nipigon,L** Can
7K5 **Nipissing,L** *R* Can
20B3 **Nipomo** USA

Nipton Oasis

19C3 Nipton USA
29C1 Niquelândia Brazil
62B1 Nirmal India
61C2 Nirmāli India
41E2 Niš Serbia, Yugos
67E4 Nisāb Yemen
53C5 Nishinoomote Japan
50G4 Nishino-shima / Japan
54B3 Nishino-shima / Japan
54A4 Nishi-suidō Str S Korea
54B4 Nishiwaki Japan
4D2 Niskibi R Can
10L3 Nisling R Can
77E1 Nissan Is PNG
10M3 Nisutlin R Can
7L4 Nitchequon Can
27K8 Niterói Brazil
34D4 Nith R Scot
57B4 Nitibe Indon
43D3 Nitra Czech
12C3 Nitro USA
77J2 Niue / Pacific O
77G2 Niulakita / Tuvalu
56D2 Niut Mt Malay
77G1 Niutao / Tuvalu
36C1 Nivelles Belg
38C2 Nivernais Region, France
32L5 Nivskiy Russian Fed
62B1 Nizāmābād India
65C3 Nizana Hist Site Israel
44J4 Nizhnekamskoye Vodokhranilische Res Russian Fed
50C1 Nizhneudinsk Russian Fed
44K4 Nizhniye Sergi Russian Fed
44G5 Nizhniy Lomov Russian Fed
44G4 Nizhniy Novgorod Russian Fed
44J3 Nizhniy Odes Russian Fed
44K4 Nizhniy Tagil Russian Fed
49L3 Nizhnyaya Tunguska R Russian Fed
44G2 Nizhnyaya Zolotitsa Russian Fed
64C2 Nizip Turk
73C5 Njoko R Zambia
73D4 Njombe Tanz
72B3 Nkambé Cam
71F4 Nkawkaw Ghana
73D5 Nkhata Bay Malawi
72B3 Nkongsamba Cam
70C3 N'Konni Niger
61D3 Noakhali Bang
10F2 Noatak USA
10G2 Noatak R USA
53C5 Nobeoka Japan
54D2 Noboribetsu Japan
29A1 Nobres Brazil
37D1 Noce R Italy
22B1 Nochistlán Mexico
22C2 Nochixtlán Mexico
17C3 Nocona USA
21A1 Nogales Sonora, Mexico
19D4 Nogales USA
22C2 Nogales Veracruz, Mexico
37D2 Nogara Italy
54B4 Nogata Japan
36C2 Nogent-en-Bassigny France
36A2 Nogent-le-Rotrou France
36B2 Nogent-sur-Seine France
44F4 Noginsk Russian Fed
53E1 Nogliki Russian Fed
28D2 Nogoyá Arg
28D2 Nogoyá R Arg
60C3 Nohar India
54D2 Noheji Japan
74C1 Nojane Botswana
54C4 Nojima-zaki C Japan
63E3 Nok Kundi Pak
3H2 Nokomis L Can
72B3 Nola CAR
44H4 Nolinsk Russian Fed
14E2 Nomans Land / USA
22B1 Nombre de Dioz Mexico
10E3 Nome USA
36D2 Nomeny France
52B1 Nomgon Mongolia
54A4 Nomo-saki Pt Japan
6H3 Nonachol L Can
53B3 Nong'an China
55C2 Nong Khai Thai
74E2 Nongoma S Africa
77G1 Nonouti / Kiribati
54A3 Nonsan S Korea
74B2 Noordoewer Namibia
10F2 Noorvik USA
3C4 Nootka Sd Can
22C2 Nopala Mexico
72B4 Noqui Angola
7L5 Noranda Can
36B1 Nord Department, France
48D2 Nordaustlandet / Barents S
3E3 Nordegg Can
32F6 Nordfjord Inlet Nor
32F8 Nordfriesische Is Germany
42C2 Nordhausen Germany
32J4 Nordkapp C Nor
7N3 Nordre Strømfjord Greenland
42B2 Nordrhein Westfalen State, Germany
32G5 Nord Stronfjället Mt Sweden
49N2 Nordvik Russian Fed
35B5 Nore R Irish Rep
35F5 Norfolk County, Eng
11C3 Norfolk Nebraska, USA
13D3 Norfolk Virginia, USA
77F3 Norfolk I Aust
17D2 Norfolk L USA
xxixK5 Norfolk Ridge Pacific O
49K3 Noril'sk Russian Fed
12B2 Normal USA
17C2 Norman USA
38B2 Normandie Region, France
15C1 Norman,L USA
76D2 Normanton Aust
10N2 Norman Wells Can
44B2 Norra Storfjället Mt Sweden
15C1 Norris L USA
13D2 Norristown USA
32H7 Norrköping Sweden
32H6 Norrsundet Sweden
32H7 Norrtälje Sweden
76B4 Norseman Aust
53C1 Norsk Russian Fed
29A1 Nortelândia Brazil
xxxJ2 North S N W Europe
35E4 Northallerton Eng
76A4 Northam Aust
74D2 Northam S Africa
xxxE3 North American Basin Atlantic O
76A3 Northampton Aust
35E5 Northampton County, Eng
35E5 Northampton Eng
13E2 Northampton USA
62E2 North Andaman / Indian O
6G3 North Arm B Can
15C2 North Augusta USA
7M4 North Aulatsivik I Can
3G3 North Battleford Can
7L5 North Bay Can
18B2 North Bend USA
34D3 North Berwick Scot
14E1 North Berwick USA
7M5 North,C Can
77G4 North C NZ
10D5 North C USA
16B2 North Canadian R USA
4C3 North Caribou L Can
9E3 North Carolina State, USA
18B1 North Cascade Nat Pk USA
4E4 North Chan Can
34C4 North Chan Ire/Scot
14A1 North Collins USA
8C2 North Dakota State, USA
35F6 North Downs Eng
36A1 North Downs Upland Eng
13D2 North East USA
xxxH1 North East Atlantic Basin Atlantic O
10E3 Northeast C USA
4B2 Northern Indian L Can
33B3 Northern Ireland UK
11D2 Northern Light L Can
23L1 Northern Range Mts Trinidad
76C2 Northern Territory Aust
34D3 North Esk R Scot
14D1 Northfield Massachusetts, USA
11D3 Northfield Minnesota, USA
35F6 North Foreland Eng
36A1 North Foreland Pt Eng
10H3 North Fork R USA
4E3 North French R Can
5K3 North Head C Can
78B1 North I NZ
4B2 North Knife R Can
53B4 North Korea Republic, S E Asia
North Land = Severnaya Zemlya
17D3 North Little Rock USA
11B3 North Loup R USA
79B4 North Magnetic Pole Can
15E4 North Miami USA
15E4 North Miami Beach USA
10O3 North Nahanni R Can
20C2 North Palisade Mt USA
16B1 North Platte USA
8C2 North Platte R USA
5J4 North Pt C Can
79A North Pole Arctic
23Q2 North Pt Barbados
12C1 North Pt USA
11D3 North Raccoon R USA
33B2 North Rona / Scot
34D2 North Ronaldsay / Scot
3G3 North Saskatchewan R Can
33D2 North Sea N W Europe
3H2 North Seal R Can
62E2 North Sentinel Andaman Is
10J2 North Slope USA
6D3 North Slope Region USA
75D1 North Stradbroke / Aust
14B1 North Syracuse USA
78B1 North Taranaki Bight B NZ
14A1 North Tonawanda USA
8C3 North Truchas Peak Mt USA
4F3 North Twin I Can
34B3 North Uist / Scot
34D4 Northumberland County, Eng
76E3 Northumberland Is Aust
7M5 Northumberland Str Can
18B1 North Vancouver Can
14C1 Northville USA
35F5 North Walsham Eng
10K3 Northway USA
76A3 North West C Aust
60C2 North West Frontier Province, Pak
7M4 North West River Can
6G3 North West Territories Can
11C2 Northwood USA
35E4 North York Moors Nat Pk Eng
16C2 Norton R USA
10F3 Norton B USA
10F3 Norton Sd USA
79F1 Norvegia,C Ant
14D2 Norwalk Connecticut, USA
12C2 Norwalk Ohio, USA
32F6 Norway Kingdom, Europe
6J4 Norway House Can
7J2 Norwegian B Can
xxxH1 Norwegian Basin Norewegian S
48B3 Norwegian S N W Europe
14D2 Norwich Connecticut, USA
35F5 Norwich Eng
14C1 Norwich New York, USA
14E1 Norwood Massachusetts, USA
12C3 Norwood Ohio, USA
41F2 Nos Emine C Bulg
53D3 Noshiro Japan
41F2 Nos Kaliakra C Bulg
44J2 Nosovaya Russian Fed
43G2 Nosovka Ukraine
34E1 Noss / Scot
74B1 Nossob R Namibia
63E3 Nostrābād Iran
73E5 Nosy Barren / Madag
73E5 Nosy Bé / Madag
73F5 Nosy Boraha / Madag
73E6 Nosy Varika Madag
42D2 Notéc R Pol
6G4 Notikewin Can
40D3 Noto Italy
32F7 Notodden Nor
54C3 Noto-hantō Pen Japan
7N5 Notre Dame B Can
4E5 Nottawasaga B Can
4F3 Nottaway R Can
35E5 Nottingham County, Eng
35E5 Nottingham Eng
7L3 Nottingham I Can
11A2 Notukeu Creek R Can
70A2 Nouadhibou Maur
70A3 Nouakchott Maur
77F3 Nouméa Nouvelle Calédonie
71F3 Nouna Burkina
74C3 Noupoort S Africa
77F3 Nouvelle Calédonie / S W Pacific O
29C2 Nova América Brazil
73B4 Nova Caipemba Angola
29B3 Nova Esperança Brazil
29D3 Nova Friburgo Brazil
73B5 Nova Gaia Angola
29C3 Nova Granada Brazil
29C3 Nova Herizonte Brazil
29D3 Nova Lima Brazil
Nova Lisboa = Huambo
29B3 Nova Londrina Brazil
73D6 Nova Mambone Mozam
37C2 Novara Italy
29C1 Nova Roma Brazil
57C4 Nova Sagres Indon
7M5 Nova Scotia Province, Can
20A1 Novato USA
29D2 Nova Venécia Brazil
45E6 Novaya Kakhovka Ukraine
49R2 Novaya Sibir, Ostrov / Russian Fed
48G2 Novaya Zemlya / Russian Fed
41F2 Nova Zagora Bulg
27K4 Nove Russas Brazil
41D1 Nové Zámky Czech
44E4 Novgorod Russian Fed
37E2 Novigrad Croatia, Yugos
53E2 Novikovo Russian Fed
37C2 Novi Ligure Italy
22A1 Novillero Mexico
41F2 Novi Pazar Bulg
41E2 Novi Pazar Serbia, Yugos
41D1 Novi Sad Serbia, Yugos
45K5 Novoalekseyevka Kazakhstan
45G5 Novoanninskiy Russian Fed
53C2 Novobureyskiy Russian Fed
45G6 Novocherkassk Russian Fed
44G3 Novodvinsk Russian Fed
45D5 Novograd Volynskiy Ukraine
43F2 Novogrudok Belorussia
28E1 Novo Hamburgo Brazil
48H5 Novokazalinsk Kazakhstan
48K4 Novokuznetsk Russian Fed
79F12 Novolazarevskaya Base Ant
40D1 Novo Mesto Slovenia, Yugos
43G3 Novomirgorod Ukraine
44F5 Novomoskovsk Russian Fed
Novo Redondo = Sumbe
45F7 Novorossiysk Russian Fed
49M2 Novorybnoye Russian Fed
48K4 Novosibirsk Russian Fed
49P2 Novosibirskye Ostrova Is Russian Fed
45K5 Novotroitsk Russian Fed
45H5 Novo Uzensk Russian Fed
43E2 Novovolynsk Ukraine
44H4 Novo Vyatsk Russian Fed
45E5 Novozybkov Russian Fed
48J3 Novyy Port Russian Fed
43E2 Novy Dwór Mazowiecki Pol
44L4 Novyy Lyalya Russian Fed
44N2 Novyy Port Russian Fed
45J7 Novyy Uzen Kazakhstan
42D2 Nowa Sól Pol
17C2 Nowata USA
61D2 Nowgong India
10H3 Nowitna R USA
75D2 Nowra Aust
63C1 Now Shahr Iran
60C2 Nowshera Pak
43E3 Nowy SŞacz Pol
10M4 Noyes I USA
36B2 Noyon France
71F4 Nsawam Ghana
71H4 Nsukka Nig
74E1 Nuanetsi Zim
74E1 Nuanetsi R Zim
71G4 Nuatja Togo
72D2 Nuba Mts Sudan
66B2 Nubian Desert Sudan
28A3 Nuble R Chile
8D4 Nueces R USA
6J3 Nueltin L Can
21B1 Nueva Casas Grandes Mexico
29A3 Nueva Germania Par
23A2 Nueva Gerona Cuba
28A3 Nueva Imperial Chile
28D2 Nueva Palmira Urug
21B2 Nueva Rosita Mexico
23B2 Nuevitas Cuba
22B1 Nuevo State, Mexico
21B1 Nuevo Casas Grandes Mexico
22A1 Nuevo Ideal Mexico
21C2 Nuevo Laredo Mexico
69D4 Nugaal Region, Somalia
7N2 Nûgâtsiaq Greenland
7N2 Nûgussuaq Pen Greenland
7N2 Nûgussuaq / Greenland
77G1 Nui / Tuvalu
52A5 Nui Con Voi R Vietnam
36C3 Nuits France
61E2 Nu Jiang R China
75A2 Nukey Bluff Mt Aust
64D3 Nukhayb Iraq
77G1 Nukufetau / Tuvalu
77G1 Nukulaelae / Tuvalu
77H1 Nukunon / Tokelau Is
48G5 Nukus Uzbekistan
10G3 Nulato USA
76B4 Nullarbor Plain Aust
71J4 Numan Nig
54C3 Numata Japan
72C3 Numatinna R Sudan
53D4 Numazu Japan
51G7 Numfoor / Indon
75C3 Numurkah Aust
10F3 Nunapitchuk USA
14A1 Nunda USA
10E3 Nunivak I USA
60D2 Nunkun Mt India
10C3 Nunligran Russian Fed
53A1 Nuomin He R China
40B2 Nuoro Sardegna
63C2 Nurābād Iran
37C2 Nure R Italy
75A2 Nuriootpa Aust
60C1 Nuristan Upland Afghan
44J5 Nurlat Russian Fed
32K6 Nurmes Fin
42C3 Nürnberg Germany
75C2 Nurri,Mt Aust
56E4 Nusa Tenggara Is Indon
57B4 Nusa Tenggara Timor Province, Indon
64D2 Nusaybin Turk
10G4 Nushagak R USA
10G4 Nushagak B USA
10G4 Nushagak Pen USA
60B3 Nushki Pak
7M4 Nutak Can
10K3 Nutzotin Mts USA
7L3 Nuvukjuak Can
61B2 Nuwakot Nepal
62C3 Nuwara-Eliya Sri Lanka
74C3 Nuweveldreeks Mts S Africa
45C3 Nyac USA
14D2 Nyack USA
72D3 Nyahururu Falls Kenya
75B3 Nyah West Aust
50C3 Nyaingentanglha Shan Mts China
72D4 Nyakabindi Tanz
44L3 Nyaksimvol' Russian Fed
72C2 Nyala Sudan
61C2 Nyalam China
72C3 Nyamlell Sudan
73D6 Nyanda Zim
44G3 Nyandoma Russian Fed
72B4 Nyanga R Gabon
61D2 Nyang Qu China
73D5 Nyasa L Malawi/Mozam
55B2 Nyaunglebin Burma
44K4 Nyazepetrovsk Russian Fed
32G7 Nyborg Den
32H7 Nybro Sweden
48J3 Nyda Russian Fed
7M1 Nyeboes Land Region Can
61D1 Nyenchentanglha Range Mts China
72D4 Nyeri Kenya
73D5 Nyimba Zambia
59H2 Nyingchi China
43E3 Nyíregyháza Hung
72D3 Nyiru,Mt Kenya
32J6 Nykarleby Fin
32F7 Nykøbing Den
32G8 Nykøbing Den
32H7 Nyköping Sweden
74D1 Nyl R S Africa
74D1 Nylstroom S Africa
75C2 Nymagee Aust
32H7 Nynäshamn Sweden
75C2 Nyngan Aust
37B1 Nyon Switz
72B3 Nyong R Cam
54A3 Nyongwol S Korea
54A3 Nyongwon N Korea
38D3 Nyons France
42D2 Nysa Pol
53E1 Nysh Russian Fed
18C2 Nyssa USA
44H3 Nyukhcha Russian Fed
50F1 Nyukzha R Russian Fed
49N3 Nyurba Russian Fed
72D4 Nzega Tanz
70B4 Nzérékore Guinea
73B4 N'zeto Angola
71F4 Nzi R Ivory Coast

O

11C3 Oacoma USA
11B3 Oahe,L Res USA
20E5 Oahu,I Hawaiian Is
75B2 Oakbank Aust
20B2 Oakdale USA
11C2 Oakes USA
75D1 Oakey Aust
19B3 Oakland California, USA
11C3 Oakland Nebraska, USA
18B2 Oakland Oregon, USA
12B3 Oakland City USA
12B2 Oak Lawn USA
20B2 Oakley California, USA
16B2 Oakley Kansas, USA
15C1 Oak Ridge USA
18B2 Oakridge USA
4F5 Oakville Can
78B3 Oamaru NZ
20D2 Oasis California, USA
18D2 Oasis Nevada, USA

42

Parksville Pichilemu

18B1 **Parksville** Can
18D2 **Park Valley** USA
62C1 **Parlākimidi** India
62B1 **Parli** India
37D2 **Parma** Italy
12C2 **Parma** USA
27K4 **Parnaiba** Brazil
27K4 **Parnaiba** *R* Brazil
41E3 **Párnon Óros** *Mts* Greece
44C4 **Pärnu** Estonia
61C2 **Paro** Bhutan
75B1 **Paroo** *R* Aust
75B2 **Paroo Channel** *R* Aust
63E2 **Paropamisus** *Mts* Afghan
41F3 **Páros** *I* Greece
19D3 **Parowan** USA
37B2 **Parpaillon** *Mts* France
28A3 **Parral** Chile
75D2 **Parramatta** Aust
8C4 **Parras** Mexico
7K3 **Parry B** Can
10O1 **Parry,C** Can
6G2 **Parry Is** Can
10O2 **Parry Pen** Can
12C1 **Parry Sound** Can
42C3 **Parsberg** Germany
6F4 **Parsnip** *R* Can
17C2 **Parsons** Kansas, USA
13D3 **Parsons** West Virginia, USA
38B2 **Parthenay** France
40C3 **Partinico** Italy
53C3 **Partizansk** Russian Fed
27H4 **Paru** *R* Brazil
22A1 **Páruco** Mexico
62C1 **Parvatipuram** India
74D2 **Parys** S Africa
17C4 **Pasadena** Texas, USA
20C3 **Pasadena** USA
57A3 **Pasangkayu** Indon
57B4 **Pasarwajo** Indon
55B2 **Pasawing** Burma
17E3 **Pascagoula** USA
41F1 **Paşcani** Rom
18C1 **Pasco** USA
36B1 **Pas-de-Calais** Department, France
32G8 **Pasewalk** Germany
3G2 **Pasfield L** Can
63D3 **Pashū'īyeh** Iran
76B4 **Pasley,C** Aust
63E3 **Pasni** Pak
28D1 **Paso de los Libres** Arg
25E4 **Paso de los Toros** Urug
25B6 **Paso Limay** Arg
20B3 **Paso Robles** USA
5H4 **Paspébiac** Can
3H3 **Pasquia Hills** Can
14C2 **Passaic** USA
42C3 **Passau** Germany
25E3 **Passo de los Libres** Arg
22B1 **Passo del Toro** *Mt* Mexico
37D1 **Passo di Stelvio** *Mt* Italy
37D1 **Passo di Tonale** Italy
28E1 **Passo Fundo** Brazil
29C3 **Passos** Brazil
37B2 **Passy** France
26C4 **Pastaza** *R* Peru
28C3 **Pasteur** Arg
6H4 **Pas,The** Can
26C3 **Pasto** Colombia
10F3 **Pastol B** USA
37D2 **Pasubio** *Mt* Italy
56D4 **Pasuruan** Indon
43E1 **Pasvalys** Lithuania
60C4 **Pātan** India
61C2 **Patan** Nepal
75B3 **Patchewollock** Aust
78B1 **Patea** NZ
78B2 **Patea** *R* NZ
40C3 **Paterno** Italy
14C2 **Paterson** USA
78A3 **Paterson Inlet** *B* NZ
60D2 **Pathankot** India
11A3 **Pathfinder Res** USA
60D2 **Patiāla** India
26C6 **Pativilca** Peru
41F3 **Pátmos** *I* Greece
61C2 **Patna** India
64D2 **Patnos** Turk
49N4 **Patomskoye Nagor'ye** *Upland* Russian Fed
27L5 **Patos** Brazil
29C2 **Patos de Minas** Brazil
28B2 **Patquia** Arg
41E3 **Pátrai** Greece
44L3 **Patrasuy** Russian Fed
29C2 **Patrocinio** Brazil
72E4 **Patta** *I* Kenya
57A4 **Pattallasang** Indon
55C4 **Pattani** Thai
20B2 **Patterson** California, USA
17D4 **Patterson** Louisiana, USA
10M3 **Patterson,Mt** Can
20C2 **Patterson Mt** USA
14A2 **Patton** USA
3C2 **Pattullo,Mt** Can
27L5 **Patu** Brazil
61D3 **Patuakhali** Bang
21D3 **Patuca** *R* Honduras
22B2 **Patzcuaro** Mexico
38B3 **Pau** France
10O2 **Paulatuk** Can
27K5 **Paulistana** Brazil
74E2 **Paulpietersburg** S Africa
17C3 **Pauls Valley** USA
55B2 **Paungde** Burma
60D2 **Pauri** India
32H5 **Pauskie** Nor
29D2 **Pavão** Brazil
37C2 **Pavia** Italy
48J4 **Pavlodar** Kazakhstan
10F4 **Pavlof V** USA
10F4 **Pavlov B** USA
44K4 **Pavlovka** Russian Fed
44G4 **Pavlovo** Russian Fed
45G5 **Pavlovsk** Russian Fed
37D2 **Pavullo nel Frigano** Italy
56D3 **Pawan** *R* Indon
17C2 **Pawhuska** USA
14A3 **Paw Paw** USA
14E2 **Pawtucket** USA
16B1 **Paxton** USA
56B3 **Payakumbuh** Indon
37B1 **Payerne** Switz
18C2 **Payette** USA
7L4 **Payne,L** Can
11D2 **Paynesville** USA
28D2 **Paysandu** Urug
36A2 **Pays d'Auge** Region, France
36A2 **Pays-de-Bray** Region, France
36A2 **Pays de Caux** Region, France
36A2 **Pays d'Ouche** Region, France
41E2 **Pazardzhik** Bulg
37E2 **Pazin** Croatia, Yugos
3E2 **Peace** *R* Can
15E4 **Peace** *R* USA
3E2 **Peace River** Can
19D3 **Peach Springs** USA
35E5 **Peak District Nat Pk** Eng
75A1 **Peake** *R* Aust
13F1 **Peaked Mt** USA
75C2 **Peak Hill** Aust
51G7 **Peak Mandala** *Mt* Indon
35E5 **Peak,The** *Mt* Eng
19E3 **Peale,Mt** USA
17D3 **Pearl** *R* USA
20E5 **Pearl City** Hawaiian Is
20E5 **Pearl Harbor** Hawaiian Is
17F4 **Pearsall** USA
74D3 **Pearston** S Africa
6H2 **Peary Chan** Can
73D5 **Pebane** Mozam
41E2 **Peć** Serbia, Yugos
29D2 **Peçanha** Brazil
17D4 **Pecan Island** USA
32L5 **Pechenga** Russian Fed
44K2 **Pechora** Russian Fed
44J2 **Pechora** *R* Russian Fed
44J2 **Pechorskaya Guba** *G* Russian Fed
44J2 **Pechorskoye More** *S* Russian Fed
40D3 **Pecoraro** *Mt* Italy
16B3 **Pecos** USA
16B3 **Pecos** *R* USA
43D3 **Pécs** Hung
56G7 **Pedang Endau** Malay
65B1 **Pedhoulas** Cyprus
75A1 **Pedirka** Aust
29D2 **Pedra Azul** Brazil
29C3 **Pedregulho** Brazil
23B3 **Pedro Cays** *Is* Caribbean
25C2 **Pedro de Valdivia** Chile
29B2 **Pedro Gomes** Brazil
29A3 **Pedro Juan Caballero** Par
28C3 **Pedro Luro** Arg
22C1 **Pedro Mentova** Mexico
62C3 **Pedro,Pt** Sri Lanka
28D1 **Pedro R Fernandez** Arg
75B2 **Peebinga** Aust
34D4 **Peebles** Scot
15D2 **Pee Dee** *R* USA
14D2 **Peekskill** USA
35C4 **Peel** Eng
10M2 **Peel** *R* Can
6J2 **Peel Sd** Can
75A1 **Peera Peera Poolanna** *L* Aust
3F2 **Peerless L** Can
51G7 **Peg Arfak** *Mt* Indon
78B2 **Pegasus B** NZ
10B2 **Pegtymel'** *R* Russian Fed
61E4 **Pegu** Burma
56B3 **Pegunungan Barisan** *Mts* Indon
56D2 **Pegunungan Iran** *Mts* Malay Indon
76C1 **Pegunungan Maoke** *Mts* Indon
56E3 **Pegunungan Meratus** *Mts* Indon
56D2 **Pegunungan Muller** *Mts* Indon
56D3 **Pegunungan Schwanet** *Mts* Indon
56B3 **Pegunungan Tigapuluh** *Mts* Indon
55B2 **Pegu Yoma** *Mts* Burma
28C3 **Pehuajó** Arg
32K7 **Peipsi Järv** *L* Estonia
32K7 **Peipus, Lake** *L* Russian Fed
29B1 **Peixe** *R* Mato Grosso, Brazil
29B3 **Peixe** *R* Sao Paulo, Brazil
52D3 **Pei Xian** China
56C4 **Pekalongan** Indon
55C5 **Pekan** Malay
56B2 **Pekanbaru** Indon
12B2 **Pekin** USA
Peking = Beijing
55C5 **Pelabohan Kelang** Malay
71E1 **Pelagie Is** Mediterranean S
57C3 **Pelau Pelau Boö** *Is* Indon
56E4 **Pelau Pelau Kangean** *Is* Indon
56D4 **Pelau Pelau Karimunjawa** *Arch* Indon
57C4 **Pelau Pelau Maisel** *Is* Indon
57C4 **Pelau Pelau Penyu** *Is* Indon
56E4 **Pelau Pelau Postilyon** *Is* Indon
57B3 **Pelau Pelau Salabangka** *Is* Indon
41E1 **Peleaga** *Mt* Rom
49N4 **Peleduy** Russian Fed
12C2 **Pelee I** Can
76B1 **Peleng** *I* Indon
10L4 **Pelican** USA
11D2 **Pelican L** USA
74A1 **Pelican Pt** S Africa
41D2 **Pelješac** *Pen* Croatia, Yugos
28C3 **Pellegrini** Arg
32J5 **Pello** Fin
10M3 **Pelly** *R* Can
7J3 **Pelly Bay** Can
10L3 **Pelly Crossing** Can
10M3 **Pelly Mts** Can
28E2 **Pelotas** Brazil
25F3 **Pelotas** *R* Brazil
65B3 **Pelusium** *Hist Site* Egypt
37B2 **Pelvoux** Region, France
44L3 **Pelym** *R* Russian Fed
56C4 **Pemalang** Indon
56B3 **Pematang** Indon
56A2 **Pematangsiantar** Indon
73E5 **Pemba** Mozam
72D4 **Pemba** *I* Tanz
3D3 **Pemberton** Can
11C2 **Pembina** USA
3E3 **Pembina** *R* Can
4F4 **Pembroke** Can
15C2 **Pembroke** USA
35C6 **Pembroke** Wales
28A3 **Pemuco** Chile
14E1 **Penacook** USA
56E2 **Penambo Range** *Mts* Malay
29B3 **Penápolis** Brazil
39A2 **Peñarroya** Spain
39B1 **Penarroya** *Mt* Spain
39A1 **Peña Trevina** *Mt* Spain
72B3 **Pende** *R* Chad
10N4 **Pendelton,Mt** Can
71G3 **Pendjari** *R* Benin
18C1 **Pendleton** USA
18C1 **Pend Oreille** *R* USA
27L6 **Penedo** Brazil
4F5 **Penetanguishene** Can
60D5 **Penganga** *R* India
52D5 **P'eng hu Lieh tao** *Is* Taiwan
52E2 **Penglai** China
52B4 **Pengshui** China
51G7 **Pengunungan Maoke** *Mts* Indon
5H4 **Peninsule de Gaspé** *Pen* Can
23C4 **Península de la Guajiri** *Pen* Colombia
23E4 **Península de Paria** *Pen* Ven
55C5 **Peninsular Malaysia** Malay
22B1 **Penjamo** Mexico
37E3 **Pennabilli** Italy
62B2 **Penner** *R* India
34D4 **Pennine Chain** *Mts* Eng
14C3 **Penns Grove** USA
9F2 **Pennsylvania** State, USA
14B1 **Penn Yan** USA
7M3 **Penny Highlands** *Mts* Can
13F1 **Penobscot** *R* USA
13F2 **Penobscot B** USA
75B3 **Penola** Aust
76C4 **Penong** Aust
23A5 **Penonomé** Panama
35D4 **Penrith** Eng
15B2 **Pensacola** USA
79E **Pensacola Mts** Ant
56E2 **Pensiangan** Malay
77F2 **Pentecost** *I* Vanuatu
3E4 **Penticton** Can
34D2 **Pentland Firth** *Chan* Scot
34D4 **Pentland Hills** Scot
44H5 **Penza** Russian Fed
35C6 **Penzance** Eng
49S3 **Penzhina** *R* Russian Fed
49S3 **Penzhinskaya Guba** *B* Russian Fed
12B2 **Peoria** USA
56B3 **Perabumulih** Indon
55C5 **Perak** *R* Malay
56B2 **Perawang** Indon
29A3 **Perdido** *R* Brazil
26C3 **Pereira** Colombia
29B3 **Pereira Barreto** Brazil
45G6 **Perelazovskiy** Russian Fed
10H4 **Perenosa B** USA
43G2 **Pereyaslav** Ukraine
53D2 **Pereyaslavka** Russian Fed
28C2 **Pergamino** Arg
37E3 **Pergola** Italy
7L4 **Péribonca** *R* Can
66D4 **Perim** *I* Yemen
38C2 **Périqueux** France
21E4 **Perlas Arch de** *Is* Panama
44K4 **Perm'** Russian Fed
Pernambuco = Recife
27L5 **Pernambuco State**, Brazil
75A2 **Pernatty Lg** Aust
41E2 **Pernik** Bulg
36B2 **Péronne** France
22C2 **Perote** Mexico
38C3 **Perpignan** France
20D4 **Perris** USA
15C2 **Perry** Florida, USA
15C2 **Perry** Georgia, USA
14A1 **Perry** New York, USA
17C2 **Perry** Oklahoma, USA
6H3 **Perry River** Can
12C2 **Perrysburg** USA
16B2 **Perryton** USA
10G4 **Perryville** Alaska, USA
17E2 **Perryville** Missouri, USA
4F5 **Perth** Can
13D2 **Perth** Can
34D3 **Perth** Scot
14C2 **Perth Amboy** USA
37A3 **Pertuis** France
26D6 **Peru** Republic, S America
12B2 **Peru** USA
xxixP5 **Peru Basin** Pacific O
xxxE6 **Peru-Chile Trench** Pacific O
40C2 **Perugia** Italy
28D1 **Perugorria** Arg
40D2 **Peruzic** Croatia, Yugos
64D2 **Pervari** Turk
44G5 **Pervomaysk** Russian Fed
45E6 **Pervomaysk** Ukraine
44K4 **Pervoural'sk** Russian Fed
37E3 **Pesaro** Italy
20A2 **Pescadero** USA
Pescadores = P'eng-hu Lieh-tao
40C2 **Pescara** Italy
37D2 **Peschiera** Italy
37D3 **Pescia** Italy
60C2 **Peshawar** Pak
41E2 **Peshkopi** Alb
12B1 **Peshtigo** USA
44F4 **Pestovo** Russian Fed
65C2 **Petah Tiqwa** Israel
19B3 **Petaluma** USA
36C2 **Pétange** Lux
22B2 **Petatlán** Mexico
73D5 **Petauke** Zambia
4F4 **Petawawa** Can
12B2 **Petenwell L** USA
75A2 **Peterborough** Aust
4F5 **Peterborough** Can
35E5 **Peterborough** Eng
14E1 **Peterborough** USA
34E3 **Peterhead** Scot
7M1 **Petermann Gletscher** *Gl* Greenland
76B3 **Petermann Range** *Mts* Aust
25B5 **Peteroa** *Mt* Chile/Arg
3G2 **Peter Pond L** Can
10M4 **Petersburg** Alaska, USA
13D3 **Petersburg** Virginia, USA
4F2 **Petite Rivière de la Baleine** *R* Can
3E2 **Petitot** *R* Can
5H3 **Petitsikapau L** Can
60C4 **Petlād** India
22C2 **Petlalcingo** Mexico
21D2 **Peto** Mexico
28A2 **Petorca** Chile
12C1 **Petoskey** USA
65C3 **Petra** *Hist Site* Jordan
79G2 **Petral** *Base* Ant
49N2 **Petra, Ostrov** *I* Russian Fed
19E3 **Petrified Forest Nat Pk** USA
27K5 **Petrolina** Brazil
48H4 **Petropavlovsk** Kazakhstan
50J1 **Petropavlovsk-Kamchatskiy** Russian Fed
29D3 **Petrópolis** Brazil
45H5 **Petrovsk** Russian Fed
49M4 **Petrovsk Zabakal'skiy** Russian Fed
50D1 **Petrovsk Zabaykal'skiy** Russian Fed
44E3 **Petrozavodsk** Russian Fed
74D2 **Petrus** S Africa
74D2 **Petrusburg** S Africa
74C3 **Petrusville** S Africa
49T3 **Pevek** Russian Fed
44H2 **Peza** *R* Russian Fed
36D2 **Pfälzer Wald** Region, Germany
42B3 **Pforzheim** Germany
60D2 **Phagwara** India
74E1 **Phalaborwa** S Africa
60C3 **Phalodi** India
36D2 **Phalsbourg** France
62A1 **Phaltan** India
55B4 **Phangnga** Thai
55C3 **Phanom Dang** *Mts* Camb
55D3 **Phan Rang** Viet
55D3 **Phan Thiet** Viet
17F4 **Pharr** USA
3H2 **Phelps L** Can
15D1 **Phelps L** USA
15B2 **Phenix City** USA
55B3 **Phet Buri** Thai
55D3 **Phiafay** Laos
17E3 **Philadelphia** Mississippi, USA
14C2 **Philadelphia** Pennsylvania, USA
11B3 **Philip** USA
Philippeville = Skikda
36C1 **Philippeville** Belg
51F5 **Philippine S** Pacific O
51F5 **Philippines** Republic, S E Asia
xxviiiH4 **Philippine Trench** Pacific O
74D3 **Philippolis** S Africa
18D1 **Philipsburg** Montana, USA
13D2 **Philipsburg** Pennsylvania, USA
10J2 **Philip Smith Mts** USA
74C3 **Philipstown** S Africa
57F7 **Phillipine S** Phil
7K1 **Phillips B** Can
16C2 **Phillipsburg** Kansas, USA
14C2 **Phillipsburg** New Jersey, USA
7L2 **Philpots Pen** Can
55C3 **Phnom Penh** Camb
19D4 **Phoenix** Arizona, USA
14B1 **Phoenix** New York, USA
77H1 **Phoenix** *Is* Pacific O
14C2 **Phoenixville** USA
55C1 **Phong Saly** Laos
Phra Nakhon = Bangkok
55C2 **Phu Bia** *Mt* Laos
55D3 **Phu Cuong** Viet
55B4 **Phuket** Thai
61B3 **Phulbāni** India
55C2 **Phu Miang** *Mt* Thai
55D2 **Phu Set** *Mt* Laos
55D1 **Phu Tho** Viet
55D4 **Phu Vinh** Viet
32K6 **Phyäselkä** *L* Fin
37C2 **Piacenza** Italy
75D1 **Pialba** Aust
75C2 **Pian** *R* Aust
37D2 **Pianoro** Italy
40C2 **Pianosa** *I* Italy
40D2 **Pianosa** *I* Italy
43E2 **Piaseczno** Pol
29D1 **Piata** Brazil
41F1 **Piatra-Neamt** Rom
27K5 **Piaui** State, Brazil
37E2 **Piave** Italy
37E1 **Piave** *R* Italy
72D3 **Pibor** *R* Sudan
72D3 **Pibor Post** Sudan
36B2 **Picardie** Region, France
17E3 **Picayune** USA
37B2 **Pic de Rochebrune** *Mt* France
28A2 **Pichilemu** Chile

Pichi Mahuida Port Hedland

28C3 **Pichi Mahuida** Arg
22D2 **Pichucalco** Mexico
35E4 **Pickering** Eng
7J4 **Pickle Lake** Can
70A1 **Pico** *I* Açores
37C1 **Pico Bernina** *Mt* Switz
23C5 **Pico Bolivar** *Mt* Ven
39C1 **Pico de Anito** *Mt* Spain
21B3 **Pico del Infiernillo** *Mt* Mexico
23C3 **Pico Duarte** *Mt* Dom Rep
27K5 **Picos** Brazil
39B1 **Picos de Europa** *Mt* Spain
75D2 **Picton** Aust
78B2 **Picton** NZ
72B1 **Pic Toussidé** *Mt* Chad
28A3 **Picún Leufú** *R* Arg
29C3 **Piedade** Brazil
20C2 **Piedra** USA
28B4 **Piedra de Aguila** Arg
20B3 **Piedras Blancas,Pt** USA
21B2 **Piedras Negras** Mexico
12B1 **Pie I** Can
32K6 **Pieksämäki** Fin
32K6 **Pielinen** *L* Fin
37B2 **Piemonte** Region, Italy
74D2 **Pienaarsrivier** S Africa
11B3 **Pierre** USA
43D3 **Pieztany** Czech
74E2 **Pietermaritzburg** S Africa
74D1 **Pietersburg** S Africa
37D3 **Pietrasanta** Italy
74E2 **Piet Retief** S Africa
45C6 **Pietrosu** *Mt* Rom
41F1 **Pietrosul** *Mt* Rom
37E1 **Pieve di Cadore** Italy
51H6 **Pigailoe** *I* Pacific O
3F3 **Pigeon L** Can
17D2 **Piggott** USA
28C3 **Pigüé** Arg
22D2 **Pijijapan** Mexico
4C3 **Pikangikum** Can
7J4 **Pikangikum L** Can
16A2 **Pikes Peak** USA
74B3 **Piketberg** S Africa
12C3 **Pikeville** USA
7O3 **Pikiutaleq** Greenland
59F2 **Pik Kommunizma** *Mt* Tajikistan
72B3 **Pikounda** Congo
59G1 **Pik Pobedy** *Mt* China/ Kirgizia
28D3 **Pila** Arg
42D2 **Pila** Pol
25E3 **Pilar** Par
25D2 **Pilcomayo** *R* Arg/Par
74E1 **Pilgrim's Rest** S Africa
60D3 **Pilibhit** India
43D2 **Pilica** *R* Pol
75E3 **Pillar,C** Aust
41E3 **Pilos** Greece
18C1 **Pilot Knob Mt** USA
20D1 **Pilot Peak** *Mt* USA
10G4 **Pilot Point** USA
10F3 **Pilot Station** USA
17E3 **Pilottown** USA
27G4 **Pimenta** Brazil
55C4 **Pinang** *I* Malay
23A2 **Pinar del Rio** Cuba
28B2 **Pinas** Arg
36C1 **Pinche** Belg
3F4 **Pincher Creek** Can
27J4 **Pindaré** *R* Brazil
41E3 **Pindhos** *Mts* Greece
17D3 **Pine Bluff** USA
16B1 **Pine Bluffs** USA
5L4 **Pine,C** Can
11D2 **Pine City** USA
76C2 **Pine Creek** Aust
14B2 **Pine Creek** *R* USA
20C1 **Pinecrest** USA
20C2 **Pinedale** California, USA
18E2 **Pinedale** Wyoming, USA
4B3 **Pine Falls** Can
20C2 **Pine Flat Res** USA
44G3 **Pinega** Russian Fed
44H3 **Pinega** *R* Russian Fed
14B2 **Pine Grove** USA
15C3 **Pine Hills** USA
3G2 **Pinehouse L** Can
15D1 **Pinehurst** USA
15E4 **Pine I** USA
17D3 **Pineland** USA
15C3 **Pinellas Park** USA
20B3 **Pine Mt** USA
3F1 **Pine Point** Can
11B3 **Pine Ridge** USA
4C4 **Pine River** USA
37B2 **Pinerolo** Italy
17D3 **Pines,Lo'the** USA
17D3 **Pineville** USA
52C3 **Pingdingshan** China
52B5 **Pingguo** China
52B2 **Pingliang** China
52B2 **Pingluo** China
52D4 **Pingtan Dao** *I* China
52E5 **P'ing tung** Taiwan
52A3 **Pingwu** China
52B5 **Pingxiang** Guangxi, China
52C4 **Pingxiang** Jiangxi, China
27J4 **Pinheiro** Brazil
28E2 **Pinheiro Machado** Brazil
56A2 **Pini** *I* Indon
41E3 **Piniós** *R* Greece
57B2 **Pinjang** Indon
76A4 **Pinjarra** Aust
3D2 **Pink Mountain** Can
75B3 **Pinnaroo** Aust
Pinos,I de = Isla de la Juventud
20C3 **Pinos,Mt** USA
19B3 **Pinos,Pt** USA
22C2 **Pinotepa Nacional** Mexico
57A3 **Pinrang** Indon
45D5 **Pinsk** Belorussia
28C1 **Pinto** Arg
44H3 **Pinyug** Russian Fed
19D3 **Pioche** USA
40C2 **Piombino** Italy
49K2 **Pioner, Ostrov** *I* Russian Fed
18D1 **Pioneer Mts** USA
44L3 **Pionerskiy** Russian Fed
43D2 **Piotrków Trybunalski** Pol
34F2 **Piper** *Oilfield* N Sea
20D2 **Piper Peak** *Mt* USA
11C3 **Pipestone** USA
4C3 **Pipestone** *R* Can
28D3 **Pipinas** Arg
5M4 **Pipmudcan, Réservoir** *Res* Can
12C2 **Piqua** USA
29B4 **Piquiri** *R* Brazil
29C2 **Piracanjuba** Brazil
29C3 **Piracicaba** Brazil
29C3 **Piraçunúnga** Brazil
29C3 **Pirai do Sul** Brazil
41E3 **Piraiévs** Greece
29C3 **Pirajuí** Brazil
37E2 **Piran** Slovenia, Yugos
29B2 **Piranhas** Brazil
29D2 **Pirapora** Brazil
28D1 **Piratina** *R* Brazil
28E2 **Piratini** *R* Brazil
41E2 **Pirdop** Bulg
29C2 **Pirenópolis** Brazil
29C2 **Pires do Rio** Brazil
41E3 **Pírgos** Greece
Pirineos = Pyrénées
38B3 **Pirineos** *Mts* Spain
27K4 **Piripiri** Brazil
36D2 **Pirmasens** Germany
41E2 **Pirot** Serbia, Yugos
60C2 **Pīr Panjāl Range** *Mts* Pak
57C3 **Piru** Indon
20C3 **Piru Creek** *R* USA
37D3 **Pisa** Italy
26C6 **Pisco** Peru
14C1 **Piseco** USA
42C3 **Písek** Czech
60B2 **Pishin** Pak
20B3 **Pismo Beach** USA
25C3 **Pissis** *Mt* Arg
37D3 **Pistoia** Italy
39B1 **Pisuerga** *R* Spain
18B2 **Pit** *R* USA
26C3 **Pitalito** Colombia
xxixN6 **Pitcairn** *I* Pacific O
32H5 **Pite** *R* Sweden
32J5 **Piteå** Sweden
41E2 **Piteşti** Rom
49L4 **Pit Gorodok** Russian Fed
36B2 **Pithiviers** France
44E3 **Pitkyaranta** Russian Fed
34D3 **Pitlochry** Scot
44M2 **Pitlyar** Russian Fed
28A3 **Pitrutquén** Chile
77H5 **Pitt** *I* NZ
3C3 **Pitt I** Can
20B1 **Pittsburg** California, USA
17D2 **Pittsburg** Kansas, USA
5G4 **Pittsburg** New Hampshire, USA
13D2 **Pittsburgh** USA
12A3 **Pittsfield** Illinois, USA
14D1 **Pittsfield** Massachusetts, USA
14C2 **Pittston** USA
75D1 **Pittsworth** Aust
20C3 **Piute Peak** *Mt* USA
61B2 **Piuthan** Nepal
53D1 **Pivan'** Russian Fed
20C3 **Pixley** USA
37D1 **Pizzo Redorta** *Mt* Italy
32B2 **Pjórsá** Iceland
26B5 **Pjura** Peru
5L4 **Placentia** Can
7N5 **Placentia B** Can
20B1 **Placerville** USA
36D2 **Plaine d'Alsace** *Plain* France
36B1 **Plaine des Flandres** *Plain* France/Belg
70C2 **Plaine du Tidikelt** *Desert* Region
36C2 **Plaine Lorraine** Region, France
16B2 **Plains** USA
11C3 **Plainview** Nebraska, USA
16B3 **Plainview** Texas, USA
20B2 **Planada** USA
27H7 **Planalto de Mato Grosso** *Plat* Brazil
27L5 **Planalto do Borborema** *Plat* Brazil
26B1 **Planalto do Mato Grosso** *Mts* Brazil
77E1 **Planet Deep** PNG
11C3 **Plankinton** USA
17C3 **Plano** USA
15E4 **Plantation** USA
15C3 **Plant City** USA
39A1 **Plasencia** Spain
44L5 **Plast** Russian Fed
53D3 **Plastun** Russian Fed
71H4 **Plateau** State, Nig
71G3 **Plateau de Dadango** Togo
36C3 **Plateau de Langres** *Plat* France
37A2 **Plateau De St Christol** Region, France
70C2 **Plateau du Tademait** Alg
36D2 **Plateau Lorrain** *Plat* France
38C2 **Plateaux de Limousin** *Plat* France
39C2 **Plateaux du Sersou** *Plat* Alg
23C5 **Plato** Colombia
45J7 **Plato Ustyurt** *Plat* Kazakhstan
65B1 **Platres** Cyprus
11C3 **Platte** USA
16B1 **Platte** *R* USA
12A2 **Platteville** USA
13E2 **Plattsburgh** USA
17C1 **Plattsmouth** USA
42C2 **Plauen** Germany
44F5 **Plavsk** Russian Fed
22B2 **Playa Azul** Mexico
26B4 **Playas** Ecuador
22C2 **Playa Vincente** Mexico
39A1 **Plaza de Moro Almanzor** *Mt* Spain
20B2 **Pleasanton** California, USA
17F4 **Pleasanton** Texas, USA
14C3 **Pleasantville** USA
12B3 **Pleasure Ridge Park** USA
55D3 **Pleiku** Viet
78C1 **Plenty,B of** NZ
11B2 **Plentywood** USA
44G3 **Plesetsk** Russian Fed
43D2 **Pleszew** Pol
7L4 **Pletipi,L** Can
41E2 **Pleven** Bulg
41D2 **Pljevlja** Montenegro, Yugos
41D2 **Ploče** Bosnia & Herzegovina, Yugos
43D2 **Płock** Pol
38B2 **Ploërmel** France
41F2 **Ploieşti** Rom
36D3 **Plombières-les-Bains** France
44C5 **Płońsk** Pol
41E2 **Plovdiv** Bulg
18C1 **Plummer** USA
10G3 **Plummer,Mt** USA
73C6 **Plumtree** Zim
20B1 **Plymouth** California, USA
35C6 **Plymouth** Eng
12B2 **Plymouth** Indiana, USA
14E2 **Plymouth** Massachusetts, USA
14C2 **Plymouth** Pennsylvania, USA
14E2 **Plymouth B** USA
35C6 **Plymouth Sd** Eng
35D5 **Plynlimon** *Mt* Wales
42C3 **Plzeň** Czech
42D2 **Pniewy** Pol
71F3 **Pô** Burkina
37E2 **Po** *R* Italy
71G4 **Pobé** Benin
53E2 **Pobedino** Russian Fed
18D2 **Pocatello** USA
43G2 **Pochinok** Russian Fed
22C2 **Pochutla** Mexico
29D1 **Poções** Brazil
13D3 **Pocomoke City** USA
29A2 **Poconé** Brazil
29C3 **Pocos de Caldas** Brazil
37D2 **Po di Volano** *R* Italy
49L3 **Podkamennaya Tunguska** *R* Russian Fed
44F4 **Podol'sk** Russian Fed
43F3 **Podol'skaya Vozvyshennost'** *Upland* Ukraine
44E3 **Podporozh'ye** Russian Fed
44G3 **Podyuga** Russian Fed
74B2 **Pofadder** S Africa
37D3 **Poggibonsi** Italy
60A2 **Poghdar** Afghan
53C3 **Pogranichnyy** Russian Fed
57B3 **Poh** Indon
53B4 **P'ohang** S Korea
79G9 **Poinsett,C** Ant
75C2 **Point** Aust
23E3 **Pointe-à-Pitre** Guadeloupe
5H4 **Pointe aux Anglais** Can
38B2 **Pointe de Barfleur** *Pt* France
5J4 **Pointe de l'Est** *C* Can
4F3 **Pointe Louis XIV** *C* Can
72B4 **Pointe Noire** Congo
72A3 **Pointe Pongara** *Pt* Gabon
75B3 **Point Fairy** Aust
23L1 **Point Fortin** Trinidad
10E2 **Point Hope** USA
6G3 **Point L** Can
10F2 **Point Lay** USA
14C2 **Point Pleasant** New Jersey, USA
12C3 **Point Pleasant** W Virginia, USA
37B2 **Point St Bernard** *Mt* France
38C2 **Poitiers** France
38B2 **Poitou** Region, France
36A2 **Poix** France
60C3 **Pokaran** India
75C1 **Pokataroo** Aust
61B2 **Pokhara** Nepal
49O3 **Pokrovsk** Russian Fed
19D3 **Polacca** USA
43D2 **Poland** Republic, Europe
14C1 **Poland** USA
4E3 **Polar Bear Prov Park** Can
45E8 **Polath** Turk
64B2 **Polatli** Turk
57B3 **Poleang** Indon
57A3 **Polewali** Indon
71J4 **Poli** Cam
37A1 **Poligny** France
49P4 **Poliny Osipenko** Russian Fed
65B1 **Polis** Cyprus
41E2 **Políyiros** Greece
62B2 **Pollāchi** India
57F8 **Polollo Is** Phil
43F2 **Polonnye** Ukraine
43F1 **Polotsk** Belorussia
18D1 **Polson** USA
45E6 **Poltava** Ukraine
40D1 **Pölten** Austria
44K3 **Polunochoye** Russian Fed
16A3 **Polvadera** USA
44E2 **Polyarnyy** Murmansk, Russian Fed
49Q2 **Polyarnyy** Yakutskaya, Russian Fed
44L2 **Polyarnyy Ural** *Mts* Russian Fed
xxixL4 **Polynesia** *Region* Pacific O
26C5 **Pomabamba** Peru
29D3 **Pomba** *R* Brazil
20D3 **Pomona** USA
17C2 **Pomona Res** USA
15E4 **Pompano Beach** USA
14C2 **Pompton Lakes** USA
17C2 **Ponca City** USA
23D3 **Ponce** Puerto Rico
15E4 **Ponce de Leon B** USA
62B2 **Pondicherry** India
7L2 **Pond Inlet** Can
5K3 **Ponds,I of** Can
39A1 **Ponferrade** Spain
72C3 **Pongo** *R* Sudan
74E2 **Pongola** *R* S Africa
62B2 **Ponnāni** India
61D3 **Ponnyadoung Range** *Mts* Burma
3F3 **Ponoka** Can
48F3 **Ponoy** Russian Fed
44G2 **Ponoy** *R* Russian Fed
38B2 **Pons** France
29E2 **Ponta da Baleia** *Pt* Brazil
70A1 **Ponta Delgada** Açores
29E1 **Ponta do Mutá** *Pt* Brazil
72B4 **Ponta do Padrão** *Pt* Angola
29D3 **Ponta dos Búzios** *Pt* Brazil
29B4 **Ponta Grossa** Brazil
37A1 **Pontailler-sur-Saône** France
29C3 **Pontal** Brazil
36C2 **Pont-à-Mousson** France
29A3 **Ponta Pora** Brazil
38D2 **Pontarlier** France
37D3 **Pontassieve** Italy
4F3 **Pontax** *R* Can
17D3 **Pontchartrain,L** USA
37A1 **Pont d'Ain** France
29A1 **Ponte de Pedra** Brazil
40C2 **Pontedera** Italy
40B2 **Ponte Lecca** Corse
39A1 **Pontevedra** Spain
12B2 **Pontiac** Illinois, USA
12C2 **Pontiac** Michigan, USA
56C3 **Pontianak** Indon
38B2 **Pontivy** France
36B2 **Pontoise** France
17E3 **Pontotoc** USA
37C2 **Pontremoli** Italy
36B2 **Pont-sur-Yonne** France
35D6 **Pontypool** Wales
35D6 **Pontypridd** Wales
35E6 **Poole** Eng
Poona = Pune
75B2 **Pooncarie** Aust
75B2 **Poopelloe,L** Aust
10G3 **Poorman** USA
26C3 **Popayán** Colombia
36B1 **Poperinge** Belg
75B2 **Popilta L** Aust
11A2 **Poplar** USA
4B3 **Poplar** *R* Can
3G4 **Poplar** *R* USA
17D2 **Poplar Bluff** USA
17E3 **Poplarville** USA
76D1 **Popndetta** PNG
22C2 **Popocatepetl** *Mt* Mexico
10F4 **Popof** *I* USA
72B4 **Popokabaka** Zaïre
51H7 **Popondetta** PNG
41F2 **Popovo** Bulg
29C3 **Poraiba** *R* Brazil
29C1 **Porangatu** Brazil
60B4 **Porbandar** India
3B3 **Porcher I** Can
29C1 **Porcos** *R* Brazil
10K2 **Porcupine** *R* USA/Can
3H3 **Porcupine Hills** Can
37E2 **Pordenone** Italy
40C1 **Poreč** Croatia, Yugos
29B3 **Porecatu** Brazil
32J6 **Pori** Fin
78B2 **Porirua** NZ
32H5 **Porjus** Sweden
53E1 **Poronay** *R* Russian Fed
53E2 **Poronaysk** Russian Fed
44E3 **Porosozero** Russian Fed
37B1 **Porrentruy** Switz
37D3 **Porretta** Italy
32K4 **Porsangen** *Inlet* Nor
32F7 **Porsgrunn** Nor
35B4 **Portadown** N Ire
12B2 **Portage** USA
4B4 **Portage la Prairie** Can
11B2 **Portal** USA
3D4 **Port Alberni** Can
39A2 **Portalegre** Port
16B3 **Portales** USA
74D3 **Port Alfred** S Africa
3C3 **Port Alice** Can
14A2 **Port Allegany** USA
17D3 **Port Allen** USA
18B1 **Port Angeles** USA
23B3 **Port Antonio** Jamaica
35B5 **Portarlington** Irish Rep
17D4 **Port Arthur** USA
34B4 **Port Askaig** Scot
36A2 **Port-Audemer** France
75A2 **Port Augusta** Aust
23C3 **Port-au-Prince** Haiti
12C2 **Port Austin** USA
62E2 **Port Blair** Andaman Is
75B3 **Port Campbell** Aust
61C3 **Port Canning** India
7M5 **Port Cartier** Can
78B3 **Port Chalmers** NZ
15E4 **Port Charlotte** USA
14D2 **Port Chester** USA
3B3 **Port Clements** Can
12C2 **Port Clinton** USA
13D2 **Port Colborne** Can
75E3 **Port Davey** Aust
23C3 **Port-de-Paix** Haiti
55C5 **Port Dickson** Malay
74E3 **Port Edward** S Africa
29D2 **Porteirinha** Brazil
12C2 **Port Elgin** Can
74D3 **Port Elizabeth** S Africa
34B4 **Port Ellen** Scot
23N2 **Porter Pt** St Vincent
20C2 **Porterville** USA
76D4 **Port Fairy** Aust
72A4 **Port Gentil** Gabon
17D3 **Port Gibson** USA
10H4 **Port Graham** USA
18B1 **Port Hammond** Can
68E7 **Port Harcourt** Nigeria
3C3 **Port Hardy** Can
7M5 **Port Hawkesbury** Can
76A3 **Port Hedland** Aust

Punta San Antonio Ravānsar

8B4 Punta San Antonio Pt Mexico
28D3 Punta Sur Arg
28A2 Punta Topocalma Chile
57B4 Puntjak Ranakah Mt Indon
14A2 Punxsutawney USA
57D3 Puper Indon
52C4 Puqi China
46J3 Pur R Russian Fed
17C2 Purcell USA
10G2 Purcell Mt USA
3E3 Purcell Mts Can
28A3 Purén Chile
16B2 Purgatoire R USA
61C3 Puri India
62B1 Pūrna India
61C2 Pūrnia India
55C3 Pursat Camb
22B1 Puruandro Mexico
26F4 Purus R Brazil
17E3 Purvis USA
56C4 Purwokerto Indon
48J3 Pur R Russian Fed
56D4 Purworejo Indon
60D5 Pusad India
53B4 Pusan S Korea
44E4 Pushkin Russian Fed
44F3 Pushlakhta Russian Fed
43F1 Pustoshka Russian Fed
28A2 Putaendo Chile
61E2 Putao Burma
78C1 Putaruru NZ
52D4 Putian China
14E2 Putnam USA
14D1 Putney USA
62B3 Puttalam Sri Lanka
42C2 Puttgarden Germany
26C4 Putumayo R Ecuador
56D2 Putussibau Indon
32K6 Puulavesl L Fin
18B1 Puyallup USA
38C2 Puy de Sancy Mt France
28A4 Puyehue Chile
78A3 Puysegur Pt NZ
73C4 Pweto Zaïre
35C5 Pwllheli Wales
44F3 Pyal'ma Russian Fed
44E2 Pyaozero, Ozero L Russian Fed
55B2 Pyapon Burma
49K2 Pyasina R Russian Fed
45G7 Pyatigorsk Russian Fed
61E4 Pyinmana Burma
54A2 Pyŏktong N Korea
54A3 Pyonggang N Korea
54A3 Pyŏnggok-dong S Korea
54A3 P'Yŏngsann N Korea
54A3 P'yongt'aek S Korea
53B4 P'yŏngyang N Korea
75B3 Pyramid Hill Aust
5J2 Pyramid Hills Can
19C2 Pyramid L USA
78A2 Pyramid,Mt NZ
38B3 Pyrénées Mts France
43F1 Pytalovo Russian Fed
55B2 Pyu Burma

Q

65C2 Qabatiya Israel
67E3 Qabr Hūd Yemen
65D3 Qā'el Hafīra Mud Flats Jordan
65D3 Qa'el Jinz Mud Flats Jordan
7O3 Qagssimiut Greenland
50C3 Qaidam Pendi Salt Flat China
63E1 Qaisar Afghan
65D2 Qa Khanna Salt Marsh Jordan
63E2 Qala Adras Kand Afghan
72D2 Qala'en Nahl Sudan
63E2 Qala Nau Afghan
60B2 Qalat Afghan
65D1 Qal'at al Hisn Syria
65C1 Qal'at al Marqab Hist Site Syria
66D2 Qal'at Bīshah S Arabia
64E3 Qal'at Sālih Iraq
50C3 Qamdo China
69E3 Qandala Somalia
69B2 Qara Egypt
45H8 Qareh Dāgh Mts Iran
63B2 Qaṛe Shīrīn Iran
67E1 Qaryat al Ulyā S Arabia
65D3 Qasr el Kharana Jordan
63E3 Qasr-e-Qand Iran
69B2 Qasr Farafra Egypt
65D2 Qaṭana Syria
67F1 Qatar Emirate, Arabian Pen
65D3 Qatrāna Jordan
69B2 Qattâra Depression Egypt
63D2 Qāyen Iran
63C1 Qazvīn Iran
66B1 Qena Egypt
63B1 Qeydār Iran
63C3 Qeys I Iran
45H8 Qezel Owzan R Iran
65C3 Qeziot Israel
53A3 Qian'an China
53A2 Qian Gorlos China
52B5 Qian Jiang R China
52E1 Qian Shan Upland China
52E3 Qidong China
52B4 Qijiang China
63E3 Qila Ladgasht Pak
60B2 Qila Saifullah Pak
52A2 Qilian China
50C3 Qilian Shan China
52B3 Qin'an China
52E2 Qingdao China
53B2 Qinggang China
52A2 Qinghai Province, China
50C3 Qinghai Hu L China
52D3 Qingjiang Jiangsu, China
52D4 Qingjiang Jiangxi, China
52B3 Qing Jiang R China
52C2 Qingshuihe China
52B2 Qingshui He R China
52B2 Qingtonxia China
52B2 Qingyang China
53B3 Qingyuan Liaoning, China
52D4 Qingyuan Zhejiang, China
59G2 Qing Zang Upland China
52B5 Qingzhou China
52D2 Qinhuangdao China
52B3 Qin Ling Mts China
55E2 Qionghai China
52A3 Qionglai Shan Upland China
55D1 Qiongzhou Haixia Str China
53A2 Qiqihar China
65C2 Qiryat Ata Israel
65C3 Qiryat Gat Israel
65C2 Qiryat Shemona Israel
65C2 Qiryat Yam Israel
67F3 Qishn Yemen
65C2 Qishon R Israel
66C2 Qishran I S Arabia
49K5 Qitai China
53C2 Qitaihe China
53C2 Qixing He R China
52C4 Qiyang China
52B1 Qog Qi China
45J8 Qolleh-ye-Damavand Mt Iran
63C1 Qolleh-ye Damavand Mt Iran
63C2 Qom Iran
63C2 Qomisheh Iran
Qomolangma Feng = Everest,Mt
65D1 Qornet es Saouda Mt Leb
7N3 Qôrnoq Greenland
63B1 Qorveh Iran
63D3 Qotābad Iran
45H8 Qotūr R Iran
14D1 Quabbin Res USA
74C2 Quaggablat S Africa
14C2 Quakertown USA
55C3 Quam Phu Quoc I Viet
16C3 Quanah USA
55D2 Quang Ngai Viet
55D2 Quang Tri Viet
55D4 Quan Long Viet
52D5 Quanzhou Fujian, China
52C4 Quanzhou Guangxi, China
11B1 Qu'Appelle Can
6H4 Qu' Appelle R Can
28D2 Quarai R Urug
28D2 Quaral Brazil
67G2 Quarayyāt Oman
69D4 Quardho Somalia
71F3 Quarkoye Burkina
19D4 Quartzsite USA
3C3 Quatsino Sd Can
63D1 Quchan Iran
75C3 Queanbeyan Aust
5G4 Québec Can
7L4 Quebec Province, Can
29C2 Quebra-Anzol R Brazil
28D2 Quebracho Urug
25F3 Quedas do Iguaçu Brazil/Arg
14C3 Queen Anne USA
3C3 Queen Bess,Mt Can
3B3 Queen Charlotte Can
3B3 Queen Charlotte Is Can
3B3 Queen Charlotte Sd Can
3C3 Queen Charlotte Str Can
6H1 Queen Elizabeth Is Can
79G9 Queen Mary Land Region, Ant
6H3 Queen Maud G Can
79E Queen Maud Mts Ant
14D2 Queens Borough New York, USA
51F8 Queens Ch Aust
75B3 Queenscliff Aust
76D3 Queensland State, Aust
75E3 Queenstown Aust
78A3 Queenstown NZ
74D3 Queenstown S Africa
14B3 Queenstown USA
73B4 Quela Angola
73D5 Quelimane Mozam
16A3 Quemado USA
71G4 Quémé R Benin
28C3 Quemuquemú Arg
4C4 Quentico Prov Park Can
28D3 Quequén Arg
28D3 Quequén R Arg
22B1 Querétaro Mexico
22B1 Queretaro State Mexico
3D3 Quesnel Can
3D3 Quesnel L Can
60B2 Quetta Pak
21C3 Quezaltenango Guatemala
57F8 Quezon City Phil
73B5 Quibala Angola
73B4 Quibaxe Angola
26C2 Quibdó Colombia
38B2 Quiberon France
73B4 Quicama Nat Pk Angola
29A4 Quiindy Par
52A4 Quijing China
28A2 Quilima Chile
28C2 Quilino Arg
26D6 Quillabamba Peru
26E7 Quillacollo Bol
38C3 Quillan France
3H3 Quill Lakes Can
28A2 Quillota Chile
75B1 Quilpie Aust
28A2 Quilpué Chile
73B4 Quimbele Angola
28C1 Quimili Arg
38B2 Quimper France
38B2 Quimperlé France
19B3 Quincy California, USA
12A3 Quincy Illinois, USA
14E1 Quincy Massachusetts, USA
28B2 Quines Arg
10F4 Quinhagak USA
55D3 Qui Nhon Viet
39B2 Quintanar de la Orden Spain
28A2 Quintero Chile
28C2 Quinto R Arg
28A3 Quirihue Chile
73B5 Quirima Angola
75D2 Quirindi Aust
73E5 Quissanga Mozam
73D6 Quissico Mozam
26C4 Quito Ecuador
27L4 Quixadá Brazil
74D3 Qumbu S Africa
75A2 Quorn Aust
66B1 Qus Egypt
67F4 Quṣayir Oman
66B1 Quseir Egypt
7N3 Qutdligssat Greenland
Quthing = Moyeni
52B3 Qu Xian Sichuan, China
52D4 Qu Xian Zhejiang, China
55D2 Quynh Luu Viet
52C2 Quzhou China
61D2 Qūzū China

R

32J6 Raahe Fin
34B3 Raasay I Scot
34B3 Raasay,Sound of Chan Scot
67F4 Raas Caseyr C Somalia
40C2 Rab I Croatia, Yugos
56E4 Raba Indon
42D3 Rába R Hung
66B4 Rabak Sudan
71A2 Rabat Mor
76E1 Rabaul PNG
65C3 Rabba Jordan
3H2 Rabbit Lake Can
66C2 Rabigh S Arabia
37B2 Racconigi Italy
7N5 Race,C Can
14E1 Race Pt USA
65C2 Rachaya Leb
42C3 Rachel Mt Germany
55D3 Rach Gia Viet
12B2 Racine USA
66D4 Radā' Yemen
43F3 Rădăuţi Rom
12B3 Radcliff USA
12C3 Radford USA
60C4 Radhanpur India
23L1 Radix,Pt Trinidad
43E2 Radom Pol
43D2 Radomsko Pol
43F2 Radomyshl' Ukraine
37E1 Radstadt Austria
43E1 Radviliẓkis Lithuania
3H4 Radville Can
6G3 Rae Can
61B2 Rãe Bareli India
7K3 Rae Isthmus Can
6G3 Rae L Can
78C1 Raetihi NZ
28C2 Rafaela Arg
65C3 Rafah Egypt
72C3 Rafai CAR
64D3 Rafhā Al Jumaymah S Arabia
63D2 Rafsanjān Iran
72C3 Raga Sudan
23Q2 Ragged Pt Barbados
40C3 Ragusa Italy
57B3 Raha Indon
66C4 Rahad R Sudan
66D4 Raheita Eth
60C3 Rahimyar Khan Pak
63C2 Rāhjerd Iran
28D2 Raíces Arg
62B1 Rāichur India
61B3 Raigarh India
75B3 Rainbow Aust
15B2 Rainbow City USA
3E2 Rainbow Lake Can
18B1 Rainier USA
18B1 Rainier,Mt USA
11D2 Rainy R USA
4C4 Rainy L Can
10H3 Rainy P USA
11D2 Rainy River Can
61B3 Raipur India
62C1 Rājahmundry India
56D2 Rajang R Malay
60C3 Rajanpur Pak
62B3 Rājapālaiyam India
60C3 Rājasthan State, India
60D3 Rājgarh India
60D4 Rājgarh State, India
60C4 Rājkot India
61C3 Rājmahāl Hills India
61B3 Raj Nāndgaon India
60C4 Rājpīpla India
61C3 Rajshahi Bang
60D4 Rajur India
78B2 Rakaia R NZ
56C4 Rakata I Indon
59G3 Raka Zangbo R China
43E3 Rakhov Ukraine
63E3 Rakhshan R Pak
67F3 Rakhyūt Oman
74C1 Rakops Botswana
43F2 Rakov Belorussia
15D1 Raleigh USA
65C4 Ram Jordan
65C2 Rama Israel
65C3 Ramallah Israel
62B3 Rāmanāthapuram India
50H3 Ramapo Deep Pacific O
4E4 Ramore Can
65C2 Ramat Gan Israel
36D2 Rambervillers France
36A2 Rambouillet France
61C3 Rāmgarh Bihar, India
60C3 Rāmgarh Rajosthan, India
63B2 Rāmhormoz Iran
65C3 Ramla Israel
67G2 Ramlat Al Wahibah Region, Oman
67E3 Ramlat as Sab'atayn Region, Yemen
19C4 Ramona USA
60D3 Rāmpur India
60D4 Rāmpura India
61D4 Ramree I Burma
45J8 Rāmsar Iran
35C4 Ramsey Eng
14C2 Ramsey USA
35C6 Ramsey I Wales
35F6 Ramsgate Eng
65D2 Ramtha Jordan
76D1 Ramu R PNG
56E1 Ranau Malay
28A2 Rancagua Chile
3B1 Rancheria R Can
11A3 Ranchester USA
61C3 Rānchi India
61B3 Rānchi Plat India
74D2 Randburg S Africa
32F7 Randers Den
74D2 Randfontein S Africa
14A1 Randolph New York, USA
13E2 Randolph Vermont, USA
20D3 Randsburg USA
78B3 Ranfurly NZ
61D3 Rangamati Bang
16A1 Rangely USA
78B2 Rangiora NZ
78C1 Rangitaiki R NZ
78B2 Rangitate R NZ
78C1 Rangitikei R NZ
55B2 Rangoon Burma
61C2 Rangpur India
62B2 Rānībennur India
61C3 Rānīganj India
7J3 Rankin Inlet Can
75C2 Rankins Springs Aust
60B4 Rann of Kachchh Flood Area India
55B4 Ranong Thai
56A2 Rantauparapat Indon
57A3 Rantepao Indon
12B2 Rantoul USA
29B1 Ranuro R Brazil
53C2 Raohe China
36D2 Raon-l'Etape France
77H3 Raoul I NZ
37C2 Rapallo Italy
28A2 Rapel R Chile
7M3 Raper,C Can
11B3 Rapid City USA
12B1 Rapid River USA
13D3 Rappahannock R USA
57A3 Rappang Indon
37C1 Rapperswil Switz
14C2 Raritan B USA
66C2 Ras Abū Dāra C Egypt
66C2 Ra's Abu Madd C S Arabia
66C2 Ras Abu Shagara C Sudan
64D2 Ra's al 'Ayn Syria
67G2 Ra's al Hadd C Oman
67G1 Ras al Kaimah UAE
67E4 Ra's al Kalb C Yemen
67G1 Ras-al-Kuh C Iran
67G3 Ra's al Madrakah C Oman
66D3 Ras Andadda C Eth
67G3 Ra's ash Sharbatāt C Oman
66C3 Ra's Asis C Sudan
66D3 Ra's at Tarfā C S Arabia
67E1 Ra's az Zawr C S Arabia
66C2 Rās Bânas C Egypt
65B3 Ras Burûn C Egypt
66C4 Ras Dashan Mt Eth
67G3 Ra's Duqm Oman
63B2 Ra's-e-Barkan Pt Iran
63E3 Ra's-e-Fasteh C Iran
65A3 Râs el Barr C Egypt
64A3 Râs el Kenâyis Pt Egypt
65C4 Ras el Nafas Mt Egypt
65B4 Rās El Sudr C Egypt
65C4 Ras en Naqb Upland Jordan
67F3 Ra's Fartak C Yemen
66B1 Râs Ghârib Egypt
72D2 Rashad Sudan
66C2 Ras Hadarba C Egypt
65C3 Rashādīya Jordan
64B3 Rashîd Egypt
63B1 Rasht Iran
65C1 Ra's ibn Hāni C Syria
63E3 Ra's Jaddi C Pak
67G2 Ra's Jibish C Oman
63E3 Rāsk Iran
66C3 Ra's Kasar C Sudan
72E2 Ras Khanzira C Somalia
60B3 Ras Koh Mt Pak
65B4 Rās Matarma C Egypt
67F4 Ra's Momi C Socotra
66B1 Râs Muhammad C Egypt
70A2 Ras Nouadhibou C Maur
63E3 Ra's Nuh C Pak
63E3 Ra's Ormara C Pak
67F3 Ra's Sharwayn C Yemen
50J2 Rasshua I Russian Fed
67F4 Ra's Shu'ab C Socotra
71E1 Rass Kaboudia Pt Tunisia
45G5 Rasskazovo Russian Fed
67E1 Ra's Tanāqib C S Arabia
67F1 Ra's Tannūrah S Arabia
42B3 Rastatt Germany
66D3 Ra's 'Tsa C Yemen
Ras Uarc = Cabo Tres Forcas
65C4 Ras Um Seisaban Mt Jordan
69E3 Ras Xaafuun C Somalia
60C3 Ratangarh India
55B3 Rat Buri Thai
60D3 Rath India
42C2 Ratherow Germany
34B4 Rathlin I N Ire
10B6 Rat I USA
10B6 Rat Is USA
60C4 Ratlām India
62A1 Ratnāgiri India
62C3 Ratnapura Sri Lanka
43E2 Ratno Ukraine
16B2 Raton USA
37D1 Rattenberg Austria
32H6 Rättvik Sweden
3B2 Ratz,Mt Can
57C2 Rau I Indon
56F7 Raub Malay
28D3 Rauch Arg
78C1 Raukumara Range Mts NZ
29D3 Raul Soares Brazil
32J6 Rauma Fin
61B3 Raurkela India
63B2 Ravānsar Iran

Rāvar **Rolândia**

63D2 **Rāvar** Iran
43E2 **Rava Russkaya** Ukraine
14D1 **Ravena** USA
37E2 **Ravenna** Italy
42B3 **Ravensburg** Germany
76D2 **Ravenshoe** Aust
35F4 **Ravenspurn** *Oilfield* N Sea
60C2 **Ravi** *R* Pak
60C2 **Rawalpindi** Pak
64D2 **Rawāndiz** Iraq
42D2 **Rawicz** Pol
76B4 **Rawlinna** Aust
8C2 **Rawlins** USA
25D6 **Rawson** Arg
61E2 **Rawu** China
56D3 **Raya** *Mt* Indon
62B2 **Rāyadurg** India
62C1 **Rāyagada** India
65D2 **Rayak** Leb
7N5 **Ray,C** Can
53B2 **Raychikhinsk** Russian Fed
66D3 **Raydah** Yemen
63D3 **Rāyen** Iran
20C2 **Raymond** California, USA
18D1 **Raymond** Can
14E1 **Raymond** New Hampshire, USA
18B1 **Raymond** Washington, USA
75D2 **Raymond Terrace** Aust
17F4 **Raymondville** USA
10H2 **Ray Mts** USA
22C1 **Rayon** Mexico
67F3 **Raysūt** Oman
63B1 **Razan** Iran
43G3 **Razdel'naya** Ukraine
53C3 **Razdol'noye** Russian Fed
41F2 **Razgrad** Bulg
41F2 **Razim** *L* Rom
35E6 **Reading** Eng
14C2 **Reading** USA
6G3 **Read Island** Can
14D1 **Readsboro** USA
28B2 **Real de Padre** Arg
28C3 **Realicó** Arg
69B2 **Rebiana** *Well* Libya
69B2 **Rebiana Sand Sea** Libya
32L6 **Reboly** Russian Fed
53E2 **Rebun-tō** *I* Japan
76B4 **Recherche,Arch of the** *Is* Aust
43G2 **Rechitsa** Belorussia
27M5 **Recife** Brazil
74D3 **Recife,C** S Africa
29E2 **Recifes da Pedra Grande** *Arch* Brazil
77F2 **Récifs D'Entrecasteaux** Nouvelle Calédonie
36D1 **Recklinghausen** Germany
28D1 **Reconquista** Arg
28C1 **Recreo** Arg
11C2 **Red** *R* Can/USA
17D3 **Red** *R* USA
55C4 **Redang** *I* Malay
14C2 **Red Bank** New Jersey, USA
15B1 **Red Bank** Tennessee, USA
5K3 **Red Bay** Can
3G3 **Redberry L** Can
19B2 **Red Bluff** USA
16B3 **Red Bluff L** USA
35E4 **Redcar** Eng
3F3 **Redcliff** Can
75D1 **Redcliffe** Aust
75B2 **Red Cliffs** Aust
16C1 **Red Cloud** USA
3F3 **Red Deer** Can
3F3 **Red Deer** *R* Can
3H3 **Red Deer** *R* Saskatchewan, Can
3H3 **Red Deer L** Can
18B2 **Redding** USA
11C3 **Redfield** USA
16C2 **Red Hills** USA
9D2 **Red L** USA
7J4 **Red Lake** Can
11C2 **Red Lake** *R* USA
20D3 **Redlands** USA
14B3 **Red Lion** USA
18E1 **Red Lodge** USA
18B2 **Redmond** USA
20D3 **Red Mountain** USA
17C1 **Red Oak** USA
38B2 **Redon** France
20C4 **Redondo Beach** USA
10H3 **Redoubt V** USA
52B5 **Red River Delta** Vietnam
58B3 **Red Sea** Africa/Arabian Pen
10N3 **Redstone** *R* Can
4C3 **Red Sucker L** Can
3F3 **Redwater** Can
3G4 **Redwater** *R* USA
11D3 **Red Wing** USA
20A2 **Redwood City** USA
11C3 **Redwood Falls** USA
12B2 **Reed City** USA
20C2 **Reedley** USA
18B2 **Reedsport** USA
13D3 **Reedville** USA
78B2 **Reefton** NZ
64C2 **Refahiye** Turk
17F4 **Refugio** USA
29E2 **Regência** Brazil
42C3 **Regensburg** Germany
70C2 **Reggane** Alg
40D3 **Reggio di Calabria** Italy
37D2 **Reggio Nell'Emilia** Italy
41E1 **Reghin** Rom
3H3 **Regina** Can
63E2 **Registan** Region, Afghan
22A1 **Regocijo** Mexico
74B1 **Rehoboth** Namibia
13D3 **Rehoboth Beach** USA
65C3 **Rehovot** Israel
26E1 **Reicito** Ven
15D1 **Reidsville** USA
35E6 **Reigate** Eng
36B2 **Reims** France
11D3 **Reinbeck** USA
3H2 **Reindeer** *R* Can
3H2 **Reindeer L** Can
39B1 **Reinosa** Spain
14B3 **Reisterstown** USA
74D2 **Reitz** S Africa
6H3 **Reliance** Can
18E2 **Reliance** USA
71C1 **Relizane** Alg
75A2 **Remarkable,Mt** Aust
56D4 **Rembang** Indon
63D3 **Remeshk** Iran
36D2 **Remiremont** France
36D1 **Remscheid** Germany
14C1 **Remsen** USA
37A2 **Rémuzat** France
12B3 **Rend L** USA
42B2 **Rendsburg** Germany
4F4 **Renfrew** Can
56B3 **Rengat** Indon
28A2 **Rengo** Chile
43F3 **Reni** Ukraine
72D2 **Renk** Sudan
7O2 **Renland** *Pen* Greenland
75B2 **Renmark** Aust
77F2 **Rennell** *I* Solomon Is
38B2 **Rennes** France
19C3 **Reno** USA
37D2 **Reno** *R* Italy
14B2 **Renovo** USA
14D1 **Rensselaer** USA
18B1 **Renton** USA
57B4 **Reo** Indon
71F3 **Réo** Burkina
63E1 **Repetek** Turkmenistan
43G2 **Repki** Ukraine
29C3 **Represa de Furnas** *Dam* Brazil
29C2 **Represa Três Marias** *Dam* Brazil
18C1 **Republic** USA
16C1 **Republican** *R* USA
33B3 **Republic of Ireland** NW Europe
7K3 **Repulse Bay** Can
4F4 **Réservoir Baskatong** *Res* Can
13D1 **Réservoir Cabonga** *Res* Can
4F4 **Réservoir Decelles** *Res* Can
7L4 **Réservoir de La Grande 2** *Res* Can
7L4 **Réservoir de La Grande 3** *Res* Can
7L4 **Réservoir de La Grande 4** *Res* Can
4F4 **Réservoir Dozois** *Res* Can
7L5 **Réservoir Gouin** *Res* Can
5G4 **Réservoir Pipmouacane** *Res* Can
63C1 **Reshteh-ye Alborz** *Mts* Iran
52A2 **Reshui** China
25E3 **Resistencia** Arg
41E1 **Resita** Rom
7J2 **Resolute** Can
78A3 **Resolution I** NZ
7M3 **Resolution Island** Can
74E2 **Ressano Garcia** Mozam
5H4 **Restigouche** *R* Can
28E1 **Restinga Seca** Brazil
28B2 **Retamito** Arg
36C2 **Rethel** France
41E3 **Réthimnon** Greece
xxviiiD6 **Reunion** *I* Indian O
39C1 **Reus** Spain
37C1 **Reuss** *R* Switz
36E2 **Reutlingen** Germany
37D1 **Reutte** Austria
44K4 **Revda** Russian Fed
3E3 **Revelstoke** Can
21A3 **Revillagigedo** *Is* Mexico
10M4 **Revillagigedo I** USA
36C2 **Revin** France
65C3 **Revivim** Israel
61B3 **Rewa** India
60D3 **Rewari** India
18D2 **Rexburg** USA
32A2 **Reykjavik** Iceland
14A2 **Reynoldsville** USA
21C2 **Reynosa** Mexico
38B2 **Rezé** France
43F1 **Rezekne** Latvia
44L4 **Rezh** Russian Fed
37C1 **Rhätikon** *Mts* Austria/Switz
65C1 **Rhazīr** Republic, Leb
36E1 **Rheda Wiedenbrück** Germany
42B2 **Rhein** *R* W Europe
42B2 **Rheine** Germany
37B1 **Rheinfielden** Switz
38D2 **Rheinland Pfalz** Region, Germany
37C1 **Rheinwaldhorn** *Mt* Switz
Rhine = Rhein
14D2 **Rhinebeck** USA
12B1 **Rhinelander** USA
37C2 **Rho** Italy
13E2 **Rhode Island** State, USA
14E2 **Rhode Island Sd** USA
Rhodes = Ródhos
74D1 **Rhodes Drift** *Ford* S Africa
18D1 **Rhodes Peak** *Mt* USA
38C3 **Rhône** *R* France
35D5 **Rhyl** Wales
27L6 **Riachão do Jacuipe** Brazil
39A1 **Ria de Arosa** *B* Spain
39A1 **Ria de Betanzos** *B* Spain
39A1 **Ria de Corcubion** *B* Spain
39A1 **Ria de Lage** *B* Spain
39A1 **Ria de Sta Marta** *B* Spain
39A1 **Ria de Vigo** *B* Spain
60C2 **Riāsi** Pak
39A1 **Ribadeo** Spain
29B3 **Ribas do Rio Pardo** Brazil
73D5 **Ribauè** Mozam
35D5 **Ribble** *R* Eng
29C3 **Ribeira** Brazil
29C3 **Ribeirão Prêto** Brazil
26E6 **Riberala** Bol
37E3 **Riccione** Italy
13D2 **Rice L** Can
12A1 **Rice Lake** USA
29D1 **Richao de Santana** Brazil
74E2 **Richard's Bay** S Africa
10L2 **Richards I** Can
17C3 **Richardson** USA
3F2 **Richardson** *R* Can
10L2 **Richardson Mts** Can
19D3 **Richfield** USA
14C1 **Richfield Springs** USA
20C3 **Richgrove** USA
5J4 **Richibucto** Can
18C1 **Richland** USA
12C3 **Richlands** USA
20A2 **Richmond** California, USA
74C3 **Richmond** Cape Province, S Africa
12C3 **Richmond** Kentucky, USA
74E2 **Richmond** Natal, S Africa
75D2 **Richmond** New South Wales, Aust
78B2 **Richmond** NZ
76D3 **Richmond** Queensland, Aust
13D3 **Richmond** Virginia, USA
78B2 **Richmond Range** *Mts* NZ
14C1 **Richmondville** USA
4F5 **Rideau Lakes** Can
15C2 **Ridgeland** USA
14A2 **Ridgway** USA
11B1 **Riding Mountain Nat Pk** Can
23D4 **Riecito** Ven
37D1 **Rienza** *R* Italy
42C2 **Riesa** Germany
25B8 **Riesco** *I* Chile
74C2 **Riet** *R* S Africa
40C2 **Rieti** Italy
37B3 **Riez** France
39B2 **Rif** *Mts* Mor
16A2 **Rifle** USA
43E1 **Riga** Latvia
44C4 **Riga,G of** Estonia/Latvia
63D3 **Rīgān** Iran
18D2 **Rigby** USA
18C1 **Riggins** USA
7N4 **Rigolet** Can
32J6 **Riihimaki** Fin
40C1 **Rijeka** Croatia, Yugos
54D3 **Rikuzen-Tanaka** Japan
71H3 **Rima** *R* Nig
3F3 **Rimbey** Can
32H7 **Rimbo** Sweden
37E2 **Rimini** Italy
41E1 **Rîmnicu Vîlcea** Rom
5H4 **Rimouski** Can
22B1 **Rincón de Romos** Mexico
32F7 **Ringkøbing** Den
28A3 **Riñihue** Chile
57A4 **Rinja** *I* Indon
72A3 **Rio Benito** Eq Guinea
26E5 **Rio Branco** Brazil
28E2 **Rio Branco** Urug
29C4 **Rio Branco do Sul** Brazil
17F4 **Rio Bravo** Mexico
21B1 **Rio Bravo del Norte** *R* USA/Mexico
29B3 **Rio Brilhante** Brazil
28A4 **Rio Bueno** Chile
26D1 **Riochacha** Colombia
29C3 **Rio Claro** Brazil
23L1 **Rio Claro** Trinidad
28C3 **Rio Colorado** Arg
28C2 **Rio Cuarto** Arg
27L6 **Rio de Jacuipe** Brazil
29D3 **Rio de Janeiro** Brazil
29D3 **Rio de Janeiro** State, Brazil
28D2 **Rio de la Plata** *Estuary* Arg/Urug
25C8 **Rio Gallegos** Arg
25C8 **Rio Grande** Arg
28E2 **Rio Grande** Brazil
22B1 **Rio Grande** Mexico
23A4 **Rio Grande** Nic
21D3 **Rio Grande** *R* Nicaragua
21B2 **Rio Grande** *R* USA/Mexico
17F4 **Rio Grande City** USA
22B1 **Rio Grande de Santiago** Mexico
27L5 **Rio Grande do Norte** State, Brazil
28E1 **Rio Grande do Sul** State, Brazil
xxxG6 **Rio Grande Rise** Atlantic O
23C4 **Riohacha** Colombia
38C2 **Riom** France
26C4 **Riombamba** Ecuador
26E7 **Rio Mulatos** Bol
29C4 **Rio Negro** Brazil
28B4 **Rio Negro** State, Arg
25F3 **Rio Pardo** Brazil
28C2 **Rio Tercero** Arg
26F6 **Rio Theodore Roosevelt** *R* Brazil
25B8 **Rio Turbio** Arg
3G2 **Riou L** Can
29B2 **Rio Verde** Brazil
22B1 **Rio Verde** Mexico
29B2 **Rio Verde de Mato Grosso** Brazil
12C3 **Ripley** Ohio, USA
15B1 **Ripley** Tennessee, USA
12C3 **Ripley** West Virginia, USA
35E4 **Ripon** Eng
20B2 **Ripon** USA
53E2 **Rishiri-tō** *I* Japan
65C3 **Rishon le Zion** Israel
14B3 **Rising Sun** USA
36A2 **Risle** *R* France
32F7 **Risør** Nor
62E2 **Ritchie's Arch** Andaman Is
7N3 **Ritenbenk** Greenland
20C2 **Ritter,Mt** USA
18C1 **Ritzville** USA
28B2 **Rivadavia** Arg
28A1 **Rivadavia** Chile
28C3 **Rivadavia Gonzalez Moreno** Arg
37D2 **Riva de Garda** Italy
26A1 **Rivas** Nic
28C3 **Rivera** Arg
28D2 **Rivera** Urug
20B2 **Riverbank** USA
70B4 **River Cess** Lib
20C2 **Riverdale** USA
14D2 **Riverhead** USA
75B3 **Riverina** Aust
71H4 **Rivers** State, Nig
78A3 **Riversdale** NZ
74C3 **Riversdale** S Africa
20D4 **Riverside** USA
3C3 **Rivers Inlet** Can
4B3 **Riverton** Can
78A3 **Riverton** NZ
18E2 **Riverton** USA
37A2 **Rives** France
15E4 **Riviera Beach** USA
7L4 **Rivière aux Feuilles** *R* Can
5G2 **Rivière aux Mélèzes** *R* Can
5H3 **Rivière aux Outardes** *R* Can
7M4 **Rivière de la Baleine** *R* Can
5G4 **Rivière du Lièvre** *R* Can
5H4 **Rivière-du-Loup** Can
7M4 **Rivière du Petit Mècatina** *R* Can
5F2 **Rivière Innuksuac** *R* Can
5G1 **Rivière Lepellé** *R* Can
5H4 **Rivière Pentecôte** Can
5F1 **Rivière Povungnituk** *R* Can
5G1 **Rivière Vachon** *R* Can
36C2 **Rivigny-sur-Ornain** France
54A2 **Riwon** N Korea
67E2 **Riyadh** S Arabia
64D1 **Rize** Turk
52D2 **Rizhao** China
65C1 **Rizokaipaso** Cyprus
32F7 **Rjukan** Nor
7K2 **Roanes Pen** Can
38C2 **Roanne** France
15B2 **Roanoke** Alabama, USA
13D3 **Roanoke** Virginia, USA
13D3 **Roanoke** *R* USA
15D1 **Roanoke Rapids** USA
19D3 **Roan Plat** USA
18D2 **Roberts** USA
19C3 **Roberts Creek Mt** USA
32J6 **Robertsforz** Sweden
17D2 **Robert S Kerr Res** USA
74B3 **Robertson** S Africa
70A4 **Robertsport** Lib
7L5 **Roberval** Can
75B2 **Robinvale** Aust
3H3 **Roblin** Can
3E3 **Robson,Mt** Can
17F4 **Robstown** USA
21A3 **Roca Partida** *I* Mexico
xxxG5 **Rocas** *I* Atlantic O
27M4 **Rocas** *I* Brazil
37D2 **Rocca San Casciano** Italy
28E2 **Rocha** Urug
35D5 **Rochdale** Eng
29B2 **Rochedo** Brazil
38B2 **Rochefort** France
12B2 **Rochelle** USA
6G3 **Rocher River** Can
75B3 **Rochester** Aust
35F6 **Rochester** Eng
11D3 **Rochester** Minnesota, USA
14E1 **Rochester** New Hampshire, USA
14B1 **Rochester** New York, USA
3C1 **Rock** *R* Can
12B2 **Rock** *R* USA
12B2 **Rockford** USA
3G4 **Rockglen** Can
15C2 **Rock Hill** USA
15D2 **Rockingham** USA
12A2 **Rock Island** USA
5H5 **Rockland** Maine, USA
12B1 **Rockland** Michigan, USA
75B3 **Rocklands Res** Aust
15C3 **Rockledge** USA
17F4 **Rockport** USA
11C3 **Rock Rapids** USA
11A3 **Rock River** USA
11A2 **Rock Springs** Montana, USA
16B3 **Rocksprings** Texas, USA
18E2 **Rock Springs** Wyoming, USA
78B2 **Rocks Pt** NZ
75C3 **Rock,The** Aust
14D2 **Rockville** Connecticut, USA
12B3 **Rockville** Indiana, USA
14B3 **Rockville** Maryland, USA
13F1 **Rockwood** USA
16B2 **Rocky Ford** USA
4E4 **Rocky Island L** Can
15D1 **Rocky Mount** USA
3F3 **Rocky Mountain House** Can
16A1 **Rocky Mountain Nat Pk** USA
8B1 **Rocky Mts** Can/USA
10F3 **Rocky Pt** USA
42C2 **Rødbyhavn** Den
5K3 **Roddickton** Can
28B2 **Rodeo** Arg
38C3 **Rodez** France
41F3 **Ródhos** Greece
41F3 **Ródhos** *I* Greece
40D2 **Rodi Garganico** Italy
41E2 **Rodopi Planina** *Mts* Bulg
76A3 **Roebourne** Aust
74D1 **Roedtan** S Africa
36D1 **Roer** *R* Neth
36C1 **Roermond** Neth
36B1 **Roeselare** Belg
7K3 **Roes Welcome Sd** Can
43F2 **Rogachev** Belorussia
17D2 **Rogers** USA
12C1 **Rogers City** USA
20D3 **Rogers L** USA
12C3 **Rogers,Mt** USA
18D2 **Rogerson** USA
4F3 **Roggan L** Can
4F3 **Roggan** *R* Can
74B3 **Roggeveldberge** *Mts* S Africa
18B2 **Rogue** *R* USA
60B3 **Rohn** Pak
60D3 **Rohtak** India
43E1 **Roja** Latvia
29B3 **Rolândia** Brazil

St Helena Sd San Ignacio

15C2 **St Helena Sd** USA
75E3 **St Helens** Aust
35D5 **St Helens** Eng
18B1 **St Helens** USA
18B1 **St Helens,Mt** USA
38B2 **St Helier** Jersey
37B1 **St Hippolyte** France
36C1 **St-Hubert** Belg
7L5 **St-Hyacinthe** Can
12C1 **St Ignace** USA
12B1 **St Ignace I** Can
35C6 **St Ives** Eng
11D3 **St James** Minnesota, USA
17D2 **St James** Missouri, USA
3B3 **St James,C** Can
5G4 **St Jean** Can
5J3 **St Jean** *R* Can
38B2 **St Jean-d'Angely** France
37A1 **St-Jean-de-Losne** France
37B2 **St-Jean-de-Maurienne** France
4G4 **St Jérôme** Can
18C1 **St Joe** USA
37E1 **St Johann im Pongau** Austria
7M5 **Saint John** Can
5K3 **St John B** Can
5K4 **St John,C** Can
13F1 **St John** *R* USA Can
19E4 **St Johns** Arizona, USA
7N5 **St John's** Can
12C2 **St Johns** Michigan, USA
15C3 **St Johns** *R* USA
13E2 **St Johnsbury** USA
14C1 **St Johnsville** USA
13E1 **St-Joseph** Can
17D3 **St Joseph** Louisiana, USA
12B2 **St Joseph** Michigan, USA
17D2 **St Joseph** Missouri, USA
23L1 **St Joseph** Trinidad
12C2 **St Joseph** *R* USA
12C1 **St Joseph I** Can
17F4 **St Joseph I** USA
7J4 **St Joseph,L** Can
37B1 **St Julien** France
38C2 **St-Junien** France
36B2 **St-Just-en-Chaussée** France
34A3 **St Kilda** *I* Scot
23E3 **St Kitts-Nevis** *Is* Caribbean
5G4 **St Laurent** Can
37A1 **St-Laurent** France
7M5 **St Lawrence** *R* Can
7M5 **St Lawrence,G of** Can
10D3 **St Lawrence I** USA
13D2 **St Lawrence Seaway** Can/USA
13F1 **St Leonard** Can
5K3 **St Lewis Sd** Can
38B2 **St Lô** France
3G3 **St Louis** Can
70A3 **St Louis** Sen
12A3 **St Louis** USA
36D3 **St-Loup-sur-Semou** France
23E4 **St Lucia** *I* Caribbean
74E2 **St Lucia,L** S Africa
34E1 **St Magnus** *B* Scot
38B2 **St Malo** France
37A2 **St Marcellin** France
5H3 **Ste Marguerite** *R* Can
73E6 **Ste Marie** *C* Madag
36D2 **Ste-Marie-aux-Mines** France
18C1 **St Maries** USA
23E3 **St Martin** *I* Caribbean
4B3 **St Martin,L** Can
37B2 **St-Martin-Vésubie** France
76D1 **St Mary,Mt** PNG
75A2 **St Mary Peak** *Mt* Aust
75E3 **St Marys** Aust
13D2 **St Marys** USA
35B7 **St Marys** *I* UK
15C2 **St Marys** *R* USA
5L4 **St Mary's B** Can
5L4 **St Mary's,C** Can
76E1 **Saint Mathias Group** *Is* PNG
10D3 **St Matthew I** USA
5G4 **St Maurice** *R* Can
37A3 **St-Maximin** France
36C2 **Ste-Menehould** France
10F3 **St Michael** USA
14B3 **St Michaels** USA
37B2 **St-Michel** France
36C2 **St-Mihiel** France
37C1 **St Moritz** Switz
38B2 **St-Nazaire** France
36C1 **St-Niklaas** Belg
36B1 **St-Omer** France
5H4 **St Pacôme** Can
5H4 **St Pascal** Can
3F3 **St Paul** Can
11D3 **St Paul** Minnesota, USA
16C1 **St Paul** Nebraska, USA
10D4 **St Paul** *I* USA
5K3 **St Paul** *R* Can
70A4 **St Paul** *R* Lib
71G4 **St Paul,C** Ghana
5H4 **St Paul du Nord** Can
11D3 **St Peter** USA
15C3 **St Petersburg** USA
7N5 **St Pierre** *I* Can
13E1 **St Pierre,L** Can
36B1 **St-Pol-Sur-Ternoise** France
42D3 **St Pölten** Austria
36B2 **St Quentin** France
38D3 **St Raphaël** France
73E5 **St Sébastien** *C* Madag
5H4 **St Siméon** Can
15C2 **St Simons I** USA
5H4 **St Stephen** Can
15C2 **St Stephen** USA
5G4 **Ste Thérèse-de-Blainville** Can
10O3 **Ste Thérèse,L** Can
4E5 **St Thomas** Can
37B3 **St-Tropez** France
36C1 **St Truiden** Belg
36A2 **St-Valéry-en-Caux** France
36A1 **St-Valéry-sur-Somme** France
11C2 **St Vincent** USA
73E6 **St Vincent** *C* Madag
23E4 **St Vincent** *I* Caribbean
75A2 **St Vincent,G** Aust
36D1 **St-Vith** Germany
36D2 **St Wendel** Germany
51H5 **Saipan** *I* Pacific O
60B2 **Saiydabad** Afghan
26E7 **Sajama** *Mt* Bol
74C3 **Sak** *R* S Africa
53D5 **Sakai** Japan
54B4 **Sakaidi** Japan
54B3 **Sakaiminato** Japan
64D3 **Sakākah** S Arabia
11B2 **Sakakawea,L** USA
4F3 **Sakami** *R* Can
73C5 **Sakania** Zaïre
73E6 **Sakaraha** Madag
45E7 **Sakarya** *R* Turk
43E1 **Sakasleja** Latvia
53D4 **Sakata** Japan
71G4 **Saketél** Benin
53E1 **Sakhalin** *I* Russian Fed
53E1 **Sakhalinskiy Zaliv** *B* Russian Fed
50F4 **Sakishima gunto** *Is* Japan
74C3 **Sakrivier** S Africa
70A4 **Sal** *I* Cape Verde
45G6 **Sal** *R* Russian Fed
32H7 **Sala** Sweden
28D1 **Saladas** Arg
28D3 **Saladillo** Arg
28C2 **Saladillo** *R* Arg
28D3 **Salado** *R* Buenos Aires, Arg
28B3 **Salado** *R* Mendoza/San Luis, Arg
25D3 **Salado** *R* Sante Fe, Arg
71F4 **Salaga** Ghana
55C3 **Sala Hintoun** Camb
72B2 **Salal** Chad
67F3 **Şalālah** Oman
28A2 **Salamanca** Chile
22B1 **Salamanca** Mexico
39A1 **Salamanca** Spain
14A1 **Salamanca** USA
72B3 **Salamat** *R* Chad
51H7 **Salamaua** PNG
65B1 **Salamis** *Hist Site* Cyprus
56E2 **Salang** Indon
32H5 **Salangen** Nor
25C2 **Salar de Arizaro** Arg
25C2 **Salar de Atacama** *Salt Pan* Chile
26E7 **Salar de Coipasa** *Salt Pan* Bol
26E8 **Salar de Uyuni** *Salt Pan* Bol
37C2 **Salasomaggiore** Italy
44K5 **Salavat** Russian Fed
76C1 **Salawati** *I* Indon
57B4 **Salayar** Indon
xxixO6 **Sala y Gomez** *I* Pacific O
28C3 **Salazar** Arg
38C2 **Salbris** France
10J3 **Salcha** *R* USA
74B3 **Saldanha** S Africa
65D2 **Saldhad** Syria
28C3 **Saldungaray** Arg
43E1 **Saldus** Latvia
75C3 **Sale** Aust
71A2 **Salé** Mor
57C2 **Salebabu** *I* Indon
44M2 **Salekhard** Russian Fed
12B3 **Salem** Illinois, USA
62B2 **Salem** India
14E1 **Salem** Massachusetts, USA
14C3 **Salem** New Jersey, USA
14D1 **Salem** New York, USA
18B2 **Salem** Oregon, USA
12C3 **Salem** Virginia, USA
56D4 **Salembu Besar** *I* Indon
32G6 **Salen** Sweden
40C2 **Salerno** Italy
35D5 **Salford** Eng
41D1 **Salgót** Hung
43D3 **Salgótarjan** Hung
27L5 **Salgueiro** Brazil
16A2 **Salida** USA
41F3 **Salihli** Turk
73D5 **Salima** Malawi
32K6 **Salimaa** *L* Fin
17C2 **Salina** Kansas, USA
19D3 **Salina** Utah, USA
40C3 **Salina** *I* Italy
22C2 **Salina Cruz** Mexico
26E8 **Salina de Arizato** Arg
28B3 **Salina Grande** *Salt pan* Arg
28B4 **Salina Gualicho** *Salt pan* Arg
28B2 **Salina La Antigua** *Salt pan* Arg
29D2 **Salinas** Brazil
22B1 **Salinas** Mexico
20B2 **Salinas** USA
20B2 **Salinas** *R* USA
28B3 **Salinas de Llancaneb** *Salt Pan* Arg
28C1 **Salinas Grandes** *Salt Pan* Arg
16A3 **Salinas Peak** *Mt* USA
17D3 **Saline** *R* Arkansas, USA
16B2 **Saline** *R* Kansas, USA
23M2 **Salines,Pt** Grenada
20D2 **Saline V** USA
27J4 **Salinópolis** Brazil
37A1 **Salins** France
35E6 **Salisbury** Eng
13D3 **Salisbury** Maryland, USA
15C1 **Salisbury** North Carolina, USA
7L3 **Salisbury I** Can
35E6 **Salisbury Plain** Eng
32K5 **Salla** Fin
28C1 **Salladillo** *R* Arg
37B2 **Sallanches** France
17D2 **Sallisaw** USA
7L3 **Salluit** Can
61B2 **Sallyana** Nepal
63A1 **Salmas** Iran
32L6 **Salmi** Russian Fed
18C1 **Salmo** Can
18D1 **Salmon** USA
18C1 **Salmon** *R* USA
3E3 **Salmon Arm** Can
18C1 **Salmon River Mts** USA
32J6 **Salo** Fin
37D2 **Salò** Italy
38D3 **Salon-de-Provence** France
Salonica = Thessaloníki
41E1 **Salonta** Rom
32K6 **Salpausselka** Region, Fin
28B2 **Salsacate** Arg
45G6 **Sal'sk** Russian Fed
65C2 **Salt** Jordan
74C3 **Salt** *R* S Africa
19D4 **Salt** *R* USA
25C2 **Salta** Arg
25C2 **Salta** State, Arg
21B2 **Saltillo** Mexico
18D2 **Salt Lake City** USA
28C2 **Salto** Arg
28D2 **Salto** Urug
26D3 **Salto Angostura** *Waterfall* Colombia
29E2 **Salto da Divisa** Brazil
29B3 **Salto das Sete Quedas** Brazil
26F2 **Salto del Angel** *Waterfall* Ven
25E2 **Salto del Guaira** *Waterfall* Brazil
26D4 **Salto Grande** *Waterfall* Colombia
19C4 **Salton S** USA
29B4 **Saltos do Iguaçu** *Waterfall* Arg
60C2 **Salt Range** *Mts* Pak
23H2 **Salt River** Jamaica
15C2 **Saluda** USA
57B3 **Salue Timpaus** *Str* Indon
62C1 **Sālūr** India
37B2 **Saluzzo** Italy
27L6 **Salvador** Brazil
17D4 **Salvador,L** USA
22B1 **Salvatierra** Mexico
67F2 **Salwah** Qatar
55B1 **Salween** *R* Burma
45H8 **Sal'yany** Azerbaijan
12C3 **Salyersville** USA
37E1 **Salzach** *R* Austria
42C3 **Salzburg** Austria
37E1 **Salzburg** Province, Austria
42C2 **Salzgitter** Germany
37E1 **Salzkammergut** *Mts* Austria
42C2 **Salzwedel** Germany
50C1 **Samagaltay** Russian Fed
57F9 **Samales Group** *Is* Phil
23D3 **Samaná** Dom Rep
64C2 **Samandaği** Turk
60B1 **Samangan** Afghan
54D2 **Samani** Japan
65A3 **Samannûd** Egypt
57G8 **Samar** *I* Phil
44J5 **Samara** Russian Fed
76E2 **Samarai** PNG
56E3 **Samarinda** Indon
58E2 **Samarkand** Uzbekistan
64D3 **Sāmarrā'** Iraq
57F8 **Samar S** Phil
61B3 **Sambalpur** India
56C2 **Sambas** Indon
73F5 **Sambava** Madag
60D3 **Sambhal** India
56E3 **Samboja** Indon
43E3 **Sambor** Ukraine
36B1 **Sambre** *R* France
53B4 **Samch'ŏk** S Korea
54A4 **Samch'ŏnp'o** S Korea
54A3 **Samdŭng** N Korea
72D4 **Same** Tanz
37C1 **Samedan** Switz
36A1 **Samer** France
73C5 **Samfya** Zambia
67F4 **Samhah** *I* Yemen
55B1 **Samka** Burma
55C1 **Sam Neua** Laos
77H2 **Samoan Is** Pacific O
41F3 **Sámos** *I* Greece
56A2 **Samosir** *I* Indon
41F2 **Samothráki** *I* Greece
28C2 **Sampacho** Arg
57A3 **Sampaga** Indon
57B3 **Sampara** *R* Indon
56D3 **Sampit** Indon
56D3 **Sampit** *R* Indon
17D3 **Sam Rayburn Res** USA
55C3 **Samrong** Camb
42C1 **Samsø** *I* Den
54A2 **Samsu** N Korea
64C1 **Samsun** Turk
57D4 **Samulaki** Indon
71F3 **San** Mali
55D3 **San** *R* Camb
43E2 **San** *R* Pol
66D3 **Şan'ā'** Yemen
72B3 **Sanaga** *R* Cam
25C4 **San Agustín** Arg
57G9 **San Agustin,C** Phil
10F5 **Sanak I** USA
57C3 **Sanana** Indon
57C3 **Sanana** *I* Indon
63B1 **Sanandaj** Iran
20B1 **San Andreas** USA
16A3 **San Andres Mts** USA
21C3 **San Andrés Tuxtla** Mexico
16B3 **San Angelo** USA
40B3 **San Antioco** Sardegna
40B3 **San Antioco** *I* Medit S
28C1 **San Antonio** Arg
28A2 **San Antonio** Chile
16A3 **San Antonio** New Mexico, USA
57F7 **San Antonio** Phil
16C4 **San Antonio** Texas, USA
20B2 **San Antonio** *R* California, USA
17F4 **San Antonio** *R* Texas, USA
39C2 **San Antonio Abad** Spain
21D2 **San Antonio,C** Cuba
16B3 **San Antonio de Bravo** Mexico
23A2 **San Antonio de los Banos** Cuba
28C4 **San Antonio Este** Arg
20D3 **San Antonio,Mt** USA
28B4 **San Antonio Oeste** Arg
20B3 **San Antonio Res** USA
20B2 **San Ardo** USA
28D3 **San Augustin** Arg
28B2 **San Augustin de Valle Féril** Arg
60D4 **Sanawad** India
22B1 **San Bartolo** Mexico
21A3 **San Benedicto** *I* Mexico
17F4 **San Benito** USA
20B2 **San Benito** *R* USA
20B2 **San Benito Mt** USA
20D3 **San Bernardino** USA
28A2 **San Bernardo** Chile
19C4 **San Bernardo Mts** USA
22A1 **San Blas** Mexico
15B3 **San Blas,C** USA
28A3 **San Carlos** Chile
22C1 **San Carlos** Mexico
26B1 **San Carlos** Nic
57F7 **San Carlos** Phil
28E2 **San Carlos** Urug
19D4 **San Carlos** USA
25B6 **San Carlos de Bariloche** Arg
50F4 **San-chung** Taiwan
44H4 **Sanchursk** Russian Fed
28A3 **San Clemente** Chile
20D4 **San Clemente** USA
19C4 **San Clemente I** USA
28C2 **San Cristóbal** Arg
21C3 **San Cristóbal** Mexico
26D2 **San Cristóbal** Ven
77F2 **San Cristobal** *I* Solomon Is
21E2 **Sancti Spíritus** Cuba
74D1 **Sand** *R* S Africa
56D3 **Sandai** Indon
56E1 **Sandakan** Malay
37E1 **San Daniele del Friuli** Italy
34D2 **Sanday** *I* Scot
16B3 **Sanderson** USA
3G2 **Sandfly L** Can
19C4 **San Diego** USA
64B2 **Sandikli** Turk
61B2 **Sandīla** India
4E4 **Sand Lake** Can
32F7 **Sandnes** Nor
32G5 **Sandnessjøen** Nor
32D3 **Sandø** Faroes
73C4 **Sandoa** Zaïre
43E2 **Sandomierz** Pol
37E2 **San Donà di Piave** Italy
61D4 **Sandoway** Burma
10F4 **Sand Point** USA
18C1 **Sandpoint** USA
38D2 **Sandrio** Italy
3B3 **Sandspit** Can
17C2 **Sand Springs** USA
76A3 **Sandstone** Aust
11D2 **Sandstone** USA
52C4 **Sandu** China
12C2 **Sandusky** USA
32H6 **Sandviken** Sweden
14E2 **Sandwich** USA
5K3 **Sandwich B** Can
3H2 **Sandy Bay** Can
7J4 **Sandy L** Can
4C3 **Sandy Lake** Can
28C2 **San Elcano** Arg
29A3 **San Estanislao** Par
8B3 **San Felipe** Baja Cal, Mexico
28A2 **San Felipe** Chile
22B1 **San Felipe** Guanajuato, Mexico
23D4 **San Felipe** Ven
39C1 **San Feliu de Guixols** Spain
28A2 **San Fernando** Chile
22C1 **San Fernando** Mexico
57F7 **San Fernando** Phil
39A2 **San Fernando** Spain
23E4 **San Fernando** Trinidad
20C3 **San Fernando** USA
26E2 **San Fernando** Ven
22C1 **San Fernando** *R* Mexico
15C3 **Sanford** Florida, USA
13E2 **Sanford** Maine, USA
15D1 **Sanford** N Carolina, USA
9E4 **Sanford** USA
10K3 **Sanford,Mt** USA
28C2 **San Francisco** Arg
23C3 **San Francisco** Dom Rep
20A2 **San Francisco** USA
20A2 **San Francisco B** USA
21B2 **San Francisco del Oro** Mexico
22B1 **San Francisco del Rincon** Mexico
20D3 **San Gabriel Mts** USA
60C5 **Sangamner** India
12B3 **Sangamon** *R* USA
51H5 **Sangan** *I* Pacific O
49O3 **Sangar** Russian Fed
62B1 **Sangāreddi** India
56E4 **Sangeang** *I* Indon
20C2 **Sanger** USA
52C2 **Sanggan He** *R* China
56D2 **Sanggau** Indon
72B3 **Sangha** *R* Congo
60B3 **Sanghar** Pak
57C2 **Sangihe** *I* Indon
37E2 **San Giorgio di Nogaro** Italy
55B3 **Sangkhla Buri** Thai
56E2 **Sangkulirang** Indon
62A1 **Sāngli** India
72B3 **Sangmélima** Cam
8B3 **San Gorgonio Mt** USA
16A2 **Sangre de Cristo** *Mts* USA
28C2 **San Gregorio** Arg
28D2 **San Gregorio** Urug
20A2 **San Gregorio** USA
60D2 **Sangrūr** India
74E1 **Sangutane** *R* Mozam
28A4 **Sanico** Arg
25E3 **San Ignacio** Arg

San Isidro Savona

57F8 **San Isidro** Phil
26D2 **San Jacinto** Colombia
19C4 **San Jacinto Peak** *Mt* USA
28A3 **San Javier** Chile
28D1 **San Javier** Misiones, Arg
28D2 **San Javier** Sante Fe, Arg
28D1 **San Javier** *R* Arg
53D4 **Sanjō** *I* Japan
25H2 **San João del Rei** Brazil
20B2 **San Joaquin** *R* USA
20B2 **San Joaquin Valley** USA
16B2 **San Jon** USA
26B1 **San José** Costa Rica
21C3 **San José** Guatemala
57F7 **San Jose** Luzon, Phil
57F8 **San Jose** Mindoro, Phil
20B2 **San Jose** USA
8B4 **San José** *I* Mexico
26F7 **San José de Chiquitos** Bol
28D2 **San José de Feliciano** Arg
28B2 **San José de Jachal** Arg
28C2 **San José de la Dormida** Arg
28A3 **San José de la Mariquina** Chile
8C4 **San José del Cabo** Mexico
28D2 **San José de Mayo** Urug
22B1 **San José de Raices** Mexico
25G2 **San José do Rio Prêto** Brazil
21B2 **San Joseé del Cabo** Mexico
54A3 **Sanju** S Korea
28B2 **San Juan** Arg
23D3 **San Juan** Puerto Rico
28B2 **San Juan** State, Arg
23L1 **San Juan** Trinidad
20B3 **San Juan** USA
26E2 **San Juan** Ven
23B2 **San Juan** *Mt* Cuba
28B2 **San Juan** *R* Arg
20B3 **San Juan** *R* California, USA
22C2 **San Juan** *R* Mexico
21D3 **San Juan** *R* Nicaragua/Costa Rica
19D3 **San Juan** *R* Utah, USA
22C2 **San Juan Bautista** Mexico
25E3 **San Juan Bautista** Par
20B2 **San Juan Bautista** USA
21D3 **San Juan del Norte** Nic
23D4 **San Juan de los Cayos** Ven
22B1 **San Juan de loz Lagoz** Mexico
22B1 **San Juan del Rio** Mexico
21D3 **San Juan del Sur** Nicaragua
22C2 **San Juan Evangelista** Mexico
18B1 **San Juan Is** USA
16A2 **San Juan Mts** USA
22C2 **San Juan Tepozcolula** Mexico
25C7 **San Julián** Arg
28C2 **San Justo** Arg
44E4 **Sankt Peterburg** Russian Fed
72C4 **Sankuru** *R* Zaïre
20A2 **San Leandro** USA
28E1 **San Leopoldo** Brazil
64C2 **Sanliurfa** Turk
28C2 **San Lorenzo** Arg
26C3 **San Lorenzo** Colombia
24C3 **San Lorenzo** Ecuador
20B2 **San Lucas** USA
28B2 **San Luis** Arg
28B2 **San Luis** State, Arg
19D4 **San Luis** USA
22B1 **San Luis de la Paz** Mexico
28D1 **San Luis del Palma** Arg
20B3 **San Luis Obispo** USA
20B3 **San Luis Obispo B** USA
22B1 **San Luis Potosi** Mexico
22B1 **San Luis Potosi** State, Mexico
20B2 **San Luis Res** USA
40B3 **Sanluri** Sardegna
22D2 **San Magallanes** Mexico
26E2 **San Maigualida** *Mts* Ven
28D3 **San Manuel** Arg
28A2 **San Marcos** Chile
22C2 **San Marcos** Mexico
17C4 **San Marcos** USA
37E3 **San Marino** Republic, Europe
28B1 **San Martin** Catamarca, Arg
28B2 **San Martin** Mendoza, Arg
79G3 **San Martin** *Base* Ant
28A4 **San Martin de los Andes** Arg
37D2 **San Martino di Castroza** Italy
22C2 **San Martin Tuxmelucan** Mexico
20A2 **San Mateo** USA
27G7 **San Matias** Brazil
52C3 **Sanmenxia** China
21D3 **San Miguel** El Salvador
20B3 **San Miguel** USA
20B3 **San Miguel** *I* USA
22B1 **San Miguel del Allende** Mexico
28D3 **San Miguel del Monte** Arg
25C3 **San Miguel de Tucumán** Arg
52D4 **Sanming** China
8B3 **San Nicolas** *I* USA
28C2 **San Nicolás de los Arroyos** Arg
74D2 **Sannieshof** S Africa
70B4 **Sanniquellie** Lib
43E3 **Sanok** Pol
23B5 **San Onofore** Colombia
20D4 **San Onofre** USA
57F8 **San Pablo** Phil
20A1 **San Pablo B** USA
28D2 **San Pedro** Buenos Aires, Arg
70B4 **San Pédro** Ivory Coast
25D2 **San Pedro** Jujuy, Arg
25E2 **San Pedro** Par
19D4 **San Pedro** *R* USA
20C4 **San Pedro Chan** USA
8C4 **San Pedro de los Colonias** Mexico
21D3 **San Pedro Sula** Honduras
40B3 **San Pietro** *I* Medit S
21A1 **San Quintin** Mexico
28B2 **San Rafael** Arg
20A2 **San Rafael** USA
20C3 **San Rafael Mts** USA
37B3 **San Remo** Italy
16C3 **San Saba** *R* USA
28D2 **San Salvador** Arg
24B2 **San Salvador** El Salvador
22B1 **San Salvador** Mexico
23C2 **San Salvador** *I* Caribbean
25C2 **San Salvador de Jujuy** Arg
71G3 **Sansanné-Mango** Togo
39B1 **San Sebastian** Spain
37E3 **Sansepolcro** Italy
40D2 **San Severo** Italy
20B3 **San Simeon** USA
26E7 **Santa Ana** Bol
21C3 **Santa Ana** Guatemala
20D4 **Santa Ana** USA
20D4 **Santa Ana Mts** USA
16C3 **Santa Anna** USA
28A3 **Santa Bárbara** Chile
21B2 **Santa Barbara** Mexico
20C3 **Santa Barbara** USA
20C4 **Santa Barbara,I** USA
20B3 **Santa Barbara Chan** USA
20C3 **Santa Barbara Res** USA
20C4 **Santa Catalina** *I* USA
20C4 **Santa Catalina,G of** USA
25F3 **Santa Catarina** State, Brazil
23B2 **Santa Clara** Cuba
20B2 **Santa Clara** USA
20C3 **Santa Clara** *R* USA
25C8 **Santa Cruz** Arg
26F7 **Santa Cruz** Bol
28A2 **Santa Cruz** Chile
57F8 **Santa Cruz** Phil
25B7 **Santa Cruz** State, Arg
20A2 **Santa Cruz** USA
20C4 **Santa Cruz** *I* USA
77F2 **Santa Cruz** *Is* Solomon Is
19D4 **Santa Cruz** *R* USA
29E2 **Santa Cruz Cabrália** Brazil
20C3 **Santa Cruz Chan** USA
70A2 **Santa Cruz de la Palma** Canary Is
23B2 **Santa Cruz del Sur** Cuba
70A2 **Santa Cruz de Tenerife** Canary Is
73C5 **Santa Cruz do Cuando** Angola
29C3 **Santa Cruz do Rio Pardo** Brazil
28E1 **Santa Cruz do Sul** Brazil
20A2 **Santa Cruz Mts** USA
28D2 **Santa Elena** Arg
26F3 **Santa Elena** Ven
28C2 **Santa Fe** Arg
28C2 **Santa Fe** State, Arg
16A2 **Santa Fe** USA
29B2 **Santa Helena de Goiás** Brazil
52B3 **Santai** China
25B8 **Santa Inés** *I* Chile
28B3 **Santa Isabel** La Pampa, Arg
28C2 **Santa Isabel** Sante Fe, Arg
77E1 **Santa Isabel** *I* Solomon Is
28D2 **Santa Lucia** Urug
20B2 **Santa Lucia** USA
19B3 **Santa Lucia Range** *Mts* USA
70A4 **Santa Luzia** *I* Cape Verde
28C1 **Santa Margarita** Arg
20B3 **Santa Margarita** USA
8B4 **Santa Margarita** *I* Mexico
20D4 **Santa Margarita** *R* USA
37C2 **Santa Margherita** Italy
28E1 **Santa Maria** Brazil
23C4 **Santa Maria** Colombia
20B3 **Santa Maria** USA
70A1 **Santa Maria** *I* Açores
28E2 **Santa Maria** *R* Brazil
16A3 **Santa Maria** *R* Chihuahua, Mexico
22C1 **Santa Maria** *R* Queretaro, Mexico
29D1 **Santa Maria da Vitória** Brazil
22B1 **Santa Maria del Rio** Mexico
26D1 **Santa Marta** Colombia
20C3 **Santa Monica** USA
20C4 **Santa Monica B** USA
29D1 **Santana** Brazil
28D2 **Santana do Livramento** Brazil
26C3 **Santander** Colombia
39B1 **Santander** Spain
39C2 **Santañy** Spain
20C3 **Santa Paula** USA
29B3 **Santa Porto Helena** Brazil
27K4 **Santa Quitéria** Brazil
37E2 **Santarcangelo di Romagna** Italy
27H4 **Santarem** Brazil
39A2 **Santarém** Port
29B2 **Santa Rita do Araguaia** Brazil
28E1 **Santa Rosa** Brazil
20A1 **Santa Rosa** California, USA
21D3 **Santa Rosa** Honduras
28C3 **Santa Rosa** La Pampa, Arg
28B2 **Santa Rosa** Mendoza, Arg
16B3 **Santa Rosa** New Mexico, USA
28B2 **Santa Rosa** San Luis, Arg
20B3 **Santa Rosa** *I* USA
21A2 **Santa Rosalía** Mexico
18C2 **Santa Rosa Range** *Mts* USA
28C1 **Santa Sylvina** Arg
27L5 **Santa Talhada** Brazil
29D2 **Santa Teresa** Brazil
40B2 **Santa Teresa di Gallura** Sardegna
28E2 **Santa Vitoria do Palmar** Brazil
20B3 **Santa Ynez** *R* USA
20B3 **Santa Ynez Mots** USA
15D2 **Santee** *R* USA
37D2 **Santerno** *R* Italy
37C2 **Santhia** Italy
28A2 **Santiago** Chile
23C3 **Santiago** Dom Rep
22A1 **Santiago** Mexico
26B2 **Santiago** Panama
57F7 **Santiago** Phil
26C4 **Santiago** *R* Peru
39A1 **Santiago de Compostela** Spain
23B2 **Santiago de Cuba** Cuba
28C1 **Santiago del Estero** Arg
25D3 **Santiago del Estero** State, Arg
20D4 **Santiago Peak** *Mt* USA
27K7 **Santo** State, Brazil
77F2 **Santo** Vanuatu
29B3 **Santo Anastatácio** Brazil
28E1 **Santo Angelo** Brazil
70A4 **Santo Antão** *I* Cape Verde
29B3 **Santo Antonio da Platina** Brazil
29E1 **Santo Antônio de Jesus** Brazil
29A2 **Santo Antônio do Leverger** Brazil
22B1 **Santo Dominco** Mexico
23D3 **Santo Domingo** Dom Rep
29C3 **Santos** Brazil
29D3 **Santos Dumont** Brazil
19C4 **Santo Tomas** Mexico
28D1 **Santo Tomé** Arg
25B7 **San Valentin** *Mt* Chile
28A2 **San Vicente** Chile
22B1 **San Vicente** Mexico
37E2 **San Vito al Tagliamento** Italy
73B4 **Sanza Pomba** Angola
28D1 **São Borja** Brazil
29C3 **São Carlos** Brazil
29C1 **São Domingos** Brazil
27H5 **São Félix** Mato Grosso, Brazil
29D3 **São Fidélis** Brazil
29D2 **São Francisco** Brazil
27L5 **São Francisco** *R* Brazil
28D1 **São Francisco de Assis** Brazil
25G3 **São Francisco do Sul** Brazil
28E2 **São Gabriel** Brazil
29C2 **São Gotardo** Brazil
73D4 **Sao Hill** Tanz
29D3 **São João da Barra** Brazil
29C3 **São João da Boa Vista** Brazil
29C1 **São João d'Aliança** Brazil
29D2 **São João da Ponte** Brazil
29D3 **São João del Rei** Brazil
29D2 **São João do Paraíso** Brazil
29C3 **São Joaquim da Barra** Brazil
70A1 **São Jorge** *I* Açores
28E2 **São José do Norte** Brazil
29C3 **São José do Rio Prêto** Brazil
29C3 **São José dos Campos** Brazil
29C4 **São José dos Pinhais** Brazil
29A2 **São Lourenço** *R* Brazil
28E2 **São Lourenço do Sul** Brazil
27K4 **São Luis** Brazil
28E1 **Sao Luis Gonzaga** Brazil
29C2 **São Marcos** *R* Brazil
29D2 **São Maria do Suaçui** Brazil
29E2 **São Mateus** Brazil
29D2 **São Mateus** *R* Brazil
70A1 **São Miguel** *I* Açores
29B1 **São Miguel de Araguaia** Brazil
38C2 **Saône** *R* France
70A4 **São Nicolau** *I* Cape Verde
29D1 **São Onofre** *R* Brazil
29C3 **São Paulo** Brazil
29B3 **São Paulo** State, Brazil
28E1 **São Pedro do Sul** Brazil
24H3 **São Pedro e São Paulo** *Is* Brazil
27K5 **São Raimundo Nonato** Brazil
29C2 **São Romão** Brazil
29C3 **São Sebastia do Paraiso** Brazil
28E2 **São Sepé** Brazil
29B2 **São Simão** Goias, Brazil
25G1 **São Simão, Barragem de** *Res* Brazil
29C3 **São Simão** Sao Paulo, Brazil
70A4 **São Tiago** *I* Cape Verde
70C4 **São Tomé** *I* W Africa
70C4 **São Tomé and Principe** Republic, W Africa
70B2 **Saoura** *Watercourse* Alg
29A1 **Saouriuiná** *R* Brazil
29C3 **São Vicente** Brazil
70A4 **São Vincente** *I* Cape Verde
41F2 **Sápai** Greece
57C3 **Saparua** Indon
56E4 **Sape** Indon
71H4 **Sapele** Nig
53E3 **Sapporo** Japan
40D2 **Sapri** Italy
32G7 **Saprsborg** Nor
17C2 **Sapulpa** USA
63B1 **Saqqez** Iran
45H8 **Sarāb** Iran
41D2 **Sarajevo** Bosnia & Herzegovina, Yugos
63E1 **Sarakhs** Iran
45K5 **Saraktash** Russian Fed
49K4 **Sarala** Russian Fed
13E2 **Saranac L** USA
13E2 **Saranac Lake** USA
41E3 **Sarandë** Alb
28E1 **Sarandi** Brazil
28D2 **Sarandi del Yi** Urug
28D2 **Sarandi Grande** Urug
57G9 **Sarangani Is** Phil
44L3 **Saranpaul'** Russian Fed
44H5 **Saransk** Russian Fed
37C2 **Saranza** Italy
71H4 **Sara Peak** *Mt* Nig
44J4 **Sarapul** Russian Fed
15E4 **Sarasota** USA
41F1 **Sărat** Rom
43F3 **Sarata** Ukraine
11A3 **Saratoga** USA
14D1 **Saratoga Springs** USA
56D2 **Saratok** Malay
45H5 **Saratov** Russian Fed
45H5 **Saratovskoye Vodokhranilishche** *Res* Russian Fed
64A2 **Saraykoy** Turk
63E3 **Sarbāz** Iran
63D2 **Sarbīsheh** Iran
37D1 **Sarca** *R* Italy
69A2 **Sardalais** Libya
63B1 **Sar Dasht** Iran
40B2 **Sardegna** *I* Medit S
Sardinia = Sardegna
32H5 **Sarektjåkkå, Mt** Sweden
66C4 **Sarenga** Eth
60C2 **Sargodha** Pak
72B3 **Sarh** Chad
63C1 **Sārī** Iran
65C2 **Sarida** *R* Isreal
64D1 **Sarikamiş** Turk
76D3 **Sarina** Aust
37B1 **Sarine** *R* Switz
60B1 **Sar-i-Pul** Afghan
69B2 **Sarīr** Libya
69A2 **Sarir Tibesti** *Desert* Libya
53B4 **Sariwŏn** N Korea
38B2 **Sark** *I* UK
64C2 **Şarkişla** Turk
51G7 **Sarmi** Indon
25C7 **Sarmiento** Arg
32G6 **Särna** Sweden
37C1 **Sarnen** Switz
4E5 **Sarnia** Can
43F2 **Sarny** Ukraine
60B2 **Sarobi** Afghan
56B3 **Sarolangun** Indon
41E3 **Saronikós Kólpos** *G* Greece
37C2 **Saronno** Italy
41F2 **Saros Körfezi** *B* Turk
44M2 **Saroto** Russian Fed
7N2 **Sarqaq** Greenland
36D2 **Sarralbe** France
36D2 **Sarrebourg** France
36D2 **Sarreguemines** France
36D2 **Sarre-Union** France
39B1 **Sarrion** Spain
60B3 **Sartanahu** Pak
40B2 **Sartène** Corse
36A3 **Sarthe** Department, France
38B2 **Sarthe** *R* France
65D1 **Sārūt** Syria
63E3 **Sarvan** Iran
45J6 **Sarykamys** Kazakhstan
48H5 **Sarysu** *R* Kazakhstan
61B3 **Sasarām** India
53B5 **Sasebo** Japan
6H4 **Saskatchewan** Province, Can
6H4 **Saskatchewan** *R* Can
3G3 **Saskatoon** Can
49N2 **Saskylakh** Russian Fed
74D2 **Sasolburg** S Africa
44G5 **Sasovo** Russian Fed
70B4 **Sassandra** Ivory Coast
70B4 **Sassandra** *R* Ivory Coast
40B2 **Sassari** Sardegna
42C2 **Sassnitz** Germany
37D2 **Sassuolo** Italy
28C2 **Sastre** Arg
54A4 **Sasuna** Japan
62A1 **Sātāra** India
6G2 **Satellite B** Can
56E4 **Satengar** *Is* Indon
32H6 **Säter** Sweden
15C2 **Satilla** *R* USA
44K4 **Satka** Russian Fed
60D2 **Satluj** *R* India
61B3 **Satna** India
60C4 **Sātpura Range** *Mts* India
41E1 **Satu Mare** Rom
28D2 **Sauce** Arg
32F7 **Sauda** Nor
58C3 **Saudi Arabia** Kingdom, Arabian Pen
36D2 **Sauer** *R* Germany/Lux
36D1 **Sauerland** Region, Germany
32B1 **Sauðárkrókur** Iceland
12B2 **Saugatuck** USA
14D1 **Saugerties** USA
3C3 **Saugstad,Mt** Can
11D2 **Sauk Center** USA
12B2 **Sauk City** USA
4E4 **Sault Ste Marie** Can
12C1 **Sault Ste Marie** USA
51G7 **Saumlaki** Indon
38B2 **Saumur** France
73C4 **Saurimo** Angola
23M2 **Sauteurs** Grenada
41D2 **Sava** *R* Serbia, Yugos
77H2 **Saval'i** *I* Western Samoa
71G4 **Savalou** Benin
45H9 **Savan** *R* Iran
15C2 **Savannah** Georgia, USA
15B1 **Savannah** Tennessee, USA
15C2 **Savannah** *R* USA
55C2 **Savannakhet** Laos
23B3 **Savanna la Mar** Jamaica
4C3 **Savant L** Can
7J4 **Savant Lake** Can
55D2 **Savarane** Laos
71G4 **Savé** Benin
73D6 **Save** *R* Mozam
63C2 **Sāveh** Iran
36D2 **Saverne** France
37B2 **Savigliano** Italy
36B2 **Savigny** France
44G3 **Savinskiy** Russian Fed
37E3 **Savio** *R* Italy
38D2 **Savoie** *Region* France
37C2 **Savona** Italy

Savonlinna Sharpsburg

32K6 **Savonlinna** Fin
10D3 **Savoonga** USA
37E2 **Savudrija Rtič** *Pt* Croatia, Yugos
32K5 **Savukoski** Fin
57B4 **Savu S** Indon
55A1 **Saw** Burma
57C3 **Sawai** Indon
60D3 **Sawai Mādhopur** India
56B2 **Sawang** Indon
55C2 **Sawankhalok** Thai
54D3 **Sawara** Japan
16A2 **Sawatch Mts** USA
5H3 **Sawbill** Can
10J2 **Sawtooth Mt** USA
18C2 **Sawtooth Range** *Mts* USA
76B2 **Sawu** *I* Indon
14A2 **Saxton** USA
71G3 **Say** Niger
60B1 **Sayghan** Afghan
67G3 **Sayh Hajmah** Oman
67F2 **Sayhūt** Yemen
45H6 **Saykhin** Kazakhstan
50D2 **Saynshand** Mongolia
16C2 **Sayre** Oklahoma, USA
14B2 **Sayre** Pennsylvania, USA
22C2 **Sayula** Mexico
22A1 **Sayulita** Mexico
45J7 **Say-Utes** Kazakhstan
14D2 **Sayville** USA
3C3 **Sayward** Can
42C3 **Sázava** *R* Czech
39C2 **Sbisseb** *R* Alg
35D4 **Scafell Pike** *Mt* Eng
34E1 **Scalloway** Scot
34D2 **Scapa Flow** *Sd* Scot
13D2 **Scarborough** Can
35E4 **Scarborough** Eng
23E4 **Scarborough** Tobago
34B2 **Scarp** *I* Scot
40B1 **Schaffhausen** Switz
42C3 **Scharding** Austria
36D1 **Scharteberg** *Mt* Germany
7M4 **Schefferville** Can
36B1 **Schelde** *R* Belg
19D3 **Schell Creek Range** *Mts* USA
14D1 **Schenectady** USA
16C4 **Schertz** USA
36C1 **Schiedam** Neth
37D2 **Schio** Italy
36D1 **Schleiden** Germany
42B2 **Schleswig** Germany
42B2 **Schleswig Holstein** State, Germany
14C1 **Schoharie** USA
76D1 **Schouten Is** PNG
36E2 **Schramberg** Germany
7K5 **Schreiber** Can
19C3 **Schurz** USA
14C2 **Schuylkill** *R* USA
14B2 **Schuylkill Haven** USA
42B3 **Schwabische Alb** *Upland* Germany
74B2 **Schwarzrand** *R* Namibia
36E2 **Schwarzwald** *Mts* Germany
42B3 **Schwarzwald** *Upland* Germany
10G2 **Schwatka Mts** USA
37D1 **Schwaz** Austria
42C2 **Schweinfurt** Germany
74D2 **Schweizer Reneke** S Africa
42C2 **Schwerin** Germany
37C1 **Schwyz** Switz
40C3 **Sciacca** Italy
35B7 **Scilly Isles** *Is* UK
12C3 **Scioto** *R* USA
11A2 **Scobey** USA
75D2 **Scone** Aust
7Q2 **Scoresby Sd** Greenland
xxxF7 **Scotia Ridge** Atlantic O
xxxF7 **Scotia S** Atlantic O
34C3 **Scotland** Country, UK
79F7 **Scott** *Base* Ant
74E3 **Scottburgh** S Africa
3C3 **Scott,C** Can
16B2 **Scott City** USA
79G6 **Scott I** Ant
7L2 **Scott Inlet** *B* Can
3G2 **Scott L** Can
18B2 **Scott,Mt** USA
76B2 **Scott Reef** Timor S
11B3 **Scottsbluff** USA
15B2 **Scottsboro** USA
75E3 **Scottsdale** Aust
19D4 **Scottsdale** USA
14C2 **Scranton** USA
11C3 **Scribner** USA
37D1 **Scuol** Switz
Scutari = Shkodër
74C3 **Seacow** S Africa
4B2 **Seal** Can
6J4 **Seal** *R* Can
75B3 **Sea Lake** Aust
5K3 **Seal Bight** Can
19D3 **Searchlight** USA
17D2 **Searcy** USA
20D3 **Searles** USA
20B2 **Seaside** California, USA
18B1 **Seaside** Oregon, USA
14C3 **Seaside Park** USA
18B1 **Seattle** USA
57B5 **Seba** Indon
13E2 **Sebago L** USA
56B2 **Sebanga** Indon
20A1 **Sebastopol** USA
58B4 **Sebderat** Eth
43F1 **Sebez** Russian Fed
13F1 **Seboomook L** USA
15E4 **Sebring** USA
37D2 **Secchia** *R* Italy
78A3 **Secretary I** NZ
17D2 **Sedalia** USA
36C2 **Sedan** France
10E5 **Sedanka** *I* USA
78B2 **Seddonville** NZ
65C3 **Sede Boqer** Israel
65C3 **Sederot** Israel
70A3 **Sédhiou** Sen
65C3 **Sedom** Israel
19D4 **Sedona** USA
74B2 **Seeheim** Namibia
79E **Seelig,Mt** Ant
36A2 **Sées** France
71B2 **Sefrou** Mor
78B2 **Sefton,Mt** NZ
55C5 **Segamat** Malay
44E3 **Segezha** Russian Fed
39B2 **Segorbe** Spain
70B3 **Ségou** Mali
Segovia = Coco
39B1 **Segovia** Spain
39C1 **Segre** *R* Spain
10D6 **Seguam** *I* USA
10D6 **Seguam Pass** USA
70B4 **Séguéla** Ivory Coast
70A2 **Seguia el Hamra** *Watercourse* Mor
17C4 **Seguin** USA
28C2 **Segundo** *R* Arg
56E2 **Seguntur** Indon
39B2 **Segura** *R* Spain
60B3 **Sehwan** Pak
16C2 **Seiling** USA
36D2 **Seille** *R* France
32J6 **Seinäjoki** Fin
11D2 **Seine** *R* Can
38C2 **Seine** *R* France
36B2 **Seine-et-Marne** Department, France
36A2 **Seine-Maritime** Department, France
72D4 **Sekenke** Tanz
72D2 **Sek'ot'a** Eth
18B1 **Selah** USA
51G7 **Selaru** *I* Indon
56E4 **Selat Alas** *Str* Indon
56C3 **Selat Bangka** *Str* Indon
56B3 **Selat Berhala** *B* Indon
51G7 **Selat Dampier** *Str* Indon
56C3 **Selat Gaspar** *Str* Indon
56E4 **Selat Lombok** *Str* Indon
56A3 **Selat Mentawi** *Str* Indon
56E4 **Selat Sape** *Str* Indon
57B4 **Selat Sumba** *Str* Indon
56C4 **Selat Sunda** *Str* Indon
57C4 **Selat Wetar** *Chan* Indon
57D3 **Selawati** *I* Indon
10F2 **Selawik** USA
10G2 **Selawik** *R* USA
10F2 **Selawik L** USA
35E5 **Selby** Eng
11B2 **Selby** USA
41F3 **Selçuk** Turk
10H4 **Seldovia** USA
74D1 **Selebi Pikwe** Botswana
53C1 **Selemdzha** *R* Russian Fed
53C1 **Selemdzhinsk** Russian Fed
49Q3 **Selennyakh** *R* Russian Fed
36D2 **Selestat** France
7Q3 **Selfoss** Iceland
11B2 **Selfridge** USA
72C1 **Selima Oasis** Sudan
43G1 **Selizharovo** Russian Fed
6J4 **Selkirk** Can
34D4 **Selkirk** Scot
3E3 **Selkirk Mts** Can
15B2 **Selma** Alabama, USA
20C2 **Selma** California, USA
15B1 **Selmer** USA
37A1 **Selongey** France
39B2 **Selouane** Mor
10M3 **Selous,Mt** Can
56C3 **Selta Karimata** *Str* Indon
28C1 **Selva** Arg
26D5 **Selvas** Region, Brazil
18C1 **Selway** USA
76D3 **Selwyn** Aust
3H1 **Selwyn L** Can
6E3 **Selwyn Mts** Can
56D4 **Semarang** Indon
44G4 **Semenov** Russian Fed
10A5 **Semichi Is** USA
10G4 **Semidi Is** USA
45F5 **Semiluki** Russian Fed
11A3 **Seminoe Res** USA
17C2 **Seminole** Oklahoma, USA
16B3 **Seminole** Texas, USA
15C2 **Seminole,L** USA
48K4 **Semipalatinsk** Kazakhstan
57F8 **Semirara Is** Phil
63C2 **Semirom** Iran
10B6 **Semisopochnoi** *I* USA
56D2 **Semitau** Indon
63C1 **Semnān** Iran
36C2 **Semois** *R* Belg
22C2 **Sempoala** Hist Site, Mexico
56E2 **Semporna** Malay
26E5 **Sena Madureira** Brazil
73C5 **Senanga** Zambia
17E3 **Senatobia** USA
53E4 **Sendai** Honshū, Japan
53C5 **Sendai** Kyūshū, Japan
60D4 **Sendwha** India
14B1 **Seneca Falls** USA
14B1 **Seneca L** USA
16A3 **Senecu** Mexico
70A3 **Senegal** Republic, Africa
70A3 **Sénégal** *R* Maur/Sen
74D2 **Senekal** S Africa
57B3 **Sengkang** Indon
27L6 **Senhor do Bonfim** Brazil
40C2 **Senigallia** Italy
40D2 **Senj** Croatia, Yugos
50F4 **Senkaku Gunto** *Is* Japan
53C3 **Senlin Shan** *Mt* China
36B2 **Senlis** France
72D2 **Sennar** Sudan
7L5 **Senneterre** Can
36D2 **Senones** France
36B2 **Sens** France
41E1 **Senta** Serbia, Yugos
72C4 **Sentery** Zaïre
3D3 **Sentinel Peak** *Mt* Can
60D4 **Seoni** India
Seoul = Soul
78B2 **Separation Pt** NZ
54A3 **Sep'o** N Korea
55D2 **Sepone** Laos
29A2 **Sepotuba** *R* Brazil
7M4 **Sept-Iles** Can
72B1 **Séquédine** Niger
20C2 **Sequoia Nat Pk** USA
65C1 **Serai** Syria
57C3 **Seram** *I* Indon
56C4 **Serang** Indon
56C2 **Serasan** *I* Indon
41D2 **Serbia** *Republic* Yugos
37D2 **Serchio** *R* Italy
45G5 **Serdobsk** Russian Fed
36B3 **Serein** *R* France
55C5 **Seremban** Malay
72D4 **Serengeti Nat Pk** Tanz
73D5 **Serenje** Zambia
43F3 **Seret** *R* Ukraine
44H4 **Sergach** Russian Fed
53C3 **Sergeyevka** Russian Fed
48H3 **Sergino** Russian Fed
27L6 **Sergipe** State, Brazil
44F4 **Sergiyev Posad** Georgia
56D2 **Seria** Brunei
56D2 **Serian** Malay
41E3 **Sérifos** *I* Greece
5H2 **Sérigny** *R* Can
37C2 **Serio** *R* Italy
69B2 **Serir Calanscio** *Desert* Libya
36C2 **Sermaize-les-Bains** France
7P3 **Sermilik** Greenland
44J5 **Sernovodsk** Russian Fed
44L4 **Serov** Russian Fed
74D1 **Serowe** Botswana
39A2 **Serpa** Port
44F5 **Serpukhov** Russian Fed
29A3 **Serra Amamba** Par
29B1 **Serra Azul** Brazil
29C3 **Serra da Canastra** *Mts* Brazil
39A1 **Serra da Estrela** *Mts* Port
29C3 **Serra da Mantiqueira** *Mts* Brazil
29B2 **Serra da Mombuca** Brazil
29B2 **Serra das Furnas** *Mts* Brazil
29C1 **Serra de Arrajas** *Mts* Brazil
29B4 **Serra de Fartura** *Mts* Brazil
29A3 **Serra de Maracaju** *Mts* Brazil
29A2 **Serra de São Jeronimo** Brazil
28D1 **Serra do Boquairao** *Mts* Brazil
29D2 **Serra do Cabral** *Mt* Brazil
27G5 **Serra do Cachimbo** *Mts* Brazil
29B2 **Serra do Caiapó** *Mts* Brazil
28E2 **Serra do CanguŞcu** *Mts* Brazil
29B3 **Serra do Cantu** *Mts* Brazil
29D3 **Serra do Caparaó** *Mts* Brazil
27K7 **Serra do Chifre** Brazil
29D2 **Serra do Espinhaço** *Mts* Brazil
28D1 **Serra do Espinilho** *Mts* Brazil
29C2 **Serra do Jibão** *Mts* Brazil
29C3 **Serra do Mar** *Mts* Brazil
29B3 **Serra do Mirante** *Mts* Brazil
27H3 **Serra do Navio** Brazil
29C3 **Serra do Paranapiacaba** *Mts* Brazil
29D1 **Serra do Ramalho** *Mts* Brazil
29B1 **Serra do Roncador** *Mts* Brazil
27G6 **Serra dos Caiabis** *Mts* Brazil
29B3 **Serra dos Dourados** *Mts* Brazil
29D1 **Serra do Sincora** *Mts* Brazil
26F6 **Serra dos Parecis** *Mts* Brazil
29C2 **Serra dos Pilões** *Mts* Brazil
29B2 **Serra do Taquaral** *Mts* Brazil
29B2 **Serra Dourada** *Mts* Brazil
29C1 **Serra Dourada** *Mts* Brazil
28E2 **Serra Encantadas** *Mts* Brazil
27G6 **Serra Formosa** *Mts* Brazil
29D2 **Serra Geral** *Mts* Bahia, Brazil
29B4 **Serra Geral** *Mts* Parona, Brazil
29C1 **Serra Geral de Goiás** *Mts* Brazil
29C2 **Serra Geral do Parana** *Mts* Brazil
41E2 **Sérrai** Greece
21D3 **Serrana Bank** *Is* Caribbean
39B1 **Serrana de Cuenca** *Mts* Spain
16B4 **Serranias del Burro** *Mts* Mexico
29B2 **Serranópolis** Brazil
26F3 **Serra Pacaraima** *Mts* Brazil/Ven
26F3 **Serra Parima** *Mts* Brazil
27H3 **Serra Tumucumaque** Brazil
36B2 **Serre** *R* France
37A2 **Serres** France
28B2 **Serrezuela** Arg
27L6 **Serrinha** Brazil
29D2 **Serro** Brazil
29B3 **Sertanópolis** Brazil
52A3 **Sêrtar** China
57D4 **Serua** *I* Indon
74D1 **Serule** Botswana
56A2 **Seruwai** Indon
56D3 **Seruyan** *R* Indon
53B1 **Seryshevo** Russian Fed
4D3 **Seseganaga L** Can
73B5 **Sesfontein** Namibia
73C5 **Sesheke** Zambia
37B2 **Sestriere** Italy
37C2 **Sestri Levante** Italy
53D3 **Setana** Japan
38C3 **Sète** France
29D2 **Sete Lagoas** Brazil
71D1 **Sétif** Alg
66C4 **Setit** *R* Sudan
54C3 **Seto** Japan
54B4 **Seto Naikai** *S* Japan
71A2 **Settat** Mor
35D4 **Settle** Eng
39A2 **Setúbal** Port
37A1 **Seurre** France
45H7 **Sevan, Ozero** *L* Armenia
45E7 **Sevastopol'** Ukraine
7K4 **Severn** *R* Can
35D5 **Severn** *R* Eng
44G3 **Severnaya Dvina** *R* Russian Fed
49L1 **Severnaya Zemlya** *I* Russian Fed
44L3 **Severnyy Sos'va** *R* Russian Fed
44K3 **Severnyy Ural** *Mts* Russian Fed
49M4 **Severo-Baykalskoye Nagorye** *Mts* Russian Fed
45F6 **Severo Donets** *R* Ukraine
44F3 **Severodvinsk** Russian Fed
48H3 **Severo Sos'va** *R* Russian Fed
44L3 **Severoural'sk** Russian Fed
19D3 **Sevier** *R* USA
19D3 **Sevier Desert** USA
19D3 **Sevier L** USA
39A2 **Sevilla** Spain
Seville = Sevilla
41F2 **Sevlievo** Bulg
70A4 **Sewa** *R* Sierra Leone
10J3 **Seward** Alaska, USA
17C1 **Seward** Nebraska, USA
10E2 **Seward Pen** USA
3E2 **Sexsmith** Can
68K8 **Seychelles,Is** Indian O
32C1 **Seyðisfjörður** Iceland
64C2 **Seyhan** Turk
45F5 **Seym** *R* Russian Fed
49R3 **Seymchan** Russian Fed
75C3 **Seymour** Aust
14D2 **Seymour** Connecticut, USA
12B3 **Seymour** Indiana, USA
16C3 **Seymour** Texas, USA
37B2 **Seyne** France
37E2 **Sežana** Slovenia, Yugos
36B2 **Sézanne** France
71E2 **Sfax** Tunisia
41F1 **Sfînto Gheorghe** Rom
42A2 **'s-Gravenhage** Neth
52B3 **Shaanxi** Province, China
72C4 **Shabunda** Zaïre
59F2 **Shache** China
79G9 **Shackleton Ice Shelf** Ant
60B3 **Shadadkot** Pak
63C2 **Shādhām** *R* Iran
20C3 **Shafter** USA
35D6 **Shaftesbury** Eng
71G4 **Shagamu** Nig
4D2 **Shagamu** *R* Can
25J8 **Shag Rocks** *Is* South Georgia
63B2 **Shāhabād** Iran
56F7 **Shah Alam** Malay
65D2 **Shahbā** Syria
63D2 **Shahdap** Iran
61B3 **Shahdol** India
63B1 **Shāhīn Dezh** Iran
63D2 **Shāh Kūh** Iran
63E2 **Shahrak** Afghan
63D2 **Shahr-e Bābak** Iran
Shahresa = Qomisheh
63C2 **Shahr Kord** Iran
45J8 **Shahsavār** Iran
44L3 **Shaim** Russian Fed
62B1 **Shājābād** India
60D3 **Shājahānpur** India
60D4 **Shājāpur** India
53E2 **Shakhtersk** Russian Fed
45G6 **Shakhty** Russian Fed
44H4 **Shakhun'ya** Russian Fed
71G4 **Shaki** Nig
11D3 **Shakopee** USA
54D2 **Shakotan-misaki** *C* Japan
10F3 **Shaktoolik** USA
44K4 **Shamary** Russian Fed
72D3 **Shambe** Sudan
14B2 **Shamokin** USA
16B2 **Shamrock** USA
14C1 **Shandaken** USA
20B3 **Shandon** USA
52D2 **Shandong** Province, China
52C5 **Shangchuan Dao** *I* China
52C1 **Shangdu** China
52E3 **Shanghai** China
52C3 **Shangnan** China
73C5 **Shangombo** Zambia
52D4 **Shangra** China
52B5 **Shangsi** China
52C3 **Shang Xian** China
53B2 **Shangzhi** China
33B3 **Shannon** *R* Irish Rep
3H2 **Shannon L** Can
52D3 **Shanqiu** China
53B3 **Shansonggang** China
50G1 **Shantarskiye Ostrova** *I* Russian Fed
52D5 **Shantou** China
52C2 **Shanxi** Province, China
52D3 **Shan Xian** China
52C5 **Shaoguan** China
52E4 **Shaoxing** China
52C4 **Shaoyang** China
34D2 **Shapinsay** *I* Scot
65D2 **Shaqqā** Syria
67E3 **Shaqqat aj Kharitah** Region, S Arabia
67E1 **Shaqra'** S Arabia
67E4 **Shaqrā'** Yemen
67E3 **Sharawrah** S Arabia
52A1 **Sharhulsan** Mongolia
54D2 **Shari** Japan
63D1 **Sharifābād** Iran
67G1 **Sharjah** UAE
76A3 **Shark B** Aust
63D1 **Sharlauk** Turkmenistan
65C2 **Sharon,Plain of** Israel
14B3 **Sharpsburg** USA

Sharya **Sirsi**

44H4 **Sharya** Russian Fed
72D3 **Shashamenē** Eth
74D1 **Shashani** *R* Zim
74D1 **Shashe** *R* Botswana
52C3 **Shashi** China
18B2 **Shasta L** USA
18B2 **Shasta,Mt** USA
65D1 **Shathah at Tahtā** Syria
64E3 **Shaṭṭ al Gharrat** *R* Iraq
65C3 **Shaubak** Jordan
3G4 **Shaunavon** Can
20C2 **Shaver L** USA
14C2 **Shawangunk Mt** USA
12B2 **Shawano** USA
17C2 **Shawnee** Oklahoma, USA
11A3 **Shawnee** Wyoming, USA
5G4 **Shawinigan** Can
52D4 **Sha Xian** China
76B3 **Shay Gap** Aust
65D2 **Shaykh Miskīn** Syria
66D4 **Shaykh 'Uthmān** Yemen
44F5 **Shchekino** Russian Fed
45F5 **Shchigry** Russian Fed
45E5 **Shchors** Ukraine
48J4 **Shchuchinsk** Kazakhstan
12B2 **Sheboygan** USA
72E3 **Shebele** *R* Eth
72B3 **Shebshi** *Mts* Nig
53E2 **Shebunino** Russian Fed
5J4 **Shediac** Can
10K2 **Sheenjek** *R* USA
34B4 **Sheep Haven** *Estuary* Irish Rep
35F6 **Sheerness** Eng
5J5 **Sheet Harbour** Can
65C2 **Shefar'am** Israel
15B2 **Sheffield** Alabama, USA
35E5 **Sheffield** Eng
14A2 **Sheffield** Pennsylvania, USA
16B3 **Sheffield** Texas, USA
5K3 **Shekalika Bay** Can
60C2 **Shekhupura** Pak
3C2 **Shelagyote Peak** *Mt* Can
5H5 **Shelburne** Can
14D1 **Shelburne Falls** USA
12B2 **Shelby** Michigan, USA
18D1 **Shelby** Montana, USA
15C1 **Shelby** N Carolina, USA
12B3 **Shelbyville** Indiana, USA
15B1 **Shelbyville** Tennessee, USA
11C3 **Sheldon** USA
10M3 **Sheldon,Mt** Can
5J3 **Sheldrake** Can
10H4 **Shelikof Str** USA
3G3 **Shellbrook** Can
18D2 **Shelley** USA
75D2 **Shellharbour** Aust
78A3 **Shelter Pt** NZ
18B1 **Shelton** USA
64E1 **Shemakha** Azerbaijan
17C1 **Shenandoah** USA
13D3 **Shenandoah** *R* USA
14A3 **Shenandoah Mt** USA
13D3 **Shenandoah Nat Pk** USA
71H4 **Shendam** Nig
66B3 **Shendi** Sudan
44G3 **Shenkursk** Russian Fed
52C2 **Shenmu** China
52E1 **Shenyang** China
52C5 **Shenzhen** China
60D3 **Sheopur** India
43F2 **Shepetovka** Ukraine
14B3 **Shepherdstown** USA
75C3 **Shepparton** Aust
36A1 **Sheppey,I of** Eng
7K2 **Sherard,C** Can
35D6 **Sherborne** Eng
70A4 **Sherbro I** Sierra Leone
5G4 **Sherbrooke** Can
14C1 **Sherburne** USA
66B3 **Shereik** Sudan
60C3 **Shergarh** India
17D3 **Sheridan** Arkansas, USA
11A3 **Sheridan** Wyoming, USA
17C3 **Sherman** USA
3H2 **Sherridon** Can
42B2 **s-Hertogenbosh** Neth
10M4 **Sheslay** Can
3B2 **Sheslay** *R* Can
33C1 **Shetland** *Is* Scot
45J7 **Shevchenko** Kazakhstan
53C1 **Shevli** *R* Russian Fed
11C2 **Sheyenne** USA
11C2 **Sheyenne** *R* USA
63C3 **Sheyk Sho'eyb** *I* Iran
50J2 **Shiashkotan** *I* Russian Fed
60B1 **Shibarghan** Afghan
53D4 **Shibata** Japan
54D2 **Shibetsu** Japan
69C1 **Shibin el Kom** Egypt
65A3 **Shibîn el Qanâtir** Egypt
4D3 **Shibogama L** Can
54C3 **Shibukawa** Japan
14B2 **Shickshinny** USA
52C2 **Shijiazhuang** China
60B3 **Shikarpur** Pak
47H4 **Shikoku,I** Japan
54B4 **Shikoku-sanchi** *Mts* Japan
54D2 **Shikotsu-ko** *L* Japan
44G3 **Shilega** Russian Fed
61C2 **Shiliguri** India
50E1 **Shilka** Russian Fed
50E1 **Shilka** *R* Russian Fed
14C2 **Shillington** USA
61D2 **Shillong** India
44G5 **Shilovo** Russian Fed
54B4 **Shimabara** Japan
54C4 **Shimada** Japan
53B1 **Shimanovsk** Russian Fed
53D4 **Shimizu** Japan
54C4 **Shimoda** Japan
62B2 **Shimoga** India
53C5 **Shimonoseki** Japan
54C3 **Shinano** *R* Japan
67G2 **Shināş** Oman
63E2 **Shindand** Afghan
14A2 **Shinglehouse** USA
4D4 **Shingleton** USA
53D5 **Shingū** Japan
54D3 **Shinjō** Japan
53D4 **Shinminato** Japan
65D1 **Shinshār** Syria
72D4 **Shinyanga** Tanz
53E4 **Shiogama** Japan
54C4 **Shiono-misaki** *C* Japan
52A5 **Shiping** China
5J4 **Shippegan** Can
14B2 **Shippensburg** USA
16A2 **Shiprock** USA
67E3 **Shiqāq al Ma'ātif** Region, Yemen
52B3 **Shiquan** China
54D3 **Shirakawa** Japan
54C3 **Shirane-san** *Mt* Japan
54C3 **Shirani-san** *Mt* Japan
63C3 **Shīraz** Iran
65A3 **Shirbīn** Egypt
54D2 **Shiriya-saki** *C* Japan
63C2 **Shīr Kūh** Iran
54C3 **Shirotori** Japan
63D1 **Shirvān** Iran
10F5 **Shishaldin V** USA
10E2 **Shishmaref** USA
10E2 **Shishmaref Inlet** USA
52B2 **Shitanjing** China
12B3 **Shively** USA
60D3 **Shivpuri** India
65C3 **Shivta** *Hist Site* Israel
19D3 **Shivwits Plat** USA
73D5 **Shiwa Ngandu** Zambia
52C3 **Shiyan** China
52B2 **Shizuishan** China
54C3 **Shizuoka** Japan
41D2 **Shkodër** Alb
43G2 **Shkov** Belorussia
49L1 **Shmidta, Ostrov** *I* Russian Fed
75D2 **Shoalhaven** *R* Aust
54B4 **Shobara** Japan
62B2 **Shoranūr** India
62B1 **Shorāpur** India
19C3 **Shoshone** California, USA
18D2 **Shoshone** Idaho, USA
18E2 **Shoshone** *R* USA
18D2 **Shoshone L** USA
19C3 **Shoshone Mts** USA
18E2 **Shoshoni** USA
45E5 **Shostka** Ukraine
66C4 **Showak** Sudan
19D4 **Show Low** USA
17D3 **Shreveport** USA
35D5 **Shrewsbury** Eng
35D5 **Shropshire** County, Eng
53B2 **Shuangcheng** China
52E1 **Shuanglia** China
53C2 **Shuangyashan** China
45K6 **Shubar-Kuduk** Kazakhstan
5J4 **Shubenacadie** Can
10J2 **Shublik Mts** USA
44N2 **Shuga** Russian Fed
52D2 **Shu He** *R* China
52A4 **Shuicheng** China
60C3 **Shujaabad** Pak
60D4 **Shujālpur** India
53B3 **Shulan** China
50C2 **Shule He** China
10G5 **Shumagin Is** USA
41F2 **Shumen** Bulg
44H4 **Shumerlya** Russian Fed
52D4 **Shuncheng** China
10G2 **Shungnak** USA
52C2 **Shuo Xian** China
63D3 **Shūr Gaz** Iran
73C5 **Shurugwi** Zim
3E3 **Shuswap L** Can
44G4 **Shuya** Russian Fed
10H4 **Shuyak I** USA
61E3 **Shwebo** Burma
55B2 **Shwegyin** Burma
61E3 **Shweli** *R* Burma
63E3 **Siahan Range** *Mts* Pak
60A2 **Siah Koh** *Mts* Afghan
60C2 **Sialkot** Pak
Sian = Xi'an
57G9 **Siarao, I** Phil
57F9 **Siaton** Phil
57C2 **Siau** *I* Indon
43E1 **Šiauliai** Lithuania
44K5 **Sibay** Russian Fed
74E2 **Sibayi L** S Africa
40D2 **Šibenik** Croatia, Yugos
56A3 **Siberut** *I* Indon
60B3 **Sibi** Pak
53C3 **Sibirtsevo** Russian Fed
72B4 **Sibiti** Congo
72D4 **Sibiti** *R* Tanz
41E1 **Sibiu** Rom
11C3 **Sibley** USA
57A2 **Siboa** Indon
56A2 **Sibolga** Indon
61D2 **Sibsāgār** India
56D2 **Sibu** Malay
57F9 **Sibuguay B** Phil
72B3 **Sibut** CAR
56E1 **Sibutu Pass** Malay/Phil
57F8 **Sibuyan** *I* Phil
57F8 **Sibuyan S** Phil
52A3 **Sichuan** Province, China
40C3 **Sicilia** *I* Medit S
40C3 **Sicilian** *Chan* Italy/Tunisia
Sicily = Sicilia
26D6 **Sicuari** Peru
60C4 **Siddhapur** India
62B1 **Siddipet** India
61B3 **Sidhi** India
69B1 **Sidi Barrani** Egypt
71B1 **Sidi bel Abbès** Alg
71A2 **Sidi Kacem** Mor
34D3 **Sidlaw Hills** Scot
79F5 **Sidley,Mt** Ant
18B1 **Sidney** Can
11B2 **Sidney** Montana, USA
16B1 **Sidney** Nebraska, USA
14C1 **Sidney** New York, USA
12C2 **Sidney** Ohio, USA
15C2 **Sidney Lanier,L** USA
Sidon = Säida
29B3 **Sidrolândia** Brazil
43E2 **Siedlce** Pol
36D1 **Sieg** *R* Germany
36D1 **Siegburg** Germany
36D1 **Siegen** Germany
37A1 **Sielle** *R* France
55C3 **Siem Reap** Camb
40C2 **Siena** Italy
36C3 **Siene** *R* France
43D2 **Sierpc** Pol
22C2 **Sierra Andrés Tuxtla** Mexico
28B3 **Sierra Auca Mahuida** *Mts* Arg
16A3 **Sierra Blanca** USA
28B4 **Sierra Blanca** *Mts* Arg
28B4 **Sierra Colorada** Arg
39B1 **Sierra de Albarracin** *Mts* Spain
39B2 **Sierra de Alcaraz** *Mts* Spain
28B1 **Sierra de Ancasti** *Mts* Arg
28B2 **Sierra de Cordoba** *Mts* Arg
28B1 **Sierra de Famantina** *Mts* Arg
39A1 **Sierra de Gredos** *Mts* Spain
39A2 **Sierra de Guadalupe** *Mts* Spain
39B1 **Sierra de Guadarrama** *Mts* Spain
39B1 **Sierra de Guara** *Mts* Spain
39B1 **Sierra de Gudar** *Mts* Spain
22C2 **Sierra de Juárez** *Mts* Mexico
28C3 **Sierra de la Ventana** *Mts* Arg
39C1 **Sierra del Codi** *Mts* Spain
28D1 **Sierra del Imán** *Mts* Arg
28B2 **Sierra del Morro** *Mt* Arg
28B3 **Sierra del Nevado** *Mts* Arg
21B2 **Sierra de los Alamitos** *Mts* Mexico
39B2 **Sierra de los Filabres** *Mts* Spain
22B1 **Sierra de los Huicholes** *Mts* Mexico
22C2 **Sierra de Miahuatlán** *Mts* Mexico
22B1 **Sierra de Morones** *Mts* Mexico
39A2 **Sierra de Ronda** *Mts* Spain
28B2 **Sierra de San Luis** *Mts* Arg
39B2 **Sierra de Segura** *Mts* Spain
22C1 **Sierra de Tamaulipas** *Mts* Mexico
39B1 **Sierra de Urbion** *Mts* Spain
28B2 **Sierra de Uspallata** *Mts* Arg
28B1 **Sierra de Valasco** *Mts* Arg
28B2 **Sierra de Valle Fértil** *Mts* Arg
22B1 **Sierra de Zacatécas** *Mts* Mexico
22C2 **Sierra de Zongolica** *Mts* Mexico
28C2 **Sierra Grande** *Mts* Arg
70A4 **Sierra Leone** Republic, Africa
70A4 **Sierra Leone,C** Sierra Leone
57F7 **Sierra Madre** *Mts* Phil
22B2 **Sierra Madre del Sur** *Mts* Mexico
20B3 **Sierra Madre Mts** USA
21B2 **Sierra Madre Occidental** *Mts* Mexico
22B1 **Sierra Madre Oriental** *Mts* Mexico
28B2 **Sierra Malanzan** *Mts* Arg
8C4 **Sierra Mojada** Mexico
39A2 **Sierra Morena** *Mts* Spain
39B2 **Sierra Nevada** *Mts* Spain
19B3 **Sierra Nevada** *Mts* USA
26D1 **Sierra Nevada de santa Marta** *Mts* Colombia
28B2 **Sierra Pié de Palo** *Mts* Arg
19D4 **Sierra Vista** USA
37B1 **Sierre** Switz
29A3 **Siete Puntas** *R* Par
41E3 **Sifnos** *I* Greece
71B1 **Sig** Alg
44E2 **Sig** Russian Fed
56A3 **Sigep** Indon
43E3 **Sighetu Marmaţiei** Rom
41E1 **Sighişoara** Rom
56A1 **Sigli** Indon
32B1 **Siglufjörður** Iceland
36E2 **Sigmaringen** Germany
26A1 **Siguatepeque** Honduras
39B1 **Sigüenza** Spain
70B3 **Siguiri** Guinea
60D4 **Sihora** India
64D2 **Siirt** Turk
50C3 **Sikai Hu** *L* China
3D2 **Sikanni** *R* Can
60D3 **Sīkar** India
60B2 **Sikaram** *Mt* Afghan
70B3 **Sikasso** Mali
57B4 **Sikeli** Indon
17E2 **Sikeston** USA
41F3 **Síkinos** *I* Greece
41E3 **Sikionía** Greece
61C2 **Sikkim** State, India
49O3 **Siktyakh** Russian Fed
39A1 **Sil** *R* Spain
37D1 **Silandro** Italy
22B1 **Silao** Mexico
57F8 **Silay** Phil
61D3 **Silchar** India
4C2 **Silcox** Can
70C2 **Silet** Alg
61B2 **Silgarhi** Nepal
64B2 **Silifke** Turk
65D1 **Silinfah** Syria
59G2 **Siling Co** *L* China
41F2 **Silistra** Bulg
44A3 **Siljan** *L* Sweden
32F7 **Silkeborg** Den
37E1 **Sillian** Austria
17D2 **Siloam Springs** USA
17D3 **Silsbee** USA
72B2 **Siltou** *Well* Chad
43E1 **Šilute** Lithuania
64D2 **Silvan** Turk
29C2 **Silvania** Brazil
60C4 **Silvassa** India
11D2 **Silver Bay** USA
19C3 **Silver City** Nevada, USA
16A3 **Silver City** New Mexico, USA
18B2 **Silver Lake** USA
20D2 **Silver Peak Range** *Mts* USA
14B3 **Silver Spring** USA
3C3 **Silverthrone Mt** Can
75B2 **Silverton** Aust
16A2 **Silverton** USA
37D1 **Silvretta** *Mts* Austria/Switz
56D2 **Simanggang** Malay
55C1 **Simao** China
63B2 **Simareh** *R* Iran
41F3 **Simav** Turk
41F3 **Simav** *R* Turk
4F5 **Simcoe,L** Can
10G5 **Simeohof** *I* USA
56A2 **Simeulue** *I* Indon
45E7 **Simferopol'** Ukraine
41F3 **Simi** *I* Greece
61B2 **Simikot** Nepal
60D2 **Simla** India
16B2 **Simla** USA
36D1 **Simmern** Germany
20C3 **Simmler** USA
74B3 **Simonstown** S Africa
3C3 **Simoom Sound** Can
38D2 **Simplon** *Mt* Switz
37C1 **Simplon** *P* Switz
6C2 **Simpson,C** USA
76C3 **Simpson Desert** Aust
10N2 **Simpson L** Can
3B2 **Simpson Peak** *Mt* Can
7K3 **Simpson Pen** Can
32G7 **Simrishamn** Sweden
50J2 **Simushir** *I* Russian Fed
56A2 **Sinabang** Indon
72E3 **Sina Dhaqa** Somalia
64B4 **Sinai** *Pen* Egypt
22A1 **Sinaloa** State, Mexico
37D3 **Sinalunga** Italy
26C2 **Sincelejo** Colombia
15C2 **Sinclair,L** USA
60D3 **Sind** *R* India
60B3 **Sindh** *Region* Pak
41F3 **Sindirği** Turk
61C3 **Sindri** India
53E2 **Sinegorsk** Russian Fed
39A2 **Sines** Port
72D2 **Singa** Sudan
55C5 **Singapore** Republic, S E Asia
55C5 **Singapore,Str of** S E Asia
56E4 **Singaraja** Indon
36E3 **Singen** Germany
72D4 **Singida** Tanz
61E2 **Singkaling Hkamti** Burma
56C2 **Singkawang** Indon
75D2 **Singleton** Aust
56B3 **Singtep** *I* Indon
55B1 **Singu** Burma
74E1 **Singuédeze** *R* Mozam
54A3 **Sin'gye** N Korea
54A2 **Sinhŭng** N Korea
40B2 **Siniscola** Sardgena
57B4 **Sinjai** Indon
64D2 **Sinjár** Iraq
60B2 **Sinkai Hills** *Mts* Afghan
66C3 **Sinkat** Sudan
59G1 **Sinkiang** Autonomous Region, China
36E1 **Sinn** *R* Germany
27H2 **Sinnamary** French Guiana
54A3 **Sinnyong** S Korea
64C1 **Sinop** Turk
54A2 **Sinpa** N Korea
54A2 **Sinp'o** N Korea
54A3 **Sinp'yong** N Korea
41E1 **Sintana** Rom
56D2 **Sintang** Indon
17F4 **Sinton** USA
39A2 **Sintra** Port
26C2 **Sinú** *R* Colombia
53A3 **Sinŭiju** N Korea
43D3 **Siofok** Hung
37B1 **Sion** Switz
11C3 **Sioux City** USA
11C3 **Sioux Falls** USA
4C3 **Sioux Lookout** Can
57F9 **Sipalay** Phil
23L1 **Siparia** Trinidad
53A3 **Siping** China
4B3 **Sipiwesk L** Can
79F3 **Siple** *Base* Ant
79F5 **Siple I** Ant
57F8 **Sipocot** Phil
56A3 **Sipora** Indon
15B2 **Sipsey** *R* USA
22A1 **Siqueros** Mexico
57F9 **Siquijor** *I* Phil
62B2 **Sira** India
40D3 **Siracusa** Italy
61C3 **Sirajganj** Bang
3D3 **Sir Alexander,Mt** Can
71G3 **Sirba** *R* Burkina
67F2 **Sīr Banī Yās** *I* UAE
76C2 **Sir Edward Pellew Group** *Is* Aust
41F1 **Siret** *R* Rom
10N3 **Sir James McBrien,Mt** Can
62B2 **Sir Kālahasti** India
3D3 **Sir Laurier,Mt** Can
64D2 **Şirnak** Turk
60C4 **Sirohi** India
62C1 **Sironcha** India
60D4 **Sironj** India
41E3 **Siros** *I* Greece
20C3 **Sirretta Peak,Mt** USA
63C3 **Sirri** *I* Iran
60C3 **Sirsa** India
3E3 **Sir Sandford,Mt** Can
62A2 **Sirsi** India

Split L

Swakop

4B2 **Split L** Can
37C1 **Splügen** Switz
18C1 **Spokane** USA
12A1 **Spooner** USA
41F3 **Sporádhes** *Is* Greece
18C2 **Spray** USA
42C2 **Spree** *R* Germany
74B2 **Springbok** S Africa
5K4 **Springdale** Can
17D2 **Springdale** USA
16B2 **Springer** USA
19E4 **Springerville** USA
16B2 **Springfield** Colorado, USA
12B3 **Springfield** Illinois, USA
14D1 **Springfield** Massachusetts, USA
11C3 **Springfield** Minnesota, USA
17D2 **Springfield** Missouri, USA
12C3 **Springfield** Ohio, USA
18B2 **Springfield** Oregon, USA
15B1 **Springfield** Tennessee, USA
13E2 **Springfield** Vermont, USA
74D3 **Springfontein** S Africa
5J4 **Springhill** Can
19C3 **Spring Mts** USA
74D2 **Springs** S Africa
14A1 **Springville** New York, USA
19D2 **Springville** Utah, USA
14B1 **Springwater** USA
18D2 **Spruce Mt** USA
35F5 **Spurn Head** *C* Eng
33D3 **Spurn Head** *Pt* Eng
18B1 **Spuzzum** Can
3D4 **Squamish** Can
49R3 **Sredhekolymsk** Russian Fed
49S4 **Sredinnyy Khrebet** *Mts* Russian Fed
44F5 **Sredne-Russkaya Vozvyshennost'** *Upland* Russian Fed
49M3 **Sredne Sibirskoye Ploskogorye** *Tableland* Russian Fed
44K4 **Sredniy Ural** *Mts* Russian Fed
55D3 **Srepok** *R* Camb
50E1 **Sretensk** Russian Fed
55C3 **Sre Umbell** Camb
62C1 **Srīkākulam** India
59G5 **Sri Lanka** Republic, S Asia
60C2 **Srīnagar** Pak
62A1 **Srīvardhan** India
42D2 **Sroda** Pol
34C2 **Stack Skerry** *I* Scot
42B2 **Stade** Germany
34B3 **Staffa** *I* Scot
35D5 **Stafford** County, Eng
35D5 **Stafford** Eng
14D2 **Stafford Springs** USA
Stalingrad = Volgograd
3D2 **Stalin,Mt** Can
74B3 **Stallberg** *Mt* S Africa
7J1 **Stallworthy,C** Can
43E2 **Stalowa Wola** Pol
14D2 **Stamford** Connecticut, USA
14C1 **Stamford** New York, USA
16C3 **Stamford** Texas, USA
74B1 **Stampriet** Namibia
74D2 **Standerton** S Africa
12C2 **Standish** USA
18D1 **Stanford** USA
74E2 **Stanger** S Africa
20B2 **Stanislaus** *R* USA
41E2 **Stanke Dimitrov** Bulg
75E3 **Stanley** Aust
25E8 **Stanley** Falkland Is
18D2 **Stanley** Idaho, USA
11B2 **Stanley** N Dakota, USA
62B2 **Stanley Res** India
Stanleyville = Kisangani
21D3 **Stann Creek** Belize
50F1 **Stanovoy Khrebet** *Mts* Russian Fed
37C1 **Stans** Switz
75D1 **Stanthorpe** Aust
34B3 **Stanton Banks** *Sand-bank* Scot
16B1 **Stapleton** USA
43E2 **Starachowice** Pol
41E2 **Stara Planiná** *Mts* Bulg
44E4 **Staraya Russa** Russian Fed
41F2 **Stara Zagora** Bulg
42D2 **Stargard** Pol
17E3 **Starkville** USA
42C3 **Starnberg** Germany
43D2 **Starogard Gdanski** Pol
43F3 **Starokonstantinov** Ukraine
35D6 **Start Pt** Eng
45F5 **Staryy Oskol** Russian Fed
14B2 **State College** USA
14C2 **Staten I** USA
15C2 **Statesboro** USA
15C1 **Statesville** USA
13D3 **Staunton** USA
32F7 **Stavanger** Nor
36C1 **Stavelot** Belg
45G6 **Stavropol'** Russian Fed
75B3 **Stawell** Aust
42D2 **Stawno** Pol
18B2 **Stayton** USA
16A1 **Steamboat Springs** USA
10F3 **Stebbins** USA
10K3 **Steele,Mt** Can
14B2 **Steelton** USA
3E2 **Steen** *R* Can
3E2 **Steen River** Can
18C2 **Steens Mt** USA
7N2 **Steenstrups Gletscher** *Gl* Greenland
6H2 **Stefansson I** Can
74E2 **Stegi** Swaziland
37D1 **Steinach** Austria
4B4 **Steinbach** Can
32G6 **Steinkjer** Nor
74B2 **Steinkopf** S Africa
3D3 **Stein Mt** Can
74C2 **Stella** S Africa
5J4 **Stellarton** Can
74B3 **Stellenbosch** S Africa
22C2 **Stemaco** Mexico
36C2 **Stenay** France
42C2 **Stendal** Germany
45H8 **Stepanakert** Azerbaijan
11C2 **Stephen** USA
78B2 **Stephens,C** NZ
75B2 **Stephens Creek** Aust
12B1 **Stephenson** USA
10M4 **Stephens Pass** USA
7N5 **Stephenville** Can
16C3 **Stephenville** USA
10F4 **Stepovak B** USA
74D3 **Sterkstroom** S Africa
16B1 **Sterling** Colorado, USA
12B2 **Sterling** Illinois, USA
16C2 **Sterling** Kansas, USA
11B2 **Sterling** N Dakota, USA
16B3 **Sterling City** USA
12C2 **Sterling Heights** USA
44K5 **Sterlitamak** Russian Fed
3F3 **Stettler** Can
12C2 **Steubenville** USA
4B3 **Stevenson L** Can
12B2 **Stevens Point** USA
6D3 **Stevens Village** USA
3B2 **Stewart** Can
19C3 **Stewart** USA
10L3 **Stewart** *R* Can
10L3 **Stewart Crossing** Can
78A3 **Stewart I** NZ
77F1 **Stewart Is** Solomon Is
6E3 **Stewart River** Can
14B3 **Stewartstown** USA
11D3 **Stewartville** USA
74D2 **Steyn** S Africa
74D3 **Steynsburg** S Africa
42C3 **Steyr** Austria
74C3 **Steytlerville** S Africa
37D3 **Stia** Italy
10L4 **Stika** USA
3B2 **Stikine** *R* Can
10M4 **Stikine Ranges** *Mts* Can
11D2 **Stillwater** Minnesota, USA
17C2 **Stillwater** Oklahoma, USA
19C3 **Stillwater Range** *Mts* USA
4E4 **Stimson** Can
16B2 **Stinett** USA
75A2 **Stirling** Aust
34D3 **Stirling** Scot
36E3 **Stockach** Germany
14D1 **Stockbridge** USA
42D3 **Stockerau** Austria
32H7 **Stockholm** Sweden
35D5 **Stockport** Eng
20B2 **Stockton** California, USA
35E4 **Stockton** Eng
16C2 **Stockton** Kansas, USA
17D2 **Stockton L** USA
35D5 **Stoke-on-Trent** Eng
4E4 **Stokes Bay** Can
32A2 **Stokkseyri** Iceland
32G5 **Stokmarknes** Nor
49P2 **Stolbovoy, Ostrov** *I* Russian Fed
32K8 **Stolbtsy** Belorussia
43F2 **Stolin** Belorussia
14C3 **Stone Harbor** USA
34D3 **Stonehaven** Scot
17C3 **Stonewall** USA
10H3 **Stony** *R* USA
5K3 **Stony I** Can
3J2 **Stony L** Can
4E3 **Stooping** *R* Can
32H5 **Storavan** *L* Sweden
32G6 **Støren** Nor
75E3 **Storm B** Aust
11C3 **Storm Lake** USA
34B2 **Stornoway** Scot
43F3 **Storozhinets** Ukraine
14D2 **Storrs** USA
32G6 **Storsjön** *L* Sweden
32H5 **Storuman** Sweden
11A3 **Story** USA
3H4 **Stoughton** Can
14E1 **Stoughton** USA
36A1 **Stour** *R* Eng
35F5 **Stowmarket** Eng
53C1 **Stoyba** Russian Fed
34B4 **Strabane** N Ire
75E3 **Strahan** Aust
42C2 **Stralsund** Germany
74B3 **Strand** S Africa
32F6 **Stranda** Nor
32H7 **Strängnäs** Sweden
34C4 **Stranraer** Scot
38D2 **Strasbourg** France
13D3 **Strasburg** USA
20C2 **Stratford** California, USA
4E5 **Stratford** Can
14D2 **Stratford** Connecticut, USA
78B1 **Stratford** NZ
16B2 **Stratford** Texas, USA
35E5 **Stratford-on-Avon** Eng
75A3 **Strathalbyn** Aust
34C4 **Strathclyde** Region, Scot
3F3 **Strathmore** Can
13E1 **Stratton** USA
12B2 **Streator** USA
37C2 **Stresa** Italy
40D3 **Stretto de Messina** *Str* Italy/Sicily
40D3 **Stroboli** *I* Italy
28C4 **Stroeder** Arg
34D2 **Stromness** Scot
32D3 **Strømø** Faroes
17C1 **Stromsburg** USA
32H6 **Stromsund** Sweden
32G6 **Ströms Vattudal** *L* Sweden
34D2 **Stronsay** *I* Scot
35D6 **Stroud** Eng
14C2 **Stroudsburg** USA
41E2 **Struma** *R* Bulg
35C5 **Strumble Head** *Pt* Wales
41E2 **Strumica** Macedonia, Yugos
43E3 **Stryy** Ukraine
43E3 **Stryy** *R* Ukraine
75B1 **Strzelecki Creek** *R* Aust
15E4 **Stuart** Florida, USA
11C3 **Stuart** Nebraska, USA
3D3 **Stuart** *R* Can
10F3 **Stuart I** USA
3D3 **Stuart L** Can
37D1 **Stubaier Alpen** *Mts* Austria
32H8 **Stubice** Pol
55D3 **Stung Sen** Camb
55D3 **Stung Treng** Camb
4C2 **Stupart** *R* Can
40B2 **Stura** *R* Italy
79G7 **Sturge I** Ant
12B2 **Sturgeon Bay** USA
4F4 **Sturgeon Falls** Can
4C4 **Sturgeon L** Can
12B3 **Sturgis** Kentucky, USA
12B2 **Sturgis** Michigan, USA
11B3 **Sturgis** S Dakota, USA
76B2 **Sturt Creek** *R* Aust
75B1 **Sturt Desert** Aust
74D3 **Stuttemeim** S Africa
17D3 **Stuttgart** USA
42B3 **Stuttgart** Germany
32A1 **Stykkishólmur** Iceland
43F2 **Styr'** *R* Ukraine
49M4 **Styudyanka** Russian Fed
29D2 **Suaçuí Grande** *R* Brazil
66C3 **Suakin** Sudan
54A3 **Suan** N Korea
52E5 **Su-ao** Taiwan
28C2 **Suardi** Arg
56C2 **Subi** *I* Indon
41D1 **Subotica** Serbia, Yugos
45D6 **Suceava** Rom
22C2 **Suchixtepec** Mexico
26E7 **Sucre** Bol
29B2 **Sucuriú** R, Brazil
72C2 **Sudan** Republic, Africa
4E4 **Sudbury** Can
35F5 **Sudbury** Eng
72C3 **Sudd** *Swamp* Sudan
27G2 **Suddie** Guyana
65B4 **Sudr** Egypt
72C3 **Sue** *R* Sudan
10M4 **Suemez I** USA
64B4 **Suez** Egypt
64B3 **Suez Canal** Egypt
64B4 **Suez,G of** Egypt
14C2 **Suffern** USA
35F5 **Suffolk** County, Eng
13D3 **Suffolk** USA
13E2 **Sugarloaf Mt** USA
75D2 **Sugarloaf Pt** Aust
3H3 **Suggi L** Can
49R3 **Sugoy** *R* Russian Fed
67G2 **Suhār** Oman
50D1 **Sühbaatar** Mongolia
60B3 **Sui** Pak
53C2 **Suibin** China
52C2 **Suide** China
53C3 **Suifenhe** China
53B2 **Suihua** China
53B2 **Suileng** China
52B3 **Suining** China
36C2 **Suippes** France
33B3 **Suir** *R* Irish Rep
52C3 **Sui Xian** China
52E1 **Suizhong** China
60C3 **Sujāngarh** India
56C4 **Sukabumi** Indon
56D3 **Sukadana** Borneo, Indon
56C4 **Sukadana** Sumatra, Indon
53E4 **Sukagawa** Japan
56D3 **Sukaraya** Indon
44F5 **Sukhinichi** Russian Fed
44G4 **Sukhona** *R* Russian Fed
45G7 **Sukhumi** Georgia
7N3 **Sukkertoppen** Greenland
7N3 **Sukkertoppen Isflade** *Gl* Greenland
32L6 **Sukkozero** Russian Fed
60B3 **Sukkur** Pak
62C1 **Sukma** India
53D2 **Sukpay** *R* Russian Fed
73B6 **Sukses** Namibia
54B4 **Sukumo** Japan
3D2 **Sukunka** *R* Can
45F5 **Sula** *R* Russian Fed
60B3 **Sulaiman Range** *Mts* Pak
34B2 **Sula Sgeir** *I* Scot
57B3 **Sulawesi** *I* Indon
57B3 **Sulawesi Sulatan** Prov, Indon
57B3 **Sulawesi Tengah** Prov, Indon
57B3 **Sulawesi Tenggara** Prov, Indon
57B3 **Sulawesi Utara** Prov, Indon
64E3 **Sulaymānīyah** Iraq
71H4 **Suleja** Nig
34C2 **Sule Skerry** *I* Scot
41F1 **Sulina** Rom
32H5 **Sulitjelma** Nor
26B4 **Sullana** Peru
17D2 **Sullivan** USA
3C3 **Sullivan Bay** Can
3F3 **Sullivan L** Can
36B3 **Sully-sur-Loire** France
40C2 **Sulmona** Italy
17D3 **Sulphur** Louisiana, USA
17C3 **Sulphur** Oklahoma, USA
17C3 **Sulphur Springs** USA
4E4 **Sultan** Can
45E8 **Sultan Dağlari** *Mts* Turk
61B2 **Sultānpur** India
57F9 **Sulu Arch** Phil
51E6 **Sulu S** Philip
36E2 **Sulz** Germany
25D3 **Sumampa** Arg
56A2 **Sumatera** *I* Indon
57B4 **Sumba** *I* Indon
56E4 **Sumbawa** *I* Indon
56E4 **Sumbawa Besar** Indon
73D4 **Sumbawanga** Tanz
34E2 **Sumburgh Head** *Pt* Scot
56D4 **Sumenep** Indon
45H7 **Sumgait** Azerbaijan
73B5 **Sumbe** Angola
50H3 **Sumisu** *I* Japan
3E4 **Summerland** Can
5J4 **Summerside** Can
3B2 **Summer Str** USA
6F4 **Summit Lake** Can
19C3 **Summits Mt** USA
78B2 **Sumner,L** NZ
54B4 **Sumoto** Japan
15C2 **Sumter** USA
45E5 **Sumy** Ukraine
18D1 **Sun** *R* USA
54D2 **Sunagawa** Japan
54A3 **Sunan** N Korea
14B2 **Sunbury** USA
28C2 **Sunchales** Arg
28C1 **Suncho Corral** Arg
53B4 **Sunch'ŏn** N Korea
53B5 **Sunch'ŏn** S Korea
11B3 **Sundance** USA
61B3 **Sundargarh** India
61C3 **Sunderbans** *Swamp* India
34E4 **Sunderland** Eng
3F3 **Sundre** Can
13D1 **Sundridge** Can
32H6 **Sundsvaall** Sweden
56E3 **Sungaianyar** Indon
56B3 **Sungaisalak** Indon
56F6 **Sungai Siput** Malay
56F6 **Sungei Petani** Malay
57A4 **Sungguminasa** Indon
18C1 **Sunnyside** USA
19B3 **Sunnyvale** USA
12B2 **Sun Prairie** USA
49N3 **Suntar** Russian Fed
63E3 **Suntsar** Pak
18D2 **Sun Valley** USA
53B2 **Sunwu** China
71F4 **Sunyani** Ghana
44E3 **Suojarvi** Russian Fed
54B4 **Suō-nada** *B* Japan
32K6 **Suonejoki** Fin
61C2 **Supaul** India
19D4 **Superior** Arizona, USA
17C1 **Superior** Nebraska, USA
12A1 **Superior** Wisconsin, USA
12B1 **Superior,L** USA/Can
55C3 **Suphan Buri** Thai
64D2 **Süphan Dağ** Turk
51G7 **Supiori** *I* Indon
57C2 **Supu** Indon
66D3 **Sūq 'Abs** Yemen
64E3 **Suq ash Suyukh** Iraq
65D1 **Suqaylibīyah** Syria
52D3 **Suqian** China
Suqutra = Socotra
67G2 **Sūr** Oman
44H5 **Sura** *R* Russian Fed
56D4 **Surabaya** Indon
54C4 **Suraga-wan** *B* Japan
56D4 **Surakarta** Indon
65D1 **Sūrān** Syria
75C1 **Surat** Aust
60C4 **Sūrat** India
60C3 **Sūratgarh** India
55B4 **Surat Thani** Thai
60C4 **Surendranagar** India
14C3 **Surf City** USA
48J3 **Surgut** Russian Fed
62B1 **Suriāpet** India
38D2 **Sürich** Switz
57G9 **Surigao** Phil
55C3 **Surin** Thai
27G3 **Surinam** Republic, S America
20B2 **Sur,Pt** USA
35E6 **Surrey** County, Eng
37C1 **Sursee** Switz
69A1 **Surt** Libya
32A2 **Surtsey** *I* Iceland
56B3 **Surulangan** Indon
37B2 **Susa** Italy
54B4 **Susa** Japan
54B4 **Susaki** Japan
19B2 **Susanville** USA
37D1 **Süsch** Switz
10J3 **Susitna** *R* USA
14C2 **Susquehanna** USA
14B3 **Susquehanna** *R* USA
14C2 **Sussex** USA
35E6 **Sussex West** Eng
3C2 **Sustut Peak** *Mt* Can
74C3 **Sutherland** S Africa
16B1 **Sutherland** USA
60C2 **Sutlej** *R* Pak
19B3 **Sutter Creek** USA
12C3 **Sutton** USA
4E3 **Sutton** *R* Can
54D2 **Suttsu** Japan
10G4 **Sutwik I** USA
77G2 **Suva** Fiji
53D4 **Suwa** Japan
43E2 **Suwałki** Pol
15C3 **Suwannee** *R* USA
65C2 **Suweilih** Jordan
53B4 **Suwŏn** S Korea
52D3 **Su Xian** China
54C3 **Suzaka** Japan
52E3 **Suzhou** China
53D4 **Suzu** Japan
54C4 **Suzuka** Japan
54C3 **Suzu-misaki** *C* Japan
48C2 **Svalbard** *Is* Barents S
43E3 **Svalyava** Ukraine
7N2 **Svartenhuk Halvø** *Region* Greenland
32G5 **Svartisen** *Mt* Nor
55D3 **Svay Rieng** Camb
32G6 **Sveg** Sweden
32G7 **Svendborg** Den
7J1 **Sverdrup Chan** Can
6H2 **Sverdrup Is** Can
53D2 **Svetlaya** Russian Fed
43E2 **Svetlogorsk** Russian Fed
32K6 **Svetogorsk** Russian Fed
41E2 **Svetozarevo** Serbia, Yugos
41F2 **Svilengrad** Bulg
43F2 **Svir'** Belrussia
44E3 **Svir'** *R* Russian Fed
42D3 **Švitavy** Czech
53B1 **Svobodnyy** Russian Fed
32G5 **Svolvaer** Nor
77E3 **Swain Reefs** Aust
77H2 **Swains** *I* American Samoa
15C2 **Swainsboro** USA
74B1 **Swakop** *R* Namibia

Tionaga Tsihombe

4E4 Tionaga Can
37D1 Tione Italy
14B1 Tioughnioga R USA
35B5 Tipperary County, Irish Rep
33B3 Tipperary Irish Rep
20C2 Tipton California, USA
17D2 Tipton Missouri, USA
62B2 Tiptūr India
22B2 Tiquicheo Mexico
41D2 Tiranë Alb
37D1 Tirano Italy
43F3 Tiraspol Moldavia
65A3 Tir'at el Ismâilîya Canal Egypt
62B2 Tirchchirāppalli India
41F3 Tire Turk
64C1 Tirebolu Turk
34B3 Tiree I Scot
41F2 Tîrgovişte Rom
41E1 Tîrgu Jiu Rom
41E1 Tîrgu Mureş Rom
60C1 Tirich Mir Mt Pak
70A2 Tiris Region, Mor
44K5 Tirlyanskiy Russian Fed
41E1 Tîrnăveni Rom
41E3 Tírnavos Greece
60D4 Tirodi India
37D1 Tirol Province, Austria
40B2 Tirso R Sardegna
62B3 Tiruchchendūr India
62B3 Tirunelveli India
62B2 Tirupati India
62B2 Tiruppattūr India
62B2 Tiruppur India
62B2 Tiruvannamalai India
3H3 Tisdale Can
17C3 Tishomingo USA
65D2 Tisīyah Syria
43E3 Tisza R Hung
61B3 Titlagarh India
41D2 Titograd Montenegro, Yugos
41E2 Titova Mitrovica Serbia, Yugos
41D2 Titovo Užice Serbia, Yugos
41E2 Titov Veles Macedonia, Yugos
72C3 Titule Zaïre
15C3 Titusville USA
35D6 Tiverton Eng
40C2 Tivoli Italy
22C2 Tixtla Mexico
22C2 Tizayuca Mexico
21D2 Tizimin Mexico
71C1 Tizi Ouzou Alg
70B2 Tiznit Mor
22B1 Tizpan el Alto Mexico
22C2 Tlacolula Mexico
22C2 Tlacotalpan Mexico
22B2 Tlalchana Mexico
22C2 Tlalnepantla Mexico
22C2 Tlalpan Mexico
22B1 Tlaltenago Mexico
22C2 Tlancualpicán Mexico
22C2 Tlapa Mexico
22C2 Tlapacoyan Mexico
22B1 Tlaquepaque Mexico
22C2 Tlaxcala Mexico
22C2 Tlaxcala State, Mexico
22C2 Tlaxiaco Mexico
10M5 Tlell Can
71B2 Tlemcem Alg
73E5 Toamasina Madag
28C3 Toay Arg
54C4 Toba Japan
60B2 Toba and Kakar Ranges Mts Pak
23E4 Tobago I Caribbean
3D3 Toba Inlet Sd Can
57C2 Tobelo Indon
4E4 Tobermory Can
34B3 Tobermory Scot
51G6 Tobi I Pacific O
3H3 Tobin L Can
19C2 Tobin,Mt USA
54C3 Tōbi-shima I Japan
48H4 Tobol R Russian Fed
57B3 Toboli Indon
48H4 Tobol'sk Russian Fed
Tobruk = Tubruq
44J2 Tobseda Russian Fed
27J4 Tocantins R Brazil
15C2 Toccoa USA
37C1 Toce R Italy
25B2 Tocopilla Chile
25C2 Tocorpuri Bol
26E8 Tocorpuri Mt Chile
26E1 Tocuyo R Ven
60D3 Toda India
57B3 Todeli Indon
37C1 Tödi Mt Switz
54B3 Todong S Korea
8B4 Todos Santos Mexico
3F3 Tofield Can
3C4 Tofino Can
77H2 Tofua I Tonga
10F4 Togiak USA
10F4 Togiak B USA
57B3 Togian I Indon
66C3 Togni Sudan
71G4 Togo Republic, Africa
52C1 Togtoh China
66C3 Tohamiyam Sudan
16A2 Tohatchi USA
57B3 Tojo Indon
10K3 Tok USA
53E3 Tokachi R Japan
54C3 Tokamachi Japan
66C3 Tokar Sudan
50F4 Tokara Retto Arch Japan
64C1 Tokat Turk
53B4 Tŏkchŏk-kundo Arch S Korea
54B3 Tok-do I S Korea
77H1 Tokelau Is Pacific O
59F1 Tokmak Kirgizia
78C1 Tokomaru Bay NZ
10M4 Toku R Can/USA
56D3 Tokung Indon
50F4 Tokuno I Japan
53C1 Tokur Russian Fed
53C5 Tokushima Japan
54B4 Tokuyama Japan
53D4 Tōkyō Japan
78C1 Tolaga Bay NZ
27H8 Toledo Brazil
28A1 Toledo Chile
39B2 Toledo Spain
12C2 Toledo USA
17D3 Toledo Bend Res USA
37E3 Tolentino Italy
73E6 Toliara Madag
26C2 Tolima Colombia
22C1 Toliman Mexico
57B2 Tolitoli Indon
37E1 Tolmezzo Italy
37E1 Tolmin Slovenia, Yugos
43F2 Tološin Belorussia
39B1 Tolosa Spain
54A4 Tolsan-do I S Korea
28A3 Toltén Chile
28A3 Toltén R Chile
22C2 Toluca Mexico
44H5 Tol'yatti Russian Fed
53C1 Tom R Russian Fed
12A2 Tomah USA
12B1 Tomahawk USA
53E3 Tomakomai Japan
56E2 Tomani Malay
53E2 Tomari Russian Fed
43E2 Tomaszów Mazowiecka Pol
22A2 Tomatlán Mexico
15B2 Tombigbee R USA
73B4 Tomboco Angola
57B3 Tomboli Indon
29D3 Tombos Brazil
70B3 Tombouctou Mali
19E4 Tombstone USA
73B5 Tombua Angola
74D1 Tomburke S Africa
28A3 Tomé Chile
39B2 Tomelloso Spain
39A2 Tomer Port
54A4 Tomie Japan
57B2 Tomini Indon
76B3 Tomkinson Range Mts Aust
49O4 Tommot Russian Fed
41E2 Tomorrit Mt Alb
48K4 Tomsk Russian Fed
14C3 Toms River USA
21C3 Tonalá Mexico
18C1 Tonasket USA
57C2 Tondano Indon
77H3 Tonga Is Pacific O
74E2 Tongaat S Africa
77H3 Tongatapu I Tonga
77H3 Tongatapu Group Is Tonga
77H3 Tonga Trench Pacific O
53B2 Tongbei China
54A2 Tongchang N Korea
52D3 Tongcheng China
52B2 Tongchuan China
52A2 Tongde China
36C1 Tongeren Belg
55E2 Tonggu Jiao I China
52A5 Tonghai China
53B2 Tonghe China
53B3 Tonghua China
53C2 Tongjiang China
53B4 Tongjosŏn-man N Korea
55D1 Tongkin,G of Viet/China
52E1 Tonglia China
52D3 Tongling China
54A3 Tongnae S Korea
75B2 Tongo Aust
28A2 Tongoy Chile
52B4 Tongren Guizhou, China
52A2 Tongren Qinghai, China
61D2 Tongsa Bhutan
55B1 Tongta Burma
50C3 Tongtian He R China
34C2 Tongue Scot
11A2 Tongue R USA
52D2 Tong Xian China
52B2 Tongxin China
53A3 Tongyu China
52B4 Tongzi China
8C4 Tónichi Mexico
72C3 Tonj Sudan
60D3 Tonk India
17C2 Tonkawa USA
55C3 Tonle Sap L Camb
36C3 Tonnerre France
54D3 Tono Japan
19C3 Tonopah USA
10J3 Tonsina USA
18D2 Tooele USA
75D1 Toogoolawah Aust
75B1 Toompine Aust
75D1 Toowoomba Aust
20C1 Topaz L USA
17C2 Topeka USA
8C4 Topolobampo Mexico
44E2 Topozero, Ozero L Russian Fed
18B1 Toppenish USA
19D4 Toppock USA
72D3 Tor Eth
41F3 Torbali Turk
63D1 Torbat-e-Heydarīyeh Iran
63E1 Torbat-e Jām Iran
10H3 Torbert,Mt USA
39A1 Tordesillas Spain
42C2 Torgau Germany
36B1 Torhout Belg
50H3 Tori I Japan
37B2 Torino Italy
72D3 Torit Sudan
29B2 Torixoreu Brazil
39A1 Tormes R Spain
3F4 Tornado Mt Can
32J5 Torne L Sweden
32H5 Torneträsk Sweden
7M4 Torngat Mts Can
32J5 Tornio Fin
28C3 Tornquist Arg
57B3 Torobuku Indon
71G3 Torodi Niger
53D1 Torom R Russian Fed
4F5 Toronto Can
44E4 Toropets Russian Fed
72D3 Tororo Uganda
64B2 Toros Dağlari Mts Turk
28E2 Torquato Severo Brazil
35D6 Torquay Eng
20C4 Torrance USA
39A2 Torrão Port
39C1 Torreblanca Spain
40C2 Torre del Greco Italy
39B1 Torrelavega Spain
39B2 Torremolinos Spain
75A2 Torrens,L Aust
28D1 Torrent Arg
21B2 Torreón Mexico
37B2 Torre Pellice Italy
77F2 Torres Is Vanuatu
76D2 Torres Str Aust
39A2 Torres Vedras Port
14D2 Torrington Connecticut, USA
11B3 Torrington Wyoming, USA
32D3 Torshavn Faroes
37C2 Tortona Italy
39C1 Tortosa Spain
63D1 Torūd Iran
43D2 Toruń Pol
33B2 Tory I Irish Rep
44E4 Torzhok Russian Fed
54B4 Tosa Japan
53C5 Tosa-shimizu Japan
53C5 Tosa-wan B Japan
37D3 Toscana Region, Italy
54C4 To-shima I Japan
32L7 Tosno Russian Fed
28C1 Tostado Arg
54B4 Tosu Japan
64B1 Tosya Turk
57B3 Totala Indon
44G4 Tot'ma Russian Fed
35D6 Totnes Eng
27G2 Totness Surinam
22C2 Totolapan Mexico
39B2 Totona Spain
28A1 Totoral Chile
28C1 Totoralejos Arg
75C2 Tottenham Aust
53C4 Tottori Japan
70B4 Touba Ivory Coast
70A3 Touba Sen
70B1 Toubkal Mt Mor
36B3 Toucy France
71F3 Tougan Burkina
71D2 Touggourt Alg
70A3 Tougué Guinea
36C2 Toul France
5H3 Toulnustouc R Can
38D3 Toulon France
38C3 Toulouse France
70B4 Toumodi Ivory Coast
55B2 Toungoo Burma
36B1 Tourcoing France
70A2 Tourine Maur
36B1 Tournai Belg
36A2 Tourouvre France
38C2 Tours France
74C3 Touws R S Africa
53E3 Towada Japan
53E3 Towada-ko L Japan
14B2 Towanda USA
20D2 Towne P USA
11B2 Towner USA
18D1 Townsend USA
76D2 Townsville Aust
63E1 Towraghondi Afghan
14B3 Towson USA
35D6 Towy R Wales
16B3 Toyah USA
54D2 Toya-ko L Japan
53D4 Toyama Japan
54C3 Toyama-wan B Japan
10D2 Toygunen Russian Fed
54C4 Toyohashi Japan
54C4 Toyonaka Japan
54B3 Toyooka Japan
53D4 Toyota Japan
71D2 Tozeur Tunisia
36D2 Traben-Trarbach Germany
64C1 Trabzon Turk
5J4 Tracadie Can
11C3 Tracy Minnesota, USA
28A3 Traiguén Chile
3E4 Trail Can
33B3 Tralee Irish Rep
35B5 Tramore Irish Rep
32G7 Tranås Sweden
55B4 Trang Thai
51G7 Trangan I Indon
75C2 Trangie Aust
28D2 Tranqueras Urug
10J2 Transalaskan Pipeline USA
79E Transantarctic Mts Ant
11C2 Transcona Can
74D3 Transkei Self-governing homeland, S Africa
74D1 Transvaal Province, S Africa
Transylvanian Alps = Muntii Carpaţii Meridionali
40C3 Trapani Italy
75C3 Traralgon Aust
70A3 Trarza Region, Maur
55C3 Trat Thai
10M2 Travaillant L Can
75B2 Traveller's L Aust
42C2 Travemünde Germany
12B2 Traverse City USA
10G2 Traverse Peak Mt USA
78B2 Travers,Mt NZ
16C3 Travis,L USA
37C2 Trebbia R Italy
42D3 Třebíč Czech
41D2 Trebinje Bosnia & Herzegovina, Yugos
42C3 Trebon Czech
28E2 Treinta y Tres Urug
25C6 Trelew Arg
32G7 Trelleborg Sweden
35C5 Tremadog B Wales
13E1 Tremblant,Mt Can
3D3 Trembleur L Can
14B2 Tremont USA
18D2 Tremonton USA
43D3 Trenčin Czech
28C3 Trenque Lauquén Arg
35E5 Trent R Eng
37D1 Trentino Region, Italy
37D1 Trento Italy
4F5 Trenton Can
17D1 Trenton Missouri, USA
14C2 Trenton New Jersey, USA
5L4 Trepassey Can
28C3 Tres Arroyos Arg
29C3 Tres Corações Brazil
29B3 Três Irmãos, Reprêsa Res Brazil
25F2 Três Lagoas Brazil
28C3 Tres Lomas Arg
28E1 Tres Passos Brazil
22D2 Tres Picos Mexico
20B2 Tres Pinos USA
29D3 Três Rios Brazil
37A3 Trets France
37C2 Treviglio Italy
37E2 Treviso Italy
36E1 Treysa Germany
37C2 Trezzo Italy
16B2 Tribune USA
62B2 Trichūr India
75C2 Trida Aust
36D2 Trier Germany
40C1 Trieste Italy
37E1 Triglav Mt Croatia, Yugos
65B1 Trikomo Cyprus
35B5 Trim Irish Rep
62C3 Trincomalee Sri Lanka
xxxG6 Trindade,I Atlantic O
26F6 Trinidad Bol
28D2 Trinidad Urug
16B2 Trinidad USA
28C3 Trinidad I Arg
23E4 Trinidad I Caribbean
23E4 Trinidad & Tobago Is Republic Caribbean
17C3 Trinity USA
8D3 Trinity R USA
7N5 Trinity B Can
10H4 Trinity Is USA
15B2 Trion USA
37B2 Triora Italy
65C1 Tripoli Leb
69A1 Tripoli Libya
41E3 Trípolis Greece
61D3 Tripura State, India
xxxH6 Tristan da Cunha Is Atlantic O
43D3 Trnava Czech
76E1 Trobriand Is PNG
5H4 Trois Pistoles Can
5G4 Trois-Rivières Can
44L5 Troitsk Russian Fed
44K3 Troitsko Pechorsk Russian Fed
53D2 Troitskoye Russian Fed
32G7 Trollhättan Sweden
32F6 Trollheimen Mt Nor
68K9 Tromelin I Indian O
74D3 Trompsburg S Africa
32H5 Tromsø Nor
20D3 Trona USA
32G6 Trondheim Nor
32G6 Trondheimfjord Inlet Nor
65B1 Troödos Range Mts Cyprus
34C4 Troon Scot
xxxJ3 Tropic of Cancer
xxxK6 Tropic of Capricorn
70B2 Troudenni Mali
3D1 Trout R Can
4F4 Trout Creek Can
3D1 Trout L Northwest Territories, Can
7J4 Trout L Ontario, Can
18E2 Trout Peak Mt USA
5K4 Trout River Can
14B2 Trout Run USA
36A2 Trouville-sur-Mer France
15B2 Troy Alabama, USA
18C1 Troy Montana, USA
14D1 Troy New York, USA
12C2 Troy Ohio, USA
14B2 Troy Pennsylvania, USA
41E2 Troyan Bulg
36C2 Troyes France
19C3 Troy Peak Mt USA
67F2 Trucial Coast Region, UAE
19B3 Truckee R USA
21D3 Trujillo Honduras
26C5 Trujillo Peru
39A2 Trujillo Spain
26D2 Trujillo Ven
19D3 Trumbull,Mt USA
75C2 Trundle Aust
7M5 Truro Can
35C6 Truro Eng
51G6 Trust Territories of the Pacific Is Pacific O
3D2 Trutch Can
16A3 Truth or Consequences USA
50C2 Tsagaan Nuur L Mongolia
50C1 Tsagan-Tologoy Russian Fed
73E5 Tsaratanana Madag
73C6 Tsau Botswana
72D4 Tsavo Kenya
72D4 Tsavo Nat Pk Kenya
11B2 Tschida,L USA
48J4 Tselinograd Kazakhstan
74B2 Tses Namibia
50D2 Tsetserleg Mongolia
71G4 Tsévié Togo
74C2 Tshabong Botswana
74C1 Tshane Botswana
45F7 Tshcikskoye Vdkhr Res Russian Fed
72B4 Tshela Zaïre
73C4 Tshibala Zaïre
72C4 Tshikapa Zaïre
72C4 Tshuapa R Zaïre
73E6 Tsihombe Madag

Tsimlyanskoye Vodokhranilishche Urziceni

45G6 **Tsimlyanskoye Vodokhranilishche** *Res* Russian Fed
Tsinan = Jinan
Tsingtao = Qingdao
73E5 **Tsiroanomandidy** Madag
3C3 **Tsitsutl Peak** *Mt* Can
43F2 **Tsna** *R* Belorussia
52B1 **Tsogt Ovoo** Mongolia
74D3 **Tsomo** S Africa
50D2 **Tsomog** Mongolia
54C4 **Tsu** Japan
54C3 **Tsubata** Japan
53E4 **Tsuchira** Japan
53E3 **Tsugaru-kaikyō** *Str* Japan
73B5 **Tsumeb** Namibia
73B6 **Tsumis** Namibia
54C3 **Tsunugi** Japan
53D4 **Tsuruga** Japan
53D4 **Tsuruoka** Japan
54C3 **Tsushima** Japan
53B5 **Tsushima** *I* Japan
Tsushima-Kaikyō = Korea Str
53C4 **Tsuyama** Japan
39A1 **Tua** *R* Port
56A2 **Tuangku** *I* Indon
45F7 **Tuapse** Russian Fed
78A3 **Tuatapere** NZ
19D3 **Tuba City** USA
25G3 **Tubarão** Brazil
65C2 **Tubas** Israel
57E9 **Tubbataha Reefs** *Is* Phil
42B3 **Tübingen** Germany
69B1 **Tubruq** Libya
14C3 **Tuckerton** USA
19D4 **Tucson** USA
25C3 **Tucumán** State, Arg
16B2 **Tucumcari** USA
28B2 **Tucunuco** Arg
26F2 **Tucupita** Ven
39B1 **Tudela** Spain
10N2 **Tudenet L** Can
64C3 **Tudmur** Syria
28C2 **Tuerto** Arg
74E2 **Tugela** *R* S Africa
75D2 **Tuggerah** *L* Aust
10H4 **Tugidak** *I* USA
57F7 **Tuguegarao** Phil
49P4 **Tugur** Russian Fed
53D1 **Tugur** *R* Russian Fed
52D2 **Tuhai He** *R* China
71F3 **Tui** *R* Burkina
10M2 **Tuktoyaktuk** Can
43E1 **Tukums** Latvia
73D4 **Tukuyu** Tanz
60B1 **Tukzar** Afghan
22C1 **Tula** Mexico
44F5 **Tula** Russian Fed
22C1 **Tulancingo** Mexico
56B3 **Tulangbawang** *R* Indon
20C2 **Tulare** USA
20C2 **Tulare Lake Bed** USA
16A3 **Tularosa** USA
26C3 **Tulcán** Colombia
45D7 **Tulcea** Rom
43F3 **Tul'chin** Ukraine
20C2 **Tule** *R* USA
73C6 **Tuli** Zim
74D1 **Tuli** *R* Zim
16B3 **Tulia** USA
10E5 **Tulik V** USA
65C2 **Tulkarm** Israel
15B1 **Tullahoma** USA
35B5 **Tullarnore** Irish Rep
38C2 **Tulle** France
37A2 **Tullins** France
17D3 **Tullos** USA
35B5 **Tullow** Irish Rep
14B1 **Tully** USA
17C2 **Tulsa** USA
64C3 **Tulūl ash Shāmīyah** *Desert Region* Syria/S Arabia
49M4 **Tulun** Russian Fed
56D4 **Tulungagung** Indon
26C3 **Tumaco** Colombia
49R3 **Tumany** Russian Fed
75C3 **Tumbarumba** Aust
26B4 **Tumbes** Ecuador
75A2 **Tumby Bay** Aust
53B3 **Tumen** China
62B2 **Tumkūr** India
63E3 **Tump** Pak
55C4 **Tumpat** Malay
60D4 **Tumsar** India
71F3 **Tumu** Ghana
75C3 **Tumut** Aust
75C3 **Tumut** *R* Aust
23L1 **Tunapuna** Trinidad
64C2 **Tunceli** Turk
73D4 **Tunduma** Zambia
73D5 **Tunduru** Tanz
41F2 **Tundzha** *R* Bulg
62B1 **Tungabhadra** *R* India
50E4 **Tung-Chiang** Taiwan
32B2 **Tungnafellsjökull** *Mts* Iceland
10N3 **Tungsten** Can
62C1 **Tuni** India
71E1 **Tunis** Tunisia
68E4 **Tunisia** Republic, N Africa
26D2 **Tunja** Colombia
14C2 **Tunkhannock** USA
10F3 **Tuntutuliak** USA
5H2 **Tunulik** *R* Can
10F3 **Tununak** USA
5J2 **Tunungayualok I** Can
28B2 **Tunuyán** Arg
28B2 **Tunuyán** *R* Arg
52D4 **Tunxi** China
20C2 **Tuolumne Meadows** USA
29B3 **Tupã** Brazil
29C2 **Tupaciguara** Brazil
28E1 **Tupanciretã** Brazil
17E3 **Tupelo** USA
43G1 **Tupik** Russian Fed
26E8 **Tupiza** Bol
20C3 **Tupman** USA
13E2 **Tupper Lake** USA
28B2 **Tupungato** Arg
25C4 **Tupungato** *Mt* Arg
61D2 **Tura** India
49M3 **Tura** Russian Fed
44L4 **Tura** *R* Russian Fed
66D2 **Turabah** S Arabia
63D1 **Turān** Iran
49L4 **Turan** Russian Fed
64C3 **Turayf** S Arabia
63E3 **Turbat** Pak
26C2 **Turbo** Colombia
41E1 **Turda** Rom
48K5 **Turfan Depression** China
48H5 **Turgay** Kazakhstan
49L5 **Turgen Uul** *Mt* Mongolia
4F3 **Turgeon** *R* Can
64A2 **Turgutlu** Turk
64C1 **Turhal** Turk
32K7 **Türi** Estonia
39B2 **Turia** *R* Spain
Turin = Torino
44L4 **Turinsk** Russian Fed
53C2 **Turiy Rog** Russian Fed
72D3 **Turkana,L** Kenya/Eth
58E1 **Turkestan** Region, C Asia
59E1 **Turkestan** Kazakhstan
64C2 **Turkey** Republic, W Asia
48G5 **Turkmenistan** *Republic* Asia
63C1 **Turkmenskiy Zaliv** *B* Turkmenistan
23C2 **Turks Is** Caribbean
32J6 **Turku** Fin
72D3 **Turkwel** *R* Kenya
20B2 **Turlock** USA
20B2 **Turlock L** USA
3C2 **Turnagain** *R* Can
78C2 **Turnagain,C** NZ
21D3 **Turneffe I** Belize
14D1 **Turners Falls** USA
36C1 **Turnhout** Belg
3G2 **Turnor L** Can
41E2 **Turnu Măgurele** Rom
41E2 **Turnu-Severin** Rom
49K5 **Turpan** China
23B2 **Turquino** *Mt* Cuba
58E1 **Turtkul'** Uzbekistan
17C2 **Turtle Creek Res** USA
3G3 **Turtle L** Can
49K3 **Turukhansk** Russian Fed
50D1 **Turuntayevo** Russian Fed
29B2 **Turvo** *R* Goias, Brazil
29C3 **Turvo** *R* São Paulo, Brazil
43E2 **Tur'ya** *R* Ukraine
17E3 **Tuscaloosa** USA
Tuscany = Toscana
14B2 **Tuscarora Mt** USA
12B3 **Tuscola** Illinois, USA
16C3 **Tuscola** Texas, USA
15B2 **Tuscumbia** USA
63D2 **Tusharik** Iran
14A2 **Tussey Mt** USA
Tutera = Tudela
62B3 **Tuticorin** India
41F2 **Tutrakan** Bulg
42B3 **Tuttlingen** Germany
77H2 **Tutulia** *I* American Samoa
22C2 **Tututepec** Mexico
50D2 **Tuul Gol** *R* Mongolia
77G1 **Tuvalu** *Is* Pacific O
49L4 **Tuvinskaya** Respublika, Russian Fed
65C4 **Tuwayilel Haj** *Mt* Jordan
66C2 **Tuwwal** S Arabia
22B2 **Tuxpan** Jalisco, Mexico
22A1 **Tuxpan** Nayarit, Mexico
22C1 **Tuxpan** Veracruz, Mexico
22C2 **Tuxtepec** Mexico
21C3 **Tuxtla Gutiérrez** Mexico
39A1 **Túy** Spain
3B2 **Tuya** *R* Can
55D3 **Tuy Hoa** Viet
64B2 **Tuz Gölü** *Salt L* Turk
64D3 **Tuz Khurmātū** Iraq
41D2 **Tuzla** Bosnia & Herzegovina, Yugos
44F4 **Tver'** Russian Fed
34D4 **Tweed** *R* Scot/Eng
75D1 **Tweed Heads** Aust
34D4 **Tweedsmuir Hills** Scot
19C4 **Twentynine Palms** USA
7N5 **Twillingate** Can
18D1 **Twin Bridges** USA
16B3 **Twin Buttes Res** USA
18D2 **Twin Falls** USA
78B2 **Twins,The** *Mt* NZ
4B4 **Twin Valley** USA
20B3 **Twitchell Res** USA
12A1 **Two Harbors** USA
18D1 **Two Medicine** *R* USA
12B2 **Two Rivers** USA
49O4 **Tygda** Russian Fed
17C3 **Tyler** USA
53E1 **Tymovskoye** Russian Fed
50F1 **Tynda** Russian Fed
34E4 **Tyne** *R* Eng
34E4 **Tyne and Wear** Metropolitan County, Eng
34E4 **Tynemouth** Eng
32G6 **Tynset** Nor
10H4 **Tyonek** USA
65C2 **Tyr** Leb
Tyre = Tyr
53C1 **Tyrma** Russian Fed
53C1 **Tyrma** *R* Russian Fed
34B4 **Tyrone** County, N Ire
16A3 **Tyrone** New Mexico, USA
14A2 **Tyrone** Pennsylvania, USA
4B3 **Tyrrel** Can
75B3 **Tyrrell,L** Aust
40C2 **Tyrrhenian S** Italy
45J7 **Tyuleni, Ostrova** *Is* Kazakhstan
48H4 **Tyumen'** Russian Fed
49O3 **Tyung** *R* Russian Fed
35C5 **Tywyn** Wales
41E3 **Tzoumérka** *Mt* Greece
74E1 **Tzaneen** S Africa

U

29D3 **Ubá** Brazil
29D2 **Ubaí** Brazil
29E1 **Ubaitaba** Brazil
72B3 **Ubangi** *R* CAR
37B2 **Ubaye** *R* France
54B4 **Ube** Japan
39B2 **Ubeda** Spain
7N2 **Ubekendt Ejland** *I* Greenland
29C2 **Uberaba** Brazil
29C2 **Uberlândia** Brazil
55D2 **Ubon Ratchathani** Thai
43F2 **Ubort** *R* Belorussia
72C4 **Ubundi** Zaïre
26D5 **Ucayali** *R* Peru
60C3 **Uch** Pak
53E3 **Uchiura-wan** *B* Japan
49P4 **Uchar** *R* Russian Fed
18A1 **Ucluelet** Can
49L4 **Uda** *R* Russian Fed
60C4 **Udaipur** India
61C2 **Udaipur Garhi** Nepal
28D3 **Udaquiola** Arg
32G7 **Uddevalla** Sweden
32H5 **Uddjaur** *L* Sweden
62B1 **Udgir** India
60D2 **Udhampur** India
37E1 **Udine** Italy
44J4 **Udmurtskaya** Respublika, Russian Fed
55C2 **Udon Thani** Thai
49P4 **Udskaya Guba** *B* Russian Fed
53C1 **Udskoye** Russian Fed
62A2 **Udupi** India
53D1 **Udyl', Ozero** *L* Russian Fed
49N2 **Udzha** Russian Fed
54C3 **Ueda** Japan
72C3 **Uele** *R* Zaïre
49U3 **Uelen** Russian Fed
42C2 **Uelzen** Germany
72C3 **Uere** *R* Zaïre
44K5 **Ufa** Russian Fed
44K4 **Ufa** *R* Russian Fed
73B6 **Ugab** *R* Namibia
72D4 **Ugaila** *R* Tanz
10H4 **Ugak B** USA
72D3 **Uganda** Republic, Africa
10G4 **Ugashik B** USA
10G4 **Ugashik L** USA
37B2 **Ugine** France
66D1 **'Uglat as Suqūr** S Arabia
53E2 **Uglegorsk** Russian Fed
44F4 **Uglich** Russian Fed
53C3 **Uglovoye** Russian Fed
44F5 **Ugra** *R* Russian Fed
34B3 **Uig** Scot
73B4 **Uige** Angola
54A3 **Ŭijŏngbu** S Korea
45J6 **Uil** Kazakhstan
18D2 **Uinta Mts** USA
54A3 **Ŭiryŏng** S Korea
54A3 **Uisŏng** S Korea
74D3 **Uitenhage** S Africa
5J2 **Uivak,C** Can
43E3 **Ujfehértó** Hung
54C4 **Uji** Japan
72C4 **Ujiji** Tanz
25C2 **Ujina** Chile
60D4 **Ujjain** India
57B4 **Ujung** Indon
76A1 **Ujung Pandang** Indon
72D4 **Ukerewe** *I* Tanz
61D2 **Ukhrul** India
44J3 **Ukhta** Russian Fed
19B3 **Ukiah** California, USA
18C1 **Ukiah** Oregon, USA
8A3 **Ukiah** USA
43E1 **Ukmerge** Lithuania
45D6 **Ukraine** *Republic* Europe
54A4 **Uku-jima** *I* Japan
50D2 **Ulaanbaatar** Mongolia
50C2 **Ulaangom** Mongolia
52C1 **Ulaan Uul** Mongolia
59G1 **Ulangar Hu** *L* China
52B1 **Ulansuhai Nur** *L* China
50D1 **Ulan Ude** Russian Fed
50C3 **Ulan Ul Hu** *L* China
28B2 **Ulapes** Arg
49Q3 **Ul'beya** *R* Russian Fed
53B4 **Ulchin** S Korea
41D2 **Ulcinj** Montenegro, Yugos
50E2 **Uldz** Mongolia
50C2 **Uliastay** Mongolia
43F1 **Ulla** Lithuania
75D3 **Ulladulla** Aust
34C3 **Ullapool** Scot
32H5 **Ullsfjorden** *Inlet* Nor
35D4 **Ullswater** *L* Eng
53C4 **Ullung-do** *I* S Korea
42C3 **Ulm** Germany
53C2 **Ul'ma** *R* Russian Fed
75A1 **Uloowaranie,L** Aust
53B4 **Ulsan** S Korea
35B4 **Ulster** Region, N Ire
57C2 **Ulu** Indon
48K5 **Ulungur He** *R* China
48K5 **Ulungur Hu** *L* China
34B3 **Ulva** *I* Scot
35D4 **Ulverston** Eng
75E3 **Ulverstone** Aust
49Q4 **Ulya** *R* Russian Fed
43G3 **Ulyanovka** Ukraine
44H5 **Ul'yanovsk** Russian Fed
16B2 **Ulysses** USA
45E6 **Uman** Ukraine
7N2 **Umanak** Greenland
61B3 **Umaria** India
60B3 **Umarkot** Pak
75A1 **Umaroona,L** Aust
18C1 **Umatilla** USA
44E2 **Umba** Russian Fed
72D4 **Umba** *R* Tanz
37E3 **Umbertide** Italy
76D1 **Umboi I** PNG
32H6 **Ume** *R* Sweden
32J6 **Umea** Sweden
74E2 **Umfolozi,R** S Africa
10H2 **Umiat** USA
74E3 **Umkomaas** *R* S Africa
67G1 **Umm al Qaiwain** UAE
67G2 **Umm as Samīm** *Salt Marsh* Oman
72C2 **Umm Bell** Sudan
66B3 **Umm Inderaba** Sudan
72C2 **Umm Keddada** Sudan
66C1 **Umm Lajj** S Arabia
72D2 **Umm Ruwaba** Sudan
67F2 **Umm Sa'id** Qatar
66B4 **Umm Saiyala** Sudan
73C5 **Umnaiti** *R* Zim
10E5 **Umnak I** USA
18B2 **Umpqua** *R* USA
60D4 **Umred** India
74D3 **Umtata** S Africa
29B3 **Umuarama** Brazil
74D3 **Umzimkulu** S Africa
74E3 **Umzimkulu** *R* S Africa
74D3 **Umzimvubu** *R* S Africa
74D1 **Umzingwane** *R* Zim
29E2 **Una** Brazil
40D1 **Una** *R* Bosnia & Herzegovina/Croatia, Yugos
14C1 **Unadilla** USA
14C1 **Unadilla** *R* USA
29C2 **Unaí** Brazil
10F3 **Unalakleet** USA
10E5 **Unalaska** *I* USA
66D1 **Unayzah** S Arabia
14D2 **Uncasville** USA
16A2 **Uncompahgre Plat** USA
74D2 **Underberg** S Africa
11B2 **Underwood** USA
44E5 **Unecha** Russian Fed
65C3 **Uneisa** Jordan
10G4 **Unga** *I* USA
7M4 **Ungava B** Can
25F3 **União de Vitória** Brazil
10F5 **Unimak Bight** USA
10F5 **Unimak I** USA
10E5 **Unimak Pass** USA
28B3 **Unión** Arg
17D2 **Union** Missouri, USA
15C2 **Union** S Carolina, USA
13D2 **Union City** Pennsylvania, USA
15B1 **Union City** Tennessee, USA
74C3 **Uniondale** S Africa
15B2 **Union Springs** USA
13D3 **Uniontown** USA
67F2 **United Arab Emirates** Arabian Pen
30E3 **United Kingdom** Kingdom, W Europe
2H4 **United States of America**
7K1 **United States Range** *Mts* Can
3G3 **Unity** Can
18C2 **Unity** USA
16A3 **University Park** USA
36D1 **Unna** Germany
61B2 **Unnāo** India
54A2 **Unsan** N Korea
34E1 **Unst** *I* Scot
57B3 **Unuana** *I* Indon
3B2 **Unuk** *R* USA
64C1 **Ünye** Turk
44G4 **Unzha** *R* Russian Fed
26F2 **Upata** Ven
73C4 **Upemba Nat Pk** Zaïre
7N2 **Upernavik** Greenland
74C2 **Upington** S Africa
20D3 **Upland** USA
77H2 **Upolu** *I* Western Samoa
3E3 **Upper Arrow L** Can
78C2 **Upper Hutt** NZ
18B2 **Upper Klamath L** USA
18B2 **Upper L** USA
35B4 **Upper Laugh Erne** *L* N Ire
23L1 **Upper Manzanilla** Trinidad
11D2 **Upper Red L** USA
14B3 **Upperville** USA
Upper Volta = Burkina
32H7 **Uppsala** Sweden
11D2 **Upsala** Can
11B3 **Upton** USA
52B1 **Urad Qianqi** China
67E1 **Urairah** S Arabia
54D2 **Urakawa** Japan
45J5 **Ural** *R* Kazakhstan
75D2 **Uralla** Aust
45J5 **Ural'sk** Kazakhstan
48G4 **Uralskiy Khrebet** *Mts* Russian Fed
29D1 **Urandi** Brazil
6H4 **Uranium City** Can
51G8 **Urapunga** Aust
16A2 **Uravan** USA
54C3 **Urawa** Japan
44L3 **Uray** Russian Fed
12B2 **Urbana** Illinois, USA
12C2 **Urbana** Ohio, USA
37E3 **Urbino** Italy
35D4 **Ure** *R* Eng
44H4 **Uren'** Russian Fed
48J3 **Urengoy** Russian Fed
53C1 **Urgal** Russian Fed
58E1 **Urgench** Uzbekistan
60B2 **Urgun** Afghan
53B1 **Urkan** *R* Russian Fed
41F3 **Urla** Turk
53C2 **Urmi** *R* Russian Fed
71H4 **Uromi** Nig
41E2 **Uroz̧evac** Serbia, Yugos
27J6 **Uruaçu** Brazil
29C1 **Uruacu** Brazil
22B2 **Uruapan** Mexico
29C2 **Urucuia** *R* Brazil
28E1 **Uruguai** *R* Brazil
28D1 **Uruguaiana** Brazil
25E4 **Uruguay** Republic, S America
25E4 **Uruguay** *R* Urug
63B1 **Urumīyeh** Iran
59G1 **Ürümqi** China
50J2 **Urup** *I* Russian Fed
49Q5 **Urup, Ostrov** *I* Russian Fed
67E3 **'Urūq al Awārik** Region, S Arabia
53A1 **Urusha** Russian Fed
60B2 **Uruzgan** Afghan
54D2 **Uryū-ko** *L* Japan
45G5 **Uryupinsk** Russian Fed
44J4 **Urzhum** Russian Fed
41F2 **Urziceni** Rom

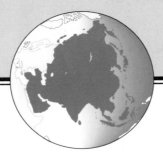

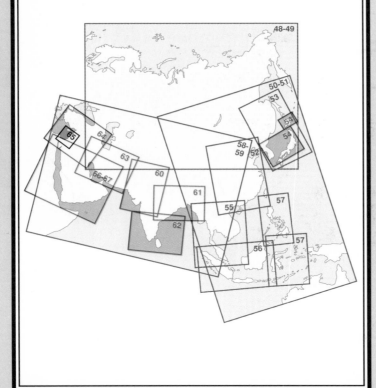

ASIA

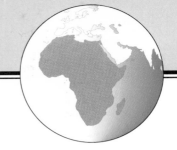

48-49
50-51
53
54
54
65
64
63
58-59
52
60
66-67
61
55
57
62
56
57

AFRICA

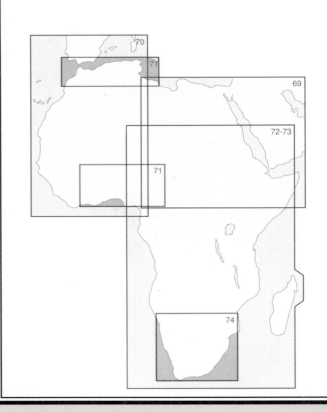

70
71
69
72-73
71
74